The *Perpendiculum*

Medieval Law and Its Practice

VOLUME 43

The titles published in this series are listed at *brill.com/mlip*

The *Perpendiculum*

Presumptions and Legal Arguments in the 12th Century

By

David De Concilio

BRILL

LEIDEN | BOSTON

ERC Advanced Grant 740611 CLCLCL (Civil Law, Common Law, Customary Law: Consonance, Divergence and Transformation in Western Europe from the late eleventh to the thirteenth centuries) 2017.

Cover illustration: *Perpendiculum*, MS Ville de Grenoble, Bibliothèque Municipale, 391 (1) Rés, fol. 161v. With kind permission on the Bibliothèque Municipale.

Library of Congress Cataloging-in-Publication Data

Names: De Concilio, David, author.
Title: The Perpendiculum : presumptions and legal arguments in the 12th century / by David de Concilio.
Description: Leiden ; Boston : Brill, 2024. | Series: Medieval law and its practice, 1873-8176 ; volume 43 | Includes bibliographical references and index.
Identifiers: LCCN 2024043083 | ISBN 9789004712751 (hardback) | ISBN 9789004713239 (ebook)
Subjects: LCSH: Presumptions (Canon law)–Early works to 1800. | Legal maxims (Canon law)–Early works to 1800.
Classification: LCC KBR100 .D43 2024 | DDC 262.9/2–dc23/eng/20240913
LC record available at https://lccn.loc.gov/2024043083

Typeface for the Latin, Greek, and Cyrillic scripts: "Brill". See and download: brill.com/brill-typeface.

ISSN 1873-8176
ISBN 978-90-04-71275-1 (hardback)
ISBN 978-90-04-71323-9 (e-book)
DOI 10.1163/9789004713239

To Emanuele Conte and John Hudson

Contents

PART 2
The Texts

Acknowledgements

This book is the result of several years of research, most of which took place during my Ph.D. program at the University of St Andrews and at Roma Tre University, under the European Research Council-funded project 'Civil Law, Common Law, Customary Law: Consonance, Divergence and Transformation in Western Europe from the Late Eleventh to the Thirteenth Centuries' (Grant Agreement no. 740611 CLCLCL). I am therefore particularly grateful to my supervisors, John Hudson and Emanuele Conte, for their constant advice, guidance, and support. Moreover, the central ideas of the book have benefited greatly from the intellectual exchange with the CLCLCL team, for which I would like to thank Dan Armstrong, Andrew Cecchinato, Cinnamon Ducasse, Will Eves, Cory Hey, Ingrid Ivarsen, Kim-Thao Le, Matthew McHaffie, Attilio Stella, and Sarah White. I would also like to thank the members of my PhD exam committee for their insightful suggestions: Caroline Humfress, Sara Menzinger, Diego Quaglioni, and Danica Summerlin.

There are many scholars who have provided invaluable help in turning my dissertation into a book: first and foremost, Gero Dolezalek and Sara Menzinger, who kindly underwent several readings of the manuscript. I am also grateful to Valeria De Fraja, Stephan Dusil, Andrea Errera, Antonia Fiori, Christophe Grellard, Irène Rosier-Catach, Corinne Leveleux-Teixeira, and Andres Winroth, for their insightful thoughts and suggestions. I would also like to express my gratitude to Susanne Lepsius and Laurent Mayali, who gave me the opportunity to perfect my research during my stays abroad as a visiting scholar at the Leopold-Wenger-Institut für Rechtsgeschichte and at the Robbins Collection of the University of California, Berkeley. I am also grateful to Frances Harty for her linguistic assistance.

I am greatly indebted to Stefania Gialdroni, who gave me the opportunity to continue this research during these years while working at the University of Padua in her European Research Council-funded project 'Migrating Commercial Law and Language (MICOLL). Rethinking *Lex Mercatoria* (11th–17th century)' (Grant Agreement no. 101002084 MICOLL). Furthermore, several field trips that made the book possible were financed by the PRIN (Progetto di Rilevante Interesse Nazionale, funded by the Italian Ministry of University and Research) 2019–2022 project 'Precetto religioso e norma giuridica: storia e dinamica di una dialettica fondativa della civiltà giuridica occidentale (secoli IV–XVII),' PI Emanuele Conte.

Finally, I am wholeheartedly thankful to my family and my partner, Cécile, for their constant support.

Preface

For the Western European legal tradition, the decades between the second half of the 12th century and the beginning of the 13th were a period of both profound change and strong consolidation. Legal teaching and learning began to spread across the continent: from Italy to England and from France to Germany, new schools were founded, some of which survive to this day. These schools introduced innovative methods of teaching and a whole new set of legal ideas and abstractions. Under the stimulus and with the active contribution of this new learning, legal practice also changed, the schools and the courts often moving at the same pace: new procedures emerged everywhere, from the Italian communes to the papal court and the secular kingdoms. These decades represent a seminal moment in the eventual establishment of the legal systems that have shaped Europe since: the continental heritage of the *ius commune* and the insular tradition of the English common law.

Over the past five years, the ERC-funded project 'CLCLCL' (Civil Law, Common Law, Customary Law: Consonance, Divergence and Transformation in Western Europe from the late 11th to the 13th centuries), led by Prof. John Hudson, has aimed to re-examine the similarities, differences, and influences between civil law and common law by looking precisely at this historical moment and digging into the roots of the division between these systems.

This book was largely conceived within that project, where I conducted my doctoral research. It is, therefore, born of a desire to shed light on the profound transformations of the late 12th and early 13th centuries by looking at the cultural milieu of the masters and schools that shaped this pivotal moment. The subject is, of course, immense and I have no ambition to explore all its facets. My research will be limited to one specific aspect: a niche work, commonly called the *Perpendiculum*, which represents an example of a literary genre invented at the time, called *brocardica*. Nevertheless, this work can provide insights into the profound transformations and strong entanglements of Western European legal culture during the long 12th century. In particular, it can inform our understanding of the legal schools of the time, helping us to reassess their cultural framework, methods, influences, and spatiality.

I am aware, however, of the difficulties involved in such a task. The roots of the 12th-century intellectual world are in many respects still to be understood, and the attempt to reconstruct its legal schools may end up chasing phantoms. This is particularly true when it comes to reconstructing an anonymous and layered text such as the *Perpendiculum*. One often has to work with a very limited number of clues: an initial, a few words, some stylistic impressions. It is possible to make suggestions, but certain proof is beyond the possibilities of the modern scholar, especially since any argument based on context runs the risk of falling into the trap of circular argumentation. The best that can be done in this regard is to make the most reasonable suggestions in the light of the evidence available to us, and to propose a reconstruction that is consistent with that evidence. From this perspective, my work, like the *Perpendiculum*, "*nec tamen vera continet ..., sed probabilia et apparentia*."[1]

1 See below, *Summula de presumptionibus*, x, 2.

Abbreviations

ACA	Arxiu de la Corona d'Aragó
AKKR	*Archiv für katholisches Kirchenrecht*
AHDE	*Anuario de Historia del Derecho Español*
Auth.	*Authenticum* (see Nov.)
B.	Burchard of Worms, *Burchardi Wormatiensis ecclesiae episcopi decretorum libri XX: Ergänzter Neudruck der Editio princeps Köln 1548*, ed. Gérard Fransen and Theo Kölzer (Aalen: Scientia Verlag, 1992)
BAV	Biblioteca Apostolica Vaticana
BIMAE	Giovanni Battista Palmieri and Augusto Gaudenzi, eds., *Bibliotheca Iuridica Medii Aevii. Scripta anecdota glossatorum*, 2nd ed., 2 vols (Bologna: Ex aedibus Angeli Gandolphi Typis Societatis Azzoguidianae, 1913–1914)
BISM	*Bullettino dell'Istituto Storico Italiano per il Medio Evo*
BM	Bibliothèque municipale
BMCL	*Bulletin of Medieval Canon Law*
BNE	Biblioteca Nacional de España
BNF	Bibliothèque Nationale de France
BNL	Bibliothèque Nationale du Luxembourg
BSB	Bayerische Staatsbibliothek
C.	Causa
c.	caput/canon
CGJC	Mario Viora, ed., *Corpus Glossatorum Juris Civilis*, 11 vols (Turin: Bottega d'Erasmo, 1966–1973)
Cod.	Paul Krüger, ed., *Corpus Iuris Civilis, II, Codex Iustinianus* (Berlin: Weidmann, 1877)
col.	column
Comp.	Emil, Friedberg, ed., *Quinque compilationes antiquae nec non collectio canonum Lipsiensis ad librorum manu sciptorum fidem recognovit et adnotatione critica* (Leipzig: Tauchnitz, 1882)
c. u.	codicological unit
D.	Distinctio (in Gratian's *Decretum*)
d.	distinctio
DBI	*Dizionario Biografico degli Italiani* (Rome: Istituto dell'Enciclopedia Italiana), online version, available at https://www.treccani.it/biografico/index.html, accessed 2022 Jul 31.

 | DOI:10.1163/9789004713239_001

DBGI	Italo Birocchi, Ennio Cortese, Antonello Mattone, Marco Nicola Miletti, Maria Luisa Carlino, Giuseppina De Giudici, and Ersilia Fabbricatore, eds., *Dizionario Biografico dei Giuristi Italiani* (*XII–XX secolo*) 2 vols (Bologna: Il Mulino, 2013)
DDC	Raoul Naz, ed., *Dictionnaire de Droit Canonique*, 7 vols (Paris: Letouzey et Ané, 1935–1965)
DGDC	Javier Otaduy Guerin, Antonio Viana Tomé, and Joaquin Sedano Rueda, eds., *Diccionario General de Derecho Canónico*, 7 vols (Pamplona: Universidad de Navarra, 2012)
DHJF	Patrick Arabeyre, Jean-Louis Halpérin, and Jacques Krynen, eds., *Dictionnaire historique des juristes français, XIIe–XXe siècle*, 2nd ed. (Paris: Press Universitaires de France, 2015)
Dig.	Theodor Mommsen and Paul Krüger, eds., *Corpus Iuris Civilis, I, Digesta* (Berlin: Weidmann, 1868)
DMLBS	Richard K. Ashdowne, David R. Howlett, and Ronald E. Latham, eds., *Dictionary of Medieval Latin from British Sources* (Oxford: Oxford University Press, 2018), available at https://logeion.uchicago.edu, accessed 2021 Sep 14
ff.	*Digesta* (see Dig.)
gl.	glossa
HB	Hofbibliothek
HLB	Hochschul- und Landesbibliothek
HMCLCP	Wilfried Hartmann and Kenneth Pennington, eds., *The History of Medieval Canon Law in the Classical Period, 1140–1234: from Gratian to the Decretals of Pope Gregory IX* (Washington, D.C.: The Catholic University of America Press, 2008)
HQLR	Helmut Coing, ed., *Handbuch der Quellen und Literatur der neueren europäischen Privatrechtsgeschichte: Erster Band; Mittelalter (1100–1500), die gelehrten Rechte und die Gesetzgebung*, 2 vols (Munich: Beck, 1973–1977)
Inst.	*Corpus Iuris Civilis, I, Institutiones*, ed. Paul Krüger (Berlin, 1868)
LexMa	Robert Auty, ed., *Lexikon des Mittelalters*, 9 vols (Munich/Zürich: Artemis Verlag/LexMA-Verlag, 1977–1999)
Lips.	Leipzig, Universitätsbibliothek, 975, *Collectio Lipsiensis*, fols. 116–153
JL	Philippe Jaffé, Samuel Löwenfeld, Ferdinand Kaltenbrunner, and Paul Eward, eds., *Regesta pontificum Romanorum*, 2 vols. (Leipzig: Veit, 1885–1888)

Nov.	Rudolf Schoell and Wilhelm Kroll, eds., *Corpus Iuris Civilis, III, Novellae* (Berlin: Weidmann, 1895)
ODNB	H.C.G. Matthew and Brian Harrison, eds., *Oxford Dictionary of National Biography*, 60 vols (Oxford: Oxford University Press, 2004), online edition, available at https://www.oxforddnb.com/, accessed 2022 Jul 31
OED	*Oxford English Dictionary* (Oxford: Oxford University Press), online edition, available at https://www.oed.com/, accessed 2022 Jul 31
ONB	Österreichische Nationalbibliothek
Phys.	Aristotle, *Physica*, ed. Fernand Bossier and Jozef Brams (Leiden: Brill, 1990)
Par. II	Paris, BNF, lat. 1566, *Collectio Parisiensis secunda*, fols. 1–54v
PL	Jacques Paul Migne, ed., *Patrologia Latina Cursus Completus*, 221 vols (Paris: Migne, 1844–1864)
q.	quaestio
RDC	*Revue de droit canonique*
RHE	*Revue d'histoire ecclésiastique*
RIDC	*Rivista Internazionale di Diritto Comune*
RSDI	*Rivista di Storia del Diritto Italiano*
SB	StaatsBibliothek
TvR	*Tijdschrift voor Rechtsgeschiedenis*
UB	Universitätsbibliothek
v.	verbum/verba
WH	Walther Holtzmann, "Walther Holtzmann Kartei," in *Stephan Kuttner Institute of* Medieval Canon Law, available at https://www.kuttner-institute.jura.uni-muenchen.de, accessed 2021 Aug 7
X.	Emil Ludwig Richter and Emil Friedberg, eds., *Decretalium Collectiones: Decretales Gregorii p. IX* (Leipzig: Tauchnitz, 1881)
ZRG Kan. Abt.	*Zeitschrift der Savigny-Stiftung für Rechtsgeschichte, Kanonistische Abteilung*
ZRG Rom. Abt.	*Zeitschrift der Savigny-Stiftung für Rechtsgeschichte, Romanistische Abteilung*

Introduction

Between the last three decades of the 12th century and the first two of the 13th, the Glossators of the Roman and canon law schools that were spreading across Western Europe were engaged in the creation of new tools and literary genres for legal teaching and argumentation. One of the most notable examples of this endeavor is the emergence of brocards, or *brocardica*. It is challenging to provide a clear definition of brocards, given the significant transformations of their structure and purpose over time. With a great deal of generalization, brocards were legal maxims for argumentation, which embodied a certain principle and equipped it with a list of the norms on said principle, often arranged according to a dialectical pattern of opposing *pro* and *contra* arguments. At a later stage, brocards were also equipped with solutions meant to solve the opposition.[1] From the 1170s onwards, collections of brocards became extremely popular, particularly in the transmontane schools of law: i.e. those schools that flourished north of the Alps, mainly in Provence, northern France, England, and the Rhineland.[2]

Among these collections, few have generated as much scholarly interest and debate as the so-called *Perpendiculum*: a canon law ensemble of *brocardica* written between 1172 and 1177 and comprising several different parts, the first of which is dedicated to legal presumptions. This interest is not surprising, given that the *Perpendiculum* represents one of the most relevant examples of the genre. Indeed, it is one of the earliest known collections of its kind and marked a pivotal turn in the development of brocards, thanks to its innovative use of rhetorical and topical techniques. On the one hand, it was the first known collection of brocards to arrange them in a *pro-contra* pattern; on the other hand, it exerted a significant influence on later works of this kind, such as the *Libellus disputatorius* of the renowned legist Pilius de Medicina, thus becoming an influential model for 12th-century jurists.

1 For a detailed account of this transformation, see David De Concilio, *Via Brocardica: The Development of Brocards and the Western European Legal Tradition (c. 1160–c. 1215)*, 2 vols (PhD dissertation: University of St Andrews, 2022), 1:52–62, and 2:7–36.

2 The definition has been introduced by Kenneth Pennington and Wolfgang P. Müller, "The Decretists: The Italian School," in *HMCLCP*, and Rudolf Weigand, "The Transmontane Decretists," in *HMCLCP*. Cf. also James A. Brundage and Melodie H. Eichbauer, *Medieval Canon Law*, 2nd ed. (London: Routledge, 2023), pp. 61ff.

 | DOI:10.1163/9789004713239_002

1 Eighty Years of Research: A Historiographical Account

For the reasons set out above, the *Perpendiculum* has attracted the attention of legal historians interested in both the development of legal argumentation and the intellectual milieu of 12th-century schools. These scholars have sought to analyze, date, and attribute the collection.

The *Perpendiculum* was first identified in 1937 by Stephan Kuttner[3] and subsequently studied by Albert Lang in two articles.[4] These studies represent the first demonstration of the relationship between brocards and rhetorical techniques and remain still fundamental works in this regard. It was Lang who named the collection '*Perpendiculum*,' deriving the name from a word used in the *explicit* of its first part, where the author refers to his work as "this plumb line" (*hoc perpendiculum*).[5] The compiler, however, did not mean to use this term as a title; rather, it was intended as a metaphor.[6] The title that he had in mind is revealed, instead, by another text attributed to him, the collection of *notabilia* "*Argumentum quod religiosi*," where he referred to the first part of the *Perpendiculum*, dedicated to presumptions, as "*Summula de presumptionibus*."[7] Consequently, Kuttner preferred to name the work in this way,[8] but Lang's choice had the advantage of providing a uniform title for the various heterogeneous parts of the ensemble, rather than just for its first section on presumptions. For this reason, the name "*Perpendiculum*" has been retained to refer to the entire collection, while its first part is usually called *Summula* or *Tractatus de presumptionibus*.

Lang was also the first to attempt to more precisely define the context of production of the *Perpendiculum*, dating it to approximately 1180 and attributing it to a Bolognese canonist who was influenced by the work of the Italian jurist

---

3 Stephan Kuttner, *Repertorium der Kanonistik (1140–1234): Prodromus corporis glossarum* (Vatican City: BAV, 1937), pp. 241–242.

4 Albert Lang, "Rhetorische Einflüsse auf die Behandlung des Prozesses in der Kanonistik des 12. Jahrhunderts," in *Festschrift Eduard Eichmann zum 70. Geburtstag dargebracht von seinen Freunden und Schülern*, ed. Martin Grabmann and Karl Hofmann (Paderborn: Schöningh, 1940); Albert Lang, "Zur Entstehungsgeschichte der Brocardasammlungen," *ZRG Kan. Abt.* 31 (1942), pp. 106–141.

5 Cf. below, *Summula de presumptionibus*, X, 2.

6 Stephan Kuttner, "Retractationes IX," in Stephan Kuttner, *Gratian and the Schools of Law. 1140–1234* (London: Variorum, 1983), p. 39.

7 Below, p. 46 n. 113.

8 Kuttner, "Retractationes IX," p. 40, and Kuttner, *Repertorium*, pp. 236, 241.

Sicardus Cremonensis.[9] In order to contextualize Lang's hypothesis, it is necessary to consider the prevailing scholarly attitudes of his time, when legal historiography was still heavily influenced by the 19th-century roots of the discipline. These had identified the birth of the medieval renaissance of law in the foundation of the civil law school in Bologna by the famous master Irnerius at the end of the 11th century.[10] Subsequently, for many decades and still at Lang's time, Bologna was regarded by scholarship as the almost exclusive center of legal innovation, with most 12th-century works attributed to this school.[11] Consequently, the effects of this Bologna-centric approach also reverberated on the history of the *Perpendiculum*.

Lang's studies constituted the foundation for the *vexata quaestio* concerning the genesis of our collection, which has engaged legal historians for over eighty years. In the 1950s, Kuttner and Rudolf Motzenbäcker contested Lang's attribution and re-examined the provenance and other characteristics of the work, situating it within the French legal milieu and anticipating its estimated composition to the 1170s.[12] At the turn of the millennium, André Gouron reconsidered the matter and sought to shed new light on the authorship and cultural context of the *Perpendiculum*, hypothesizing an Anglo-Norman origin.[13] This theory was subsequently further strengthened by Peter Landau.[14] These reconsiderations of the authorship of the text were also linked to the prevailing historiographical trends of the time, and to an increasing shift from a Bologna-centric perspective of 12th-century legal culture towards the concept of a system of 'national' legal schools across Western Europe.[15] Kuttner, Gouron, and

9 Lang, "Zur Entstehungsgeschichte," pp. 123, 135.

10 For an account, see Ennio Cortese, "Alle origini della scuola di Bologna," *RIDC* 4 (1993), pp. 7–49, repr. in Ennio Cortese, *Scritti*, 2 (Spoleto/Rome: Centro italiano di studi sull'alto Medioevo/Il Cigno Galileo Galilei, 1999).

11 On the legal historiographical trends since Savigny, see Emanuele Conte, *Diritto comune: Storia e storiografia di un sistema dinamico* (Bologna: Il Mulino, 2009), pp. 13–42.

12 Kuttner, "Réflexions sur les brocards des glossateurs," in *Mélanges Joseph de Ghellinck*, 2 (Gembloux: J. Duculot, 1951), repr. in Stephan Kuttner, *Gratian and the Schools*, no. IX, and Rudolf Motzenbäcker, *Die Rechtsvermutung im kanonischen Recht* (Munich: Zink, 1958), pp. 93–100, respectively.

13 André Gouron, "Une école de canonistes anglais à Paris. Maître Walter et ses disciples (vers 1170)," *Journal des savants* 1 (2000), pp. 47–72, repr. in André Gouron, *Pionniers du droit occidental au Moyen Âge*, no. VI. (Aldershot/Burlington: Variorum/Ashgate, 2006).

14 Peter Landau, "Walter von Coutances und die Anfänge der anglo-normannischen Rechtswissenschaft," in *Panta Rei: Studi dedicati a Manlio Bellomo*, ed. Orazio Condorelli, 3 (Rome: Il Cigno Galileo Galilei, 2004).

15 For an account of this process, see Emanuele Conte, "La France dans une 'Europe juridique'? La relation à l'Italie au 12ème siècle," *RSDI* 94, no. 2 (2021), pp. 17–37.

Landau were all engaged in a progressive re-evaluation of the transmontane centers of legal learning, contributing especially to the discovery of the 12th-century French and Anglo-Norman schools.[16] This 'national' characterization of the legal schools is one of the aspects that I will consider when addressing the origin of the *Perpendiculum*.

2 The *Perpendiculum* as a Source for the History of Presumptions

However, the *Perpendiculum* has not been solely studied in the context of the history of brocards, as it is not, in fact, merely a collection of brocards. Rather, it is a heterogeneous ensemble of diverse texts and legal devices, consisting of several parts. The first part of the collection, the *Summula de presumptionibus*, has contributed significantly to the elaboration of 12th-century Romano-canonical theories on presumptions. In recent times, the role of the collection in this regard has been meticulously examined by Antonia Fiori, who has shown the contribution of the *Summula de presumptionibus* to the development of the concept of irrebuttable presumption, called *praesumptio legis violenta* by the text. This was a presumption established by law that does not admit evidence to the contrary.[17]

16 Kuttner, *Repertorium*; Stephan Kuttner and Eleanor Rathbone, "Anglo-Norman Canonists of the Twelfth Century. An Introductory Study," *Traditio* 7 (1949), pp. 279–358, repr. in Kuttner, *Gratian and the Schools*, no. VIII. Regarding Gouron, besides his book André Gouron, *La science juridique française aux XIe et XIIe siècles: Diffusion du droit de Justinien et influences canoniques jusqu'à Gratien* (Milan: Giuffrè, 1978), he also published a great number of articles on this subject, mostly reunited now in four volumes: André Gouron, *Études sur la diffusion des doctrines juridiques médiévales* (London: Variorum, 1987); André Gouron, *Droit et coutume en France aux XIIe et XIIIe siècles* (Aldershot: Variorum, 1993); André Gouron, *Juristes et droits savants: Bologne et la France médiévale* (Aldershot\Brookfield: Variorum\Ashgate, 2000); André Gouron, *Pionniers du droit occidental au Moyen Âge* (Aldershot\Burlington: Variorum\Ashgate, 2006). For Landau, see—among the others—Peter Landau, "The Origins of Legal Science in England in the Twelfth Century: Lincoln, Oxford and the Career of Vacarius," in *Readers, Texts and Compilers in the Earlier Middle Ages: Studies in Medieval Canon Law in Honour of Linda Fowler-Magerl*, ed. Martin Brett and Kathleen G. Cushing (London: Routledge, 2017); Peter Landau, "The Origin of the Regula iuris 'Quod omnes tangit' in the Anglo-Norman School of Canon Law during the Twelfth Century," *BMCL* 32 (2015), pp. 19–35; cf. also the literature cited below, p. 20 n. 12.

17 Antonia Fiori, "Praesumptio violenta o iuris et de iure? Qualche annotazione sul contributo canonistico alla teoria delle presunzioni," in *Der Einfluss Der Kanonistik Auf Die Europäische Rechtskultur*, 1, *Zivil- und Zivilprozessrecht*, ed. Orazio Condorelli, Franck Roumy, and Mathias Schmoeckel (Cologne: Böhlau Verlag, 2009).

On this point, it is worth setting out a brief overview of the concept of presumptions here, since this term has often been employed with different theoretical and practical meanings.[18] In the common understanding of the word, a presumption is defined as "the action of taking for granted or presuming something; ... a belief based on available evidence," or "grounds or reason for presuming or believing; presumptive evidence." In legal terms, it can be understood as "a supposition that the court allows or requires to be made."[19] It is also defined as "the act of believing that something is true without having any proof" or "a belief that something is true because it is likely, although not certain."[20] However, upon examination of these broad definitions,[21] it becomes evident that they share certain common features: i) the presumption is a belief or supposition; ii) it is grounded in a parameter of likelihood; iii) it is justified in the absence or scarcity of other evidence.

In legal terms, the use of a presumption can be regarded as a substitute for proof: a role that it has played since Roman times[22] and that also characterized it in the 12th century.[23] In the case of a judicial matter that is open do doubt, the most direct outcome is the removal of the doubt through the acquisition of proof. Nevertheless, there are instances when this is either not possible or not

18 Cf. Richard H. Helmholz and W. David H. Sellar, "Presumptions in Comparative Legal History," in *The Law of Presumptions: Essays in Comparative Legal History*, ed. Richard H. Helmholz and W. David H. Sellar (Berlin: Duncker & Humblot, 2009), pp. 11–13.

19 *OED*, s.v. "presumption," available at www.oed.com/view/Entry/150903, accessed 2021 Jan 25

20 *Cambridge Dictionary*, s.v. "presumption," available at www.dictionary.cambridge.org/dictionary/english/presumption, accessed 2021 Jan 25.

21 Cf. Raymundo Gama, "Presumptions and Fictions: A Collingwoodian Approach," in *Legal Fictions in Theory and Practice*, ed. Maksymilian Del Mar and William Twining (Cham: Springer, 2015), pp. 355–356.

22 See Guido Donatuti, "Le 'praesumptiones iuris' come mezzi di svolgimento del diritto sostanziale romano," *Rivista di Diritto Privato* 3, no. 1 (1933), pp. 161–206, repr. in Guido Donatuti, *Studi di diritto romano*, 1 (Milan: Giuffrè, 1976).

23 It was considered a kind of *probatio ficta* or *quasi probatio*: Jean-Philippe Lévy, *La hiérarchie des preuves dans le droit savant du Moyen-Âge depuis la renaissance du droit romain jusqu'à la fin du XIVe siècle* (Paris: Librairie du Recueil Sirey, 1939), pp. 27 and 84. Simon de Bisignano, *Summa in Decretum Simonis Bisinianensis*, ed. Pier V. Aimone-Braida (Vatican City: BAV, 2014), v. *modus probationis*, to C.2 q.1 c.7, distinguishes between two modes of proof: the legitimate proof ("*legitima probatione*") and the means used in place of proof ("*loco probationis*"), such as the presumption ("*suspicio*"). Later procedural literature included the presumption in the *species probationum*: Lévy, *La hiérarchie*, p. 25; cf. Richard M. Fraher, "Conviction According to Conscience: The Medieval Jurists' Debate Concerning Judicial Discretion and the Law of Proof," *Law & History Review* 7 (1989), pp. 23–88, especially 33, 37, 40–48, 52; Massimo Vallerani, "I fatti nella logica del processo medievale: Note introduttive," *Quaderni Storici* 36 (2001), pp. 665–693, 682.

convenient, because the necessary evidence cannot be provided, is insufficient, or the search for it would require an excessive expenditure of effort. Consequently, the issue of the presumption is therefore that of doubt,[24] which in the Romano-canonical procedure usually coincided with the absence of direct evidence in the form of testimony or documents. In such instances, a system of presumptions serves an alternative to proof, enabling the resolution of doubt, the establishment of truth, and the reaching of a verdict.[25] This is explicitly stated in the incipit of the *Perpendiculum*, which illustrates how presumptions are "very necessary during trials, especially whenever we dispute about uncertainties."[26]

In other words, a presumption replaces proof about the facts under investigation with a supposition of what the facts could be, usually (but not always) based on other facts. In order for this supposition to be valid, it must have a sufficient level of credibility. Consequently, the presumption must follow a logical inferential reasoning process, which provides its rationale and strength.[27] The presumption is, therefore, the outcome of that reasoning process,[28] which aims to solve a doubtful matter by establishing a truth that, due to its inherent likelihood, does not require proof because it is stronger than a mere conjecture. In this light, the *Summula de presumptionibus* was designed to provide logical legal arguments (*loci argumentorum*) in the form of brocards to justify the establishment of presumptions on uncertain facts based on certain ones. Consequently, the work was entirely centered around the concept of what a fact is and the various shapes that the uncertainty around a fact could take.

Finally, it is crucial to note that, despite presumptions being mainly a substitute for proofs, they are not only that. When they are strong enough, their primary procedural outcome is to invert the burden of proof or even establish

---

24 Cf. Hanns Hohmann, "Presumptions in Roman Legal Argumentation," in *Proceedings of the Ontario Society for the Study of Argumentation Conference, 4 (2001): Argumentation and its Applications; University of Windsor, May 17–19, 2001*, ed. Hans v. Hansen, Robert C. Pinto, Christopher W. Tindale, J. Anthony Blair, and Ralph H. Johnson, pp. 1–14, available online at https://scholar.uwindsor.ca/ossaarchive/OSSA4/papersandcommentaries/61/, accessed 2022 Aug 01, 1; Adolfo Giuliani, "Civilian Treatises on Presumptions, 1580–1620," in *The Law of Presumptions*, p. 24. For a detailed account on the intellectual frame around the concept of doubt, see James Q. Whitman, *The Origins of Reasonable Doubt: Theological Roots of the Criminal Trial* (New Haven: Yale University Press, 2008), pp. 115–124.

25 Giuliani, "Civilian Treatises," p. 23.

26 See below, *Summula de presumptionibus*, I, 1.

27 On the limits to the standardization of the parameter of verisimilitude behind this reasoning, see De Concilio, *Via Brocardica*, 1:178–182.

28 Giuliani, "Civilian Treatises," pp. 24–25.

a judicial truth that contrasts with the factual one, not admitting evidence to the contrary. In a legal historical perspective, the *Summula de presumptionibus* is notable for its significant contribution to the establishment of the concept of a legal irrebuttable presumption (*praesumptio legis violenta*).

By publishing a full rendition of the text of the *Summula* for the first time, this book aims to help historians better understand the development of the Romano-canonical procedure, which was strongly grounded in presumptive reasonings,[29] as well as the argumentative and logical techniques employed by the legal schools of the period, based on the use of *loci loicales* in form of brocards.

3 The Reasons for a New Investigation

We have briefly seen the reasons why the *Perpendiculum* is a significant text for the historiographical understanding of legal learning in 12th-century Western Europe and how it has attracted the attention of scholars for the past eighty years. However, despite this long historiographical tradition, the collection requires re-examination today for two main reasons.

Firstly, no comprehensive and detailed studies have so far been carried out on the text of the work itself. Until now, the knowledge of the *Perpendiculum* was based on the few passages of the *Summula de presumptionibus* that had been edited by Kuttner and Lang in their studies. The consequence of this incomplete textual availability was twofold. Firstly, it restricted access to only a limited portion of the work, as the *Summula* represents merely a fraction of the ensemble. Secondly, it prevented a comprehensive understanding of the *Summula* itself, as the previously edited part did not include the *loci* and allegations.

Indeed, an edition of the *Summula de presumptionibus* has been advocated by legal historians for a long time. In 1990, Gérard Fransen announced his intention to publish it,[30] but unfortunately, he passed away before completing the

29 I will address this matter in David De Concilio, "Imputer l'intention dans les procédures romano-canoniques. Réflexions sur la théorie des présomptions autour du Concile du Latran IV," in *Intention, imputation, responsabilité Autour du concile du Latran IV*, ed. I. Rosier-Catach, R. Eckert, C. Grellard, and C. Leveleux-Teixeira, forthcoming.

30 Gérard Fransen, "Canonistica minora," in *'Houd voet bij stuk', Xenia iuris historiae G. van Dievoet oblata*, ed. Fred Stevens and Dirk Van den Auweele (Leuven: Katholieke Universiteit Leuven, Faculteit der Rechtsgeleerdheid, Afdeling Romeins, Recht en Recht-

task. Subsequently, two decades ago, André Gouron announced that the task was about to be completed by a "brave enough legal historian,"[31] but nothing came of it. Consequently, the publication of such an edition continued to represent one of the *desiderata* of European medieval legal history up to the present day.

The reasons for this desire are readily apparent. The *Summula* was a highly influential work—both in terms of the development of legal theories on presumptions and the utilization of topical argumentation in the form of brocards. Consequently, a full knowledge of the text of the *Summula* can facilitate the study of the history of legal concepts, and specifically of the development of the Romano-canonical system of presumptions, thus carrying on the work conducted by Motzenbäcker, Gouron, and Fiori. Furthermore, an accessible version of the other two parts is necessary to understand the formation of brocards as a genre and the argumentation techniques followed in the 12th-century legal schools. This will make it possible to revise (and challenge) the current historiography on this point, as it is still grounded in the excellent but outdated studies of Kuttner and Peter Weimar.[32]

Moreover, a comprehensive analysis of the text of the *Perpendiculum* is also necessary to understand the broader context of 12th-century legal doctrines and methods. Indeed, legal historians have repeatedly highlighted the strong textual connections between the *Summula* and several other juristic products

---

geschiedenis, 1990), repr. in Gérard Fransen, *Canones et Quaestiones: Évolution des doctrines et système du droit canonique*, (Goldbach: Keip, 2002), 1.1:34: "*Aux fol. 44–49ᵛ se lit un traité assez répandu sur les présomptions «Hic locus frequens in iudiciis est» dont on prépare l'édition.*"

31 Gouron, "Une école de canonistes," p. 63.

32 The only two comprehensive studies of brocards published to date are Stephan Kuttner, "Réflexions," and Peter Weimar, "Argumenta brocardica," *Studia Gratiana* 14 (1967), pp. 91–123, which remain the fundamental starting point for any research on the subject. Since then, new individual studies have been carried on some of the 12th-century collections of brocards: see Matthias Schwaibold, *Brocardica 'Dolum per subsequentia purgari': Eine englische Sammlung von Argumenten des römischen Rechts aus dem 12. Jahrhundert* (Frankfurt am Main: Klostermann, 1985); Matthias Schwaibold, "Wer sucht, der findet," *Rechtshistorisches Journal* 4 (1985), pp. 202–214; Hans van de Wouw, "Brocardica Dunelmensia," *ZRG Rom. Abt.* 108 (1991), pp. 234–278. Some more general works on brocards, instead, still rely on Kuttner's and Weimar's studies from a legal-historical perspective: Lisa Isola, *Venire contra factum proprium: Herkunft und Grundlagen eines sprichwörtlichen Rechtsprinzip* (Frankfurt am Main: Peter Lang GmbH, Internationaler Verlag der Wissenschaften, 2017), pp. 15–40; Daniele Velo Dalbrenta, *Brocardica: Una introduzione allo studio e all'uso dei brocardi. Principi di filosofia forense* (Milan: Franco Angeli, 2007), pp. 21–22.

of the time. These include the canon law *Summae* of Simon de Bisignano and Sicardus Cremonensis, the *Libellus disputatorius* of the civilian jurist Pilius de Medicina, and a number of other smaller glosses, *ordines iudiciarii*, and *tractatus* produced both by Roman and canon lawyers, in Italy as in France. Nevertheless, scholars have not yet succeeded in fully elucidating the precise nature of these relationships. In order to achieve this, it is necessary to examine the sources in greater detail, with the aid of a modern edition. Once this issue (i.e. establishing which work influenced the others) has been resolved, it will be possible to gain new insights into the process of development of legal thought in 12th-century schools and the circulation of doctrines and texts in those milieux.

Finally, clarifying these textual relationships would give us new insights into the landscape of 12th-century schools of law. In fact, we have seen that scholars had conflicting opinions on the geographical location of the *Perpendiculum* between the two sides of the Alps. In order to dispel these doubts, it is necessary to place its tradition in a spatial dimension that goes beyond the 'national' characterization of the legal schools conventionally emphasized by historiography, and to frame it within a wider area that encompasses the cathedral schools of northern France, England, and western Germany. This is indeed an area that clearly influenced the production and dissemination of our collection, a common cultural milieu[33] that scholars have defined as 'transmontane schools.'[34] In order to unveil both the spatial dimension of the diffusion of the *Perpendiculum* and the wider intellectual horizon in which it was conceived, these transmontane schools must in turn be placed in relation to the Italian schools of law that flourished in the period.

In short, I will broadly argue that an examination of the geographical and intellectual pattern of the *Perpendiculum* and its related works can provide a picture of the deep connections within the network of schools that flourished at the time both in Italy and beyond the Alps, thus suggesting the existence

33 On the fact that these regions can be regarded as a single cultural environment, not only legally, see C. Stephen Jaeger, *The Envy of Angels: Cathedral Schools and Social Ideals in Medieval Europe, 950–1200* (Philadelphia: University of Pennsylvania Press, 1995), pp. 15–16; Richard W. Southern, *Scholastic Humanism and the Unification of Europe*, 2 vols (Oxford: Blackwell, 1995–2001), 1:163, 267. On the role of the English schools in this milieu in particular, see Richard W. Southern, "The Place of England in the Twelfth-Century Renaissance," *History. The Journal of the Historical Association* 45 (1960): 201–216, repr. in Richard W. Southern, *Medieval Humanism and Other Studies* (Oxford: Blackwell, 1970), and Rodney M. Thomson, "England and the Twelfth-Century Renaissance," *Past & Present* 101 (1983), pp. 3–21, who circumscribes Southern's reconstruction.

34 See above, p. 1 n. 2.

of a common Western European legal culture as early as in the 12th century. In particular, the study of the *Perpendiculum* will help us to overcome the conventional historiographical vision of 12th-century learned law in terms of center vs. periphery, which, although constantly challenged, still very much dominates our common understanding.

4 Sources

In light of the context set out above, this study will focus on that part of the Western legal tradition that has often been called "learned law:" that is, the theories and doctrines produced by masters who taught in universities and legal schools, where works such as the *Perpendiculum* were produced. The adjective 'learned' perhaps conveys a reductive idea of this complex set of doctrines, which was in fact often also followed by the legal practice,[35] but as a term it concisely encapsulates the theories and concepts concerned, so I will use it in this study. More specifically, I will deal in general terms with the doctrines and literature that developed around the two main legal systems of Continental Europe during the Middle Ages: civil law (i.e. Roman law: two terms that I will use interchangeably here) and canon law. Together, these two bodies of law constituted the so-called *ius commune*, a complex of universally valid norms and principles that complemented the many particular laws (*iura propria*) of local medieval polities and institutions. The *Perpendiculum* and other primary sources that we will examine will mostly contain references to these two legal systems, sometimes together with passages from Lombard law (the legal customs and laws of the old kingdom of Italy), or non-legal sources that were considered moral *auctoritates* at the time, such as the Bible.

Speaking of these sources, a caveat must be made. In studying the *Summula* and other related 12th-century juristic works, we will often come across concepts, formulations, and definitions that made a profound contribution to the legal thought of the time, especially with regard to the treatment of presumptions. Sometimes I will present these as "the earliest" or "one of the earliest" examples of their kind. It is worth bearing in mind that this does not necessarily mean that we are dealing with something that had been newly invented in these works: in all likelihood, hardly anything new was formulated for the first

35 Cf. Kenneth Pennington, "Learned Law, Droit Savant, Gelehrtes Recht: The Tyranny of a Concept," *Syracuse Journal of International Law and Commerce* 20 (1994), pp. 205–215.

time in works such as *summae*, *ordines*, or *brocardica*. These genres often concocted concepts that they extracted from the layers of glosses that had been introduced into legal teaching by masters and written in the margins of the texts of Gratian's *Decretum* and the *Corpus Iuris Civilis*. And yet, we still know very little about the teaching and rhetorical techniques of the 12th century, compared to the vast (much of which is still unexplored) marginal glosses in the bulky books of Roman and canon law that we have. Only the brief writing *on* and *outside* these books have been studied in detail, while the main source of knowledge, the glosses, remain largely overlooked.[36] Therefore, the chronological claims that I will make in this study with regard to certain theoretical formulations must be understood only in terms of our current knowledge and in the awareness that the vast mass of unedited material remains to be studied: in other words, within the *corpus clausus* of our sources.

Again, with regard to chronological claims, it is important to clarify the criteria used to date some of the sources in this study. As they are anonymous and mostly consist only of allegations from Gratian's *Decretum*, many of the sources analysed in this book are extremely difficult to date with certainty, including the *Perpendiculum* itself. In many cases, one of the few clues is the mention of some papal decretals, especially those issued by Alexander III during his pontificate (1159–1181). On the one hand, these references certainly provide a *terminus post quem*, since logically a work (or its specific recension) could not have been written before the decretals it cites. On the other hand, they also help to circumscribe the *terminus ante quem*, given the lack of references to later sources. Of course, the compilers worked from copies and collations of material circulating in their area, and it often took time for the new *ius decretalium* to be incorporated into these works; moreover, authors from the last decades of the 12th century often referred to older material, not only to the most recent sources. Therefore, the fact that a particular work does not cite decretals after a certain one does not necessarily mean that a particular text was written by the end of the pontificate of the pope who wrote it. It does, however, suggest that the work was written not too many years later. Moreover, the impression that certain

---

36 Most scholars who have worked on glosses have collected those with a specific *siglum*, like Rudolf Weigand, *Die Glossen zum Dekret Gratians*, 2 vols (Rome: Libreria Ateneo Salesiano, 1991), or excerpted glosses on a particular topic, like Azo, *Glosse preaccursiane alle istituzioni: Strato azzoniano*, ed. Severino Caprioli et al., 2 vols (Rome: Istituto Storico Italiano per il Medio Evo, 1984–2004). Recently, a major contribution has been made by Tammo Wallinga, *The Casus Codicis of Wilhelmus de Cabriano* (Frankfurt am Main: Klostermann, 2005).

works were produced in the 1170s or early 1180s on the basis of the decretals they cite is often reinforced by the fact that these decretals are cited without any reference to the systematic collections that began to be used from the 1180s. This approach to dating anonymous 12th-century canon law works is not new and has been conventionally used by well-established scholars.[37] However, many of these chronological attributions remain speculative and, although probable and based on our best knowledge, must be taken *cum grano salis*.

5 Map of the Book

On the basis of these premises, we can finally turn our attention to the *Perpendiculum*. This study is divided into two main parts, which will proceed as follows.

Part 1 contains an analytical study of the text and consists of four chapters.

In chapter 1, I will outline the manuscript tradition of the *Perpendiculum* and its textual composition, as well as its content, method, and purpose. After examining the three main parts that make up the ensemble, I will focus on the texts inserted in and appended to it.

Chapter 2 will be devoted to the context and scope of the *Perpendiculum*: first, I will examine its significance and influence on 12th-century legal thought, particularly with regard to the development of brocards and the Glossators' theory of presumptions. I will then consider the textual relationship of the *Perpendiculum* to similar sources, of both canon and Roman law, from both sides of the Alps; this comparison will include some of the most influential canon law *Summae* of the period, as well as other legal works textually related to the *Perpendiculum*. Through this, we will better understand the literary context in which our collection was produced.

Chapter 3 will delve more deeply into the history of the work and the questions that historiography has tried to answer. Through a careful textual analysis, I will offer suggestions regarding its dating, paternity, and intellectual milieu.

Finally, in chapter 4, I will make some brief concluding remarks on the importance of the *Perpendiculum* and its school for the history of 12th-century legal thought. I will emphasize the role of this collection and its related texts

37 Cf. for example the dating proposed by Weigand for the glosses of the canonist W.: below, p. 59.

in the establishment of a legal theory of presumptions, as well as its fortunes among jurists on both sides of the Alps. I will also argue that the *Perpendiculum* represents an explanatory paradigm of the shifting historiographical understanding of the Western legal tradition. Indeed, the existence of a group of texts which share common characteristics in terms of style, technique, subject matter, and textual references, and that were produced in both northern France and Italy, offers some significant insights into the historical and intellectual relationship between these two prominent legal milieux, and it highlights the existence of a common Western European legal culture.

The second part of the book will present the primary sources on which the study is based. First, I will outline the editorial criteria used for the various texts and a description of the manuscripts in which the *Perpendiculum* is found. The reader will then find the text of the first three parts of the work; for the first two—the *Summula de presumptionibus* and a group of 26 brocards which was probably intended as an appendix to the *Summula*—the book provides an edition and a translation. In addition, the second part is accompanied by a synoptic table of its brocards to help the reader to visualize the textual differences between the different manuscripts. With regard to the third part of the ensemble, a different choice has been made: for reasons that will be explained later,[38] I will not provide a complete edition, but rather a critical table of contents of the rubrics of its brocards. As for Part II, it is intended to be read with the help of a synoptic table to accompany those brocards that appear in more than one manuscript.

Furthermore, after the third part of the *Perpendiculum*, the reader will find some additional texts: the *Perpendiculum* is an ensemble of argumentative devices, and several smaller works were interspersed between its three main parts. The pure diversity of this collection shows the modern reader the argumentation techniques used by 12th-century jurists, so I have decided to include the editions of those texts that appear in more than one manuscript.[39]

38 See below, pp. 125–126.

39 See below, p. 126.

PART 1

The Analysis of the Work

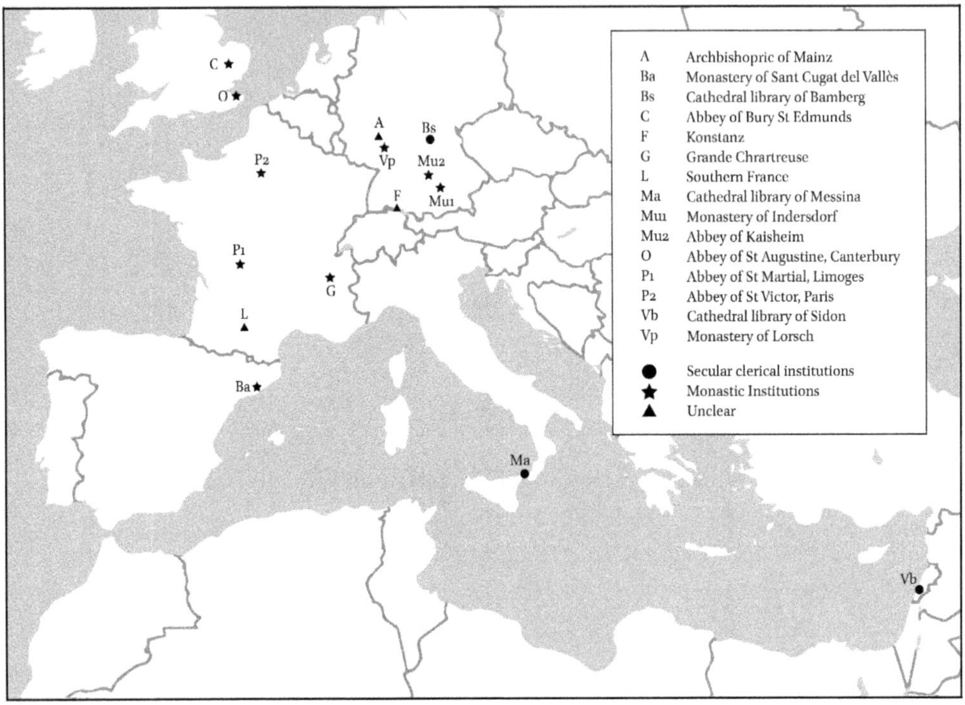

Map of the earliest known place of provenance of the manuscripts of the *Perpendiculum*

CHAPTER 1

The Work: The *Perpendiculum* and Its Text

Now that we have defined the scope of this study, it is time to take a closer look at the *Perpendiculum*, starting with its textual tradition and composition. In this chapter, I will examine the surviving manuscripts of the *Perpendiculum* (1), then I will analyze its three main parts (2), the other small texts that have been interspersed between them (3), and finally some works appended to the ensemble (4).

1 A European Text: The Manuscript Tradition of the *Perpendiculum*

The text of the *Perpendiculum* survives in 15 known manuscripts:[1]

A Aschaffenburg, HB, Perg. 26, fols. 214va–217va; 200^{rc}–201ra (A1).
Ba Barcelona, ACA, Cugat 55, fols. 44ra–48vb.
Bs Bamberg, SB, Can. 17 (P.I.11), fol. 95va.
C Cambridge, Pembroke College, 101, fols. 61vb–68ra.
F Fulda, HLB, 100 D. 10, fols. 80ra–81^{vd}.
G Grenoble, BM, 391 (1) Rés., fols. 161va–163^{rc}.
L Leipzig, UB, Rep. II 117, fols. 1ra–10rb.
Ma Madrid, BNE, 421 (C.4.1), fols. 3ra–13ra.
Mu1 Munich, BSB, Clm. 7622, fols. 47va–52vb.
Mu2 Munich, BSB, Clm. 8013, fols. 115^{v}–117vb.
O Oxford, University College, 117, fol. 145(bis)$^{ra-vb}$.
P1 Paris, BNF, lat. 4720A, fols. 30vb–36vb.
P2 Paris, BNF, lat. 14606, fols. 166va–167^{vc}.
Vb Vatican City, BAV, Borgh. 287, fols. 1ra–8va.
Vp Vatican City, BAV, Pal. lat. 653, fols. 113ra–117^{rc}.

The most important aspect of the manuscripts to be studied is their provenance, as this can provide important insights into the cultural and intellectual environment in which the *Perpendiculum* circulated.

---

1 Kuttner, *Repertorium*, p. 241; Stephan Kuttner, "An Interim Checklist of Manuscripts," *Traditio* 11 (1955), pp. 439–448, 447; Stephan Kuttner, "An Interim Checklist of Manuscripts (III)," *Traditio* 13 (1957), pp. 467–471, 470; Stephan Kuttner, "Annual Report," *Traditio* 19 (1963), pp. 509–516, 511; Kuttner, "Retractationes IX," p. 40. For descriptions of the manuscripts, see below, pp. 131–198.

 | DOI:10.1163/9789004713239_003

The first general consideration in this regard concerns the institutional setting from which they came. We can see that all the codices belonged to ecclesiastical institutions: the majority to monasteries (Ba, C, G, Mu1, Mu2, O, P1, P2, and Vp), while three of them were in cathedrals (Bs, Ma, and Vb); for three other copies of the *Perpendiculum* (A, F, and L) it is not possible to identify the precise origin, but they ended up in both secular clerical (A) and monastic (F, L) institutions.

If we look at the geographic origin of our codices, we can see that they were distributed throughout Western Europe. Two manuscripts (C and O) are of English origin and both come from Benedictine abbeys: Bury St Edmunds and St Augustine in Canterbury; the first manuscript is also the only copy of the work that contains another text that can be attributed to the same author, the *notabilia "Argumentum quod religiosi."*[2] Three other copies (G, P1, and P2) are certainly French. One of them comes from a royal abbey in Paris, which also had important ties with the Anglo-Norman realm: Saint-Victor (P2);[3] another belongs to a place historically linked to the Angevin kingdom: the abbey of Saint-Martial of Limoges (P1);[4] the third manuscript comes from the monastery of Grande Chartreuse, north of Grenoble (G),[5] i.e. from southern France, an area that often served as a link between the North and the Italian schools. It is noteworthy that two of these French manuscripts, G and P1, show very strong similarities in both Parts I and II, and could be derived from the same archetype. We can probably add a fourth manuscript to this French group: L. This codex is made up of different units, most of which are from southern Germany; however, the unit containing the *Perpendiculum* can be considered either Italian or southern French on the basis of its rounded script.[6] I

---

2 See below, pp. 44–46.

3 On the role of Saint-Victor as intermediary between the kingdoms of France and England in the second half of the 12th century, see Rolf Grosse, "Entre cour et cloître: Saint-Victor et les Capétiens au XIIe siècle," in *L'école de Saint-Victor de Paris: Influence et rayonnement du Moyen Âge à l'époque moderne*, ed. Dominique Poirel (Turnhout: Brepols, 2010), pp. 95–100.

4 Limoges, like the rest of the Limousin, passed to the Angevins in 1152 through the marriage of Eleanor of Aquitaine to Henry Plantagenet, Duke of Normandy, Count of Anjou, and future king of England. On the dissemination of legal knowledge at Saint-Martial, see Danica Summerlin, *The Canons of the Third Lateran Council of 1179: Their Origins and Reception* (Cambridge: Cambridge University Press, 2019), pp. 178–180.

5 Gouron, "Une école de canonistes," p. 63 n. 37, following a hypothesis of Hermann Kantorowicz, suggested that the manuscript derives from an archetype brought to the Grande Chartreuse at the beginning of the 13th century and written before 1185 by the jurist Pierre Fouquois. See also André Gouron, "Notes sur les collections de quaestiones reportatae chez les civilistes du XIIe siècle," in *Houd voet bij stuk*, repr. in Gouron, *Droit et coutume*, no. VI, p. 61.

6 See below, pp. 170 ff.

tend to agree with this second possible origin for two reasons: firstly, because its variants, especially in the *Summula*, are similar to those of G; secondly, because the script, although very similar to that of Bologna, shows some signs of transalpine influences.[7] Three copies (Ba, Ma, and Vb) of the *Perpendiculum* are of Mediterranean origin, although they are closely linked to the Norman and French milieux. The first (Ma) was produced in the cathedral library of Messina and ended up in Madrid after the city's revolt of 1672–1678 and the War of the Spanish Succession;[8] Ma seems to be the oldest surviving codex of the *Perpendiculum*, having been produced in the last quarter or last two decades of the 12th century. The second manuscript (Vb) is a 13th-century codex from the Outremer, i.e. from the crusader states imbued with French culture:[9] more specifically, from the cathedral library of Sidon, in modern Lebanon,[10] from where it was transferred to the papal library after the abolition of the local Latin bishopric.[11] The only Spanish manuscript of the *Perpendiculum* (Ba) is

---

7 For example, in most instances the word '*qui*' is spelled or abbreviated as 'q' with a superscript 'i;' an Italian scribe, instead, would consistently abbreviate '*qui*' as 'q' with a crossbar. On these aspects, cf. Albert Derolez, *The Palaeography of Gothic Manuscript Books: From the Twelfth to the Early Sixteenth Century* (Cambridge: Cambridge University Press, 2003), pp. 68, 109.

8 The manuscript came into Spanish hands in 1678, when the Viceroy Francisco de Benavides, Count of Santisteban del Puerto, regained control of Messina and, in retaliation against the rebellious city, confiscated the library of its cathedral chapter. Like the other Latin and Greek codices in this library, it was entrusted to the next viceroy, Juan Francisco Pacheco y Téllez-Girón, 4th Consort Duke of Uceda, who included it in his personal library and took it with him to Spain in 1696. In 1711, the manuscript was confiscated by the Crown, along with the rest of Uceda's estate, when he sided with the Austrians in the War of the Spanish Succession. See Anna Tedesco, "Juan Francisco Pacheco v duca di Uceda, uomo politico e mecenate tra Palermo, Roma e Vienna nell'epoca della guerra di successione Spagnola," in *La pérdida de Europa : la guerra de sucesión por la Monarquía de España*, ed. Antonio Alvarez-Ossorio Alvariño, Bernardo José García García, and Virginia León Sanz (Madrid: Fundación Carlos de Amberes, 2007), pp. 499–500. See also below, p. 174 n. 27.

9 The possible French origin of the copyist of this manuscript (or its model) could also be suggested by a codicological element. In fact, in brocard no. 226 of Part III ("*Aliquis obligatus ere alieno*:" below, p. 391), the scribe placed the letter 'h' in front of the word '*aes*:' this suggests that he could not pronounce the sound associated with this letter phonetically, and therefore could not remember which Latin words required an 'h' and which did not. Therefore, he was probably French, Italian, or Spanish.

10 Gouron, "Une école de canonistes," p. 67, asserts that this manuscript has "*des liens avec l'Angleterre*."

11 See Anneliese Maier, "Die Handschriften der 'Ecclesia Sidonensis'," in *Ausgehendes Mittelalter: Gesammelte Aufsätze zur Geistesgeschichte des 14. Jahrhunderts*, ed. Anneliese Maier and Agostino Paravicini Bagliani, 3 (Rome: Edizioni di storia et letteratura, 1977); Miriam

also linked to French culture and it comes from the monastery of Sant Cugat del Vallès. However, the largest group of manuscripts (A, Bs, F, Mu1, Mu2, and Vp) seems to come from the German area, which was culturally influenced by northern France and the Anglo-Norman world:[12] two from the Rhine valley (A and Vp) and four from southern Germany (Bs, F, Mu1, and Mu2). Again, most of them certainly come from ecclesiastical institutions: we can mention the archbishopric of Mainz, the monastery of Lorsch, the cathedral library of Bamberg, and the monastery of Indersdorf. Of course, for most of the manuscripts it cannot be taken for granted that they were copied in the ecclesiastical institutions from which they came. Regarding the manuscripts in this group, it is worth noting that F has many similarities in its variants with those of Ma, suggesting that they may have derived from the same archetype.[13]

This geographical picture suggests a wide distribution of the *Perpendiculum* in the religious centers of the transmontane legal environment, as well as in the southernmost regions linked politically and culturally to the French and Norman territories: the kingdom of Sicily and the crusader states. This undoubtedly helps to characterize and identify the origin and circulation of the *Perpendiculum*, reinforcing the idea of its French origins. However, it is significant that

---

Rita Tessera, "Dalla liturgia del Santo Sepolcro alla biblioteca di Sidone: Note sulla produzione libraria latina di Oltremare nel secolo XII–XIII," *Aevum* 79, no. 2 (May–August 2005), pp. 413–415.

12 Linda Fowler-Magerl, *Ordines Iudiciarii and Libelli De Ordine Iudiciorum (From the Middle of the Twelfth to the End of the Fifteenth Century)* (Turnhout: Brepols, 1994), pp. 95–99; Ronald G. Witt, *The Two Latin Cultures and the Foundation of Renaissance Humanism in Medieval Italy* (Cambridge: Cambridge University Press, 2012), pp. 343–345. The Parisian and Anglo-Norman influence in the German legal schools has been studied by Peter Landau, *Die Kölner Kanonistik des 12. Jahrhunderts: Ein Höhepunkt der europäischen Rechtswissenschaft* (Badenweiler: Bachmann, 2008); Peter Landau, "Simon von Bisignano, Sikard von Cremona und die Mainzer Kanonistik der Barbarossazeit: Zur Biographie des Simon von Bisignano und zur Forschungsgeschichte," *BMCL* 28 (2008), pp. 119–144; Peter Landau, "The School of Canon Law in Cologne during the 12th Century," in *Proceedings of the Thirteenth International Congress of Medieval Canon Law: Esztergom, 3–8 August 2008*, ed. Peter Erdö and Szabolcs Anzelm Szuromi (Vatican City: BAV, 2010); Peter Landau, "Gerard Pucelle und die Dekretsumme Reverentia sacrorum canonum: Zur Kölner Kanonistik im 12. Jahrhundert," in *Mélanges en l'honneur d'Anne Lefebvre-Teillard*, ed. Bernard d'Alteroche et al. (Paris: Éditions Panthéon-Assas, 2010).

13 However, as we shall see, the *Perpendiculum* is an open text whose manuscripts can only be compared to a limited extent, making it difficult to trace them back to the same antigraph. For example, both F and Ma contain a significant variant in the allegations of Part II, citing the decretal *Sicut Romana* (below, p. 35); moreover, they both follow roughly the same order of brocards in Part III, containing the groups I have named β, ζ, ε, and η (below, p. 38); nevertheless, to this sequence Ma also adds the groups γ, δ, and ζ.

none of the manuscripts seem to come from northern Italy: the heart of Bolognese legal culture,[14] considering that we know for certain that the work was directly known in the 1180s in this area, since it was used and directly referenced to by Pilius de Medicina in his *Libellus disputatorius* (1181–1185).[15] This apparent contradiction could be resolved by hypothesizing that the absence of northern Italian manuscripts is due to the lack of surviving copies and not to the lack of circulation. This, in turn, could be explained by the fact that in the Italian schools the *Perpendiculum* must have been quickly replaced by the most up-to-date brocardic collections, such as the *Libellus* itself, while its use lasted longer in peripheral areas, such as Germany, where most of the manuscripts come from.

The geographical origin of the *Perpendiculum* is revealed not only by the provenance of its manuscripts, but also by the other texts that accompany it in the codices. Many of the manuscripts are miscellaneous books containing a majority of works from the Parisian, Anglo-Norman, and Colognian schools, with a minor presence of Provençal or Bolognese content.[16] These elements may suggest that the geographical origin of the *Perpendiculum* lies in the transmontane schools, but they also reveal the cultural influences and interests of its readers, who seem to have been much more in contact with the legal production of transmontane decretists than that of Bolognese jurists. Moreover, the types of texts that we often find in these miscellaneous manuscripts show that the compilers of the different versions of the *Perpendiculum* were particularly interested in collecting all kinds of rhetorical and dialectical devices for teaching and argumentation: not only *brocardica*, but also other similar genres, like *quaestiones*[17] and *distinctiones*.[18]

---

14 As we shall see, there is a manuscript, L, which has been considered to be possibly Italian, but I believe that a southern French origin is more likely.

15 Pilius used the *Summula* as a direct model for his work and explicitly mentioned it, thus testifying not only to his knowledge but also to a certain circulation of the *Perpendiculum* in the Po valley: see below, pp. 77–80.

16 Cf. below, pp. 131–198.

17 The word *quaestio* is an umbrella term that covers several different genres within the medieval schools, which generally involved the confrontation of divergent opinions on a controversial passage and the resolution of the controversy through the use of dialectics. The *quaestio*, like the brocard, introduced a doubtful case and then listed sets of arguments, *pro* and *contra* two opposing solutions. On the *quaestio* in the legal schools of the time, see Gérard Fransen, "Les questions disputées dans les facultés de Droit," in *Les questions disputées et les questions quodlibétiques dans les facultés de Théologie, de Droit et de Médecine*, ed. Bernardo Carlos Bazàn, John W. Wippfel, Gérard Fransen, and Danielle Jacquart (Turnhout: Brepols, 1985), repr. in Fransen, *Canones et Quaestiones*, 1.2; Annal-

1.1 *A Closer Look: The Three Main Parts of the* Perpendiculum

The *Perpendiculum* is a composite and heterogeneous text. We could define it as 'alluvial,' borrowing a geological term: a multilayered product resulting from the progressive sedimentation of different materials brought by the many streams of 12th-century legal science, resulting in a highly fertile soil.

Conventionally, legal historians have distinguished two parts of the work: the *Summula de presumptionibus*—which, as anticipated, is a monographic treatise on legal presumptions structured in the form of brocards—and the rest, which is considered to be an unsystematic collection of brocards. On closer examination, however, the material of this second part can again be divided into two main groups: Part II, which is a set of 26 *pro-contra* brocards intended to be an appendix to the *Summula*, and Part III, which is a miscellaneous and heterogeneous collection of arguments that varies greatly from one manuscript to another.[19] Thus, we can roughly identify three main parts, but this division is often blurred: initially, because the first two parts were probably intended to be a single work; and also because later compilers often intertwined and merged Parts II and III with several other external materials that have not yet been analyzed and were originally alien to the ensemble. This second aspect gives us a clear example of the method of the milieu in which the *Perpendiculum* was compiled, characterized by the collection of works in the 'alluvial' creation of *textes vivants*, used both for teaching and argumentation.

Regarding the manuscripts, a first group of ten (A, Ba, C, G, L, Ma, Mu1, P1, Vb, and Vp) contains all three main parts of the work. In two of them (A and Ba), a fragment of the *Summula* is repeated elsewhere in an interpolation (designated A1, fols. 200^{rc}–201ra, and Ba1, fols. 47va–48rb, respectively). A second group (F, O, and P2) consists of some series of brocards from the second and third parts, plus a small fragment of the *Summula* transmitted by F. Finally, Mu2 contains only the *Summula* and Bs is only a fragment of its incipit.

---

isa Belloni, *Le questioni civilistiche del secolo XII* (Frankfurt am Main: Klostermann, 1989); Peter Weimar, "Die legistische Literatur der Glossatorenzeit," in *HQLR*, 1:142, 144–146, 222–226, 245–249; Knut Wolfgang Nörr, "Die Kanonistische Literatur," in *HQLR*.

18 On the *distinctio* as a method, see below, p. 23 n. 23. On legal *distinctiones* as a genre, see Emil Seckel, *Distinctiones glossatorum: Studien zur Distinktionen-Literatur der romanistischen Glossatorenschule* (Berlin: Verlag von Otto Liebmann, 1911); Erich Genzmer, "Vorbilder für die Distinctionen der Glossatoren," in *Acta Congressus Iuridici Internationalis VII saeculo a decretalibus Gregorii IX et XIV a Codice Iustiniano promulgatis*, 2 (Rome: Libraria Pont. Inst. Utriusque Iuris, 1935).

19 As noted by Motzenbäcker: see Kuttner, "Retractationes IX," p. 40.

1.2 *Part I:* Summula de presumptionibus

The first part of the *Perpendiculum* is the most interesting for the history of legal thought because of its classification of presumptions and the rhetorical techniques it uses; it is therefore the part that has received the most attention from scholars. It is a treatise on legal presumptions that combines the genre of *summula* with brocards.[20] Its name comes from its anonymous author, who refers to it as *Summula de presumptionibus* in another work, the collection of *notabilia "Argumentum quod religiosi,"*[21] which is appended to the *Perpendiculum* in C.[22]

In a short introduction (I), the author illustrates the different types of uncertainty that can lead to the establishment of a legal presumption regarding a fact. These uncertainties are logically categorized, according to two pairs of criteria, following the method of *distinctio*.[23] Firstly, the uncertainty may concern an extrinsic or intrinsic fact: the former corresponds to a factual question, i.e. the inquiry into the external historical fact; the latter has to do with the inner, subjective question, i.e. the inquiry into all that concerns the subjective and internal elements of human conduct and that in modern terms we call the psychological element of the fact. Secondly, the uncertainty may depend either on the substance[24] or on the quality of the fact: the former means the very existence of the fact in question, while the latter corresponds to its circumstances.

---

20 Kuttner, "Réflexions," p. 787.

21 Below, pp. 44–46.

22 Kuttner, *Repertorium*, pp. 236, 241.

23 The *distinctio* was a method of scholastic knowledge common to all fields of medieval learning, which in logic corresponded to the exegetical technique of *divisio*, which involved separating the logical parts of a concept in order to specify its various applications. In the field of law, this method used a process of division and subdivision of legal matters according to a binary logic, thus hierarchically classifying the rules from the general to the specific, emphasizing the analogies and the differences between them, and resolving the antinomies by relying on the logical distinction between *genus* and *species*. See Christoph Meyer, *Die Distinktionstechnik in der Kanonistik des 12. Jahrhunderts: Ein Beitrag zur Wissenschaftsgeschichte des Hochmittelalters* (Leuven: Leuven University Press, 2000); Gerhard Otte, *Dialektik und Jurisprudenz: Untersuchungen zur Methode der Glossatoren* (Frankfurt am Main: Klostermann, 1971), pp. 73–97; Andrea Errera, *Il concetto di scientia iuris dal XII al XIV secolo: Il ruolo della logica platonica e aristotelica nelle scuole giuridiche medievali* (Milan: Giuffrè, 2003), pp. 1–42; Andrea Errera, "The Role of Logic in the Legal Science of the Glossators and Commentators," in *A Treatise of Legal Philosophy and General Jurisprudence*, 7, *The Jurists' Philosophy of Law from Rome to the Seventeenth Century*, ed. Peter Stein and Andrea Padovani (Dordrecht: Springer, 2007), pp. 82–89.

24 Or essence: the *Summula* uses the two words interchangeably. Cf. Otte, *Dialektik*, pp. 50–51.

It is worth noting that both pairs correspond to concepts of Aristotelian philosophy,[25] and the opposition substance/quality derives from his *Categories*.[26] The combination of these criteria leads to four different types of legal uncertainty:

Type of uncertainty	Definition given by the *Summula*	Meaning
On the substance of an extrinsic fact	*Extrinseci facti essentia*	Whether the material fact happened or not
On the quality of an extrinsic fact	*Extrinseci facti qualitas*	The circumstances of the material fact
On the substance of an intrinsic fact	*Intrinseci facti substantia*	Subsistence or not of the psychological element of the fact
On the quality of an intrinsic fact	*Intrinseci facti qualitas*	The circumstances of the psychological element of the fact

The author of the *Summula* then adds a fifth group of cases based on uncertainty about a law or a document and its interpretation, where he adopts the criteria of harmonizing conflicting opinions established by canon law and the rhetorical tradition.[27] As Lang has shown, this division reflects the adoption of the rhetorical system of *status* or *controversiae*,[28] and is a clear example of the influence of the liberal arts on the author of the *Perpendiculum*.

After the introduction, the *Summula* devotes a section to each of the five groups of cases outlined (II–VI). For the first four groups (i.e. those concerning uncertainty about facts), our author writes a short introductory paragraph in which he gives some examples of the cases that can be attributed to this category.

25 Michael J. Zimmerman and Ben Bradley, "Intrinsic vs. Extrinsic Value," in *The Stanford Encyclopedia of Philosophy* (*Spring 2019 Edition*), ed. Edward N. Zalta, available at https://plato.stanford.edu/archives/spr2019/entries/value-intrinsic-extrinsic/, accessed 2021 Aug 29.

26 See Aristotle, *Categories and De Interpretatione*, ed. and trans. John Ackrill (Oxford: Clarendon Press, 1963), pp. 5–12 and 24–31. Cf. Otte, *Dialektik*, pp. 59–72.

27 Lang, "Rhetorische Einflüsse," p. 80.

28 Lang, "Rhetorische Einflüsse," pp. 75–77. In particular, the first case (*extrinseci facti essentia*) coincides with the rhetorical *status coniecturalis*, while the second (*extrinseci facti qualitas*) coincides with the *status generis*. The third and fourth cases (about the intrinsic fact), on the other hand, do not find a strict correspondence in the *status* theory. The fifth, however, corresponds to the *status legalis* or *controversia legitima*.

For example, uncertainty about the essence of an extrinsic fact means that it is doubtful whether the fact occurred or not, while uncertainty about the quality of an extrinsic fact refers to its characteristics (e.g., whether the fact is just or unjust). After these brief, discursive illustrations, the text lists a group of criteria for each of these categories, according to which one can presume from the fact: for example, the quality of a fact can be presumed according to the place in or the time at which the fact happened. These criteria are explicitly defined as *loci*: a heuristic rhetorical technique for uncovering arguments.[29] This is an extremely significant aspect, since the classification of presumptions according to the *loci* from which they originate will be one of the characteristics of later juristic works on the subject, and therefore one of the most influential aspects of the *Summula* on the legal treatment of presumptions.[30] In addition, these *loci* are sometimes arranged in columns in the manuscripts,[31] showing a tendency towards graphic displays. Finally, for each of these *loci* the work gives a brocard, thus collecting all the possible legal sources (*argumenta*) *pro* and *contra* this *locus*. It is important to note that in order to be used as legal arguments, these *loci* must derive their validity and legitimacy from the legal sources. What the *Summula* does, therefore, is to validate the use of certain topics on the basis of logic (*loci loicales*) in order to establish a presumption,

---

29 *Loci* or Topics (from Greek *τόποι*) were devices used to develop and identify the necessary arguments for disputation. "As it is easier to find a hidden thing when you know the place where you should look for it—Cicero and Boethius said—similarly it is easier to find an argument when you know its place (*locus*):" Cicero, *Topica*, ed. Wilhelm Friedrich (M. Tullii Ciceronis scripta quae manserunt omnia) 1:2 (Leipzig: Teubner, 1912), 7, 426.30–34 and Boethius, *In Ciceronis Topica*, ed. and trans. Eleonore Stump (Ithaca, NY: Cornell University Press, 1988) 1, 280.12–14. In order to indicate where to look for arguments, the topical technique grouped them under commonplaces or propositions, which, as we have seen, are called *loci* (or *sedes*) *argumentorum*. On Topics in general, see Eleonore Stump, *Dialectic and Its Place in the Development of Medieval Logic* (Ithaca, NY: Cornell University Press, 1989), and Eleonore Stump, "Topics: Their Development and Absorption into Consequences," in *The Cambridge History of Later Medieval Philosophy*, 1, *From the rediscovery of Aristotle to the disintegration of Scholasticism, 1100–1600*, ed. Norman Kretzmann, Anthony Kenny, Jan Pinborg, and Eleonore Stump (Cambridge: Cambridge University Press, 1982); Sten Ebbesen, "Ancient Scholastic Logic as the Source of Medieval Scholastic Logic," in Kretzmann et al., *The Cambridge History*, 1; Niels Jørgen Green-Pedersen, *The Tradition of the Topics in the Middle Ages: The Commentaries on Aristotle's and Boethius' "Topics"* (Munich: Philosophia Verlag, 1984); Otte, *Dialektik*, pp. 186–224. For the legal use of *loci*, cf. Otte, *Dialektik*, pp. 61–72. The influence of rhetorical *loci* on the early collections of brocards, including the *Perpendiculum*, has been studied by Lang, "Rhetorische Einflüsse."

30 See below, pp. 77–80.

31 For example, in Mu2 and Vp.

by listing all the legal sources that have made use of them.[32] It is worth anticipating here that the use of *loci* in the *Summula* shows various elements of innovation that make it a stepping stone in the development of legal argumentation and in the consolidation of brocards as a literary genre, as I will show later in this study.[33]

There are several possible concurrent elements which may have influenced the *Perpendiculum* in this approach, leading to the consideration of circumstances for the classification of facts. The first is expressly acknowledged by the author himself when he deals with the quality of the extrinsic fact; in fact, most of the *loci* on this point are expressly derived from C.23 q.8 c.14: a passage from John Chrysostom's homily on the Gospel of Matthew. There, on the basis of some biblical examples, the Father of the Church recommends that, in order to impute a homicide, not only the act itself, but also its circumstances, including the time, the cause, the intention, and the differences, should be carefully examined.[34]

The second potential element of influence is the decretal *Sicut dignum* of Pope Alexander III, addressed to Bishop Bartholomew of Exeter and dated to the same years as the *Summula*, between 1171 and 1173. Here the pontiff, in response to the murder of Thomas Becket and with the intent of prosecuting not only the material authors but also the moral instigator of the deed, King Henry II, stated that the evaluation of a crime must take into account its

32 See De Concilio, *Via Brocardica*, 1:41–43, 1:52–54, and 2:7–16.

33 See below, pp. 49–51.

34 Cf. C.23 q.8 c.14: "*Occidit Finees hominem, et reputatum est illi ad iusticiam. Abraham uero, non solum homicida, uerum etiam patricida (quod certe est grauius) effectus Deo magis placuit. Petrus uero geminum fecit homicidium: fuit tamen opus spirituale, quod factum est. Non solum igitur respiciamus ad opera, sed ad tempus, et ad causam, et ad uoluntatem, personarum quoque differentiam, et quantacumque alia ipsis operibus acciderunt, diligentissime requiramus. Non enim possumus aliter ad ueritatem peruenire*". Here, John Chrysostom gives three examples. The first is that of Phineas, a Jewish priest who was displeased with the immorality with which the Moabites and Midianites had successfully seduced the Israelites into sexual intercourse with them and into worshipping Baal-peor, which had led to a plague sent by God to punish his people. Therefore, Phineas personally executed an Israelite man and a Midianite woman while they were together in the man's tent, thus ending the plague (Num. 25:1–9). The second example is that of Abraham, who was prepared to sacrifice his own son (Gen. 22:1–19). Finally, with regard to Saint Peter, he refers to the episode of Ananias and Sapphira, who sold their land in order to donate the proceeds to Peter for the needs of the Church, but secretly withheld some of the money: knowing this, Peter condemned the couple for lying to God, and they died immediately, struck by divine punishment (Act 5:1–11).

circumstances, such as age, sex, condition, place and time, as well as the *animum*.[35] However, since it is not possible to establish with certainty the chronological precedence between the decretal and the *Summula*, the influence of the former on the latter remains a hypothesis.

Finally, and more generally, the way in which the *Summula* deals with uncertain facts was influenced by the contemporary intellectual focus on the psychological element in the imputation of facts. Indeed, from the beginning of the 12th century, medieval theologians, especially in France, turned their attention to psychological introspection and the subjective sphere of the individual,[36] which led to a growing interest in the concept of intentionality and its inquiry in order to determine the nature of human actions.[37] From the analysis of these elements in sins, this interest quickly spread to canon law in order to determine the moral qualification of an act.[38] The *Summula*, with its categorization of facts, responded precisely to this interest, since presumptions were indeed the

---

35 See *Sicut dignum est* (JL 12180 = WH 929 = X. 5.12.6): "*Sane, quum vir literatus et sapiens et discretus et in his plurimum exercitatus exsistas, plenius nosti, quod in excessibus singulorum non solum quantitas et qualitas delicti, sed aetas, scientia, et sexus atque conditio delinquentis sunt attendenda, et non solum secundum praedicta, sed secundum locum et tempus, quo delictum committitur, unicuique poenitentia debet indici, quum, sicut tu ipse non ignoras, idem excessus magis sit in uno quam in alio puniendus*". Cfr. Lotte Kéry, "Non enim homines de occultis, sed de manifestis iudicant. La culpabilité dans le droit pénal de l'Église à l'époque classique," *RDC* 80 (2003), pp. 311–336, 322 ff.; Lotte Kéry, *Gottesfurcht und irdische Strafe: Der Beitrag des mittelalterlichen Kirchenrechts zur Entstehung des öffentlichen Strafrechts* (Cologne: Böhlau, 2006), p. 386 f.

36 Colin Morris, *The Discovery of the Individual, 1050–1200* (Toronto: University of Toronto Press, 1972), pp. 76–79, explained this with the centrality of the intellectual desire of the time for self-knowledge.

37 See Odon Lottin, *Psychologie et morale aux XIIe et XIIIe siècles*, 6 vols (Louvain/Gembloux: César/Duculout, 1946–1960), 4:309–486; Sara Menzinger, "Finzioni dei canoni: Natura, realtà e finzione nella canonistica del XII secolo," *Reti Medievali Rivista* 21 (2020), pp. 203–241, published online: March 29, 2020, DOI: 10.6092/1593-2214/6727, p. 206; Sara Menzinger, *Finzioni del diritto medievale* (Macerata: Quodlibet, 2023).

38 Cf. Stephan Kuttner, *Kanonistische Schuldlehre von Gratian bis auf die Dekretalen Gregors IX: Systematisch auf Grund der handschriftlichen Quellen dargestellt* (Vatican City: BAV, 1935); Kéry, *Gottesfurcht*. This can be seen, for example, in the Christian contribution to the development of the concept of *mens rea* as a requirement for criminal liability, which implies an inquiry into the intention of the accused: David McIlroy, "Christianity, mens rea and the boundaries of criminal liability," in *Christianity and Criminal Law*, ed. Mark Hill et al. (London: Routledge, 2020). At the same time, questions were being asked about whether people should be punished for their intentions or private opinions: Gillian R. Evans, *Law and Theology in the Middle Ages* (London: Routledge, 2002), p. 143, who links this issue question to concerns about occult crimes, i.e. crimes that could not be easily proven, such as sexual offences. See also Elizabeth Papp Kamali, *Felony and the Guilty Mind in Medieval England* (Cambridge: Cambridge University Press, 2020).

most effective procedural tool for investigating the psychological element.[39] The moral debate on the role of intention in determining the nature of will and actions is echoed in several passages of the *Perpendiculum*: not only in the *Summula*, but also in several brocards of Part II.[40]

Returning to the structure of the *Summula*, after the treatment of presumptions relating to uncertain facts (II–V), the work goes on to analyze the uncertainty arising from a law or a document (VI). This section is remarkable in several aspects. First of all, unlike the previous parts, it is not divided into *loci* or *pro-contra* brocards: instead, it takes a discursive form in order to explain the possible criteria of interpretation. This, in turn, is extremely relevant because it explicitly describes the logical method used by jurists in distinguishing between different cases. On the case of a new controversy on the interpretation of the law which had never been resolved before, the *Summula* provides a long gloss instructing the lawyer on how to defeat an adversary in court, referring to the criteria established by Isidore of Seville and incorporated into the *Decretum* as D.4 c.2.[41] If, on the other hand, the uncertainty in the interpretation of the law is due to the conflicting opinions of previous jurists, the *Summula* outlines a hierarchy of criteria that the reader should follow: first, the opinion of the elders; secondly, that of the majority or of the best men; finally, in case of conflict between the majority and the strongest authorities, the former should be followed.

After the section on interpretation, the treatment of presumptions on three other subjects is added to the *Summula*, in three additional parts: one on the validity of documents in which some falsehood is found (VII); another on the ownership of goods in possession of a priest, in dispute between the latter and the Church (VIII); and one on the cases in which a presumption does not admit evidence to the contrary (IX). This last part, as we shall see, is the most significant for the history of legal thought because of its innovative theorizations. It is noteworthy that these three sections differ in structure and style from the previous ones: although they follow a brocardic pattern, like sections II–V, the

39 I will deal with this in detail in De Concilio, "Imputer l'intention."

40 Below, *Summula de presumptionibus*, III, 5, and in entire sections IV and V; Part II, brocards nos. 3–5 and 7–10. I have addressed this matter in David De Concilio, "Soggettività e qualificazione del fatto. L'indagine del factum intrinsecum tra diritto e teologia nel XII secolo: due casi di studio e spunti per una ricerca," *Historia et Ius* 22 (2022), paper 9, pp. 1–42, repr. in *Tra diritto e religione. Dialoghi e influenze nella storia giuridica*, ed. Marta Cerrito and Francesco Di Chiara (Rome: Historia et Ius, 2023).

41 On the textual problems of this passage, see below, pp. 73–74.

organization of these brocards is different: they do not represent *loci loicales*, but rather groups of legal arguments, and unlike the previous parts, these arguments are clearly divided into two groups of *pro-contra* sources.

At the end of the work, a final statement expresses the author's purpose and method. This plumb line (*perpendiculum*), he says, does not contain truths, but *probabilia* and *apparentia*: a statement that, as I have shown elsewhere, tells us much about the conceptual framework behind scholastic and legal argumentation, which conceived judicial truth as the most probable truth among different degrees of probability.[42] Moreover, the author claims that he wrote the work for the benefit of the orator in a disputation, to establish legal presumptions for and against each case. Finally, he also states that he did not distinguish explicitly between *pro* and *contra argumenta*: it is rather up to the reader to diligently identify the nature of the allegations.[43]

The concluding section of the *Summula* is significant in many respects. Firstly, the use of the word '*perpendiculum*' (plumb line, but also mason's rule or carpenter's square)[44] as a descriptive image for his work is an interesting choice. In the absence of explanations, we can only guess at the intention behind this word by looking at the use of the term in medieval literature. There, we find that the word '*perpendiculum*' (similarly to '*norma*' and '*regula*')[45] was sometimes used in a figurative sense, meaning a "guide to correctness," just as an actual plumb line was a guide for a mason;[46] moreover, a figurative use of the word can be traced back to antiquity.[47] Perhaps the most significant examples of this use are provided by two ecclesiastical writings. The first is *De rerum naturis* (or

---

42 See De Concilio, *Via Brocardica*, 1:175–182.

43 See below, *Summula de presumptionibus*, X, 3. As we have seen, however, the author did in fact make a clear distinction between *pro* and *contra* in sections VII–X.

44 Cf. DMLBS, s.v. "perpendiculum."

45 Cf., for example, Isidore of Seville, *Etymologiarum sive Originum*, ed. Wallace M. Lindsay (Oxford: Clarendon Press, 1911), VI, xvii, 1–2: "*Canon autem Graece, Latine regula nuncupatur. Regula autem dicta, quod recte ducit, nec aliquando aliorsum trahit. Alii dixerunt regulam dictam vel quod regat, vel quod normam recte vivendi praebeat, vel quod distortum parvumque quid corrigat.*" For a translation, see Isidore of Seville, *The Etymologies of Isidore of Seville*, ed. and trans. Stephen A. Barney, Jennifer Beach, W.J. Lewis, Oliver Berghof, and Muriel Hall (Cambridge: Cambridge University Press, 2006).

46 See DMLBS, s.v. "perpendiculum." The example cited included several passages in the work of Aldhelm, bishop of Sherborne (d. 709), as well as a passage from John of Oxnead (d. c. 1293), which testifies to the longevity of this figure of speech.

47 Cf. Egidio Forcellini et al., eds., *Lexicon totius Latinitatis*, 6 vols, 2nd ed. (Padua: Typis Seminarii, 1940), s.v. "perpendiculum;" Charlton T. Lewis and Charles Short, eds., *A Latin*

De Universo), written in 847 A.D. by the Frankish monk Rabanus Maurus. In a chapter on carpentry tools, Rabanus writes about measuring instruments: the square (*norma*), the rule (*regula*), and the plumb line (*perpendiculum*). Following the example of Isidore of Seville,[48] Rabanus explains that if everything is not done with these tools, the building will be faulty.[49] Rabanus also gives an allegorical interpretation of the tools: his whole work, he says, has been composed according to the rule of righteous faith and the plumb line of sound doctrine.[50] The analogy is later adopted by a political work called *Perpendiculum* (or *Polypticum*) by Atto, bishop of Vercelli (c. 885–961 A.D.), written between 952 and 958 A.D.[51] Under the influence of Rabanus,[52] in one of the glosses to the only manuscript, the title of Atto's work is explained as a metaphor: the *perpendiculum* is a measuring instrument (*normam*), and if everything on a building site is not done with it, the building will be full of defects.[53] We can try to apply these useful insights into the rhetorical use of the word to the *Summula* by linking them to the methodological indications that the author gives in the conclusions. The '*perpendiculum*' (i.e. the *Summula*) could then be the measuring instrument that allows the orator, like a mason, to avoid making mistakes when constructing the arguments for legal disputation. Although it is impossible to go beyond speculation, the choice of the word '*perpendiculum*' in the *Summula* draws a comparison between the scholastic method of disputation and architecture which modern scholarship has also attempted to establish.[54] It is also

---

Dictionary (Oxford: Oxford University Press, 1879; repr. 1933), s.v. "perpendiculum;" Alexander Souter, ed., *A Glossary of Later Latin to 600 A.D.* (Oxford: Clarendon Press, 1949), s.v. "perpendiculum."

48 Isidore of Seville, *Etymologiarum*, XIX, xviii, 1–2.

49 Rabanus Maurus, *De rerum naturis*, PL 111:9–612, XXI, xi, 1–2.

50 Rabanus Maurus, *De rerum naturis*, XXI, xi, 2: "*ut omnia opera nostra secundum sanctarum Scripturarum traditionem et regulam rectae fidei, perpendiculumque sanae doctrinae faciamus.*"

51 See Atto of Vercelli, *Polipticum quod appellatur Perpendiculum*, ed. and trans. Giacomo Vignodelli, 2 vols (Florence: SISMEL-Edizioni del Galluzzo, 2019); Giacomo Vignodelli, *Il filo a piombo: il Perpendiculum di Attone di Vercelli e la storia politica del regno italico* (Spoleto, 2011).

52 Cf. Atto, *Polipticum*, 2:72–73.

53 Atto, *Polipticum*, 1:229: "*Perpendiculum: normam. Perpendiculum quidem est quod semper adtenditur, denique in fabrica, nisi omnia ad perpendiculum fiant, cuncta mendosa construuntur. Perpendiculum namque aeditor et hunc vult appellare libellum, in quo noxia redarguere et honesta sanccire disponit.*" An Italian translation is given in Atto, *Polipticum*, 2:7.

54 Erwin Panofsky, *Gothic Architecture and Scholasticism* (Latrobe: Archabbey Press, 1951); Charles Radding and William Clark, *Medieval Architecture, Medieval Learning: Builders and Masters in the Age of Romanesque and Gothic* (New Haven/London: Yale University

significant that, while the other two architectural words used by Isidore and Rabanus (*norma* and *regula*) have retained a figurative legal meaning to this day (norm and rule), '*perpendiculum*' has not, and our collection is allegedly the only work in which the term is used in a legal sense.

The second element of great significance that we find at the end of the *Summula* are the brief methodological indications given by its author. They constitute one of the earliest—if not the earliest—descriptions of the *pro-contra* brocardic method that we know of. The author of the *Summula* states that he did not apply dialectical argumentation to legal sources in order to reach an objective and certain interpretation—as was done, we might add, in other *pro-contra* genres that sought to resolve the opposition, such as the *quaestio*; he wanted to produce, in his own words, *probabilia et apparentia*. Moreover, the fact that the author dedicates the *Summula* to the "orator more than the judge" tells us that the aim of these *probabilia* was eminently practical: to train lawyers in the normative sources and to enable them to argue dialectically for and against each case in the courtroom, which was what practice required.[55] Indeed, it is the specific choice of the word '*orator*' instead of '*rhetor*' that tells us that the main target of the *Summula* was the lawyer, thus implying a forensic connotation of the purpose of the work.[56] And in order to argue both ways, it was necessary for lawyers to treat the sources not as the embodiment of an absolute truth, but rather as repositories of two opposing probabilities. In turn, the reason for this practical necessity and this relativistic approach, both in courts and in the schools, lies in the very design of the Romano-canonical procedure, which was based on a dialectical structure of two opposing positions: as *ars opponendi et respondendi*, where the aim is not to reveal an absolute truth, but rather to establish a relative one, based on the activity of the two parties.[57]

Press, 1994); Emanuele Conte, "Il Digesto fuori dal Digesto," in *Interpretare il Digesto: Storia e metodi*, ed. Antonio Padoa-Schioppa and Dario Mantovani (Pavia: IUSS Press, 2014), p. 280.

55 More extensively on this point, see De Concilio, *Via Brocardica*, 1:209–213.

56 Cf. the difference between the two figures drawn by Gaius Marius Victorinus, *Commenta in Ciceronis Rhetorica*, ed. Thomas Riesenweber (Berlin: De Gruyter, 2013), p. 3, lines 17–20: "*Dicendum etiam uidetur, quae distantia sit inter rhetorem, sophistam et oratorem. Rhetor est, qui docet litteras atque artes tradit eloquentiae; sophista est, apud quem dicendi exercitium discitur; orator est, qui in causis priuatis ac publicis plena et perfecta utitur eloquentia.*"

57 On the *ordo iudicii* as *ordo eloquendi*, see Alessandro Giuliani, *Il concetto di prova: Contributo alla logica giuridica* (Milan: Giuffrè, 1961), pp. 115–158; Alessandro Giuliani, "L'ordo

Nevertheless, the *Summula*'s 'practical' outlook should not lead us to underestimate the abstract and theoretical significance of the work. In fact, this remarkable feat implies a deep and systematic knowledge of the normative sources, which was equally necessary to draw from them both the arguments for disputation and new legal concepts.[58] In other words, the *Summula de praesumptionibus* demonstrates how the new canon law science provided clerics with the legal reasoning—what Boureau defined as "judicial abstraction"[59]—for their practical and intellectual aims.[60]

In light of what we have seen so far, the *Summula* seems to consist of three different layers, which differ in style, structure, and argumentation techniques: one on the uncertainties of facts (II–VI), one on the interpretation of laws and documents (VII), and one on other types of presumptions considered relevant by the author (VIII–IX). This gives the impression that the *Summula* is the result of an 'alluvial' process of collection of topics on presumptions, although they were all included in the same editorial project from the beginning, as evidenced by the fact that all the sections appear in all the manuscripts of the *Summula* (except fragments), and that they were framed by an introduction and a conclusion.

Finally, with regard to the legal allegations, we can see that the *Summula* cites mostly sources of canon law, which of course usually come from Gratian's

---

iudiciarius medioevale," *Rivista di diritto processuale* 43 (1988), pp. 598–614; Alessandro Giuliani, "Osservazioni sulla procedura nel metodo dialettico: dalla tradizione aristotelica a quella medievale," in *L'educazione giuridica. 6. Modelli storici della procedura continentale; 2. Dall'ordo iudicarius al codice di procedura*, ed. Alessandro Giuliani and Nicola Picardi (Napoli: Ed. Scientifiche Italiane, 1994).

58 Alain Boureau, *L'Empire du livre: Pour une histoire du savoir scolastique (1200–1380)* (Paris: Belles Lettres, 2007), pp. 183–184, highlighted how these two aspects were complementary in scholastic culture: universal abstractions required empirical verifications, and casuistry aspired to universality.

59 Alain Boureau, *La loi du royaume: Les moines, le droit et la construction de la nation anglaise (XIe–XIIIe siècles)* (Paris: Belles Lettres, 2001), pp. 18–19.

60 Cf. also Conte, *Diritto comune*, p. 38 and Conte, "La France," pp. 33 ff. A similar use of normative sources has been highlighted by Emanuele Conte, "Ordo iudicii et regula iuris: Bulgarus et les origines de la culture juridique (XIIe siècle)," in *Frontières des savoirs en Italie à l'époque des premières universités*, ed. Joel Chandelier and Aurélien Robert (Rome: École française de Rome, 2015), pp. 171–175, and especially 173–174, who suggested that the Rhenish reception of Bulgarus's *regulae iuris*, adapted by Bertrandus Metensis in a similar commentary, could be explained by the need to provide the Cologne school with universal propositions extracted from the body of Justinian's codification, according to the composite approach of that cultural milieu.

Decretum; it is worth noting that, of the hundreds of allegations in this work, not a single one refers to a *palea*, that is, to one of the later additions to the *Concordia*.[61] This element is consistent with the possible time and place of composition of the *Summula*, i.e. the French schools of the 1170s. In fact, *paleae* are largely absent from the French manuscripts of the *Decretum* copied in this period, and most of them seem to have been introduced in Bologna in the 1180s.[62]

Moreover, the *Summula* sometimes uses canons that were not included in Gratian's work, citing the *Decretum* (1012–1023) of Burchard of Worms.[63] With regard to this last work, we should not be particularly surprised to find it among our author's sources: at that time, Burchard's collection was still in circulation and in use, especially in episcopal contexts.[64]

---

61 Two *paleae* are cited by only a minority of manuscripts: D.23 c.13 by G, L, and Mu2 on IV, 7.7; C.16 q.1 c.45 by C on V, 7.7. For the analysis of the *paleae* to Gratian's *Decretum* see Jürgen Buchner, *Die Paleae im Dekret Gratians: Untersuchung ihrer Echtheit* (Rome: Pontificium Athenaeum Antonianum, 2000).

62 Although manuscript studies of the tradition of the *Decretum* do not allow for more precise paleographical evaluations in this respect, on this point in general see Anders Winroth, "Sankt Gallen, Stiftsbibliothek, 673 in Context: Twelfth-Century Transformations and Abbreviations of Gratian's Decretum," in *Creating and Sharing Legal Knowledge in the Twelfth Century: Sankt Gallen, Stiftsbibliothek, 673 and Its Context*, ed. Stephan Dusil and Andreas Thier (Leiden: Brill, 2022); John C. Wei, "Gratian's Decretum in France and Halberstadt," in *Rechtshandschriften des deutschen Mittelalters: Produktionsorte und Importwege*, ed. Patrizia Carmassi and Gisela Drossbach (Wiesbaden: Harrassowitz, 2015); John C. Wei, *Π-group (P-group)*, available at https://web.archive.org/web/20210415052423/https://sites.google.com/site/repertoriumiuriscanonici/home/gratian/p-group, accessed 2024 May 29; Rudolf Weigand, "Paleae und andere Zusätze in Dekrethandschriften mit dem Glossenapparat Ordinaturus Magister," AKKR 159 (1990), pp. 448–463.

63 Burchard of Worms, *Burchardi Wormatiensis ecclesiae episcopi decretorum libri XX: Ergänzter Neudruck der Editio princeps Köln 1548*, ed. Gérard Fransen and Theo Kölzer (Aalen: Scientia Verlag, 1992). A forthcoming new edition is planned by the project *Burchards Dekret Digital* of the University of Kassel.

64 Greta Austin, *Shaping Church Law Around the Year 1000. The Decretum of Burchard of Worms* (Farnham: Ashgate, 2009), pp. 20–29. See also Hartmut Hoffmann and Rudolf Pokorny, *Das Dekret des Bischofs Burchard von Worms: Textstufen—frühe Verbreitung—Vorlagen* (Munich: Monumenta Germaniae Historica, 1991); Detlev Jasper, "Burchards Dekret in der Sicht der Gregorianer," in *Bischof Burchard von Worms. 1000–1025*, ed. Wilfried Hartmann (Mainz: Selbstverlag der Gesellschaft für Mittelrheinische Kirchengeschichte, 2000); Peter Landau, "Vorgratianische Kanonessammlungen bei Dekretisten und in frühen Dekretalensammlungen," in *Proceedings of the Eighth International Congress of Medieval Canon Law: San Diego, University of California at La Jolla, 21–27 August 1988*, ed. Stanley Chodorow (Vatican City: BAV, 1992).

The few citations that do not come from canon law are either Roman norms from the *Corpus Iuris Civilis* (Code and Digest) or moral *auctoritates* such as the Bible. Marginal glosses, which include references to the Gospels and to concepts from the *artes liberales*, are rare in the manuscripts.[65]

1.3 *Part II:* Brocarda "Introductis publica utilitate"

Returning to the subdivision of the *Perpendiculum*, its second part is a set of 26 *pro-contra* brocards which immediately follows the *Summula* in ten out of eleven manuscripts containing the latter. This element may suggest that the two parts were meant to circulate together and were probably written in close succession.

Moreover, the textual tradition of this part is fairly uniform: the majority of manuscripts (A, Ba, F, L, Ma, Mu1, Vb, and Vp) place the 26 brocards in the same order. The only exceptions in this group are the interpolation of another brocard in Ma (between nos. 12 and 13) and the repetition of brocard no. 7 in the third part of the *Perpendiculum* in two manuscripts (F and Ma, as nos. 86 and 79, respectively). Two other manuscripts (G and P1) follow the same progressive order of the brocards, but twelve of them (nos. 3, 4, 6–8, 12–14, and 23–26) are missing. In P1, however, the missing brocards in Part II (except for no. 26) are inserted in Part III, at nos. 92–103: we can assume that the scribe of P1, after copying from a manuscript derived from the same archetype used for G,[66] used a second antigraph to integrate the missing parts.[67]

There are four manuscripts that do not follow the above order. In manuscript C, for example, the order of the brocards in Part II is almost completely different, except for the first and last two brocards, and it is interspersed with two small series of brocards from Part III. Something similar can be said for two other manuscripts, O and P2, where we can note three main aspects: firstly, the brocards belonging to Part II do not follow the standard order; secondly,

65 On fol. 114^{r}, Vp cites Lk 18, Lk 11:5 and Paul's letters; on fol. 114^{v}, the rhetorical system of circumstances (Durant W. Robertson jr., "A Note on the Classical Origin of 'Circumstances' in the Medieval Confessional," *Studies in Philology* 43, no. 1 (1946), pp. 6–14) and a reference to Cicero's system of *attributa personarum* (Cicero, *De inventione*, ed. and trans. Harry M. Hubbell (Cambridge, Massachusetts: Harvard University Press/London: Heinemann, 1949), I.24.34).

66 That G and P1 derive from the same archetype is confirmed by a careful analysis of their significant variants, both in Parts I and II, which also supports the idea of a common geographical provenance: see above, p. 18.

67 This is not the only manuscript in which the scribe of the *Perpendiculum* seems to have used and collated different antigraphs: the same can also be hypothesized for Vb, as mentioned below, p. 38.

they appear in sequences alternating with brocards from Part III; thirdly, some brocards are missing (only one in O, fourteen in P2). Furthermore, it should be noted that O contains only the rubrics of the brocards, without the allegations and mostly without the *contraria*, which reveals a very different editorial project: the collection of maxims, rather than arguments. Finally, in the small fragment A1, we find only one brocard from Part II.[68]

The standard order of the brocards seems to follow, at least in part, a logical criterion by subject: interspersed with rubrics on different subjects, we find groups of brocards linked by the same themes: intention and will (nos. 3–5), consent and agreement (nos. 7–10), ignorance (nos. 11–14),[69] and the validity of acts (18–21). This suggests that, unlike Part III, the brocards in Part II were not randomly grouped and were intended to circulate together: another clue that strengthens the idea of an editorial project.

Moreover, like the *Summula*, Part II cites only Gratian's *Decretum* and no later sources of canon law, with the notable exception of an allegation transmitted by F and Ma which refers to the decretal *Sicut Romana ecclesia* (JL 12293 = WH 944), or rather to one of the parts into which this decretal was divided by the collections of the time (beg. "*Preterea*" = 1 Comp. 1.21.6 = X. 1.29.5),[70] cited by these two manuscripts as "some extravagant decretal to the bishop of Sens."[71]

The study of Part II of the *Perpendiculum* is significant in many ways. On the one hand, the relative uniformity of its manuscript tradition, which I have just outlined, suggests a possible common and standardized editorial project

68 I have called A1 a small fragment of eight brocards, seven of which belong to Part III, interpolated in the *Quaestiones Aschaffenburgenses* of the same manuscript (see below, pp. 93 and 133–134), on fols. 200^{rc}–201ra.

69 On the problem of ignorance and its excusability, see Odon Lottin, *Psychologie et morale*, 3:56–92; Christophe Grellard, *La possibilità dell'errore: Pensare la tolleranza nel Medioevo* (Canterano: Aracne, 2020), pp. 21–52; Christophe Grellard, "Que m'est-il permis d'ignorer? La foi, l'ignorance et les limites acceptables de l'orthodoxie," in *Genèses antiques et médiévales de la foi*, ed. Christophe Grellard, Philippe Hoffman, and Laurent Lavaud (Paris: Institut d'études Augustiniennes, 2020); Christophe Grellard, "L'erreur invincible et le problème sceptique à la fin du Moyen Age," in *Irrtum—Error—Erreur*, ed. Andreas Speer and Maxime Mauriège (Berlin: de Gruyter, 2018); Christophe Grellard, "Systèmes de pensées et de croyances médiévaux," *Annuaire de l'École pratique des hautes études* (EPHE), *Section des sciences religieuses* 125 (2018), pp. 293–300.

70 On this point, see [Pier V. Aimone Braida], *Prolegomena*, in Simon de Bisignano, *Summa in Decretum*, pp. LXXIV–LXXV.

71 See below, *Perpendiculum*, Part II, no. 26.24.

between Parts I and II, if not a common paternity. On the other hand, one of its brocards, which I have numbered as 17, offers several clues as to the origin, textual tradition, and intellectual connections of the collection.[72]

This "brocard" is more precisely a short text on acquisitive prescription[73] and is the only discursive passage in Part II.[74] The text is introduced by the phrase: "In these last chapters, note, my dearest, what you have asked." The significance of this sentence is twofold: firstly, the words "last chapters" clearly link Part II with the *Summula*; secondly, the expression "my dearest" suggests that the author was addressing his work to someone in particular. Certainly, the *Summula* is full of recommendations and exhortations in the second person singular, but this could also be a rhetorical device; however, the use of the vocative adjective "*karissime*" and the mention of a specific request suggest otherwise, although we will never know who the addressee of the collection was.

The most interesting aspect of brocard no. 17, however, is its relationship to another text: a gloss signed "Jo." attributed to the Bolognese canonist Ioannes Faventinus (fl. 1171–1190).[75] Ioannes's gloss is very similar to the text of the *Perpendiculum*: the incipit is identical, word for word, and both texts contain the same allegations.[76] However, the version given by Part II is much longer

---

72 See below, *Perpendiculum*, Part II, no. 17.

73 On acquisitive prescription in medieval times, see Harry Dondorp, David Ibbetson, and Eltjo J.H. Schrage, eds., *Limitation and Prescription: A Comparative Legal History* (Berlin: Duncker & Humblot, 2019), and especially Harry Dondorp, "Limitation and Prescription in Justinian's Corpus Iuris Civilis," Ibid.; Emanuele Conte, "Lapse of Time in Medieval Laws: Procedure, Prescription, Presumptions, Custom," Ibid.; and Harry Dondorp, "Prescription and Limitation in Medieval Canon Law," Ibid.

74 See below, *Perpendiculum*, Part II, no. 17.

75 On Ioannes, see Andrea Bettetini, "Giovanni da Faenza (Johannes Faventinus)," in *DBGI*, 1:1013–1014; Norbert Höhl, "Wer war Johannes Faventinus? Neue Erkenntnisse zu Leben und Werk eines bedeutendsten Dekretisten des 12. Jahrhunderts," in Chodorow, *Proceedings San Diego*.

76 Rudolf Weigand, "Die Glossen des Johannes Faventinus zur Causa 1 des Dekrets und ihr Vorkommen in späteren Glossenapparaten," AKKR 157 (1988), pp. 73–107, 86–87 no. 15, v. *gravamen … ex usu* to C.1 q.1 c.124: "*Idest non consuescat, uel ex usu, scilicet preterito quasi ratione prescriptionis angarias sacerdotibus non imponat. Cum enim de aliquarum rerum prescriptione agitur inspiciendum est utrum communi iure talia a talibus possideri ualeant nec ne. Primo casu sola longe usurpationis detentione currit prescriptio ut infra xvi. Q. iii. et iiii. per totum, saluo eo quod de limitibus dicitur C. e. Q. e. Licet* (*et C.*) *Jnter memoratos* (*C.16 q.3 cc.5,6*). *Secundo casu non currit; prescriptio enim ius creatum aduocat, nouum autem non creat* (*ut*) *infra xxxiii. Q. v. Quod deo* (*c.4*) *et di. c. Contra morem* (*D.100 c.8*) *et supra di. xxiii. Jllud autem* (*c.5*) *et infra xvi. Q. i. C. ult* (*c.68*) *et Q. iii. § Potest etiam* (*p.c.15*) *et Q. vii. Decimas* (*c.1*) *et infra e. Q. iii. Quesitum* (*c.4*). *Jn his omnibus et* (*in*) *aliis infinitis casibus prescriptio euanescit, quia non est proditum ius commune scriptum uel non scriptum, quo tales talia ualeant possidere. Jo.*"

than the gloss because it provides examples of the kind of goods that could be acquired by *praescriptio*. Moreover, in contrast to the gloss, the text of Part II has a clear *pro-contra* structure; finally, they end with different formulations. Despite the obvious differences, the striking similarities between these two texts cannot be ignored: later in the study I will analyze their possible implications.[77]

Finally, this piece is a very interesting text not only because of the relationship between the *Perpendiculum* and Ioannes Faventinus, but also because of its legal content, since it attempts to set some limits on the possibility of acquiring a right or a thing by prescription. A certain thing or right—the brocard explains—can only be acquired by prescription if it is held by someone who has a common right[78] to hold things of the same kind: in other words, only if it is held by possession and not by mere detention. For example, a priest can acquire by prescription the right to collect tithes, but a layman certainly cannot. This was a highly topical issue for 12th-century practice, as the consolidation of secular powers at that time led to the questioning of several factual situations of possession and detention of wealth.[79]

1.4 *Part III:* Brocarda "Levius punitur" *or* "Principium spectandum"

Part III was probably composed a few years after the rest, and while Parts I and II have a relatively uniform tradition, we conveniently use its name to refer to an agglomeration of arguments whose number, order, and content vary exceptionally from one manuscript to another. This should therefore not be considered as a definite, standardized, and closed work, but rather as a work in progress, an 'alluvial,' open, and non-definitive group of texts:[80] a "*texte vivant*," to use a term dear to legal historians.[81]

77 See below, pp. 67–71.

78 Here, the term "*ius commune*" can be understood as a synonym for the combination of *ius naturale* and *ius gentium*, as opposed to *ius civile*, following a tradition going back to Ulpian: v. Dig. 1.1.6pr; cf. also Ennio Cortese, *La norma giuridica: Spunti teorici nel diritto comune classico* (Milan: Giuffrè, 1964; repr. Rome: Senato della Repubblica, 2020), p. 64 and Ibid., n. 75.

79 See, for example, the widespread use of acquisitive prescription to justify the creation of bonds of serfdom in 12th- and 13th-century Italy: Emanuele Conte, *Servi medievali: Dinamiche del diritto comune* (Rome: Viella, 1996), *passim*.

80 Gouron, "Une école de canonistes," p. 64, suggested that it could be the result of a 'laboratory' of students in the same school.

81 It was Stephan Kuttner, "Notes on the Roman Meeting, on Planning and Method," *Traditio* 11 (1955), pp. 431–439, 437 who was the first to use this expression for many works of the Glossators: "We have frequently to do with works that have undergone multiple recension, rewriting, and enlargement at the hand of the author and/or his students."

Many of these texts recur in other manuscripts and often circulated together. Looking at these recurring patterns, it is possible to identify some small and relatively standard series of brocards that appear in the same order in different manuscripts. Hence, in an attempt to shed some light on their tradition, I have divided this recurring content into eleven series of brocards.[82] On the basis of these sets, we can also outline a major distinction between two groups of manuscripts: those beginning with α (beg.: *"Levius punitur qui commissum sponte confitetur;"* mss. A, G, L, Mu1, and P1) and those beginning with β (beg.: *"Principium spectandum;"* mss. Ba, F, Ma, and O; the mss. A1 and P2 begin with the same group but with different brocards). The three exceptions, which begin with different series, are C, Vb, and Vp.

If we look carefully at these eleven series and at the brocards that appear only in one manuscript, we can draw some conclusions about the origin of the text. The general impression is that Part III consists of several collections of arguments of different origins. These collections, which often circulated together in the transmontane schools, were appended to the *Perpendiculum* by different compilers, each of whom inserted the texts according to his needs and the sources at his disposal.[83] In some cases, the groups of texts recur relatively frequently; in the case of P1 and Vb, it seems that the scribes had different copies of the *Perpendiculum* on their hands, containing partly different groups of brocards, which they decided to collate.[84]

Regarding Part III as transmitted by P1 and Vb, there are other notable considerations. Firstly, in both manuscripts this part is considerably longer than in the others, and they contain large series of brocards not found in any other manuscript, thus illustrating the great variety of the tradition. As for P1, there is also a long group of brocards (beg. *"Nullus archidiaconus"*) interspersed between those of Part III (fols. 33va–35vb), which, because of its characteristics, can be considered a separate collection rather than part of the ensemble.[85] As far

82 The series are identified by the letters α, β, γ, δ, ε, ζ, η, θ, κ, λ, μ: see below, p. 127.

83 This method corresponds to what has been defined as the "user's perspective," i.e. collections of normative texts arranged according to the needs and objectives of their users: Conte, *Diritto comune*, p. 55.

84 As far as P1 is concerned, this is suggested by the fact that the brocards missing from Part II (which follows the same tradition as G) have been interpolated later, between β and μ. In Vb, on the other hand, many rubrics are repeated in more than one group (sometimes in a different form), which could suggest that the scribe of the Sidonian manuscript collated more than one copy without paying attention to the repetitions.

85 See below, pp. 43–44.

as Vb is concerned, we can date the final compilation of this variant not too many years after the early 1180s.[86] Apart from its length (partly due to the many repetitions), this codex is remarkable because it is the only manuscript that contains the entire ensemble of works textually linked to the *Perpendiculum* and attributed by Gouron to the same author.[87]

The characteristics outlined above lead to some suggestions. Firstly, the open and dynamic nature of the text shows how our contemporary notion of authorship is, in many contexts, alien to the medieval mentality: an aspect emphasized by the anonymity of many of these transmontane authors.[88] Secondly, the extremely layered composition of the collection(s) is evidence of an encyclopedic culture typical of their transmontane ecclesiastical context.[89] The compilers of the third part of the *Perpendiculum*, as is common for the earliest collections of brocards in the second half of the 12th century,[90] were interested in collecting as many *argumenta* as possible, without any systematic purpose: their main concern was the creation of broad repositories for legal disputation. In this respect, the authors of Part III seem to have had a different approach from that of the author of the *Summula*, which was much more homogeneous.

This last consideration is confirmed by the heterogeneous nature of Part III: while the first two parts are consistently characterized by a *pro-contra* structure and a common style, this part is a combination of arguments with and without *contraria*, according to the fashion typical of the earliest collections

86 First, because this manuscript occasionally cites papal decretals of Alexander III (d. 1181), as already noted by Kuttner, "Réflexions," p. 773 n. 24, but none of the later pontiffs: cf. the argument above, pp. 11–12. Second, because its brocard no. 182 refers to C.35 q.6 c.2 as "*decreto Celestini*:" this text is a *palea*, and the fact that it is not cited as part of the *Decretum* suggests that, at the time of the composition of this variant, it was not still incorporated into Gratian's work, hence before the 1180s.

87 See below, pp. 94–95.

88 Cf. Sara Menzinger, "Riflessioni sul rapporto tra autore e testo nella produzione giuridica medievale," *Historia et ius* 11 (2017), paper 23, pp. 1–18.

89 This attitude is well illustrated by the motto of the school of St Victor: "Learn everything. You will see that nothing is useless; there is no pleasure in a restricted science." See Hugh of St Victor, *Hugonis de Sancto Victore Didascalicon De studio legendi. A Critical Text*, ed. Charles H. Buttimer (Washington, D.C.: The Catholic University Press, 1939), VI, 3, p. 115 (= PL 176:801A); translation by Dominique Poirel, "Reading and Educating Oneself in the 12th: Hugh of Saint-Victor's Didascalicon," in *A Companion to Twelfth-Century Schools*, ed. Cédric Giraud (Leiden: Brill, 2020), p. 113. On the maxim, cf. Dominique Poirel, "'Apprends tout': Saint-Victor et le milieu des Victorins à Paris, 1108–1330," in *Lieux de savoir*, ed. Christian Jacob, 1 (Paris: Albin Michel, 2007).

90 See De Concilio, *Via Brocardica*, 1:52–54, and 2:7–16.

of brocards.[91] We should also consider the presence of many other short non-brocardic texts that circulated together with the *Perpendiculum*, often interspersed between its three main parts, or appended to it, often in more than one manuscript and in the same order: *distinctiones, notae, tractatus*. The *Perpendiculum* can therefore be understood as an ensemble of dialectical and rhetorical legal devices, consisting of many works, rather than as a single work of brocards. We could apply to this collection (as well as to many other late 12th-century brocardic collections) the same label of "*recueils factices*" that has been used to describe the haphazard and irregular modes of composition of the collections of *quaestiones* of the period.[92] These characteristics make the *Perpendiculum* a work at the turning point of the profound transformations that the brocardic genre underwent during this period. The earliest collections of *brocardica* were, in fact, mostly repositories of legal arguments of various kinds, containing not only brocards in the strict sense, but also any text that their compilers considered useful for disputation: *distinctiones, notabilia*, etc.; it is only from the 1170s and 1180s that the genre took its stable form, thanks to more systematic compilations of legal maxims with *pro-contra* arguments.[93] As far as the *Perpendiculum* is concerned, while its first two parts more closely resemble a homogeneous and coherent work of the kind that would be produced in the last two decades of the century, the third part and the other interpolated pieces are still a patchwork, very similar to the earliest examples of the genre.

91 Ibid.

92 Gérard Fransen, "La structure des 'Quaestiones disputatae' et leur classement," *Traditio* 23 (1967), pp. 516–534, repr. in Fransen, *Canones et Quaestiones*, 1.2, p. 517. On the limits of this definition, see Orazio Condorelli, "Note su formazione e diffusione delle raccolte di quaestiones disputatae in diritto canonico (secoli XII–XIV)," in *Juristische Buchproduktion im Mittelalter*, ed. Vincenzo Colli (Frankfurt am Main: Klostermann, 2002), p. 398. On collections of *quaestiones*, in addition to the literature cited above, p. 21 n. 17, see Manlio Bellomo, *I fatti e il diritto tra le certezze e i dubbi dei giuristi medievali (secoli XIII–XIV)* (Rome: Il Cigno Galileo Galilei, 2000); Manlio Bellomo, "'Factum' e 'ius': Tra le certezze e i dubbi del pensiero giuridico medievale," *RIDC* 6 (1996), pp. 21–45, repr. in Bellomo, *Medioevo edito e inedito*, 2 (Rome: Il Cigno Galileo Galilei, 1997); Manlio Bellomo, "Legere, repetere, disputare: Introduzione ad una ricerca sulle 'quaestiones' civilistiche," in Manlio Bellomo, *Aspetti dell'insegnamento giuridico nelle Università medievali. Le 'quaestiones disputatae'* (Reggio Calabria: Parallelo 38, 1974), repr. in Bellomo, *Medioevo edito e inedito*, 1; André Gouron, "La diffusion des premiers recueils de Questions Disputées: Des civilistes aux canonistes," in *Studia in honorem eminentissimi cardinalis Alphonsi M. Stickler*, ed. Rosalio Castillo Lara (Rome: Libreria Ateneo Salesiano, 1992); Hermann Kantorowicz, "The Quaestiones Disputatae of the Glossators," *TvR* 16 (1939), pp. 1–67, repr. in Hermann Kantorowicz, *Rechtshistorische Schriften* (Karlsruhe: C.F. Müller, 1970).

93 See below, pp. 49–51. Cf. De Concilio, *Via Brocardica*, 1:52–63.

2 A Mosaic of Works: The Other Texts Inserted in the *Perpendiculum*

This brief description of the main division of the *Perpendiculum* gives us an idea of its complexity, but in the manuscript tradition of the work we can also identify various texts inserted in its three main parts, in manuscripts A, G, L, Mu1, P1, and Vb. In these codices, for example, a particular group of brocards in Part II or III is followed by other texts (glosses, *distinctiones*, or even other collections of arguments), after which the standard group of brocards resumes, only to be interspersed with new external material.

2.1 *The* distinctio "Ad movendum varie iudicem"

The first of these interposed texts is a short piece already identified by Kuttner,[94] who initially described it as a series of *notabilia* characterized by the method of the *distinctio*, but later noted that it could be better described as a proper *distinctio*.[95] Until now, historiography has referred to this *distinctio* as "*Delicto coram iudice*," after the incipit of the text; however, the work itself contains its own rubric in almost all copies: "*Ad movendum varie iudicem*," which therefore seems a more appropriate title.

This rubric explains well the content of the text, which could be more precisely defined as a brief instruction on rhetorical tactics in disciplinary or criminal cases before the courts: like the *Summula*, it is addressed to an audience of practitioners and explains how to plead before a judge. It illustrates four ways for pleading, divided according to the purpose of the pleader: to ask forgiveness for a criminal; to increase the punishment; to persuade the judge to apply procedural law and the rule of equity; to induce the offended party to remit the offence out of favor.[96] For each of these cases, the *distinctio* gives a rubric, arranged in an ordinal form ("*in primo casu*," "*in secundo casu*," etc.).[97] For each rubric, the *distinctio* lists a series of arguments, mostly from the *Decretum*, but with a reference to the Gospel of Matthew and one to the Lord's Prayer.

---

94 Kuttner, *Repertorium*, p. 234, who erroneously considered this text and the collection "*Hec sunt que suadent*" (below, pp. 47–48) to be part of the same work (cf. Kuttner, "Retractationes IX," p. 40).

95 Kuttner, *Repertorium*, p. 234; Kuttner, "Réflexions," p. 774 n. 31; Kuttner, "Retractationes IX," p. 40; see also Lang, "Rhetorische Einflüsse," p. 84, and Gouron, "Une école de canonistes," p. 66.

96 "*Delinquenti veniam implorare; contra ipsum exasperare vindictam; assidentes iudici iustitie ordinem et equitatis suadere normam; lesum inducere ut remittat gratis offensam.*" See below, pp. 393–395.

97 Gouron, "Une école de canonistes," pp. 50, 61, 66, identified this preference for enumeration in some other works produced by an Anglo-Norman school of canon law active in Paris in the 1170s. We shall return to this aspect.

"Ad movendum varie iudicem" appears in five of the manuscripts in the ensemble: in one of them (Vb), it is copied three times: twice in full, plus a fragment of the incipit. In two of our codices, it is inserted in Part III: P1 and Vb. In the other two cases, the *distinctio* follows the *Perpendiculum* after Part III: G and again in Vb. Finally, in two cases the text is interpolated between Parts II and III: L and Mu1.

2.2 *The Roman Law Gloss* "In multis"

Although many of the works and legal sources contained in the *Perpendiculum* are from canon law, there are occasionally some civil law texts that are copied. The most common example is a very short text on the legal status of women, which almost faithfully reproduces the gloss "*in multis*" to Dig. 1.5.9, that is a passage by Papinianus on the restrictions on women's legal capacity under Roman law: "*In multis iuris articulis deterior est conditio feminarum quam masculorum.*"[98] Both the gloss and the text illustrate the areas of law in which the status of women is limited, using various legal arguments from the Digest, the Code, and the Institutes. However, the version of the gloss contained in the *Perpendiculum* and that transmitted by the ordinary gloss to the Digest differ in some aspects: in the former, the allegations are appended at the end, in a random order, while in the latter they are inserted in an orderly fashion after each *articulus*; moreover, the *Perpendiculum* mentions only 12 areas of limitation, as opposed to 18 in the ordinary gloss; finally, one of the areas listed in our text (*magistratus susceptio*) does not appear in the gloss.

The areas on restriction of women's status listed by the text concern both procedural matters and aspects relating to the sphere of family law and the transmission of family property, with a particular focus on forms of personal representation and public office. According to the gloss, women cannot act as judges or arbitrators; they cannot be appointed tutors or curators, they are unable to file someone else's will or guarantee someone else's debts; they cannot adopt, be witnesses to a will, act as accusers or informers; finally, women cannot be attorneys or magistrates and they are forbidden from appearing

98 Cf. Accursius, "Glossa ordinaria ad Digestum vetus," in Nicolaus Bevilacqua (ed.), *Pandectarum, seu digestorum Iuris Ciuilis* (Venice: Bevilacqua, 1569), 1:33, v. *in multis* to Dig. 1.5.9; the text as it appears in the *glossa ordinaria* has also been edited by Beatrice Pasciuta, "La costruzione del genere nel diritto medievale: norme e dottrina," *RSDI* 95 (2022), pp. 1–21, 4 n. 10. This gloss will be eventually consecrated to success by Guillaume Durand in his *Speculum iudiciale*: cf. Guillelmus Durantis. *Speculum iuris*, 2 vols (Basel: apud Ambrosium et Aurelium, 1574; repr. Aalen: Scientia-Verlag, 1975), 1:153. See also Pasciuta, "La costruzione," p. 5 n. 11, and Élisabeth Schneider, "L'interprétation des termes d'homme ou de personne en droit savant, source d'inégalité," *Droit et cultures* 69 (2015), pp. 89–112.

before the magistrate in someone else's interest.[99] This text is found in five manuscripts (A, G, L, Mu1, and P1) between Parts II and III: in three of them it comes immediately after the former (A, G, and P1), while in L and Mu1 it is preceded by the *distinctio "Ad movendum varie iudicem."*

2.3 *The Texts Inserted in Both G and P1*

G and P1 are two manuscripts that clearly come from the same archetype, as they show many points of contact. One of these is the interpolation of two very small texts in Part III, immediately after the gloss *"In multis:"* a short brocard with Roman law allegations on the possibility of punishing what the law does not hold (beg.: *"Punitur quod factum iure non tenuit"*) and a canon law distinction on the consequences of denunciation (beg.: *"Denuntiatio inducit dolum"*).[100]

2.4 *The Text Inserted in P1:* Brocardica "Nullus archidiaconus"

In addition to the short texts also transmitted by G, manuscript P1 interpolates a large collection of 219 brocards into Part III, beginning with *"Nullus archidiaconus"* (fols. 33va–35vb). These brocards are mostly without oppositions and are characterized by the frequent use of *decretales extravagantes* in the allegations. Of the decretals that we can identify with certainty, the majority were issued by Alexander III (1159–1181), most of them to English prelates. The *extravagantes* are not the only source cited from this period: the collection mentions the canons of the Third Lateran Council (1179) five times and the Sixth Council of Tours (1163) once. The date of composition of the collection can also be determined from the incipits identified, which could refer to some decretals issued by Lucius III (1181–1185). Therefore, on the one hand, his pontificate (1181–1185) represents the *terminus ante quem* of the work; on the other hand, the fact that the collection does not cite later decretals suggests that it was probably composed not too many years after that date.[101] In conclusion, then, we can place the compilation of *Nullus archidiaconus* more than a decade after the rest of the *Perpendiculum*, in the 1180s.

Moreover, the *extravagantes* and the conciliar canons are not the only sources that distinguish this collection from the *Perpendiculum*, in which it is included. Brocard no. 179 cites another collection of decretals, using the strange expression *"decretali Girardi."* Obviously, *Girardus* cannot be the author of the decretals, so it must be the name of the compiler of a collection. Unfortunately,

99 See below, p. 396.
100 See below, p. 397.
101 See above, pp. 11–12.

this element does not help much in solving the mystery of Gerard's identity. It is known that the Anglo-Norman master Gerardus Pucella (c. 1177–1184) wrote a *Summa super decretalia*, which is unfortunately lost.[102] It is therefore possible that the brocard refers to his work, although this hypothesis remains speculative. In any case, this collection of brocards testifies to the fact that the *Perpendiculum* underwent many changes and additions by its users several years after its first redaction.

2.5 *The Texts Inserted in Mu1*

As we have just seen, not all small texts inserted into the *Perpendiculum* appear in more than one copy. Like P1, Mu1 contains a variety of material not found in any other codex. The first addition is on fol. 51rb, where there is a series of three canon law *distinctiones*: the first concerns ignorance (beg.: "*Sciendum est quod ignorantia alia est pena alia culpa*"), the second revolves around the case of a serf ordained as a priest (beg.: "*Servus aut ordinatur domino sciente aut nesciente*"),[103] while the third deals with the serfs owned by Jews (beg.: "*Mancipia Iudeorum aut semper fuerunt infidelia*").[104] A second addition is found on fol. 52^{ra-b}, where there is a treatise on the *arbor consanguinitatis* (beg.: "*Compositionis arboris causa hec est*"), while another civilian *distinctio* is appended to Part III, on fol. 52rb (beg.: "*Iure humano inutilis est promissio*").

3 Texts Appended to the Third Part of the *Perpendiculum*

Among the manuscripts of the *Perpendiculum*, two of them (C and Vb) contain, after Part III, some works that are not included in the ensemble but are closely related to it.

3.1 *The* notabilia "Argumentum quod religiosi" *and* "Argumentum contra religiosos"

The first works of great significance for their relationship to the *Perpendiculum* are two related collections of *notabilia*,[105] contained in C (fols. 56^{r}–61va) and Vb (fol. 10^{rc-vb}), called "*Argumentum quod religiosi*" and "*Argumentum contra*

102 Kuttner and Rathbone, "Anglo-Norman Canonists," p. 303.

103 Cf. Nov. 123 c.17 = D.54 c.20.

104 Cf. D.54 c.13.

105 *Notabilia* were arguments that derived from *notae*, i.e. marginal glosses used to draw the reader's attention to a particular point in the legal text. Some of these *notae* were used to summarize in a short maxim the concepts contained in the text and were used as a

religiosos," respectively.[106] While Kuttner considered them to be two independent works,[107] Gouron believed them to be variants of the same collection.[108] Aware that it is always difficult to draw a line between the two when dealing with the fluid nature of many medieval legal collections, I believe that on close textual examination, Kuttner's interpretation is preferable. There are certainly similarities in the content of some rubrics and in the structure of the work: both collections, for example, follow the order of the *Decretum*. However, the divergences are extremely significant: most of the *notabilia* on the first part of the *Decretum* are different; moreover, *Argumentum quod religiosi* also covers the second part of Gratian's work, which is the main subject of this collection, while *Argumentum contra religiosos* is limited to the first part of the *Concordia*. The two texts also seem to differ in style and structure. While the one in the Borghese manuscript consists only of *notabilia* and, in keeping with the genre, usually has only one allegation to support each short sentence,[109] the *Argumentum quod religiosi* is something of a hybrid work: the rubrics often have several

---

tool of legal argumentation: hence the name (*argumenta*) *notabilia*. In this case, therefore, the *notabile* can be identified with the *argumentum* it embodies. These *notabilia*, which at first were mere glosses of notable arguments, sometimes, like brocards, embodied a legal maxim or rule. On this genre, see Kuttner, *Repertorium*, pp. 232–233; Kuttner, "Réflexions," p. 770; Weimar, "Argumenta," p. 110; Alfons M. Stickler, "Sacerdotium et Regnum nei decretisti e nei primi decretalisti: Considerazioni metodologiche di ricerca e testi," *Salesianum* 15 (1953), pp. 5–42, 9. It is worth noting that brocards seem to derive from later *notabilia*, which were expanded by adding other parallel allegations, thus becoming repositories of arguments: when these repositories included the opposite allegations, or when two opposite *notabilia* were combined, we have the emergence of brocards: Kuttner, *Repertorium*, p. 233; Weimar, "Argumenta," pp. 110–111; Peter Weimar, "Die legistische Literatur und die Methode des Rechtsunterrichts der Glossatorenzeit," *Ius Commune* 2 (1969), pp. 43–83, 60–61, and the literature cited on n. 52; see also the late 11th- early 12th-century collection of *notabilia* edited by Giuseppe Speciale, "Studio sui notabilia del codice Assisi 220," *Quaderni catanesi di studi classici e medievali* 17 (1987), pp. 157–214.

106 See Kuttner, *Repertorium*, pp. 236–237. The *notabilia* "*Argumentum quod religiosi*" have been recently studied by Bruce Brasington, "'A Minor Literary Genre': Examination of Selected 12th Century Canonistic Argumenta/Notabilia," in *Proceedings of the Fifteenth International Congress of Medieval Canon Law: Paris, 17–23 July 2016*, ed. Florence Demoulin-Auzary, Nicolas Laurent-Bonne, and Franck Roumy (Vatican City: BAV, 2022), pp. 1161–1165.

107 Kuttner, *Repertorium*, pp. 236–237.

108 Gouron, "Une école de canonistes," p. 68.

109 In terms of structure, this type of *notabilia* is similar to two 13th-century collections. The first is the *Notabilium fragmenta Borghesiana* (Vatican City, BAV, Borgh. 261, fols. 129–134^v: cf. Kuttner, *Repertorium*, p. 237), which collect maxims on selected passages from the second and third parts of the *Decretum* in the form of short sentences from the texts cited. The second is the *Notabilia "Ad instantem quorumdam*," probably written before 1215, in which each chapter of the *Decretum* and each paragraph added by Gratian are provided with a

allegations and contain *contraria*.[110] For this reason, the relationship of each work to the *Perpendiculum* must be considered separately.

The text transmitted by C, *Argumentum quod religiosi*, can be attributed with certainty to the author of the core structure of the *Perpendiculum*. Firstly, two *notabilia* in *Argumentum quod religiosi* contain internal references to an equal number of brocards in the second part of the *Perpendiculum*,[111] referred to as "*concordantiae nostrae*."[112] Secondly, in this collection we find an explicit reference to the *Summula de presumptionibus*, which is called exactly the same.[113] It is also worth noting that *Argumentum quod religiosi* contains a reference to Thomas Becket as "*beatus*," which could not have been possible before 1173: an element that has been used to try to date and contextualize both this collection and the *Perpendiculum*.[114]

On the other hand, the collection preserved in Vb, *Argumentum contra religiosos*, differs significantly from that contained in C, also in terms of its relationship with the *Perpendiculum*, since it does not contain any of the internal references mentioned above. Considering these two elements, we can hypothesize that the two works are only partially related and have two different authors. The relationship between *Argumentum contra religiosos* and the *Perpendiculum* can therefore be reduced to the fact that the two works circulated together and possibly in the same environment: in fact, in Vb, the collection follows the third part of the *Perpendiculum*, after the *distinctio* "*Ad movendum varie iudicem*" and the *distinctiones* "*Hec sunt que suadent*," that we are about to examine.

---

notabile, so that the whole work is a collection of excerpts of the relevant legal sentences from the *Decretum* for those who cannot afford a copy of the text: Kuttner, *Repertorium*, pp. 237–239.

110 See also Brasington, "'A Minor Literary Genre'," pp. 1162–1163.

111 The two brocards cited are Part II, nos. 12 and 16. However, C is one of the few manuscripts that does not follow the standard organization of the text in this part: the brocards of Part II are in fact in a completely different order and mixed with those of groups β and ε of Part III. The two brocards cited in *Argumentum quod religiosi* therefore correspond to nos. 27 and 3 of C, respectively.

112 C, fol. 56ra, to D.4 c.6, and fol. 56rb, to D.8 c.2. In both cases the reference is "*in concordantiis nostris sub eadem nota*." The term "*concordantiae*" (concordances) is also used several times in the *Summula* to refer both to *pro-contra* brocards and to brocards in general; this word is common among medieval jurists, who used it in the sense of parallel allegations: cf., for example, Nino Tamassia and Giovanni Battista Palmieri, eds., *Iohannis Bassiani Libellus de ordine judiciorum*, BIMAE, 2:229–248, 220 § 69, and below, p. 86 n. 161.

113 C, fol. 56ra, to D.3 c.4: "*Cap. Erit autem* (*D.4 c.2*). *Ad quod hoc cap. valeat, in summula de presumptionibus explanatur*." Cf. Kuttner, "Réflexions," p. 775.

114 On this point and on the possible objections, see below, pp. 90–91.

3.2 *The Set of* distinctiones "Hec sunt que suadent"

Manuscript Vb contains a series of canon law *distinctiones* beginning with "*Hec sunt que suadent ne spoliatus restituatur*."[115] The text probably dates from the 1170s or early 1180s, as can be deduced from several elements. The first is the allegation of a decretal of Alexander III in the first *distinctio* of the series,[116] which could suggest that it was composed shortly after the end of his pontificate (1181).[117] Secondly, the fact that the decretal is cited without reference to any systematic collection suggests that the *distinctiones* could not have been composed long after the proliferation of this type of work in the 1180s. Finally, the parallels between some of the *distinctiones* and a group of glosses signed with the initial 'W.', written in the second half of the 1170s, help to identify a *terminus post quem*.[118]

As to the origin of the collection, it is worth noting its author's penchant for enumeration: of the 101 distinctions, 27 are introduced by statements such as "*tria sunt*," "*quatuor sunt*," and "*quinque sunt*." As mentioned earlier, this predilection for numbering, which is also found in the *distinctio* "*Ad movendum varie iudicem*" and in other works that we will examine later, has been suggested as characteristic of the Parisian canon law school,[119] but it cannot be considered as an exclusive feature of that area and seems to be common among

115 Kuttner, *Repertorium*, p. 234, at first erroneously considered this text to be part of the *distinctio* "*Ad movendum varie iudicem*" which precedes it in the manuscript; later (Kuttner, "Retractationes IX," p. 40) he more correctly reported it as a different text.

116 The decretal is not cited by the *distinctio*, which says only "*c. Alexandri extravaganti*," but the text without omissions is reported in a parallel gloss: "*ut in extravaganti decreto c. Abbas*" (JL 14131 = WH 6): cf. Weigand, *Die Glossen zum Dekret*, 2:638 no. 11.

117 See above, pp. 11–12.

118 Cf. below, pp. 59–66. Although it cannot be established with certainty whether the glosses predate the *distinctiones*, it is unlikely that much time elapsed between their respective compilations.

119 Gouron, "Une école de canonistes," pp. 50, 61, 66. On the Parisian schools in general, see André Gouron, "Une école ou des écoles? Sur les canonistes français (vers 1150–vers 1210)," in *Proceedings of the Sixth International Congress of Medieval Canon Law: Berkeley, California, 28 July–2 August 1980*, ed. Stephan Kuttner and Kenneth Pennington (Vatican City: BAV, 1985), repr. in Gouron, *Pionniers*, no. VIII; André Gouron, "Canon Law in Parisian Circles Before Stephan of Tournai's Summa," in Chodorow, *Proceedings San Diego*; Anne Lefebvre-Teillard, "Du Décret aux décrétales: L'enseignement du droit canonique au sein de l'école parisienne (fin XIIe–début XIIIe s.)," in *Les débuts de l'enseignement universitaire à Paris (1200–1245 environ)*, ed. Jacques Verger and Olga Weijers (Turnhout: Brepols, 2013); Peter Landau, "Master Peter of Louveciennes and the Origins of the Parisian School of Canon Law around 1170," in *Proceedings of the Fourteenth International Congress of Medieval Canon Law: Toronto, 5–11 August 2012*, ed. Joseph Goering, Stephan Dusil, and Andreas Thier (Vatican City: BAV, 2016).

theologians, under the influence of the *artes liberales*: thus, it perhaps reveals more about the intellectual background of its author than about its geographical provenance.

The collection *"Hec sunt que suadent"* has not received much attention from legal historians,[120] but it is relevant for its relationship with the *Perpendiculum*. Certain elements suggest a link between the two works: apart from their presence in the same codex, some of the *distinctiones* also appear in the *Perpendiculum*. This is the case of the very first two distinctions in the collection (fol. 8vb), which are parallel to two brocards in Part III.[121] Moreover, *distinctio* no. 29 bears obvious echoes of the first brocard in Part II.[122]

However, in order to fully investigate this point and the relationship between the *distinctiones "Hec sunt que suadent"* and the *Perpendiculum*, we need to place the former in the context of a group of 12th-century canon law glosses signed with the initial 'W.' that I mentioned earlier: I will discuss them in the next chapter,[123] where I will examine the *Perpendiculum* in its wider context, both intellectual and textual.

---

120 Rudolf Weigand, "W.-Glossen zum Dekret Gratian," in *Ministerium Iustitiae: Festschrift für Heribert Heinemann zur Vollendung des 60. Lebensjahres*, ed. André Gabriels and Heinrich J.F. Reinhardt (Essen: Ludgerus-Verlag, 1985), and Weigand, *Die Glossen zum Dekret*, 2:633–644, included some of the *distinctiones* in his edition of the parallel glosses of master W.; Gouron, "Une école de canonistes," p. 66, incidentally mentioned the collection in his study of the Parisian Anglo-Norman school of law.

121 D. no. 1 corresponds to α19, while d. no. 2 to α1.

122 Gouron, "Une école de canonistes," p. 65.

123 Cf. below, pp. 59–66.

CHAPTER 2

The *Perpendiculum* in Its Context

After a brief examination of our work from a textual point of view, we can look at the *Perpendiculum* in its context, in order to shed some light on the intellectual milieu in which it was produced. This, as we shall see, makes it possible to analyze the question of the origin and paternity of our collection. In fact, the *Perpendiculum* is not an isolated work, and many links can be established with other juristic works of its time, especially with regard to its first part: the *Summula de presumptionibus*. In this chapter, I will address the influence of the *Summula* on the legal culture of its time from both a theoretical and a textual point of view. First, I will consider the importance of the *Perpendiculum* for the development of brocards as a genre and for the 12th-century theory of legal presumptions; then, I will examine the textual connections between the *Summula* and other contemporary works (1170s) dealing with the same subject to establish a clear relationship between them. Finally, I will analyze other works produced in the 1180s which bear the traces of a manifest influence of the *Perpendiculum*.

1 The Importance of the *Summula* for the Development of Brocards

As I have already mentioned, the *Summula de presumptionibus* is extremely significant in many respects. One of these is its original and peculiar hybrid structure and its extensive use of rhetorical tools, which make it an important testimony to the development of new argumentative techniques in the legal field and to the creation of brocards as a literary genre.

The first element of innovation is the use that the *Summula* makes of the technique of *loci*, which, as we have seen, are topics based on logic and supported by normative sources.[1] This feature is common to most of the earliest brocardic collections produced in the second half of the 12th century.[2]

In fact, the earliest brocardic collections, just like the *Summula*, consisted only of sentences (*rubricae*) and sets of legal references attached to them (*argumenta*). In both cases, the rubric was not intended to express an independent

1 See above, pp. 25–26.

2 Andrea Errera, "Aristotele, i "Topica" e la scienza giuridica medievale," *Angelicum* 85, no. 1 (2008), pp. 341–362, 352.

 | DOI:10.1163/9789004713239_004

legal maxim, but only to anticipate and explain the content of the arguments attached to it, which is precisely the heuristic function of rhetorical *loci*. Brocardic collections of this kind can therefore be described as repositories of *loci argumentorum*, collections of legal arguments.[3] In the *Summula*, this approach is still evident if one looks at the way its rubrics are formulated: "*ex loco*," "*ex tempore*," etc. However, what distinguishes the *Summula* from other, earlier collections of this kind is the much more refined nature of the *loci loicales* used here. Andrea Errera, who has studied this type of argumentation, has made this point about the *Libellus disputatorius* of Pilius de Medicina,[4] showing that while most of the earlier collections followed the logical pattern of the *distinctio*, this work shows a knowledge of syllogistic technique that suggests the influence of the new Aristotelian logic.[5] This technique consisted of the articulation of Topics in a syllogistic form, defined *modi presumendi*, which makes these Topics more elaborate than mere *loci loicales*. However, it has been shown that Pilius took the articulation into *modi* from the *loci* of the *Summula de presumptionibus*.[6] Thus, Errera's reflections on the Aristotelian influence on the way the *Libellus* treats topical argumentation can be extended and ultimately traced back to the *Summula*.

Moreover, the use of brocardic argumentation in the *Summula de presumptionibus* can be considered innovative compared to the earliest collections of brocards for another reason. The earliest brocardic works did not make consistent use of the *pro-contra* opposition that generally characterizes the genre: this is the case, for example, for collections such as the so-called *Brocardica "Dolum"* and the *Brocardica Dunelmensia*.[7] The first collection of brocards to use the *pro-contra* pattern throughout is probably the *Summula de presumptionibus*, although, unlike later collections, it does not make the oppositions between the arguments explicit in its text, as its anonymous author states in the conclusions of the work.[8] Borrowing directly from the *Summula*, this *procontra* structure was then adopted by later collections such as Pilius's *Libellus disputatorius*, which popularized this new method in the Italian schools; the *Summula* thus represents a turning point in the diffusion of *pro-contra* brocards as a tool of legal argumentation, and indirectly an influential model for

3 See De Concilio, *Via Brocardica*, 1:41–43 and 1:52–62.
4 See below, pp. 77–80.
5 Errera, "Aristotele," pp. 354–356.
6 See below, p. 79.
7 See Schwaibold, *Brocardica Dolum*, pp. 102–104, and van de Wouw, "Brocardica Dunelmensia," pp. 235–236, respectively.
8 See below, *Summula de presumptionibus*, x, 3.

further transformations of the brocardic genre.[9] Finally, in the *Perpendiculum* we also find one of the earliest (if not the earliest) examples of a brocard with a *solutio contrariorum*, as the *Summula* (VIII, 4) solves the issue of the ownership of goods in possession of a priest, in dispute between the latter and the Church, by adopting a distinction from Burchard's *Decretum*, based on whether it is certain that the priest had possessions before ordination or not.

2 The Importance of the *Summula* for the Glossators' Theory on Presumptions

The original contribution of the *Summula de presumptionibus* to the legal culture of its time is not limited to the brocardic genre: the work is also one of the first examples of the canon law interest in presumptions, and it was extremely influential among several jurists of its time. It is therefore worth spending a few pages on the importance of the *Summula* in the elaboration of 12th-century legal theory on presumptions. Before doing so, however, it is necessary to outline the historical process that led to the elaboration of this theory.

2.1 *A 12th-Century Product: The Theory of Presumptions*

The creation of a proper system of legal presumptions in the Western European legal tradition can be traced back to Justinian's codification. Until then, Roman law had no such system, since classical Roman procedure lacked a proper doctrine of evidence.

This was the natural consequence of the classical Roman system of litigation, which consisted of two stages: a procedure *in iure* and one *apud iudicem*. The first stage took place before the magistrate, who took note of the case and sent the litigants to the *iudex*: a private person appointed to settle the case. This procedure included the participation of lawyers, but not the discussion of evidence. The second stage, on the other hand, took place before the *iudex*, who examined the pleadings and the evidence presented: it did not involve lawyers, but the parties were often assisted by orators in order to convince the judge. Because of this strict division of tasks between lawyers *in iure* and rhetors *apud iudicem*, rhetoric and techniques of persuasion played a central role in the factual examination of the dispute, rather than the need to prove individual legal positions through the law of evidence.[10]

9 For a detailed account of this historical process, see De Concilio, *Via Brocardica*, 1:52–62 and 2:7–36.

10 See Max Kaser, *Das römische Zivilprozessrecht*, 2nd ed. (Munich: Beck, 1996), pp. 361–369, and especially 362.

Classical Roman jurists did not, therefore, concern themselves extensively with the means and problems of evidence, although they did sometimes, under the influence of rhetoric, use a kind of legal reasoning that we would call presumption. These inferential procedures were used by jurisconsults as principles for interpreting substantive law: this can be seen from several passages that have survived in the Digest.[11] However, no normative value could be ascribed to these inferential mechanisms of legal interpretation. Thus, in classical Roman times presumptions were left to rhetoric, from which they originated; and yet we do not find any discussion on presumptions among Roman rhetoricians, even though their field of application is uncertainty, which is precisely the realm of rhetoric.[12]

It was only in the post-classical period, during the Principate, that both parts of the trial began to take place before a judge who was a state official, in the so-called *cognitio extraordinaria*. As a result, the Roman judge began to be bound by fixed legal rules for the assessment of evidence, and an evidentiary procedure began to emerge. For this reason, presumptive tools also began to find their way into post-classical legal language. Finally, with the codification of Justinian, these evidentiary principles became fixed legal rules, transforming the classical inferential processes into true presumptions in the legal sense.[13] We can therefore consider Justinian as the first to establish a system of presumptions based on classical material. However, this system, built on the casuistic basis of the *iura*, still lacked a theoretical systematization and even an explicit definition.[14] Indeed, if we look at the presumptions in the *Corpus Iuris Civilis*,

---

11 For an account of presumptions in Roman times, cf. Kaser, *Das römische Zivilprozessrecht*, pp. 597–599; Hohmann, "Presumptions in Roman Legal Argumentation;" Guido Donatuti, "Le praesumptiones iuris in diritto romano (loro origine)," *Annali della Facoltà di giurisprudenza della R. Università di Perugia* 42 (1931), pp. 1–112, repr. in Donatuti, *Studi di diritto romano*, 1; Donatuti, "Le 'praesumptiones iuris' come mezzi"; Contardo Ferrini, "Le presunzioni in diritto romano," *Rivista italiana per le scienze giuridiche* 14 (1892), pp. 258–294, repr. in *Opere di Contardo Ferrini*, ed. Emilio Albertario, 3 (Milan: Hoepli, 1929). See also Antonio Sánchez-Gil, *La presunzione di validità dell'atto giuridico nel diritto canonico* (Milan: Giuffrè, 2006), pp. 11–27; Eduardo Labandeira, *Las presunciones en derecho canónico* (Pamplona: Universidad de Navarra, 1967), pp. 23–29.

12 Hanns Hohmann, "Presumption in Legal Argumentation: From Antiquity to the Middle Ages," in *Proceedings from the 1999 Ontario Society for the Study of Argumentation Conference, 3 (1999): Argumentation at The Century's Turn; held at Brock University*, ed. Hans V. Hansen, Christopher W. Tindale, and Elmar Sveda, available online at https://scholar.uwindsor.ca/ossaarchive/OSSA3/papersandcommentaries/28/, accessed 2022 Aug 01, § 1.

13 See Kaser, *Das römische Zivilprozessrecht*, pp. 595–599.

14 Motzenbäcker, *Die Rechtsvermutung*, p. 7; Francisco Cuena Boy, "Presunciones (DCH)," *Max Planck Institute for European Legal History Research Paper Series*, 2018–06 (2018), pp. 1–25, 2.

we see that they are scattered throughout the books,[15] with no single treatment in any particular place: this can probably be explained by the fact that, in keeping with the Roman mentality, presumptions were not considered to be a subject for jurists, but rather for rhetoricians.

The necessary systematization was first provided by the medieval jurists who, on the basis of the *Corpus Iuris Civilis*, developed a proper theory of presumptions, which can therefore be considered a product of the 11th and 12th centuries.[16]

In the 12th century, legists and canonists were engaged in classifying presumptions according to various criteria, following the method of *distinctio*.[17] This process was gradual: it began in the second half of the 12th century with the *Summa Trecensis*[18] and ended at the beginning of the 13th century, with Tancred's *ordo iudiciarius* (1214–1216).[19] It is precisely Tancred's definition, which

15 In the Institutes, for example, there are no rules on presumptions. In the Digest, we find a few scant mentions: Dig. 22.3 reads "*de probationibus et praesumptionibus*," but it only contains some passages on presumptions at the end of the title, as an appendix to proofs (Dig. 22.3.24–25). Some other examples are found in other titles: e.g., Dig. 4.2.23pr. Many presumptions were concerned with the meaning of a particular phrase in wills: Dig. 29.2.30.4; Dig. 31.1.67.10; Dig. 32.1.33.2; Dig. 32.1.73.3; Dig. 33.7.18.3; Dig. 34.3.28.2; D.40.5.24.8; D.40.7.40.7; D.43.4.3.3. Some parallel statements on wills are found in the Code: Cod. 6.27.5.16 and Cod. 4.19.15. Sometimes, the term '*praesumptio*' was used for a legal fiction, as in Cod. 5.13.1.1.13a and Cod. 8.14.7. In the Code, however, title 4.19 "*de probationibus*," unlike Dig. 22.3, does not expressly add the words "*et praesumptionibus*," but it does give some examples of presumptions: Cod. 4.19.6; Cod. 4.19.12; Cod. 4.19.15; Cod. 4.19.23.

16 On this point, see André Gouron, "Aux racines de la théorie des présomptions," *RIDC* 1 (1990), pp. 99–109, repr. in Gouron, *Droit et coutume*, no. VII, p. 99; Motzenbäcker, *Die Rechtsvermutung*, p. 44. I will deal only with the treatment of presumptions in the schools of canon and civil law: for the use of presumptions in England, developed under the influence of continental learned law, see David J. Seipp, "Presumptions in Early English Common Law," in Helmholz et al., *The Law of Presumptions*, and Richard H. Helmholz, "The Law of Presumptions and the English Ecclesiastical Courts," in Helmholz et al., *The Law of Presumptions*.

17 See the fundamental study of Fiori, "Praesumptio," pp. 78–81.

18 The earliest *Summa* to Justinian's Code, known as *Trecensis*, was at first erroneously attributed to Irnerius by Fitting in his edition: see Hermann Fitting, ed., *Summa Codicis des Irnerius* (Berlin: Guttentag, 1894); in the 1980s, Gouron ascribed the work to a Provençal jurist called Geraudus: André Gouron, "L'auteur et la patrie de la Summa Trecensis," *Ius Commune* 12 (1984), pp. 1–38; André Gouron, "L'élaboration de la 'Summa Trecensis'," in *Sodalitas: Scritti in onore di Antonio Guarino*, ed. Vincenzo Giuffrè, 8 (Napoli: Jovene, 1985).

19 See Fiori, "Praesumptio," p. 78; Gouron, "Aux racines"; and Motzenbäcker, *Die Rechtsvermutung*, pp. 133–134. On the *ordo iudiciarius* as a genre, see Alfons M. Stickler, "Ordines

became a point of reference for later jurists,[20] that we can use to understand the characteristics of the Glossators' concept of presumption: "an argument for believing a fact which arises from the proof of another fact."[21] According to this definition, which is close to our modern understanding, presumption consists of an inferential reasoning that establishes a conjectural truth about an unknown fact from a known one. It therefore coincides with the rhetorical concept of *argumentum*,[22] i.e. "a reason that produced belief regarding a thing in doubt,"[23] "a method of proving what is not certain by means of what is certain."[24]

However, Tancred's definition is only the end of a long development. The civilian jurists of the Provençal school were the first to deal with this construct, categorizing presumptions according to their origin.[25] The main civilian distinction, rooted in the *Summa Codicis* (c. 1168) of Placentinus (d. c. 1182),[26] was between a *praesumptio facti*, made directly by the judge (hence also called *praesumptio iudicis*) and a *praesumptio iuris* (or *legis* or *legitima*), made by the

---

judiciarii," in DDC 6 (1957): 1132–1143; Knut Wolfgang Nörr, "Ordo Iudiciorum und Ordo Iudiciarius," *Studia Gratiana* 11 (1967), pp. 327–343, repr. in Knut Wolfgang Nörr, *Iudicium est actus trium personarum: Beiträge zur Geschichte des Zivilprozessrechts in Europa* (Goldbach: Keip, 1993); Linda Fowler-Magerl, *Ordo iudiciorum vel ordo iudiciarius: Begriff und Literaturgattung* (Frankfurt am Main: Klostermann, 1984); Fowler-Magerl, *Ordines*; Bruce Brasington, *Order in the Court: Medieval Procedural Treatises in Translation* (Leiden: Brill, 2016).

20 Fiori, "Praesumptio," p. 78.

21 Tancred of Bologna, *Ordo iudiciarius*, ed. Friedrich Bergmann, in *Pillii, Tancredi, Gratiae libri de iudiciorum ordine*, ed. Friedrich Bergmann (Göttingen: Vandenhoeck et Ruprecht, 1842), p. 257: "*Praesumptio est argumentum ad credendum unum factum surgens ex probatione ulterior facti.*"

22 Bernardus Papiensis, *Bernardus Papiensis Faventini episcopi Summa decretalium*, ed. Ernst A.T. Laspeyres (Regensburg: Manz, 1860), p. 50: "*Praesumptio est argumentum movens aliquatenus iudicem ad credendum.*" Cf. Gama, "Presumptions," p. 351; Giuliani, "Civilian Treatises," pp. 41–42; Sánchez-Gil, *La presunzione*, pp. 15–16.

23 "*Ratio rei dubiae faciens fidem*:" Cicero, *Topica*, 2.8, 426.35–37. The translation used is by Toivo J. Holopainen, *Dialectic and Theology in the Eleventh Century* (Leiden: Brill, 1996), p. 137.

24 "*Ratio per ea quae certa sunt fidem dubiis adferens*:" Quintilianus, *Institutio Oratoria*, ed. and trans. Harold E. Butler, 2 (Cambridge, Massachusetts: Harvard University Press, 1921), v, x, 8.

25 Gouron, "Aux racines," pp. 102–106. On traces of civilian presumptions before Placentinus, see Motzenbäcker, *Die Rechtsvermutung*, pp. 46–58.

26 On this jurist, see Ennio Cortese, "Piacentino," in DBGI, 2:1568–1571; Emanuele Conte, "Piacentino," in DBI 83 (2015), available at https://www.treccani.it/enciclopedia/piacentino_(Dizionario-Biografico)/, accessed 2022 Jul 31.

law.[27] This distinction became very popular with both legists and canonists; the latter sometimes changed the terminology, calling *praesumptio legis* also "*praesumptio canonis*," and *praesumptio facti* "*praesumptio iudicis*." Instead, canonists divided the presumption into three categories, according to the intensity of its influence on the judgement. The first was the *praesumptio temeraria*, which was irrelevant to the judgement; the second was the *praesumptio probabilis*, which required a purgatory oath to be dismissed; the third was the *praesumptio violenta*, which led directly to the judgement.[28] The *praesumptio violenta* was in turn divided according to its source, the judge or the law. Of particular interest is the *praesumptio legis violenta* (also called *iuris et de iure* or *necessaria*): a presumption established by the law so strong that it does not admit evidence to the contrary and leads directly to the verdict: it is in this context that we can frame the role of the *Summula de presumptionibus*. In fact, this work combined the canon law concept of *praesumptio violenta* with the Placentinian distinction of presumptions between *facti* and *iudicis*.

2.2 *The Role of the* Perpendiculum *in the Theory of Presumptions*

As will be seen in this study, the *Summula de presumptionibus* became a very popular work in the late 12th century, influencing the juristic treatment of presumptions in many ways. For example, its original classification of presumptions into *loci* became a staple point in the matter, shaping not only the work of contemporaries such as Pilius de Medicina and Sicardus of Cremona,[29] but also—more than forty years later—Tancred's *ordo iudiciarius*,[30] which in turn

---

27 See Gouron, "Aux racines," pp. 105–106; André Gouron, "Placentinus 'Herold' der Vermutungslehre?," in *Festschrift zum 65. Geburtstag und zur Emeritierung von Professor Dr. Hans Kiefner: Herausgegeben von Freunden, Kollegen und Mitarbeitern*, ed. Ulrike Brüning and Thomas Hoeren (Münster: Institut für Kirchenrecht, 1994), repr. in Gouron, *Juristes*, no. VIII; Fiori, "Praesumptio," pp. 79, 81–82.; Motzenbäcker, *Die Rechtsvermutung*, pp. 58–62. The use of *praesumptio iudicis* is also found in Gratian's *Decretum*: Labandeira, *Las presunciones*, pp. 30–31.

28 Fiori, "Praesumptio," pp. 79–80, 86–101.

29 See below, pp. 75–76 and 77–80.

30 Tancred, *Ordo iudiciarius*, p. 257 f., lines 14–12: "*Surgit autem praesumptio multipliciter: ex persona, ut C.31. q.2. c. Lotharius. 4. (pr.) Dig. quod. met. caus. 4, 2. l. non est verisimile. 23. (pr.); ex loco, ut X.1. de praesumt. 2, 16. c. quanto. 9. (X. 2.23.8) X.2. de sponsalib. 4, 1. c. tertio 8. (X. 2.23.13); ex tempore, ut X. 2. de sponsal. 4, 1. c. ad id quod. 7. (X. 4.1.21); ex aetate, ut X.3. de praesumt. 2, 14. c. cum in iuventute. 2.(X. 2.23.15); et ex multis aliis causis et modis, sicut per concordantias in hoc titulo positas evidenter probatur.*" Not only does Tancred use, directly or indirectly, the same scheme as the *Summula*: he also adopts the same language. In fact, he uses the word "*concordantias*," which the *Summula* commonly uses to refer to its own brocards (see above, p. 46 n. 112). Of course, at first sight Tancred seems to be referring here

became the point of reference on the subject. From this point of view, however, one of the most important elements in the *Perpendiculum* is the aforementioned classification of presumptions into *temeraria*, *probabilis*, and *violenta*. In fact, the *Summula* is one of the earliest sources known to us to introduce the concept of a presumption established by law which does not admit evidence to the contrary,[31] and perhaps the first, as far as we know, to define it as *praesumptio legis violenta*: it does so in the ninth section of the work, where it deals with uncertainty in the interpretation of a law or a document.[32] Our author first distinguishes between a presumption of the judge (*iudicis ex facto*) and a presumption of the law (*legis*), clearly influenced by Placentinus's civilian distinction.[33] He then states that in the first case, i.e. when the judge presumes something from a fact, the presumption is *violenta* if it leads to the decision but admits evidence to the contrary. He then moves on to the second source of presumption and introduces a distinction between two types of *praesumptio legis*: one that admits contrary evidence and another (*legis violenta*) that does not and leads to the judgement. The author specifies that the latter occurs when the *praesumptio legis* is so strong that a judge can impose a punishment on the basis of what is presumed.[34] The *Perpendiculum* is unlikely—contrary to previous historiographical understanding—to be the first work to introduce the concept of an irrebuttable presumption established by law, possibly anticipated by the *Summa* of Ioannes Faventinus, written in 1171.[35] However, the *Summula* certainly contributed to the success of this concept. It is the first work to distinguish between two different types of *praesumptiones legis*, one that admits evidence to the contrary and one that does not. The combination of the Placentinian distinction and the criteria of canon law, rooted in both Ioannes Faventinus and the *Perpendiculum*, was soon perfected by Simon de Bisignano and Pilius de Medicina.[36] As we shall see, the *Summula de presump-*

to his own parallel *pro-contra* allegations ("as is clearly proved by the concordances contained in this title"); but there is no trace of such concordances in this part of the *Ordo*, and the reference could perhaps be understood as something borrowed from the *Summula*.

31 Although it is difficult to establish the exact chronology without doubt, the only other two works of the first half of the 1170s known to us where we find such a concept are some glosses signed with the initial 'W.' and a gloss attributed to Ioannes Faventinus: see below, pp. 63–66 and 68–69, respectively.

32 Cf. below, *Summula de presumptionibus*, IX, 1–3. See also Fiori, "Praesumptio," pp. 94–96.

33 To the point that Gouron, "Aux racines," pp. 107–108, initially believed that the *Summula* belonged to his entourage.

34 Fiori, "Praesumptio," pp. 94–96; Motzenbäcker, *Die Rechtsvermutung*, pp. 98–100.

35 Cf. below, pp. 68–69.

36 Cf. below, pp. 71–73 and 79–80.

tionibus and its treatment of presumptions are closely linked to the work of many other jurists of the second half of the 12th century. Before analyzing these connections, however, it is worth looking a little more closely at the legal reasoning behind the elaboration offered by the *Summula*, by examining the three canon law *sedes materiae* of this distinction.

2.3 Praesumptio facti *and* legis*: The Canon Law* sedes materiae

Among the several allegations provided by the *Summula* and other related works in differentiating between the various types of presumption, we can identify three *loci* that constitute its *sedes materiae*.

The *sedes materiae* for the *praesumptio facti*, i.e. a presumption established by the judge on a casuistic basis and which can be refuted by evidence, is C.7 q.1 c.3. Importantly, this canon is not mentioned by the *Summula*, which does not provide any allegation for the *praesumptio facti*, preferring to focus only on the *legis*. Nevertheless, it is worth analyzing it to better understand the juridical reasoning on this point provided by other works of canon law.

This chapter is a decretal from Gregory I to Clement, bishop and primate of Byzacena. It deals with the case of a priest called Adeodatus, who was absent from his church for two months. Presuming that Adeodatus had violated his priestly duty of not leaving his parish, his chorbishop,[37] Quincianus, replaced him and ordained another priest. Adeodatus then appealed to the Pope, citing illness as the reason for his prolonged absence. On this basis, Pope Gregory in this decretal urged Clement to investigate the case and, if Adeodatus was found to be justified in his absence, to restore him to his position.[38] C.7 q.1 c.3

37 The phenomenon of rural bishops was common in North Africa at that time: see Leslie Dossey, *Peasant and Empire in Christian North Africa* (Berkeley: University of California Press, 2010), pp. 125–144.

38 C.7 q.1 c.3: "*Presentium latoris Adeodati querelam, qui se sui presbiteratus loco incongrue dicit expulsum, licet subditae tibi textus explanet petitionis, tamen paulo iudicauimus apertius retexendam. Asserit namque a Quinciano fratre et coepiscopo nostro in loco suo quibusdam se suis ordinandis negotiis relaxatum, egritudinisque causa per duorum mensium spatium suue se ecclesiae defuisse; cuius rei occasionem captantem predictum fratrem nostrum alium loco eius presbiterum illic ordinasse. Hortamur itaque fraternitatem tuam, ut causam eius sollicite districteque perquiras, et, si manifestae egritudinis causa, sicut dicitur, ecclesiae suae eum defuisse repereris, nullum ei ex ordinatione alterius presbiteri permittas preiudicium generari, sed in loco suo eum fac sine aliqua dubietate restitui. Et infra: §. 1. Illud autem karitatem tuam specialiter ammonemus, ut, si uera fuerit huius suggestio, atque in suo ordine fuerit restitutus, de presbitero, qui in loco eius ordinatus est, subtiliter districteque esse sollicitus debeas. Et si quidem sine datione aliqua ad eundem ordinem uenit, ut in symoniacam heresim non potuisset incidere, in aliam quamcumque ecclesiam uacantem eum*

thus became the *sedes materiae* for the *praesumptio facti*, because it allowed for the possibility that evidence might overcome Quincianus's presumption against Adeodatus.

As for the *praesumptio legis*, we have seen that it can be divided into two types: one that admits contrary evidence and one that does not. For the former, the *Perpendiculum* does not provide a *sedes materiae*. For the latter, however, the *Summula* offers two legal arguments.

The first is D.54 c.15: another letter from Pope Gregory I, this time to Fortunatus, bishop of Naples. The chapter deals with Jewish authority over Christian slaves. First, the Pope emphasizes that slaves owned by Jews who decide to become Christians must be freed, according to the general legal principle that forbids Jews from owning Christian slaves. Gregory then introduces a distinction between two different cases. If the slave who decides to convert had been bought for the sole purpose of resale, the merchant has three months to find a Christian buyer. If, on the other hand, the slave remains in the merchant's possession after three months, the merchant must release him: in effect, he is be considered to have acquired the slave for his own use and not for resale, in violation of the law.[39] It is clear how this consequence acts as a presumption against the merchant, and because it is established directly by the normative text, the canonists considered it to be a *praesumptio legis* and therefore irrebuttable.

---

uolumus ordinari. Sin autem in eum quippiam (quod auertat Dominus) tale fuerit repertum, ipso etiam presbiteratus priuetur ordine, quem non causa replendae necessitatis ecclesiae, sed sola conprobatur ambitione suscepisse." Cf. Gregory the Great, *Registrum epistularum: Libri I–VII*, ed. Dag Norbeg (Turnhout: Brepols, 1982), IV, 13, p. 231.

39 D.54 c.15: "*Fraternitatem uestram oportet esse sollicitam, si de Iudeorum seruitio non solum Iudeus, sed etiam quisquam paganorum fieri uoluerit Christianus, postquam uoluntas eius fuerit patefacta, ne hunc sub quolibet ingenio uel argumento cuipiam Iudeorum uenundandi facultas sit; sed is, qui ad Christianam conuerti fidem desiderat, defensione uestra in libertatem modis omnibus uendicetur. §. 1. Hi uero, quos huiuscemodi oportet seruos amittere, ne forsitan utilitates suas irrationabiliter existiment inpediri, sollicita uos hoc conuenit consideratione seruare, ut, si paganos, quos mercimonii causa de externis finibus emerint, infra tres menses, dum emptor, cui uenditi fuerant, non inuenitur, fugere ad ecclesiam forte contigerit, et uelle se dixerint Christianos fieri, uel etiam extra ecclesiam hanc talem uoluntatem prodiderint, pretium eorum a Christiano scilicet emptore percipiant. Si autem post prefinitos tres menses quisquam huiuscemodi seruorum Iudaicorum uelle suum dixerit, et fieri uoluerit Christianus, nec aliquis eum postmodum emerit, nec dominus qualibet occasionis specie hunc audeat uenundare, sed ad libertatis proculdubio premia perducatur, quia hunc non ad uendendum, sed ad sibi seruiendum dicitur conparasse.*" Cf. Gregory the Great, *Registrum epistularum*, VI, 29, p. 401.

Finally, C.11 q.1 c.25, the second chapter which became a *sedes materiae* on irrebuttable presumption, is much more straightforward. This canon is taken from the Third Council of Orléans of 538 A.D., which condemned the conspiracy of clerics against their superiors and established that in such a case the presumption against them could not be refuted in any way.[40]

It is important to keep these legal passages in mind because they will be crucial to understanding the reasoning behind the elaboration of the *praesumptio legis* provided by some other canon law works we are about to examine, which were written in the 1170s and are closely linked to the *Perpendiculum*.

3 Contemporary Works with Textual Links to the *Perpendiculum*

The *Perpendiculum* shows some textual similarities with other works of its time, particularly in terms of the conceptualization and classification of presumptions. This leads to the question of the relationship between these works and whether the *Perpendiculum* influenced or was influenced by them. This question, in turn, has implications for the attribution and origin of the work, as well as for the definition of its cultural milieu. In the following pages, I will examine all the texts produced in the 1170s by other authors that can be linked to the *Perpendiculum*, highlighting their points of contact and their divergences.

3.1 *The Glosses of* magister W. (*mid-1170s*)

One of the texts associated with the *Perpendiculum* is a group of 31 glosses to the *Decretum*, written by a jurist who signed himself with the initial 'W.' This set of glosses is particularly significant because, together with the *Summula de presumptionibus*, it is one of the earliest known examples of canon law interest in legal presumptions.

These glosses were edited by Weigand,[41] who dated them to the mid-1170s, since the decretals cited in them have no reference to systematic collections, and the most recent of them dates from 1173–1174.[42] In an attempt to identify the

40 C.11 q.1 c.25: "*Si qui clericorum* (*ut nuper in multis locis per superbiam diabolo instigante actum fuisse perpatuit*) *rebelli auctoritate se in unum coniuratione intercedente collegerint, aut sacramenta inter se data, aut cartulam conscriptam fuisse patuerit, nullis excusationibus presumptio labetur …*"

41 Weigand, "W.-Glossen," and Weigand, *Die Glossen zum Dekret*, 2:633–644.

42 Cf. above, pp. 11–12.

mysterious author of the glosses, Weigand hypothesized a link with the Bolognese school, whose members are often quoted in the same apparatuses.[43]

However, Gouron ruled out Weigand's Bolognese hypothesis because four glosses use the *pro-contra* brocardic method, which he said was absent from the Bolognese teaching during that decade.[44] He hypothesized an Anglo-Norman origin for W.'s glosses, based on two considerations. First, because they deal extensively with legal presumptions and fictions,[45] which were very popular among Anglo-Norman jurists at the time. Secondly, because the style used by W., who was accustomed to presenting his arguments by enumerating points (*tria sunt, quatuor faciunt*, etc.), is also attested by an allegedly Anglo-Norman *ordo iudiciarius* produced in the Parisian school in the same years.[46] As we will see in the next chapter, these elements led Gouron to identify master W. with the author of other legal works written in northern France during the same period, including the *Perpendiculum*.[47]

There are, however, some objections to Gouron's arguments. Firstly, the canon law interest in presumptions and fictions was not exclusive to the transmontane schools: it was also widespread among Italian jurists of the 1170s. Secondly, the predilection for enumeration cannot be considered an exclusive stylistic feature of the Parisian school, as no one has established that it was not used anywhere else. Rather, it seems to be an indication of W.'s theological background, since at that time, under the influence of the *artes liberales*, differentiation by numbering seemed to be very common in theological works.

Finally, Sara Menzinger has recently shown that, on closer examination, it is difficult to establish with certainty the geographical origin of W.'s glosses, since they reflect both French and Italian elements, as well as both theological and canon law knowledge.[48] On the one hand, Gouron's hypothesis is supported by the themes of W.'s glosses (fictions, presumptions, and intentionality, which were much in vogue in northern France),[49] their grammatical taste, and their

43 Weigand, *Die Glossen zum Dekret*, 2:643–644.

44 Gouron, "Une école de canonistes," p. 60. It should be noted, however, that very little of the Bolognese teaching of the time has actually been studied, compared to the amount of unexplored marginal glosses that we have.

45 Cf. Weigand, *Die Glossen zum Dekret*, 2:633–644, glosses nos. 5, 5a, 5b, 6, 6a, 6b, 10, 10a, 14, 16, 17, 24.

46 Gouron, "Une école de canonistes," pp. 60–61.

47 Ibid.

48 Menzinger, *Finzioni del diritto*, pp. 123–125.

49 Menzinger, "Finzioni dei canoni," pp. 206–209. On the attention to intentionality in the French theological schools, cf. also De Concilio, "Soggettività e qualificazione," pp. 20–27.

circulation in the Parisian and Anglo-Norman schools.[50] On the other hand, Menzinger stressed the early reception of W.'s work in the glosses of the Bolognese canonist Ioannes Faventinus,[51] and the influence on W. himself of the theologian and canonist Gandulphus,[52] active in Bologna between 1160 and 1170. Later in this book, I will devote some space to the question of a possible common authorship of the *Summula* and W.'s glosses, as well as to that of the geographical provenance of the latter,[53] since they are central to understanding the *Perpendiculum* as a case study of the intellectual milieu of the 12th-century legal schools. However, I will leave this problem aside for the moment, since it is necessary to analyze more closely the affinities between W.'s glosses and the galaxy of texts related to the *Perpendiculum*.

A relevant point is the relationship between W.'s glosses and the collection of *distinctiones "Hec sunt que suadent,"* which we examined in the previous chapter.[54] In that work, out of 101 distinctions, 14 coincide with an equal number of W.'s glosses;[55] although the degree of agreement between the two texts varies, the connection is obvious. Since the glosses are dated between 1173/4 and 1179, a similar period can be hypothesized for the set of *distinctiones*. We can therefore assume with some plausibility that W.'s glosses and the *distinctiones "Hec sunt que suadent"* are products of the same legal context, if not of the same author. As is usual in the development of 12th-century legal texts, it is likely that the 12 parallel distinctions were incorporated into the collection by extrapolation from the glosses; however, we do not have enough elements to exclude the reverse.

---

50 Menzinger, "Finzioni dei canoni," p. 219.

51 Menzinger, *Finzioni del diritto*, pp. 124–125 and 148–172.

52 On Gandulphus, see Gandulphus, *Magistri Gandulphi Bononiensis sententiarum libri quatuor*, ed. Johannes Wilhelm von Walter (Vienna: Aemilius Haim, 1924); Hans Van de Wouw, "Gandulphus von Bologna," in *LexMA* 4 (1989): 1105; Menzinger, *Finzioni del diritto*, pp. 40–54 and 124–125.

53 See below, pp. 93–105.

54 See above, pp. 47–48.

55 Here, I will use 'H' and 'W' to indicate the distinctiones *"Hec sunt que suadent"* and W.'s glosses, respectively. I have numbered the former according to their order in Vb; for the latter, instead, I follow the numbering established by Weigand, *Die Glossen zum Dekret*, 2:633–644. The parallel passages are: H 1 = W 11; H 6 = W 12; H 8 = W 21; H 9 = W 22; H 25 = W 3 and 3a; H 27 = W 8, H 29 = W 13; H 39 = W 25; H 43 = W 14; H 44 = the end of W 14; H 48 = W 20; H 57 = W 10; H 82 = W 2; H 90 = W 4. Seven of these parallel passages had already been noted by Weigand, *Die Glossen zum Dekret*, 2:637–642, but his numbering of H's distinctions is different.

In addition, another work must be added to the list of texts associated with W.'s glosses: a collection of 32 *distinctiones* (beg.: "*Tria sunt que faciunt ut aliquis sine sua culpa*"), written around the second half of the 1170s[56] and contained in the manuscript Rome, Biblioteca Casanatense, 1105. It is difficult to place the work geographically: on the one hand, it contains a brief reference to England,[57] but in the Casanatense manuscript (of probable Italian origin) it is accompanied by the works of Italian authors with strong transmontane ties, such as Ioannes Faventinus and Simon de Bisignano,[58] both of whom have more than one connection with W., having borrowed his treatment of presumptions and fictions in their *Summae*.

In any case, the *distinctiones* "*Tria sunt que faciunt*" are similar in style to the other writings of W., since they show the same tendency to enumerate, usually expressed here by numbering the distinctions (i.e. d. i., d. ii., d. iii., etc.); more importantly, they contain several textual parallels with both W.'s glosses and "*Hec sunt que suadent*."[59] Therefore, this collection of *distinctiones* can be considered as another product of W.'s circle, although some differences suggest that it could be a later creation of the same school.

In conclusion, the textual parallels identified so far between the works that can be attributed to W.'s school are as follows:

56 The work has never received much attention from historiography, apart from the record of its existence given by Kuttner, *Repertorium*, p. 235, who erroneously identified it as '*notabilia*.' The *terminus ante quem* can probably be established before the 1180s by a reference in d. 12 to C.35 q.6 c.2 as "*decreto Celestini*:" see the considerations above, p. 39 n. 86; this dating is confirmed by the fact that the *distinctiones* refer only to the *Decretum*, without citing any decretal (see above, pp. 11–12). The *terminus ante quem*, on the other hand, can be deduced from the fact that this work must be later than W.'s glosses: see below, p. 65.

57 D. 19: "*Movende religionis quandoque inregulariter factum toleratur, ut di. xlv. De iudeis, quando ius dispensatur, sicut quando permissum Anglicis ne a religione excideret consanguineis copulari.*"

58 This manuscript, produced in the middle of the 13th century, is of Italian origin and appears to be a luxury product with illustrations and illuminations. The codex, a single editorial project, contains the *Summa* of Ioannes Faventinus (1ra–201va), this set of *distinctiones* (201vb–202vb), and an unfinished copy of the *Summa* of Simon de Bisignano (203ra–226vb). Cf. [Aimone Braida], *Prolegomena*, pp. XVIII–XIX.

59 In addition to the initials H and W (see above, p. 61 n. 55), to show these parallels I will use the letter T to indicate "*Tria sunt que faciunt*:" T 10 = H 92; T 15 = W 10 = H 57; T 24 = W 21 = H 8; T 28 = H 54. As for H, I have established the numerical order in T according to the order of the *distinctiones* in the manuscript.

Glosses signed by W. (numbered by Weigand)	*Distinctiones "Hec sunt que"* (numbered by me)	*Distinctiones "Tria sunt"* (numbered by me)
2	82	
3/3a	25	
4	90	
8	27	
10	57	15
11	1	
12	6	
13	29	
14	43–44	
20	48	
21	8	24
22	9	
25	39	
	54	28
	92	10

In this light, we can say that W.'s glosses are related to a work connected with the *Perpendiculum*, namely the *distinctiones "Hec sunt que suadent,"* probably by the same author or school. But what about the relationship of the glosses to the *Perpendiculum* itself? Gouron has highlighted some connections, the most significant of which is W.'s gloss no. 16, which deals with the case of the irrebuttable presumption,[60] a matter which, as we have seen, is addressed by the *Summula de presumptionibus*.[61] However, in the gloss the matter is only alluded to and there is no coherent explanation or reference to the term *praesumptio violenta*, whereas in the *Summula* the point is treated in a much more explicit and complete way. Other minor affinities with the *Perpendiculum* are found in W.'s glosses nos. 13 and 11: like their parallel *distinctiones* in *"Hec sunt que suadent"* (correspondingly nos. 1 and 29), these

60 Cf. Weigand, *Die Glossen zum Dekret*, 2:640, no. 16, v. *patuerit*, to C.11 q.1 c.25: "*Argumentum quod ex quo presumptio inducitur probatio in contrarium non admittitur ut hic et supra di. liiii. Fraternitatem* (c.15) *et infra xxxii. Q. i. Dixit Dominus* (c.2). *Set contrarium reperitur infra xxxv. Q. iii. Extraordinaria pollutio* (c.11). *W.*"

61 Gouron, "Une école de canonistes," p. 65.

glosses show parallels or connections with brocard no. α19 in Part III and brocard no. 1 in Part II, respectively.[62]

However, if there are some elements of connection between W.'s work and the *Perpendiculum*, there are also divergences that cannot be easily dismissed, especially on the most important matter in the *Summula*, namely the classification of legal presumptions. W.'s glosses contain the canon law tripartite division of legal presumptions into *temeraria*, *probabilis*, and *violenta*,[63] which seems to be the earliest known attestation of this formulation.[64] The tripartition also appears in two other works of W.'s school: the *distinctiones "Hec sunt que suadent"*[65] and *"Tria sunt que faciunt."*[66] However, there are some minor differences in the four texts as regards the classification adopted. As far as W.'s

---

62 See above, p. 48.

63 Weigand, *Die Glossen zum Dekret*, 2:640, no. 10, v. *suspitionis*, to C.2 q.1 c.13: *"Presumptio quandoque est temeraria ut hic et infra vi. q. i. C. Oues* (c.9) *et infra xi. Q. iii. C. Graue* (c.74) *et supra xxxiii. di. c. Habuisse* (c.7) *et hec semper repudianda est. Quandoque probabilis ut infra e. C. et e. Q. c. Si peccauerit* (c.19), *Q. iiii. C. Presbiter si a plebe* (q.5 c.13) *et hec inducit purgationem. Quandoque est uera uel uiolenta ut infra xxxii. Q. i. C. Dixit Dominus* (c.2) *et hec inducit sententiam. W."* See also Ibid., no. 10a: *"Suspitio alia dicitur temeraria ut hic et ut infra e. q. iii. Consuluisti* (q.5 c.20) *et supra di. xxxiii. Habuisse* (c.7), *alia probabilis ut de sacerdote habetur qui infamabatur a populo et tunc debet purgare innocenciam suam et sic dicitur probabilis ut infra e. q. iii. Presbiter* (q.5 c.5 et 13). *Alia dicitur uera et necessaria ut de eo qui inuenit uxorem suam cum alio in lectulo, non tamen commiscentes. Tunc si hoc probare per legitimos testes poterit ex tali suspitione potest eam dimittere ut infra e. Q. Si peccauerit* (c.19) *et infra xxxii. Q. i. Dixit* (c.2). *W."*

64 Fiori, "Praesumptio," p. 86, gives Simon's *Summa* as the probable first example of the appearance of the tripartition, but this is later than W.'s glosses: see below, pp. 71–72. This has also been noted by Menzinger, *Finzioni del diritto*, pp. 210–211.

65 *Distinctiones "Hec sunt que suadent,"* as found in Vb, fol. 9[va], d. 57: *"Suspitio seu presumptio alia est temeraria, C. ii. q. i. Primo* (C.2 q.1 c.13), *Multi* (C.2 q.1 c.18) *'id est', C. vi. q. i. c. Oves* (C.6 q.1 c.9), *C. xi. q. iii. In cunctis* (C.11 q.3 c.52), *D. xxxii. c. Habuisse* (D.33 c.7); *alias est probabilis, C. ii. q. v. Presbiter* (C.2 q.5 c.13), *C. vii. q. ii. c. Nuper* (C.7 q.2 c.2); *alias* (male etas) *violenta, C. xxxi. q. i. Si quis clericorum* (C.11 q.1 c.25), *Quicumque litem* (C.11 q.1 c.35), *C. xxiii. q. i. Paratus* (C.23 q.1 c.2). *Prima reprobatur, secunda inducit purgationem, tertia iuditium exigit. Sed contra C. ii. q. i. Si peccaverit* (C.2 q.1 c.19)."

66 *Distinctiones "Tria sunt que faciunt,"* as found in Rome, Biblioteca Casanatense, 1105, fol. 202[ra], d. 15: "*Ad presumptione. Presumptio alia temeraria, alias probabilis, alias violenta. Temeraria quandoque habetur ratione spuspicantis presumentis, puta si quendam quis viderat cum mulier semel loquentem unum, sinistrum aliquod suspicatur; quandoque ratione infamis, puta si ex maledicorum conficitionibus aliquis infametur. Probabilis quandoque ratione verisimilis indicii, puta si aliquis ex verisimilibus indiciis infametur pro tali, postea quis ad purgationem cogi, ut in B. Habetur* (B.9 c.32); *quandoque ratione communis approbationis, puta sinister rumor de aliquo publice apud omnis pervenerit. Violenta quandoque habetur ex iure, ut xi. q. v. Si qui clericorum* (C.11 q.1 c.25), *quandoque ex certa ratione, ut ii. ca. q. i. Si peccaverit* (C.2 q.1 c.19)."

glosses are concerned, gl. no. 10 enunciates the distinction and briefly explains its effects; in addition, gl. no. 10a provides a few examples of the *praesumptio probabilis* and *violenta* (there called *necessaria*: a term later used by Tancred to indicate the *praesumptio legis violenta*).[67] In the *distinctiones "Hec sunt que suadent"* (d. 57), the tripartition resembles gl. no. 10: there are no examples, only the explanation of the effects. In "*Tria sunt que faciunt*" (d. 15), on the other hand, the definition is much more elaborate (although it contains fewer allegations) and seems to be a later production, perhaps by another jurist in the same milieu: the first two types of presumption are provided with examples, and each of the three types is subdivided into two subcategories. It is also interesting to note that in this distinction the concept of *praesumptio probabilis* is borrowed directly from Burchard's *Decretum* 9:32, as in Rufinus.[68] Most importantly, unlike the other works of W.'s school, "*Tria sunt que faciunt*" combines the tripartite division with the distinction, first introduced by the *Summula de presumptionibus*, between two types of *praesumptio violenta*, defined here as "*ex iure*" (which corresponds to *praesumptio legis violenta*) and "*ex certa ratione*" (which seems to correspond to *praesumptio iudicis violenta*).

Despite the differences, the tripartition of presumptions is present in all the works that can be certainly attributed to W.'s school. If, on the other hand, we look at the *Summula de presumptionibus*, we find no trace of this distinction. The only classification of presumptions is the division *iudicis/legis* and the definition of *praesumptio legis violenta*, while there is no mention of the other two types, *temeraria* and *probabilis*. This suggests that the author of the *Summula* may not have known the tripartite division (and thus of W.'s works), otherwise he would probably have included it in his monographic work. In turn, we do not find in W.'s texts the distinction between *praesumptio iudicis* and *legis* made in the *Summula*, which reinforces the idea of the absence of direct influence between the two authors,[69] except for the *distinctiones* "*Tria sunt que faciunt*," which could therefore be a later work, written after the civilian distinction had become popular among canonists. Regarding the main point of contact, which is the presence of the definition of *praesumptio violenta* in both W.'s works and the *Summula*, it is difficult to establish a chronological precedence beyond doubt, and therefore to determine which work was the first to introduce this expression. We know that W.'s glosses were written in the mid-

67 Cf. Fiori, "Praesumptio," pp. 78–81.

68 Ibid., pp. 84–85.

69 This objection, rightly raised by Gouron, "Une école de canonistes," p. 62, with regard to the relationship between the glosses and Simon's *Summa*, can logically be used here to question the relationship between W.'s glosses and the *Summula de presumptionibus*.

1170s, probably between 1173 and 1174, while the period of composition of the *Summula* is more uncertain and can only be placed between 1172 and 1177 on the basis of the textual evidence we have.[70] Returning to the comparison between the two works, another small but significant difference in the treatment of presumptions between W.'s glosses and the *Summula* is that in the latter we do not find the distinction between *praesumptiones per presens* and *per preteritum* which appears in the former.[71]

Finally, although not a decisive argument, another element of divergence between W.'s glosses and the *Summula* is their treatment of a subject similar to that of presumptions: legal fictions.[72] While the glosses show a great predilection for this subject and play a fundamental role in its theorization,[73] the *Summula* does not deal with *fictiones* at all. In conclusion, we can say that the *Summula*, despite some minor affinities, seems to diverge from W.'s glosses in its main characteristics.

---

70 See below, pp. 90–93.

71 Cf. Weigand, *Die Glossen zum Dekret*, 2:634–635, nos. 5–5b.

72 Some 12th-century jurists noticed a proximity between presumptions and fictions. Apart from W.'s interest in both subjects, the two devices were partly assimilated by Pilius, who in the last part of the first book of his *Libellus* moved from presumptions to legal fictions, since as one can presume against the truth, so one establishes fictions; see Pilius de Medicina, *Libellus Pylei Disputatorius: Liber Primus*, ed. Jürgen Meyer-Nelthropp (PhD dissertation: University of Hamburg, 1958), p. 443: "*Exposuimus supra de presumpcionibus secundum factorum varietates. set quia sicut contra veritatem presumitur ita et fingitur de iuris fictionibus disseramus.*" This proximity is particularly evident in the case of violent legal presumptions and was noted by medieval jurists; some of them, like Azo and his school, even identified the *praesumptio legis violenta* as a legal fiction: Fiori, "Praesumptio," pp. 99–106. In fact, both are held to be true even in the face of evidence to the contrary. But if the two devices are similar in practice, they are certainly different in terms of logic: Fiori, "Praesumptio," pp. 75–77; Yan Thomas, "Fictio legis. L'empire de la fiction romaine et ses limites médiévales," *Droits* 21 (1995), pp. 17–63, 18; Franco Todescan, *Diritto e realtà: Storia e teoria della fictio iuris* (Padua: CEDAM, 1979), pp. 87–88. While the *praesumptio legis violenta* denies what *might* be true, fictions are explicitly false. This was noted by the jurists of the time, who regarded the irrebuttable presumption as a legal declaration about doubtful matters, and fictions as certain falsehoods: Todescan, *Diritto e realtà*, pp. 168–184; Fiori, "Praesumptio," pp. 105–106. Moreover, in the *artes*, both tools can be traced back to the same reasoning: a presumption corresponded to a rhetorical *argumentum*, and in turn, in the grammatical and rhetorical tradition, there was a partial conceptual and terminological overlap between *argumentum* and *fictio*. This can be seen in legal and narrative terms, "to describe the narration of what *could* have been done rather than what was actually done:" Matthew Kempshall, *Rhetoric and the Writing of History, 400–1500* (Manchester: Manchester University Press, 2014), pp. 337–342, 388; Ernst R. Curtius, *European Literature and the Latin Middle Ages*, trans. Willard R. Trask (New York: Pantheon Books, 1953), pp. 452–455.

73 Menzinger, "Finzioni dei canoni", and Menzinger, *Finzioni del diritto*.

3.2 *The Work of Ioannes Faventinus* (1171–1175)

The picture around the anonymous works related to the *Perpendiculum* is beginning to take shape: the ensemble itself shows some textual similarities with a group of texts (W.'s glosses, the *distinctiones "Hec sunt que suadent," "Tria sunt que faciunt,"* and *"Ad movendum varie iudicem"*) that are closely related. However, our collection also has many points of contact with some of the major works produced by well-known jurists of the time, which I will examine in the following pages. Most of these connections have already been highlighted (though not always resolved) in previous literature on the *Perpendiculum*, as in the cases of Simon de Bisignano and Sicardus Cremonensis.[74] However, there is another prominent canonist whose work shows clear parallels with the *Perpendiculum*, but who has been overlooked by previous studies on the subject, which have failed to notice these similarities: the Bolognese decretist Ioannes Faventinus.

We know little about Ioannes, who studied and taught in Bologna in the early 1170s and became bishop of Faenza in 1177. Around 1171, he compiled a *Summa* on the *Decretum*, drawing extensively on the works of Rufinus and Stephen of Tournai, while in the following years (1172–1175) he wrote a large number of glosses on Gratian's work,[75] which belong to what Weigand has defined as the sixth gloss composition, dating from the early 1170s.[76] With regard to these glosses, we have already seen how one of them has a clear correspondence with brocard no. 17 of the second part of the *Perpendiculum* on the acquisitive prescription, although the latter contains a longer version.[77] This element certainly testifies to a link between the two authors, but it does not allow us to establish their relationship beyond doubt. On the one hand, it would be possible to assume that the *Perpendiculum* was influenced by Ioannes and not vice versa, for two reasons: firstly, because the version contained in the latter is shorter than the former; secondly, because this text on acquisitive prescription dealt with a particularly sensitive issue in Italian society at the time. On the other hand, the opposite cannot be ruled out with certainty. Moreover, this parallel passage establishes a link between Ioannes and Part II, but does not tell us any-

74 See below, pp. 71–74 and 75–76.

75 See the literature cited above, p. 36 nn. 75–76, and Norbert Höhl, *Die Glossen des Johannes Faventinus zur Pars I des Decretum Gratiani: Eine literargeschichtliche Untersuchung* (PhD dissertation: Universität Würzburg, 1987).

76 Rudolf Weigand, "The Development of the Glossa ordinaria to Gratian's Decretum," in *HMCLCP*, p. 63.

77 See above, pp. 35–37.

thing directly about the relationship between the former and the *Summula*: although it is likely that Part II was intended from the outset as an appendix to Part I and was compiled by the same author, this assumption will remain a hypothesis. However, the relationship between Ioannes and the *Perpendiculum* is not limited to his glosses and Part II respectively, but also includes the *Summa* of the bishop of Faenza and the *Summula de presumptionibus*.

The most significant connection between Ioannes's *Summa* and the *Perpendiculum* is to be found in the very heart of the *Summula*: the concept of *praesumptio legis violenta*. The canon law idea of a presumption established by law which does not admit evidence to the contrary, is regarded by scholars as a concept that finds its earliest attestations in the *Summula de presumptionibus*, in the work of W., and in the *Summa* of Simon de Bisignano (c. 1177–1179),[78] the latter being considered the first occurrence of this idea in a canon law *Summa*.[79] On the contrary, an embryonic stage of this concept, albeit without the term '*violenta*' to indicate such a presumption, can already be found in the *Summa* of Ioannes at the beginning of the decade.

It is not too surprising that legal historians have overlooked this occurrence: although Ioannes was the most cited canonist before Huguccio, his *Summa* has not yet been published in a modern edition, and modern scholars have often regarded his work as unoriginal because of its heavy indebtedness to Rufinus and Stephen of Tournai. However, a closer look at Ioannes's work reveals unexpected traits of innovation, as in this case.

The occasion is the norm which would become the *sedes materiae* on irrebuttable presumption: C.11 q.1 c.25. Ioannes examines the apparent contradiction between this passage and C.7 q.1 c.3: as we have seen, while the former establishes a presumption that does not admit proof to the contrary, the latter recognizes the possibility that evidence could overcome a presumption.[80] In his *Summa*, the future bishop of Faenza resolves the apparent contradiction by distinguishing between the two cases: the presumption against Adeodatus in C.7 q.1 c.3 is a *praesumptio facti*, which stands until proven otherwise; whereas that of C.11 q.1 c.25 is a *praesumptio legis*, which therefore does not admit contrary evidence.[81] In this way, albeit with different words and in a much shorter

78 In this sense, see Fiori, "Praesumptio," pp. 89–91 and 94–96.

79 See below, p. 71.

80 See above, pp. 57–59.

81 Ioannes Faventinus, *Summa decretorum*, as found in Madrid, BNE, 421, fol. 117rb, v. *nullis excusationibus* to C.11 q.1 c.25: "*supra C. vii. q. ii. Presentium* (C.7 q.1 c.3) *contra, sed ibi contra sacerdotem erat presumptio facti cui standum erat nisi in contrarium probaretur. Hic est presumptio legis contra quam probatio non admittitur.*"

version, Ioannes proposes the same model that we have found in the *Summula*: after borrowing Placentinus's civilian distinction, he draws a differentiation between the consequences of these two types of presumption, in what seems to be the earliest occurrence of the concept (but not the term) of *praesumptio legis violenta*.

However, Ioannes's contribution on presumptions is not limited to his *Summa*. The Bolognese jurist returns to the concept of irrebuttable presumption in two glosses to the same canon. In the first, he gives a long list of legal arguments on irrebuttable presumptions, citing not only the *Decretum* but also the Code, the Digest, and the *Lex Lombarda*.[82] In the second, Ioannes delves more deeply into the distinction between *praesumptio facti* and *legis*, again opposing their cases. Ioannes explains that in the case of C.11 q.1 c.25 it is the canon that presumes and establishes a punishment, and therefore there is no place for evidence to the contrary. In C.7 q.1 c.3, on the other hand, it is the bishop who presumes and imposes a punishment, and therefore there is a place for evidence to the contrary. In other words, the latter is a presumption of fact against the priest, which must be adhered to only in the absence of evidence to the contrary, while the former is a presumption of law, which is irrebuttable.[83]

In short, we can see how both the *Perpendiculum* and Ioannes Faventinus introduce the concept of *praesumptio legis violenta*, following the Placentinian model of distinguishing between *praesumptio legis* and *facti*. The *Summula*, however, treats the subject more generally and in more detail: it distinguishes between two different types of *praesumptio legis*, one irrebuttable and the other not, and for the former it explicitly uses the adverb '*violenter*;' furthermore, while the *sedes materiae* is again C.11 q.1 c.25, in the *Perpendiculum* there

82 See MS Munich, BSB, Clm. 28175, fol. 140v, v. *nullis excusationibus* to C.11 q.1 c.25. This manuscript is one of the richest examples of Ioannes's glosses and has been dated to the late 12th or early 13th century (before 1215) by Rudolf Weigand, "Die Dekretanhänge in den Handschriften Heiligenkreuz 44, Pommersfelden 142 und München 28175," *BMCL* 13 (1983), pp. 1–25; see also Weigand, *Die Glossen zum Dekret*, 2:861–864; Weigand, "The Development of the Glossa ordinaria," p. 63.

83 MS Munich, BSB, Clm. 28175, fol. 140v, v. *nullis excusationibus* to C.11 q.1 c.25: "*Supra vii. q. ii. Presentium* (C.7 q.1 c.3) *contra. Solutio. Hic canon presumit et penam statuit et idcirco locus essem probationi in contrarium. Ibi vero episcopus presumit et penam statuit, idcirco est* (cum *non* praem. et exp.) *locus probationi in contrarium. Vel sic quod idem est, sed in contra sacerdotem erat presumptio facti, cui standum est nisi in contrarium probetur, et hic est presumptio legis, contra quam probatio non ammittitur. Jo.*" It is worth noting that the scribe mistakenly wrote the adverb '*non*' after the second occurrence of the word '*locus*' and then expunged it, whereas it should have been placed before the first '*locus*.'

is no trace of C.7 q.1 c.3 among the *contraria*. In Ioannes, the definition is shorter and closely linked to the casuistic opposition between C.11 q.1 c.25 and C.7 q.1 c.3; moreover, in his treatment the *praesumptio legis* always seems to be irrebuttable, and perhaps for this reason he does not feel the need to use the term '*violenta*' or '*violenter*.' Despite the undeniable textual differences, however, we are faced with two of the earliest testimonies to the concept of irrebuttable legal presumption. Of course, since Ioannes's version is shorter and less elaborate than the *Summula*'s, these differences could suggest that the two jurists arrived at the theoretical elaboration of this type of presumption independently of each other; however, it is also possible that one of the two authors took it from the other. In the latter case, the obvious question would be whether the *Summula* was influenced by Ioannes or vice versa. Once again, however, it is impossible to establish this beyond doubt. Since Ioannes's version is less elaborate than the *Summula*, if there was indeed an influence, we could imagine that the author of the latter took it from the Bolognese canonist and expanded it.[84] If the contrary were true, Ioannes would have had no reason to summarize the longer argument of the *Summula* instead of using it as a whole, nor to omit the distinction between two different types of *praesumptio legis*, or the term '*violenta*'/'*violenter*.'

However, in order to clarify the relationship between the two authors, we should consider the other connecting element that we have seen: the parallels between brocard no. 17 of Part II and the gloss of Ioannes. Contrary to the formulations of the irrebuttable presumption, where an independent elaboration cannot be ruled out, in this case the direct influence of one of the two jurists on the other is beyond doubt. Moreover, since Ioannes's text is shorter, it could have been written earlier, otherwise he could have borrowed from the examples of the *Perpendiculum*.

In conclusion, Parts I and II of the *Perpendiculum* could have been influenced by both the *Summa* and the glosses of Ioannes Faventinus, although the opposite interpretation cannot be ruled out; nor, with regard to the *Summula*, can an

84 Of course, relying on this kind of argument is not always decisive: even if a shorter text often appears to be older than a longer version, the opposite is also possible, as Motzenbäcker shows with regard to the relationship between the *Summula* and the *Summa* of Sicardus Cremonensis: see below, p. 76. However, while in the latter case the shortest text appears to be the most elaborate, in the case of the relationship between Ioannes Faventinus's *Summa* and the *Perpendiculum*, the former is *both* shorter and less elaborate, thus strengthening the idea of chronological precedence.

independent process by the two authors be excluded. What is certain, however, is there is more than a hint of correlation between the two. Moreover, another element can be added to this possible connection: the attribution of the *Perpendiculum* to Ioannes by the scribe of one of its surviving manuscripts, Ma: a point I will come to later,[85] after examining the relationship of the *Perpendiculum* to other jurists of the time.

3.3 *The* Summa *of Simon de Bisignano (1177–1179)*

One of the most important works that can be linked to the *Perpendiculum* is the *Summa* on the *Decretum* by the canonist Simon de Bisignano (fl. 1174–1179),[86] written c. 1177–1179.[87] This work has many parallels with the texts examined so far, making it difficult to clarify the relationship of dependence between them.

Starting from comparison with the work of master W., as we have seen, both the glosses and the *distinctiones "Hec sunt que suadent"* contain the tripartition of the legal presumption into *temeraria, probabilis,* and *violenta*. The same distinction is also presented, for the first time in a canon law *summa,* by Simon, and the two texts show many similarities.[88] It seems clear that there is a direct influence between them, and this obviously raises the question of whether Simon influenced W., or vice versa. Gouron noted that the formulation in W.'s gloss must be earlier,[89] because if W. had been dependent on Simon's work, he would probably have used Simon's distinction between *praesumptio canonis* and *praesumptio hominis* in his glosses,[90] as it appears instead in another, later

---

85 See below, pp. 104–105.

86 See Orazio Condorelli, "A proposito della Summa in Decretum di Simone da Bisignano edita da Pier V. Aimone Braida," *BMCL* 32 (2015), pp. 37–55, and Martin Bertram, "Simon of Apulia: Randbemerkungen zu der Edition der Dekretsumme des Simon von Bisignano," *Mittelalter: Interdisziplinäre Forschung und Rezeptionsgeschichte* 18 (2017), pp. 1–27.

87 Kuttner, *Repertorium*, p. 149. On Simon's *Summa*, see also Josef Juncker, "Die Summa des Simon von Bisignano und seine Glossen," *ZRG Rom. Abt.* 15 (1926), pp. 326–500.

88 Simon de Bisignano, *Summa in Decretum*, v. *modus probationis* to C.2 q.1 c.7, lines 41–45: "*Suspicio autem alia probabilis, alia temeraria, alia certa, alia violenta. Temeraria omnis repellenda est ut infra C.e. q.v Primo* (C.2 q.1 c.13), *Multi* (C.2 q.1 c.18). *Probabilis purgationem inducit, infra C.e. q.iiii. Presbiter si* (C.2 q.5 c.13). *Certa veritati preiudicat. Si ergo per temerariam suspicionem fuerit aliquis condempnatus, sententia debet irritari. Similiter si per probabilem.*" Cf. Fiori, "Praesumptio," p. 89; Motzenbäcker, *Die Rechtsvermutung*, pp. 100–104.

89 Gouron, "Une école de canonistes," p. 62.

90 Simon de Bisignano, *Summa in Decretum*, v. *Si quis clericorum ... rebelli auctoritate* to C.11 q.1 c.25, lines 92–96: "*Unde hic generaliter colligitur quod ubi canon presumit et penam super presumptum statuit non admittitur probatio in contrarium, ut supra d. liiii. Fraternitatem* (D.54 c.15). *Ubi homo presumit, probatio in contrarium admittitur, licet presumptioni*

product of W.'s school: the *distinctiones 'Tria sunt que faciunt.'*[91] More recently, Sara Menzinger has shown how the way the two works deal with legal fictions confirms this impression,[92] and that Simon relied on W.'s glosses, both directly and through the work of Ioannes Faventinus, which in turn represents the earliest reception of W.'s theories on fictions in Italy.[93]

Leaving aside W.'s glosses, we can see how the treatment of legal presumptions in Simon's *Summa* shows possible connections with both the *Summula de presumptionibus* and the work of Ioannes Faventinus. On the subject of irrebuttable presumptions, in the commentary to C.11 q.1 c.25, Simon's work makes the distinction between *praesumptio canonis* and *hominis*: this is the equivalent, in different words, of the Placentinian concept, which is also expressed by the author of the *Summula* when he distinguishes between *praesumptio legis* and *iudicis*, and by Ioannes when he speaks of *praesumptio legis* and *facti*.

At this point, the question naturally arises: did Simon take this distinction from Ioannes or from the *Summula*? We know for certain that Simon used Ioannes's work, as Sara Menzinger has shown with regard to his treatment of fictions.[94] Furthermore, while the *Summula* distinguishes between two types of *praesumptio legis* (one which allows contrary evidence and one which does not), Simon in this passage, like Ioannes, speaks only of the irrebuttable *praesumptio legis* and does not use the term '*violenta*' in relation to this chapter.[95] Therefore, while previous scholarship has assumed that Simon borrowed his comment to C.11 q.1 c.25 from the *Perpendiculum*,[96] it seems more likely that he took it from Ioannes's *Summa*.

However, this does not necessarily mean that Simon did not know and use the *Summula de presumptionibus*; on the contrary: textual analysis gives us many reasons to believe that he did. Firstly, there is another passage in his *Summa* dealing with irrebuttable presumptions where he seems to follow the *Perpen-*

---

addidisset penam, ut supra C.vii. q.i. Presentium (C.7 q.1 c.3) ..." Here I follow the *lectio* given by the manuscript Augsburg, Staats- und Stadtbibliothek, I, which reads "*homo*;" Aimone's edition, instead, prefers the variant "*vero non*" given by the other manuscripts, despite the fact that the *Codex augustanus* often gives better *lectiones*: see [Aimone Braida], *Prolegomena* p. xv. Cf. above, p. 64, n. 63.

91 See above, p. 64 n. 66.

92 Menzinger, "Finzioni dei canoni," p. 223, n. 78.

93 Menzinger, *Finzioni del diritto*, pp. 207–219.

94 Ibid., pp. 207–219.

95 As we have seen, he uses it instead to comment on C.2 q.1 c.7, following W.'s model.

96 Cf. Motzenbäcker, *Die Rechtsvermutung*, pp. 101–102.

diculum: commenting on D.54 c.15,[97] which is the other *sedes materiae* on the subject, Simon distinguishes two types of *praesumptio canonis*, depending on whether a punishment is established on the basis of what is presumed or not. In the first case, the *praesumptio canonis* does not admit contrary evidence, while in the second it does: it is precisely the conceptual equivalent of the distinction made by the *Summula* with regard to the *praesumptio legis*.

Of course, one might object that these parallels do not prove that Simon used the *Summula*, but merely suggest that the two texts were related: is it possible, perhaps, that the author of the *Perpendiculum* used Simon's work and not vice versa? This question has already been raised by previous scholarship. In Simon's *Summa*, the requirement of establishing a punishment for the irrebuttable presumption is particularly emphasized and more precisely formulated than in the *Perpendiculum*. For this reason, Motzenbäcker has convincingly argued that Simon's formulation seems to go beyond the version of the *Summula*, and so the latter should be considered as the earlier of the two works, from which Simon borrowed the content of his own, more complete elaboration.[98] A further element in favor of the precedence of the *Perpendiculum* is the fact that, unlike Simon's *Summa*, it does not use W.'s tripartition of presumptions: if the *Summula* had been written after the *Summa*, its author would have been aware of this distinction and would probably have used it in his monographic work.

There is, however, another passage which must be considered in order to define the relationship between Simon's *Summa* and the *Summula de presumptionibus* and which, if we were to confirm the latter's precedence, would prove that Simon knew and used the *Perpendiculum*. Both works contain a long gloss on the characteristics of the law,[99] the text of which is almost identical. Lang hypothesized that the original gloss came from Simon's work and that the author of the *Summula* relied on it.[100] In her study of the *praesumptio violenta*,

---

97 Simon de Bisignano, *Summa in Decretum*, v. *Fraternitatem … ad seruiendum sibi dicitur comparasse* to D.54 c.15, lines 2–6: "*Cum canon contra aliquem presumit ita quod aut penam statuat tamquam super certo aut non, cum itaque presumit ita quod penam statuat, tunc non admittitur probatio in contrarium, ut hic dicitur et infra C.xi. q.i. Si quis clericorum* (C.11 q.1 c.25)."

98 Motzenbäcker, *Die Rechtsvermutung*, p. 102.

99 Simon de Bisignano, *Summa in Decretum*, v. *Erit autem lex honesta* to D.4 c.2; cf. below, *Summula de presumptionibus*, VI, 8–19. On this gloss, which comes from Isidore through Gratian, see Diego Quaglioni, *La giustizia nel medioevo e nella prima età moderna* (Bologna: Il Mulino, 2004), p. 47.

100 Lang, "Rhetorische Einflüsse," p. 80.

Antonia Fiori shared Lang's opinion and observed that the author of the *Perpendiculum* had faithfully copied the gloss's internal references (i.e. '*infra*' and '*supra*') to Simon's *Summa*.[101] On this point, it should be noted that in most manuscripts of the *Summula* the word '*infra*' is repeatedly used instead of '*in*' in this passage, but only in two of these cases does the textual tradition of Simon's *Summa* use the same term. Instead, in the other passages where Simon uses the word '*infra*,' we do not find it in the *Summula*. Moreover, there is a relevant divergence in the gloss after VI, 18 ("*Manifesta*"): the *Summula*, after quoting C.32 q.1 c.2, adds two other allegations to the same *locus* and then moves directly to VI, 19 ("*Non privato commodo*"). Instead, Simon interpolates here a comparison with the need for clarity in oaths, introduced by his typical phrase, "*Hinc collige*."[102] The absence of this entire passage in the version reported by the *Summula*, as well as the presence of other minor differences in the choice of words and sometimes in the allegations, does not support the thesis of a scribe so faithful as to mechanically copy even internal references. Moreover, as Fiori acknowledges, apart from the gloss to D.4 c.2, a general impression of Simon's dependence on the *Perpendiculum* remains.[103] In conclusion, Simon's work shows a clear connection with, and seems to be dependent on, all the works examined so far: the *Summula de presumptionibus*, Ioannes's *Summa*, and W.'s glosses.

4 Works Directly Influenced by the *Perpendiculum*

If authors of the 1170s, such as Simon de Bisignano, still leave some room for doubt as to their chronological and textual relationship with the *Perpendiculum* (i.e. whether they were influenced by it or vice versa), other legal works produced between the late 1170s and the 1180s undoubtedly show a direct influence of the *Summula*, both in their treatment of the *praesumptio legis* and in their structure, dealing as they do with presumptions in the form of brocards

101 Fiori, "Praesumptio," p. 85.

102 Simon de Bisignano, *Summa in Decretum*, v. *et quia poterat* to D.4 c.2, lines 19–25: "*Hinc collige posse cogi eos qui iurant se audiuisse ab antecessoribus suis consanguinitatem esse inter hunc et illam, ita debere iurare se hoc audiuisse ab antiquioribus suis et antiquitus, scilicet ante initium huius litis, propter fraudem quorundam qui triduo ante iudicium faciunt sibi a predecessoribus suis computari parentelam, arg. infra d.l. Vt constitueretur (D.50 c.25). Aperta enim debet iuratio esse ne per obscuritatem in captionem contineat.*" Apart from the *Summa*, the expression "*Hinc collige*" is often found in his glosses: Rudolf Weigand, "Die Glossen des Simon von Bisignano," AKKR 161 (1992), pp. 362–395.

103 Fiori, "Praesumptio," p. 85.

and *loci argumentorum*. It is worth briefly examining these works to understand the extent of the influence of the *Summula* on Western European legal literature.

4.1 *The* Summa *of Sicardus Cremonensis (1179–1181)*

About two years after Simon's work, between 1179 and 1181, another Italian canonist produced a *Summa in Decretum* which bears strong resemblance to the *Summula de presumptionibus*: Sicardus Cremonensis (c. 1155–1215).[104] His work therefore raises the usual questions about its relationship with the *Perpendiculum* and makes it necessary to devote a few words to it.

While it was for many years attributed to the Bolognese school, Stephan Kuttner (who initially agreed with this hypothesis)[105] convincingly demonstrated that Sicardus's *Summa* had little in common with the Italian schools in terms of style and structure, and that the Bolognese jurists never cited it. Following this line of argument, Kuttner attributed the work to the so-called French school of canon law. The elements that support this theory are the geographical origin of the *Summa*, written by Sicardus while he was teaching in Mainz,[106] its stylistic features, such as the use of rhetoric and the combination of different genres, its use of French canon law works, and its influence on French jurists.[107]

The points of contact between Sicardus's *Summa* and the *Perpendiculum* show an unmistakable relationship. Firstly, we find here the distinction between *praesumptio legis* and *facti*, which we have already seen.[108] However, Sicardus may have borrowed it from Simon, whose work had a profound influence on him.[109] There are, nonetheless, more substantial arguments in favor of a direct relationship between Sicardus and the *Perpendiculum*. As Lang has shown, the whole matter of legal presumptions in Sicardus's work is almost identical to that of the *Summula*. The incipit, the division of facts according to four criteria, and the various categories according to which the presumptions can be established are the same.[110]

---

104 On Sicardus, cf. Antonia Fiori, "Sicardo da Cremona," in *DBGI*, 2:1859–1860.

105 Kuttner, *Repertorium*, pp. 150–153.

106 The Rhenish schools of canon law seem to be linked to the Anglo-Norman jurists active in northern France: see above, p. 20 n. 12. Cf. also Kuttner, *Repertorium*, pp. 171, 179, n. 3, 216.

107 Kuttner, "Réflexions," pp. 783–787.

108 Cf. Sicardus Cremonensis, *Summa in Decretum*, as found in Munich, BSB, Clm. 8013, fol. 49^{v}, to C.6 q.5: "*Est autem praesumptio: legis, ut C. ad macedonianum l. ult., hec nequit infringi; facti, ut D. quod metus causa l. Non, huic potest obviam iri.*" Cf. Motzenbäcker, *Die Rechtsvermutung*, pp. 104–108.

109 Cf. Kuttner, *Repertorium*, p. 151.

110 Cf. Lang, "Rhetorische Einflüsse," pp. 85–87.

Again, the central question is whether the *Summula* influenced Sicardus, or vice versa. Lang hypothesized dependence of the *Summula* on Sicardus's *Summa*, and that the latter must be older for two reasons: because its version of the text is shorter, and because the *Perpendiculum* contains brocards of a later type compared with the style of the occasional *pro-contra* structure of the *Summa*.[111] However, Motzenbäcker argued convincingly that it was the *Perpendiculum* that influenced Sicardus's *Summa*; in response to the first of Lang's stylistic observations, Motzenbäcker gave the example of another passage in Sicardus's *Summa* where the author borrowed Placentinus's text on proofs and presented it in a shorter version. With regard to the second argument, he did not consider it decisive, and stressed that the dialectical arguments in Sicardus's *Summa* already contained some *solutiones*, and thus showed a more elaborate form than the brocards of the *Summula*.[112] Apart from these considerations, Motzenbäcker's hypothesis rests mainly on the relationship that the *Summula* itself has with Simon's work: if the former is older than the latter, and the latter is older than Sicardus's work, then there is no room for doubt.[113] Since this syllogism seems to be textually sound, I can reasonably agree with Motzenbäcker that both Simon and Sicardus borrowed from the *Summula* as a model.

4.2 *The* Speculum iuris canonici *of Peter of Blois (c. 1180)*

Another jurist active in the French schools who seems to have been directly influenced by the *Perpendiculum* is the Anglo-Norman cleric Peter of Blois the younger—not to be confused with the more famous archdeacon of Bath.[114] Around 1180, when he was a canon at Chartres (1176–1181), Peter wrote a collection of *distinctiones* hybridized with the *pro-contra* brocardic method, called *Speculum iuris canonici*, which consists of 60 chapters dealing with various propositions of canon law, which Peter defines at times as *generalia*, *regulae*, or *quaestiones*.

In one of these chapters, the *Speculum* makes a distinction between the two types of *praesumptio legis* that clearly echoes that of the *Summula*. Using a slightly different terminology, Peter explains that when the law makes a presumption, it either imposes a conditional penalty on the basis of that

111 Lang, "Rhetorische Einflüsse," pp. 85–92; Lang, "Zur Entstehungsgeschichte," pp. 125–141.

112 Motzenbäcker, *Die Rechtsvermutung*, p. 93, n. 1.

113 Ibid.

114 A. Lambert, "Blois (Pierre de)," in *DDC* 2 (1937): 925–926, and Charles Lefebvre, "Pierre de Blois," in *DDC* 6 (1957): 1472; see also Richard W. Southern, "The Necessity for Two Peters of Blois," in *Intellectual Life in the Middle Ages: Essays Presented to Margaret Gibson*, ed. Lesley Smith and Benedicta Ward (London: Hambledon Press, 1992).

presumption, or makes an absolute presumption. In the first case, the presumption does not admit evidence to the contrary, while in the second it does.[115]

From the text of this distinction alone, it is not possible to determine whether Peter borrowed it directly from the *Summula* or used an intermediate source such as Simon's *Summa*. However, the similarities between the *Perpendiculum* and the *Speculum* are not limited to the treatment of the *praesumptio legis*, which suggests a possible direct influence of our collection on Peter's work. Thus, brocards nos. 7, 11, 21, and 23 in Part II of the *Perpendiculum* parallel chapters 31, 15, 44, and 53 of the *Speculum*, while brocards β5 and β7 in Part III resemble chapters 54 and 52 of the *Distinctiones*.

4.3 *The* Libellus disputatorius *of Pilius de Medicina (1181–1185)*

Although most of the textual connections of the *Perpendiculum* can be identified in canon law works, perhaps the most remarkable example of its importance is to be found in its influence on some civil law works produced in the Italian 'minor schools' of the Po valley between the late 1170s and the 1180s. The term 'minor schools,' which I have chosen to use, was coined by Ennio Cortese to refer to the (mainly Italian) schools of law that proliferated during the 12th century outside the Bolognese model, with their own characteristics and approaches, which can be summarized as a greater interest in legal practice, the influence of the *artes liberales*, and the study of different types of law.[116] Among these Italian schools, the most emblematic case the of direct influence

115 See Peter of Blois, *Petri Blesensis opusculum de distinctionibus in canonum interpretatione adhibendis, sive ut auctor voluit 'Speculum iuris canonici,'* ed. Gottlieb Reimer (Berlin: Reimer, 1837), c.14, pp. 36–39, and especially p. 37: "*Ius enim, i. e. lex, vel canon, aliquid quando presumit, et super presumpto aliquid statuit, ut in premissis exemplis, quandoque absolute presumit. Ubi super presumpto aliquid statuit, probationem in contrarium non admittit, ut in premissis exemplis. Ubi autem aliquid absolute presumit, super presumpto non constituendo aliquam penam conditionaliter imponit, tunc probatio in contrarium admittitur* …" Cf. Motzenbäcker, *Die Rechtsvermutung*, pp. 108–110.

116 Cf. Ennio Cortese, *Il Rinascimento giuridico medievale*, 2nd ed. (Rome: Il Cigno Galileo Galilei, 1996), especially pp. 27–30; Cortese, *Il diritto*, 2:103–143. The adjective 'minor' is not used to indicate lesser importance, but simply as a form of respect for the *alma mater*, Bologna. Among English-speaking scholars, the concept has been adopted by Anders Winroth, "Law Schools in the Twelfth Century," in Bernard d'Alteroche et al., *Mélanges Lefebvre-Teillard*, and Anders Winroth, "Law Schools and Legal Education," in *The Cambridge History of Medieval Canon Law*, ed. Anders Winroth and John C. Wei (Cambridge: Cambridge University Press, 2022), p. 265, as well as by Jason Taliadoros, *Law and Theology in Twelfth-century England: The Works of Master Vacarius (c. 1115/1120–c. 1200)* (Turnhout: Brepols, 2007), p. 3.

of the *Perpendiculum* is certainly the *Libellus disputatorius* of the famous master Pilius de Medicina (fl. 1175–c. 1210).[117]

Along with the *Brocardica* of Otto Papiensis (second half of the 12th c.),[118] Pilius's *Libellus* is the first collection of *pro-contra* brocards produced in northern Italy. The work is a systematic collection of *loci* from the *Corpus Iuris Civilis*, organized to serve as arguments in legal disputations. Pilius produced two recensions of this book: the first (c. 1181–1185) was intended for use by legal practitioners,[119] while the second (c. 1195) was addressed to students.[120]

Pilius's *Libellus disputatorius* is divided into three books, the first of which is devoted to legal presumptions and is directly influenced by the *Summula de*

---

117 For a partial edition of this work, see Pilius de Medicina, *Libellus Pylei Disputatorius*. On Pilius, see Emanuele Conte, "Pillio da Medicina," in *DBI* 83 (2015), available at https://www.treccani.it/enciclopedia/pillio-da-medicina_(Dizionario-Biografico)/, accessed 2022 Jul 31; Ennio Cortese, "Pillio," in *DBGI*, 2:1587–1590; Peter Weimar, "Pilius, Bologneser Zivilrechtslehrer (um 1150—nach 1207)," in *LexMA* 6 (1993): 2159.

118 On this collection, see Schwaibold, "Wer sucht," and Weimar, "Argumenta," pp. 119–121. Cf. also David De Concilio, "Moneta e cultura giuridica: Un brocardo di Azzone nella costruzione del diritto pecuniario medievale," *TvR* 87 (2019), pp. 384–426. On Otto, see Luca Loschiavo, "Ottone da Pavia," in *DBGI*, 2:1475; Peter Weimar, "Otto Papiensis," in *LexMA* 6 (1993): 1585.

119 This recension contains no *solutiones contrariorum* and was written between 1181 and 1185, during the years of *otium* between Pilius's move to Modena and the beginning of his teaching there. In his proem to Placentinus's *Summa* on the *Tres Libri*, edited by Friedrich Carl von Savigny, *Geschichte des römischen Rechts im Mittelalter*, 4, 2nd ed. (Heidelberg: Mohr, 1850; repr. Aalen: Scientia-Verlag, 1986), pp. 312–315, Pilius himself tells us that after three years of teaching in Bologna he moved to Modena, but was forced to delay the beginning of his teaching there for two years because of an oath he had taken in the *Alma Mater*. It was during these two years that Pilius completed his *Libellus*. Since the first document attesting to his presence in Modena dates from 1181, his move must have taken place shortly before that date: see Conte, "Pillio."

120 After the redaction of the first recension, Pilius became enthusiastic about using the *pro-contra* method in his teaching: between 1186 and 1195 he wrote a collection of *quaestiones* for his classes. In 1195, becoming more aware of the didactic importance of dialectical discussion for the legal training of his students, he wrote this second recension of his *Libellus*. The main aim of this edition was to reform the teaching of law by introducing a method based on reasoning rather than memory: Cortese, *Il diritto*, 2:152. As Pilius himself said in the preface to the second recension, he expected to reduce the duration of legal studies from ten to four years. In this second recension, Pilius added a prologue to the work, but also *solutiones contrariorum* to his *generalia* and references to his *quaestiones*: cf. Belloni, *Le questioni civilistiche*, pp. 53–54; Ugo Nicolini, *Pilii Medicinensis quaestiones sabbatinae: Introduzione all'edizione critica* (Modena; Università degli Studi, 1933), pp. 24, 26–27; Kuttner, "Réflexions," p. 770. On the basis of these cross-references, Belloni suggested that Pilius intended the two works to be complementary in the education of his students.

presumptionibus in many respects.[121] First, from a technical point of view, Pilius borrowed the same articulation in rhetorical *loci*, here defined as *modi*.[122] Moreover, in these *modi* he followed the categories of the *Summula*, from the distinctions of extrinsic/intrinsic—substance/quality to the various criteria according to which a presumption can be made. Thus, Pilius borrowed the entire model of the first book of the *Libellus* from the *Summula*, including its structure in *pro-contra* brocards, which represents a fundamental innovation in the development of the genre.[123] He replaced the canon law allegations with references to Roman law, developed and expanded the brocards, and added many new categories and digressions, but the core structure is clearly the same.[124]

The clearest textual evidence of Pilius's direct reliance on the *Summula*, however, is to be found in the incipit of the first book of the *Libellus*, where the jurist mentions "that treatise which is called *De presumptionibus* by the common people," which is "very useful and necessary ... especially when at some time it happens to have doubts about uncertainties."[125] This passage, which is undoubtedly a reference to the *Summula*, testifies not only to Pilius's direct knowledge of this work, but also to its circulation and popularity in northern Italy in the first half of the 1180s.

Another aspect that shows Pilius's dependence on the *Summula* is the theoretical way in which he treats legal presumptions. This point has been examined in detail,[126] so I will limit myself to outlining the main parallels. Following the model of the *Summula*, Pilius distinguishes between a *praesumptio facti* and a *praesumptio iuris*, and divides the latter into two: one that admits evidence to the contrary and one that does not.[127] In his definition of legal presumptions, however, Pilius shows knowledge not only of the *Summula*, but also of the canon law tripartition elaborated by the transmontane decretists.

121 Pilius's reliance on the *Summula* has been emphasized since Lang, "Zur Entstehungsgeschichte," pp. 139–141. Cf. Kuttner, "Réflexions," p. 775.

122 On the use of rhetoric in Pilius, cf. Hanns Hohmann, "Rhetoric in Medieval Legal Education: Libellus Pylei Disputatorius," *Disputatio 4 Discourses of Power: Grammar and Rhetoric in the Middle Ages* (1999), pp. 59–73. On Topics in the form of *modi arguendi*, see Severino Caprioli, ed., *Modi arguendi: Testi per lo studio della retorica nel sistema del diritto comune* (Spoleto: Centro Italiano di Studi sull'Alto Medioevo, 2006).

123 See above, pp. 49–51.

124 Kuttner, "Réflexions," p. 775.

125 Pilius, *Libellus*, p. 3: "*tractatum illum esse utilissimum et pernecessarium, qui de presumpcionibus vulgo intitulatur.*" Cf. below, *Summula de presumptionibus*, I, 1.

126 Motzenbäcker, *Die Rechtsvermutung*, pp. 62–65; Fiori, "Praesumptio," pp. 82, 98–99.

127 Fiori, "Praesumptio," pp. 98–99.

In fact, he was the first legist to supplement the civilian categorization with the canon law one. The latter was adapted to the civilian procedure by removing the reference to the *purgatio canonica* as the result of the *praesumptio probabilis*.[128]

It should also be noted that the influence of the *Summula de presumptionibus* on the first book of the *Libellus* should not be understood as a dependence on a limited part of Pilius's work. Rather, the *Libellus* is entirely built around its book on legal presumption, which is the core of the work and its very raison d'être:[129] one could say that the *Libellus* is intended to be primarily a work on presumptions (and the related matter of fictions). This is evidenced, for example, by the space that this theme occupies in the whole work,[130] as well as by the fact that the *Libellus* was commonly known, with a metonymy, as *De presumptionibus*.[131]

4.4 *The* Tractatus de operibus (*1174–1190*)

A direct influence of the *Perpendiculum* on the canon law production of its time is found not only in the major works of great jurists such as Simon, Sicardus, and Pilius, but also in smaller, anonymous works that are much less known to historiography. This is the case of a treatise contained in one of the manuscripts of the *Perpendiculum*, Ba, in a codicological unit of clear Anglo-Norman origin,[132] which I have called *Tractatus de operibus*.[133]

The subjects dealt with in the *Tractatus de operibus* suggest that the text was intended as a manual of procedure for ecclesiastical judges. In fact, it can be divided into two parts: the first illustrates the different types of presumption that can be drawn from an internal act (i.e. the psychological element), while the second deals with external acts (i.e. the historical fact); the former, in turn, is divided into different types of evidence (testimony, *fama*, and documents) and legal privileges. I will focus my attention on the first part, because it shows sig-

128 Fiori, "Praesumptio," pp. 98–99.

129 Cf. Kuttner, "Réflexions," p. 775.

130 For example, in Vienna, ONB, Cvpl. 2157, the *Libellus* extends from fol. 36^{r} to fol. 87^{v}. Almost two-thirds of the work consists of the first book, *De presumptionibus* (fols. 36^{r}–68rb), while the second (*De iudiciis*, fols. 68rb–77rb) and the third (which "*non habet certam materiam sed multiplices et varios in se disputandi articulos continet*," fols. 77rb–87va) each consist of 10 folios.

131 Kuttner, "Réflexions," pp. 775–776.

132 See below, pp. 138–140.

133 See De Concilio, "Soggettività e qualificazione," which deals with the treatise in detail. There, the reader will also find a detailed textual analysis and edition of this work.

nificant similarities with the *Summula de presumptionibus*,[134] suggesting that the *Tractatus de operibus* was strongly influenced by it.

As we have seen, the author of this treatise, like the author of the *Summula*, examines the different types of presumption that can be made about a fact.[135] In both works, we have the division of the fact according to extrinsic/intrinsic and essence/circumstances;[136] their combination gives us four different criteria according to which one can presume, which are mirrored in the two texts:

Category	Definition given by the *Summula*	Definition given by the *Tractatus*	Meaning
On the substance of an extrinsic fact	*Extrinseci facti essentia*	*Opus exterior*	Whether the material fact happened or not
On the quality of an extrinsic fact	*Extrinseci facti qualitas*	*Exterioris operis accidentia*	The circumstances of the material fact
On the substance of an intrinsic fact	*Intrinseci facti substantia*	*Opus interior*	Subsistence or not of the psychological element of the fact
On the quality of an intrinsic fact	*Intrinseci facti qualitas*	*Interioris operis accidentia*	The circumstances of the psychological element of the fact

Whereas the *Summula* begins by examining the extrinsic fact, the *Tractatus* begins with the intrinsic.[137] Moreover, unlike the *Perpendiculum*, the *Tractatus* does not proceed in an orderly fashion according to the subdivisions of the act, but rather wavers. It first lists the criteria according to which consent

134 As noted by James A. Brundage, "Some Canonistic Quaestiones in Barcelona," *Manuscripta* 15 (1971), pp. 67–76, 75.

135 While the *Summula* speaks of fact (*factum*), the *Tractatus* uses the word 'action' (*opus*). Despite the terminological differences, there is a substantial correspondence between the two: indeed, it is clear that the kind of *factum* analyzed by the *Perpendiculum* is a fact derived from human conduct, and indeed in the *Summula* the two words are conceptually interchangeable. On this point, see De Concilio, "Soggettività e qualificazione," pp. 14–17.

136 The first is *extrinsecum/intrinsecum* in the *Summula* and *exterior/interior* in the *Tractatus*, while the second is *substantia/qualitas* and *opus/accidentia operis*, respectively.

137 See De Concilio, "Soggettività e qualificazione," p. 16; Fransen, "Canonistica minora," p. 36.

may or may not be presumed,[138] then the cases which, according to the examples given by the author in the introduction, have to do with the *accidentia* of the extrinsic fact, i.e. the reason which could affect the validity of consent.[139] The treatise then returns to the analysis of the *opus interior* itself, which deals with cases other than consent.[140] After this analysis, the manuscript contains a brocard dealing with a different subject, namely the problem of the judge's conscience.[141] While the examination of the intrinsic fact that we have outlined is strikingly similar in the *Summula* and the *Tractatus*, the same cannot be said for the extrinsic fact. Here, the *Tractatus* does not follow the presumptive model of the *Perpendiculum*, but is organized according to the main means of evidence: testimony, repute, and documents.

Despite the partial dissimilarities, the connection between the *Tractatus de operibus* and the *Summula de presumptionibus* is obvious. However, in order to confirm that the latter influenced the former, we need to date the *Tractatus*.[142] That the treatise was more recent is suggested by its allegations: unlike the *Summula*, the *Tractatus* occasionally cites papal decretals (as "*decretum extra*"). The *terminus post quem* can therefore be established on the basis of the most recent of these decretals, *Sicut Romana ecclesia* (JL 12293 = WH 944 = X. 1.3.1), which can be dated to 1173–1174.[143] The *terminus ante quem*, on the other hand, can

138 The first four, namely the quality of the person ("*ex persona*"), crying ("*ex fletu*"), clamor ("*ex clamore*"), flight ("*ex fuga*"), are also found in the *Summula* under "*exterioribus signis*" (IV, 9). Then, in the *Tractatus*, there is a specific argument about the betrothed woman who could break the betrothal but did not, which is not present in the *Summula*. The two following criteria (silence and lack of contradiction) are parallel to IV, 6 of the *Summula*, but have a different formulation and partly different allegations. The following categories concern coercion (which is also the subject of IV, 8 of the *Summula*, although there is no direct connection between the two) and the presumption of consent from salutation.

139 Reluctance, fear and coercion, anger, passion, deception. Then, there are other factors that may (or may not) alter the validity of consent: withdrawal of consent, simulation, conditional consent; finally, the treatise lists some states of mind that alter consent, such as fear and inebriation.

140 Fear, for example, can be presumed from personal characteristics, place, and sex; repentance from external actions; will from the same *loci* examined for consent. Incidentally, the treatise moves again from the action to its circumstances, examining the nature that the will can have, good or bad.

141 "*Quod potius factum conscientiam quam allegata debeat iudicari.*" It is unclear whether this brocard was originally part of the work or not: cf. De Concilio, "Soggettività e qualificazione," pp. 19–20.

142 On this point, cf. De Concilio, "Soggettività e qualificazione," pp. 12–14.

143 In De Concilio, "Soggettività e qualificazione," p. 13, I had mistakenly considered another decretal cited, WH 932, as to be the most recent, attributing it to Lucius III (1181–1185) and

be inferred from the fact that the *Tractatus* uses the same expression "*extra*" to refer to two *paleae* of Gratian's *Decretum*: *Quicumque* (C.27 q.2 c.8)[144] and *Venter* (D.35 c.5).[145] The reason for this may be that when the *Tractatus* was written, the presence of these *paleae* in the manuscripts of the *Decretum* was still fragmentary, and they were probably not yet found in some of the codices circulating in the northern schools; therefore, the author of the *Tractatus* felt the need to emphasize their foreign origin with the word "*extra*." If we look at this practice in other sources, we can see that *Quicumque* was still referred to as "*extra*" in Parisian and Anglo-Norman works between 1185 and 1188:[146] this is the case of the French *Summae* "*Tractaturus Magister*" (Reims, 1182),[147] "*Permissio quedam*" (1185–1186),[148] and *Lipsiensis* (1186),[149] as well as of the two *Summae* attributed to Honorius of Kent, "*De iure canonico tractaturus*" (c. 1188)[150] and *Summa decretalium quaestionum* (written shortly afterwards).[151] It is first

---

dating the text accordingly. However, while this decretal is indeed attributed to this pontiff from 1 Comp. 5.2.6 onwards, in earlier collections (Par. II 26.4 and Lips. 1.15) it is instead reported as "*ex decretis Iulii*" and therefore attributed to Pope Julius. The most recent decretal must therefore be WH 944.

144 Rudolf Weigand, "Fälschungen als Paleae im Dekret Gratians," in *Fälschungen im Mittelalter: Internationaler Kongress der Monumenta Germaniae Historica, München, 16.–19. September 1986*, ed. Detlev Jasper, 2 (Hannover: Hahnsche Buchhandlung, 1988), p. 312, and Rudolf Weigand, "Die frühen kanonistischen Schulen und die Dekretabbreviatio Omnebenes," AKKR 155 (1986), pp. 72–91, 85–87, showed that the canon was probably forged by the decretist Omnibene, bishop of Verona, in his *Abbreviatio Decreti* (1156), in order to find an argument against conditional marriage. The circulation of this text in his time seems to have been fragmentary.

145 This time we have a different style of citation: the presence of the passage in the *Decretum* is clearly stated ("*D. xxxv.*"), but it is followed by the word "*extra*." This could mean that the text was already included in the *Decretum*, but the scribe wanted to emphasize its character as a *palea*. In any case, the inclusion of this *palea* preceded that of *Quicumque*: for example, the *Summa Parisiensis* (late 1160s) quotes this text in full, which means that it was probably already included in the *Decretum* as a *palea*, but that it was still not found in most copies: Terence P. McLaughlin, ed., *The Summa Parisiensis on the Decretum Gratiani* (Toronto: Pontifical Institute of Mediaeval Studies, 1952), p. XII. In his *Summa*, Simon de Bisignano also cites *Venter* as part of the *Decretum*: cf. Simon de Bisignano, *Summa in Decretum*, v. *Est luxuria* to D.2 de cons. c.83, line 453.

146 Rudolf Weigand, *Die bedingte Eheschließung im kanonischen Recht*, 1 (Munich: Max Hueber, 1963), pp. 181–195.

147 Cf. Peter Landau, "Die Dekretsumme 'Tractaturus magister' und die Kanonistik in Reims in der zweiten Hälfte des 12. Jahrhunderts," *ZRG Kan. Abt.* 131 (2014), pp. 132–152.

148 Cf. below, p. 149.

149 Cf. below, p. 85 n. 159.

150 Cf. below, p. 88.

151 Cf. Weigand, "The Transmontane Decretists," p. 198.

mentioned as a *palea* is in the *Summa* of Huguccio (1188–1190).[152] From these elements, it is reasonable to place the *terminus ante quem* of our treatise at the end of the 1180s. This period can be confirmed on two other grounds: firstly, the fact that the decretals cited in this work are referred to only by their incipit, without reference to a particular collection; secondly, the dating of the other texts in the same codicological unit, the *Quaestiones Barcinonenses II* and *III*.[153] We can therefore reasonably assume that the *Tractatus* was composed between the mid-1170s and mid-1180s, before the increasing popularity of systematic collections of decretals, and in any case between 1174 and 1190. This dating would fit well with its relationship to the *Perpendiculum*: indeed, it is reasonable to think that the *Summula* influenced the *Tractatus* and not vice versa: otherwise the former would have used the more detailed categories of the latter.

5 Later Fortunes of the *Summula*'s Distinction on the *praesumptio legis*

In the previous pages, we have examined the works which show traces of a direct influence of the *Perpendiculum* between the late 1170s and the 1180s. This is only a part of a larger number of legal texts which, in that period, borrowed the *Summula*'s model for the treatment of the *praesumptio violenta*. For many of these works, however, it is impossible to determine with certainty whether they took this model directly from our collection or from a mediated source such as Simon's *Summa*. Whatever the source, what is certain is the success of this elaboration, rooted in the *Perpendiculum*, among both Italian and French jurists. It is therefore worth examining it briefly.

5.1 *Ioannes Bassianus and the* praesumptio ex qualitate facti

As we have already seen, the bipartition of the *praesumptio legis* contained in the *Summula* had a strong reception both in the French milieu and in the Italian 'minor schools,' and among legists as well as canonists. This double circulation is well illustrated by a group of texts that share a very similar formulation when distinguishing between the two types of *praesumptio legis*.

In the Roman law schools of the Po valley, this is attested by a *distinctio* transmitted by two manuscripts: Cambridge, Trinity College, B.1.29,[154] fol. 212ʳ, and

152 Hence, it was probably added to the *Decretum* shortly before: Weigand, "The Transmontane Decretists," pp. 106, 205.

153 Below, pp. 138–139.

154 "Ct" in the collation below, p. 86 n. 160.

Vatican City, BAV, Chigi E.VII.218,[155] fol. 83ra, as part of the so-called *Collectio Chisiana I*.[156] In the latter, the *distinctio* is attributed to Ioannes Bassianus (2nd half of the 12th c.),[157] through the *siglum* 'Jo.'

The same distinction also appears in an *ordo iudiciarius* beginning with "*Olim edebatur*," which was certainly composed after 1177 and whose origin is disputed between Italy and the Anglo-Norman world.[158] Moreover, its text largely parallels with that of a passage in the Anglo-Norman *Summa Lipsiensis*: a canon law work on Gratian's *Decretum*, written in Paris in 1186,[159] which

155 Extremely miscellaneous, this manuscript contains several brocardic works (and more generally collections of arguments, including *quaestiones* and *distinctiones*), as well as various materials from the so-called 'minor schools' of the Po valley, both of Roman and Lombard law; it is worth mentioning the *Brocarda Lombarde*, Otto's *Brocarda*, Pilius's *Libellus disputatorius*, some writings of Ioannes Bassianus, the solutiones of Azo's brocards and Vaccella's *Argumenta*: see De Concilio, *Via Brocardica*, 2:15–16.

156 Seckel, *Distinctiones*, p. 389, f).

157 Ennio Cortese, "Bassiano (Bosiano, Boxiano), Giovanni," in *DBGI*, 1:191–193; Peter Weimar, "Johannes Bassianus," in *LexMA* 5 (1991): 556–557.

158 The *ordo* "*Olim*" was already known to 19th-century legal historians, who attributed it to Otto Papiensis: Savigny, *Geschichte des römischen Rechts*, pp. 379–383. In 1892, however, Giovanni Tamassia and Giovanni Battista Palmieri published an edition of the manuscript Padua, Biblioteca Universitaria, 1745, which they believed to contain a long and coherent work by Ioannes Bassianus, edited by them under the title *Libellus de ordine judiciorum*: see Tamassia and Palmieri, *Iohannis Bassiani Libellus*. In reality, this codex was a miscellaneous manuscript containing, among many other works, the *ordo* "*Olim*." This was corrected by Emil Seckel, "Ueber neuere Editionen juristischer Schriften aus dem Mittelalter I," *ZRG Rom. Abt.* 21 (1900), pp. 212–338, 306–324, who returned to the traditional attribution to Otto. This attribution was later questioned by Kuttner and Rathbone, "Anglo-Norman Canonists," pp. 290–291, and Knut Wolfgang Nörr, "Die Literatur zum gemeinen Zivilprozess," in *HQLR*, 1:388, who suggested an Anglo-Norman origin, reviving a theory already put forward in the 19th century by Exupère Caillemer, "Le droit civil dans les provinces anglo-normandes au XIIe siècle," *Mémoires de l'Académie nationale des Sciences, Arts et Belles-Lettres de Caen* 1883 (1883), pp. 157–226, 185–187. The detailed study of Fowler-Magerl, *Ordo iudiciorum*, pp. 76–80, in turn, re-established the hypothesis of Otto's paternity. In response, the Anglo-Norman theory was revived by André Gouron, "Qui a écrit l'ordo 'Olim edebatur'?," *Initium* 8 (2003), pp. 64–84, repr. in Gouron, *Pionniers*, no. XIII, who attributed it to the master Rodoicus Modicipassus. Finally, this suggestion has recently been challenged by Bertram, "Rodoicus Modicipassus," pp. 140–142, who once again restored Otto's attribution. Gero Dolezalek, however, maintains strong doubts that the Otto who compiled the *Ordo* was Otto Papiensis, since the manuscript tradition of the work suggests an Anglo-Norman origin: cf. Fowler-Magerl, *Ordo iudiciorum*, p. 78.

159 See Kuttner, *Repertorium*, pp. 196–198; Kuttner and Rathbone, "Anglo-Norman Canonists," p. 290. The work has been attributed to the Anglo-Norman jurist Rodoicus Modicipassus by Peter Landau, "Rodoicus Modicipassus—Verfasser der Summa Lipsiensis?," *ZRG Kan. Abt.* 92 (2006), pp. 340–354, 342–344, although this hypothesis has recently been challenged by Martin Bertram, "Rodoicus Modicipassus und der Praecentor von Sens. Wer

draws its material on presumptions from various sources, including Peter of Blois, Sicardus, Placentinus, and Simon de Bisignano.

It is worth examining the differences and similarities between the various formulations of this distinction. In Ioannes's *distinctio*[160] and in the *ordo*,[161] the text is almost parallel. Both distinguish between a *praesumptio legis ex qualitate facti* (based on the circumstances of the fact), which can be refuted, and a *praesumptio legis* properly speaking, which establishes a consequence from the presumption and is irrebuttable. The same distinction, with a slightly different formulation, is found in the *Summa Lipsiensis*, where, unlike the other two texts and more similarly to the *Perpendiculum*, it is preceded by a differentiation between *praesumptio iudicis* and *praesumptio iuris* (so called and not '*legis*').[162]

---

war der Verfasser der Dekretsummen 'Omnis qui iuste iudicat' (Lipsiensis), 'Et est sciendum' und des Ordo iudiciarius 'Olim edebatur'?," *Mittelalter: Interdisziplinäre Forschung und Rezeptionsgeschichte* 3 (2020), pp. 120–153.

160 "*Quandoque presumit lex* [lex presumit *tr.* Ct] *ex qualitate facti* [facto Ct] *et* [tunc *add.* Ct] *probatio admittitur in contrarium, unde dictum est: "tamdiu presumptioni statum quamdiu in* [*om.* Ct] *contrarium non* [*om.* Ct] *probatur* [probetur Ct]," *ut D. de iure dotium l. Nuptura* (Dig. 23.3.57) *et D. quod metus causa l. Non est verisimile* (Dig. 4.2.23pr), *C. de donationibus l. Si* [*om.* Ct] *preses* [presens Ct] (Cod. 8.53.8) *et C. de probationibus l. Sive* (Cod. 4.19.13.1). *§ Quandoque lex presumit et statuit nec admittitur probatio in contrarium, et hoc: ex rigore scripture, ut C. de arbitris* (Cod. 2.55.4) *l. Ne in arbitris* [l. ... arbitris *om.* Ct] *et C. de contrahenda* [et committenda *add.* Ct] *stipulatione l. i.* (Cod. 8.37.1) *et D. de verborum obligationibus l. Sciendum* [Si eodem Ct] (Dig. 45.1.30); *favore ultime voluntatis, ut C. de institutionibus et substitutionibus l. Generaliter* (Cod. 6.25.7pr), *§* [*om.* Ct] *Cum autem* (Cod. 6.25.7.1) *et C. de inofficioso* [officioso Ct] *testamento l. Si mater* (Cod. 3.28.3); *similiter favore dotis, ut C. de rei uxorie actione* (Cod. 5.13). *Jo.* [*om.* Ct]."

161 Tamassia and Palmieri, *Iohannis Bassiani Libellus*, p. 236, § 373–374: "*Format autem lex quandam presumptionem ex qualitate facti et admittitur probatio in contrarium, unde dicitur «tamdiu presumptioni statur donec probetur contrarium,» ut D. de iure dotium l. Nuptura (Dig. 23.3.57); et C. de donationibus inter virum et uxorem l. Etiam (Cod. 5.16.6); et C. de probationibus l. Sive (Cod. 4.19.16). Quoniam vero presumptum format et super presumpto statuit nec in contrarium admittur probatio (que presumptio legis a quibusdam dicitur); hanc alias vigor scripture inducit, ut C. de arbitris l. Ne in arbitris (Cod. 2.46.4); alias favore ultime voluntatis, ut C. de institutionibus et substitutionibus l. Generaliter § cum autem (Cod. 6.25.6.1); alias dotis, ut C. de rei uxorie actione l. I et II (Cod. 5.13.1 et 2); alias eam inducit odium vel coniurationum, vel conspirationum, ut in Decretis ca. XI q. I c. Si qui clericorum (C.11 q.1 c.25) cum omnibus concordantiis suis.*" Here, I have slightly departed from Tamassia's and Palmieri's edition, which in the last sentence wrongly reads "*coniurationem*" and "*conspirationem*" instead of their respective plural genitive forms.

162 Rudolf Weigand et al., eds., *Summa 'Omnis qui iuste iudicat' sive Lipsiensis*, 5 vols (Vatican City: BAV, 2007–2018), 1:258, v. *dicitur* to D.54 c.15: "*id est presumitur. Et est presumptio iuris contra quam non admittitur probatio in contrarium. Et nota quod est presumptio iudicis et*

However, whereas the text in the *Lipsiensis* ends here, both Ioannes's distinction and the *ordo "Olim"* list the reasons for the irrefutability of the legal presumption: the rigorous interpretation of a writing and the preferential treatment accorded to testaments and dowries. The *ordo "Olim"* adds a further reason to explain the irrebuttable presumption based on C.11 q.1 c.25, namely the aversion to plots and conspiracies.[163]

From this brief examination it is clear how the formulation offered by this group of texts clearly borrows, either directly or indirectly, the model of the *Perpendiculum*. However, there are also some notable elements of novelty.

Firstly, these works specify when a legal presumption can be rebutted: when it is established by the circumstances of a fact (*ex qualitate facti*); in the *Summula*, on the other hand, this was only a residual category, defined merely in opposition to the *praesumptio legis violenta*. This element, moreover, echoes the formulation of another product of the school of Ioannes Bassianus: the *ordo iudiciorum "Sapientiam,"*[164] which distinguishes the *praesumptio legis* between a presumption *iuris et de iure*, which is irrebuttable, and a presumption *super facto*, which is not.[165]

Secondly, we can no longer find an explicit reference to the establishment of a punishment as a condition for the irrebuttable presumption. In fact, all the texts simply say that a presumption is of this kind when the law "*statuit*" or "*super presumpto statuit*," without mentioning the word '*penam*,' as was the

contra hanc admittitur probatio, ut vii q.i Presentium (C.7 q.1 c.3). *Est presumptio iuris et hec duplex est quia quandoque format presumptionem ex qualitate facti, unde dicitur: 'Standum est presumptioni, donec probetur in contrarium'; quandoque statuit super presumpto et tunc non admittitur probatio in contrarium, et infra lxxvii Si expositus* (D.87 c.9), *infra xi q.i Si qui clericorum* (C.11 q.1 c.25)."

163 See above, p. 59.

164 The author of this *ordo* (perhaps Azo or one of his pupils) repeatedly refers to Ioannes as "*magister meus.*" Jean-Marie Carbasse, "L'ordo iudiciorum Sapientiam affectant omnes," in *Confluence des droits savants et des pratiques juridique. Actes du colloque de Montpellier (12–14 décembre 1977)* (Milan: Giuffrè, 1979), believed that the work was written after the *Compilatio prima* (1182–1192), while Fowler-Magerl, *Ordo*, pp. 130–133, dated it before 1191.

165 Christian Coppens, ed., "Libellus de ordine iudiciorum," in *Voortschrijdend Procesrecht. Ein historische Verkenning*, ed C.H. van Rhee, F. Stevens, and Ernest Persoons (Leuven: Universitaire Pers Leuven, 2001), pp. 270–271: "*Sunt presumtiones quedam contra quas non admittitur probatio in contrarium. Has presumtiones appellat magister meus iuris et de iure … Sunt alie presumtiones contra quas admittitur probatio in contrarium. Hee appellari possunt presumtiones super facto, ut ff. Quod metus causa l. ult.* (Dig. 4.2.23) *ff. de iure dotium. Nuptura (Dig. 23.3.57). Presumtiones tales varie sunt et multe sparse in lege, et que non possunt temere diffiniri. Ecce enim ex facto cuiuslibet contra eum presumitur.*"

case in the *Summula* and in the other works examined so far. This paved the way for the idea that a presumption is irrebuttable only because it is qualified as such by a legal provision.[166]

In light of these elements, it is not difficult to disentangle the chronological relationship between these texts. As far as the *ordo "Olim"* is concerned, it would not be unreasonable to imagine that its author took this categorization from Ioannes and his school, in which the formulation seems to be well established, both in the *distinctio* and in the *ordo "Sapientiam."* As for the relationship between Ioannes's *distinctio* and the *Summa Lipsiensis*, and thus between the Roman and canon law elaborations on this point, it is more difficult to establish a clear connection. Of course, if we date Ioannes's distinction before the *ordo "Olim,"* we could assume that it is also earlier than the *Lipsiensis*, but for the time being any further curiosity on this point will remain unsatisfied. In any case, these connections certainly underline the deep entanglement between the late 12th-century legal schools, where the circulation of knowledge seems to have overcome disciplinary, geographical, and authorial boundaries with extreme rapidity. This is also borne out by some further evidence of the direct or indirect circulation of the theory of presumptions established by the *Summula de presumptionibus* in both the Italian and Anglo-Norman schools of canon and civil law.

5.2 *Further Evidence of Popularity*

Apart from the *Lipsiensis*, further evidence of the spread of the model provided by the *Perpendiculum* among Anglo-Norman canonists is offered by the canon law *Summa "De iure canonico tractaturus"* (c. 1185–1191), attributed to Honorius of Kent (fl. c. 1185–d. c. 1210/1213) who studied in Paris during these years. In his commentary on D.54 c.15, Honorius refers to the theory which qualifies the presumption against the Jewish merchant who does not sell a Christian slave within three months (D.54 c.15) as an irrebuttable *praesumptio iuris*. The English jurist, however, departs from this theory and states that in a similar case anyone who is willing to prove the contrary should be admitted.[167]

---

166 Fiori, "Praesumptio," pp. 96–98; see also Motzenbäcker, *Die Rechtsvermutung*, pp. 110–114.

167 See Honorius of Kent, *Magistri Honorii Summa 'De iure canonico tractaturus'*, ed. Rudolf Weigand et al., 3 vols (Vatican City: BAV, 2004–2010), p. 179, v. *si autem* to D.54 c.15: "*Si autem venditur et presumitur et hec est presumptio iuris, ubi non admitteretur Iudeus probare in contrarium, quia ius super presumpto penam statuit, arg. xi q.i Si qui clericorum* (C.11 q.1 c.25). *Nobis autem videtur in consimili casu quolibet admitti volentem in contrarium probare, licet difficilius hic, quam ut Iudex presumat, arg. vii q.i Presuntium* (C.7 q.1 c.3)."

Among the Italian minor schools of Roman law, on the other hand, another trace of the influence of the *Perpendiculum* is found in the same Chigi manuscript that contains Ioannes's *distinctio*, in a passage of the so-called *Distinctiones Chisianae II*,[168] no. 19, which differentiates presumptions according to the theory of *status*, following the model established by the *Summula*.[169]

Further evidence of the popularity of the *Summula* is found in the collection of brocards "*Argumentum quod voluntas*,"[170] copied in Italy between 1189 and 1208,[171] which is dependent on the *Perpendiculum*. Firstly, most of the brocards in the second part of the *Perpendiculum* also appear in the first five rubrics of this collection;[172] secondly, the sixth rubric of this work, "*de presumptionibus*," draws heavily on the structure of the *Summula* and echoes its brocard on the *praesumptio legis violenta*.[173]

Of course, all the works examined so far present a picture of a very complicated network of ideas, texts, authors, and schools that are somehow related to the *Perpendiculum* and to each other. Nevertheless, this complex network can help us to answer some questions about our collection, namely its dating and its author, which I will examine in the next chapter.

---

168 A table of contents is provided by Gustav Pescatore, *Beiträge zur mittelalterlichen Rechtsgeschichte*, 2 (Berlin: Prager Verlag, 1889), pp. 120–121.

169 Vatican City, BAV, Chigi E.VII.218, fol. 97vb, beg.: "*Presumptio distinguitur alias ex causa, alias ex loco, alias ex tempore, alias ex persona.*"

170 Contained in the manuscript Luxembourg, BNL, 139, fols. 279va–281rb. Cf. Kuttner, "Retractationes IX," p. 42; Weimar, "Argumenta," p. 122.

171 Thomas Falmagne and Luc Deitz, *Die Echternacher Handschriften bis zum Jahr 1628 in den Beständen der Bibliothèque Nationale de Luxembourg sowie der Archives diocésaines de Luxembourg, der Archives nationales, der Section historique de l'Institut grand-ducal und des Grand Séminaire de Luxembourg*, 2 (Wiesbaden: Harrassowitz, 2009), pp. 298–307, 300, 302.

172 There are the following correspondences between the brocards of "*Argumentum quod voluntas*" and Part II of the *Perpendiculum*: 1 = 4; 2 = 3; 4 = 10; 7 = 8; 9 = 23; 12 = 8; 15 = 19; 17 = 18; 19 = 21; 20 = 22; 34 = 12; 35 = 14; 36 = 11. There are also some parallels with the manuscript tradition of Part III.

173 See De Concilio, *Via Brocardica*, 2:27–28.

CHAPTER 3

The Dating and the Author of the *Perpendiculum*

In the previous pages, we have analyzed the *Perpendiculum* and the main works textually linked to it, trying to establish what relationships exist between them. In doing so, we have provided the necessary information to deal with the question of the origin of the *Perpendiculum*, which scholars have been trying to answer since Lang's studies. In the following pages, I will attempt to provide a partial answer to this question, in light of the historiography on the subject. I will examine its dating, authorship, and provenance. Then, in the next chapter, I will draw some conclusions and suggest interpretations of its meaning in light of this analysis.

1 The Dating of the Work

Lang believed that the *Perpendiculum* was written in the 1180s: his hypothesis was based on the assumption that both Sicardus's and Simon's works influenced the *Summula de presumptionibus*: as we have seen, Kuttner and Motzenbäcker reconsidered this relationship. The latter, assuming that the *Summula* predates Simon's *Summa* (1177–1179), established the year 1177 as the *terminus ante quem* for its composition. For the *terminus post quem* he proposed 1170, on the grounds of the clear influence on it of the theory on presumption expressed in Placentinus's *Summa Codicis* (c. 1168)[1] and the *Summa Coloniensis* (1169).[2] Motzenbäcker's hypothesis, which places the *Perpendiculum* in the 1170s, fits well with the evidence we have, such as the absence of any reference to papal decretals and the very short time span between all the other works related to it.

This reconstruction also convinced Gouron, who shortened the hypothetical period by proposing 1173 as the *terminus post quem*.[3] This hypothesis was advanced in the light of the collection of *notabilia* "*Argumentum quod religiosi*,"

1 Cf. Placentinus, *Placentini Summa Codicis*, ed. Nicolaus Rhodius (Mainz: Schoeffer, 1536; repr. Turin: Bottega d'Erasmo, 1962).

2 Motzenbäcker, *Die Rechtsvermutung*, p. 93, n. 1. On the *Summa Coloniensis*, see Gérard Fransen, ed., *Summa 'Elegantius in iure divino' seu Coloniensis* (Vatican City: BAV, 1986); while Fransen attributed it to northern France, Landau, *Die Kölner Kanonistik*, pp. 15–18, has suggested that it originated in Cologne. For the treatment of presumptions in this work, see Motzenbäcker, *Die Rechtsvermutung*, p. 92.

3 Gouron, "Une école de canonistes," p. 65; cf. also Gouron, "Aux racines," p. 107.

 | DOI:10.1163/9789004713239_005

in which, as we have seen, there is a reference to Thomas Becket as *beatus*,[4] which would not have been possible before 1173. However, there are two objections to this. Firstly, the *terminus post quem* of the *notabilia* does not necessarily apply to the *Perpendiculum*, despite their close relationship: it is plausible that the *Summula* was written before the *notabilia*, since the latter refers to the former.[5] Secondly, the word "*beatus*" does not necessarily come from the author and could just as well be an addition by the copyist.

This last consideration leads us to another aspect that we should bear in mind when dating the *Perpendiculum*: the time frame of the *Summula* does not necessarily apply to the other parts of the work. So far, historiographical interest in our text has been almost exclusively on Part I, the *Summula*. This is partly, of course, because of its particular importance for the theory of legal presumptions and the success of the work. But I think it is also due to two other equally important reasons: the complicated textual tradition of its other parts, which has discouraged any attempt to deal with it, and the intrinsic difficulty of a textual study of brocardic collections. It therefore seems necessary to test whether the dating proposed for the *Summula* can be applied to Parts II and III.

The only attempt to date the rest of the *Perpendiculum* was made by André Gouron. He considered the different parts[6] to have been composed in roughly the same years, with only a slight difference in time.[7] As we have seen, the uniform tradition of the ensemble comes to an abrupt end in Part III, which is characterized by an extreme variety of brocards from one manuscript to another. This element suggested to Gouron that we were dealing with an unfinished work: he hypothesized that the master author of the *Summula* was only able to standardize a first set of brocards (Part II), while a workshop of pupils continued the work in different ways (Part III).[8]

I am not entirely convinced by this explanation. Certainly, the difference between Parts II and III is striking, but it does not seem to be due solely to the lack of uniformity in the manuscript tradition. On closer inspection, Part II seems to be tightly related to the *Summula*: it contains only *pro-contra* brocards

4 MS C, fol. 59vb, to C.24 (*male* C.20) q.1: "*Arg. pro papa Alexandro usque c. Alienus* (c.19). *Arg. sume de beato Thoma*," noted by Gouron, "Une école de canonistes," p. 65. Cf. Kuttner, "Réflexions," p. 788, and André Gouron, "Aux racines," p. 107.

5 Cf. Gouron, "Une école de canonistes," p. 65.

6 Which he thought were two, not realizing the significant differences between Parts II and III.

7 Because of the presence of some decretals of Alexander III in the unsystematic part, while the *Summula* cites only the *Decretum*: Gouron, "Une école de canonistes," p. 64.

8 Gouron, "Une école de canonistes," p. 64.

and cites only Gratian's *Decretum*; moreover, the text of its brocard no. 17[9] suggests that it was a definite set of arguments intended to be an appendix to the *Summula*. Part III, on the other hand, is a miscellaneous collection of various arguments, including other types of legal texts. The difference therefore seems to be above all editorial. Perhaps this divergence could be explained by understanding Part III more as a *texte vivant*, made up of many pieces inserted by the various compilers of its manuscripts, rather than as an attempt to complete an unfinished, closed work produced by a single school.[10] This explanation would fit well with the absence of the modern notion of authorship,[11] which is particularly evident in the production of canon law knowledge in the 1170s, which is characterized by a number of anonymous works and the collation of different texts. Moreover, this interpretation is easily reconciled with the nature of the early collections of brocards, which were more like repositories of legal arguments than systematic works. Rather than distinguishing between the scholarly work of a master and that of his pupils, one could speak of the work of various compilers aimed to collect as many arguments as possible for legal practice.

Given these historiographical premises, it is possible to make some reflections on the dating of the various parts of the *Perpendiculum*.

With regard to the *Summula*, Motzenbäcker's hypothesis is convincing as far as the *terminus ante quem* is concerned: if, as I believe, the *Summula* predates Simon's *Summa*, it must have been written before 1177. As for the *terminus post quem*, some further observations should be made. The dating proposed so far (1170) is based on the influence of the Placentinian distinction of presumptions on the *Summula*; and yet I have tried to show (although it is not possible to exclude the opposite with certainty) that our work probably borrowed this elaboration from the *Summa* of Ioannes Faventinus (1171). I will therefore propose a slightly shorter period for the composition of the *Summula*: between 1172 and 1177.

Regarding Part II and its explicit connection to Part I, it is plausible, as Gouron argued, that the two were intended to circulate together very early and certainly before the end of the 1170s, as suggested by the absence of references to papal decretals in both parts. Again, the relationship to the *Summa* of Ioannes Faventinus provides a useful element for dating the work. If, as I

9 See above, pp. 36–37; below, *Perpendiculum*, Part II, no. 17.

10 Medieval legal production is rich in this type of works: Menzinger, "Riflessioni," p. 2.

11 Cf. Menzinger, "Riflessioni," *passim*, and Lesley Smith, *The Glossa Ordinaria: The Making of a Medieval Bible Commentary* (Leiden: Brill, 2019), pp. 33–38.

believe, it is brocard no. 17 of Part II that was borrowed from Ioannes and not vice versa, then this section of the *Perpendiculum* must have been compiled after Ioannes's glosses, which date from between 1172 and 1175.

Finally, for Part III, it is difficult to establish a single date for the entire text, given the heterogeneous tradition of the various sets of *argumenta*. The ensemble is certainly of an 'alluvial' nature, but the addition of this part occurred quite early. For example, the group of texts called β, which marks the beginning of Part III in five manuscripts (and contains parallels to *"Hec sunt que suadent"*), was certainly established by 1179. Indeed, eight brocards from this group are interpolated into the *Quaestiones Aschaffenburgenses*, a collection contained in A and compiled between 1174 and 1179:[12] I have marked the interpolation as A1. Further evidence of this is the fact that, apart from the later ensemble interpolated into P1 (*"Nullus archidiaconus"*),[13] we do not find many decretals and the few that are cited date from no later than the pontificate of Alexander III, without reference to any systematic collection.[14]

In conclusion, the three parts of the *Perpendiculum* seem to have been made in a short succession of years in the 1170s, confirming the suggestion made by André Gouron.

2 The Problem of the Authorship

Now that we have established the chronology of the *Perpendiculum*, we can draw some conclusions about its paternity. After Lang's first attempts, Gouron revived the question in two separate studies. In the 1980s, while working on the reconstruction of Provençal law schools, he attributed the *Perpendiculum* to the circle of Gui Francesc, a contemporary of Placentinus who taught in Montpellier.[15] Later, when he began to work on the Parisian law schools, Gouron revised his theory and attributed the work to a group of Anglo-Norman canonists working in Paris.[16] Today, this last hypothesis is the starting point for any discussion on the subject.

12 See below, pp. 133–134.

13 See above, pp. 43–44.

14 Cf. Gouron, "Une école de canonistes," p. 64, n. 40.

15 Gouron, "Aux racines," pp. 107–108. On Gui Francesc, see André Gouron, "Autour de Placentin à Montpellier: Maître Gui et Pierre de Cardona," in *Mélanges G. Fransen*, ed. Stephan Kuttner and Alfons M. Stickler, 1 (Rome: Libreria Ateneo Salesiano, 1976), and André Gouron, "Qui était l'énigmatique maître G?," *Journal des savants* 3–4 (1990), pp. 269–289, repr. in Gouron, *Droit et coutume*, no. XIV.

16 Gouron, "Une école de canonistes," pp. 47–72, and especially 65–66.

2.1 *The Waltherus Hypothesis*

In a very detailed study, Gouron collected a number of textual clues that he believed linked several works together: similarity of style, use of rhetoric and examples, tendency towards certain themes and settings. He therefore hypothesized that this group of works should be attributed to the same author, whom he associated with a school of canon law active between 1160 and 1180.

The first work attributed to this circle by the French scholar is the first 16 chapters of an *ordo iudiciarius* called "*Tractaturi de iudiciis*,"[17] which Gouron himself called "*Tractaturi A*." He analyzed the relationship between *Tractaturi A* and the other works circulating with it in its four manuscripts, namely a treatise on civilian actions (*Summa legum*), a treatise on prescriptions, and a small formulary of 14 libels. Gouron has convincingly demonstrated that these works form part of an ensemble linked by common features: the aim of describing Roman legal procedure for canonists, and the constant use of methods borrowed from rhetoric, such as the use of enumeration and *pro-contra* argumentation.[18] Gouron then turned to the question of the ensemble's origin. On the basis of textual evidence,[19] he suggested that *Tractaturi* and the *Summa legum* were written in a Parisian school of canon law, dating *Tractaturi A* to c. 1165–1166 and the rest to 1170–1177.[20] Furthermore, on the basis of textual elements and references to England, he identified the author of *Tractaturi A* as an English or Anglo-Norman jurist repeatedly referred to in the ensemble as *magister Waltherus*,[21] to whom he also attributed the formulary of libels.[22] The rest of the ensemble, he suggested, was the product of one of Waltherus's pupils.[23]

---

17 Discovered by Johann Friedrich von Schulte, "Über die Summa Legum des Codex Gottwicensis Nr. 38 aus dem XII. Jahrhundert," *Sitzungsberichte der philosophisch-historischen Klasse der kaiserlichen Akademie der Wissenschaften in Wien* 57 (1868), pp. 433–460, the ensemble was edited by Carl Gross, ed., *Incerti auctoris Ordo judiciarius, pars summae legum et Tractatus de praescriptione: Nach einer Göttweiger (Stiftsbibliothek, saec.12. ex.) und einer Wiener (Hofbibliothek, saec.13. ex.) Handschrift* (Innsbruck: Verlag von Wagner'schen Universitäts-Buchhandlung, 1870). For more information, see Fowler-Magerl, *Ordo*, pp. 58–64.

18 Gouron, "Une école de canonistes," pp. 49–50.

19 For example, a reference to the birth of King Philip II of France (*Tractaturi A*), an *episcopus Parisiensis* (*Summa legum*), and an example mentioning Saint-Denis and the war in Normandy (*Summa legum*): cf. Ibid., p. 51.

20 Ibid., pp. 52–53.

21 Ibid., pp. 52, 56. Cf. also Landau, "Walter von Coutances," pp. 185–186.

22 Gouron, "Une école de canonistes," pp. 56–58; there are indeed a number of references to a *Waltherus/Gualterus* in the text. Fowler-Magerl, *Ordo*, pp. 58 ff., had attributed the formulary to the Bolognese school. The formulary also circulates as a separate work in Vb, which also contains the *Perpendiculum* and the other works we have examined.

23 Gouron, "Une école de canonistes," pp. 52–56, 58–60.

In the remainder of his study of the subject, Gouron suggested that other works belonged to the school of master Waltherus. In particular, he attributed to him the glosses signed W. which we have already analyzed. The arguments in favor of these suggestions are the tendency of both texts to enumerate, the common use of the *pro-contra* opposition, and the interest in legal presumptions.[24] Gouron therefore suggested that the *siglum* W. should be resolved as belonging to Waltherus.

The suggestion that W. is Waltherus led Gouron to identify the workshop of this master as the place of production of the *Perpendiculum*. The main argument for this attribution is "*l'étroite parenté, allant parfois jusqu'à une identité dans les contenus, qui relie le Perpendiculum aux gloses siglées W.*"[25] On this basis, he made the same hypothesis for the *distinctiones "Hec sunt que suadent"* and "*Ad movendum varie iudicem*," reinforced by their tendency to enumerate. Before analyzing the validity of this identification, it is worth examining its subsequent historiographical fortunes.

2.2 *From Waltherus to Walter of Coutances*

Despite his attempt to reconstruct the work of Waltherus, Gouron was unable to discover the real identity behind this name.[26] A few years later, Landau, who was studying Anglo-Norman canon law schools and the production of English decretals, made a final effort to identify the author of the *Perpendiculum*. Based on Gouron's study, he tried to show that the mysterious Walter could be Walter of Coutances, an Anglo-Norman prelate active in the late 12th century.[27] Gouron had already ruled out this hypothesis, since there was no evidence that Walter was a canonist, nor was there any information about him before 1191.[28]

Landau attempted to overcome Gouron's objection by providing biographical information on Walter of Coutances, in order to show the compatibility between him and the characteristics of *magister* Waltherus. The picture that emerges is that of a Cornish prelate, probably of Norman origin, who climbed the ecclesiastical ladder and made his way in the entourage of the Angevin kings.[29] The first point Landau tried to make was that Walter's biography did

24 Ibid., pp. 60–67. In fact, the fifteenth chapter of the *ordo "Tractaturi"* is devoted to presumptions, one of the earliest indications of canonical interest in the subject.

25 Ibid., p. 65.

26 Ibid., pp. 67–72.

27 Landau, "Walter von Coutances," pp. 183–204.

28 Gouron, "Une école de canonistes," p. 70.

29 Canon (1169) and treasurer (1177) of Rouen cathedral, he was already archdeacon of Oxford in 1175, and later that year he appears at the court of King Henry II as *sigillarius*. In the fol-

not contradict the hypothesis that he was, in the relevant years, in the same environment in which the *Perpendiculum* and the other works attributed to Waltherus were produced. Thus, he hypothesized a period of teaching in Paris between 1165 and 1174—where he could have written *Tractaturi* before becoming part of Henry II's household—and that after 1175 he continued his legal work in Oxford, where Landau suggests he wrote the glosses.[30]

Secondly, Landau tried to show that Walter of Coutances had a solid legal background, contrary to what Gouron claimed,[31] and convincingly presented some evidence for this, such as references in Walter's letters and elements of his career.[32] Landau also suggested that Walter played a role in the production of the decretal collections *Rotomagensis Prima* and *Secunda*, which seems plausible as he was archbishop of Rouen at the time.[33]

Many of Landau's arguments for Walter's canon law training are persuasive. However, some perplexities can be raised about what Landau considered to be his "*wichtigste Indiz*:"[34] the attribution to Walter of one of the most important English collections of decretals, known as the *Appendix Concilii Lateranensis*.[35]

---

lowing decade, the king's favor marked his success: in 1183 Walter was elected bishop of Lincoln and in 1184 archbishop of Rouen. After many diplomatic missions on behalf of the monarchy, he followed King Richard I to Messina in 1190, to go on the crusade. Walter remained there until the spring of 1191, when he was sent back to enforce the king's will in England. After the disgrace of William Longchamp, he held the office of justiciar from September 1191 until the end of 1193. Walter negotiated the release of King Richard from captivity in Germany, then returned to Normandy, where he was repeatedly at odds with the king and the city of Rouen. He died there in 1207. Cf. Landau, "Walter von Coutances," pp. 188–196. See also: Peter A. Poggioli, *From Politician to Prelate: The Career of Walter of Coutances, Archbishop of Rouen, 1184–1207* (PhD dissertation: Johns Hopkins University, 1984); Ralph V. Turner, "Coutances, Walter de," in *ODNB* 13 (Oxford, 2004): 712–714.

30 Cf. Landau, "Walter von Coutances," pp. 188–196. Elsewhere, Landau suggested that Walter may have contributed to the beginnings of the studies in Oxford: Landau, "The Origins of Legal Science in England," pp. 178–179.

31 Landau, "Walter von Coutances," pp. 196–204.

32 Ibid., pp. 196–197: in a letter to Bartholomew of Exeter, Walter cites canon law and seems to allude to himself as being trained *in utroque*. In another letter to Henry the Young King, he cites both secular and canon law. He was also appointed as arbitrator in a dispute between the archbishop of Canterbury and Christ Church in 1189. Landau finds further evidence in a personal plea to Celestin III and an exchange of letters with Innocent III. He was also a papal judge-delegate on five occasions.

33 Ibid., pp. 200–201.

34 Ibid.

35 Giovanni Domenico Mansi, ed., "Appendix Concilii Lateranensis," in *Sacrorum Conciliorum nova et amplissima collectio*, ed. Giovanni Domenico Mansi (Florence/Venice: Zatta, 1778), 22:248–453. Defined by Kuttner and Rathbone, "Anglo-Norman Canonists," p. 283,

Landau suggested that the collection had been written in Lincoln[36] and that Walter of Coutances could therefore have been its author, completing it in Lincoln where he was bishop in 1184.[37] However, this point is far from accepted by scholars, who barely agree on the English provenance of this work. A major criticism of Landau's attribution came from Martin Brett, who pointed out that the Lincoln manuscript—Landau's main clue—does not appear in the catalogues of the Lincoln library, which was started in 1160 and continued until the late 13th century.[38] This objection is not conclusive, but it does suggest that the manuscript arrived in Lincoln later than Walter.

Despite the doubtful attribution of the *Appendix*, Landau's reconstruction seems convincing in showing that Walter of Coutances had legal knowledge and that he was active in the years of Waltherus's work. However, he did not prove that the mysterious Waltherus *was* in fact Walter of Coutances, only that there is no reason to believe that he was not.

There is another element that seems to fit Landau's reconstruction but which has not been taken into account: the manuscript Ma of the *Perpendiculum*. From the paleographic analysis of this codex, we know that it comes from the cathedral library of Messina, where it was copied in the last two decades of the 12th century.[39] This element makes us think of Walter of Coutances: he was

as "the fountainhead of the main decretal tradition," as the modern name suggests, the *Appendix* (at least in its vulgate edition) is a systematic collection that begins with the canons of the Third Lateran Council of 1179, followed by 49 titles: cf. Charles Duggan, "English Canonists and the 'Appendix Concilii Lateranensis'," *Traditio* 18 (1962), pp. 459–468, 459; Charles Duggan, *Twelfth-century Decretal Collections and Their Importance in English History* (London: Athlone Press, 1963), pp. 51–57. The work is the result of a series of different stages and can be dated to c. 1181–1185: Duggan, "English Canonists," p. 459; Landau, "Walter von Coutances," p. 198. Its provenance, at least as far as its first recension is concerned, is today believed to be English: Duggan, "English Canonists," pp. 460–462. See also Walther Holtzmann, *Studies in the Collections of Twelfth-century Decretals*, ed. Christopher R. Cheney and Mary G. Cheney (Vatican City: BAV, 1979), pp. 116–134; Peter Landau, "Die Entstehung der systematischen Dekretalensammlungen und die europäische Kanonistik des 12. Jahrhunderts," *ZRG Kan. Abt.* 65 (1979), pp. 120–148.

36 Landau, "Walter von Coutances," p. 198; Landau, "Die Entstehung," p. 130. His opinion is based on two considerations: a) the only English manuscript belongs to the Lincoln cathedral library; b) the second most recent decretal in the collection is a letter from Pope Lucius III to the bishopric of Lincoln.

37 Landau, "Walter von Coutances," pp. 198–200.

38 Martin Brett, "English Law and Centres of Law Studies in the Later Twelfth Century," in *Archbishop Eystein as Legislator: The European Connection*, ed. Tore Iversen (Trondheim: Tapir, 2011), p. 101.

39 Cf. above, p. 19 and below, pp. 174–176.

in Messina between 1190 and 1191,[40] and if he really was the author of the *Perpendiculum*, the text could have been copied by the cathedral chapter during his stay. However, as we have seen, in Ma there is an attribution of the work to Ioannes Faventinus, written at the time of copying and probably by the scribe himself: this element would hardly fit in with this suggestive reconstruction. This apparent clue must therefore be rejected, and the presence of the *Perpendiculum* in Messina must be explained simply by the influence of the Norman world on intellectual life in Sicily in the second half of the 12th century.[41]

In conclusion, the paucity of elements at our disposal makes it impossible to prove whether Walter of Coutances was Waltherus or not. Moreover, Landau's hypothesis, although suggestive, depends on the idea that Gouron's attribution of the *Perpendiculum* is well-founded. It is therefore time to try to test this reconstruction.

2.3 *Analyzing Gouron's Syllogism*

Gouron's attribution of the *Perpendiculum* to Waltherus is a point that needs to be addressed. In summary, the whole hypothesis is based on the following syllogism: Waltherus is W.; W. is the author of the *Perpendiculum*; therefore Waltherus is the author of the *Perpendiculum*. We will see that on closer analysis Gouron's syllogism is not convincing and that three groups of works and three different authors (W., Waltherus, and the anonymous compiler of the *Summula*) can be identified. To validate this conclusion, we need to examine both the major and minor premises.

---

40 Cf. above, p. 95 n. 29.

41 On this topic, see Valeria De Fraja, "Le prime fonti di Gioacchino da Fiore Libri e intellettuali nel Regno di Sicilia," *BISM* 116 (2014), pp. 93–129, 109–115, 118–122; Jean-Marie Martin, "L'immigrazione normanna, inglese e francese nel regno normanno di Sicilia," in *Studi in onore di Salvatore Tramontana*, ed. Errico Cuozzo (Ariano Irpino: Elio Sellino, 2003), pp. 286–289; Charles H. Haskins, "England and Sicily in the Twelfth Century," *The English Historical Review* 26, no. 103 (1911), pp. 433–447; Evelyn Jamison, "Alliance of England and Sicily in the Second Half of the 12th Century," *Journal of the Warburg and Courtauld Institutes* 6 (1943), pp. 20–32; L.J.A. Loewenthal, "For the Biography of Walter Ophamil, Archbishop of Palermo," *The English Historical Review* 87, no. 342 (1972), pp. 75–82; Graham A. Loud, "Il regno normanno-svevo visto dal regno d'Inghilterra," in *Il Mezzogiorno normanno-svevo visto dall'Europa e dal mondo mediterraneo: Atti delle tredicesime giornate normanno-sveve; Bari, 21–24 ottobre 1997*, ed. Giosuè Musca (Bari: Dedalo, 1999); Margaret Schlauch, "Literary Exchange Between Angevin England and Sicily," *Romanic Review* 14 (1923), pp. 168–188; Ralph V. Turner, "Les Anglo-Normands et la Sicilie," *Études Normandes* 35, no. 3 (1986), pp. 39–60; Vincenzo Roberto Imperia, *I vescovati nella Sicilia normanna (secc. XI–XII): Potestà normative e competenze giurisdizionali in un territorio multiculturale* (Palermo: Palermo University Press, 2022), pp. 67–71, 154–157, and 217–220.

With regard to the major premise, the strongest argument in favor of identifying Waltherus and W., apart from the fortunate coincidence of the initials,[42] is the tendency to enumerate and distinguish. It is a strong point, but even if we do not find such an intense use of enumeration in other decretists' glosses, it is not uncommon in the canon law works of this period, especially in the Parisian circle,[43] but also among theologians, under the influence of the *artes liberales*. It cannot, therefore, be considered as sufficient proof of a common paternity.[44] Above all, the question of identification does not seem to be settled when we consider the way in which the two works deal with legal presumptions. It is true that the *ordo "Tractaturi A"* is early evidence of the canon law interest in the subject, but the treatment given here is neither very long nor particularly innovative, lacking the aspects that characterize the treatment of legal presumptions in W.'s glosses.[45] It has been suggested that this striking divergence could be explained by the fact that *Tractaturi* is a youthful work.[46] This

42 This does not seem to be a decisive argument: a quick look at the known personalities of the time, both jurists and other scholars, shows that the name Waltherus, both in its English and French versions (Walter and Gauthier) is extremely common in this geographical area.

43 For example, cf. Simon de Bisignano, *Summa in Decretum*, to: D.1 c.1, line 157 (MSS Ba and A); D.2 c.1, line 36; D.4 c.1, line 81; D.24 c.5, line 16 (MS A); D.64 c.36, line 91; C.6 p.q.1, line 48; C.16 q.1 c.36, line 101; C.27 a.q.1, line 39; C.28 q.1 c.9, line 102; C.35 q.10 c.1, line 3. The predilection for enumeration in this cultural area can also be seen in the *distinctiones "Tria sunt consideranda in electione,"* copied in the late 12th century in the margins of the pre-Gratian material in Oxford, Bodleian Library, Barlow 37 (fol. 1v), and edited by Michael D. Elliot, ed., *Wigorniensis D (Barlow 37)*, available at http://individual.utoronto.ca/michaelelliot/manuscripts/texts/transcriptions/wigorniensisD.pdf, accessed 2020 Aug 28. This work is clearly linked to the Parisian circle of the *Summa Monacensis* (below, p. 112 n. 32), as first hypothesized by Stephan Kuttner, "The Decretal Presbiterum (JL 13912)—A Letter of Leo IX," *BMCL* 5 (1975), pp. 133–135, 134, n. 8, and recently demonstrated by Tatsushi Genka, "The Distinctiones Tria consideranda sunt in electione in the Oxford, Bodleian MS Barlow 37," *BMCL* 36 (2019), pp. 275–297. The fact that these *distinctiones* are not linked to the author(s) of our works, but simply attest to a shared predilection for enumeration, can be confirmed by the lack of textual similarities. For example, the first *distinctio* of the group, which refers to elections, does not appear in the group of *distinctiones* dedicated to the same subject in the set *"Hec sunt que suadent"* (Vb, nos. 15–17, fol. 8vd).

44 This argument was, to some extent, unconsciously put forward by Gouron himself, "Une école de canonistes," p. 67, who noticed that "*on est en droit de se demander si la passion pour les chiffres et les comptes, caractéristique commune à ces deux parties, n'est pas un trait propre aux écrivains anglais et français: je suis frappé par la présence de la même tendance dans la série Quatuor sunt quae mandato—tout à fait indépendante de l'œuvre de Walter, et sûrement plus ancienne.*"

45 Cf. Fiori, "Praesumptio," p. 83.

46 Landau, "Walter von Coutances," p. 202.

explanation seems overly modern, since medieval legal works were not conceived as complete and final products: instead, authors were accustomed to returning to their works over many years to improve and expand upon them.[47] It seems strange, therefore, that the author of the glosses and the *Summula* did not include his innovative treatment of presumptions in his *ordo* at a later date. Another element that could strengthen the hypothesis of the same paternity is the fact that the formulary contained in the ensemble of *Tractaturi* also appears in Vb, next to a work that clearly belongs to W., like the *distinctiones "Hec sunt que suadent."* However, the formulary is in a different codicological unit from the *Perpendiculum*, which excludes any original editorial project of the scribe. Finally, if we exclude the single occurrence of the formulary in Vb, the manuscript tradition of the ensemble *Tractaturi* never intersects with that of the other two groups of works, i.e. the *Perpendiculum* and W.'s glosses, which instead circulate together at times. In view of these difficulties, the hypothesis of identification of Waltherus with W. seems hard to accept, although there are not enough elements to exclude it with absolute certainty. It therefore remains for us to analyze the minor premise of Gouron's syllogism.

There is no denying that W.'s glosses and the ensemble of the *Perpendiculum* have some similarities, but we have also seen differences: is this compatible with a common paternity? First of all, we should distinguish between the *Summula* and the rest of the work. As far as the former is concerned, in my opinion, the elements we have examined do not suggest a strong relationship. There is only a limited point of textual contact, but stylistically the *Summula* is not characterized by the main characteristic that united the other texts, namely the tendency to enumerate. This profound difference is confirmed by the fact that the only other work that can be attributed with certainty to the author of the *Summula*, the *notabilia "Argumentum quod religiosi,"* does not show this stylistic feature. Like the author of the *Summula*, W. makes use of *pro-contra* argumentation, but this seems to have been a common feature of the transmontane canonists of the 1170s. Finally, the lack of theoretical links in the way the two works categorize legal presumptions supports the idea that there was

47 This is evidenced by the constant presence of multiple redactions in medieval legal works: Menzinger, "Riflessioni," p. 2. One need only think of the case of Pilius's *Libellus*. The fact that the creation of later redactions can be the result of a rethinking of the author's own work with the aim of incorporating new theories has been proposed by Emanuele Conte and Sara Menzinger, *La Summa Trium Librorum di Rolando da Lucca (1195–1234): Fisco, politica, scientia iuris* (Rome: Viella, 2012), pp. XVIII–XX, with regard to the *Summa* of Rolandus de Lucca.

no direct mutual influence between them. In fact, if we assume that W. was also the author of the *Perpendiculum*, given the popularity that the tripartite classification of presumptions enjoyed among jurists, it is difficult to understand why he did not include this classification in his monographic work on presumptions, focusing instead only on the *praesumptio violenta*.[48] This lack of direct influence between the two texts has two main consequences. On the one hand, W. and the author of the *Summula* should probably be considered as two different authors. On the other hand, it is plausible that these two different jurists did not know each other, although they were active in the same years. Otherwise, if we hypothesize the chronological precedence of the glosses, it would be difficult to understand why the author of the *Summula* did not use the tripartition of the presumptions, which became extremely popular.[49] Conversely, if we assume that the *Summula* is earlier, we could not explain why W. did not know it, given the great influence it exerted.

However, the relationship between W.'s work and the third part of the *Perpendiculum* is another matter: there are some undeniable connections between the texts. This is shown by the occasional insertion of two *distinctiones* in Part III, as well as by the strong similarities between W.'s style and that of the distinction "*Ad movendum varie iudicem*."

These two contrasting elements could be reconciled by hypothesizing that the *Perpendiculum* and W.'s work, although the products of two different authors, often circulated together in the same milieu. This, of course, does not necessarily mean that they were produced in the same context—since, as we have seen, it is difficult to ascribe W.'s work with certainty to a specific school—but rather that both were read by the same readers in the transmontane circles from which the surviving manuscripts of the *Perpendiculum* come. This common circulation could also explain the direct influence that both works had on Simon's *Summa*. In other words, it seems plausible that, after compiling the *Summula*, the transmontane jurists who were engaged in collecting the *argumenta* which eventually constituted the third part of the *Perpendiculum*, began to bring together other works of this kind available in those schools, both of Italian and transmontane origin. In this 'alluvial' process, the works of master

48 Moreover, in this case the absence cannot be explained by considering the *Summula* as a work of youth, as Landau did with *Tractaturi*: the proximity in time makes it impossible to explain the absence of a second recension. This has also been noted by Menzinger, *Finzioni del diritto*, pp. 122–123.

49 Unless, of course, we imagine that the author of the *Summula* was aware of W.'s distinction and deliberately excluded it because he did not agree with it. This seems unlikely, however, since there is not much to disagree with in the tripartition, which was conceived as a description of the existing system of presumptions.

W. were occasionally interpolated in the brocards collected in the school of the *Perpendiculum*. This originally alien nature of W.'s materials is confirmed by two facts: firstly, we find them only in a minority of 13th-century manuscripts (A, G, L, Mu1, P1, and Vb), while we find no traces of them in Ma, allegedly the oldest codex of the *Perpendiculum*, or in C, which contains the only other text that can be attributed with certainty to the author of the *Summula*. Secondly, with the exception of Vb, we can only find traces of W. in the form of short, interpolated fragments.

The main objection to this reconstruction is represented by Vb. In fact, this codex is quite remarkable. It contains a large number of works which Gouron attributed to the author of the *Summula*: not only the *Perpendiculum* and the *notabilia "Arg. contra religiosos,"* but also some texts more clearly linked to W., such as the distinctions *"Hec sunt que suadent"* and the formulary of libels circulating in the ensemble of "*Tractaturi*." It could therefore easily appear as a kind of collection of Walter's works. However, some observations should be made. Firstly, this is one of the latest versions of the *Perpendiculum*, in which most of the errors have been corrected and the number of allegations has been increased; more than any other manuscript, Vb testifies to the habit of collecting legal arguments from several sources. I therefore believe that it represents precisely the 'alluvial' process of encounter between the two authors that I have proposed. Secondly, as I have already mentioned, the formulary of libels, which could strengthen the idea of an authorial collection, is part of a different codicological unit.

In conclusion, I think that Gouron's syllogism, which identifies *magister* Waltherus with W. and with the author of the *Summula de presumptionibus*, does not find the necessary textual elements to confirm it, and that it is difficult to imagine the same paternity. In view of these perplexities, I will treat Waltherus, W., and the anonymous author of the *Summula* as three separate persons.

2.4 *Different Authors, Common Features*

In summary, three authors and as many groups of works can be identified. The first is Waltherus and his school, where *Tractaturi A* and the rest of its ensemble were produced. The second is W., to whose circle we can attribute Weigand's glosses and some sets of *distinctiones*: *"Ad movendum varie iudicem," "Hec sunt que suadent,"* and "*Tria sunt que faciunt*" (composed a little later). Finally, there is the author of the *Summula de presumptionibus*, in whose circle we can place the core structure of the *Perpendiculum* and the *notabilia "Argumentum quod religiosi."* The first two groups are united by a similar style, but they treat the subject of presumptions in very different ways. The second and third groups, on the other hand, are linked by some textual clues and occasional common circulation, but not by style or treatment of presumptions. By inference, the first and third groups are unrelated. Moreover, both the second and third groups influenced authors such as Simon and Sicardus, whose works do not show any relationship with Waltherus.

However, it is important to stress that, despite the unconvincing nature of Gouron's hypothesis about *magister* Walter, all the texts examined so far share certain features. Firstly, they are products whose style shows a strong influence of the *Trivium*, such as the tendency to enumerate and the use of rhetorical and dialectical tools like brocards and *distinctiones*. Most importantly, all these works are united as the earliest examples (so far known) of canon law interest in legal presumptions. I believe that these elements are not coincidences, but that they suggest that all these works were either born or had their main circulation in the same environment: the legal schools of northern France and the Paris basin. Other clues, as well as the obvious similarities, strengthen this geographical attribution. With regard to the activity of Waltherus and the ensemble of *Tractaturi*, we have already seen how their textual references ascribe them to a Parisian school of Anglo-Norman jurists.[50] As far as master W. is concerned, it is difficult to prove whether he was a French jurist influenced by (and influencing) the Bolognese school, or vice versa.[51] However, this uncertainty is in itself of great importance, since it highlights the strong intellectual links between these two milieux. As far as the author of the *Summula de presumptionibus* is concerned, in the course of this study we have seen many elements that support attribution to the schools of the Paris basin and possibly some Anglo-Norman links:[52] the grammatical taste, the use of the rhetorical doctrine of *loci*, the reference to Thomas Becket in his *notabilia*, the provenance and circulation of its surviving manuscripts, the absence of *paleae* among its allegations.

However, in order to confirm this general impression and attribute the *Perpendiculum* to the French milieu, we must first face another possible objection that could radically relocate its paternity and origin. In fact, even having examined

50 See above, p. 94.
51 See above, pp. 59–61.
52 The "intellectual osmosis" between the French and Anglo-Norman milieux is highlighted by Conte, "La France," pp. 24–25.

the previous historiographical attempts to identify the author of the *Perpendiculum*, there is one last attribution that must be considered.

2.5 *The Oldest Attribution: Scribal Mistake or Actual Author?*

Lang, Gouron, and Landau are not the only ones who have tried to identify the author of *Summula de presumptionibus*. Although ignored by scholars, a much older attribution has been made, more than eight hundred years ago. In fact, the allegedly oldest manuscript of the *Perpendiculum*, Ma, attributes the collection to Ioannes Faventinus, probably in the hand of the scribe himself, and in any case at the time of copying, i.e. in the last two decades of the 12th century.[53] Taken on its own, this attribution could easily be dismissed as a scribal error, possibly explained by the fact that the antigraph from which the copy was made contained Ioannes's *Summa*, which follows the ensemble in Ma (fols. 25–199), and that this misled the copyist about the full content of the text. However, the strong textual links between the *Perpendiculum* and the work of Ioannes in both Parts I and II[54] force us to ask whether this attribution is perhaps something more than a mistake. In other words, is it possible that Ma's scribe was right and that the similarities between the *Perpendiculum* and the work of Ioannes should not just be interpreted as the former quoting the latter, but rather as the bishop of Faenza quoting himself?

The hypothesis is certainly suggestive, but there are some objections that are not easy to dismiss. The differences in the treatment of the irrebuttable *praesumptio legis*, which I have already examined, are certainly one of them: if Ioannes were the author of the *Summula*, why would he not use the distinction between two different types of *presumptiones legis* contained in the latter, nor the term '*violenta*'/'*violenter*?'

Moreover, we have seen how the *Perpendiculum* seems to ignore W.'s tripartition of presumptions. We know from Sara Menzinger's studies that Ioannes knew W.'s work, having read and quoted his glosses on fictions.[55] Therefore, assuming that the bishop of Faenza was the author of the *Summula*, it would be difficult to explain why he did not include W.'s elaboration in this monographic work on the subject.[56]

A more compelling objection is perhaps rooted in the manuscript tradition of the *Perpendiculum*: all of its manuscripts, with the exception of the very

53 Ma, fol. 3^{r}: "*Opus magistri Iohannis facentini.*"

54 See above, pp. 67–71.

55 Menzinger, *Fnzioni del diritto*, pp. 207–219.

56 Cf. above, p. 101 n. 49.

same Ma, seem to have originated and circulated beyond the Alps, while there is no evidence of diffusion in Bologna or northern Italy. If the author of the collection had been a Bolognese canonist like Ioannes, whose *Summa* and glosses were widely read in the Peninsula, the existence of an Italian manuscript tradition would have been more likely.

Finally, the hypothesis of Ioannes as the author of the collection contrasts with the general impression that the *Perpendiculum* originated in northern France.

Be that as it may, the link between Ioannes and the *Perpendiculum* is extremely important for the history of legal thought and learning in the 12th century, because it represents an additional element that testifies to the deep interactions between the French and Italian schools of law in the 12th-century. In the following pages, I will explore this significance and its historiographical implications.

CHAPTER 4

Conclusions: The *Perpendiculum* between France and Italy

The conclusions we can draw from the picture we have sketched so far are twofold.

First, the legal milieu of the *Perpendiculum* and its related works reinforces the idea of the existence of a transregional (or transnational) group of jurists between Paris and Bologna, active in the 1170s and influential in France, Italy, England, Spain, and western Germany. From the analysis of our works, we can see how this group of scholars was, in many respects, highly significant for the history of 12th-century legal thought and learning. Indeed, it shows a precocious canon law interest in legal presumptions, and its elaboration of these matters enjoyed great popularity throughout the Western European legal world. Moreover, these works played a crucial role in the spread of the brocardic method and scholastic techniques of argumentation in both canon and civil law texts, encouraging their adoption in many works of their time and the hybridization of different genres.

Above all, this trans-regional group of works tells the story of the intertwined interaction between the Parisian and Italian jurists of the time: a story of deep connections, rapid circulation, mutual influences, and blurred boundaries. Master W. and his namesakes, whose provenance cannot be determined, are a clear example of this.

As we shall see, from both these perspectives the *Perpendiculum* represents a significant case that could challenge conventional historiographical understandings of 12th-century legal learning and help to reshape the spatial and intellectual boundaries set by scholarship on the elaboration of both legal concepts and literary genres.

Therefore, in these last pages of this study, I will examine these two aspects and draw some illustrative conclusions, summarizing—without claiming to be exhaustive[1]—the fortunes of the theory of presumptions elaborated by Ioannes Faventinus, W., and the *Summula de presumptionibus*. First, I will consider the influence of Bolognese and Provençal ideas on the Parisian school in this respect; then, I will give some examples of the close links between this

1 In this respect, Fiori, "Praesumptio" is a comprehensive starting point.

 | DOI:10.1163/9789004713239_006

school and Bologna; finally, I will recapitulate the circulation of the Parisian texts in Italy.

1 Southern Ideas in Northern France

If my geographical attribution of the *Summula de presumptionibus* is confirmed, the elaboration of the Parisian ecclesiastical school of law would be fundamental for the diffusion of the canon law theory of presumptions.[2] However, the interest of the Parisian masters in this subject cannot be isolated from the intellectual winds blowing through the other schools of law of the time.

1.1 *A Melting Pot of Ideas*

The contribution to the theory of presumptions made by the *Perpendiculum* and the other northern French texts that we have examined certainly has some original features, but it was also influenced by ideas from the south, due to the privileged position of its milieu. Thanks to the flourishing schools of its city, which attracted masters, texts, and students from all over the continent, Paris could in fact benefit from a direct cultural exchange with the other main areas of the 'medieval legal renaissance:'[3] northern Italy and southern France.[4]

Indeed, the theories of presumption developed in the Parisian schools were deeply influenced by the intellectual products of the Provençal civilian milieu,[5] where the first known works on the subject were written.[6] One of the first works to show an interest in legal presumptions, the Anglo-Norman *Tractaturi A*, draws on the Provençal *Summa Trecensis*[7] and the work of Rogerius (c. 1110–1162),[8] an Italian jurist who taught in Provence.[9] More significantly, in

2 This has been emphasized, for example, by Fiori, "Praesumptio," p. 86.

3 The expression is borrowed from Cortese, *Il Rinascimento*.

4 Cf. Conte, "La France," pp. 25–26.

5 The spread of Provençal texts in the Parisian school, emphasized by Gouron, "Qui était," pp. 284–287, is attested, for example, by the number of works by this school found in the manuscripts of the *Perpendiculum*.

6 Gouron, "Aux racines." It should be noted, however, that the pre-Rogerian and pre-Placentinian Bolognese glosses have not yet been fully studied, and it is therefore impossible to attribute the paternity of the civilian theory of presumption to these masters with certainty.

7 See above, p. 53 n. 18.

8 See Luca Loschiavo, "Rogerio," in *DBI* 88 (2017), available at https://www.treccani.it/enciclopedia/rogerio_(Dizionario-Biografico)/, accessed 2023 May 10; Ennio Cortese, "Rogerio," in *DBGI*, 2:1716–1717.

9 On these influences on *Tractaturi A*, see Gouron, "Une école de canonistes," p. 52.

the *Summula de presumptionibus* the concept of irrebuttable presumption is based on the civilian distinction between *praesumptio legis* and *iudicis* elaborated by another Italian jurist, Placentinus, who taught in Montpellier and who in turn based his *Summa Codicis* on that of Rogerius.[10] In this respect, it makes little difference whether the *Summula* adopted Placentinus's distinction directly (as scholars have hitherto thought) or, as I believe, through the work of Ioannes Faventinus: it still testifies to the circulation and influence of legal ideas coming from both Bologna and Provence in the northern French schools of law.

At about the same time as the writing of the *Summula*, other influential ideas on the subject were certainly coming from Bologna to Paris, as can be seen from W.'s glosses, which for the first time conceptualized the gradation of presumptions into *temeraria*, *probabilis*, and *violenta*. Again, we do not yet know whether W. was a Bolognese or a Parisian master,[11] but this does not drastically affect the relevant fact at hand: that is, the deep, reciprocal, and rapid intellectual exchange between the two main Western European centers of learning. If he belonged to the French school, he would be an example both of Bolognese influence in Paris (as evidenced by his reception of Gandulphus's theories)[12] and, conversely, of the rapid spread of transmontane texts in Italy (as his gloss on fictions is used by Ioannes Faventinus no more than two years after their redaction).[13] If, on the other hand, he were a Bolognese, the fact that his main impact and circulation can be located among the transmontane works would still indicate the rapid and extraordinary reception of the Italian jurists in northern France. And, as we shall see, what determined this reception was the encounter between W.'s glosses and the *Summula de presumptionibus*.

The picture that emerges is that of a flourishing center of legal knowledge in Paris, in rapid and constant contact with the theoretical innovations developed in the schools of Provence and northern Italy, and where the ideas of civil law were read and applied by the masters of canon law. This reception, however, was far from unoriginal: through W. and the *Perpendiculum*, it gave birth to a fruitful elaboration that circulated widely in the transmontane schools and finally returned to Italy, as we will see in these pages.

---

10 See above, p. 54.

11 See above, pp. 59–61.

12 Menzinger, *Finzioni del diritto*, pp. 40–54 and 124–125.

13 Ibid., pp. 124 and 147–172.

1.2 *The Theory of Presumptions in Northern France*

Between the second half of the 1170s and the end of the 1180s, the categorizations of canon law presumptions introduced by W.'s glosses and the *Summula de presumptionibus* enjoyed great popularity, especially in the ecclesiastical schools of law of the Paris basin and northern France, where interest in the subject seems to have been particularly strong. Thus, for example, the bipartition of the *praesumptio legis* introduced by the *Perpendiculum* was taken up by the *Tractatus de operibus*, which we have already examined and which was largely based on its model.[14]

Moreover, at the end of the 1170s, the treatment of the *praesumptio violenta* elaborated by the *Summula* and by Ioannes Faventinus was merged with the canon law tripartition of presumptions conceptualized by W., as attested for the first time by the *Summa in Decretum* of Simon de Bisignano.[15] Thereafter, as we have seen, Simon's new theoretical formulation became very influential among canonists and was taken up especially in the Parisian and Anglo-Norman schools of northern France, as testified by works such as the *Speculum* of Peter of Blois, the *Summa Lipsiensis*, and the *Summa "De iure canonico tractaturus."*[16] Thus, by adopting and merging the conceptualization of presumptions offered by his three models, Simon de Bisignano finally consecrated them to success among the transmontane decretists. This success, in turn, gives us a picture of a Parisian legal milieu particularly interested in the further refinement of this procedural device. Elsewhere, I have tried to provide some insights into the possible reasons for the great popularity of presumptions among the ecclesiastical jurists of northern France, linking it to the development of the new Romano-canonical procedure as well as to the scholastic discovery of new logical and argumentative tools.[17] However, it is not the role of this success in Parisian and Anglo-Norman jurisprudence that is relevant here, but rather how it reveals the complex reality of intellectual and spatial relationships between the two legal worlds of Western Europe in the 12th-century: those of the transmontane and Italian schools of law. In the following pages, I will try to explore precisely this entangled relationship by focusing on the reception of the *Perpendiculum* by authors who can be placed at the crossroads between these worlds.

---

14 See above, pp. 80–84.

15 See above, p. 71 nn. 88 and 90, p. 73 n. 97.

16 Fiori, "Praesumptio," p. 96. See also above, pp. 76–77, 86, and 88.

17 See De Concilio, *Via Brocardica*, 1:143–184; see also De Concilio, "Imputer l'intention."

2 Paris and Bologna: So Far and Yet So Close

The story told by the *Perpendiculum* is one of contamination, entanglement, and mixtures; it is a story that unfolds in several places, linking the cradle of this work, the Paris basin, with the beating heart of medieval jurisprudence: Bologna. The exemplary narrative of this story is the reception of the *Summula de presumptionibus* in the hands of certain jurists whose lives and works form a bridge between these worlds.

The first (chronologically and in terms of importance) is Simon de Bisignano, whose *Summa*, as we have seen, takes up the distinction between the two types of *praesumptio legis* drawn by the *Perpendiculum* and combines it with both Ioannes's distinction and master W.'s tripartition.[18] However, as we shall see, Simon also embodies a strong link between the legal schools on either side of the Alps.

2.1 *From Norman Apulia to Angevin England: Simon de Bisignano*

The early circulation of Simon de Bisignano's *Summa* among Anglo-Norman canonists was noted seventy-five years ago by Kuttner and Rathbone;[19] nevertheless, the Italian origin of this work, and more precisely its affiliation to the Bolognese school, was for a long time taken for granted. In the 1990s, however, this assumption was challenged, first by Rudolf Weigand, who noted the scarce circulation of Simon's *Summa* among Bolognese jurists,[20] and then by Peter Landau, who highlighted the influence of this work in northern France, especially on the author of the Anglo-Norman *Summa Lipsiensis* (written a few years later). Consequently, Landau attempted to place Simon as an author in the Parisian or Rhenish schools;[21] however, the lack of certain elements in this suggestion led Orazio Condorelli to repropose the Bolognese hypothesis.[22] Finally, Martin Bertram has recently found a solution to the dilemma, convincingly demonstrating that Simon de Bisignano should be identified with the prelate Simon de Apulia (d. 1223),[23] dean of York and later bishop of Exeter.[24] Bertram's

---

18 See above, pp. 71–73.

19 Kuttner and Rathbone, "Anglo-Norman Canonists," p. 334.

20 Weigand, *Die Glossen zum Dekret*, 2:615.

21 Landau, "Simon von Bisignano," and [Peter Landau], *Presentazione*, in Simon de Bisignano, *Summa in Decretum*, pp. V–VI. A comprehensive account of the relationship between the two works is provided by [Aimone Braida], *Prolegomena*, pp. XCII–CV.

22 Condorelli, "A proposito della Summa," pp. 43–45.

23 See Frank Barlow, "Apulia, Simon of," in *ODNB*, published online: May 24, 2007, DOI: 10.1093/ref:odnb/94380.

24 Bertram, "Simon of Apulia," especially pp. 31–38.

identification is supported by the episcopal *acta* of Exeter, which state that around the 1220s Bishop Simon surrounded himself with fellow villagers from Bisignano.[25] He also emphasized that eight of the eleven surviving manuscripts of Simon's *Summa* are from either England or northern France, while only three are Italian.[26]

This new identification helps us to shed new light on the relationship between Simon's *Summa* and the works circulating in the Parisian schools examined so far; this relationship, in turn, may provide some additional insights into the open question of the place of production of Simon's work. As Bertram points out, even if we can identify Simon de Bisignano with Simon de Apulia, we do not know whether he wrote his *Summa* in Italy or when he had already moved to Northern Europe.[27]

From this point of view, the textual and chronological dependence of Simon's *Summa* on the *Summula de presumptionibus* is particularly significant. As we have seen, the two works share common characteristics in style (the tendency towards graphic representation and enumeration), method (the use of *pro-contra* brocards and dialectics), and content (their parallel passages and the interest in presumptions and fictions). These elements show that Simon was well acquainted with the intellectual products of the Parisian school, and it is certainly easier to imagine such direct knowledge of the *Summula* if we place the redaction of Simon's *Summa* after he went north, thus setting the date of his move before 1179. However, these affinities cannot be a decisive argument, as we cannot completely rule out the possibility that Simon came across the *Summula* during his stay in Italy. While we have no evidence of the *Perpendiculum* circulating south of the Alps during this decade, its popularity in the Peninsula just a few years later is widely attested.[28]

A similar line of thought can be followed regarding Simon's use of W.'s glosses on presumptions. In one respect, this could strengthen the idea of an Anglo-Norman redaction of the *Summa* and certainly testifies to the rapid circulation of texts between the schools, since about four years would have passed between the compilation of the glosses and their inclusion in Simon's work. However,

25 Ibid., p. 37.

26 Ibid., pp. 3–12. It is also worth noticing that one of these three Italian manuscripts, the Rome, Casanatense, 1105, contains the *distinctiones "Tria sunt que faciunt,"* which can be attributed to W.'s school and thus to another author who, like Simon, is disputed between the Parisian and Bolognese schools: see above, p. 62.

27 Bertram, "Simon of Apulia," pp. 38–39.

28 See below, pp. 113–114.

we must bear in mind that the geographical attribution of W.'s glosses is still uncertain and that Simon may have become aware of them during his time in Bologna, where they were already circulating.[29]

The strongest clue that might place Simon's journey northwards before 1179 is rather the relationship between his work and another text deeply influenced by the *Perpendiculum*: the *Summa in Decretum* of Sicardus Cremonensis, written in Mainz between two and four years later.

2.2 *Italian Roots, French Influences: Other Works on the Edge*

We have already seen how Sicardus's treatment of legal presumptions is based both on Simon's model and on a direct knowledge of the *Summula de presumptionibus*, and how Stephan Kuttner has shown the geographical affinity between this work, which he attributed to the French school,[30] and the *Perpendiculum*. More precisely, we could say that Sicardus's *Summa* is the work of an Italian jurist, which reflects the profound influence of the so-called transmontane schools, which were active in that culturally complex geographical-legal area that encompassed both the Angevin and the Capetian kingdoms, as well as the western edge of the Holy Roman Empire.[31] Certainly, Sicardus's transmontane influence shows more than a hint of Parisian and Anglo-Norman connections, which are not limited to his relationship with the *Perpendiculum* and Simon's *Summa*, or to his interest in the methods and topics favored by these schools, such as dialectical argumentation and presumptions. For example, he relies heavily on the *Summa "Inperatorie maiestati"* (c. 1172): a work with a penchant for distinctions, formerly attributed to Carinthia,[32] but now ascribed to the Parisian school,[33] in which we find many Anglo-Norman echoes.[34] We should also not forget the role played by Parisian and Anglo-Norman canonists in the Rhineland,[35] where Sicardus wrote his *Summa*.

---

29 See above, pp. 59–61.

30 Kuttner, "Réflexions," pp. 783–787.

31 Cf. above, p. 1 n. 2.

32 Winfried Stelzer, "Die Summa Monacensis ('Summa Inperatorie maiestati') und der Neustifter Propst Konrad von Albeck," *Mitteilungen des Instituts für Österreichische Geschichtsforschung* 88 (1980), pp. 94–112.

33 Landau, "Master Peter of Louveciennes," pp. 386–390, who attributed it to Peter of Louveciennes and dated it to c. 1172.

34 For example, a reference to King Henry II (Stelzer, "Die Summa," p. 104, n. 40) and an influence on later Anglo-Norman texts such as the *Speculum* of Peter of Blois.

35 See the literature cited above, p. 20 n. 12.

The influence of the Parisian theory of presumptions on works at the crossroads between the transmontane and Italian schools is not, however, limited to the *Summae* of Simon and Sicardus. For example, another work influenced by the *Perpendiculum* (perhaps through the mediation of Ioannes Bassianus) and disputed between the Anglo-Norman milieu and the Peninsula is the *ordo "Olim edebatur"* (composed after 1177), in which we find a treatment of the *praesumptio legis* that echoes the *Summula*.[36] As we have seen, the history of the attribution of this work is a vivid example of shifting historiographical trends, as well as of the difficulty of distinguishing between Italian and transmontane influences in late 12th-century legal literature.[37]

Moreover, it should be remembered that the distinction of the *Summula* between *praesumptio violenta legis* and *iudicis* was adopted, albeit in different terms, by a later product of W.'s school: the *distinctiones "Tria sunt que faciunt,"* which we have already examined.[38]

In this section, we have focused on the close links between the Bolognese and Parisian milieux through the influence of the *Summula de presumptionibus* on some works and authors that can be considered as a cultural *trait d'union* of these schools. In fact, all the works examined here are characterized either by their uncertain localization (showing both Italian and French elements), or by their great cultural hybridization. To some degree, this shows that the historiographical boundaries between national schools belie a more blurred reality, in which the legal products of northern France and the Po Valley were strongly contaminated and subject to mutual influences. But it also highlights the direct impact of the *Perpendiculum* on both sides of the Alps. In the following pages, I will focus on this last aspect as another example of the great intellectual exchange that the Western European legal schools experienced during the late 12th century.

3 From Paris to Italy

The reception of the *Summula de presumptionibus* among Italian jurists in the 1180s is one of the best examples of both the influence of the Parisian school beyond its borders and the deep connections between the legal cultures on

36 See above, pp. 85–88.
37 See above, p. 85 n. 158.
38 See above, p. 64 n. 66.

either side of the Alps, both in terms of the theory of presumptions and the development of brocards as a legal literary genre.

The most significant case in this respect is the adoption of the model of the *Summula* by Pilius's *Libellus disputatorius* (c. 1181–1185). We have already examined the influence of the *Perpendiculum* on the work of this Modenese jurist: the structure in *loci*, the direct reference to the *Summula*, the theoretical treatment of presumptions.[39] Moreover, the role of the *Perpendiculum* in the compilation of the *Libellus* cannot be limited to the subject of legal presumptions: it is also fundamental to the spread of *pro-contra* brocards in Italian schools. In fact, Pilius borrowed the dialectical structure of his brocardic work from the *Summula*, which is the first example of the consistent use of this method in a collection of legal arguments. Before the *Perpendiculum*, as we have seen, the earliest brocardic collections do not show a consistent use of dialectical opposition, and the adoption of this method by the *Libellus disputatorius* makes it one of the earliest Italian works of this kind to implement the *pro-contra* structure, together with another product of the same milieu and of clear transmontane influence, Otto's *Brocardica* (1180s).[40] Thus, by adopting the method of the *Summula*, Pilius's *Libellus* opened the way for the spread of the brocardic genre in northern Italy, for its use as a systematic explanatory tool, for its adoption in the civilian schools, and, above all, for the development of its final form, complete with *solutiones contrariorum*.[41]

Although Pilius de Medicina is the most important, he is not the only example of the influence of the *Perpendiculum* among Italian legists. We find several other traces of the use of its theory of presumptions in the so-called Italian minor schools of the Po valley, such as the works of Ioannes Bassianus, which testify, directly or indirectly, to the theoretical influence and widespread popularity of the *Summula de presumptionibus* south of the Alps, explicitly recorded by Pilius himself.[42] In turn, this influence—and, more generally, this journey from Paris to the Peninsula—makes it possible to consider the *Perpendiculum* as an explanatory case study that rethinks the conventional historiographical paradigm of 12th-century Western European legal learning.

39 See above, pp. 77–80.

40 See De Concilio, *Via Brocardica*, 2:24–25.

41 For the historical transformation of brocards and the adoption of *solutiones contrariorum*, see: De Concilio, *Via Brocardica*, 1:52–62, 2:7–36; Weimar, "Argumenta."

42 See above, p. 79 n. 125.

4 Rethinking Historiographical Boundaries: The *Perpendiculum* as a Case Study

In these pages, I have presented the *Perpendiculum* as an example of the complex and entangled relationship between the Western European legal schools of the late 12th century, both in terms of its reception by legists and canonists on either side of the Alps, and in terms of the wider intellectual context in which its theory of presumptions can be placed. The picture that emerges is one of an interconnected intellectual and legal milieu, sharing interests (legal presumptions) and methods (brocardic argumentation), linking northern and southern schools, canon and Roman lawyers: Ioannes Faventinus, Waltherus, W., the author of the *Summula*, Simon, Sicardus, Pilius, Ioannes Bassianus, and the Anglo-Norman canonists.

From this perspective, for a research that aims to use the *Perpendiculum* as a case study to shed light on the milieu of the 12th-century schools and their influence on Western legal culture, the questions of paternity, chronological dependence, and geographical attribution of the various works are of secondary importance.

The long-term study of the relationship between schools, authors, and texts, has been at the center of historiographical research for many years. This is the result of several factors. First, the enduring myth of the authorial text, rooted in the approach that legal historiography has followed since its beginnings, when Savigny conceived his *Geschichte des römischen Rechts im Mittelalter* as a biographical work of literary history.[43] Secondly, this issue was also an attempt to understand the mutual influences between different 'national' schools at a time when national legal traditions were of great interest to historiography. From this perspective, for example, the chronological precedence of W.'s glosses over a 'Bolognese' author like Simon was not only significant in terms of their biographical and authorial relationship, but also asserted the early influence of the Parisian legal school over the Italian one, or vice versa. In the same way, the attribution of the work of a particular jurist, be it W. of Simon, to either the Italian or the Parisian milieu, was also the subject of debate because it appealed to the narrative of national legal traditions.

43 Cf. Hermann Kantorowicz, *Studies in the Glossators of the Roman Law: Newly Discovered Writings of the Twelfth Century* (Cambridge: Cambridge University Press, 1938), p. 213; Menzinger, "Riflessioni;" Conte, *Diritto comune*, p. 18.

This biographical and geographical focus of legal historiography has shaped the scholarly debate on the *Summula de presumptionibus* and its related texts. And in this respect, the *Perpendiculum* is an explanatory paradigm of these historiographical tendencies. We have seen how, in the first half of the 20th century, the *Summula*, like several other works, was attributed to a Bolognese environment. As with the general shift in historiographical focus from Bologna to France, the *Perpendiculum* moved beyond the Alps in a second stage, as part of the wider reassessment of the importance of France in legal learning. Finally, the recent interest in the Anglo-Norman schools of canon law is well represented by Gouron's attribution of the work to Anglo-Norman circles in Paris.

I must confess that even the genesis of this book was not exempt from these historiographical tendencies and national narratives: indeed, the initial research hypothesis of this study was the Anglo-Norman nature of the *Perpendiculum*, and initially, in the doctoral thesis on which this work is based, I stressed this element in contrast to the Bolognese tradition.[44] However, the more I worked on these texts, the more I realized the difficulty of attributing with certainty a particular text or author to a particular school: a difficulty that I have tried to illustrate in the previous pages. Is W. Bolognese or Parisian? And Simon's *Summa*? And the *ordo* "*Olim*?" The reason why it is so difficult to answer these questions is not only because of the lack of biographical information or textual clues: it is above all because, despite all our national attributions, we can hardly identify any major point of divergence between these schools, which seem to have more in common than they differ.

Later, I came to understand that these national narratives inevitably fail to emphasize the most important point that emerges from the study of the *Perpendiculum*: the image of a common Western European legal culture, consisting of a network of schools that transcends conventional historiographical boundaries and encompasses both sides of the Alps and even England.[45] The existence of this milieu has been more consciously noticed by legal historians in recent decades and has been called by various names.[46] If we keep this in

44 See De Concilio, *Via Brocardica*, 1:135–136.

45 On the 12th-century legal schools, see also Anders Winroth, "Law Schools in the Twelfth Century," and Winroth, "Law Schools and Legal Education."

46 For example, Harold J. Berman, *Law and Revolution*, 2 vols (Cambridge, Massachusetts: Belknap Press, 1983), calls it "Western legal tradition," while Sara Menzinger, "Legal Profession," in *A Cultural History of Law in the Middle Ages*, ed. Emanuele Conte and Laurent Mayali, 2 (London: Bloomsbury Academic, 2019), p. 130, speaks of a "unified experience of learned law between the twelfth and thirteenth centuries" in the European centers of learning.

mind, we can separate biographical literary history from cultural and intellectual history by highlighting the common cultural and legal environment that links works and authors from Paris and Italy.

Of course, I do not wish to underestimate literary history, nor the importance of studying the authorial and geographical attribution of works: a prosopographical and institutional approach is necessary in order to historically frame the circulation of knowledge in its context, and I have tried to deal with this by disentangling the complex web of textual relationships in the most plausible way given the elements at our disposal. The interpretations offered are not always certain beyond doubt, but in terms of intellectual history, these doubts do not alter the central point of this study, which underlines the importance of going *beyond* the necessary prosopographical dimension.

In fact, these attributions, while important, are of secondary relevance compared to the common trajectories of our texts: by freeing ourselves from the biographical obsession with authorship, we can focus our attention on what these texts suggest to us: in the 1170s there is a school of law in Paris, to which some of our texts belong, in close and rapid dialogue with the law schools in Bologna and Italy, to which other texts belong. The jurists of these two schools used a common pool of theoretical constructs and textual passages and were deeply involved in a pioneering use of presumptions and brocards; they were also interested in the same subjects and often shared masters, ideas, and texts. This is the true significance of the *Perpendiculum* as a case study for the history of 12th-century legal thought and for our understanding of the circulation of knowledge in that period, from which some conclusions can be drawn.

The central point to be considered is the rapid, twofold, and widespread circulation of innovative texts, methods, and authors between the Parisian and Italian schools:[47] we have seen, for example, that no more than four years can have passed between W.'s glosses and Simon's *Summa*, and no more than another four years between the latter and Sicardus's work. This rapid circulation should lead us to question conventional historiographical assumptions and boundaries about 12th-century schools, both spatially and conceptually.

With regard to spatial boundaries, on the one hand, as I have already said, this circulation highlights the inadequacy of the scholarly concept of 'national' schools in the face of a much more complex and interconnected reality. On the other hand, it points to the limits of the historiographical understanding of 12th-century legal learning in Western Europe: although this extraordinary cir-

47 This has been highlighted by Conte, "La France."

culation between schools has of course already been noted in the literature, it has not led to a complete rethinking of the conventional historiographical narrative. This narrative is based on a circular model of the diffusion of knowledge, with Bologna and the Italian schools at the center and the rest at the periphery. Orazio Condorelli, for example, with regard to the use of Simon's *Summa* by the transmontane canonists of the 1180s, acknowledges "*i rapidissimi e intensi processi di irradiazione della scienza canonistica su base europea.*"[48] And yet his words are not casual: 'irradiance' implies a circular propagation from a center, whereas if we look at the spread of the canon law theory of presumptions, we see a wavering movement between the two sides of the Alps: rather than concentric, the propagation of learned legal thought seems to have been multipolar.

This circulation of knowledge challenges not only geographical borders, but also conceptual and conventional boundaries between disciplines. For example, the influence of the *Perpendiculum* on legists such as Pilius and Ioannes Bassianus reinforces our awareness of their already widely attested knowledge and use of sources of canon law.[49] This, in turn, urges us to reconsider the sharp distinction between the use of canon law and civil law. We are still far from the late phenomenon of the *utrumque ius*, i.e. the combination of these two laws as two distinct legal systems participating in the *ius commune*. However, it shows that in the 12th century the mentality that Francesco Calasso defined as *utraque lex*, as the knowledge of both Roman and canon law,[50] was a reality not only in the transmontane legal world, but also among Italian legists, whose claim to the self-sufficiency of Roman law ("*omnia in corpore iuris inveniuntur*")[51] seems to

48 Condorelli, "A proposito della Summa," p. 43.

49 Cf. Nicolini, *Pilii Medicinensis*, p. 79, and more recently Conte, "Pillio." The latter also studied this aspect in his forthcoming research: Emanuele Conte, "Verona 1187. Pillius and the Monks of Canterbury," under publication in the *Studies in Honour of Anne Duggan*.

50 Francesco Calasso, *Medio Evo del diritto: 1. Le fonti* (Milan: Giuffrè, 1954), pp. 232–233, defined in this way the alternate use of both Roman and canon legal rules according to need, without considering them as part of a systematic body of norms. Cf. also Ennio Cortese, "Lex, aequitas, utrumque ius nella prima civilistica," in *Lex et iustitia nell'utrumque ius: Radici antiche e prospettive attuali; Atti del 7. Colloquio internazionale romanistico-canonistico (12–14 maggio 1988)*, ed. Americo Ciani and Giovanni Diurni (Vatican City: Libreria Editrice Vaticana, 1989), repr. in Cortese, *Scritti*, 2; Cortese, *Il diritto*, 1:385–388, and 2:57–58, 80–81; Conte, "Il Digesto," pp. 279–280. More precisely, in the *utraque lex*, Roman law (identified as human law) is paired with natural law as an expression of divine law, which included but was not limited to canon law.

51 The sentence is later and comes from Accursius, "Glossa ordinaria ad Digestum vetus," v. *notitia*, to Dig. 1.1.10.2. On this claim, see Cortese, *Il Rinascimento giuridico*, pp. 30 ff.; Luca

be more a matter of principle than of fact. This is certainly more evident in the Italian minor schools, to which Pilius and Ioannes Bassianus belonged, where attention to forensic practice (and thus to the contamination of laws) seems to have been stronger.[52]

For all these reasons, a study of the *Perpendiculum* is not just a study of the history of legal literature, nor just a window into the Glossators' theory of presumption and argumentation techniques. It is, first and foremost, a case of great value for understanding the world of the 12th-century schools of law and the circulation of their knowledge, which shaped the Western legal tradition.

Loschiavo, "Lo studio e l'insegnamento del ius civile nel secolo XII," in *Pietro Lombardo. Atti del XLIII Convegno storico internazionale. Todi, 8–10 ottobre 2006* (Spoleto: Fondazione Centro italiano di studi sull'alto Medioevo, 2007), pp. 97, 108–110; Manlio Bellomo, "Una nuova figura intellettuale: il giurista," in *Il secolo XI: Una svolta?*, ed. Cinzio Violante and Johannes Fried (Bologna: Il Mulino, 1993), repr. in Bellomo, *Medioevo edito e inedito*, 2, pp. 13–14.

52 Cf. above, p. 77.

PART 2

The Texts

CHAPTER 1

Prolegomena to the Texts

This second part of the book presents the textual reconstruction of the *Perpendiculum* and other texts closely related to it. First of all, it is necessary to clarify the criteria adopted for the presentation of the text and the edition.

1 List of the Manuscripts

For the reader's convenience, some information on the manuscript tradition of the work given in the first part of this study has also been repeated here. The *Perpendiculum* survives in 15 manuscripts:

A	Aschaffenburg, HB, Perg. 26, fols. 214va–217va; 200^{rc}–201ra (A1).
Ba	Barcelona, ACA, Cugat 55, fols. 44ra–48vb.
Bs	Bamberg, SB, Can. 17 (P.I.11), fol. 95va.
C	Cambridge, Pembroke College, 101, fols. 61vb–68ra.
F	Fulda, HLB, 100 D. 10, fols. 80ra–81^{vd}.
G	Grenoble, BM, 391 (1) Rés., fols. 161va–163^{rc}.
L	Leipzig, UB, Rep. II 117, fols. 1ra–10rb.
Ma	Madrid, BNE, 421 (C.4.1), fols. 3ra–13ra.
Mu1	Munich, BSB, Clm. 7622, fols. 47va–52vb.
Mu2	Munich, BSB, Clm. 8013, fols. 115^{v}–117vb.
O	Oxford, University College, 117, fol. $145(\text{bis})^{ra-vb}$.
P1	Paris, BNF, lat. 4720A, fols. 30vb–36vb.
P2	Paris, BNF, lat. 14606, fols. 166va–167^{vc}.
Vb	Vatican City, BAV, Borgh. 287, fols. 1ra–8va.
Vp	Vatican City, BAV, Pal. Lat. 653, fols. 113ra–117^{rc}.

The entire *Summula* is found in 11 manuscripts (A, Ba, C, G, L, Ma, Mu1, Mu2, P1, Vb, and Vp). In one of them (Ba), part of the *Summula* is repeated elsewhere in the manuscript and has been indicated as Ba1. Fragments are also found by Bs (incipit) and F (explicit).

Part II, on the other hand, appears in 13 manuscripts: A, Ba, C, F, G, L, Ma, Mu1, O, P1, P2, Vb, and Vp.

Finally, brocards belonging to Part III survive in 13 manuscripts: A (plus A1), Ba, C, F, G, L, Ma, Mu1, O, P1, P2, Vb, and Vp.

 | DOI:10.1163/9789004713239_007

2 Editorial Decisions

Two major editorial decisions have been made regarding the textual reconstruction of the *Perpendiculum*.

2.1 *Reconstruction of the Manuscript Tradition*

The first concerns the problem of archetype. Certainly one of the aims of an edition of a text should be to identify the various strands of its textual tradition.[1] However, I believe that this principle of textual criticism is not easily applied to the *Perpendiculum*, and more generally to the late 12th- and early 13th-century collections of brocards.[2] As noted earlier, the *Perpendiculum*, like many other works of this genre, is a *texte vivant*. Even the most stable part of its text, the *Summula*, is an extremely stratified work, with many interventions over time and space. Any attempt at a philological reconstruction of its textual tradition should take into account all the elements of this ensemble: its three main parts, the rubrics, the individual allegations, and the many small texts interspersed within it; this makes the reconstruction of a *stemma codicum* according to traditional criteria extremely difficult. Such an analysis is an enormous task, and hardly a fruitful one: the surviving copies of the *Perpendiculum* have been constantly contaminated by textual variants from other strands of the tradition, as can be seen in manuscripts that clearly collated more than one source, such as P1 and Vb. For these reasons, in editing the *Perpendiculum* we should abandon the idea of the existence of a single original text. As I noted a few years ago with regard to the *Brocardica* of Otto-Azo,[3] the nature of the brocardic collections—inherently open and collective, as shown by the multiple reworkings and 'alluvial' formation of the texts—should lead us to reconsider our understanding of the relationship between text and authorship. Contrary to the biographical approach once adopted by the history of medieval legal literature, the modern notion of 'authorship' cannot easily be applied to the medieval scholastic mentality.[4] This is not to question the possibility or the opportunity of a philological reconstruction of the text, but rather to stress the need to take these peculiarities into account when producing a critical edition.

---

1 For the basic principles of textual criticism, see Hermann Kantorowicz, *Einführung in die Textkritik: Systematische Darstellung der textkritischen Grundsätze für Philologen und Juristen* (Leipzig: Dieterich, 1921).

2 I have already made similar remarks for the collection of Otto-Azo: De Concilio, "Moneta," pp. 405–406.

3 Ibid., p. 406.

4 Cf. Menzinger, "Riflessioni," pp. 1–10.

This has two main consequences. The first is that I have decided not to proceed with the preparation of a *stemma codicum*, as there is little point in doing so. A similar decision had already been taken in the past by another scholar who was faced with the difficulties inherent in editing a collection of brocards: Matthias Schwaibold in his reconstruction of the so-called *Brocardica "Dolum per subsequentia purgari."*[5] The second consequence, at least as far as the allegations are concerned, is the impossibility of choosing one main manuscript to be identified as the 'correct' one and to consider the others as mere variants. In this respect, I have decided, for purely practical reasons, to take Vb as the base manuscript for the edition of Parts I and II. This codex represents a later version of the work, in which most of the errors have been corrected and the number of allegations has been expanded. It is therefore probably the most complete textual basis from which to compare the variants.

In the case of obvious errors in the base manuscript or uncertain readings, variants from the other manuscripts have been adopted. With regard to the collation of Part III, however, it is impossible not only to identify one manuscript as the 'correct' one, but also to choose a stable base, given the large number of variants and the lack of a common textual basis. For this reason, I have adopted the criterion of the most common variant.

2.2 *Results of the Edition*

The second editorial decision regarding the reconstruction of the text concerns the outputs presented to the reader and, ultimately, the opportunity of an edition itself.

For the first two parts of the work—the *Summula de presumptionibus* and the 26 appended brocards—both an edition and a translation are presented. This has been made possible, despite the impossibility of reconstructing an original text, by the existence of a relatively stable tradition and the presence of discursive parts, which are worthy of translation. A very different approach has been taken to Part III. Here, the greater diversity of the textual tradition prevents us from doing the same. Indeed, as we have seen, this part (which is the longest in most manuscripts) is characterized by an enormous diversity between the different manuscripts in terms of length, brocards, rubrics, and allegations, to the point that it is very difficult to identify even a common textual basis. While a complete edition of the entire collection of brocards would certainly be desirable, this variety—which can be explained by the very nature of the work, which was intended to be an 'open text' subject to change—makes it extremely onerous and, to some extent, defeats the very purpose of such

5 See Schwaibold, *Brocardica Dolum*, pp. 32–37.

an enormous task. Furthermore, the possibility of translation is thwarted by the structure of the text itself, which consists only of individual, independent sentences and abbreviated legal references. At the same time, at least a partial structural representation of the rest of our collection is necessary. I have therefore decided to provide a critical table of contents for the brocards of Part III: that is, a list of the rubrics of all the brocards, with the collation of their variants and the order in which they appear in the manuscripts, but without the allegations. Although not ideal, this solution is sufficient to fulfill the purpose of this study: to understand the textual tradition of the *Perpendiculum* and to show in detail its content and the way it deals with legal argumentation. A complete edition of the allegations, on the other hand, could certainly be helpful to those readers interested in understanding the legal reasoning and argumentation behind the individual brocards, but would add little to our point of view. For this reason, the complete publication of the allegations is not included in this work: those who are particularly interested in exploring the depths of the argumentative logic of the ensemble will have to find their answers in the many manuscripts of the *Perpendiculum* available online, whose references are given in the bibliography.

Finally, an edition has also been included for those texts that have been interpolated into the third part of the *Perpendiculum* in the tradition of more than one manuscript: the *distinctio "Ad movendum varie iudicem,"* the gloss *"In multis,"* and the two small texts preserved by both G and P1. The reason for this is that, although on closer examination they are independent works, they can be helpful in giving the reader an idea of the intricate textual tradition of the *Perpendiculum*, which is, after all, an ensemble of argumentative devices. Instead, I have omitted those works that are only interposed into a single manuscript for various reasons. Firstly, their presence does not appear to be significant for the tradition of the work; moreover, in the case of the small texts transmitted by Mu1, they would not be relevant to the reader, while in the case of the *Brocardica "Nullus archidiaconus"* inserted in P1, the excessive length of the work puts it beyond the scope of this study.

3 Presentation of Text

Other minor decisions have been made regarding the presentation of the text.

3.1 *Structure of the Text*

Instead of the traditional line numbering, it has been decided to divide the text into paragraphs to construct the critical apparatus and to facilitate citations. The paragraphs numbers, as well as all other editorial additions, have been inserted between 〈 〉. In the footnotes, the paragraphs are indicated by the section sign §.

The collation of the alternative variants is provided in the critical apparatus, generally following the indications given by Kuttner,[6] updated in accordance with the most recent uses for the presentation of critical editions of medieval legal texts. The abbreviations used in the critical apparatus follow the traditional Latin standard.

Furthermore, some specific remarks must be made about the structure of the different parts of the *Perpendiculum*.

As far as Part I is concerned, the original text of the *Summula* does not contain any kind of internal subdivision. However, as we have seen, it can be divided thematically into eight sections, plus an introduction and a conclusion. I have decided to adopt this division and to distinguish between the different thematic parts by giving each of them a heuristic title and a number. They have been inserted between 〈 〉 like the other editorial additions.

As for Part II, since the brocards follow the same order in seven of its manuscripts, I have decided to adopt this order and numbering in the edition. Where a brocard is missing or follows a different order in a particular manuscript, this is indicated after the rubric.

For Part III, the greater complexity of its tradition requires further specifications. The great variety of brocards in the various manuscripts makes it impossible to compile a uniform list for this part according to a single order. As explained in the study, 11 groups of brocards have been identified (called α, β, γ, δ, ε, ζ, η, θ, κ, λ, and μ), according to the frequency of their repeated appearance in the same order in different manuscripts. For each of these groups I have prepared a table of contents; the order and numbering of the brocards within each table is based on their most common order in the textual tradition. For each brocard, the corresponding number in each manuscript is given after the rubric. Where the brocard has a *pro-contra* structure or an internal subdivision, the *contrarium* and the beginning of the internal rubrics are also given with their collation. After the tables of these groups, a table has been provided for each manuscript, listing all the brocards that appear only in its individual tradition. Apart from these specifications, I have used the same criteria as for Parts I and II.

For the convenience of the reader, I have included synoptic tables for Part II and for the brocards of Part III which appear in more than one manuscript.

---

6 Stephan Kuttner, "Notes on the Presentation of Text and Apparatus in Editing Works of the Decretists and Decretalists," *Traditio* 15 (1959), pp. 452–464.

3.2 *Legal References and Allegations*

As brocards are repositories of legal arguments, the allegations are an integral part of the brocardic genre on which the work is based, and not mere references to an external text. It has therefore been considered appropriate to place the identification of the citations between round brackets ( ) in the body of the text, rather than in footnotes, in order to facilitate comparison with the source cited.[7] For this reason, since the allegations have been integrated into the main text, I do not provide an *apparatus fontium*. A second set of footnotes is included only to provide more detailed explanations of textual references, translation choices, or peculiarities of manuscript tradition that cannot be briefly explained in the critical apparatus.

Since the *Perpendiculum* has an 'alluvial' nature and its manuscripts often collate several sources, sometimes a single hand repeats the same allegation twice in the same manuscript (and sometimes in two different places); at other times, a text appears more than once in the same manuscript (for example, the *distinctio "Ad movendum varie iudicem"* in Vb): in such cases, the repetitions have been indicated by giving the following variants with a subscripted number after the siglum of the manuscripts (e.g., A_1 or Vb_1).

As far as Parts I and II are concerned, one of the difficulties in choosing a basic manuscript is that there are several allegations that appear in only one or a handful of codices. In order to be consistent with the base manuscript, the allegations that do not appear in Vb should not be included in the text but should be noted in the critical apparatus. However, this would often cause difficulties for the reader and make the apparatus burdensome because of the large number of allegations of this kind. I have therefore preferred to include them in the main text, with a reference to those manuscripts which do not include them in the apparatus.

After the reference to the number and the incipit of the *Distinctio*/*Causa*, the *Summula* usually quotes the exact words in the text of the canon from which the argument is to be drawn: for example, when the *Summula* says "*D. lxxxi. In omnibus certus quis*," this means that the words "*certus quis*" are to be found in the text of D.81 c.26. Only rarely, in some manuscripts, is this indicated by the abbreviation "v." ('*verbum*'/'*verba*'). To help the reader distinguish these references, they are enclosed in double quotation marks " " as any other direct quotation.

---

7 In this regard, I have decided to depart from the traditional style suggested by Kuttner, "Notes on the Presentation," pp. 461–464, and to follow the suggestion of Menzinger, "Riflessioni," pp. 7–8.

Sometimes the allegations in Vb differ from Friedberg's critical edition of the *Decretum* or Mommsen's edition of the *Corpus Iuris Civilis*. In these cases, if at least one other manuscript reports the reference 'correctly,' it has been preferred and included in the main text instead of the one transmitted by Vb. If, on the other hand, none of the manuscripts gives the 'correct' reference, the 'wrong' version has been retained in the main text, while the 'correct' one has been given in the *apparatus* as part of the collation, followed by the initials Fr (ed. Friedberg) or Mo (ed. Mommsen).

3.3 *Abbreviations*

Some decisions have been made concerning the abbreviation of the normative sources cited. The various abbreviations for the word '*Distinctio*' have been standardized as 'D.'; similarly, the different abbreviations for '*Causa*' and '*capitulum*' have been standardized as 'C.' and 'c.,' respectively; finally, all abbreviations for '*argumentum*'/'*argumenta*' ('ar.,' 'arg.,' etc.) have been standardized as 'arg.,' and all abbreviations for '*verbum*'/'*verba*' as 'v.' For the Digest I have used the common abbreviation 'ff.' (probably a corruption of a capital 'D.'),[8] regardless of the shape of the 'd.' with a horizontal abbreviation stroke used in the manuscripts. The abbreviation for Burchard's *Decretum* is 'B.' The books of the Bible are referred to by their standard English abbreviations.

On the other hand, as regards the resolution of the abbreviated words within the text, in case of uncertainty they have been presented by placing the doubtful letters between 〉〈. Passages impossible to resolve have been indicated with an obelus †.

3.4 *Orthography*

The use of punctuation, capitalization, and spelling has been adapted to reflect current usage and the most common forms. In particular:

- the use of 'u' and 'v' has been normalized to the current use;
- the use of 'i' and 'j' has been adapted to the current use;
- 'ci' before a vowel has been usually transcribed as 'ti;'
- 'np' has been generally transcribed as 'mp;'
- double consonants have been kept only when they correspond to the current use;
- the use of 'h' has been normalized;
- the use of 'd' and 't' has been brought into agreement with the most common forms;

8 See Hermann Fitting, "Ueber die Entstehung des Zeichens ff für die Digesten," *Zeitschrift für Rechtsgeschichte* 12 (1876), pp. 300–301; Adolf Stölzel, "Nochmals die Abkürzung ff für die Abkürzung D.," *Zeitschrift für Rechtsgeschichte* 13 (1878), pp. 399–400.

- 'y' has been usually replaced by 'i;'
- different spellings of the same words have been standardized and mere slips of the pen have been omitted;
- the different ways of writing numbers (i.e., with Roman numbers or with Arabic numerals) have been standardized. Roman numbers are always lower case and followed by a dot;
- the Roman numbers corresponding to 4 and 9 have been adapted to the modern usage ('iv.' and 'ix.') in order to facilitate reading and avoid confusion, even when the manuscripts use the oldest forms 'iiii.' and 'viiii.';
- the presence of pilcrows in some manuscripts, as well as the presence of section signs and other superfluous marks, has been omitted in the collation for the sake of readability; the use of § in the text has been retained only when referring to the citation of internal passages of legal sources.

3.5 *Translation*

Finally, in the English translation of the Latin text of Parts I and II, words have sometimes been added to make the sentence more understandable; these appear within square brackets [ ]. Where, on the other hand, the words added are implicit in the Latin, or are repeated more than once in English for the sake of clarity, brackets have not been used. In the case of allegations, the choice of translation depends on the nature of the passage. Often, after the citation of the legal source, the text refers to the specific words from which the legal argument can be made: these citations have not been translated, as they do not contain a meaningful sentence, but merely a textual and technical reference. More rarely, and only in the case of sources other than the *Decretum*, such as the Bible or Burchard's work, does the *Perpendiculum* quote a complete passage; in these cases, a translation is given. In the case of biblical quotations, I have chosen to use the Douay-Rheims translation because it is often closer to the literal Latin, although I have sometimes adapted it to reflect the slight differences between the passages quoted in the *Perpendiculum* and the Vulgate.

CHAPTER 2

Manuscript Descriptions

A description of the manuscripts of the *Perpendiculum* is a useful companion to the analysis of its text and a scholarly expectation when embarking on an edition. It not only gives us an insight into the circulation and tradition of the work. Above all, it is a necessary tool for understanding the cultural milieu in which the *Perpendiculum* was produced and used, and it has told us much in this regard.

For this reason, I have tried to provide as detailed descriptions as possible. Ideally, this would have meant examining all the codices in person. However, this was often not possible. With a few exceptions, I have had to rely on digital images and sometimes microfilms. Of course, these means are usually sufficient to analyze the content of the manuscripts but tell us too little about their material aspects. In this respect, I have often had to rely on previous catalogue descriptions, many of which are very old and provide little detail. For these reasons, the accuracy and depth of the detail and the amount of information in the descriptions vary from manuscript to manuscript.

A Aschaffenburg, HB, Perg. 26

Century	13th *in.*–14th *in.*
Catalogues	Josef Hofmann and U. Hermann Hauke, *Die Handschriften der Stiftsbibliothek und der Stiftskirche zu Aschaffenburg* (Aschaffenburg: Geschichts- und Kunstverein, 1978), pp. 53–56.
Material	Parchment. 24,5 × 17,5. I + 227 fols. The MS consists of 6 originally independent units, probably already united in the 15th century.
Provenance	Archbishopric of Mainz: this can be deduced from the places mentioned (Esselborn on the front paste-down, Lengfeld on 194^r).
Ownership	In the 16th century the MS was owned by the collegiate church of Aschaffenburg (mark on 1^r upper edge).
Binding	Wooden boards with brown leather cover with clasps, 15th century.
Paste-downs	On the front, a fragment of a sacramentary (14th century), followed by a note about a purchase of oil, mentioning the village of Esselborn in the district of Alzey-Worms. On the rear, the last fol. has been used as paste-down.

 | DOI:10.1163/9789004713239_008

I *Fols. 1–94*

Foliation: 94 fols. Collation: i–xi^{8}, xii^{6}. 18×12. 2 columns. 40–42 lines. Hand: gothic minuscule (13th century). Rubrication: headings in red; page titles, §§, and Lombard majuscules at the beginning of each chapter, alternately in red and blue; at the beginning of the book there are some larger initials with floral decoration in the opposite color.

1ra–94vb Guillelmus Durantis, *Repertorium aureum iuris canonici* (fragment).

Prologue	*Reverendo in Christo patri ac domino Matheo*
Rubric	*〉Incipit repertorium〈*
Incipit	*Prothoplasti rubigine humana* (1ra)
Explicit	ends with lib. v tit. 3: *An medicus possit vendere sanitatem dominus //.*
Literature	Knut Wolfgang Nörr, "Die Kanonistische Literatur," in *HQLR*, 1:380.
Editions	Guillelmus Durantis, *Repertorium aureum corpore iuris canonici* (Rome: Schencbecher, 1474).

II *Fols. 95–165*

Foliation: 71 fols. Collation: xiii^{8}, xiv^{6}, xv^{8}, xvi^{8} (wants 7), xvii^{8}, xviii^{4} (wants 3,4), xix–xxii^{8}. 16,5×12. 2 columns. 36 lines. Hand: gothic minuscule by two hands. Without rubrication.

95ra–165vb Bartholomaeus Brixiensis, *Casus decretorum* (fragment).

Prologue	*〈Q〉uoniam suffragantibus antiquorum laboribus*
Incipit	*〈H〉umanum genus. Casus iste sic ponitur* (95rb)
Colophon	*Expliciunt casus decretorum etc.*
Literature	Nörr, "Die Kanonistische Literatur," p. 371.
Editions	Bartholomaeus Brixiensis, *Casus decretorum*, ed. Nikolaus Kessler (Basel: Kessler, 1489).

III *Fols. 166–193*

Foliation: 28 fols. Collation: xxiii–xxv^{8}, xxvi^{4}. 18×13,5. 2 columns. 39 lines. Hand: gothic minuscule by one hand, corresponding to the second hand of the previous text. Rubricated.

166ra–193vb Guilelmus Accursii, *Casus institutionum* (Lib. II.9–IV.28).

Incipit	*// exemplum est si peto a iudice* (174ra).
Explicit	*supra. De legatis § Sed non usque.*
Colophon	*Expliciunt casus domini Whilhelmi filii Accursii. Deo gracias.*
Literature	Weimar, "Die legistische Literatur der Glossatorenzeit," in *HQLR*, 1:221.

IV *Fols. 194–217*

Foliation: 24 fols. Collation: xxvii–xxix^{8}. 20,5×12–13. 2 columns. Except for fols. 197^{r}–207^{r} and 210^{r}–214^{r}, in three columns. Alternating number of lines, c. 50. Hand: gothic minuscule (13th century). Without rubrication. This unit seems to be an ensemble linked to the Parisian school and composed between 1175 and 1180.[1]

194ra–196va *Summa Codicis* (Cod. 3.31–41).
Possibly produced in Paris in the 1180s.
Incipit // *ad fatalitatem ut si forte res periit*
Explicit *aquiline directe arbitraria est et perpetua.*
Literature Hans van de Wouw, "Notes on the Aschaffenburg Manuscript Perg. 26," *BMCL* 3 (1973), pp. 97–107, 98.
Editions Sample in van de Wouw, "Notes," pp. 101–102.

197ra–207^{v} *Quaestiones Aschaffenburgenses.*
A collection of canon law *quaestiones* from the Parisian school, compiled c. 1174–1179. Written by a different hand than the *Summa*. Fransen divides the collection into two parts: the first contains q.1–14, the second q.15–86. The first group of *quaestiones* generally follows a three-column lay-out, with the solution in the center and the arguments on either side. In the second part, instead, some questions are written in long lines. Nine *quaestiones* from the second part also appear in the *Quaestiones Barcinonenses breves*.[2] Between q.21 and 22 there is a *distinctio* and a *Summula de induciis*, extracted from the *Summa Decreti* of Stephen of Tournai.
Gouron believes that the mention of a *magister Gido, Ga., Gaid.*, and *G* here refers to Gui Francesc, thus testifying to the diffusion of Provençal texts in the Parisian school.
Between q.10 and 11 (200^{rc}–201ra) there are eight brocards from the third part (except no. 6 A1, which is from Part II) of the *Perpendiculum*, which I have marked with the *siglum* A1. The texts are confused with the allegations of the *distinctiones*, and perhaps they are used as allegations themselves; more precisely, they are found in these positions: 1 A1: 200^{rc}; 2 A1: 200^{rc}, 200^{vc}; 3 A1: 200va, 201ra; 4, 5 and 6 A1: 200vb; 7 A1: 200^{vc}; 8 A1: 201ra.
Incipit ⟨*S*⟩*criptor quidam magistro suo iure* (197rb)
Explicit *prius polluit per adulterium.*

1 Gouron, "Notes sur les collections," p. 62.
2 See below, p. 140.

Literature van de Wouw, "Notes," pp. 98–99; Gouron, "Qui était," pp. 284–287.
Editions Gérard Fransen, "Quaestiones Aschaffenburgenses," *BMCL* 16 (1986), pp. 71–86, repr. in Fransen, *Canones et Quaestiones*, 1.2; sample ed. by van de Wouw, "Notes," pp. 102–103.

207^{v}–210ra *Quaestiones.*
Written in two columns, in a different hand from the previous *quaestiones*, it is a collection of five texts by different authors: nos. 1 and 3 are by Placentinus, no. 2 is anonymous, nos. 4 and 5 are by Bulgarus.
Incipit *Quaeritur an heres cautioni de restituenda usus nomine legata renuntiare possit*
Explicit *dum iudex fare veritatem non potuit.*
Literature van de Wouw, "Notes," p. 99.

210ra–214rb *Quaestiones dominorum bononiensium* (*Collectio Aschaffenburgensis*).
A collection of 44 *quaestiones*, written in three columns. Some are attributed to Bolognese masters, but most are anonymous. The collection is related to the *Collectio Gratianopolitana* contained in our manuscript G.
Literature van de Wouw, "Notes," p. 100. Gouron, "Notes," p. 62.
Editions sample in van de Wouw, "Notes," pp. 103–106.

214va–217va *Perpendiculum.*
214va–216ra *Summula de presumptionibus.*
Incipit *⟨H⟩ic locus in iudiciis frequens est et pernecessarius*
Explicit *quam propter prolixitatem distinguere non curavi.*
216ra–217rb Part II.
Incipit *Introductis publica auctoritate renuntiare non licet*
Explicit *Si romanorum dicendo omnia.*
217rb *Glossa de conditione feminarum.*
Incipit *In multis iuris articulis deterior est conditio feminarum quam masculorum*
Explicit *ff. de accusatoribus Qui accusare.*

217rb–217va Part III.
Incipit *Levius punitur qui commissum sponte confitetur*
Explicit *D. xcv. Illud ubi nam quibus.*
217vb Blank.

V *Fols. 218–227*

Foliation: 10 fols. Collation: xxx^{10}. 19,5×12,5–13. 2 columns. 55–62 lines. Hand: gothic minuscule with two hands (second hand between fol. 223ra and 224vb), pearl script. Quotations are underlined. Without rubrication.

218ra–227vb *Summa in Decretum* (fragment).
A work in the Bolognese style, written around 1180, it is related to the so-called *Summa Casinensis*. It is divided into three parts:
218ra–224vb C.12 q.1 c.28–C.12 q.2 c.73.
Incipit *//sicut hii. Signatur contrarium*
Explicit *ut in predicto exemplo et xvii. Q. iv. Questi. Consensu concilii.*
225ra Petrus Cantor, *Commentarius ad epistulas Pauli* (fragment of the incipit, by a third hand, in the first 13 lines).
225ra–227rb C.12 q.1 a.c.1–c.23.
Incipit *In precedenti causa ostendit magister qualiter clerici*
Explicit *victum et tegumentum et dicitur alias xvi. Q. i. Si cupis.*
Literature van de Wouw, "Notes," p. 100.
Editions sample in van de Wouw, "Notes," pp. 106–107.

Ba Barcelona, ACA, Cugat 55

Century 12th *ex.*–13th *in.*

Catalogues Francesc X. Miguel Rosell, "Catàleg dels llibres manuscrits de la Biblioteca del Monestir de Sant Cugat del Vallès existents a l'Arxiu de la Corona d'Aragó," *Butlletí de la Biblioteca de Catalunya* 8 (1928–1932), pp. 143–240, 232–235; Gérard Fransen, "Manuscrits canoniques conservés en Espagne (II)," *RHE* 49 (1954), pp. 152–156, repr. in Fransen, *Canones et Quaestiones*, 1.1.

Material Parchment. 24,5×16. III + 148 fols. The manuscript is a miscellany made up of 9 codicological units. At least the first 6 codicological units are of French origin. Its main contents are ten sets of *quaestiones* (*Barcinonenses I–X*).

Provenance Benedictine monastery of Sant Cugat del Vallès.

Binding In parchment (19th century).

I *Fols. 1–26*

Foliation: 26 fols. 24,5 × 16. 2 columns, 50 lines. Hand: gothic minuscule. Rubricated. Initials in red at the beginning of each paragraph. At the beginning of the text there is a larger initial in red and black with a geometric texture and zoomorphic decoration. Some glosses in the margins.

1^r–26^v Iulianus, *Novellarum Epitome*.

Title *Liber novellarum Iustiniani continens quamdam expositionem legum et quasdam questiones iuris* (on the edge).

In the margin *Liber autenticorum translatus fuit de greco in latinum de verbo in verbum; liber novellarum de sententia ad sententiam.*

Rubric *In nomine domini. Incipit liber novellarum domini Iustiniani.*

Incipit *In digestis et in constitutionibus didicimus parentibus quidem et liberis*

Colophon *Explicit liber novellarum domini Iustiniani imperatoris semper augusti.*

Literature Wolfgang Kaiser, *Die Epitome Iuliani: Beiträge zum römischen Recht im frühen Mittelalter und zum byzantinischen Rechtsunterricht* (Frankfurt am Main: Klostermann, 2004).

Editions Iulianus, *Iuliani Epitome Latina Novellarum Iustiniani*, ed. Pietro Fiorelli and Anna Maria Bartoletti Colombo (Florence: Università degli studi di Firenze, Dipartimento di teoria e storia del diritto, 1996).

II *Fols. 27–43*

Foliation: 17 fols. 24,5 × 16. 2 columns, 50 lines. Hands: gothic minuscule. Rubricated (except for fols. 43^{rb-v}) with §§, initial strokes at the beginning of the paragraphs. From 40va also underlining. At the beginning of the text there is a larger Lombard-style initial in red.

27^r–43rb Bertrandus Metensis, *Commentarius De regulis iuris*.

A treatise of Anglo-Norman origin: Bertrandus, Bishop of Metz (*sed.* 1180–1212) was a member of the circle of the Anglo-Norman master

Gerardus Pucella, who was associated with the Cologne school of canon law.

Prologue *Universus tractatus veteris sapientie legum in pandectis continetur*

Incipit *Regula est que rem que est breviter etc.*

Explicit *Pretor habet honoris possessionem loco heredis, id est ille, cui pretor dat honoris possessionem, habetur pro herede sive experiatur sive conveniatur.*

Literature Gero Dolezalek, "Zur Datierung des Kommentars 'De regulis iuris' von Bertrandus Metensis," *Ius Commune* 11 (1984), pp. 31–36; Stephan Kuttner, "Bertram of Metz," *Traditio* 13 (1957), pp. 501–505.

Editions Bertrandus Metensis, *Bertrandus Metensis de regulis iuris*, ed. Severino Caprioli (Perugia: Università di Perugia, 1981).

43^{rb-v} Rodoicus Modicipassus, *Quaestiones Barcinonenses I*.

A single canon law *quaestio disputata* by Rodoicus (or Rotbertus) Modicipassus, an Anglo-Norman canonist.[3] The *quaestio*, written between 1192 and 1200, is related to the *quaestiones Barcinonenses IV*, which consist of another *quaestio* by the same author.

Incipit *Quidam episcopus, auctoritate apostolica factus archiepiscopus*

Explicit *›Sententia magistri Rotberti Modicipassus.‹ Si monachi tacuerunt ... C. de prescriptione xxx annorum Male agitur, Cum notissimi.*

Literature Brundage, "Some Canonistic Quaestiones," pp. 67–76.

Editions James A. Brundage, "The Quaestiones of Rotbertus Modicipassus in a Barcelona Manuscript," *Studies in Medieval Culture* 5 (1975), pp. 87–95; Fransen, "Canonistica minora," pp. 47–52.

III *Fols. 44–49*

Foliation: 6 fols. 24,5 × 16. 2 columns, 47 lines. Hand: gothic minuscule. Rubrication for each brocard (except fols. 47va–48rb), large Lombard-style initials mark the beginning of the paragraphs (only for the *Summula*). Rubricated diagrams (fols. 48^{rb-vb}).

3 See Landau, *Rodoicus*; Landau, "The Origin of the Regula iuris," pp. 27–31, now questioned by Bertram, "Rodoicus Modicipassus;" cf. also Stephan Kuttner, "Rodoicus ou Rotbertus Modicipassus (Parvipassus)," in *DDC* 7 (1965): 701–702.

44^{r}–48^{v} *Perpendiculum.*

44ra–45va *Summula de presumptionibus.*

Incipit *Hic locus frequens in iudiciis est pernecessarius*

Explicit *quod propter prolixitatem distinguere non curavi.*

45va–47ra Part II.

Incipit *Introductis publica utilitate renunciare non licet*

Explicit *Causa iii. Q. viii. Omnia.*

47ra–47va Part III.

First series, nos. 1–12.

Incipit *Principium spectandum*

Explicit *Causa xviii. Q. viii. Occidit ad causam.*

47va–48rb *Summula de presumptionibus* (fragment, from III, 5.1 to V, 10.4). An interpolated fragment indicated as Ba1.

Incipit *// Causa xxii. Q. ii. Ne quis qui non habet cor duplex*

Explicit *D. xxxv. Sexto, D. l. Liberos qui.*

48^{rb-vb} Part III.

Second series, from no. 13.

Incipit *// Causa xvii. Q. iv. Sunt qui*

Text *Ob delictorum emendationem et animi*

Explicit *multa prohibentur.*

49^{rv} Blank.

IV ***Fols. 50–58***

Foliation: 9 fols. 24,5×16. 2 columns, 54 lines. Hand: gothic minuscule: three hands (fols. 50^{r}–54^{v}, 54^{v}–57^{v}, 58^{r}). Rubrication: large Lombard-style initials mark the beginning of the *quaestiones* (only fols. 50^{r}–54^{v}), initial strokes at the beginning of the paragraphs. *Solutiones* underlined. No rubrication on fol. 58^{r}.

50^{r}–54^{v} *Quaestiones Barcinonenses II.*

Eighteen canon law *quaestiones disputatae*, without rubrics. The *quaestiones* have been carefully amended, often by underlining. All the *quaestiones*, except the first, have the *siglum* S. The collection was allegedly compiled in the early 1180s, probably in an English context. Fransen, who edited the collection, did not attempt to solve the initial, and limited himself to suggesting Sicardus Cremonensis as a possible author, but excluded Simon de Bisignano "*car nous sommes dans un contexte d'œuvres françaises et non bolon-*

aises."[4] In the light of the recent identification of Simon de Bisignano with Simon de Apulia,[5] this conclusion may need to be reconsidered and the attribution re-examined.

Incipit *Quandam uxorem lapsam in adulterium maritus de adulterio accusavit*

Explicit *unde cum Christus prior sit tempore in hoc pignore pocior est et iure. S.*

Literature Brundage, "Some Canonistic Quaestiones," pp. 67–76.

Editions Fransen, "Les questions disputées de Maitre S.," pp. 331–343.

54v–56va *Quaestiones decretales* (*Barcinonenses III*).

Compiled for class discussion in the early 1180s: references to the Third Lateran Council.

Incipit *Queritur quare votum sollempne*

Explicit *solet queri.*

Literature Fransen, "Les questions disputées de Maitre S.," p. 331.

Editions Brundage, "Some Canonistic Quaestiones," pp. 67–76; Gérard Fransen, "Quaestiones decretales dans un manuscrit espagnol," in *Sine invidia communico: Opstellen aangeboden aan Prof. Dr. A.J. de Groot*, ed. Paul L. Nève and Emile Christian Coppens, 2nd ed. (Nijmegen: Gerard Noodt Instituut, Katholieke Universiteit Nijmegen, 1987), repr. in Fransen, *Canones et Quaestiones*, 1.2.

56vb–57rb *Tractatus de operibus.*

Incipit *Cum de opere exteriori dubitatur*

Explicit *Respondit Dominus Nec ego te condempnabo. Adaptatio patet.*

Literature Fransen, "Les questions disputées de Maitre S.," p. 331; De Concilio, "Soggettività e qualificazione."

Editions Fransen, "Canonistica minora," pp. 36–42; De Concilio, "Soggettività e qualificazione."

---

4 Gérard Fransen, "Les questions disputées de Maitre S.," in *Satura Roberto Feenstra sexagesimum quintum annum aetatis complenti ab alumnis collegis amicis oblata*, ed. Johan Albert Ankum, Johannes Emil Spruit, and Felix B.J. Wubbe (Fribourg: Éditions universitaires, 1985), repr. in Fransen, *Canones et Quaestiones*, 1.2, pp. 332–333.

5 See above, pp. 110–111.

57rb–va *Sermo sive arenga.*
Incipit *Nemo accendit lucernam*
Explicit *et vocari ad hominibus rabbi.*
Literature Fransen, "Les questions disputées de Maitre S.," p. 331.
Editions Fransen, "Canonistica minora," pp. 42–44.

57va–b *Quaestio disputata.*
Incipit *Quidam paterfamilias habuit filium*
Explicit *per xl. annos moram fecit.*
Literature Fransen, "Les questions disputées de Maitre S.," p. 331.
Editions Fransen, "Canonistica minora," pp. 44–47.

58r Rodoicus Modicipassus, *Questiones Barcinonenses IV.*
A single canon law *quaestio disputata* by the Anglo-Norman canonist Rodoicus (or Rotbertus) Modicipassus, written between 1192 and 1200. The *quaestio* is related to the *quaestiones Barcinonenses I*, which consist of a single *quaestio* by the same author.
Incipit *Prior cuiusdam canonice regularis que suberat domino pape*
Explicit *quia temere renunciando deliquit.*
Literature Brundage, "Some Canonistic Quaestiones," pp. 67–76.
Editions Brundage, "The Quaestiones," pp. 87–95; Fransen, "Canonistica minora," pp. 52–54.

58v Blank.

V *Fols. 59–66*

Foliation: 8 fols. 24,5 × 16. 3 columns, 59 lines (fols. 59–62r), 2 columns, 61 lines (fols. 62v–66). Hand: gothic minuscule. Rubrication: large Lombard-style initials mark the beginning of the *quaestiones.*

59r–62r *Quaestiones decretales* (*Barcinonenses V seu breves*).
Possibly written around 1160. They have some similarities with the *Quaestiones Aschaffenburgenses II.* Classical three-column lay-out, with the *quaestio* in the center and the allegations on either side. The first of each group of allegations in the left column is rubricated.
Incipit *Accidit ut in quibusdam*
Explicit *si sue petitionis probata apparuerint testimonia.*
Literature Brundage, "Some Canonistic Quaestiones," pp. 67–76.
Editions Gérard Fransen, "Quaestiones Barcinonenses breves," BMCL 15 (1985), pp. 31–49, repr. in Fransen, *Canones et Quaestiones*, 1.2.

62ᵛ–66ʳᵃ *Quaestiones decretales* (*Barcinonenses* VI).

Six canon law *quaestiones* compiled after the *quaestiones Barcinonenses* V, probably c. 1168–1172. Lay-out in two columns. The allegations are often arranged in two smaller columns. This collection corresponds to the *quaestiones Lipsenses* IV.1 and *Bambergenses* II.2.[6]

Incipit *Apostolicus adversiis imperatoris effrenatam licentiam*

Explicit *nam si a generalibus excommunicatione omnes illas personas secludimus.*

Literature Gérard Fransen, "Les 'Questiones' des canonistes II," *Traditio* 13 (1957), pp. 481–501, repr. in Fransen, *Canones et Quaestiones*, 1.2, p. 497; Brundage, "Some Canonistic Quaestiones," pp. 67–76.

Editions Gérard Fransen, "États différents d'une meme Question disputée," ZRG *Kan. Abt.* 68 (1982), pp. 136–152, repr. in Fransen, *Canones et Quaestiones*, 1.2, and ZRG *Kan. Abt.* 74 (1988), pp. 141–167.

66ᵛ Blank.

VI *Fols. 67–90*

Foliation: 24 fols. 24,5 × 16. 1 column, 53 lines (fols. 67–89). Hand: gothic minuscule. Rubrication: large Lombard-style initials and red underlining mark the beginning of paragraphs (only fol. 67ʳ); on the other folios, there is blank space for initials.

67ʳ–89ʳ *Summa in Decretum "Et est sciendum."*

A French commentary on the *Decretum*, written in Sens during the pontificate of Lucius III (1181–1185). Landau attributed the work to Rodoicus Modicipassus, but this has recently been challenged by Bertram.

Incipit ›Secundum Bartolomeum‹ *Humanum genus duobus regitur naturali scilicet iure et moribus. Et est sciendum*

Explicit *vel consuetudine generali defenderetur.*

Literature Bertram, "Rodoicus Modicipassus;" Peter Landau, "Der Dekretglossenapparat Et est sciendum–ein Werk des Kanonisten Rodoicus Modicipassus," *RIDC* 24 (2013), pp. 19–26; Brundage, "Some Canonistic Quaestiones," pp. 67–76.

Editions several excerpts, based on the manuscript Stuttgart, Würtembergische Landesbibliothek, hist. fol. 419, fols.

6 See below, pp. 172 and 150 respectively.

34–48rb, and 49, in Franz Gillmann, "Die Dekretglossen des Cod. Stuttgart. Hist. F. 419," AKKR 107 (1927), pp. 192–250, repr. in *Gesammelte Schriften zur klassischen Kanonistik von Franz Gillmann*, ed. Rudolf Weigand, 1 (Würzburg: Echter, 1988), no. 14.

89^{v}–90^{rv} Blank.

VII *Fols. 91–96*

Foliation: 6 fols. 23,5 × 14,5. 1 column, 55 lines (fols. 92–95). Hand: gothic minuscule. No rubrication.

92^{r}–93^{r} *Florilegium legum.*

Excerpts from Bulgarus, Rogerius, and others, mainly on procedure.

Incipit *Si quis vocatus ad iudicium conveniendus lege Cornelia de siccariis*

Explicit *postea appellare poterit, scilicet x. diebus transactis.*

93^{v}–94^{r} *Tractatus de actionum varietate.*

A work composed in northern Italy at the end of the 11th century. In this manuscript, it is the first part of a *compendium* which includes the following *Tractatus de prescriptionibus* and *de actionibus*, probably written in southern France in the middle of the 12th century.

Incipit *De actionum varietate et earum vita seu longitudine*

Explicit *studuimus strictim obtemperare.*

Literature Fowler-Magerl, *Ordo*, pp. 160–163; Fowler-Magerl, *Ordines*, p. 74; Stephan Kuttner in Hermann Kantorowicz, *Studies in the Glossators*, p. 348, addition no. 326; André Gouron, "Le traité 'De actionum varietate', la version du manuscrit de Barcelone (A.C.A. San Cugat 55) et la 'Glossa Coloniensis' aux institutes (manuscrit de Cologne H.A. W 328)," *Initium* 2 (1997), pp. 373–390, repr. in Gouron, *Pionniers*, no. II.

Editions A later recension of this work is edited in Hermann Fitting, *Juristische Schriften des früheren Mittelalters* (Halle: Buchhandlung des Waisenhauses, 1876), pp. 62–69 and 128–131.

94ra *Catalogus prescriptionum.*

This text is a catalogue of prescriptions from Rogerius's circle, although perhaps not written by Rogerius himself.

Incipit *Est prescriptio trium dierum*

Explicit *nisi in libertate ut de usur. 1 Cum in rem.*

Literature Fowler-Magerl, *Ordo*, pp. 169–170.

Editions Rogerius, *Catalogus prescriptionum*, in *Octavum volumen tractatuum e variis iuris interpretibus collectorum* (Lyon: Regnault, 1549; repr. Turin: Bottega d'Erasmo, 1970 (CGJC 5:6)), fol. 92vb.

94^{r}–95^{v} Geraudus (?), *Tractatus de natura actionum*.

A treatise on actions, which Gouron attributes to the Provençal jurist Geraudus, author of the *Summa Trecensis*. It is noteworthy that it also appears in Bs (47^{v}–49^{v}). Here the first part of the *tractatus* is omitted. In this manuscript it forms part of a *compendium*, together with the two previous works.

Incipit *Actio nihil aliud est*

Explicit *que in ytalicis contractibus oriuntur.*

Literature Fowler-Magerl, *Ordo*, pp. 165–167. André Gouron, "'Primo tractavit de natura actionum Geraudus': Studium bononiense, glossateurs et pratique juridique dans la France méridionale," in *Chiesa, diritto e ordinamento della societas Christiana nei secoli XI e XII: Atti della nona Settimana internazionale di studio; Mendola, 28 agosto–2 settembre 1983* (Milan: Vita e Pensiero, 1986), repr. in Gouron, *Droit et coutume en France*, no. I.

Editions Fitting, *Juristische Schriften*, pp. 56–62, 117–127.

96^{rv} Blank.

VIII ***Fols. 97–138***

Foliation: 42 fols. 24,5×16. 2 columns, 51 lines (fols. 97–138). Hand: gothic minuscule. Rubrication: large Lombard-style initials mark the beginning of each *quaestio* (in 3 *quaestiones* of fol. 97^{r} and on fols. 98–102); on fol. 97^{rv} the other *quaestiones* have a blank space left for the initial. On fol. 138^{rv} there is no rubrication, but §§ mark the beginning of each paragraph.

97^{ra-vb} *Quaestiones Barcinonenses VII.*

A collection of 20 civilian texts without solutions, related to the *Quaestiones dominorum Bononiensium*. "*Oto*" (Papiensis) is mentioned in the first *quaestio*.

Incipit *⟨T⟩itius castellum suum seio dedit in feudum*

Explicit *sed ea presente et non contradicente stipulati sunt.*

Literature Brundage, "Some Canonistic Quaestiones," pp. 67–76.

98^{r}–102vb *Quaestiones Barcinonenses VIII.*
A collection of canon law *quaestiones* compiled in the late 12th century.
Incipit *De eo qui preter voluntatem*
Explicit *privilegium non habuerat expoliatus.*
Literature Brundage, "Some Canonistic Quaestiones," pp. 67–76.

102vb–137^{v} *Quaestiones Barcinonenses IX.*
This collection of canon law shows similarities with the *Quaestiones Bambergenses II.*
Incipit *Quidam testes probant Bertam esse filiam Martini*
Explicit *Isti de speciali concessione super talem.*
Literature Gérard Fransen, "Les 'Questiones' des canonistes III," *Traditio* 19 (1963), pp. 516–531, repr. in Fransen, *Canones et Quaestiones*, 1.2; Brundage, "Some Canonistic Quaestiones," pp. 67–76.

138^{ra-vb} *Quaestiones Barcinonenses X.*
It is actually a single canon law *quaestio* compiled in Paris after 1234. The text is parallel to q.1. of the *Quaestiones Neapolitanae.*
Incipit *Ex consuetudine longa abbas quidam*
Explicit *item est de veteri.*
Literature Brundage, "Some Canonistic Quaestiones," pp. 67–76.
Editions Gérard Fransen, "Les 'Quaestiones Neapolitanae'," *BMCL* 6 (1976), pp. 29–46, repr. in Fransen, *Canones et Quaestiones*, 1.2.

IX *Fols. 139–148*

Foliation: 10 fols. 24,5×16. 2 columns, 59 lines (fols. 139–148). Hand: gothic minuscule. Rubricated, with red initials at the beginning of the paragraphs (except for fols. 141–146, where only the first column is rubricated).

139ra–140rb Hugolinus de Sesso, *Tractatus de appellationibus.*
Rubric *⟩Incipit tractatus domini Hugolini de appellatione⟨*
Incipit *Appellationis usus quam sit frequens quam necessarius*
Explicit *et mirum est quomodo bonus Alexander tertius dormitavit.*
Colophon *Explicit tractatus appellationis.*
Literature Fowler-Magerl, *Ordo*, p. 243.
Editions Gonzalo Martínez Diez, "Tres lecciones del siglo XII del Estudio general de Palencia," *AHDE* 61 (1991), pp. 391–449.

140rb–141ra Hugolinus de Sesso, *Tractatus de recusatione iudicum.*

Rubric ›*Incipit tractatus domini Ugolini de recusatione iudicum*‹

Incipit *Quia suspecti et inimici iudicis*

Explicit *et sententiando partem facit.*

Colophon *Explicit.*

Literature Fowler-Magerl, *Ordo*, pp. 223–224.

Editions Martínez Diez, "Tres lecciones," pp. 391–449.

141ra–146ra Hugolinus de Sesso, *Tractatus de testibus.*

Rubric *Incipit de testibus secundum Ugolinum*

Incipit *Lecturi capitulum de testibus ad euidentiam dicendorum*

Explicit *ordinet et emendet.*

Literature Fowler-Magerl, *Ordo*, pp. 223–224.

Editions Martínez Diez, "Tres lecciones," pp. 391–449.

146^{v}–148^{r} Bernardus Papiensis, *Summa titulorum Decretalium* (fragment).

Incipit *In nomine Domini*

Explicit *et occulte.*

Editions Bernardus Papiensis, *Summa decretalium.*

Bs Bamberg, SB, Can. 17 (P.I.11)

Century 13th *in.*

Catalogues Friedrich Leitschuh and Hans Fischer, *Katalog der Handschriften der Königlichen Bibliothek zu Bamberg*, revised ed. (Wiesbaden: Harrassowitz, 1966), pp. 880–884; "Bamberg, Staatsbibliothek Bamberg, Msc.Can.17," in *Handschriften Portal*, available at https://resolver.staatsbibliothek-berlin.de/HSP0004E4F500000000, accessed 2024 Jan 20; Karl-Georg Pfändtner and Stefanie Westphal, *Die Handschriften des 13. und 14. Jahrhunderts der Staatsbibliothek Bamberg: Mit Nachträgen von Handschriften und Fragmenten des 10. und 12. Jahrhunderts*, 2 (Wiesbaden: Harrassowitz, 2015) pp. 8–9. The content is also analyzed by Peter Landau, "Lehrbuch contra Fälschung: Die Bamberger Anfänge der europäischen Strafrechtswissenschaft und die Würzburger Güldene Freiheit," *Deutsches Archiv für Erforschung des Mittelalters* 62, no. 2 (2006), pp. 505–536.

Material Parchment. 25,4 × 18,5. I + 184 + I fols. This miscellaneous manuscript consists of 10 codicological units and can be divided into

	two main parts (c. u. I and c. u. II–X); its pieces were already united before the current binding.
Provenance	Franconia.
Ownership	Bamberg, cathedral library.
Binding	Current binding made in 1611.
Paste-downs	Paper.

I *Fols. 1–54*

Foliation: 54 fols. Collation:[7] i–v^{8}, vi^{10}, vii$^{6 \text{ (wants 5–6)}}$. 2 columns, 42 lines. Hand: gothic minuscule. Rubrication: illuminated initial letter with floral motifs; small red initials at the beginning of each paragraph.

1^{r} Blank.

There are various annotations. Some mnemonic verses (*"Loyces arguta cinifarum cuspis acuta* ..."), and fragments from Rufinus's *Summa Decreti* and Peter of Blois's *Speculum iuris canonici*, as well as a commentary on Aristotle's *De memoria et reminiscentia.*

1vb–47ra *Collectio Decretalium* (*Bambergensis*).

A French systematic collection of decretals compiled in France during or shortly after the pontificate of Lucius III (1181–1185).

Rubric	*De symonia et ne merces pro ecclesie consecratione*
Incipit	*Cum sit Romana*
Explicit	*a sanguine et ydolotito. Finis.*
Literature	Walter Deeters, *Die Bambergensisgruppe der Dekretalensammlungen des 12. Jahrhunderts* (PhD dissertation: University of Bonn, 1956), pp. 247–323; Landau, "Lehrbuch," pp. 506–507.
Editions	Emil Friedberg, ed., *Die Canones-Sammlungen zwischen Gratian und Bernhard von Pavia* (Leipzig: Tauchnitz, 1897), pp. 84–115.

47va Geraudus (?), *Summa Codicis Trecensis* (excerpt).

Literature	Fowler-Magerl, *Ordo*, p. 165; Gouron, "L'auteur et la patrie;" Gouron, "L'élaboration."
Editions	Geraudus, "Summa Trecensis."

47va–54vb Compendium "*Cum de criminalibus quaestionibus.*"

A compendium written in middle of the 12th century for the cathedral school of Bamberg, consisting of several texts:

7 Information on the collation of the manuscript, only partially provided by the catalogues, has been kindly supplied by Prof. Dr Bettina Wagner.

47va–49va Geraudus (?), *Tractatus de natura actionum.*

A treatise on actions, attributed by Gouron to the Provençal jurist Geraudus, author of the *Summa Trecensis.* It also appears in Ba (94^{r}–95^{v}). This MS also contains the well-known *Prologus* (incipit: *Quoniam eorum desideriis*). This is at the end, however.

Rubric	*Quedam utilia sunt ista de actionibus*
Incipit	*Actiones sunt legitime persecutiones*
Explicit	*fructus quoque restituuntur.*
Literature	Fowler-Magerl, *Ordo*, pp. 165–167. Gouron, "Primo tractavit;" Landau, "Lehrbuch," p. 507.
Editions	Fitting, *Juristische Schriften*, pp. 56–62, 117–127.

49va–50vb *Ordo iudiciorum criminalium.*

Composed around 1160.

Rubric	*De criminalibus causis*
Incipit	*Cum de criminalibus quaestionibus*
Explicit	*sine competentis iudicis auctoritate imponunt.*
Literature	Fowler-Magerl, *Ordo*, pp. 57, 165; Fowler-Magerl, *Ordines*, p. 74; Landau, "Lehrbuch," pp. 507–508.
Editions	Johann Friedrich von Schulte, "De criminalibus causis (aus dem Bamberger Codex P. I. 11)," in *I. Constitutio Constantini ad Ablavium. II. De criminalibus causis: Festschrift zur Feier des 22. Dezember 1888, an welchem vor 50 Jahren Geheimerat Prof. Dr. Bernhard Windscheid in Bonn zum Doctor iuris utriusque promoviert wurde …*, ed. Johann Friedrich von Schulte (Bonn: Universitäts-Buchdruckerei von Carl Georgi, 1888).

50vb–51rb *Quaestiones legitimae (Bambergensia).*

The work is related to the southern French *Exceptiones Petri*, a civilian work from the early 12th century.

Incipit	*Queritur ad exhibendum actio*
Explicit	*ex empto agendum non dubitamus.*
Literature	Landau, "Lehrbuch," p. 508.
Editions	Fitting, *Juristische Schriften*, pp. 172–173.

51rb–52vb *Tractatus de actionum varietate.*

A version of the *tractatus "De actionum varietate et earum vita",*[8] composed around 1160.

Rubric *De vita actionum*

Incipit *›D‹e actionum uarietate earumque longitudine cognosci*

Explicit *contra extraneos detentatores xxx. annis tolluntur.*

Literature Fowler-Magerl, *Ordo*, p. 164; Landau, "Lehrbuch," p. 509.

Editions Fitting, *Juristische Schriften*, pp. 174–180.

52vb–54vb *Vocabularium.*

A 12th-century lexicon of legal terms.

Incipit *Non de fide instrumentorum*

Explicit *postliminium habent qui //*

Literature Max Conrat, *Geschichte der Quellen und Literatur des römischen Rechts im früheren Mittelalter* (Leipzig: Hinrichs, 1891), p. 619, n. 7; Landau, "Lehrbuch," p. 509.

II *Fols. 55–74*

Foliation: 20 fols. Collation: viii–ix^8, x^4. 2 columns, 42 lines. Hand: gothic minuscule. No rubrication.

55ra–63va *Ordo iudiciarius (Bambergensis).*

Probably written in an Anglo-Norman context (England or Ireland), after 1186. The work shows links with the *Summa Lipsiensis.*

Incipit *›Q‹uia iudiciorum quedam sunt preparatoria*

Explicit *Quid ergo, et xix. Q.iii. Mandamus.*

Literature Fowler-Magerl, *Ordo*, pp. 105–106; Brasington, *Order in the court*, pp. 197–275; Wiesław Litewski, *Der römisch-kanonische Zivilprozeß nach den älteren ordines iudiciarii*, 1 (Kraków: Wydawnictwo Uniwersytetu Jagiellonskiego, 1999), p. 40; Landau, "Lehrbuch," p. 510.

Editions Johann Friedrich von Schulte, ed., *Der ordo iudiciarius des Codex Bambergensis P I 11, Wiener SitzB. 70* (Vienna: Gerold, 1872), pp. 289–326.

63va–74vb Petrus Blesensis, *Distinctiones "Speculum iuris canonici."*

Sixty chapters on various canon law arguments, written by the Anglo-Norman Peter of Blois the Younger during his time at Char-

8 See above, p. 142.

tres (c. 1176–1181). The work uses the brocardic method and has some points of contact with the *Perpendiculum*.

Prologue ⟩*P*⟨*rometheus in Caucasi montis cacumine*
Incipit *Potentissima pars est uniuscuiusque*
Explicit *nisi dispensatio contra faciat.*
Literature Kuttner, *Repertorium*, pp. 220–222; Landau, "Lehrbuch," p. 510.
Editions Peter of Blois, *Opusculum*.

III *Fols. 75–95*

Foliation: 21 fols. Collation: xi–xii^{8}, xiii$^{6\ (\text{wants } 6)}$. 2 columns, 54–66 lines. Hand: gothic minuscule, different hand. No rubrication.

75ra–94ra *Summa Decreti* (*olim Distinctiones Halenses*).
Composed in the French school, c. 1185–1186, perhaps in Provence.
Incipit *Permissio quedam est provida*
Explicit *quandocumque vult poterit retractare.*
Literature Kuttner, *Repertorium*, pp. 192–194; Landau, "Lehrbuch," pp. 510–511; Tatsushi Genka, "Die Hallenser Handschrift ULB Ye 20 52 im Licht der Überlieferung der Summa Permissio quedam zum Dekret Gratians," in Carmassi and Drossbach, *Rechtshandschriften des deutschen Mittelalters*.

94ra–95ra *Summa Decreti: Appendix.*
The *Summa "Permissio quedam"* is followed by an appendix of various texts (*summulae, distinctiones, contraria*) by the same author.
Incipit *Sciendum est quod argumentatio*
Explicit *utile propter inutile remouetur.*
Literature Stephan Kuttner, "Notes on Manuscripts," *Traditio* 17 (1961), pp. 533–534, 533.

95va *Summula de presumptionibus* (fragment).
The manuscript contains, after the previous appendix, only a short fragment of the *incipit* of the *Summula de presumptionibus*, which ends abruptly with II, 3.3.
Incipit ⟩*H*⟨*ic locus frequens in iudiciis est et pernecessarius*
Explicit *c. eadem q. eadem.* //

IV *Fols. 96–118*

Foliation: 23 fols. Collation: xiv–xv^{8}, xvi$^{6\ (\text{wants } 6)}$, xvii^{2}. 2 columns (fols. 96–103), 3 columns (fols. 104–116), 59–62 lines. Hand: gothic minuscule; different hands. No rubrication.

96ra–103vb *Distinctiones Decretorum* (*Summa Gallicana-Bambergensis*).
A collection of French *distinctiones* composed after 1178, mostly excerpted from the *Summa "Inperatorie maiestati."* There is a first fragment here, while a second one is on fols. 178ra–180vb.
Incipit *Consuetudo aliquando constitutionem perimit*
Explicit *dispar cultus.*
Literature Kuttner, *Repertorium*, p. 219; Landau, "Lehrbuch," p. 511.

104^{r}–110^{r} *Quaestiones Decretalium* (*Bambergenses II.1*).
A probably French collection compiled before 1191, identified by Kuttner in his *Repertorium* and then divided into two groups by Fransen: this is the first group. The series runs parallel to the *Quaestiones Lipsienses II.*[9]
Incipit *Presbiter quidam clericum suum*
Explicit *nemini enim dolus suus prodesse debebit.*
Literature Kuttner, *Repertorium*, pp. 246–247; Gérard Fransen, "Les 'Questiones' des canonistes: Essai de dépouillement et de classement (I)," *Traditio* 12 (1956), pp. 566–592, repr. in Fransen, *Canones et Quaestiones*, 1.2; Landau, "Lehrbuch," p. 512.
Editions Fransen, "Les 'Questiones' des canonistes II," pp. 481–501.

110^{v}–116^{r} *Quaestiones Decretalium* (*Bambergenses II.2*).
This is the second group of the *quaestiones Bambergenses II*. This part corresponds to the *quaestiones Lipsienses IV.1* and the *Barcinonenses VI.*[10] It is also related to the *Lipsienses III.2.*[11]
Incipit *Apostolicus aduersus effrenem*
Explicit *fratribus quoque consentientibus commissam.*
Literature Kuttner, *Repertorium*, pp. 246–247; Fransen, "Les 'Questiones' des canonistes I," pp. 566–592.
Editions Fransen, "Les 'Questiones' des canonistes II," pp. 481–501.

116^{v}–117^{r} Blank.

117^{v}–118^{r} *Versus de Causis in Decreto Gratiani.*
Verses summarizing some of the causes of the *Decretum.*

---

9 See below, pp. 170–171.
10 See below, p. 172, and above, p. 141, respectively.
11 See below, p. 172.

Incipit *Tertia restituit*
Explicit *medio removetur et uno.*

118^v Blank.

V *Fols. 119–126*

Foliation: 8 fols. Collation: xviii^8. 3 columns (fols. 119–120^r), 2 columns (fols. 120^v–126), 53–63 lines. Hand: gothic minuscule; different hands. No rubrication.

119^r *Quaestiones Decretalium* (*Bambergenses I.1*).
Probably a French collection compiled c. 1175–1178, identified by Kuttner in his *Repertorium* and then divided into three groups by Fransen: this is the first group.
Incipit *Tema. Vacante quadam parrochia, parrochiani*
Explicit *cum nullus heres sue sit.*
Literature Kuttner, *Repertorium*, p. 246; Fransen, "Les 'Questiones' des canonistes II," pp. 481–501.
Editions Fransen, "Les 'Questiones' des canonistes I," pp. 566–592.

119^r–120^r *Quaestiones Decretalium* (*Bambergenses I.2*).
This is the first part of the second group of the *quaestiones Bambergenses I*.
Incipit *Tema. Quidam plebanus uacante ecclesia quadam*
Explicit *ab hereditate repellendus.*
Literature Kuttner, *Repertorium*, p. 246; Fransen, "Les 'Questiones' des canonistes I," pp. 566–592.
Editions Fransen, "Les 'Questiones' des canonistes II," pp. 481–501.

120va–123rb *Quaestiones Decretalium* (*Bambergenses I.3*).
This is the third group of the *quaestiones Bambergenses I* and is closely related to the *Bambergenses III.2* in the same manuscript and the *Lipsienses I*.[12]
Incipit *Quidam laicus forte*
Explicit *unde Moyses, cum uideret Egiptiacum cum Iudeo concantantem //*
Literature Kuttner, *Repertorium*, p. 246; Fransen, "Les 'Questiones' des canonistes II," pp. 481–501.
Editions Fransen, "Les 'Questiones' des canonistes," pp. 566–592.

12 See below, p. 171.

123va–126rb *Quaestiones Decretalium* (*Bambergenses I.2*).
This is the second part of the second group of the *quaestiones Bambergenses I*.

Incipit	*Monachi capellam cuiusdam ecclesie*
Explicit	*ad hereditatis suffragium.*
Literature	Kuttner, *Repertorium*, p. 246; Fransen, "Les 'Questiones' des canonistes I," pp. 566–592.
Editions	Fransen, "Les 'Questiones' des canonistes II," pp. 481–501.

VI ***Fols. 127–138***

Foliation: 12 fols. Collation: xix^{8}, xx^{4}. 2 columns, 37–51 lines. Hand: gothic minuscule; different hands (fols. 127–134; 135–138). No rubrication, except fols. 135–137: initial strokes, small red initials and marginal words circled in red.

127ra–133va *Quaestiones Decretalium* (*Bambergenses III.1*).
A probably French collection compiled before 1191, identified by Kuttner in his *Repertorium* and then divided into four groups by Fransen: this is the first group.

Incipit	*Quidam discipulus artis*
Explicit	*omnino manducare noluit.*
Literature	Kuttner, *Repertorium*, p. 247; Fransen, "Les 'Questiones' des canonistes I," pp. 566–592; Fransen, "Les 'Questiones' des canonistes II," pp. 481–501.
Editions	Fransen, "La structure."

134^{rv} Blank.

135ra–137^{v} *Quaestiones Decretalium* (*Bambergenses III.2*).
This is the first part of the second group of the *quaestiones Bambergenses III*. It is closely related to the *Lipsienses I*.[13]

Incipit	*Quodam religioso sacerdote*
Explicit	*qui eas possidet.*
Literature	Kuttner, *Repertorium*, p. 247; Fransen, "Les 'Questiones' des canonistes II," pp. 481–501.
Editions	Fransen, "Les 'Questiones' des canonistes," pp. 566–592.

138^{rv} Blank.

13 See below, p. 171.

VII *Fols. 139–162*

Foliation: 24 fols. Collation: xxi–xxiii^{8}. 2 columns, 46–47 lines (fols. 139–146), 55–57 lines (fols. 147–162). Hand: gothic minuscule; different hands (fols. 139–146, 147–162). No rubrication, except for fols. 139–146: initial strokes, small red initials and marginal words circled in red.

139ra–146vb *Quaestiones Decretalium* (*Bambergenses III.2*).

This is the second part of the second group of the *quaestiones Bambergenses III*, with some parallels with the *Lipsienses* III.1.[14]

Incipit *Thema. Uxor cuiusdam diuortium querens*

Explicit *quod ipsi imponitur.*

Literature Kuttner, *Repertorium*, p. 247; Fransen, "Les 'Questiones' des canonistes II," pp. 481–501.

Editions Fransen, "Les 'Questiones' des canonistes," pp. 566–592.

147ra–162rb Pseudo-Rufinus, *Summa in Decretum*, (fragment).

A commentary on the second and third parts of the *Decretum*, composed c. 1165–1175 and copied out of Rufinus's *Summa*.

Incipit *Condicio ecclesiastice religionis*

Explicit *tamen ad solam † conversationem //*

Literature Kuttner, *Repertorium*, pp. 132–133; Landau, "Lehrbuch," p. 512.

Editions partly in Rufinus, *Die Summa magistri Rufini zum Decretum Gratiani*, ed. Johann Friedrich von Schulte (Giessen: E. Roth, 1892).

162^{v} Blank.

VIII *Fols. 163–169*

Foliation: 7 fols. Collation: xxiv$^{8 \text{ (wants 8)}}$. 3 columns (fols. 163–166); 2 columns (fols. 167–169), 51–65 lines. 25,5 × 18,8. Hand: gothic minuscule; different hands (fols. 163–166; 167; 168; 169). No rubrication.

163^{r}–166^{v} *Quaestiones Decretalium* (*Bambergenses III.3*).

This is the third group of the *quaestiones Bambergenses III*.

Incipit *Queritur si sacerdos sit reus*

Explicit *cum nullus heres supersit.*

Literature Kuttner, *Repertorium*, p. 247; Fransen, "Les 'Questiones' des canonistes II," pp. 481–501.

Editions Fransen, "Les 'Questiones' des canonistes I," pp. 566–592.

14 See below, p. 171.

167$^{ra–vb}$ *Commentarius in Epistolas Pauli.*
A theological commentary.
Incipit *Quod est aliud sacramentum*
Explicit *quibus se conformauit apostolus ut lucri faceret et de his hic agit S.*

168$^{ra–vb}$ *Commentarius ad Aristotelis opus "De memoria et reminiscentia."*
A logical commentary.
Incipit *Idest: Singulum istorum caput reliqua duo*
Explicit *iudicat enim intellectus de utrisque.*

169$^{ra–vb}$ *Commentarius ad Sententias Petri Lombardi* (fragment).
A theological commentary.
Incipit *⟩S⟨tatuit Moyes terminos circa montem*
Explicit *Contradictores, id est inquisitores vel calupniatores.*

IX *Fols. 170–177*

Foliation: 8 fols. Collation: xxv^8. 2 columns (fols. 170, 176^v–177); 2 columns (fols. 171–176^v), 37–57 lines. 25,5 × 18,8. Hand: gothic minuscule; different hands (fols. 170; 171–177). Rubrication: small red initials and strokes.

170$^{ra–vb}$ *Quaestiones Theologiae.*
Incipit *Aliquid debetur soli Deo, et aliquis exhibet illud alii*
Explicit *si ante lapsum, quis eis hoc reuelauit, si post lapsum, miseri fuerint.*

171^r–177vb *Quaestiones Decretalium* (*Bambergenses III.4*).
This is the fourth group of the *quaestiones Bambergenses III.*
Incipit *Quidam clericus cuidam militi*
Explicit *et quodammodo se tranquille se habere non prodesset.*
Literature Kuttner, *Repertorium*, p. 247; Fransen, "Les 'Questiones' des canonistes I," pp. 566–592; Fransen, "Les 'Questiones' des canonistes II," pp. 481–501.
Editions Fransen, "La structure," pp. 516–534.

X *Fols. 178–184*

Foliation: 7 fols. Collation: xxvi$^{8\ (\text{wants } 8)}$. 2 columns, 60 lines. 25,5 × 18,8. Hand: gothic minuscule. No rubrication.

178ra–179vb *Distinctiones Decretorum* (*Summa Gallicana-Bambergensis*).
This is the second fragment, the first one being on fols. 96ra–103vb.
Incipit *Videndum est quid sit excommunicatio et que species eius*
Explicit *liberis dicit solet.*
Literature Kuttner, *Repertorium*, p. 219.

179vb–180vb *Tractatus de consanguinitate et affinitate.*
Incipit *Quoniam consanguinitatis quasi*
Explicit *dirimitur contractum.*

180vb–184^{v} *Compendium.*

180vb–182ra *Ordo iudiciarius.*
Composed in Reims or Amiens c. 1171.
Incipit *In principio de ordine*
Explicit *idest iudicis arbitrio reseruate.*
Colophon *Explicit.*
Literature Fowler-Magerl, *Ordo*, pp. 88–91; Fowler-Magerl, *Ordines*, p. 75; Landau, "Lehrbuch," pp. 512–513.
Editions Friedrich Kunstmann, "Über den ältesten Ordo iudiciarius mit Rücksicht auf Magistri Ricardi Anglici ordo iudiciarius …" *Kritische Überschau der deutschen Gesetzgebung und Rechtswissenschaft* 2 (1854), pp. 10–29.

182ra–183rb *Distinctiones ad quaestiones disputatas.*
Incipit *Utrum liceat iuramentis paganorum fidem tenere*
Explicit *fornicationis causa uxorem dimittere non potest.*

183^{rb-vb} *Tractatus de probationibus.*
Written by Bertrandus Metensis in the mid-12th century.
Incipit ⟩*S*⟨*epenumero in iudiciis*
Explicit *et hec sufficiant.*
Literature Fowler-Magerl, *Ordo*, pp. 219–220; Fowler-Magerl, *Ordines*, p. 75; Landau, "Lehrbuch," p. 513.
Editions Agathon Wunderlich, "Beiträge zur Literaturgeschichte des Prozesses im 12 u. 13. Jahrhundert," *Zeitschrift für geschichtliche Rechtwissenschaft* 2 (1842), pp. 92–98.

183vb–184ra *Tractatus de foro competenti.*
Incipit *Eorum que possidentur a clericis alia sunt ecclesiastica, alia propria seu patrimonialia*

	Explicit	*a suo episcopo potest condempnari, a quo et potest ordinari.*
184ra	*Nota de emphyteotico iure.*	
	Incipit	*Videndum est aliquid de emphiteosi*
	Explicit	*secundum dies uxoris protendetur emphiteosis.*
184^{ra-b}	*Tractatus de lege diocesana.*	
	Incipit	*Quid sit lex diocesiana*
	Explicit	*in quo sit legi diocesiane obnoxia.*
184^{rb-va}	*Tractatus de obligationibus.*	
	Incipit	*Quoniam ex contractu nascitur obligatio*
	Explicit	*ex omnibus his obligationibus actiones nascuntur.*
184va	*Notabile de testamenti factione.*	
	Incipit	*Quinque sunt que impediunt*
	Explicit	*potestas, puta in filio familias et in servo.*
184va	*Notabile de accusatione clericorum.*	
	Incipit	*Quinque suggerunt ne laici*
	Explicit	*ut et ipsi eos non admittant.*
184va	*Tractatus de appellationibus.*	
	Incipit	*Quid sit appellatio*
	Explicit	*etiam post datam sententiam potest appellare.*
184vb	*Nota de usucapione.*	
	Incipit	*Usucapio est acquisitio dominii*
	Explicit	*horum enim, si quid defuerit, usucapio* ⟨*non*⟩ *procedit.*
184vb	*Tractatus de praescriptionibus.*	
	This small *tractatus* depends on the *Summa decreti* of Stephen of Tournai. Part of the *compendium* starting at 180vb.	
	Incipit	*Prescriptio est exceptio causam trahens ex tempore*
	Explicit	*et que sint ad prescriptionem nessaria.*
	Literature	Fowler-Magerl, *Ordo*, p. 171; Fowler-Magerl, *Ordines*, p. 75; Landau, "Lehrbuch," pp. 513–514.
184vb	*Definitio testamenti.*	
	Incipit	*Textamentum est novissime voluntatis*
	Explicit	*alias fieri velit.*

C Cambridge, Pembroke College, 101

Century 12th *ex.*–13th.

Catalogues Rodney M. Thomson, *A Descriptive Catalogue of the Medieval Manuscripts owned by Pembroke College, Cambridge* (Cambridge: Brewer, 2022), pp. 61–62; Montague Rhodes James, *A Descriptive Catalogue of the Manuscripts in the Library of Pembroke College, Cambridge* (Cambridge: Cambridge University Press, 1905; repr. 2009), pp. 94–95; Kari Anne Rand Schmidt, *The Index of Middle English Prose: Handlist XVIII; Manuscripts in the Library of Pembroke College, Cambridge and the Fitzwilliam Museum* (Cambridge: D.S. Brewer, 2006), p. 2.

Material Parchment. 29×20. I + 131 fols. The manuscript is a miscellany and is made up of 7 codicological units bound together at an early date.

Provenance Benedictine abbey of Bury St Edmunds (except perhaps VI, possibly from the abbey of St Benet's at Hulme): until the 15th century, fols. 1–93, together with the MS Ipswich Central Library, 6, fols. 1–176, formed the abbey's MS 65.[15]

Ownership William Smart (d. 1599), portreeve of Ipswich, by whom given to Pembroke.

Binding Leaf of an *Organon* (13th–14th century).

Paste-downs On the front, a table of contents lists those of c. u. I and of MS Ipswich, Central Library, 6, fols 1^r–176^r.

I *Fols. 1–24*

Foliation: 24 fols. Collation: i–iii^8. 21×14. 2 columns, 65–70 lines. Hand: anglicana (fols 1^r–6^v); gothic minuscule (fols 9^r–24^v). Rubricated with small red and green initials.

1^r–6^v Petrus Comestor, *Compilatio sermonum.*

Incipit *Ex Egypto vocavi*

Explicit *tributum auri frequenter deo solvere.*

7^r–8^v Blank.

15 Richard Sharpe, "Reconstructing the Medieval Library of Bury St Edmunds: The Lost Catalogue of Henry of Kirkstead," in *Bury St Edmunds: Medieval Art, Architecture, Archaeology and Economy*, ed. in Antonia Gransden (London: British Archaeological Association, 1998), p. 215.

9^r–24^v Gregory the Great, *Moralia in Iob*.
Incipit *Nomen virginis Maria*
Explicit *quia illa eos pena saciat, que mentem ecclesie.*
Editions Gregory the Great, *Moralia in Iob*, ed. Marc Adriaen (Turnhout: Brepols, 1979).

II *Fols. 25–40*

Foliation: 16 fols. Collation: iv–v^8. 24,5×16. 48 lines. Hand: gothic minuscule (same of VI). Red underlining and highlighting.

25^r–40^v *Distinctiones*.
Distinctions on various subjects, organized in diagrams. Mostly theological.
Incipit *Christus capud ecclesie*

III *Fols. 41–55*

Foliation: 15 fols. Collation: vi^4, vii^{14} (wants 12–14). 22,5×11. 72 lines. Hand: gothic minuscule (fols. 41^r–50^v), anglicana (several, fols. 51^r–55^v). Rubricated.

41^r–46^v Petrus Lombardus, *Libri sententiarum* (*excerpta*).
Incipit *In hoc tractatu non solum pium lectorem*
Explicit *de quo non penitet aliquis.*
Literature Philip W. Rosemann, *The Story of a Great Medieval Book: Peter Lombard's Sentences* (Peterborough, Ontario: Broadview Press, 2007), n. 15.
Editions Peter Lombard, *Libri sententiarum*, PL 192:519–964.

47^r–54^r Rogerius Salesburiensis, *Commentarius ad Psalmos* (incomplete).
A commentary on Psalms 1–28 by Roger of Salisbury (fl. 1160). Fols. 51^v–52^v are blank.
Incipit *Beatus vir*
Explicit *rubeus ut fervidi sicut in caritate.*
Literature Thomas D. Hardy, *Descriptive Catalogue of Materials Relating to the History of Great Britain and Ireland: to the End of the Reign of Henry VII*, 2 (London: Longman, 1862), p. 284, no. 385.

54^v Blank.
55^r *Adnotatio*.
55^v Blank.

IV *Fols. 56–68*

Foliation: 15 fols. Collation: viii^8 ix^8 (wants 6–8). 22×14,5. 3 columns, 55 lines. Hand: gothic minuscule. No rubrication.

56^{r}–61va *Notabilia.*

Incipit *Arg. quod religiosi*

Explicit *Nota raptam que alii desponsata … Arg. Contra capitulo ultimo.*

Literature Above, pp. 44–46; Brasington, "'A Minor Literary Genre,'" pp. 1159–1165.

Editions Samples in Brasington, "'A Minor Literary Genre,'" pp. 1159–1165.

61^{v}–68^{r} *Perpendiculum.*

61vb–63^{rc} *Summula de presumptionibus.*

Rubric *De presumptionibus.*

Incipit *Hic locus in iudiciis frequens*

Explicit *quod propter prolixitatem distinguere non curavi.*

63^{rc-va} Part II (nos. 1–4).

A first series of 4 brocards from Part II.

Incipit *Introductis publica autoritate renunciare non licet*

Explicit *Numerus te nullus.*

63^{va-b} Part III (nos. 1–3).

A first group of 3 brocards from Part III, interpolated into Part II.

Incipit *Testes esse cogendos ad testimonium dicendum*

Explicit *C. xxxvi. C. Secunda.*

63vb–64rb Part II (nos. 5–14).

A second group of 10 brocards from Part II.

Incipit *Metus vel iussus principis*

Explicit *Quisquis pro aliquo.*

64^{rb-vb} Part III (nos. 4–10).

A second series of 7 brocards from Part III, interpolated into Part II.

Incipit *Que ex causa statute sunt causam non excedunt*

Explicit *C. xxxii. Q. ii. Mulier.*

64vb–65va Part II (nos. 15–26).

A third and last group of 12 brocards from Part II.

Incipit *Rati habitio et sequens consensus retrahitur*

Explicit *Ad mensam omnem fidelem.*

65va–68ra Part II (nos. 11–95).
A third and final series of 85 brocards from Part III.
Incipit *Nec recte factum mutatur neque recte susceptum*
Explicit *D. lx. Quid autem.*

68^{v} Blank.

V *Fols. 69–85*

Foliation: 17 fols. Collation: x^{10} xi$^{8\ (\text{wants } 8)}$. 19,5×9,5. 2 columns, 48 lines. Hand: gothic minuscule. Red or blue initials.

69^{r}–83ra *Constitutiones Lateranensis concilii quarti.*
The text includes the canons of the Fourth Lateran Council, the canons on the recovery of the Holy Land, and a sermon of Innocent III.
Incipit *Firmiter credimus et simpliciter confitemur*
Explicit *magis uidebitur expedire.*
Editions Antonio García y García, ed., *Constitutiones Concilii quarti Lateranensis una cum Commentariis glossatorum* (Vatican City: BAV, 1981).

83^{ra-b} *Expositio vocabularum.*
An explanation of 17 Anglo-Saxon legal terms in Anglo-Norman, in a 13th-century hand.
Incipit *Sak est curt et iustise*
Explicit *Forstal. Force faire en real chemin.*
Editions Tony Hunt, *Teaching and Learning Latin in Thirteenth-century England*, 1 (Cambridge: D.S. Brewer, 1991), p. 54.

83^{v}–85^{v} Blank.

VI *Fols. 86–93*

Foliation: 8 fols. Collation: xii^{8}. 22×14,5. 2 columns, 66 lines. Hand: gothic minuscule (same of II). Rubrication: red and green initials.

86^{r}–91^{v} Stephanus de Lingua-Tonante, *Expositio super Genesim* (unfinished).
A biblical work of Stephen Langton (c. 1150–1228), archbishop of Canterbury.
Incipit *Moralis expositio Magistri S. Archiepiscopi super Genesim*
Explicit *sed quia debet infirmari caritate //*
Editions Gilbert Dahan, "L'Exégèse de l'histoire de Caïn et Abel du XIIe au XIVe siècle en Occident: Textes," *Recherches de théologie ancienne et médiévale* 49 (1982), pp. 21–89.

92^v *Adnotatio.*
Reference to the abbey of St Benet at Hulme, Norfolk.
Incipit *Deu mayntene ceste eglise et tute seinte eglise*
Explicit *et det eis vitam eternam. Amen.*

93^r Blank.

93^v *Versus mnemotechnici.*
Incipit *Humano more crux presens edidit ore*
Explicit *Iudicastis bene mutastis non bene.*

VII *Fols. 94–131*

Foliation: 38 fols. Collation: xiii^{10}, xiv–xv^{8}, xvi^{12}. 22,5 × 14,5. 3 columns, 50 lines. Hand: gothic minuscule. Rubrication: red or blue initials.

94^r–131^r *Interpretationes nominum Hebraicorum.*
Incipit *Aaz apprehendes*
Explicit *Zuzim, consiliatores eorum.*
Literature Giovanna Murano, "Chi ha scritto le interpretationes hebraicorum nominum?," in *Etienne Langton, prédicateur, bibliste, théologien*, ed. Louis-Jacques Bataillon et al. (Turnhout: Brepols, 2010).

131^v *Additiones.*
An addition to the text on fol. 120^v.

F Fulda, HLB, 100 D. 10

Century	13th *in.*
Catalogues	Regina Hausmann, *Die Historischen, Philologischen und Juristischen Handschriften der Hessischen Landesbibliothek Fulda bis zum Jahr 1600. B 1–25, C 1–18.68, D1–48. Beschrieben von Regina Hausmann* (Wiesbaden: Harrassowitz, 2000), pp. 127–131.
Material	Parchment. 36 × 23. 127 fols. The manuscript is a miscellany. It consists of 9 codicological units. Three of them (II, V, VII), including the *Perpendiculum*, were collated later from an older manuscript (mid-13th century).
Provenance	Constance (references to Chur and Constance, fols. 117^v–118^r). Probably originally from northern France.
Ownership	Weingarten: note of property *"Monasterii Weingartensis 1638"* (fol. 2^r).
Binding	Wooden boards with leather cover with clasps.
Paste-downs	Parchment (fols. 1 and 127).

1rv *Breviarium.*
Fragment with lections and hymns for the feast of St Augustine, used as paste-down.
Editions Société des Bollandistes, ed., *Bibliotheca hagiographica Latina antiquae et mediae aetatis*, 2 vols (Bruxelles: Société des Bollandistes, 1898–1901), 2:785; Guido Maria Dreves, Clemens Blume, and Henry Marriott Bannister, eds., *Analecta hymnica*, 55 vols (Leipzig: Fues's Verlag/Reisland, 1886–1922), 52:110–112, nos. 117–118.

I *Fols. 2–7*

Foliation: 6 fols. Collation: $i^6 + ii^1$. 2 columns, 42 lines. Hand: gothic minuscule. Rubrication: in the text, alternating blue and red Lombard initials with floral motifs at the beginning of each paragraph; rubricated paragraph titles. In the apparatus, red initials at the beginning of each paragraph, glossed words underlined.

2r–7v Innocent IV, *Novellae cum apparatu eiusdem.*
Incipit *Cum in multis iuris articulis*
Explicit *eum sententia requiritur.*
Literature Stephan Kuttner, "Die Konstitutionen des ersten allgemeinen Konzils von Lyon," *Studia et documenta historiae et iuris* 6 (1940), pp. 70–131, repr. in Stephan Kuttner, *Medieval Councils, Decretals and Collections of Canon Law: Selected Essays* (London: Variorum, 1980), no. XI; Peter-Josef Kessler, "Untersuchungen über die Novellen-Gesetzgebung Papst Innozenz IV (I)," *ZRG Kan. Abt.* 31 (1942), pp. 142–320.
Editions Justus Henning Böhmer, ed., *Corpus Iuris Canonici*, 2 vols (Halle: Orphanotropheus, 1747), appendix III, 2:351–367.

II *Fols. 8–9*

Foliation: 2 fols. Collation: iii^2. 2 columns, 36 lines. Hand: gothic minuscule. No rubrication, but blank space left for capital letters at the beginning of each paragraph.

8r–9v Innocent IV, *Novellae cum apparatu Goffredi de Trano.*
A collection of 8 *novellae.*
Incipit *⟩S⟨tatuimus ut si quis electionem*
Explicit *aliis legittimis actibus nichilomnis admittatur.*
Apparatus *In formam obicitur cum dicitur electionem ... S. de clerico excomunicato vel deposito minori. Apostolice. G.*
Literature Kuttner, *Die Konstitutionen*; Kessler, *Untersuchungen.*
Editions *Corpus Iuris Canonici*, 2, appendix III, pp. 351–367.

III *Fols. 10–45*

Foliation: 36 fols. Collation: iv–vii^8, viii^4. 2 columns, 68 lines. Hand: gothic minuscule. Rubrication: as for c. u. I, alternating blue and red Lombard initials with floral motifs at the beginning of each paragraph; rubricated paragraph titles.

10^r–45^v Ambrosius Bononiensis, *Summa super titulis decretalium.*

Incipit *Formavit deus hominem ad ymaginem et similitudinem suam*

Explicit *et regnat deus vivus per eterna secula amen.*

Literature Kuttner, *Repertorium*, pp. 392–393; José-Antonio Martín Avedillo, "La 'Summa super titulis decretalium' del canonista Ambrosius," ZRG *Kan. Abt.* 54 (1968), pp. 57–94; José-Antonio Martín Avedillo, "Estado actual de la investigación sobre el canonista Ambrosius," in *Proceedings of the Third International Congress of Medieval Canon Law: Strasbourg, 3–6 September 1968*, ed. Stephan Kuttner (Vatican City: BAV, 1971).

Editions Martín Avedillo, "La Summa."

IV *Fols. 46–69*

Foliation: 24 fols. Collation: ix–xi^8. 2 columns, 75 lines (fols. 46–58), 66 lines (fols. 59–69). Hand: gothic minuscule. Without rubrication. Blank space left for Lombards (fols. 59–69).

46^r–58^v Damasus, *Quaestiones* (fragment).

Incipit *// et non obesse. XXII. Q. v. hoc videtur*

Colophon *Expliciunt quaestiones. Deo gratias.*

Literature Kuttner, *Repertorium*, pp. 426–428.

59^r–69^r *Quaestiones Fuldenses.*

A series of canon law *quaestiones* that combines texts borrowed from the *Quaestiones Bambergenses II* (qq.1–32)[16] with a set signed by the Bolognese canonist Tancred (qq.33–43).

Incipit ⟩Q⟨*uatuor clerici erant in quadam domo manentes*

Explicit *a petitione mulieri absolvo. T.*

Literature Kuttner, *Repertorium*, p. 430.

Editions Fransen, "Les 'Questiones' des canonistes III," pp. 516–531.

69^v Blank.

16 See above, p. 150.

v *Fols. 70–71*

Foliation: 2 fols. Collation: xii². 2 columns, 44 lines. Hand: gothic minuscule. Without rubrication. Blank space left for Lombards (fol. 70ʳ).

70ʳ–71ᵛ Innocent IV, *Novellae cum apparatu eiusdem.*

A collection of 4 *novellae* (28, 29, 32, 41).

Incipit *Dilecto filio Andree capellano nostro*

Explicit *repete que no. Infra de verb. sig. Olim tibi* (X. 5.40.16).

Apparatus *Cum in multis iuris ... derogari.*

Literature Kuttner, *Die Konstitutionen*, pp. 70–131; Kessler, *Untersuchungen*, pp. 142–320.

Editions *Corpus Iuris Canonici*, 2, appendix III, pp. 351–367.

VI *Fols. 72–79*

Foliation: 8 fols. Collation: xiii8. 3 columns, 68 lines (fols. 72–78ʳ), 52 lines (fols. 78ᵛ–79). Hand: gothic minuscule. Rubricated brocards. Initial strokes at the beginning of each *contrarium* and *solutio*; red diagrams marking the arguments. No rubrication on fols. 78ᵛ–79ᵛ.

72ʳ–78ʳ Damasus, *Brocarda.*

Rubric *Incipiunt brocarda magistri Damasi.*

Incipit *Arg. Ignorantiam excusare in his que iuris sunt*

Colophon *Laus tibi sit Christe quoniam liber explicit iste.*

Literature Kuttner, *Repertorium*, p. 419; De Concilio, *Via Brocardica*, 2:30–31.

78ᵛ–79ᵛᵃ Wernerus Sorotensis, *Decretum versificatum.*

This text contains only the versified rubrics of the work.

Incipit *Di. I. ut videat quisque divinum ius hominisque*

Explicit *Neupmate donato concludit fine beato.*

Literature Alfons M. Stickler, "Iter Helveticum," *Traditio* 14 (1958), pp. 475–477; Miroslav Bohácek, "Un manuscrit intéressant du 'Compendium' de Werner von Schussenried," *Traditio* 18 (1962), pp. 472–482.

VII *Fols. 80–87*

Foliation: 8 fols. Collation: xiv–xv⁴. 4 columns, 75 lines (fols. 80–81), 86 lines (fols. 82–87). Hand: gothic minuscule. Rubrication (fols. 80–81): red Lombard initials at the beginning of each rubric; red diagrams for the arguments. No rubrication (fols. 82–87), blank space left for Lombard initials.

80ʳ–81ᵛ *Perpendiculum.*

80ʳᵃ *Summula de presumptionibus* (fragment).

Explicit *Hec de presumptionibus licet minus ... quod propter prolixitatem distinguere non curavi.*

80ra–80^{vc} Part II.
Incipit *Introductuctis publica utilitate renuntiare non licet*
Explicit *nec deinde adiuto nec ipse videtur exceptus.*
80^{vc}–81^{vd} Part III.
Incipit *Principium spectandum ut*
Explicit *D. XLI. C. I. Que omnibus.*

82^{r}–87va *Brocarda.*
A collection of brocards composed after 1185.
Incipit *›A‹rgumentum a minori per negationem*
Explicit *VIII q. I Qui episcopatum.*
Literature De Concilio, *Via Brocardica*, 2:12; Kuttner, *Repertorium*, p. 235; Kuttner, "Retractationes IX," p. 41; Knut Wolfgang Nörr, *Zur Stellung des Richters im gelehrten Prozess der Frühzeit: Iudex secundum allegata non secundum conscientiam iudicat* (Munich: Beck, 1967), p. 51, n. 2; Hubert Müller, *Der Anteil der Laien an der Bischofswahl: Ein Beitrag zur Geschichte der Kanonistik von Gratian bis Gregor IX.* (Amsterdam: B.R. Grüner, 1977), pp. 108–109; Weimar, *Argumenta*, p. 122.

87va Appendix: *Nota.*
Incipit *Nota. Hec persone non debent admitti in testimonium*
Explicit *que sint ille persone quere VI. Q. I. infames.*
Literature Kuttner, *Repertorium*, p. 235, n. 1.

VIII *Fols. 88–111*

Foliation: 24 fols. Collation: xvi–xviii^{8}. 2 columns, 69 lines. Hand: gothic minuscule. Rubrication: underlined words at the beginning of each paragraph; blank space left for Lombard initials; rubricated titles (fols. 96–98). Fol. 111 is torn, missing the first part of fol. 111ra and almost the entire fol. 111rb.

88^{r}–96ra *Casus ad Compilationem I.*
Incipit *›C‹anonum. Canones debent ab omnibus observari*
Explicit *qui querit scire qui adest interrogat ille.*
Literature Kuttner, *Repertorium*, p. 400.

96ra–102va *Casus ad Compilationem II.*
Incipit *›P‹reterea. Quesivit Anchontanus episcopus quid esset faciendum de lege*
Explicit *in ipso pretextu contentis.*
Literature Kuttner, *Repertorium*, pp. 40–41.

102vb–110rb Vincentius Hispanus, *Casus ad Compilationem III*.
Incipit *Cum omnes. In prima parte istius capituli reprobatur invidia*
Explicit *pro monasterio sancti Bertini.*
Literature Kuttner, *Repertorium*, pp. 403–404; Kuttner, "Notes," p. 539.

110rb–111rb *Casus ad Constitutiones Lateranensis concilii quarti* (*Casus Fuldenses*).
Incipit *Firmiter. Dividitur capitulum in tres partes*
Literature Kuttner, *Repertorium*, pp. 405–406; Kuttner, "Notes," p. 539; García y García, *Constitutiones Concilii quarti*, pp. 467–481.
Editions García y García, *Constitutiones Concilii quarti*, pp. 483–490.

IX *Fols. 112–127*

Foliation: 16 fols. Collation: xix^4, xx^8, xxi^4. 2 columns, 64 lines (fols. 112–114), 67 lines (fols. 115–126). Hand: gothic minuscule. No rubrication, except for fols. 112–114, where there are rubrics at the beginning of each paragraph.

112^r–114va Damasus de Bononia (?), *Ordo iudiciarius*.
Incipit *//ff. de interrogata actione*
Explicit *potest etiam advocatus rei actorem interrogare.*
Literature Fowler-Magerl, *Ordo*, pp. 126–127; Kuttner, *Repertorium*, p. 428, n. 3.
Editions Pseudo-Damasus, *Die "Summa de ordine iudiciario" des Magister Damasus*, ed. Ludwig Wahrmund (Innsbruck: Wagner, 1926; repr. Aalen: Scientia Verlag, 1962), p. 26.

115^r–126^v Tancredus Bononiensis, *Ordo iudiciarius* (incomplete).
Incipit *Assiduis postulationibus me karissimi socii*
Text there is an interruption between *partium eligi debet//* (115vb) and *// et respondendo in hunc modum* (116^r)
Explicit *ad rudium instructionem breviter dixisse sufficiat* (126^v).
Literature Fowler-Magerl, *Ordo*, pp. 128–130.
Editions Tancred, *Ordo iudiciarius*.

G Grenoble, BM, 391 (1) Rés

Century 13th *in*.
Catalogues Paul Fournier, Edmond Maignien, and Auguste Prudhomme, *Catalogue général des manuscrits des bibliothèques publiques de*

France: Départements, 7, *Grenoble* (Paris: Éditions du Centre national de la recherche scientifique, 1889), pp. 206–207.

Material: Parchment. 33,1 × 22,5. 164 fols. The manuscript is a miscellany.

Provenance: The Grande Chartreuse. The manuscript is thought to have been written before 1185 by the jurist Pierre Fouquois from an archetype brought there at the beginning of the 13th century.[17]

Binding: Wood, covered with sheepskin.

Foliation: 164 fols. Collation:[18] i^{2}, $ii–v^{10}$, vi^{14}, vii^{6}, viii^{14}, ix^{6}, x^{14}, xi^{6}, xii^{14}, xiii^{6}, xiv^{14}, xv^{6}, xvi^{2}, xvii^{4}, $xviii–xix^{8}$. Hand: gothic minuscule.

$1^{ra}–2^{vb}$ Justinian, *Digesta*, *"De diversis regulis iuris antiqui" et "De verborum significatione"* (fragment).

Literature: Peter Stein, "The Digest Title 'De diversis regulis iuris antiqui' and the General Principles of Law," in *Essays in Jurisprudence in Honor of Roscoe Pound*, ed. Ralph A. Newman (Westport: Greenwood Press, 1962).

Editions: Theodor Mommsen and Paul Krüger, eds., *Corpus Iuris Civilis, I, Digesta* (Berlin: Weidmann, 1868).

$3–23^{va}$ Placentinus, *Summa Institutionum.*

Incipit: *Iuris arti professionique boni*

Explicit: *de calumpnia iurare non debet.*

Editions: Placentinus, *Placentini Summa Institutionum*, ed. Nicolaus Rhodius (Mainz: Schoeffer, 1535; repr. Turin: Bottega d'Erasmo, 1973 (CGJC 1:1)); Fitting, *Juristische Schriften*, pp. 217–223.

$23^{v}–148^{vb}$ Placentinus, *Summa in IX libros Codicis.*

Incipit: *Quondam ego credidi quod sufficiat*

Explicit: *simpliciter facta omnia restituit, ut C. e. l. ult.*

Editions: Placentinus, *Summa Codicis.*

$44^{va–b}$ Placentinus, *Summula de verborum obligationibus.*

Incipit: *Quoniam verborum obligatio*

Explicit: *que ex stipulatu vocatur, ut insuper.*

$149^{r}–155^{r}$ *Quaestiones dominorum Bononiensium* (*Collectio Gratianopolitana*).

A collection of *quaestiones* from the Bolognese school of law, compiled between 1162 and 1175.

---

17 Gouron, "Une école de canonistes," p. 63, n. 37, following a hypothesis of Hermann Kantorowicz; Gouron, "Notes," p. 61.

18 Information on the collation of the manuscript was kindly provided by Emmanuelle Spagnol (BM Grenoble).

Incipit *Richardus mutuam pecuniam accepit*
Explicit *ratio etatis quam senatus.*
Literature Belloni, *Le questioni civilistiche*; Gouron, "Notes," pp. 57–61.
Editions Giovanni Battista Palmieri, ed., *Quaestiones dominorum Bononiensium: Collectio Parisiensis*, BIMAE, 1: 235–264.

155^{r}–156^{v} Ioannes Faventinus (?), *Quaestiones* (*I*).
Incipit *Prior consensu fratrum*

157ra–160vb *Glossa ad Decretum Gratiani.*
A short gloss on certain terms in Gratian's *Decretum.*
Incipit *Divinarum et humanarum constitutionem*
Explicit *distancie gradus aucmentat.*

161^{r-v} Ioannes Faventinus (?), *Quaestiones* (*II*).
Explicit *ecclesia possit constituere.*

161^{v}–163^{r} *Perpendiculum.*

161^{v}–162rd *Summula de presumptionibus.*
Incipit *Hic locus in iudiciis frequens est*
Explicit *Hec de presumptionibus licet minus … quod propter prolixitatem distinguere non curavi.*

162^{rd-vc} Part II.
Incipit *Introductis publica utilitate renuntiare non licet*
Explicit *Res inter alios aucta* (sic!) … *C. i. q. vii. Qui in qualibet c. Tali.*

162^{vc-vd} *Glossa de conditione feminarum.*
The first of three short texts that appear, in the same order, also in P1. The original text begins on fol. 162^{vd}, while the copyist started from the last part of the allegations, on fol. 162^{vc}.
Allegations *ff. de tutelis l. ultima* (fol. 162^{vc})
Incipit *In multis iuris articulis deterior est conditio feminarum quam masculorum* (fol. 162^{vd})
End of allegations *ff. de accusatoribus Qui accusare* (fol. 162^{vd}).
Explicit *pro cautione magistratus. susceptione postulatione* (fol. 162^{vd}).

	162^{vd}	*Brocardum.*	
		Incipit	*Punitur quod factum iure non tenuit*
		Explicit	*C. si mancipium ita fuerit alienatum ut l. Ea.*
	162^{vd}	*Distinctio.*	
		Incipit	*Denuntiatio inducit dolum*
		Explicit	*inducit interpretationem ut C.//*
	162^{vd}–163rb	Part III.	
		Incipit	*Levius punitur qui commissum sponte confitetur*
		Explicit	*Ubi culpa non deprehenditur ... C. xxxiii. q. iii.*
	163^{rb-c}	*Distinctio.*	
		Rubric	*Ad movendum varie iudicem*
		Incipit	*Delicto coram iudice manifestato*
		Explicit	*C. xxiv. q. iv. Si illic.*
164^{rv}	Blank.		

L Leipzig, UB, Rep. II 117 (*olim* 247)

Century	13th–14th.
Catalogues	Robert Naumann, *Catalogus librorum manuscriptorum qui in Bibliotheca Senatoria civitatis Lipsiensis asservantur* (Grimma: Gebhardt, 1838), pp. 80–81, no. CCXLVII; "Leipzig, Universitätsbibliothek Leipzig, Rep. II 117 (Leihgabe Leipziger Stadtbibliothek)," in *Handschriften Portal*, available at https://resolver.staatsbibliothek-berlin.de/HSP00051F2C00000000, accessed 2024 Jan 20.
Material	Parchment and paper. 52 fols. The manuscript is a miscellany and consists of three parts, plus 2 additional units as added paper.[19]
Provenance	France and Germany.
Ownership	Benedictine monastery of St. Ulrich and Afra, Augsburg; donation note on fol. 31^r: fols. 31^r–47^v were copied by Petrus de Mergentheim in the second half of the 13th century and came to

19 The information on the codicological units, including dimensions, collation, and possible origin and dating, was kindly provided by Katrin Krum (UB Leipzig).

Augsburg in 1347 as legate of Albert, priest of the church of St. Ulrich und Afra.[20] The manuscript was still in Augsburg in the late 15th century or early 16th when the paper units were added (as indicated by the watermark: an Augsburg pine nut with a crown).

Binding Cardboard (17th century).

Paste-downs Paper. One leave on the front and one on the rear.

I *Fols. 1–12*

Parchment. Foliation: 12 fols. Collation: i^{8}, $ii^{12\ (wants\ 5–12)}$. 21,2 × 14,7. 2 columns, 43 lines (fols. 1–12). Hand: gothic minuscule. Rubrication (fols 1^{r}–10ra). 1^{r} has the number of an earlier foliation. Provenance: southern France or possibly northern Italy, 2nd quarter of the 13th century.

1^{r}–10^{r} *Perpendiculum.*

1^{r}–3va *Summula de presumptionibus.*

Incipit *⟩H⟨ic locus in iuditiis frequens et pernecessarius*

Explicit *⟩H⟨ec de presumptionibus et minus ... quam propter prolixitatem distinguere non curavi.*

3va–5rb Part II.

Incipit *Introductis publica auctoritate renuntiare non licet*

Explicit *Naturali verbo non omnia continentur ... D. xxi. Si romanorum dicendo omnia.*

5rb *Distinctio.*

Rubric *Ad movendum varie iudicem*

Incipit *Delicto coram iudice manifestato*

Explicit *C. xxiv. q. iv. Si illic.*

5^{rb-va} *Glossa de conditione feminarum.*

Incipit *In multis iuris articulis deterior est conditio feminarum quam masculorum*

Explicit *ff. de accusatoribus Qui accusare.*

5va–10rb Part III.

Incipit *Levius punitur qui commissum sponte confitetur*

Explicit *D. xxxvii. q. ii. Qui desponsata.*

10^{rb-v} *Quaestiones Lipsienses II.*

A short series of canon law *quaestiones* parallel to the *Bambergenses II.1*,[21] compiled at the end of the 12th century.

---

20 Winfried Stelzer, *Gelehrtes Recht in Österreich: Von den Anfängen bis zum frühen 14. Jahrhundert* (Vienna: Böhlaus, 1982), p. 133.

21 See above, p. 150.

Incipit	*Quidam duxit quandam suam consanguineam*
Explicit	*Queritur de hac questione ... C. xxiv. q. iii. Hec est.*
Literature	Kuttner, *Repertorium*, p. 247; Fransen, "Les 'Questiones' des canonistes I," p. 567.
Editions	Fransen, "Les 'Questiones' des canonistes II," pp. 494–495, 500–501.

11r–12v *Summa in Decretum.*

A fragmentary text allegedly composed at the beginning of the 13th century and associated with the Bolognese school.

Incipit	*Queritur cuius sint hec verba*
Explicit	*sapientia eorum devota est.*
Literature	Kuttner, *Repertorium*, p. 154; Stephan Kuttner, "General Report," *Traditio* 12 (1956), pp. 557–559, 559.

II *Fols. 13–16*

Paper. Foliation: 4 fols. Collation: iii^4. 21,5 × 14,5. Provenance: Augsburg, 15th *ex.*–16th *in.*

13r–16v Blank.

III *Fols. 17–30*

Parchment. Foliation: 14 fols. Collation: iv^6, v^8. 21,4 × 14,2. 3 columns, 60 lines (fol. 17r), 2 columns, 36 lines (fols. 17v–20r), 1 column (fols. 20v–30v). Hand: gothic minuscule. No rubrication. Provenance: France (probably southern France), 2nd half of the 12th century.

17r *Quaestiones Lipsienses III.1.*

A short series of canon law *quaestiones* compiled before 1191, related to the *Lipsienses III.2* in the same manuscript (fol. 20v) and with parallels to the second group of the *Bambergenses III.2.*[22]

Incipit	*Inter militem et viduam agebatur*
Explicit	*prosequntur iniuriam in causa criminali.*
Literature	Kuttner, *Repertorium*, p. 247.
Editions	Fransen, "Les 'Questiones' des canonistes I."

17v–20r *Quaestiones Lipsienses I.*

A collection of canon law *quaestiones* compiled between 1175–1190, closely related to the *Bambergenses I.3* and *III.2.*[23]

Incipit	*Quidam pro facinoribus*
Explicit	*absens fuit nec ne.*

---

22 See above, p. 153.

23 See above, pp. 151–153.

Literature Kuttner, *Repertorium*, p. 246.
Editions Fransen, "Les 'Questiones' des canonistes I," pp. 566–581.

20^{v} *Quaestiones Lipsienses III.2.*
This is the second unit of the *Lipsienses III*, consisting of a single canon law *quaestio*, related to the *Bambergenses II.2.*[24]
Incipit *Quidam pater familias*
Explicit *D. ix. Sane.*
Literature Kuttner, *Repertorium*, p. 247; Fransen, "Les 'Questiones' des canonistes I."
Editions Fransen, "Les 'Questiones' des canonistes II," pp. 486, 500.

21^{r}–30^{r} *Quaestiones Lipsienses IV.1.*
A collection of canon law *quaestiones* compiled before 1191 and divided by Fransen into two parts. This is the first part. The collection runs parallel to the *Bambergenses II.2.*[25]
Incipit *Ecclesie subiecte monasterio*
Explicit *Quidam se et sua ... fratibus confitentibus commissam.*
Literature Kuttner, *Repertorium*, p. 247; Fransen, "Les 'Questiones' des canonistes I," pp. 567–568.
Editions Fransen, "Les 'Questiones' des canonistes II."

30^{v} *Quaestiones Lipsienses IV.2.*
The second part of the *Lipsienses IV*, consisting of a single canon law *quaestio.*
Incipit *Monachus ab abbate institutus*
Explicit *refici poterat.*
Literature Kuttner, *Repertorium*, p. 247; Fransen, "Les 'Questiones' des canonistes I," pp. 567–568.
Editions Fransen, "Les 'Questiones' des canonistes II."

IV *Fols. 31–48*

Parchment. Foliation: 18 fols. Collation: vi^{10}, vii^{8}. 21,5 × 15,7. 2 columns, 39 lines. Hand: gothic minuscule. Rubrication: red Lombard initials with floral decorations (fols. 31–47). Provenance. Germany, 13th *ex.*–14th *in.*

31^{r}–47^{v} Ulricus de Völkermarkt, *Epitome ex decretalibus Gregorii IX.*
Rubric *Gregorii pape noni. Incipiunt excerpta decretalium domini Gregorii*
Incipit *Quoniam romana ecclesia ... auctoritate propria presumere vel etiam usurpare*

24 See above, p. 150.
25 See above, p. 150.

Colophon *Explicit opus. Petrus de Mergentheim scripsit.*
Literature Stelzer, *Gelehrtes Recht.*

48^{rv} Guido Sancti Laurentii in Lucina, presbiteri Cardinalis et Henricus XIII Bavariae Inferioris Dux, *Duae epistolae.*

The first is a letter (1267) from Guy of Burgundy, cardinal protector of San Lorenzo in Lucina (1262–1272) and apostolic legate in Germany, to Duke Henry XIII of Lower Bavaria, asking for peace with King Ottokar II of Bohemia; the second is Henry's reply.

Letterhead *Illustrissimo domino et in Christo sibi karissimo*
Incipit *Quoniam ex officio nobis iniuncte legacionis*
Explicit *Patentes litteras intimetis* (48rb).
Posterior incipit *Paternitatis vestre litteras*
Posterior explicit *ad conservacionem pace roboretur* (48vb).
Literature Werner Maleczek, "Die Urkunden des päpstlichen Legaten Guido, Kardinalpriester von S. Lorenzo in Lucina, aus den Jahren 1265 bis 1267 (Legation nach Skandinavien und Deutschland)," *Archiv für Diplomatik, Schriftgeschichte, Siegel- und Wappenkunde* 56 (2010), pp. 65–150; Jindrich Šebánek, "Die Urkunden des päpstlichen Legaten Guido im Codex Diplomaticus et Epistolaris Regni Bohemiae," in *Palaeographica, diplomatica et archivistica: Studi in onore di Giulio Battelli*, 2 (Rome: Edizioni di Storia e Letteratura, 1979); Hermann Markgraf, "Über die Legation des Guido, tit. s. Laurentii in Lucina presbyteri cardinalis, von 1265–1267," *Zeitschrift des Vereins für Geschichte (und Alterthum) Schlesiens* 5 (1863), pp. 65–106.
Editions Guido's letter has the same content of an identical letter sent to Ottokar: František Palacký, *Über Formelbücher, zunächst in Bezug auf böhmische Geschichte* (Prague: Kronberger und Řiwnač, 1842), p. 265.

V *Fols. 49–52*

Paper. Foliation: 4 fols. Collation: viii$^{6\ (\text{wants } 6)}$. The fifth leaf is the pastdown. 21,9 × 16. Provenance: Augsburg, 15th *ex.*–16th *in.*

49^{r}–52^{v} Blank.

Ma Madrid, BNE, 421 (*olim* C.4.1)

Century	12th *ex.*
Catalogues	*Inventario general de manuscritos de la Biblioteca Nacional*, 1 (Madrid: Ministerio de Educación Nacional, 1953), pp. 285–286. Cf. also Gérard Fransen, "Manuscrits canoniques (1140–1234) conservés en Espagne," *RHE* 48 (1953), pp. 224–234, repr. in Fransen, *Canones et Quaestiones*, 1.1, p. 232.
Material	Parchment. 33,9 × 20,3. 199 + II fols. The manuscript consists of two parts written by different hands, but very close in time (last quarter or last two decades of the 12th century).[26]
Provenance	Messina cathedral, chapter library (before 1679).[27]
Ownership	Library of Philip V (from 1711); Juan Francisco Pacheco Téllez Girón, IV Duque de Uceda (no later than 1692);[28] *dominus* Angelus (note on fol. 2ʳ, no later than 14th century).
Binding	Green parchment, golden decorations and monogram, characteristic of the Duke of Uceda (17th century).
Paste-downs	3 blank paper leaves on the front, 4 on the rear.
1ʳ	Paper leaf (17th century). Rubric: *Ioañis Facontini Concordantia canonum*

26 This information was provided by Valeria De Fraja, who is currently working with Elisabetta Caldelli and Francesco Siri on the catalogue of the Messina cathedral library. All the following codicological information comes from her invaluable help.

27 This hypothesis was kindly confirmed by Valeria De Fraja. The scripts in the codex suggest a Norman origin and are very close to those of the manuscripts that were certainly copied on the island, and in particular to a group that can be traced back to a Messinese *scriptorium* active in the second half of the 12th century. On this *scriptorium*, see Hugo Buchthal, "A School of Miniature Painting in Norman Sicily," in *Late Classical and Medieval Studies in Honour of Albert Mathias Friend jr.*, ed. Kurt Weitzmann et al. (Princeton, New Jersey: Princeton University Press, 1955), pp. 325–327; Angela Daneu Lattanzi, "Due sconosciuti manoscritti di epoca normanna," in *Atti del Convegno Internazionale di Studi Ruggeriani* (*Palermo 21–25 aprile 1954*), ed. Società siciliana per la storia patria, 1 (Palermo: Scuola linotypografica Boccone del povero, 1955). Cf. De Fraja, "Le prime fonti," pp. 117–118. Many codices of the library of the Duke of Uceda were brought from the former chapter library of the Messina cathredral, confiscated in 1679: see Gregorio de Andrés, "Catálogo de los manuscritos de la biblioteca del Duque de Uceda," *Revista de archivos, bibliotecas y museos* 78 (1975), pp. 5–40, 12, 25; José María Fernández Pomar, "La colección de Uceda de la Biblioteca Nacional: Nueva edición del catálogo de manuscritos," *Helmántica* 27 (1976), pp. 475–518, 478, n. 4.

28 Fernández Pomar, "La colección," p. 503; Andrés, "Catálogo," p. 25, n. 160.

2r Rubric: *De suma magistri Iohanis super concordantia. Unus de libris xii. quondam domini Angeli* (14th-century hand).[29]

I *Fols. 3–24*

Parchment. Foliation: 22 fols. 2 columns, 48 lines. Hand: gothic minuscule. Rubrication: red Lombard initials at the beginning of each paragraph, smaller red initials before each allegation.

3r–13r *Perpendiculum.*

3r–6ra *Summula de presumptionibus.*
The scribe attributed the work to Ioannes Faventinus.
Rubric *Opus magistri Iohannis facentini*
Incipit *Hic locus frequens in iudiciis est*
Explicit *quas propter prolixitatem distinguere non curavi.*

6ra–vb Part II (nos. 1–12).
Incipit *Introductis comuni utilitate ab renuntiare non licet*
Explicit *Ignorantia etiam que est ... sed nec illum eis prodest.*

6vb *Brocardum.*
A single canon law brocard interpolated into Part II.
Incipit *Quo legitime factum non est, nec nomen facti meretur*
Explicit *C. xxv. q. ii. Imperiali pro infectis.*

29 There is no certainty about the identity of *dominus Angelus.* Although we cannot go beyond mere speculation, we cannot exclude the possibility that this note might refer to the 13th-century cleric Angelo Saccano, Messinese nobleman, *doctor in utroque*, dean and vicar capitular of Messina cathedral, elected bishop of Catania in 1331: see Cajo-Domenico Gallo, *Annali della Città di Messina Capitale del Regno di Sicilia: Dal giorno di sua fondazione sino a tempi presenti*, 2 (Messina: Gaipa, 1758), p. 184, no. 5. In the sources he is often referred to as *dominus*: Stefano Di Chiara, *Memoria per la consecrazione dei vescovi di Sicilia da tenersi presente nelle attuali circostanze che rendono pericoloso e difficile l'accesso al Sommo Pontefice* (Palermo: Nella Stamperia Reale, 1813), p. 138; Barbara Maria Rita Spinella, *La Cattedrale di Santa Maria di Messina nei documenti dell'Archivio Ducale Medinaceli di Toledo (1282–1412)* (PhD dissertation: University of Catania, 2013), pp. 133, 150. However, this question cannot be answered here, and the matter requires fresh investigation, especially in the light of the documents of the Messina cathedral preserved in the Medinaceli Archive of Toledo.

6vb–8^{r} Part II (nos. 13–26).
Incipit *Invincibilis ignorantia facti excusat*
Explicit *Generali verbo non omnia continentur ... D. lxi. Miramur in cuiusquam persona.*

8rb–13ra Part III.
Although recorded otherwise in previous catalogues, the *Perpendiculum* ends here on fol. 13ra and not on fol. 24^{v}.
Incipit *Initium spectandum*
Explicit *Propter proxime dictam causam ... C. e. q. e. Qui neque regiminis et § quibus.*

13ra–24^{vc} *Brocarda.*
In the manuscript, there is no interruption between the *Perpendiculum* and this civilian collection of brocards appended to it.
Incipit *In quibus casibus ordo servetur*
Explicit *Pretium non ex re sed ex negotiatione.*
Literature Kuttner, "Retractationes IX," p. 42; De Concilio, *Via Brocardica*, 2:13.

II *Fols. 25–199*

Parchment. Foliation: 175 fols. 2 columns, 53 lines. Hand: gothic minuscule; different from the previous one. Rubrication: alternating red and blue Lombard initials at the beginning of each paragraph; underlined words; red initial strokes at the beginning of sentences. Larger red initials with floral decoration in the incipit and on fol. 26^{r}. *Distinctiones* marked by glosses in alternating red and blue letters.

25^{r}–199^{r} Ioannes Faventinus, *Summa decretorum.*
Incipit *Cum multa super concordantia discordantium canonum*
Colophon *Explicit Summa magistri Johannis.*

Mu1 Munich, BSB, Clm. 7622

Century	13th–14th.
Catalogues	Karl Halm, Georg von Laubmann, and Wilhelm Meyer, *Catalogus codicum latinorum Bibliothecae Regiae Monacensis*, 1.3 (Munich: Bibliotheca regia, 1873), p. 179.
Material	Parchment. 25,5 × 17,5. II + 52 + II fols. The MS consists of a single unit.
Provenance	Augustinian monastery of Indersdorf.
Binding	Cardboard cover, covered with white paper.
Paste-downs	2 blank paper leaves on the front, 2 on the rear.

Foliation: 52 fols. 2 columns, 55 lines. Hand: gothic minuscule. Rubrication and the beginning of each paragraph, with red Lombard initials (except for fols. 11^r–16^v, where there is no rubrication). Small pieces of parchment between fols. 17^v–18^r, 18^v–19^r, 22^v–23^r, 23^v–24^r.

1ra–46ra Udo Magister, *Summa super Sententias Petri Lombardi.*

A scholar active in Paris, Udo composed his *Summa* between 1160 and 1165.

Incipit *Sicut desidiosi et pigri*

Explicit *commendendo.*

Literature Odon Lottin, "Le Premier commentaire connu des Sentences de Pierre Lombard," *Recherches de théologie ancienne et médiévale* 11 (1939), pp. 64–71; Joseph N. Garvin, "Magister Udo: A Source of Peter of Poitiers's Sentences," *The New Scholasticism* 28 (1954), pp. 285–298; Joseph N. Garvin, "The Manuscripts of Udo's Summa super Sententias Petri Lombardi," *Scriptorium* 16 (1962), p. 376.

46rb–47rb *De essentia divina.*

Theological material. Garvin identifies the content of fol. 46^{rv} as material from Udo's *Summa* which had previously been omitted.

Literature Garvin, "The Manuscripts," p. 376.

47va–52va *Perpendiculum.*

47va–49ra *Summula de presumptionibus.*

Rubric *De presumptionibus*

Incipit *Hic locus frequens in iudiciis est*

Explicit *quod propter prolixitatem distinguere non curavi.*

49ra–50rb Part II.

Incipit *Introductis publica utilitate renuntiare non licet*

Explicit *Generali verbo non omnia continentur … D. lxi. Miramur in cuiusquam persona.*

50^{rb-va} *Distinctio.*

Rubric *Ad movendum varie iudicem*

Incipit *Delicto coram iudice manifestato*

Explicit *C. xxiv. q. iv. Si illic.*

50va *Glossa de conditione feminarum.*

Incipit *In multis et variis articulis deterior est conditio feminarum quam masculorum*

Explicit *ff. de accusatoribus Qui accusare.*

50va–51ra	Part III.	
	A first series of brocards (nos. 1–24).	
	Incipit	*Levius punitur qui commissum sponte confitetur*
	Explicit	*Principium spectandum … C. xxiii. q. v. c. Prodest qua plectendo.*
51rb	*Distinctio de ignorantia.*	
	Incipit	*Sciendum est quod ignorantia alia est pena alia culpa*
	Explicit	*xii. q. ii. Qui et humanis.*
51rb	*Nota de curialibus.*	
	Incipit	*D. li. Nota quod curiales temporaliter dicuntur*
	Explicit	*bene potest promovi.*
51rb	*Distinctio de servorum ordinatione.*	
	Incipit	*Servus aut ordinatur domino sciente aut nesciente*
	Explicit	*ut liv. Si servus.*
51rb	*Distinctio de mancipiis Iudeorum.*	
	Incipit	*Mancipia iudeorum aut semper fuerunt infidelia*
	Explicit	*quod esse non debet.*
51^{va-b}	Part III.	
	A second series brocards (nos. 25–43).	
	Incipit	*Iuxta personarum et meritorum qualitatem*
	Explicit	*Non dicitur bonum nisi debet bonum … C. e. q. vii. Hii qui necessario.*
52^{ra-b}	*Tractatus de arbore consanguinitatis.*	
	Incipit	*Compositionis arboris causa hec est*
	Explicit	*deinceps ascende ad patrium magnum tandem ad tripatrium.*
52rb	Part III.	
	A third series of brocards (nos. 44–46).	
	Incipit	*Multa iuste rogantur que iniuste effectui mancipantur*
	Explicit	*Quod reprobanda sit promissio habetur … C. v. q. i. Principatus.*
52^{rb-va}	*Distinctio de inutilitate promissionis.*	
	Incipit	*Iure humano inutilis est promissio*
	Explicit	*Romanus pontifex admittit.*

52^{va-b} Bulgarus, *Materia Institutionum.*
Incipit *Liber iste liber institutionum seu elementorum*
Explicit *quia opportet imperatoriam maiestatem etc.*
Literature Kantorowicz, *Studies in the Glossators*, pp. 65–66.
Editions Giovanni Battista Palmieri, ed., *Wernerii Summa Institutionum cum glossis Martini, Bulgari, Alberici aliorumve*, BIMAE, 1, *Additiones*, pp. 1–208, 3–6.

52vb Gervasius de Monte Sancti Eligii, *Quodlibet.*
Rubric *De verbi magistri Gervasii*
Incipit *Progenitus habebat auctem dandi benedictiones*
Explicit *in capite tuo.*
Literature Matthäus Bernards, "Zur Überlieferung mittelalterlicher theologischer Schriften: Neue Handschriften," *Recherches de théologie ancienne et médiévale* 19 (1952), pp. 327–336, 329; Palémon Glorieux, "Répertoire des Maîtres en théologie de Paris au XIIIe siècle," *Études de philosophie médiévale* 17–18 (1933), pp. 1933–1934.

52vb *Distinctio de gratia.*
Incipit *Gratia: gratis data*

52vb Nota: *De ss. Trinitate et actibus humanis.*

Mu2 Munich, BSB, Clm. 8013

Century 12th–13th.
Catalogues Halm, Laubmann, and Meyer, *Catalogus codicum*, 1.3, p. 216; Elisabeth Klemm, *Die romanischen Handschriften der Bayerischen Staatsbibliothek*, 3.2 (Wiesbaden: Reichert, 1988), pp. 196–197.
Material Parchment. 25×18. II + 117 + I fols. The MS consists of a single unit.
Provenance Cistercian imperial abbey of Keisheim.
Binding Leather cover (15th century, restored) with strings and coat of arms of Keisheim.
Paste-downs Front: one blank parchment sheet and a second, older sheet numbered I. On the rear, one blank parchment sheet.
I^{r}: unknown theological text.
Incipit // ⟩*im*⟨*ponunt onera importabilia super humeros* (Mt 25).
Explicit *Qui cum domino pater et spiritu sancto vivit et regnat per omnia † amen.*

1r–v: Philippus Eichstetensis, *Expositio super Magnificat.*

Incipit	*Illuminata illuminatrix, incontaminata Dei* (1r). Explicit: *pro penali misericor⟨dia⟩* (1v).
Edition	Andreas Bauch, *Das theologisch-aszetische Schrifttum des Eichstätter Bischofs Philipp von Rathsamhausen (1306–1322)* (Eichstätt: Verlag der Katholischen Kirche in Bayern, 1948), pp. 178–250.

Foliation: 117 fols. Collation: i^3, $ii–xiv^8$, xv^2. 1 column, 45 lines (fols. 4–115v); 2 columns, 45 lines (fols. 116–117). Hand: gothic minuscule. In the *Summa* many glosses by another hand. Rubricated: red title, red and blue initials with decoration (fols. 1–3); red Lombard initials and paragraph titles (fols. 4–117). Larger red and blue ornate initial with yellow background at the beginning of work, depicting Sicard seated (fol. 4r). The text of the *Summula* contains diagrams (fol. 115v).

1r–3r	*Sermo.*	
	Incipit	*Deus omnipotens*
	Explicit	*incolomes per tempora longiora conservet. amen.*
4r–115v	Sicardus Cremonensis, *Summa in Decretum.*	
	Rubric	*Incipit Summa decretorum Magistri Sigihardi Cremonensis Episcopi*
	Incipit	*Diligite iusticiam qui iudicatis terram*
	Explicit	ends abruptly at *quia ita dimissus abiit //*
	Literature	Kuttner, *Repertorium*, pp. 150–153.
115v–117v	*Perpendiculum* (*Summula de presumptionibus*).	
	Rubric	*De presumptionibus*
	Incipit	*Hic locus in iudiciis frequens est*
	Explicit	ends abruptly at *Contra. Pro contrario facit scriptura Origenis ... de con. D. iv. Si non sanctificatur. in fine //*

O Oxford, University College, 117

Century	12th–13th.
Catalogues	Henry O. Coxe, *Catalogus codicum MSS. qui in collegiis aulisque Oxoniensibus hodie adservantur*, 1 (Oxford: E Typographeo Academico, 1852), p. 35.
Material	Parchment. 27,5 × 18,5. IV + 156 + I fols. The MS consists of a single unit, to which miscellaneous material has been added.
Provenance	Benedictine St Augustine's abbey in Canterbury (originally of St Peter and St Paul).

Binding	Cardboard covered with leather.
Paste-downs	Front: one blank paper leaf (I) and three parchment ones (II–IV). II^r: signature of the manuscript. III^r: table of contents. IV^r: theological text, barely legible. Rear: one blank paper leaf.

Foliation: 156 fols. 2 columns (fols. 1–152^r); 3 columns (fols. 152^v–157). 37–43 lines (fols. 1–43), 31–42 lines (fols. 45–128), 34–40 lines (fols. 129–144), 41 lines (fol. 145), 38–39 lines (fol. 145bis), 46 lines (fol. 146^r), 39 lines (fols. 146^v–147), 46–55 lines (fols. 149–151), 58–62 lines (fols. 152^v–157). Hand: gothic minuscule, several hands. Rubricated: red title (fols 1^r, 45^r); large red Lombard initials (some with floral decoration; on fol. 45^r a cross shield in the center) at the beginning of each book, book incipits and explicits in red (fols. 1–128); smaller Lombard initials at the beginning of some paragraphs (fols. 1–42); red strokes at the beginning of each sentence and rubricated glosses in the margins (fols. 45–51^r); alternating blue and red Lombard initials (fols. 129–137^r; 145bis); rubricated brocards (fols. 152^v–157). Content of fols. 35^r–36va cancelled by red crosses. Diagrams on fols. 129^v–140^r. Fol. 145 is repeated in the numbering.

1^r–42^r	Augustine, *De doctrina Christiana.*	
	Rubric	*Hic incipit liber Aurelii Augustini de doctrina Christiana*
	Incipit	*Sunt precepta quedam tractandarum scripturarum*
	Explicit	*quem de sacramentis sive de philosophia scripsit.*
	Literature	B. Hoon Woo, "Augustine's Hermeneutics and Homiletics in De doctrina Christiana," *Journal of Christian Philosophy* 17 (2013), pp. 97–117.
	Editions	Augustine, *De doctrina Christiana*, ed. and trans. R.P.H. Green (Oxford: Clarendon Press, 1995).
42^v	Blank.	
43^r–44^v	Missing.	
45–122vb	Augustine, *Confessionum libri XIII.*	
	Rubric	*Incipit primus liber Confessionum Aurelii Augustini*
	Incipit	*Confessionum mearum librri* (sic) *de bonis et de malis*
	Explicit	*sit aperietur. Amen.*
	Editions	Augustine, *Confessionum libri XIII*, ed. Luc Verheijen (Aurelii Augustini opera), 1:1 (Turnhout: Brepols, 1981).

122vb–128^{r}	Augustine, *De utilitate agendae poenitentiae.*	
	Rubric	*Incipit Augustinus de penitentia*
	Incipit	*Quam sit utilis et necessaria penitentie*
	Explicit	*Magnus es domine et laudabilis es valde.*
	Editions	Augustine, *De utilitate agendae poenitentiae*, PL 39: 1549–1560.
128^{v}	Blank.	
129^{ra-b}	*Summula de matrimonio.*	
	Incipit	*He sunt cause separaccionis coniugii*
	Explicit	*nupcias. Explicit.*
	Literature	Pierre Legendre, "Miscellanea Britannica," *Traditio* 15 (1959), pp. 491–497, 494, n. 11.
129rb	*Summula de matrimonio.*	
	Incipit	*Nota fides pacciones*
	Explicit	*D. xxx. Si quis presbiter.*
129^{v}–140rb	Sicardus Cremonensis, *Summa in Decretum* (*excerpta*).	
	These excerpts often take the form of *distinctiones*, arranged in diagrams.	
	Incipit	*Multa sunt que sine summi pontificis*
	Explicit	*in sabbato carnes comedere valeamus.*
	Literature	Legendre, "Miscellanea," p. 494, n. 11; Stephan Kuttner, "Annual Report," *Traditio* 16 (1960), pp. 531–533, 533.
140^{v}–144vb	*Notabilia De excommunicatione et penitentia.*	
	Incipit	*A communione itaque ecclesie*
	Explicit	*Devota quod que maritum … C. xxvii. q. i. Devotam.*
	Literature	Legendre, "Miscellanea," p. 494, n. 11; Kuttner, *Repertorium*, p. 240.
144vb	*Notabilia.*	
	This series of *notabilia* can be distinguished from the previous one because it has been copied by a different hand.	
	Incipit	*Sine testibus tabulariis non est credendum*
	Explicit	*Uxores coruscant radiis maritorum.*
145^{r-v}	*Versus mnemotechnici.*	
	Incipit	*Ordine plana carent spoliatus*
	Explicit	*fit cum fertur vice versa.*
$145^{bisra-vb}$	*Perpendiculum* (rubrics from Parts II and III).	
	Brocards from the original text, here *notabilia* without *contraria* and allegations.	

145^{bisra} Part II.
A first series of 13 brocards, in mixed order.
Incipit *Introductis publica utilitate renunciare non licet*
Explicit *Probatio facta in seculari … plenam fidem facit.*

$145^{bisra-vb}$ Part III.
A first sequence of brocards from Part III, which also appear in other manuscripts.
Incipit *Principium spectandum esse*
Explicit *Sicut peccat qui … incidit in eius sententiam.*

145^{bisvb} Part II.
A second group of 12 brocards, in mixed order.
Incipit *Rati habitio et sequens consensus retrahitur*
Explicit *Generali verbo non omnia continentur.*

145^{bisvb} Part III.
Three brocards appended to the *Perpendiculum* that appear only in this manuscript (nos. 36–38).
Incipit *Omnes monachi cum propriam voluntatem*
Explicit *Non licet presbitero … missas canere.*

146^{ra-b} *Notabilia.*
Incipit *Reos criminum etiam de sacris locis*
Explicit *usque ad tertium gradum.*

146rb *Definitiones.*
Incipit *Cocodrillus serpens est aquaticus*
Explicit *circoncisionem gentes prepucium appellare.*

146^{va-b} Bernardus Papiensis, *Breviarium extravagantium* (fragment).
Incipit *Arbitri est proprie iudicare*
Explicit *et pastor nescit.*
Editions Friedberg, *Quinque compilationes.*

147^{ra-va} *Notabilia.*
Incipit *Sacrilegi crimen incurrit*
Explicit *debet servare illesa.*

147va–148^{r} *Adnotationes.*
On space originally left blank, some pencil annotation, almost illegible.

148^{v} Blank.

149ra–151vb	*Summa in Decretum.*	
	A French *Summa* composed c. 1175–1178.	
	Incipit	*Questio si iure naturali*
	Explicit	*constitutiones illud optinere* (breaks off at D.96)
	Literature	Kuttner, *Repertorium*, p. 181; Kuttner, "An Interim Checklist," p. 446; Kuttner, "Notes," p. 499; Kuttner and Rathbone, "Anglo-Norman canonists," p. 314, n. 66.
152ra	*Contra privilegium.*	
	Incipit	*Contra privilegium quod contrarius ratione est indultum*
	Explicit	*xvi. C. q. i. Possessores.*
152ra	*De privilegio.*	
	Incipit	*De privilegio. Quod decime singulis annis redentur*
	Explicit	*C. si adversis venditionem l. Si minor.*
152va–157^{vc}	*Brocarda Oxonica.*	
	Incipit	*Argumentandum ex superficie litere*
	Explicit	*Non sufficit quid civiliter ... § In insulam.*
	Literature	Kuttner, "Retractationes IX," p. 42; Legendre, "Miscellanea," p. 494, n. 11. See De Concilio, *Via Brocardica*, 2:11.

P1 Paris, BNF, lat. 4720A

Century	12th–13th.
Catalogues	"Latin 4720A," in *Archives et manuscrits de la Bibliothèque Nationale de France*, available at https://archivesetmanuscrits.bnf.fr/ark:/12148/cc63589v, accessed 2019 Oct 6.
Material	Parchment. III + 114 + III fols. The MS is a miscellany and consists of 6 codicological units.
Provenance	Cluniac abbey of Saint-Martial of Limoges.
Binding	Wood, covered with leather; golden decorations and emblem of the French royal library.
Paste-downs	4 blank parchment sheets on the front; the *verso* of the last paste-down front sheet, numbered as I^r, has a sheet of paper with a table of contents of the manuscript attached; 3 blank parchment sheets on the rear.

I *Fols. 1–22*

Parchment. Foliation: 23 leaves, but with a shift in numbering from fol. fol. 7bis; a small sheet of paper with a table of contents of the manuscript is attached to fol. 1^{r}. Collation:[30] i^{8}, ii^{2}, iii^{8}, iv^{5}. 13,5 × 20. Columns: 1 column (1^{r}–9^{v}); 2 columns (10^{r}–22^{v}), 26–62 lines. Hand: gothic minuscule, several hands. Rubrication: red title, rubrics, and pilcrows at the beginning of each paragraph, some initials outlined in red (1^{r}–6^{r}); no rubrication (7^{r}–22^{v}). This codicological unit dates from the 12th century.

1^{r}–5^{r} Rainerius Perusinus, *Ars notaria* (fragment).

Rubric In nomine domini amen. Ars notariae Rainerii Perusini

Incipit *)D(e his, que ab hominibus aguntur*

Explicit *Item si taceat rem //* (p. 6 of Wahrmund's edition).

Editions Rainerius Perusinus, *Die Ars Notariae des Rainerius Perusinus*, ed. Ludwig Wahrmund (Innsbruck: Wagner, 1917).

5$^{r–v}$ *De exheredatione.*

Incipit *Cause ingratitudinis quibus parentes possunt filios suos exheredare sunt xiiii.*

Explicit *ab orthodos, rectum et doxa, gloria.*

5^{v} Justinian, *Digestum vetus*, Dig. 13.6.23.

Incipit *Si commodavero tibi equum*

Explicit *commodavi qui eum laborem sustinere non potuit.*

Literature Gérard Fransen, "Questiones Lemovicenses II," *ZRG Kan. Abt.* 76 (1990), pp. 156–171, repr. in Fransen, *Canones et Quaestiones*, 1.2, p. 156.

5^{v}–6^{r} Justinian, *Digesta*, "*De diversis regulis iuris antiqui*" (*excerpta*).

Rubric *De diversis regulis iuris*

Incipit *Item vel eius est nolle qui potest et velle*

Explicit *Ytem nemo alieno nomine agere potest.*

Literature Fransen, "Questiones Lemovicenses II," p. 156.

6^{v} Blank.

7^{r}–9^{r} Arnaldus magister, *Definitiones.*

The name of Arnaldus does not appear in the text, but in the index on fol. 1^{r}. It also appears later (fol. 17^{v}). Different hand.

Incipit *(C)um velimus quasdam facere diffinitiones*

Explicit *item nota quod testamentum aliquando dicitur inofficiosum. Puta si pater //*

30 Information on the collation of the whole manuscript was kindly provided by Dr Graziella Pastore (BNF).

9^v Iohannes, *Testamentum.*
Different hand.
Incipit *Ego Iohannes immensi morbi gravedine debilitatus*
Explicit *quod iterum non reddit.*

$10^{ra}–17^{vb}$ *Compendium Sophisticorum Elenchorum.*
This work, which also mentions James of Venice's translation of the *Elenchi,* was probably composed between 1150 and 1180, possibly in Paris. Different hands.
Incipit *Cum omnis ars disserendi tres habet partes*
Explicit *ad presens suficiant*
After the work there is a supposed colophon: *Explicit hic codex Arnaldi versificantis / versificatori debetur laus meliori / versificator amans per carmina laudat amoena.*
Editions Sten Ebbesen and Yukio Iwakuma, "Compendium Sophisticorum Elenchorum (MS Paris BN 4720A)," *Cahiers de l'Institut du Moyen-Âge Grec et Latin* 60 (1990), pp. 47–112, 47–48; Sten Ebbesen, "Anonymi Parisiensis Compendium Sophisticorum Elenchorum: The Upsala Version," *Cahiers de l'Institut du Moyen-Âge Grec et Latin* 66 (1996), pp. 253–312, 257; Sten Ebbesen, "Paris 4720A: A 12th Century Compendium of Aristotle's Sophistici Elenchi," *Cahiers de l'Institut du Moyen-Âge Grec et Latin* 10 (1973), pp. 1–20.

$17^{vb}–22^{vb}$ *Fallaciae Melidunae* (*Collectio paralogismorum*).
A collection of *istantiae,* a 12th-century argumentation technique, from the school of the Melidunenses.
Incipit *Ad huiusmodi argumentum*
Explicit *est declarabunt*
Literature Iwakuma Yukio, "Two more Instantia Texts: An edition," *Zinbun* 24 (1989), pp. 13–88, 14.

II *Fols. 23–36*

Parchment. Foliation: 15 fols, but with one unnumbered leaf between fols. 30 and 31. Collation: v^7, vi^8 (1 unnumbered fol. between 1 and 2). 13,5×20. 2 columns ($23^r–36^v$), 31–53 lines. Hand: gothic minuscule, different hands. No rubrication, except for red rubrics on $30^v–31^r$.

$23^r–29^v$ *Summa Codicis* (fragment).
Incipit *⟨C⟩um de fide ac religione*
Explicit *l. Si quis ad declinandum.*
Literature Fransen, "Questiones Lemovicenses II," pp. 156–157.

30$^{r–va}$ *Quaestiones disputatae.*
Different hand.
Incipit *⟨Q⟩uidam habebat concubinam*
Explicit *Teobaldus huic cause interfuit et hec scripsit.*
Edition Gérard Fransen, "Le mariage simulé: Deux questions disputées au XIIe siècle," in *Etudes de droit et d'histoire: Melanges mgr. H. Wagnon* (Leuven: Bibliothèque Centrale de l'U.C.L., 1976), repr. in Fransen, *Canones et Quaestiones*, 2, pp. 534–538.

30va *De electione.*
Incipit *Pro iusta et canonica electione*
Explicit *fiunt iure potestatis contra pertinent ad iniuriam.*

30vb–36vb *Perpendiculum.*

30vb–31ra *Summula de presumptionibus.*
Incipit *Hic locus frequens in iudiciis est*
Explicit *quod propter prolixitatem distinguere non curavi.*

31ra–31vb Part II.
A first series of 14 brocards.
Incipit *Introductis publica utilitate renunciare non licet*
Explicit *Res inter alios acta aliis non preiudicat ... C. i. q. vii. Qui in qualibet.*

31vb *Glossa de conditione feminarum.*
The first of three short texts that appear, in the same order, also in G.
Incipit *In multis iuris articulis deterior est conditio feminarum quam masculorum*
Explicit *s. de arbitriis sanctimus.*

31vb *Brocardum.*
Incipit *Punitur quod factum iure non tenuit*
Explicit *C. Si mancipius fuerit alienatum ut l. Ea.*

31vb *Distinctio.*
Incipit *Denunciatio inducit dolum*
Explicit *inducit interpretationem ut C. de plus petitionibus.*

31vb–32ra Part III.
A first sequence of 17 brocards.
Incipit *Levius punitur qui commissum sponte confitetur*

Explicit *Ubi culpa non est, ibi ad cautelam pena imponitur ... C. xxxiii. q. iii. Dixit Sarra in visu.*

32^{ra-b} *Distinctio.*
Incipit *Delicto coram iudice manifesto*
Explicit *C. xxiv. q. iv. Si illic.*

32rb–33va Part III.
A second sequence of brocards (nos. 18–83).
Incipit *Punitur qui alias esset excusandus*
Explicit *D. lxxx. Quanto.*

33va–35vb *Brocarda.*
A long collection of 219 brocards interpolated into the *Perpendiculum*, produced between 1181 and 1190 in northern France or England.
Incipit *Nullus archidiaconus vel archipresbyter curam conferat animarum*
Explicit *Ecclesie servitores ... Infra Extra Inter Cetera.*
Literature De Concilio, *Via Brocardica*, 2:13–14.

35vb–36rb Part III.
A third sequence of brocards (nos. 84–103).
Incipit *Que statuta sunt ex causa*
Explicit *Hoc verbum ... C. xxxii. q. ii. Mulier.*

36rb–36va Part II.
A second series of 12 brocards.
Incipit *Rati habitio et sequens consensus retro trahitur*
Explicit *Generali verbo non omnia ... ad mensam omnem fidelem.*

36^{va-b} Part. III.
A third sequence of brocards (from no. 104).
Incipit *Episcopus assensu clericorum*
Explicit *Testes non nisi de visis ... Odit, Illi, non oportet, In ecclesia //*

III *Fols. 37–52*

Parchment. Foliation: 16 fols. Collation: vii–viii^{8}. 13,5×19,2. 2 columns, 41–55 lines. Hand: gothic minuscule, several hands. No rubrication.

37^{r}–44vb *Quaestiones Lemovicenses II.*
One of the earliest collections of canon law *quaestiones*. Qq. 1–18 were compiled in the 1160s at the latest. Additions were made in the 1170s and early 1180s.

Incipit *Alicui marito relaxatur pena suspendii*
Explicit *Solutio. Miles non potest … favorabilior est pars ecclesie quam militis.*
Editions Fransen, "Questiones Lemovicenses II."

44vb *De simonia.*
Incipit *Simonia est erga ea que a domino gratis instituta sunt dari*
Explicit *in ea impositione manus collata.*

44vb *Generalia.*
Three *generalia* copied *ad calcem* by a different hand. The first also appears as brocard in the *Perpendiculum* (ε37).
Incipit *Plus valet quod agitur quam quod simulate concipitur*
Explicit *Rubrica. Cum quis in alterius iure succedit, eius iure uti debet.*

45^{r}–52^{v} Iohannes Lemovicensis, *Tractatus de distinctionibus sophismatum.*
A treatise composed c. 1240. Different hand.
Incipit *Super eandem regulam fundatur hoc sophisma*
Explicit *in uno et in multis.*
Literature Lambertus Marie De Rijk, *Some Earlier Parisian Tracts on Distinctiones Sophismatum* (Nijmegen: Ingenium Publishers, 1988), p. XVI.

IV *Fols. 53–60*

Parchment. Foliation: 8 fols. Collation: ix^{8}. 12,8 × 21,5. Columns: 1 column (53^{v}–60^{v}); 2 columns (53^{r}), 36–67 lines. Hand: gothic minuscule. No rubrication.

53^{r}–60^{v} *Distinctiones.*
Incipit *Quatuor sunt affecciones animi*
Explicit *expandere religio* †
Different hands.

V *Fols. 61–70*

Parchment. Foliation: 10 fols. Collation: x^{2}, xi^{8}. 14,5 × 21. 2 columns, 45–49 lines. Hand: gothic minuscule, several hands. No rubrication.

61^{ra-vb} *Grammatica.*
Incipit *Diffinire que est conglutinacio* ⟩*duorum*⟨ *vocalium*
Explicit *Euripedem tetrasillabum.*

62ra–67rb *Introductiones Parisienses.*
An introduction to Logic (*summula loicales*). Different hand. Diagrams in the margin. The work has been attributed by de Libera to a Parisian milieu of the first decades of the 13th century.
Incipit *Introductio est brevis et aperta demonstratio in aliquam artem*

Explicit *possibilis qualitas est qualitas diu durans.*
Literature Lambertus Marie De Rijk, *Logica Modernorum: A Contribution to the History of Early Terminist Logic*, 2.1 (Assen: Van Gorcum, 1967), pp. 441–447; Alain de Libera, "Bulletin d'Histoire de la Logique Médiévale," *Revue des Sciences philosophiques et théologiques* 76 (1992), pp. 640–666, 662–663; Alain de Libera, *César et le Phénix: Distinctiones et sophismata parisiens du XIIIe siècle* (Pisa: Scuola Normale Superiore, 1999), pp. IX–XXXI.
Editions Alain de Libera, *César et le Phénix*, pp. 3–7 (extract).

67va–69vb *Distinctiones sophismatum.*
Different hand (13th century). The text belongs to the same milieu as the previous one and has parallels with the *Abstractiones* of a master called Hervaeus Sophista.[31]
Incipit *⟩N⟨otandum quod ut dicit Aristoteles*
Explicit *hominem*
Literature de Libera, "Bulletin," pp. 662–663; de Libera, *César et le Phénix*, pp. IX–XXXI.
Editions de Libera, *César et le Phénix*, pp. 11–21 (extracts).

70^{ra-vb} *Grammatica*
Incipit *aeripedem quod est pentasillabum enim hec est sillaba quoque ponit*
Explicit *non conso //*
Different hand.

VI ***Fols. 71–112***

Parchment. Foliation: 42 fols. Collation: xii^{10}, xiii^{6}, xiv^{8}, xv^{2}, xvi–xvii^{8}. 15×19. Columns: 1 column (81^{r}–103^{v}); 2 columns (71^{r}–80^{v}, 105^{r}–109^{r}), 26–50 lines. Hand: gothic minuscule, several hands. No rubrication, except for some red strokes on 81^{rv} and 94^{v}, red rubrics and small Lombard initials at the beginning of each paragraph on 96^{r}–97^{r} and 99^{r}–100^{r}.

71ra–80vb *Sermones nonnulli.*
Incipit *// In principio et cum homines inebriati fuerint per illos illecti*
Explicit *enim dixit cum veniat.*

31 On this author, see De Rijk, *Logica Modernorum*, 2.1, pp. 50–51.

81^r–95^v Aristotle, *De sophisticis elenchi cum glossis.*
Different hand.
Rubric *De sophisticis aut elenchi et de eis que videntur elenchi*
Colophon *explicit liber elenchorum.*

Editions Aristotle, *De sophisticis elenchi*, ed. Bernard G. Dod (Leiden: Brill, 1975).

96^r–103^v *Liber de ceremoniis et officiariis sancti Martialis Lemovicensis.*
Incipit *Item ex quo musce incipiunt fratres in refectorio*
Explicit *inde ignarus ut pro eo faciat.*
Different hands.
Literature Jean-Loup Lemaitre and Françoise Vielliard, "La Liève de la confrérie des premières chandelles à Limoges," *Bulletin de la Société archéologique et historique du Limousin* 129 (2001), pp. 45–113.

104^{rv} Blank.

105ra–109vb *Grammatica.*
Incipit *Duo queritur principaliter, scilicet de evocatione et conceptione*
Explicit *hoc non est ibi pleonasmos.*
Different hand.

110^r–112^r Blank.

112^v *Adnotatio.*
The note, incomplete and with the words trimmed, refers to a lawsuit.
Text *Dies post festum apostolorum Petri et Pauli est assignatum Iohanni Boyol. ad producendum te⟩stes⟨ // contra s⟩ic⟨ deponent in causam que vertitur inter eos.*

P2 Paris, BNF, lat. 14606[32]

Century 13th *in.*

Catalogues Gilbert Ouy, *Les manuscrits de l'abbaye de Saint-Victor: Catalogue établi sur la base du répertoire de Claude de Grandrue (1514)*, 2 (Turnhout: Brepols, 1999), p. 108; "Latin 14606," in *Archi-*

32 Due to the fragile condition of this codex, the BNF does not allow it to be consulted and I had to rely on the digitization available online. For this reason, it has not been possible to provide more information regarding the material aspects of the manuscript than that offered by the previous catalogues.

ves et manuscrits de la Bibliothèque Nationale de France, available at https://archivesetmanuscrits.bnf.fr/ark:/12148/cc75357s, accessed 2019 Oct 6.

Material — Parchment. 34×24. I + 168 fols. The MS consists of a single unit.

Provenance — Augustinian abbey of Saint-Victor, Paris (until 1796).

Paste-downs — Front: description of the content of the work and book curse. The same curse is repeated on I^{r} and 1^{r}.

2 columns (except fol. 167: 3 columns), 50–52 lines. Hand: gothic minuscule.

1^{r}–166va — Ioannes Faventinus, *Summa decretorum*.
The work, in combination with the *Perpendiculum*, appears also in Ma.
- Rubric: *Incipit summa magistri Iohannis Faventini super decreta Gratiani*
- Incipit: *Cum multa super concordantia discordantium canonum*
- Explicit: *Accessi portum quo mihi cursus erat.*

166va–167^{vc} — *Perpendiculum*.

$166^{va\text{–}b}$ — Part III.
A first group of 5 brocards.
- Incipit: *Qui occasionem damni dat damnum dedisse*
- Explicit: *Frustra debitum exigit ... nonne acciperis.*

166vb — Part II.
A single brocard.
- Incipit: *Generali verbo omnia non continentur*
- Explicit: *C. iii. q. viii. Omnia.*

166vb–167ra — Part III.
A second group of 3 brocards (nos. 6–8).
- Incipit: *Principium spectandum*
- Explicit: *Ordinis turbatio non irritat factum ... Econtra.*

$167^{ra\text{–}va}$ — Part II.
A second series of 11 brocards.
- Incipit: *Licitum est homini contra suum factum venire*
- Explicit: *Metus et iussus principis ... C. vii. q. i. c. Nichil quia nec perfesta.*

	167^{va-c}	Part III. A final group of 11 brocards (nos. 9–19). Incipit *Tam lege divina quam humana* Explicit *Nichil actum creditur vel irritari meretur … D. l. ii. sollicitudo.*
167^{vc}	Alexander III, *Epistola decretalis ad episcopum Lexoviensem.* Rubric *Decretum seu rescriptum alexander iii. ad episcopum Lexoviensem* Incipit *Super alia questione scilicet* Explicit *eius inimicum existere.* Edition Pierre Crabbe, ed., *Concilia omnia tam generalia quam particularia*, 1, 2nd ed., (Cologne: Quentel, 1551), pp. 892–893, c.6.	
168^{r}	Blank. Contains just the sentence: *contra i. de successoribus ab intestato … arg. ff. de annuis legatis l. i.* Parchment strip between fols. 167–168: *Nupciarum bonum usque aliud sed etiam contrahere dampna est … est malum et ipsium nubere.*	

Vb Vatican City, BAV, Borgh. 287

Century	13th–14th.
Catalogues	Anneliese Maier, *Codices burghesiani Bibliothecae Vaticanae* (Vatican City: BAV, 1952), pp. 328–330.
Material	Parchment. 29,5 × 22. 110 + I fols. The MS is a miscellany and consists of two codicological units.
Provenance	Sidon, library of the capital chapter (possessor note on fol. 110^{v}).[33]
Ownership	Papal library of Avignon (14th century).[34]

33 See above, p. 19, n. 11.

34 Maier, *Codices burghesiani*, pp. 328–330, reports the presence of the manuscript in the 1369 catalogue of the Papal library of Avignon, under the number 1426: see also Maurice Faucon, *La librairie des papes d'Avignon: Sa formation, sa composition, ses catalogues, 1316–1420; D'après les registres de comptes et d'inventaires des archives vaticanes*, 2 (Paris: Thorin, 1886–1887), p. 210.

I *Fols. 1–10*

Foliation: 10 fols. Collation: i^{10}. 4 columns (except fol. 10^{r}: 3 columns), 65 lines. Hand: gothic minuscule. Rubricated (fols 1^{r}–8va). There is at least one lost folio between 6 and 7.

1^{r}–10^{v} *Perpendiculum.*

1ra–2^{rc} *Summula de presumptionibus*
- Rubric *Incipit de presumptionibus.*
- Incipit *Hic locus in iudiciis frequens est*
- Explicit *quam propter prolixitatem distinguere non curavi.*

2^{rc}–3va Part II.
- Incipit *Introductis publica auctoritate renuntiare non licet*
- Explicit *Generali verbo non omnia continentur ... D. lxi. Miramur in cuiusquam persona.*

3va–6^{vc} Part III.
A first group of 153 brocards.
- Incipit *Episcopum que promiserit consensu clericorum*
- Explicit *Sepe aliquid irritatur ... C. xxi. q. ii. c. i.*

6^{vc} *Distinctio.*
- Rubric *Ad movendum vario modo iudicem*
- Incipit *Delicto coram iudice manifestato*
- Explicit *D. xc. Si quis contristaverit.*

6^{vc}–7rb Part III.
A second sequence of brocards (nos. 154–174).
- Incipit *Equitas et mansuetudo rigori preferetur*
- Explicit *Non dicitur posse fieri ... Nos in quemquam multi.*

7rb *Distinctio.*
- Rubric *Ad movendum vario modo iudicem*
- Incipit *Delicto coram iudice manifesto*
- Explicit *aliquando allegantes delin //*

7rb–8va Part. III.
A third sequence of brocards (from no. 175).
- Incipit *Utile pro inutile vitiatur ut.*
- Explicit *Una pena non excludit aliam ut ... C. ii. q. vii. Accusatio querendum.*

8^{va-b} *Distinctio.*
- Rubric *Ad movendum varie iudicem*
- Incipit *Delicto coram iudice manifestato*
- Explicit *C. xxiv. q. iv. Si illic.*

8vb–10rb *Distinctiones.*
Incipit *Hec sunt que suadent ne spoliatus restituatur*
Explicit *D. ii Nichil.*

10^{rc-vb} *Notabilia.*
Incipit *Arg. contra religiosos*
Explicit *Arg. quod cessante causa … c. Statuimus.*

II *Fols. 11–110*

Foliation: 100 fols. Collation: ii–xiii^{8}, xiv^{4}. 2 columns, 48 lines. Hand: gothic minuscule. Rubricated: alternating large red and green Lombard initials; red initial strokes; underlined words.

11^{r}–109va Stephanus Tornacensis, *Summa decretorum.*
Incipit *Si duos ad cenam convivas invitaveris*
Explicit *Concludit et causarum ultimam et ultimam questionem.*
Literature Herbert Kalb, *Studien zur Summa Stephans von Tournai: Ein Beitrag zur kanonistischen Wissenschaftsgeschichte des späten 12. Jahrhunderts* (Innsbruck: Universitätsverlag Wagner, 1983); Stephan Kuttner, "The Third Part of Stephen of Tournai's Summa," *Traditio* 14 (1958), pp. 502–506.
Edition Crabbe, *Concilia*, 2:892–893, c.6. Partial edition in Stephen of Tournai, *Die Summa über das Decretum Gratiani*, ed. Johann Friedrich von Schulte (Giessen: E. Roth, 1891). The prologue is edited by Kalb, *Studien*, pp. 113–120.

109^{va-b} *Summula in tractatum de poenitentia.*
Incipit *Questionis de penitentia longus est*
Explicit *Sine dilectione namque timor non nisi penam habet.*
Literature Kuttner, *Repertorium*, p. 135.

109vb–110rb *Formularium instrumentorum et libellorum.*
This formulary has been attributed to Waltherus by Gouron.
Incipit *Liber conventionalis. Ego gualterus conqueror deo et vobis Bezo*
Explicit *De libellis refutatoriis. Ego gualterus scribo … ab uxore mea in presentia talium testium.*
Literature Gouron, "Une école de canonistes," pp. 48, 56–58. Fowler-Magerl, *Ordo*, p. 59.

Vp Vatican City, BAV, Pal. lat. 653

Century	13th.
Catalogues	Enrico Stevenson, *Codices Palatini Latini Bibliothecae Vaticanae*, 1 (Rome: Ex Typographeo Vaticano, 1886), p. 232; Michael Kautz, "Vatikan, Biblioteca Apostolica Vaticana, Pal. lat. 653. Manuscript description," in *Bibliotheca Laureshamensis—digital: Virtual Monastic Library of Lorsch*, ed. Alexandra Büttner and Michael Kautz (Heidelberg, 2014), available online at https://digi.ub.uni-heidelberg.de/sammlung51/werk/pdf/bav_pal_lat_653.pdf, accessed 2019 Jul 19; Sigrid Krämer, *Handschriftenerbe des deutschen Mittelalters*, 2 (Munich: Beck, 1989), pp. 500, 715. See also Bernhard Bischoff, *Die Abtei Lorsch im Spiegel ihrer Handschriften*, 2nd ed. (Lorsch: Laurissa, 1989), p. 126.
Material	Parchment. 30,5 × 22. II + 130 + I fols. The manuscript is a miscellany and consists of 3 codicological units.
Provenance	Benedictine imperial abbey of Lorsch (65^r^).
Ownership	Schönau im Steinachtal, Odenwald (14th–15th century) (fols 1^r^, 128^r^); Heidelberg, Bibliotheca Palatina (until 1622–1623).
Binding	Cardboard cover, covered with white parchment (Rome, 1940s).
Paste-downs	Leaves of paper.

Before fol. 1 there are two other fols of parchment marked A–B.

A^r Cutting, in margin the remains of a canon law text *de electione*.

B Various notes from different hands and with different content (13th century).

B^r Incipit *Ypodromus*
Explicit *vel doles quod eras.*

B^v Incipit *urbs sacra Hierusalem dicitur atque Salem*
Explicit *cum intentione fallendi.*

I *Fols. 1–64*

Foliation: 64 fols. Collation: i–viii^8. 20,5 × 17. 2 columns, 50–56 lines. Hand: gothic minuscule. Rubrication: incipit, explicit, and rubrics in red; red Lombard letters, partly with floral decoration.

1^r–64va Bernardus Papiensis, *Breviarium extravagantium cum glossis*.
Rubric *Incipit breviarium extravagantium B. prepositi Papiensis*
Incipit *Iuste iudicate, recte iudicate, filii hominum*
Explicit *Concludit et causarum ultimam et ultimam questionem.* Added: *voti.*

Added	*Indignum est ... quis facere compellatur. Gregorius in registro. Quamdiu et ... et pastor nescit.*
Literature	Kuttner, *Repertorium*, pp. 322–344.
Edition	Friedberg, *Quinque compilationes*.

II *Fols. 65–112*

Foliation: 48 fols. Collation: ix–xiv[8]. 23×13,5. 2 columns, 50–56 lines. Hand: gothic minuscule. Rubrication: incipit, explicit, and rubrics in red; red Lombard initials. Diagrams in marginal glosses. Loss of leaves after fol. 112v.

65ra *Adnotatio: De temptatione diaboli.*

Quotes from the Bible and Church fathers on the devil's temptation of Jesus.

Rubric	*De temptacione diaboli in Xm in Luca*
Incipit	*Nisi ieiunasset temptandi occasio non adesset*
Explicit	*non est timendus diabolus, quia nihil potest nisi permissus.*

65ra–b *Adnotationes: testes de negotiis Monasterii Laureshamensi.*

Lists of witnesses for the good acquisitions of the monastery.

Incipit	*Hii sunt testes de vinea Adelradi*
Explicit	*Testes de molendino in Marbach ... pro se et uxore et filiis suis.*

65va–112ra Sicardus Cremonensis, *Summa in Decretum.*

Rubric	*Incipit summa secundum magistrum Sykardum Cremonensem episcopum*
Incipit	*〉D〈iligite iusticiam qui iudicatis terram*
Explicit	*et mei iudicium matris arbitrio derelinquo.*
Colophon	*Explicit feliciter.*
Literature	Kuttner, *Repertorium*, pp. 150–153.

112ra–vb *De Decreti Gratiani continentia.*

A summary of the first part and of the first three *causae* of the second part of the *Decretum*. The text ends abruptly, probably due to a loss of leaves.

Rubric	*Continentia prime partis Gratiani per singulas distinctiones*
Incipit	*In prima disctinctione agitur de iure naturali*
Explicit	*In hac iii. causa agitur de expoliatis ... an accusato liceat accusationem in accusatorem vertere.*

III *Fols. 113–128*

Foliation: 16 fols. Collation: xv–xvi^{8}. 24×18,5. 3 columns (fols. 113–117^{r}), 1 column (fols. 117^{v}–128), 50–56 lines. Hand: gothic minuscule. Rubrication: incipit, explicit, and rubrics in red; red Lombard initials. Diagrams in marginal glosses. Loss of leaves after fol. 112^{v}.

113^{r}–117^{r} *Perpendiculum.*

113ra–114va *Summula de presumptionibus.*

Rubric *De presuptionibus* (sic!)

Incipit *Hic locus frequens est in iudiciis*

Explicit *quam propter prolixitatem distinguere non curavi.*

114va–115^{vc} Part II.

Incipit *Introductis publica utilitate non licet et renuntiare*

Explicit *Generali verbo non omnia continentur ... omnia nichil d. non.*

Solution (!) added to the first brocard, before the rubric: *Solutio. Sub speciale est in summo pontifice, scilicet ut possit renuntiare ius que introductus ob publica utilitate.*

115^{vc}–117rb Part III.

A first group of 40 brocards from Part III.

Incipit *Plus valet quod in veritate agitur*

Explicit *Propter proxime dictam causam ... C. eadem q. eadem Qui neque regiminis et § Quibus.*

117rb *Nota de presentia verborum.*

Incipit *Nota quod quorumque verborum presentia exigitur*

Explicit *desponsaverit vel subarraverit.*

117$^{rb–c}$ Part III.

A second group of 4 brocards from Part III.

Incipit *Quod et si ecclesiasticus patronus*

Explicit *Et similiter per vim deposita sit ... D. xxxiii. Laici et Habuisse.*

117^{v}–128^{r} Petrus Blesensis, *Distinctiones "Speculum iuris canonici."*

In the rubric the work is wrongly attributed to Ivo of Chartres.

Rubric *Incipit summa concordantiarum canonum discordantium Ivonis Karnotensis*

Prologue *Prometheus in Caucasi montis cacumine*

Explicit *C. xi. q. iv. c. penultimo.*

Literature Kuttner, *Repertorium*, pp. 220–222.

Editions Peter of Blois, *Opusculum.*

CHAPTER 3

The Text of the Perpendiculum

Part I (*Summula de presumptionibus*)

⟨I.⟩ Incipit de presumptionibus

⟨1.⟩ Hic locus in iudiciis frequens est et pernecessarius, maxime quotiens super incerto disputatur. ⟨2.⟩ Incertum autem consistit circa factum extrinsecum vel intrinsecum, puta voluntatem vel consensum, et circa iuris vel cuiusque autentice scripture interpretationem. ⟨3.⟩ Item cum incertitudo circa extrinsecum vel intrinsecum factum consistit, aut est circa facti substantiam aut circa facti qualitatem. ⟨4.⟩ Cum constat de substantia operis, nunc singula ordine prosequamur.

⟨II. Circa extrinseci facti essentiam⟩

⟨1.⟩ Cum incertitudo versatur circa extrinseci facti essentiam, quid esse vel non esse, factum vel non factum, vel futurum esse vel non esse, presumitur ex locis his quos viii. sinodus ponit, D. lxxxi. c. In omnibus (D.81 c.26), puta:

⟨1.1.⟩ Ex persona agentis.

⟨1.2.⟩ Ex persona eius cum quo quid agitur.

I. *om. per totum* A Bs P1, Opus magistri Iohannis Facentini Ma ‖ Incipit *om.* C G L Mu1 Vp **1.** in iudiciis *post* frequens *tr.* Ba Bs Ma Mu1 P1, *post* est *tr.* Vp ‖ est *om.* C L ‖ pernecessarius] pernecessariis C ‖ quotiens] cum C ‖ incerto] incerte L ‖ disputatur] disputetur Ba **2.** autem *om.* Bs Mu1 P1 ‖ consistit] existit Ma ‖ circa[1]] eu (*cum abbr. signo*) *del. et corr., marg.* Mu1 ‖ extrinsecum *om.* Ba, intrinsecum Bs, extrinsecus L Mu2, intrinsecus P1 ‖ vel[1] *om.* Ba, et circa factum A Bs C G Ma Mu2 P1 Vp ‖ intrinsecum] extrinsecum Bs, intrinsecus L Mu2, e *praem. et exp.* Mu1, extrinsecus P1 ‖ puta] et circa *praem. et exp.* Bs ‖ voluntatem] voluntate A G Mu2 ‖ vel[2] *om.* Bs ‖ consensum] concessum A, consensu G Mu2 ‖ et] vel G, l. *exp.* circa Mu1 ‖ vel[3] *om.* L ‖ cuiusque] cuiuscumque A C Mu2, quocumque Ba ‖ scripture autentice *tr.* P1 ‖ interpretationem] interpretatione A, interemptionem Vp **3.** factum *post* circa[1] *tr.* Ba Bs Ma Mu1 P1 ‖ intrinsecum … extrinsecum *tr.* Ba Bs Ma L P1 ‖ extrinsecum] extrinsecus *corr.* G, extrinsecus Mu2 ‖ intrinsecum] extrinsecum Mu1, intrinsecus G Mu2 ‖ circa[2]] contra A ‖ facti[2] circa[3] *tr.* A ‖ circa[3] *om.* Bs Mu1 P1 ‖ qualitatem] voluntatem Mu2, substantiam *praem. et exp.* Vb **4.** Cum] vel P1 ‖ operis] corporis G, coeperis Mu2 ‖ singula ordine] de singulis L ‖ prosequamur ordine *tr.* Mu1 **II.1.** Primus modus *praem. marg.* G ‖ Cum] Ubi Bs Mu1 P1 ‖ versatur] versetur Ba ‖ extrinseci *om.* A Ba Bs C G L Ma Mu1 P1 Vp ‖ essentiam] esse *praem. et exp.* G ‖ quid] de Ma, quod Vp ‖ esse] esset L ‖ vel[1] non esse *om.* L ‖ vel[2] non factum *om.* Bs (*homoiotel.*) P1 ‖ vel[3] *om.* Bs C L Mu2 ‖ futurum] futurarum Vp ‖ his locis *tr.* A Ba Bs C G L Ma Mu1 Mu2 P1 Vp ‖ viii.] ix. Mu1 ‖ sinodus] sidnodus *cum* d[1] *exp.* P1 ‖ ponit *om.* A Ba Bs C G L P1 Vp, † Ma, distinxit (*post* omnibus *tr.* Mu2) Mu1 Mu2 ‖ c.—puta *om.* C L **1.2.** eius *om.* Ba ‖ quo *om.* L

 | DOI:10.1163/9789004713239_009

⟨I.⟩ Here begins [the summula] on presumptions

⟨1.⟩ The topic[1] under discussion recurs often, and it is very necessary during trials, especially whenever we dispute about uncertainties. ⟨2.⟩ An uncertainty can be about an extrinsic or intrinsic fact (for example, will or consent), and about the interpretation of the law or of any authentic document. ⟨3.⟩ Furthermore, when an uncertainty is about an extrinsic or intrinsic fact, it may be either about the substance of the fact or about its quality. ⟨4.⟩ Now we set out in order, one by one, the cases where the uncertainty depends upon the substance of a deed.

⟨II. On the essence of an extrinsic fact⟩

⟨1.⟩ When the uncertainty concerns the essence of an extrinsic fact (what is or what is not, what happened or what did not happen, or what will be or what will not be), one should presume from the topics established by the eighth synod (D.81 c.26), namely:

⟨1.1.⟩ From the person taking action.

⟨1.2.⟩ From the person in relation to whom action is taken.

1 See Stump, "Topics," p. 273: "'Topic' is the infelicitous but by now standard translation for the Latin technical term '*locus*,' designating a logical concept variously understood throughout ancient and medieval philosophy."

⟨1.3.⟩ Ex tempore.
⟨1.4.⟩ Ex loco.
⟨1.5.⟩ Ex modo agendi.
⟨1.6.⟩ Ex frequentia.
⟨1.7.⟩ Ex societate vel solitudine.
⟨1.8.⟩ Ex precedenti conversatione.
⟨1.9.⟩ Ex eo quod solet vulgo fieri.
⟨1.10.⟩ Ex etate.
⟨1.11.⟩ Ex necessitudine.
⟨1.12.⟩ Ex eo quod respondere vel innocentiam suam quis purgare subterfugit.
⟨1.13.⟩ Ex defectu indiciorum, expedientia pretermissa intelliguntur.
⟨1.14.⟩ Ex fama omnium communi.

⟨2.⟩ Ex persona agentis presumitur pro aliquo vel contra aliquem, ut:
⟨2.1.⟩ D. lxxxi. In omnibus (D.81 c.26) "certus quis."
⟨2.2.⟩ C. xii. q. i. c. i. (C.12 q.1 c.1) "probatissimo seniori."
⟨2.3.⟩ D. lxviii. Presbiteri quos (D.68 c.2) "et dubium est."
⟨2.4.⟩ C. xii. q. i. Sint manifeste (C.12 q.1 c.21) "ne sub occasione."
⟨2.5.⟩ C. xviii. q. ii. Diffinimus (C.18 q.2 c.21) "suscipiat abbatissa."
⟨2.6.⟩ C. eadem. q. eadem In decima (C.18 q.2 c.24) "patres spirituales."

1.7. *om. per totum* Bs P1 ‖ solitudine] ex *praem.* Ba, sollicitudine Mu1 **1.8.** *om. per totum* Bs P1 **1.9.** *om. per totum* Bs P1 ‖ vulgo solet *tr.* L ‖ solet] soli Ba **1.10.** *om. per totum* Bs P1 **1.11.** necessitudine] necessitate L **1.12.** quod] quid *praem.* P1 ‖ respondere] reddere C ‖ innocentiam] ignorantiam Mu2 ‖ suam *ante* innocentiam *tr.* C, *rep.* Vb, sua Vp ‖ quis] quid C, ante subterfugit *tr.* Vp ‖ purgare *post* vel *tr.* C, expurgare Vp ‖ subterfugit] subterfuit A, subterfugio C **1.13** intelliguntur] intelligentur *cum* e *exp. et corr.* Mu2 **1.14.** *post* § 2 *tr.* L ‖ Ex] E Vp ‖ omnium *om.* A C G P1 ‖ communi *om.* A C, pro quolibet contra Vp **2.** *om. per totum* Bs ‖ presumitur—ut *om.* Ma ‖ pro aliquo] reliquo Ba, id Vp ‖ aliquo] aliquio A, alioquo C ‖ vel *om.* Vp ‖ aliquem *om.* A Ba C G L Mu1 Mu2 P1 Vp ‖ ut] ubi A, *om.* G L Mu1 Mu2 P1 **2.1.** D.] quia (arg. Vp) pro et contra *praem.* L Vp, ut *praem.* Mu2 ‖ In] c. *praem.* Bs Ma P1 ‖ certus] ubi dicitur *praem.* Mu2 **2.2.** C.] Q. pro D. L, ut *praem.* Mu2, arg. pro *praem.* Vp ‖ xii.] xx. C ‖ c. i. *om.* C, Omnis etas Ma Mu2 ‖ probatissimo] proba primo A, pro baptismo L Vp, ubi dicitur *praem.* Mu2 ‖ seniori *om.* Ma **2.3.** D.] Q. (arg. Vp) pro *praem.* L Vp, ut *praem.* Mu2 ‖ lxviii.] lxvii. Vp ‖ Presbiteri] c. *praem.* Bs Ma ‖ quos] reperisti *add.* Mu2 ‖ et] ubi dicitur *praem.* Mu2, ubi *praem.* Vb **2.4.** C.] C. xx. *praem.* Bs, Q. (arg. Vp) pro *praem.* L Vp, ut *praem.* Mu2 ‖ xii.] xxii. L ‖ Sint] Sunt C ‖ ne] nec Fr, ubi dicitur *praem.* Mu2 ‖ sub occasione] † Vb **2.5.** C.] arg. (Q. et L) pro et contra *praem.* L Vp, ut *praem.* Mu2 ‖ Diffinimus] c. *praem.* Bs Mu1 P1 ‖ Diffinimus—abbatissa] † Vb ‖ suscipiat] ubi dicitur *praem.* Mu2 ‖ abbatissa *om.* L **2.6.** C.] et (arg. Vp) pro *praem.* L Vp, ut *praem.* Mu2 ‖ In] c. *praem.* Bs P1 ‖ In decima] ı⟩n⟨ udentiam Mu1 ‖ Undecima *Mu2* ‖ decima] cma *cum abbr. signo* L ‖ patres spirituales] † Vb ‖ patres] ubi dicitur *praem.* Mu2 ‖ spirituales *om.* Mu1

⟨1.3.⟩ From the time.
⟨1.4.⟩ From the place.
⟨1.5.⟩ From the course of action.
⟨1.6.⟩ From the frequency.
⟨1.7.⟩ From whether there is a group of people or an individual.
⟨1.8.⟩ From previous dealings.
⟨1.9.⟩ From what usually happens in practice.
⟨1.10.⟩ From the age.
⟨1.11.⟩ From a close relationship.
⟨1.12.⟩ From the case where somebody avoids answering in court or vindicating his innocence.
⟨1.13.⟩ From the lack of clues, one can consider that some necessary things have been omitted.
⟨1.14.⟩ From the common repute among everyone.

⟨2.⟩ From the person taking action, one should presume for someone or against someone, as in:
⟨2.1.⟩ D.81 c.26.
⟨2.2.⟩ C.12 q.1 c.1.
⟨2.3.⟩ D.68 c.2.
⟨2.4.⟩ C.12 q.1 c.21.
⟨2.5.⟩ C.18 q.2 c.21.
⟨2.6.⟩ C.18 q.2 c.24.

⟨2.7.⟩ ut C. viii. q. iii. Talia (C.8 q.3 c.1).
⟨2.8.⟩ C. xxxi. q. ii. Lotarius (C.31 q.2 c.4) “metu unius hominis.”

⟨3.⟩ Ex persona eius cum quo quid agitur.
⟨3.1.⟩ D. lxxxi. In omnibus (D.81 c.26) “certis personis.”
⟨3.2.⟩ C. xviii. q. ii. In decima (C.18 q.2 c.24) “extra eam, que preest.”
⟨3.3.⟩ C. eadem q. eadem Perniciosam (C.18 q.2 c.25) “minus religiosos.”
⟨3.4.⟩ In psalmo: “Cum sancto sanctus eris … et cum perverso perverteris” (Ps. 17:26–27).
⟨3.5.⟩ In parabolis: “Noli esse assiduus cum homine iracundo, … ne forte discas semitas eius, et sumas scandalum anime tue” (Prov 22:24–25).
⟨3.6.⟩ C. iii. q. v. De accusatoribus (C.3 q.5 c.3) “vel qui cum inimicis morantur.”
⟨3.7.⟩ C. ii. q. vii. Cum pastoris (C.2 q.7 c.58) “tales habeat testes” et c. Pervenit (C.2 q.7 c.59) “sic vice corrigere.”

2.7. *om. per totum* A Ba C L Ma Mu1 Vb Vp ‖ ut *om.* G **2.8.** *om. per totum* A Ba C L Ma Mu1 Vb Vp ‖ C.] ut *praem.* Mu2, *om.* P1 ‖ ii.] ultima G ‖ metu] ubi dicitur *praem.* Mu2 ‖ hominis *om.* P1 *add.* G Mu2 P1 **3.** *om. per totum* Bs ‖ Ex persona eius] *del. in nigro et rescripsit in rubro Mu1* ‖ quid *om.* P1 Vb ‖ agitur] agetur A, presumitur pro aliquo *add.* Mu1 **3.1.** D.] Q. (arg. Vp) pro et contra *praem.* L Vp, ut *praem.* Mu2 ‖ lxxxi.] lxxiii. *cum* ii. *exp.* Vp ‖ In] c. *praem.* Bs Ma ‖ personis certis *tr.* Vp ‖ certis] ex *praem.* A, cunctis C, et *praem.* G L, ubi dicitur et *praem.* Mu2 **3.2.** *om. per totum* G ‖ C.] arg. (Q. et L) pro contra *praem.* L Vp, *om.* Mu1, ut *praem.* Mu2 ‖ xviii.] xix. Ba Mu1, viii. Vb ‖ In decima] Undecima Mu2 ‖ In] c. *praem.* Bs P1, ubi Vb ‖ extra—preest *om.* L, † Vb ‖ extra] ubi dicitur *praem.* Mu2 ‖ eam] ea C, *om.* Vp ‖ que] quod Ma ‖ preest] potest Mu1 **3.3.** C.] Q. et pro contra *praem.* L, ut *praem.* Mu2, arg. pro et contra *praem.* Vp ‖ eadem … eadem] xviii. … ii. G ‖ Perniciosam—religiosos *om.* Bs ‖ Perniciosam] c. *praem.* P1 ‖ minus] ubi dicitur *praem.* Mu2 ‖ religiosos] † Vb, religiosis Vp **3.4.** In] ut *praem.* Mu2 ‖ psalmo] spalmo Mu1 ‖ et] cum viro innocente innocens eris *add.* P1 ‖ cum perverso] † Vb ‖ perverteris] perversus eris P1 **3.5.** In] ut *praem.* Mu2 ‖ assiduus *post* iracundo *tr.* G Mu2, iracundus *praem. et exp.* Vb ‖ iracundo homine *tr.* P1 ‖ sumas] suma A **3.6.** C.] contra *praem.* L, arg. contra *praem.* Vp, ut *praem.* Mu2 ‖ v.] i. Ba ‖ De] c. Mu1, *om.* Mu2 ‖ accusatoribus] accusationibus G Vp ‖ vel qui *om.* Ma ‖ vel] ubi dicitur *praem.* Mu2 ‖ qui cum] cum qui *tr.* A, quicumque Ba ‖ qui *om.* L, quod Vp ‖ cum *interl.* Vp ‖ inimicis] inimico G Mu2 ‖ morantur *om.* Ma **3.7.** *om. per totum* A C G Mu2 ‖ C.] pro et contra *praem.* L, arg. pro et contra *praem.* Vp ‖ Cum] c. *praem.* Mu1 P1 ‖ pastoris tales] pastorales Ba ‖ pastoris] pastor L pastoralis P1 ‖ habeat] habeant Mu1 ‖ testes] arg. pro et contra *praem.* Vp ‖ et c.] C. eadem q. eadem Ma, i. Vp ‖ c. *om.* Ba L ‖ Pervenit] ad nos *add.* Ba L Vp, ad *add.* Ma ‖ sic vice corrigere] s⟩c⟨i⟩licet⟨ ulcer⟩i⟨or L ‖ corrigere] carrigere Vp

⟨2.7.⟩ C.8 q.3 c.1.
⟨2.8.⟩ C.31 q.2 c.4.

⟨3.⟩ From the person in relation to whom action is taken.
⟨3.1.⟩ D.81 c.26.
⟨3.2.⟩ C.18 q.2 c.24.
⟨3.3.⟩ C.18 q.2 c.25.
⟨3.4.⟩ In the psalm: "With the holy, thou wilt be holy … and with the perverse thou wilt be perverted" (Ps 17:26–27).
⟨3.5.⟩ In the parable: "Be not a friend to an angry man … lest perhaps thou learn his ways, and take scandal to thy soul" (Prov 22:24–25).
⟨3.6.⟩ C.3 q.5 c.3.
⟨3.7.⟩ C.2 q.7 c.58 and C.2 q.7 c.59.

⟨3.8.⟩ C. xii. q. i. Necessaria (C.12 q.1 c.3) in fine.
⟨3.9.⟩ In evangelio: "qui male agit, odit lucem" (Jn 3:20).

⟨4.⟩ Ex tempore.
⟨4.1.⟩ D. lxxxi. In omnibus (D.81 c.26) "certo tempore."
⟨4.2.⟩ C. i. q. i. Statuimus (C.1 q.1 c.106) "crisma accepturi dent."
⟨4.3.⟩ C. i. q. i. Emendari (C.1 q.1 c.104) "nummos in conca."
⟨4.4.⟩ C. xxvii. q. i. Neque viduas (C.27 q.1 c.3) "diuturna."
⟨4.5.⟩ C. viii. q. iii. c. i. et ii. (C.8 q.3 c.1 et 2).
⟨4.6.⟩ C. xxxi. q. i. Relatum (C.31 q.1 c.4) "vivente viro," "iuramentum."
⟨4.7.⟩ ut D. xlviii. c. i. (D.48 c.1) "nam et tempore opus est."
⟨4.8.⟩ C. de postulando, Quisquis vult (Cod. 4.6.6.).
⟨4.9.⟩ D. lxxxi. Episcopus (?), Non oportet (D.81 c.28).

⟨5.⟩ Ex loco.
⟨5.1.⟩ D. lxxxi. In omnibus (D.81 c.26) "certo loco" et c. Valet (D.81 c.9) "mutatur locus."

3.8. *om. per totum* A Ba C G Ma Mu2 P1 Vb, *post §4 tr.* L ‖ C.] pro et contra *praem.* L, arg. pro et contra *praem.* Vp **3.9.** *om. per totum* A Ba C G L Ma Mu1 Mu2 P1 Vp **4.** *om. per totum* Ba ‖ tempore] loco L, presumitur aliquit pro vel contra *add.* Mu1 **4.1.** D.] pro et contra *praem.* L, ut *praem.* Mu2, arg. pro et contra *praem.* Vp ‖ In] c. *praem.* Ma Mu1 P1 ‖ certo] ubi dicitur *praem.* Mu2 **4.2.** *post §4.3 tr.* Mu1 P1 ‖ C. i. q. i.] et c. Mu1, *om.* P1 ‖ C.] contra *praem.* L, ut *praem.* Mu2, arg. contra *praem.* Vp ‖ Statuimus] c. *praem.* P1 ‖ accepturi crisma *tr.* Mu1 P1 ‖ crisma] ubi dicitur *praem.* Mu2 ‖ dent] nichil *praem.* Mu2 **4.3.** C. i. q. i.] q. (ut *praem.* Mu2, arg. contra *praem.* Vp) eadem A C G Mu2 Vp, *om.* Ba, et C. L, C. eadem q. eadem Ma ‖ Emendari] c. *praem.* Mu1 P1, placuit *add.* Mu2, Emendati Vp ‖ nummos] ubi dicitur *praem.* Mu2 ‖ conca] concam Fr, concas *et* non mittant *add.* Mu2 **4.4.** C.] contra *praem.* L, arg. contra *praem.* Vp, ut *praem.* Mu2 ‖ xxvii.] xxvi. Ma ‖ i.] ii. P1 ‖ Neque] c. *praem.* P1, nunquam Vp ‖ viduas] inclinas P1 ‖ diuturna] divina C Vp, observatione *add.* Ma, ubi dicitur *praem. et* observatione *add.* Mu2 **4.5.** C.] pro et contra *praem.* L, arg. pro et contra *praem.* Vp, ut *praem.* Mu2 ‖ viii.] vii. Vb ‖ iii.] ii. Vb ‖ et ii. *om.* Vb **4.6.** C.] contra *praem.* L, ut *praem.* Mu2, arg. *praem.* Vp ‖ xxxi.] xxii. Ma ‖ Relatum] Relatura L ‖ c. *praem.* Mu1 P1 ‖ vivente] ubi dicitur *praem.* Mu2 ‖ viro] *ante* vivente *tr.* A, curo G ‖ iuramentum] dedisse *add.* Mu2, *om.* P1 **4.7.** *om. per totum* A Ba C L Ma Mu1 P1 Vb Vp ‖ xlviii.] lviii. G ‖ i.] Quoniam multa ubi dicitur *add.* Mu2 **4.8.** *om. per totum* A Ba C L Ma Mu1 Mu2 P1 Vb Vp ‖ de postulando *male* postulavi G **4.9.** *om. per totum* A Ba C L Ma Mu1 P1 Vb Vp ‖ D.] ut *praem.* Mu2 ‖ Episcopus] Episcopum G **5.** loco] tempore Ba, modo agendi L, presumitur aliquod pro aliquo *add.* Mu1 **5.1.** *post §5.2 tr.* Mu1 P1 ‖ D.] pro et contra C. *cum* C. *exp.* L, arg. pro et contra *praem.* Vp ‖ In] de Ba G, c. *praem.* Ma P1 ‖ omnibus] deterioribus Ba ‖ certo] ubi dicitur *praem.* Mu2 ‖ loco] in *praem.* Mu2 ‖ et—locus *om.* Mu2 ‖ c. *om.* Ma ‖ mutatur locus *om.* A Ba C G L Ma Mu1 P1 Vp

---

4. The rubric is erroneously reported at II, 5 instead of *Ex loco* Ba, the titles of the rubrics from II, 4 to II, 6 are wrongly advanced by one position L

⟨3.8.⟩ C.12 q.1 c.3 at the end.
⟨3.9.⟩ In the Gospel: "he that doth evil hateth the light" (Jn 3:20).

⟨4.⟩ From the time.
⟨4.1.⟩ D.81 c.26.
⟨4.2.⟩ C.1 q.1 c.106.
⟨4.3.⟩ C.1 q.1 c.104.
⟨4.4.⟩ C.27 q.1 c.3.
⟨4.5.⟩ C.8 q.3 c.1 and 2.
⟨4.6.⟩ C.31 q.1 c.4.
⟨4.7.⟩ D.48 c.1.
⟨4.8.⟩ Cod. 4.6.6.
⟨4.9.⟩ ?, D.81 c.28.

⟨5.⟩ From the place.
⟨5.1.⟩ D.81 c.26 and c.9.

⟨5.2.⟩ C. xviii. q. ii. Diffinimus (C.18 q.2 c.21) "non cubet."
⟨5.3.⟩ C. eadem q. eadem In decima (C.18 q.2 c.24) "usque ad vestibulum."
⟨5.4.⟩ C. eadem q. eadem Perniciosam (C.18 q.2 c.25) "privata domicilia," "abscondite."
⟨5.5.⟩ D. lvi. Presbiterorum (D.56 c.1) "in cenobiis;" B. ii. Ancillas (B.2 c.114).
⟨5.6.⟩ C. xxxiv. q. i. Non satis (C.34 q.1–2 c.3).
⟨5.7.⟩ D. lxxvii. Si quis (D.77 c.8).
⟨5.8.⟩ D. xxiv. Quando episcopus (D.24 c.5).
⟨5.9.⟩ B. lib. ii. Inhibendum (B.2 c.116) "longe a mansione."
⟨5.10.⟩ D. xvi. Quod dictus (D. 16 c.14).
⟨5.11.⟩ C. xii. q. ii. Qui humanis (C.12 q.2 c.24).

⟨6.⟩ Ex modo agendi.
⟨6.1.⟩ D. lxxxi. Clericus solus (D.81 c.20) "mandet aliquid secrete."
⟨6.2.⟩ C. xviii. q. ii. Diffinimus (C.18 q.2 c.21) "secreto ad collocutionem."

5.2. de presumptionibus *add.* Ma ‖ C. *om.* L, arg. contra *praem.* Vp ‖ Diffinimus] Diffinivimus G, c. *praem.* Mu1 P1 ‖ non] ubi dicitur *praem.* Mu2 ‖ cubet] iubet C, monachus *add.* Mu2 5.3. C. eadem q. eadem] C. xviii. Q. ii. Mu1 P1 ‖ C.] contra *praem.* L, arg. contra *praem.* Vp ‖ In decima] Undecima Mu2 ‖ In] c. *praem.* P1 ‖ usque] ubi L, ubi dicitur *praem.* Mu2, v. *praem.* Vb 5.4. C.] contra *praem.* L, arg. contra *praem.* Vb ‖ Perniciosam] Perniciosum L, c. *praem.* P1 ‖ privata] ubi dicitur *praem.* Mu2 ‖ abscondite] abscondi G, *marg. cum signo* Mu2 Vp 5.5. D.] et *praem.* Ba, contra L, arg. contra pro *praem.* Vp ‖ Presbiterorum] c. per *praem. cum* per *exp.* P1 ‖ in cenobiis *om.* Mu2 ‖ B.] d. A, contra L, D. Vb ‖ ii.] lib. *praem.* Ba Ma Mu1 Mu2, lii. L, x. *praem.* P1, d. iii. Vb ‖ Ancillas *om.* A, Ancillam Mu1 5.6. *om. per totum* A Ba C L Ma Mu1 P1 Vb Vp 5.7. *om. per totum* A Ba C L Ma Mu1 P1 Vb Vp 5.8. *om. per totum* A Ba C L Ma Mu1 P1 Vb Vp ‖ xxiv.] xxiii. Mu2 5.9. *om. per totum* A Ba C L Ma Mu1 P1 Vb Vp ‖ longe] ubi dicitur *praem.* Mu2 5.10. *om. per totum* A Ba C L Ma Mu1 P1 Vb Vp 5.11. *om. per totum* A Ba C L Ma Mu1 P1 Vb Vp ‖ Qui] Quod G 6. *§ 6–6.4 post § 7.5 tr.* Vp ‖ Ex modo agendi] Ex frequentia vel longa mora L, presumatur *add.* Mu1, -a. *praem. et* Ex mutatione status ut arg. causa vii. q. i. Hoc (C.7 q.1 c.45) "precepit" *add.* Vp 6.1. D.] contra *praem.* L, arg. contra *praem.* Vp ‖ Clericus] c. *praem.* Mu1 P1 ‖ solus *om.* Mu1 P1 ‖ mandet] ubi dicitur *praem.* Mu2, mandat *et ante* solus *tr.* Vp ‖ aliquid] aliquis A L ‖ secrete] secreto L 6.2. C.] contra *praem.* L, arg. contra *praem.* Vp ‖ xviii.] viii. L ‖ Diffinimus] c. *praem.* Mu1 P1 ‖ secreto] ubi dicitur *praem.* Mu2 ‖ ad *om.* Ma ‖ collocutionem] collationem L, locutionem Ma

---

5.2. Here follows the correct title of the work, placed here instead of the beginning Ma 6. The order of II, 6 and II, 7 is inverted and the letters -a. and -b. at the beginning of the lines indicate the right order of the rubrics Vp

⟨5.2.⟩ C.18 q.2 c.21.
⟨5.3.⟩ C.18 q.2 c.24.
⟨5.4.⟩ C.18 q.2 c.25.
⟨5.5.⟩ D.56 c.1, B. 2 c.114.
⟨5.6.⟩ C.34 q.1–2 c.3.
⟨5.7.⟩ D.77 c.8.
⟨5.8.⟩ D.24 c.5.
⟨5.9.⟩ B.2 c.116.
⟨5.10.⟩ D. 16 c.14.
⟨5.11.⟩ C.12 q.2 c.24.

⟨6.⟩ From the course of action.
⟨6.1.⟩ D.81 c.20.
⟨6.2.⟩ C.18 q.2 c.21.

⟨6.3.⟩ C. xxxiii. q. v. Notificasti (C.33 q.5 c.2) "extorsisse," "sine abbate."
⟨6.4.⟩ C. xxx. q. v. Aliter (C.30 q.5 c.1) "ita peracta," "aliter presumpta."

⟨7.⟩ Ex frequentia vel mora.
⟨7.1.⟩ D. lxxxi. Clericus solus (D.81 c.20) "frequenter intret."
⟨7.2.⟩ C. xviii. q. ii. Diffinimus (C.18 q.2 c.21) "per modica et in brevi."
⟨7.3.⟩ C. eadem q. eadem In decima (C.18 q.2 c.24) "frequenter," "brevis."
⟨7.4.⟩ D. xxxiv. Quorumdam (D.34 c.1) "immoderatam familiaritatem," "mala fama."
⟨7.5.⟩ C. xxxiii. q. ii. c. i. (D.2 de pen. c.1) "et rursum."

⟨8.⟩ Ex societate vel solitudine.
⟨8.1.⟩ D. lxxxi. In omnibus (D.81 c.26) "certe solum ad solam."
⟨8.2.⟩ D. eadem Clericus solus (D.81 c.20) et c. Clerici (D.81 c.32) "et hoc non soli."
⟨8.3.⟩ C. xviii. q. ii. Diffinimus (C.18 q.2 c.21) "in presentia abbatisse."
⟨8.4.⟩ C. eadem q. eadem In decima (C.18 q.2 c.24) "cum ea sola."

6.3. *post § 6.4 tr.* A Ba C G L Ma Mu1 Mu2 Vp ‖ C.] contra *praem.* L ‖ Notificasti] c. *praem.* Mu1 P1 ‖ extorsisse] exturosisse A, excessis L, ubi dicitur *praem.* Mu2 ‖ sine] me A L ‖ abbate] iii. *add.* L **6.4.** *om. per totum* P1 ‖ C.] contra *praem.* L, arg. contra *praem.* Vp ‖ Aliter *om.* L, Nec *praem.* Mu1 ‖ ita] tamen A, ubi dicitur *praem.* Mu2 **7.** *del. et add.* vaca *interl.* Vp ‖ Ex] -b. *praem.* Vp ‖ vel *om.* Ma ‖ mora] longa *praem.* (presumitur aliquid *add.* Mu1) A Ba C L Mu1 Mu2 P1 Vp, *om.* Ma **7.1.** D.] contra *praem.* L, † Vb, arg. contra *praem.* Vp ‖ Clericus] c. *praem.* Mu1 ‖ frequenter] ubi dicitur *praem.* Mu2 ‖ intret *om.* Ba **7.2.** C.] pro *praem.* L, † Vb, arg. pro *praem.* Vp ‖ Diffinimus *om.* Mu2, c. *praem.* P1 ‖ et *om.* Ma ‖ in *om.* Vp ‖ brevi] *cum signo add.* G **7.3.** C.] r. *praem.* L, † Vb, arg. pro *praem.* Vp ‖ In decima *add. marg. cum signo* G ‖ In *om.* L, ut Vb ‖ frequenter *om.* L, ubi dicitur *praem.* Mu2 ‖ brevis] et *praem.* Ba, et in *praem. male* Ma, brevi *cum* et in *praem. et* per modica *add.* (*homoiotel.*) L **7.4.** D.] contra *praem.* L, † Vb, arg. contra *praem.* Vp ‖ xxxiv.] xxxiii. G Mu2, † Vb ‖ Quorumdam] Quarumdam L ‖ immoderatam] immoderata G, ubi dicitur *praem.* Mu2 ‖ familiaritatem] familiaritate G ‖ mala fama] *interl.* Mu2 **7.5** *om. per totum* A Ba C L Ma Mu1 P1 Vb Vp ‖ q.] di. G **8.** vel] et Mu2 ‖ solitudine] sollicitudine sepe presumitur aliquod Mu1, precedenti conversatione P1 **8.1.** D.] † Vb, arg. contra *praem.* Vp ‖ lxxxi.] † Vb ‖ In] c. *praem.* Mu1 P1 ‖ certe *om.* Mu2 ‖ solum] si solus Mu1, ubi dicitur *praem.* Mu2, solus P1 ‖ ad] et *praem.* Ma ‖ solam] solum A **8.2.** D. eadem] † Vb ‖ D.] pro contra *praem.* L, arg. pro et contra *praem.* Vp ‖ Clericus] c. *praem.* Mu1 P1 ‖ et] D. eadem Ma ‖ c. *om.* L Ma ‖ et—soli *om.* A Ba C G L Mu1 Mu2 P1 Vp ‖ et hoc *om.* Ma **8.3.** C.] pro *praem.* L, arg. pro et contra *praem.* Vp ‖ xviii.] viii. L ‖ q. ii. *om.* A Ba C G P1 Vp ‖ Diffinimus] c. *praem.* Mu1 P1 ‖ in] ubi dicitur *praem.* Mu2 ‖ presentia] *cum signo add.* G ‖ abbatisse] *interl.* Vb **8.4.** C.] contra *praem.* L, arg. pro et contra *praem.* Vp ‖ In] c. *praem.* Mu1 P1 ‖ cum] ubi dicitur *praem.* Mu2

⟨6.3.⟩ C.33 q.5 c.2.
⟨6.4.⟩ C.30 q.5 c.1.

⟨7.⟩ From the frequency or from delay.
⟨7.1.⟩ D.81 c.20.
⟨7.2.⟩ C.18 q.2 c.21.
⟨7.3.⟩ C.18 q.2 c.24.
⟨7.4.⟩ D.34 c.1.
⟨7.5.⟩ D.2 de pen. c.1.

⟨8.⟩ From whether there is a group of people or an individual.
⟨8.1.⟩ D.81 c.26.
⟨8.2.⟩ D.81 c.20 and c.32.
⟨8.3.⟩ C.18 q.2 c.21.
⟨8.4.⟩ C.18 q.2 c.24.

⟨8.5.⟩ C. vii. q. i. Qualiter (C.7 q.1 c.13) "fidelium relatione."
⟨8.6.⟩ C. ii. q. vii. Pervenit (C.2 q.7 c.59).
⟨8.7.⟩ D. xlvii. Necesse (D.47 c.8).

⟨9.⟩ Ex precedenti vel sequenti conversatione et opere.
⟨9.1.⟩ C. i. q. ultima c. Tali (C.1 q.7 c.17) "evidens."
⟨9.2.⟩ C. ii. q. i. Inprimis (C.2 q.1 c.7) "si vita vel opinio eius," in fine capituli.
⟨9.3.⟩ C. eadem q. vii. Alieni (C.2 q.7 c.23) et c. Non potest (C.2 q.7 c.24).
⟨9.4.⟩ C. xi. q. i. Si qui clericorum (C.11 q.1 c.25) "nullis excusationibus presumptio."
⟨9.5.⟩ C. xii. q. ii. Monemus (C.12 q.2 c.18) in fine capituli.
⟨9.6.⟩ D. xxvii. Quod interrogasti (D.27 c.6).
⟨9.7.⟩ D. xxviii. Quia sunt culpe (D.28 c.10) "postea," "prava" et fere per totum capitulum.
⟨9.8.⟩ D. eadem Priusquam (D.28 c.4).
⟨9.9.⟩ D. lxi. Miramur (D.61 c.5), "prior vita testimonium preberet" (p. § 4), et in eodem capitulo "notari ambitus solent" (p. § 5), et c. Episcopum (D.61 c.6) "multo."

8.5. *om. per totum* A Ba C G Ma Mu1 Mu2 P1 Vb ‖ C.] pro *praem.* L, arg. contra *praem.* Vp ‖ relatione] arg. pro et contra *add.* Vp **8.6.** *om. per totum* A Ba C L Ma Mu1 P1 Vb Vp **8.7.** *om. per totum* A Ba C L Ma Mu1 P1 Vb Vp ‖ Necesse] est etiam *add.* Mu2 **9.** *om. per totum* P1 ‖ vel sequenti *om.* L Ma ‖ et opere *om.* Ma Vp **9.1.** C.] pro *praem.* L, arg. pro *praem.* Vp ‖ i.] v. L ‖ ultima] i. L, vii. Mu1 P1 ‖ c. *om.* C L Ma, *interl.* Vb ‖ evidens] meritorum *add.* Ma, ubi dicitur *praem.* Mu2 **9.2.** C.] pro *praem.* L, arg. pro *praem.* Vp ‖ In] c. *praem.* Mu2 ‖ si—vel *om.* Mu2 ‖ opinio eius] eius opinio *tr.* Mu1, cuius opinio P1, cuiusve opinionis Mu2 ‖ in fine capituli *om.* A Ba C G L Ma Mu1 Mu2 P1 Vp **9.3.** C.] contra *praem.* L, arg. contra *praem.* Vp ‖ eadem *om.* C L, iii. Ma ‖ vii.] iv. Ma, ii. Vp ‖ Alieni] suscipere non possumus *add.* Ma, c. *praem.* Mu1 P1 ‖ et—potest *om.* Ma ‖ c. *om.* L **9.4.** C.] contra *praem.* L, arg. contra *praem.* Vp ‖ xi.] ii. Mu1 ‖ Si] c. *praem.* Mu1 P1 ‖ qui] quod Ma ‖ clericorum] clericum C ‖ nullis—presumptio *om.* A Ba C G L Ma Mu1 Mu2 P1 Vp **9.5.** C.] contra *praem.* L, arg. contra *praem.* Vp ‖ Monemus] c. *praem.* Mu1 **9.6.** *om. per totum* P1 ‖ D.] contra *praem.* L, C. Vb, arg. pro et contra *praem.* Vp ‖ xxvii.] q. rf. *add.* Vb, xxviii. Vp ‖ Quod] Qui C ‖ interrogasti] interrgogasti *cum* g[1] *exp.* A **9.7.** D.] contra *praem.* L, arg. pro *praem.* Vp ‖ xxviii.] xxix. A ‖ Quia] que G, c. *praem.* P1 ‖ culpe] depe. G ‖ postea—capitulum *om.* A Ba C G L Ma Mu1 Mu2 P1 Vp **9.8.** *om. per totum* A Ba C L Ma Mu1 P1 Vb Vp **9.9.** *om. per totum* A C ‖ D.] contra *praem.* L, arg. pro et contra *praem.* Vp ‖ Miramur] c. *praem.* Mu1 P1 ‖ prior vita] † L ‖ testimonium—capitulo *om.* Ma ‖ testimonium *om.* Ba L Vp, *ante* prior *tr.* (*et* ubi dicitur *praem.* Mu2) G Mu2 ‖ preberet *om.* G, prebet L Mu1 ‖ et—multo *om.* G Mu2 ‖ et—solent *om.* Vp ‖ in eodem capitulo *om.* Ba L ‖ ambitus—multo] a pre actus L ‖ solent] solet Ba L Mu1 P1 Vb, *om.* Ma ‖ et c. *om.* Ba, D. (arg. contra *praem.* Vp) eadem Ma Vp ‖ Episcopum] Episcoporum Ba Ma ‖ multo] ante *add.* Ba P1 Vp, ante nota probabilisque *add.* Ma, autem *add. male* Mu1

⟨8.5.⟩ C.7 1. 1 c.13.
⟨8.6.⟩ C.2 q.7 c.59.
⟨8.7.⟩ D.47 c.8.

⟨9.⟩ From previous or subsequent dealings and actions.
⟨9.1.⟩ C.1 q.7 c.17.
⟨9.2.⟩ C.2 q.1 c.7, at the end of the chapter.
⟨9.3.⟩ C.2 q.7 c.23 and c.24.
⟨9.4.⟩ C.11 q.1 c.25.
⟨9.5.⟩ C 12 q.2 c.18 at the end of the chapter.
⟨9.6.⟩ D.27 c.6.
⟨9.7.⟩ D.28 c.10 and generally through all the chapter.
⟨9.8.⟩ D.28 c.4.
⟨9.9.⟩ D.61 c.5 p. § 4 and in the same chapter p. § 5, and c.6.

⟨9.10.⟩ Arg. contra: C. viii. q. i. Hoc (C.7 q.1 c.45?) ergo ipse.

⟨9.11.⟩ D. l. Presbiteros qui immolaverunt (D.50 c.32) "si precedens eorum vita probet."

⟨9.12.⟩ C. i. q. i. Si qui a simoniacis (C.1 q.1 c.108) "si tamen eos laudabilis vita commendat."

⟨9.13.⟩ B ii. Inhibendum (B.2 c.116) "frequenter perpetratum reperitur."

⟨10.⟩ Ex eo quod fieri solet.

⟨10.1.⟩ D. xcviii. Transmarinos (D.98 c.2) "solent evenire."

⟨10.2.⟩ C. xvi. q. ii. Visis (C.16 q.2 c.1) "humani moris est."

⟨10.3.⟩ D. xcviii. Affros (D.98 c.3) "sepe probati sunt."

⟨10.4.⟩ D. xxviii. De Siracusane (D.28 c.13) "per quos ecclesiastica."

⟨10.5.⟩ C. viii. q. i. Si ergo (C.8 q.1 c.16) "que sepe."

⟨10.6.⟩ C. xvi. q. ii. c. i. (C.16 q.2 c.1) "humani."

⟨10.7.⟩ D. lxxix. Si transitus (D.79 c.10) "ut solet."

⟨10.8.⟩ D. lxiii. c. Nosse (D.63 c.12) "sepe contingere solet."

⟨10.9.⟩ C. xv. q. i. Illud (C.15 q.1 c.2) "iniuriam pati solent."

9.10. *om. per totum* A Ba C G L Ma Mu1 Mu2 P1 Vb 9.11. *om. per totum* A Ba C L Ma Mu1 P1 Vb Vp ‖ si] ubi dicitur *praem.* Mu2 ‖ probet] pmi *cum abbr. signo et ante* eorum *tr.* G 9.12. *om. per totum* A Ba C L Ma Mu1 P1 Vb Vp ‖ simoniacis] simonia non si G ‖ si] ubi dicitur *praem.* Mu2 9.13. *post §10 tr.* A C G L Ma Mu1 Mu2 Vp ‖ B.] arg. contra *praem.* Vp ‖ ii.] i. L, lib. *praem.* Ma Mu1 Mu2 ‖ Inhibendum] c. *praem.* P1 ‖ frequenter] ubi dicitur *praem.* Mu2 ‖ reperitur *om.* Ma 10. *om. per totum* Ba ‖ solet *post* quod *tr.* Ma Mu1 P1 ‖ fieri] vulgo *praem.* (*et* p⟩lerumque⟨ a⟩ccidit⟨ (?) *add. Mu1*) Ma Mu1 P1 10.1. D.] contra *praem.* L, arg. contra *praem.* Vp ‖ xcviii.] xxviii. Mu1 ‖ Transmarinos] c. *praem.* Mu1 P1 ‖ solent] solet (ubi dicitur *praem.* Mu2) G L Mu2 Vb Vp 10.2. C.] contra *praem.* L, arg. contra *praem.* Vp ‖ Visis] litteris *add.* Ma, c. i. Mu1 P1 ‖ humani] ubi dicitur *praem.* Mu2 ‖ est *om.* Ba Ma P1, illum *add.* Mu1 10.3. D.] et capitulis *praem.* Mu1, contra *praem.* L, arg. contra *praem.* Vp ‖ xcviii.] xviii. A ‖ Affros] passim *add.* Ma, c. *praem.* Mu1 P1 ‖ sepe] ubi dicitur *praem.* Mu2 10.4. *post §10.7 tr.* Ba Ma Vp ‖ D.] contra *praem.* L ‖ De] c. *praem.* P1 ‖ Siracusane] Siracusioane *cum* io *exp.* A ‖ per] ubi dicitur *praem.* Mu2 ‖ quos] quas G ‖ ecclesiastica] solet *add.* A Ba C G Mu1 Mu2 Vp soli *add. male* L, solcet P1 10.5. *om. per totum* Ba C G Ma Mu1 Mu2 P1 Vp ‖ C.] contra *marg. praem.* L ‖ que sepe] "talis," "moveri (muneri L) solet" A L 10.6. *om. per totum* A Ba C G L Ma Mu1 Mu2 P1 Vp 10.7. *om. per totum* A C G Mu2 ‖ D.] contra *marg. praem.* L, arg. contra *praem.* Vp ‖ lxxix.] lxxx. L, lxxviii. P1 ‖ Si] c. *praem.* Mu1 P1 ‖ transitus] transatus L ‖ solet] fieri *add.* Ma 10.8 *om. per totum* A Ba C G L Ma Mu2 Vb Vp 10.9. *om. per totum* A Ba C G L Ma Mu2 Vp ‖ solent] solet Mu1 Vb

---

10. The rubric is wrongly placed at 11, 11, instead of *Ex etate* Ba

⟨9.10.⟩ Argument against: C.7 q.1 c.45?
⟨9.11.⟩ D.50 c.32.
⟨9.12.⟩ C.1 q.1 c.108.
⟨9.13.⟩ B. 2 c.116.

⟨10.⟩ From what usually happens in practice.
⟨10.1.⟩ D.98 c.2.
⟨10.2.⟩ C.16 q.2 c.1.
⟨10.3.⟩ D.98 c.3.
⟨10.4.⟩ D.28 c.13.
⟨10.5.⟩ C.8 q.1 c.16.
⟨10.6.⟩ C.16 q.2 c.1.
⟨10.7.⟩ D.79 c.10.
⟨10.8.⟩ D.63 c.12.
⟨10.9.⟩ C.15 q.1 c.2.

⟨11.⟩ Ex etate.

⟨11.1.⟩ D. xxxiv. Fraternitatis (D.34 c.7) "et etas istius."

⟨11.2.⟩ C. xii. q. i. Omnis etas (C.12 q.1 c.1).

⟨11.3.⟩ D. l. Penitentes (D.50 c.63) "iuvenibus," "non facile."

⟨11.4.⟩ C. xxvii. q. i. Viduas (C.27 q.1 c.2) "perfectioris etatis."

⟨11.5.⟩ D. lxxxvi. Tanta nequitia (D.86 c.24).

⟨11.6.⟩ D. xx. c. ultimo (D.20 c.3) "quod a pluribus senioribus."

⟨11.7.⟩ C. xx. q. i. Iuvenculas (C.20 q.1 c.12).

⟨11.8.⟩ C. xviii. q. ii. Diffinimus (C.18 q.2 c.21) "cum quadam vetula."

⟨11.9.⟩ D. xxxiv. Quorumdam (D.34 c.1) "qui et iuvenis."

⟨11.10.⟩ C. xxxiii. q. ii. In adolescentia (C.33 q.2 c.14) et c. Antiqui (C.33 q.2 c.19).

⟨11.11.⟩ C. xxvi. q. vii. Tempora (C.26 q.7 c.2) "etatis senilis intuitum."

⟨11.12.⟩ D. lxxvii. Episcopus (D.77 c.6) "sane si coniugati iuvenes."

⟨11.13.⟩ D. lxxxvi. Si quid (D.86 c.23) "senioribus."

⟨11.14.⟩ C. xxxv. q. vi. Notificamus (C.35 q.6 c.3) "antiquioribus."

---

11. *om. per totum* P1 ‖ etate] eo quod solet vulgo fieri Ba **11.1.** *post § 10.7 tr.* L ‖ D.] pro *marg. praem.* L, arg. pro *praem.* Vp ‖ xxxiv.] xxxiii. L ‖ Fraternitatis] Fraternitati A Ba G L Vb, c. Fraternitas P1 ‖ et] ubi dicitur *praem.* Mu2 ‖ etas] cetas *cum* c *exp.* G ‖ istius *om.* A Ba C G L Mu1 P1 Vp, illius Ma, illius de quo agitur Mu2 **11.2.** C.] contra *marg. praem.* L, arg. contra *praem.* Vp ‖ xii.] xiii. A, ii. Mu2 ‖ q. i. Omnis etas] c. i. Mu1 P1 ‖ etas] in malum Ma **11.3.** *post § 11.10 tr.* Mu1 P1, *post § 11.14 tr.* G Mu2, *om. per totum* A Ba C L Ma Vp ‖ Penitentes] c. *praem.* Mu1 P1 ‖ iuvenibus non facile] "propter (ubi dicitur *praem.* Mu2) etatis fragilitatem" (fragilitatis Mu2) G Mu2 **11.4.** *om. per totum* A Ba C L Ma Mu1 P1 Vb Vp ‖ Viduas] c. ii. G ‖ perfectioris] ubi dicitur *praem.* Mu2 **11.5.** *om. per totum* A Ba C L Ma Mu1 P1 Vb Vp **11.6.** *post § 11.10 tr.* Mu1 P1, *om. per totum* A Ba C G L Ma Mu2 Vp ‖ xx.] xxi. Mu1, xv. P1 ‖ quod a] quia P1 ‖ senioribus] et *praem. male* Mu1 **11.7.** C.] contra *marg. praem.* L, arg. contra *praem.* Vp ‖ xx.] xxi. L ‖ q. i. *om.* L, c. Vp ‖ Iuvenculas] In vinculas L, fieri abbatissas "prohibemus" *add.* Mu2, c. *praem.* P1 **11.8.** C.] contra *marg. praem.* L, *om.* Mu1, arg. pro *praem.* Vp ‖ q. ii.] di. *exp.* q. i. L ‖ Diffinimus] c. *praem.* P1 ‖ cum *om.* G Mu2 ‖ quadam] quedam (ubi dicitur *praem.* Mu2) G Mu2 ‖ vetula] auctoritate L **11.9.** *om. per totum* P1 ‖ D.] contra *marg. et praem.* L, arg. contra *praem.* Vp ‖ xxxiv.] xxxiii. L ‖ Quorumdam] c. *praem. et* relatione *add.* Mu1 ‖ qui] ubi dicitur *praem.* Mu2 ‖ iuvenis] iuventus L, esse dicitur *add.* Mu2 **11.10.** C.] D. P1, arg. pro *praem.* Vp ‖ xxxiii.] iii. A ‖ q.] c. L ‖ In] etiam A, c. *praem.* P1 ‖ et—Antiqui *om.* A, † Ba ‖ et c.] q. eadem Ma ‖ c. *om.* C L Vp, cum G ‖ Antiqui] Ante quod Vb **11.11.** *om. per totum* A Ba C L Ma Mu1 P1 Vb Vp ‖ etatis] ubi dicitur *praem.* Mu2 **11.12.** *om. per totum* A Ba C L Ma Mu1 P1 Vb Vp ‖ sane] ubi dicitur *praem.* Mu2 ‖ si *om.* G **11.13.** *om. per totum* A Ba C G L Ma Mu2 Vp ‖ lxxxvi.] xxxxvi. *cum* x.[1] *corr.* l Mu1 ‖ Si] c. *praem.* Mu1 P1 **11.14.** *om. per totum* A Ba C G L Ma Mu2 Vp ‖ Notificamus] c. *praem.* P1

⟨11.⟩ From the age.

⟨11.1.⟩ D.34 c.7.
⟨11.2.⟩ C.12 q.1 c.1.
⟨11.3.⟩ D.50 c.63.
⟨11.4.⟩ C.27 q.1 c.2.
⟨11.5.⟩ D. 86 c.24.
⟨11.6.⟩ D.20 c.3.
⟨11.7.⟩ C.20 q.1 c.12.
⟨11.8.⟩ C.18 q.2 c.21.
⟨11.9.⟩ D.34 c.1.
⟨11.10.⟩ C.33 q.2 c.14 and c.19.
⟨11.11.⟩ C.26 q.7 c.2.
⟨11.12.⟩ D.77 c.6.
⟨11.13.⟩ D.86 c.23.
⟨11.14.⟩ C.35 q.6 c.3.

⟨12.⟩ Ex necessitudine.

⟨12.1.⟩ D. lxxxi. Feminas (D.81 c.31) “necessitudinum causas.”

⟨12.2.⟩ D. eadem Volumus (D.81 c.24) et c. Cum omnibus (D.81 c.27).

⟨12.3.⟩ D. xxxii. Interdixit (D.32 c.16).

⟨12.4.⟩ C. i. q. iii. Pervenit (C.1 q.3 c.13) “quod gravius est consanguineis.”

⟨12.5.⟩ D. xxviii. De Siracusane (D.28 c.13) “uxor vel filii.”

⟨12.6.⟩ D. lxxxix. Decenter (D.89 c.6) “sanguine propinquis.”

⟨12.7.⟩ D. lxxxvi. Non satis (D.86 c.14) “tempore.”

⟨12.8.⟩ C. xii. q. ii. Quisquis episcopus (C.12 q.2 c.19) “cognatis propriis.”

⟨13.⟩ Ex eo quod respondere, vel innocentiam suam quis purgare, vel iustis correptionibus obedire, subterfugit.

⟨13.1.⟩ D. xxxiv. Quorumdam (D.34 c.1) “rationibus non obedit.”

⟨13.2.⟩ D. lxxxi. Si quispiam (D.81 c.22).

⟨13.3.⟩ C. iii. q. ix Decrevimus (C.3 q.9 c.10) “nam manifestum.”

⟨13.4.⟩ C. iv. q. v. Quisquis (C.4 q.5 c.1) “ipse in se dampnationis sententiam.”

⟨13.5.⟩ C. xi. q. iii. c. De illis (C.11 q.3 c.109).

⟨13.6.⟩ C. xxiv. q. iii. De illicita (C.24 q.3 c.6) in fine.

---

12. necessitudine] necessitate Ba C L P1 **12.1.** D.] arg. pro *praem.* Vp ‖ Feminas] c. *praem.* Mu1 P1 ‖ necessitudinum] necessitudinem C, ubi dicitur *praem.* Mu2, necessitudine P1 **12.2.** D. eadem *om.* Ba, et c. Mu1 P1 ‖ D.] arg. pro *praem.* Vp ‖ Volumus et *om.* Ma ‖ c. *om.* Ma Mu1 Vp ‖ Cum] o. *praem. et exp.* L ‖ omnibus] “necessitatem” *add.* Vp **12.3.** *post §12.6 rep.* L ‖ D.] arg. pro *praem.* Vp ‖ xxxii.] xxvii. L, xxxi. L_1, xxxi. Mu2 ‖ Interdixit] Interdixerit A, Interdixitt *cum* t[3] *exp.* G, c. *praem.* L Mu1 P1, Interdixi Ma, † *add.* Vb **12.4.** C.] arg. contra *praem.* Vp ‖ Pervenit] c. *praem.* Mu1 P1 ‖ quod] et *praem.* Mu1 P1, ubi dicitur *praem.* Mu2, quia Vb ‖ consanguineis] † Vb **12.5.** D.] arg. contra *praem.* Vp ‖ uxor] ubi dicitur *praem.* Mu2, et *praem.* P1 ‖ vel] aut Fr, alis Ba ‖ filii] de *praem. et exp.* A **12.6.** *om. per totum* C ‖ D.] arg. contra *praem.* Vp ‖ lxxxix.] lxxxviii. Ba, lxxxii. L ‖ Decenter] c. De cetero Mu1, c. *praem.* P1 ‖ sanguine] ubi dicitur *praem.* Mu2 **12.7.** *om. per totum* A Ba G L Ma Mu1 Mu2 P1 Vb Vp **12.8.** *om. per totum* A Ba C G L Ma Mu2 Vp ‖ C. *om.* Mu1 ‖ xii.] xx. *cum* x.[2] *exp. et corr.* P1 ‖ Quisquis] c. *praem.* Mu1 **13.** respondere] responderetur G ‖ vel[1] *om.* A ‖ quis *ante* subterfugit *tr.* C P1 ‖ purgare vel[2]—obedire *om.* Ma ‖ iustis] nullis G, ult⟩imis⟨ L ‖ subterfugit *post* purgare *tr.* L, quis *praem. et exp.* Mu1 **13.1.** D.] arg. pro et contra *praem.* Vp ‖ Quorumdam] c. *praem.* P1 ‖ rationibus *post* obedit *tr.* Mu1 P1, ubi dicitur *praem.* Mu2 ‖ non obedit] nolunt L **13.2.** D.] arg. contra *praem.* Vp ‖ lxxxi.] xxxi. Mu2 Vp ‖ Si quispiam *om.* A, c. Si qui sunt Mu1 P1 **13.3.** C.] arg. contra *praem.* Vp ‖ iii.] iv. G ‖ ix.] xi. L, viii. Ma ‖ Decrevimus] c. *praem.* Mu1 ‖ nam] et iam L, ubi dicitur *praem.* Mu2, *om.* P1 ‖ manifestum] “professio” *add.* A Ba C G Vp, professio rei *add. male* Mu2, est *add.* Mu1 P1 **13.4.** *post §13.6 tr.* Mu1 P1 ‖ C.] arg. contra *praem.* Vp ‖ Quisquis] c. *praem.* Mu1 P1 ‖ ipse *om.* Ba Ma, in rem L, ubi dicitur *praem.* Mu2 ‖ se] sacri Vp ‖ sententiam *om.* A Ba C G L Mu1 Mu2 P1 Vp **13.5.** *om. per totum* A Ba C G L Ma Mu2 Vb Vp **13.6.** C. *om.* Mu1 ‖ iii.] iiii. *cum* i.[4] *exp.* A L, v. Mu2 ‖ illicita] illicito A ‖ in fine] capituli *add.* A C G L Ma Mu2 Vp, *om.* Mu1 P1

⟨12.⟩ From a close relationship.
⟨12.1.⟩ D.81 c.31.
⟨12.2.⟩ D.81 c.24 and c.27.
⟨12.3.⟩ D.32 c.16.
⟨12.4.⟩ C.1 q.3 c.13.
⟨12.5.⟩ D.28 c.13.
⟨12.6.⟩ D.89 c.6.
⟨12.7.⟩ D. 86 c.14.
⟨12.8.⟩ C.12 q.2 c.19.

⟨13.⟩ From the case where somebody avoids answering in court, vindicating his innocence, or complying with valid reproofs.
⟨13.1.⟩ D.34 c.1.
⟨13.2.⟩ D.81 c.22.
⟨13.3.⟩ C.3 q.9 c.10.
⟨13.4.⟩ C.4 q.5 c.1.
⟨13.5.⟩ C.11 q.3 c.109.
⟨13.6.⟩ C.24 q.3 c.6 at the end.

⟨13.7.⟩ B. i. Bonifacius (B.1 c.161) "et nullus dubitat quod ita iudicium nocens subterfugit, quemadmodum ut absolvatur qui est innocens querit."

⟨14.⟩ Ex defectu indiciorum, expedientia pretermissa intelliguntur.

⟨14.1.⟩ D. lxviii. Presbiteri quos (D.68 c.2).

⟨14.2.⟩ De con. D. iv. Parvulos (D.4 de cons. c.110), c. Placuit (D.4 de cons. c.111).

⟨14.3.⟩ D. eadem Cum itaque (D.4 de cons. c.112) et c. Si nulla (D.4 de cons. c.113).

⟨14.4.⟩ De con. D. i. contra Ecclesie vel altaria (D.1 de cons. c.18).

⟨15.⟩ Ex fama communi.

⟨15.1.⟩ C. xxxv. q. vi. Si duo viri (C.35 q.6 c.4) "sicut fama."

⟨15.2.⟩ C. ii. q. v. Presbiter (C.2 q.5 c.13).

⟨15.3.⟩ Q. eadem Si mala fama (C.2 q.5 c.16) et c. Habet hoc (C.2 q.5 c.6).

⟨15.4.⟩ B. ii. De presbiteris (B.2 c.236) "et non habent collegas."

13.7. i.] lib. *praem.* Ba Ma Mu2 P1, p. *praem.* Mu1 ‖ Bonifacius *om.* A ‖ et] in Ma, *om.* Mu2 ‖ nullus] nullum ius Ba ‖ quod] qui Vb ‖ subterfugit] subterfugiat *cum* a *exp.* G ‖ quemadmodum] que ad modum Ba ‖ ut absolvatur *om.* A Vb, *post* querit *tr.* L ‖ ut] si *add.* Mu1 ‖ qui] quod A Vp ‖ innocens] nocens L ‖ querit] queri L **14.** *om. per totum* P1 ‖ indiciorum] indicione *cum* ne *exp. et corr.* G ‖ expedientia pretermissa] ex defectu *praem.* A, ex obedientia Vp ‖ intelliguntur pretermissa *tr.* Mu1 **14.1.** D.] arg. pro *praem.* Vp ‖ lxviii.] lxxviii. Ma, lxxiii. G Mu2, lxix. Vp ‖ Presbiteri] c. *praem.* Mu1 P1 ‖ quos] reperisti *add.* Ma **14.2.** De con. D. iv.] D. iii. de contra Ba, D. iii. de con. P1 ‖ De] D. C Vb, arg. contra *praem.* Vp ‖ iv.] iii. A C G Mu2 Vb ‖ Parvulos *om.* A ‖ c.] et *praem.* A C G Mu1 Mu2 P1 Vp, et L, *om.* Ma **14.3.** *om. per totum* A ‖ D. eadem] *om.* Ba Mu1 P1 ‖ D.] arg. contra *praem.* Vp ‖ Cum] Eum Ba ‖ et *om.* Ma ‖ c. *om.* Ba Ma Mu1 P1 ‖ Si nulla] Similia Mu1 ‖ nulla] extant *add.* Ma **14.4.** *om. per totum* P1 ‖ de—i.] d. eadem Mu2 ‖ de] D. C Vb, D. *praem. et exp.* L, arg. contra *praem.* Vp ‖ cons.] contra Ba ‖ i.] ii. Mu1 ‖ contra *om.* A Ba C G Ma Mu1 Mu2 Vp, *interl.* Vb ‖ Ecclesie] Cum dei *praem. male* Mu2 ‖ altaria] altario Mu2 **15.** *om. per totum* P1 **15.1.** C. *om.* Mu1, arg. pro *praem.* Vp ‖ vi.] iii. G Mu2 ‖ Si] c. *praem.* Mu1 P1 ‖ viri *om.* Mu1 P1 ‖ sicut] ubi dicitur *praem.* Mu2 ‖ fama] est *add.* Ba C Ma Mu1 Mu2 P1 Vp, c. *cum abbr. signo add.* G **15.2.** C.] arg. pro *praem.* Vp ‖ v.] ii. A ‖ Presbiter] si "mala opinione" *add.* Ma, c. *praem.* Mu1 **15.3.** Q. eadem *om.* Ba L Mu1 P1, C. eadem *praem.* Ma ‖ Q.] C. Mu2, arg. pro *praem.* Vp ‖ Si] c. *praem.* A C G Mu2 Vp ‖ et c.] C. eadem q. eadem Ma ‖ Habet *post* hoc *tr.* Ma ‖ Habet *om.* Ba Mu1 P1 Vp ‖ hoc] proprium (lxx. *praem. et exp.* Mu1) *add.* A Ba C G L Ma Mu1 Mu2 P1 Vp **15.4.** ii.] lib. *praem.* Ba Ma Mu1, lib. v. Mu2 ‖ et non *om.* Ba ‖ et] ubi dicitur *praem.* Mu2 ‖ habent] hiabent *cum* i. *exp.* Vp

⟨13.7.⟩ B. 1 c.161: "And no one doubts that the guilty evades the judgement, just as he who is innocent seeks to be acquitted."

⟨14.⟩ From the lack of clues, one can understand that some necessary things have been omitted.

⟨14.1.⟩ D.68 c.2.

⟨14.2.⟩ D.4 de cons. c.110, c.111.

⟨14.3.⟩ D.4 de cons. c.112 and c.113.

⟨14.4.⟩ D.1 de cons. c.18.

⟨15.⟩ From common repute.

⟨15.1.⟩ C.35 q.6 c.4.

⟨15.2.⟩ C.2 q.5 c.13.

⟨15.3.⟩ C.2 q.5 c.16 and c.6.

⟨15.4.⟩ B. 2 c.236.

⟨16.⟩ Ecce quid circa extrinseci facti substantiam, pro aliquo vel contra aliquem presumatur, et ex quibus locis; 'factum' largissime accipe, et in singulis titulis tu ipse discerne, quid pro aliquo vel contra aliquem presumatur.

⟨III. Circa extrinseci facti qualitatem⟩

⟨1.⟩ Cum autem de facto constat, sed circa eius qualitatem incertum vertitur, quod bonum vel malum, iustum vel iniustum, hoc quoque secundum magis et minus, quam liberum vel servum, et sic de ceteris, que insunt, presumimus ex his locis, quos Iohannes Chrisostomus in illo capitulo Occidit Finees, C. xxiii. q. viii. (C.23 q.8 c.14), assignat, puta:

⟨1.1.⟩ Ex tempore.
⟨1.2.⟩ Ex loco.
⟨1.3.⟩ Ex causa.
⟨1.4.⟩ Ex voluntate.
⟨1.5.⟩ Ex personarum differentia.
⟨1.6.⟩ Ex cura vel diligentia eiusque contrario.
⟨1.7.⟩ Ex dignitate.
⟨1.8.⟩ Ex necessitudine.
⟨1.9.⟩ Ex consequentia operis et actione precedenti.
⟨1.10.⟩ Ex modo agendi.

16. circa *om.* Vp ‖ extrinseci] intrinseci A, extrinsecam Mu1 ‖ substantiam *post* pro aliquo *tr.* L ‖ contra] circa Vp ‖ et] etiam A, *om.* Mu2 ‖ quibus] quibusdam Mu2 ‖ discerne] discernere C Vp ‖ quid] quod Ma **III.1.** ii. modus *praem. marg.* G ‖ Cum] Ubi P1 ‖ de[1] *om.* C ‖ qualitatem] voluntatem C ‖ incertum veritur] dubitatur L ‖ quod] quid A C L Mu1 Mu2 Vp ‖ vel[1]] quid A ‖ vel[2] iniustum *om.* A ‖ hoc] hec G ‖ quoque] quia P1 ‖ magis] maius Ba Mu1 Mu2 Vp ‖ et[1] *om.* G, vel L Mu2 ‖ quam] quem Ba G Ma Mu1 Mu2 ‖ ceteris] decretis Mu1 ‖ insunt] sint *praem.* C, sunt Mu1 ‖ his] is L ‖ Occidit] decidit A ‖ xxiii.] xxiv. L Vp ‖ assignat *om.* A Ba C G Ma Mu2 Vp ‖ puta *om.* C, putas G **1.6.** diligentia] diligentia *cum* di *exp. et corr. marg.* neg P1 **1.7.** *om. per totum* C **1.8.** necessitudine] necessitate P1 **1.9.** consequentia] constantia Ba ‖ et actione *rep. marg.* G ‖ actione] occasione Mu2 ‖ precedenti] precedente A, precedentis L

⟨16.⟩ Here is what can be presumed about the substance of an extrinsic fact, either for or against someone, and from which topics; understand 'fact' very broadly, and distinguish for yourself, in the individual titles, what can be presumed for or against someone.

⟨III. On the quality of an extrinsic fact⟩

⟨1.⟩ When, on the other hand, the fact is certain, but there is uncertainty about its quality (whether it is good or bad, just or unjust, and this in turn also concerns a greater or lesser degree of probability, or whether the person is free or a serf, and so on about other uncertainties that are present), we presume from what John Chrysostom indicates in that chapter C.23 q.8 c.14, namely:

⟨1.1.⟩ From the time.
⟨1.2.⟩ From the place.
⟨1.3.⟩ From the cause.
⟨1.4.⟩ From the will.
⟨1.5.⟩ From the difference between persons.
⟨1.6.⟩ From care or diligence and its contrary.
⟨1.7.⟩ From the standing of a person.
⟨1.8.⟩ From a close relationship.
⟨1.9.⟩ From the consequence of a deed and from the preceding action.
⟨1.10.⟩ From the course of action.

⟨2.⟩ Ex tempore.

⟨2.1.⟩ C. xxii. q. ultima Quotiens (C.22 q.5 c.21) "non in oportuno tempore."

⟨2.2.⟩ D. liv. Fraternitatem (D.54 c.15) "post prefinitos tres menses," "quia hunc."

⟨2.3.⟩ C. xxiii. q. viii. Occidit (C.23 q.8 c.14) "ad tempus."

⟨2.4.⟩ C. xxxiii. q. iv. c. viii., ix., x., xi. (C.33 q.4 c.8, 9, 10, 11).

⟨2.5.⟩ D. lxxxvi. Non satis (D.86 c.14) "tempore."

⟨3.⟩ Ex loco.

⟨3.1.⟩ C. de his qui per metum l. i. (Cod. 7.67.1) ut "in sacro," liber vii.

⟨3.2.⟩ C. xxii. q. ultima Quotiens (C.22 q.5 c.21) "non in oportuno loco."

⟨3.3.⟩ C. xxxii. q. v. Qui viderit (C.32 q.5 c.13) "plerumque ex loco."

⟨3.4.⟩ D. lvi. Presbiterorum (D.56 c.1) "aut in cenobiis."

⟨3.5.⟩ C. xvi. q. i. Si cupis (C.16 q.1 c.5) "quid facis in urbibus."

⟨3.6.⟩ D. lxxxvi. Non satis (D.86 c.14) "loco."

---

2. *om. per totum* P1 **2.1.** C.] arg. contra *praem.* Vp ‖ Quotiens] vero *add.* Ba C G Ma Mu1 Vp, Quod L, c. *praem. et* vero *add.* P1 ‖ non] ubi dicitur *praem.* Mu2, arg. contra *add.* Vp ‖ in oportuno] inportuno L ‖ in *om.* Vb **2.2.** D.] arg. contra *praem.* Vp ‖ Fraternitatem] c. *praem.* Mu1 P1 ‖ post] ubi dicitur *praem.* Mu2, postquam A Vb ‖ prefinitos *om.* A, *marg. cum signo et* presbiteros *add. male* G, prefinitus L, finitos Vb ‖ tres] iii. Ba C G Mu2, iv. L ‖ menses tres *tr.* C Vb ‖ quia hunc] quos nunc Ba, *om.* L Ma **2.3.** C.] arg. contra *praem.* Vp ‖ xxiii.] xxiv. Vp ‖ Occidit] c. *praem.* A Mu1 ‖ ad] ubi dicitur "respiciamus" *praem.* Mu2 **2.4.** C. xxxiii.] et L ‖ C.] arg. pro *praem.* Vp ‖ xxxiii.] xxiii. G Mu2 ‖ c. viii. *om.* Mu2 ‖ ix.] et c. *praem.* Mu2 ‖ x.] et c. xix. Mu2 ‖ xi.] et (c. *add.* Mu2) *praem.* A G L Ma Mu2 Vp **2.5.** D.] arg. pro *praem.* Vp ‖ lxxxvi.] xxxvi. Vp ‖ Non] c. *praem.* Mu1 ‖ satis] est *add.* Ma ‖ tempore] ubi dicitur *praem. et* commendatur *add.* Mu2 **3.** *om. per totum* P1, Ex modo agendi *praem. et exp.* Vb **3.1.** *om. per totum* A Ba C G L Ma Mu1 Mu2 P1 Vp **3.2.** C.] arg. pro et contra *praem.* Vp ‖ Quotiens] c. *praem.* Mu1, c. *praem. et* vero *add.* P1 ‖ non] ubi dicitur *praem.* Mu2 ‖ in oportuno] inportuno L ‖ in] etiam Ba Vp **3.3.** C.] D. Ma, arg. pro et contra *praem.* Vp ‖ Qui] Quod L, c. *praem.* Mu1 P1 ‖ plerumque] † L, ubi dicitur *praem.* Mu2 **3.4.** D.] arg. pro et contra *praem.* Vp ‖ Presbiterorum] filios *add.* Ma; c. *praem.* Mu1 P1 ‖ aut] ubi dicitur *praem.* Mu2 ‖ cenobiis] Serviendi *add. male* Mu2 **3.5.** C.] arg. contra *praem.* Vp ‖ xvi.] xiii. A ‖ cupis] cupit L, esse *add.* P1 ‖ quid] quod Ma, ut dicitur *praem.* Mu2 ‖ urbibus] nobis L **3.6.** D.] arg. pro et contra *praem.* Vp ‖ Non satis] notis Ba C ‖ loco] ex *praem.* A Ba C Ma Vp, ubi dicitur *praem.* Mu2

⟨2.⟩ From the time.

⟨2.1.⟩ C.22 q.5 c.21.
⟨2.2.⟩ D.54 c.15.
⟨2.3.⟩ C.23 q.8 c.14.
⟨2.4.⟩ C.33 q.4 c.8, 9, 10, 11.
⟨2.5.⟩ D.86 c.14.

⟨3.⟩ From the place.

⟨3.1.⟩ Cod.7.67.1.
⟨3.2.⟩ C.22 q.5 c.21.
⟨3.3.⟩ C.32 q.5 c.13.
⟨3.4.⟩ D.56 c.1.
⟨3.5.⟩ C.16 q.1 c.5.
⟨3.6.⟩ D.86 c.14.

⟨4.⟩ Ex causa: 'causam' hic large accipio, ut includam necessitatem, officium, obedientiam et omnem licitam vel illicitam causam.

⟨4.1.⟩ C. xxiii. q. i. Quid culpatur (C.23 q.1 c.4) "certum non est," "ordo serviendi."

⟨4.2.⟩ C. iii. q. v. Canonica (C.3 q.5 c.6) "fides, vita et libertas nescitur;" hic ex causa contra eos presumitur favore accusati, ne innocens dampnetur.

⟨4.3.⟩ C. xxii. q. ii. Ne quis (C.22 q.2–3 c.14) "ideo non est perniciosum," "secundum autem ideo" et c. Michi autem (C.22 q.2–3 c.12).

⟨4.4.⟩ D. lxxxvi. Non satis (D.86 c.14) "causa."

⟨4.5.⟩ C. xxxii. q. iv. Dixit Sara (C.32 q.4 c.3) "sed studio."

⟨4.6.⟩ C. xxiii. q. v. De occidendis (C.23 q.5 c.8) "nisi forte."

⟨4.7.⟩ C. xxiii. q. v. Miles (C.23 q.5 c.13) et in sequentibus capitulis ⟨4.8.⟩ et C. xxiii. c. Si non licet (C.23 q.5 c.9) et consequentibus capitulis.

⟨4.9.⟩ C. xxxiii. q. v. Una sola (C.33 q.5 c.6).

---

4. *om. per totum*: P1 ‖ Ex—hic] Casum L ‖ causam] rm *cum abbr. signo* A, vero appello *add.* Mu1 ‖ hic *om.* A C Ma Mu2 Vp ‖ large] longe A ‖ accipio] accipe C L Ma, *om.* Mu1, † Vb ‖ includam] includat C, includas L Ma ‖ officium] ex officio Vp **4.1.** *§4.1–2 post §3.6 tr.* Ma ‖ C.] arg. pro et contra *praem.* Vp ‖ xxiii.] xxiv. L ‖ Quid] Qui P1 ‖ certum] ubi dicitur *praem.* Mu2 ‖ non] est *praem.* L, *om.* Mu1 P1 Vp ‖ ordo serviendi *om.* L ‖ ordo] credo C ‖ serviendi *marg.* Mu2 **4.2.** C.] arg. pro et contra *praem.* Vp ‖ iii.] xxxiii. Vp ‖ Canonica] c. *praem.* A Ba G P1, arg. pro et contra c. *praem.* Vp ‖ fides] et *add.* C Vp, *om.* Ma, ubi dicitur *praem.* Mu2, v. *praem.* Vb ‖ et *om.* Mu1 P1 ‖ nescitur *om.* Ba ‖ hic—dampnetur *om.* Ma ‖ causa *om.* Ba ‖ contra] que *praem.* L ‖ favore] a fvrce L ‖ accusati] accusari Ba, accusanti *cum* n *exp. et corr.* G, avocati L ‖ innocens] minus L ‖ dampnetur] condempnetur L **4.3.** C.] arg. pro *praem.* Vp ‖ xxii.] ii. C ‖ Ne] c. *praem.* P1 ‖ quis] arbitretur *add.* Mu1 Mu2 P1 ‖ ideo^{1}] ubi dicitur *praem.* Mu2 ‖ non est *om.* P1 ‖ perniciosum] permissum L, permitto *cum abbr. signo supra* to P1 ‖ secundum—ideo^{2} *om.* L Ma ‖ secundum] secundo C ‖ autem] ad *cum abbr. signo* Vb, arg. pro *praem.* Vp ‖ ideo^{2} et] etiam ideo C ‖ ideo^{2} *om.* Mu1 P1, mitius est *add.* Mu2 ‖ et c.] C. eadem q. eadem Ma ‖ Michi autem *om.* L Mu2, autem *praem.* Vp ‖ Michi] nichil G **4.4.** D.] arg. pro *praem.* Vp ‖ Non] c. *praem.* P1 ‖ causa] causam L, *om.* Mu1, ubi dicitur *praem.* Mu2 **4.5.** *om. per totum* C L ‖ C.] arg. pro *praem.* Vp ‖ iv.] iii. A G Vp ‖ Dixit] c. *praem.* P1 ‖ sed *om.* Mu2 ‖ studio] (arg. pro *praem. et interl.* Vp) "hanc causam" "et ideo" (publici muneris gratia privatam culpam pretexit *add.* Ma) *add.* A Ba G Ma Vp, et c. "hanc causam querende" (posteritatis et ideo *add.* P1) *add.* Mu1 P1, ubi dicitur *praem. et* "querende posteritatis" *add.* Mu2 **4.6.** C.] et Mu1, arg. *praem.* Vp ‖ xxiii.] xxxii. C, xxxiii. L P1 ‖ De] c. *praem.* P1 ‖ nisi forte] miles A, *om.* Ba C G L Ma Mu1 Mu2 P1 Vp **4.7.** *om. per totum* A Mu1 Mu2 P1 Vb ‖ C.] arg. contra *praem.* Vp ‖ xxiii.] eadem Ma, xxxiii. *cum* x.^{3} *exp.* Vp ‖ v.] eadem Ma ‖ Miles] Sileres Ba, Si *praem.* C G L Vp ‖ et *om.* Ma ‖ sequentibus] ceteris *praem.* L, cetis arg. contra *praem.* Vp ‖ capitulis similibus L **4.8.** *ante §4.6 tr.* P1, *om. per totum* A Ba C G L Ma Mu2 Vb Vp ‖ C. xxiii. *om.* Mu1 ‖ consequentibus] cum sequentibus Mu1 **4.9.** *om. per totum* A Mu2 Vb ‖ C. *om.* L, arg. pro et contra *praem* Vp ‖ xxxiii.] xxviii. L, xxiii. G P1

⟨4.⟩ From the cause: here I interpret 'cause' broadly, in order to include the necessity, the office, the obedience, and all the legitimate and illegitimate causes.

⟨4.1.⟩ C.23 q.1 c.4.

⟨4.2.⟩ C.3 q.5 c.6; from the cause, here it is presumed for the accused and against those accusers whose faith, life, and liberty are unknown, so that an innocent is not condemned.

⟨4.3.⟩ C.22 q.2–3 c.14 and c.12.

⟨4.4.⟩ D.86 c.14.

⟨4.5.⟩ C.32 q.4 c.3.

⟨4.6.⟩ C.23 q.5 c.8.

⟨4.7.⟩ C.23 q.5 c.13 and in the following chapters ⟨4.8.⟩ and C.23 q.5 c.9 and the following chapters.

⟨4.9.⟩ C.33 q.5 c.6.

⟨4.10.⟩ C. eadem q. eadem Unum solum (C.33 q.5 c.3).
⟨4.11.⟩ C. xxiii. q. viii. Occidit (C.23 q.8 c.14) “ad causam.”

⟨5.⟩ Ex voluntate, quia voluntas et propositum distinguunt maleficium.
⟨5.1.⟩ C. xxii. q. ii. Ne quis (C.22 q.2–3 c.14) “quod non habet duplex cor.”
⟨5.2.⟩ Q. eadem Beatus Paulus (C.22 q.2–3 c.5) “ipsius voluntatis.”
⟨5.3.⟩ Q. eadem Homines (C.22 q.2–3 c.3) “sed putat non pluisse periurus est.”
⟨5.4.⟩ D. lxiii. Verum (D.63 c.28 pars 4) “et idcirco destruxit.”
⟨5.5.⟩ D. l. Quantum (D.50 c.48) “voluntas,” “perniciosa.”
⟨5.6.⟩ C. xxii. q. ii. Homines (C.22 q.2–3 c.3) “nisi rea mens.”
⟨5.7.⟩ C. xv. q. i. Non est (C.15 q.1 c.10) in toto capitulo.
⟨5.8.⟩ C. xxiii. q. viii. Occidit (C.23 q.8 c.14) “sed ad voluntatem.”
⟨5.9.⟩ Q. v. eiusdem cause Cum homo (C.23 q.5 c.19) “multum distat.”
⟨5.10.⟩ C. xxii. q. v. Qui periurare paratus est (C.22 q.5 c.13).
⟨5.11.⟩ C. D. lxxxiii. Error (D.83 c.3).
⟨5.12.⟩ C. xxiii. q. v. Excommunicatorum (C.23 q.5 c.47) ubi “non enim.”

4.10. *om. per totum* A Ba C G L Ma Mu1 P1 Vb Vp **4.11.** xxiii.] xxxiii. A, xxviii. L ‖ q. viii. *om.* A ‖ Occidit] Cedit G L Mu2, Finees *add.* Ma, c. *praem.* Mu1 ‖ causam] uxorem L **5.** *om. per totum* P1 ‖ quia—maleficium *om.* Ma ‖ quia] qua C ‖ voluntas] propositum et *praem.* C ‖ distinguunt] distinguuntur C, extinguit L **5.1.** C.] arg. pro *praem.* Vp ‖ xxii.] xxx. A ‖ quis] arbitretur *add.* Mu1 Mu2 ‖ quod] quo Ba1, qui (ubi dicitur *praem.* Mu2) A Ba C L Mu1 Mu2 Vb ‖ cor (cur C) duplex *tr.* A Ba Ba1 C G L Mu1 P1 Vp **5.2.** Q. eadem *om.* Ba Ba1, et c. L Mu1 P1, C. eadem *praem.* Ma ‖ Q.] arg. pro *praem.* Vp ‖ Paulus *om.* Mu1 P1 ‖ ipsius] quantum *praem.* Mu1 P1, ubi dicitur *praem.* Mu2 **5.3.** Q. eadem *om.* Ba Ba1, et c. L Mu1 P1, C. eadem *praem.* Ma ‖ Q.] arg. contra *praem.* Vp ‖ sed] si (ubi dicitur *praem.* Mu2) A Ba Ba1 C G L Mu2 Vb Vp, *om.* Ma ‖ putat] putavit L, falsum *add.* Ma ‖ non *interl.* Mu2 ‖ pluisse] probasse Mu1 ‖ periurus est *om.* Ma ‖ periurus] per rarus L, arg. contra *praem.* Vp **5.4.** D.] arg. pro contra *praem.* Vp ‖ lxiii.] lxiv. Mu2 ‖ Verum] quia *add.* Mu2 ‖ et] ubi dicitur *praem.* Mu2 ‖ idcirco] ideo L ‖ destruxit] distruxit *cum* i^2 *exp. et corr.* G, iste *add.* Ma, destrunxit Vp **5.5.** D.] arg. pro contra *praem.* Vp ‖ l.] i. L ‖ Quantum] (c. *praem.* Mu1 P1) dicit (dixit G L Mu2) *add.* A Ba1 C G L Mu1 Mu2 Vp ‖ voluntas] ubi dicitur *praem.* Mu2 ‖ perniciosa] per ratissa L **5.6.** C.] arg. pro p. *praem. et exp.* Vp ‖ q. ii. *om.* L ‖ nisi] nisit G, ubi dicitur *praem. et* sit *add. male* Mu2 ‖ rea] ea G **5.7.** *om. per totum* Mu1 P1 ‖ C.] arg. pro *praem.* Vp ‖ xv.] xvi. *cum* i. *exp.* A, vx. L ‖ i.] v. Ba Ba1, *om.* G ‖ non] meo Ba, *om.* Ba1, vano Vp ‖ est] esse Ba Ba1 Vp ‖ in toto capitulo *om.* A Ba Ba1 C G L Mu2 Vp, “nisi propria voluntate” Ma **5.8.** C.] arg. contra *praem.* Vp ‖ xxiii.] xviii. Ba1, xxviii. L ‖ viii.] vii. Ma ‖ Occidit] Finees *add.* Ma, c. *praem.* P1 ‖ sed] et Fr, *om.* Ma Mu1, ubi dicitur *praem.* Mu2 **5.9.** Q.] et *praem.* Ba Ba1 Mu1 P1, *marg. Vb* ‖ eiusdem cause] C. eadem *et ante* Q. *tr.* C Ma Mu2, et *et ante* Q. *tr.* L, arg. pro contra *et ante* q. *tr.* Vp ‖ Cum] Eius dicit omne *praem.* Vp ‖ multum] militari Ba Ba1 Mu1, ubi dicitur *praem.* Mu2, mulctari Vp **5.10.** C.] arg. contra *praem.* Vp ‖ peiurare] peierare Ba Ba1 C G Vp, perierare L, iurare Ma ‖ paratus est *om.* L P1 ‖ est] periurus habetur *add.* Ma **5.11.** *om. per totum* A Ba C G L Mu1 Mu2 P1 Vb Vp **5.12.** *om. per totum* A Ba Ba1 C G L Ma Mu1 Mu2 P1 Vp.

⟨4.10.⟩ C.33 q.5 c.3.
⟨4.11.⟩ C.23 q.8 c.14.

⟨5.⟩ From the will, because the will and the purpose distinguish a malicious deed.

⟨5.1.⟩ C.22 q.2–3 c.14.
⟨5.2.⟩ C.22 q.2–3 c.5.
⟨5.3.⟩ C.22 q.2–3 c.3.
⟨5.4.⟩ D.63 c.28 part 4.
⟨5.5.⟩ D.50 c.48.
⟨5.6.⟩ C.22 q.2–3 c.3.
⟨5.7.⟩ C.15 q.1 c.10 in the entire chapter.
⟨5.8.⟩ C.23 q.8 c.14.
⟨5.9.⟩ C.23 q.5 c.19.
⟨5.10.⟩ C.22 q.5 c.13.
⟨5.11.⟩ D. 83 c.3.
⟨5.12.⟩ C.23 q.5 c.47.

⟨6.⟩ Ex personarum differentia.

⟨6.1.⟩ C. xxiii. q. viii. Occidit (C.23 q.8 c.14) "personarum quoque differentiam."

⟨6.2.⟩ C. eadem q. v. Cum homo (C.23 q.5 c.19).

⟨6.3.⟩ C. eadem q. v. De occidendis (C.23 q.5 c.8) "nisi forte sit miles" et c. Miles (C.23 q.5 c.13) et c. Si non licet (C.23 q.5 c.9) "his exceptis."

⟨6.4.⟩ C. v. q. v. Non omnis (C.5 q.5 c.2) "noveris furem." ⟨6.5.⟩ Ergo distingue personas.

⟨6.6.⟩ D. xxxiv. Quorumdam (D.34 c.1) "venatorem."

⟨6.7.⟩ C. xvi. q. vii. Quicumque (C.16 q.7 c.4) "de ipsa venatione sua."

⟨6.8.⟩ D. lxxxviii. Fornicari (D.88 c.10).

⟨6.9.⟩ D. lxxxvi. Non satis (D.86 c.14), Item consideranda (D.86 c.17).

⟨6.10.⟩ D. l. Clericum qui paganum (D.50 c.5).

⟨7.⟩ Ex cura vel diligentia eiusque contrario.

⟨7.1.⟩ D. l. Hii qui arborem (D.50 c.49) ⟨7.2.⟩ et c. Sepe (D.50 c.50) "voluntate vel negligentia."

---

6. *om. per totum* Ba1 P1 **6.1.** C.[1]] arg. pro contra *praem.* Vp ‖ xxiii.] xxxiii. C ‖ Occidit] c. *praem.* P1 ‖ personarum—differentiam *om.* L ‖ personarum] ubi dicitur *praem.* Mu2 ‖ quoque *om.* Mu2 Vp ‖ differentiam] differentia A C Mu1 **6.2** *post § 6.3 tr.* G L ‖ C.[2]—homo *om.* Mu2 ‖ C. eadem q. v.] et c. (*om.* L) A Ba Ba1 C G L Mu1 P1 Vp ‖ Cum homo] Sileres (C.23 q.5 c.13) *add.* Ba **6.3.** C. eadem q. v. *om.* Ba ‖ C. eadem] et L ‖ C.] arg. pro contra *praem.* Vp ‖ De] c. *praem.* Mu1 ‖ nisi] non A, ubi dicitur *praem.* Mu2 ‖ forte *om.* A Ba C G L Mu2 P1 Vb Vp ‖ et[1]—exceptis] etc. Mu2 ‖ et[1]—Miles[2] *om.* (*homoiotel.*) Mu1 P1 ‖ et[1] c.[1]] C. eadem q. eadem Ma ‖ c.[1] *om.* L ‖ Miles] Sileres Ba1, si *praem.* Ba C G Vb Vp, ei *praem.* L ‖ et[2]—exceptis *om.* A Ba Ba1 C G L Ma Vp **6.4.** C.] arg. contra *praem.* Vp ‖ omnis] omnes P1 ‖ noveris *om.* L, ubi dicitur *praem.* Mu2 ‖ furem] fur est L ‖ distingue] distinguit G **6.5.** *post § 6.6 tr.* Ba1, *om. per totum* Ba Mu1 P1 arg. contra *praem.* Vp ‖ ergo] quo Ba1, erga L ‖ distingue] distinguitur L, distinguit Mu2 ‖ personas] persanas *cum* a[1] *exp. et corr.* o A **6.6.** D.] arg. contra *praem.* Vp ‖ xxxiv.] xxxiii. A P1, xxiv. Ba Ba1, xxxii. Vp ‖ Quorumdam] c. *praem.* Ma Mu1 P1, ubi dicitur *add.* Mu2 ‖ venatorem] venatori Ba Ba1 C P1 Vp, venationi (sit deditus *add.* Mu2) G Mu1 Mu2 **6.7.** C.] arg. pro *praem.* Vp ‖ vii.] vi. L Mu2 ‖ Quicumque] Quis *cum abbr. signo supra* s L, recognoverit *add.* Ma, c. *praem.* Mu1 P1 ‖ de—sua *om.* A Mu2 ‖ ipsa *om.* Ba Ba1 C G L Ma Vb Vp ‖ sua *om.* Ba Ba1 C G L Ma Vb Vp, tsua *cum* t *exp.* P1 **6.8.** *om. per totum* G Mu2 ‖ D.] arg. pro contra *praem.* Vp ‖ lxxxviii.] lxxxiv. A L Vb, lxxxix. Ba1 ‖ Fornicari] Fornicati C, "hominibus" *add.* Ma, c. *praem.* P1 **6.9.** D.] arg. pro contra *praem.* Vp ‖ Non] c. *praem.* P1 ‖ Item consideranda *om.* Mu2 ‖ Item] De Ma, *om.* Mu1 P1 **6.10.** *om. per totum* A Ba1 C G L Ma Mu1 Mu2 P1 Vp **7.** *om. per totum* Ba1 P1 ‖ diligentia] diligentiaque *et post* eiusque *tr.* L **7.1.** D.] arg. contra *praem.* Vp ‖ Hii] c. *praem.* Mu1 P1 ‖ qui *om.* A ‖ arborem *om.* L, incidere ex neglectu *add. male* Ma, morientis cor constituto *add. male* Vb **7.2.** *post § 7.3 tr.* Ma ‖ et c.] D. eadem Ma ‖ c. *om.* L ‖ voluntate *om.* A Ba Ba1 C G L Mu1 Mu2 P1 Vp ‖ vel (ubi dicitur *praem.* Mu2) negligentia *ante* et *tr.* A Ba Ba1 C G L Mu1 Mu2 P1 Vp

⟨6.⟩ From the difference between persons.

⟨6.1.⟩ C.23 q.8 c.14.
⟨6.2.⟩ C.23 q.5 c.19.
⟨6.3.⟩ C.23 q.5 c.8 and c.13 and c.9.
⟨6.4.⟩ C.5 q.5 c.2. ⟨6.5.⟩ Therefore, distinguish persons.
⟨6.6.⟩ D.34 c.1.
⟨6.7.⟩ C.16 q.7 c.4.
⟨6.8.⟩ D.88 c.10.
⟨6.9.⟩ D.86 c.14, c.17.
⟨6.10.⟩ D.50 c.5.

⟨7.⟩ From care or diligence and from its contrary.

⟨7.1.⟩ D.50 c.49 ⟨7.2.⟩ and c.50.

⟨7.3.⟩ D. eadem Si duo (D.50 c.51) "dixerit cave."
⟨7.4.⟩ C. xxiii. q. v. Si homicidium (C.23 q.5 c.41) "invito."
⟨7.5.⟩ D. l. Clericum qui paganum (D.50 c.5) "non convenit."

⟨8.⟩ Ex dignitate.
⟨8.1.⟩ C. xxxii. q. v. Qui viderit (C.32 q.5 c.13) "ex ordine."
⟨8.2.⟩ D. xl. Non nos (D.40 c.1) "quis enim sanctum esse dubitet" et Homo (D.40 c.5).
⟨8.3.⟩ C. xxv. q. i. Nulli (C.25 q.1 c.4) "sublimitas peccatum."
⟨8.4.⟩ D. l. Quia tua (D.50 c.16) "precedit honore."
⟨8.5.⟩ D. xix. Nulli fas (D.19 c.5) "quia maioris."
⟨8.6.⟩ C. xxvii. q. i. Viduas que maioris (C.27 q.1 c.3).
⟨8.7.⟩ C. xi. q. iii. c. iii. (C.11 q.3 c.3) et c. Absit (C.11 q.3 c.14).
⟨8.8.⟩ C. i. q. iii. Salvator (C.1 q.3 c.8) "contra."
⟨8.9.⟩ C. vi. q. i. Quiescite (C.6 q.1 c.12).

7.3. D. eadem *om.* Ba Ba1 L, et c. Mu1 P1 ‖ D.] arg. pro *praem.* Vp ‖ duo] dua L, fratres *add.* Mu2 ‖ dixerit] dixit C, fratri *add.* Ma, ubi dicitur *praem.* Mu2 **7.5.** D.] arg. contra *praem.* Vp ‖ Clericum *rep. et exp.* G, c. *praem.* Mu1 P1 ‖ qui paganum *om.* L ‖ qui] quod Ma P1 ‖ non] ubi dicitur *praem.* Mu2 ‖ convenit] militibus (ecclesie *add.* Mu2) *add.* Ma Mu2, per quod ad. C. xxii. q. i. missi de. (?) *add.* Vp **8.** *om. per totum* Ba1 P1, *marg.* Vb **8.1.** *om. per totum* Mu2 ‖ C.] arg. contra *praem.* Vp ‖ xxxii.] xxii. P1, xxxiii. Vb ‖ Qui] Quod G L ‖ viderit] videtur G **8.2.** D.] arg. pro contra *praem.* Vp ‖ xl.] l. L ‖ Non nos] c. i. Mu1 P1 ‖ quis] ubi dicitur *praem.* Mu2 ‖ enim—esse *om.* Vp ‖ esse *om.* A Ba Ba1 C G L Mu2 Vb ‖ et] c. A C, c. *add.* Ba Ba1 G Mu1 P1 Vp, *om.* L, D. eadem Ma ‖ Homo] Christianus (Christiana L) *add.* A Ba Ba1 C G L Mu1 Mu2 P1 Vp, Christianus "propter altitudinem dignitatis" *add.* Ma **8.3.** Ilarius Papa: siquidem maiori reatu delinquit qui potiori honore fruit, et graviora facit vitia peccatorum sublimitas peccantium *add. marg.* Ma ‖ C.] arg. contra *praem.* Vp ‖ xxv.] xcv. Ba, xxx. L ‖ Nulli—peccatum *om.* Mu2 ‖ Nulli] fas *add.* Ma, c. *praem.* Mu1 P1 ‖ sublimitas peccatum *om.* A Ba Ba1 C G L Vp, maiori reatu Ma, qui pociori et sublimitas Mu1, quod peccatorum et sublimitas P1 ‖ peccatum] peccantium Fr **8.4.** *§ 8.4–5 post § 8.6 tr.* Ba1 ‖ D.] arg. contra *praem.* Vp ‖ l. *om.* Vp ‖ tua] tu Ba Ba1, sanctitas *add.* Mu2, sanctitas P1 ‖ precedit] precellit (ubi dicitur *praem.* Mu2) A Ba Ba1 C G L Mu2 Vb Vp, maior *praem.* Ma ‖ honore *om.* A Ba Ba1 C G L Vb Vp **8.5.** D.] arg. contra *praem.* Vp ‖ xix.] xxx. L, lxix. Mu1 ‖ Nulli fas] *om.* Ma ‖ fas] eos L, *om.* Mu1 P1 ‖ quia *rep.* Ma, ubi dicitur *praem.* Mu2 ‖ maioris] maiori C, excommunicationis *add.* Mu2 **8.6.** *post § 8.3 tr.* (*et post § 8.8 rep.* Ma) Ba Ma Mu1 P1 Vp ‖ *om. per totum* (*homoiotel.*) Mu2 ‖ C.] arg. contra *praem. Vp* ‖ Viduas] Inducias C, c. *praem.* P1 ‖ que maioris *om.* Ba Ba1 Ma Mu1 P1 Vp ‖ maioris] minoris L **8.7.** *om. per totum* Mu2 ‖ C.] arg. pro *praem.* Vp ‖ c. iii.[2] *om.* Ba1 P1 ‖ iii.[2]] iv. A, v. Mu1 ‖ et. *om.* Mu1 P1 ‖ c.[2] *om.* Mu1 **8.8.** C.] C. xxvii. q. i. Viduas (C.27 q.1 c.3) *praem.* Ma, arg. pro *praem.* Vp ‖ i.] v. L ‖ Salvator] c. *praem.* P1 ‖ contra *rep.* Ba1, *om.* L Mu1 Mu2, "quod si prefati" *add.* Vp **8.9.** *om. per totum* A Ba C Ma Mu1 P1 Vb Vp

⟨7.3.⟩ D.50 c.51.
⟨7.4.⟩ C.23 q.5 c.41.
⟨7.5.⟩ D.50 c.5.

⟨8.⟩ From the standing of a person.
⟨8.1.⟩ C.32 q.5 c.13.
⟨8.2.⟩ D.40 c.1 and c.5.
⟨8.3.⟩ C.25 q.1 c.4.
⟨8.4.⟩ D.50 c.16.
⟨8.5.⟩ D.19 c.5.
⟨8.6.⟩ C.27 q.1 c.3.
⟨8.7.⟩ C.11 q.3 c.3 and c.14.
⟨8.8.⟩ C.1 q.3 c.8.
⟨8.9.⟩ C.6 q.1 c.12.

⟨9.⟩ Ex necessitudine: hanc large intellige.

⟨9.1.⟩ C. v. q. v. Non osculatur (C.5 q.5 c.3) "semper pater."

⟨9.2.⟩ C. iii. q. v. Consanguinei (C.3 q.5 c.1) et Accusatores (C.3 q.5 c.2).

⟨9.3.⟩ C. xxxv. q. vi. Consanguineos (C.35 q.6 c.1).

⟨9.4.⟩ C. xvi. q. ii. Visis (C.16 q.2 c.1) "humani moris est," "cuius iudicio."

⟨10.⟩ Ex consequentia operis et actione precedenti.

⟨10.1.⟩ C. xxii. q. ii. Utilem (C.22 q.2–3 c.21) "in multis:" recole quod sacerdotes interfecit.

⟨10.2.⟩ C. eadem q. eadem Quod ait (C.22 q.2–3 c.18) "ut exitus docuit."

⟨10.3.⟩ C. iii. q. v. c. ii. (C.3 q.5 c.2) "ante externum diem."

⟨10.4.⟩ C. v. q. v. Non omnis (C.5 q.5 c.2) in fine.

⟨10.5.⟩ C. xxxiii. q. i. Quod interrogasti (C.33 q.1 c.1), Igitur si vir aliam (C.33 q.1 c.2).

⟨10.6.⟩ C. ii. q. vii. Querendum (C.2 q.7 c.18) "cuius sit conversationis" et c. Non potest (C.2 q.7 c.24) in fine.

---

9. *om. per totum* Ba1 P1 ‖ Necessitudine] Necessitate Ba ‖ intellige] accipe Ma **9.1.** *post § 9.2 tr.* C Mu2 ‖ C.] arg. pro contra *praem.* Vp ‖ v. *om.* Vp ‖ Non] c. *praem.* Mu1 ‖ semper pater *om.* L Mu1 Mu2 P1 ‖ pater] patet A **9.2.** C.] arg. contra *praem.* Vp ‖ v.] vi. L Mu2 ‖ Consanguinei] Et *praem. male* A, Consanguineis Ba Vp ‖ et] c. *add.* Mu1 ‖ Accusatores] accusatoas G, c. *praem et* vel testes *add.* Mu2, c. *praem.* P1 **9.3.** C.] arg. pro *praem.* Vp ‖ xxxv.] xxxvi. Mu1 ‖ q. vi. Consanguineos] c. i. Mu1 P1 **9.4.** C.] arg. contra *praem.* Vp ‖ xvi.] xxvi. L ‖ Visis] litteris *add.* Ba1 Ma, c. i. Mu1 P1, Iuris Vp ‖ humani] ubi dicitur *praem.* Mu2 ‖ est *om.* Ma ‖ cuius iudicio *om.* Mu2, etc. P1 ‖ cuius] † A, cum L, et cum Mu1 ‖ iudicio] iuris (est *praem.*) dictio Ba Ba1, *om.* Mu1 **10.** *om. per totum* Ba1 P1 ‖ precedenti actione (occasione Mu2) *tr.* G Mu2 **10.1.** C.] arg. pro *praem.* Vp ‖ Utilem] Utile est Ba1 ‖ in multis—interfecit *om.* Mu2 ‖ recole] colere P1 ‖ quod] quos C, qui A G L Vb ‖ sacerdotes] sacerdotem G Vp ‖ interfecit] interfecerit *add.* Ba Ba1 Mu1 P1, *om.* Vb **10.2.** C. eadem q. eadem] et c. L P1 ‖ C.] arg. pro *praem.* Vp ‖ Quod] Qui C L ‖ ut] ubi dicitur *praem.* Mu2 ‖ docuit] docuerit L **10.3.** C.] arg. contra *praem.* Vp ‖ v.] ii. A ‖ c. ii.] Accusatores Ma, ii°. Accusatores Mu2 ‖ ante] iram te A, ubi dicitur *praem.* Mu2, n⟩atura⟨ P1 ‖ externum] esternam P1, extremum A C Vb Vp **10.4.** C.] arg. contra pro *praem.* Vp ‖ Non] c. *praem.* Mu1 ‖ fine] capituli *add.* Ma **10.5.** xxxii.] xxiii. G Mu2 ‖ i.] v. Mu1 ‖ Quod] Qui C ‖ Igitur] ubi dicitur *praem.* Mu2, *om.* P1 ‖ si—aliam] scium L ‖ aliam] ralis *exp.* Ma **10.6.** *post § 10.7 tr.* Ba Ba1 C G L Ma Mu1 Mu2 P1, *post § 10.8 tr.* Vp ‖ C. ii. q. vii.] C. eadem q. eadem Ma Mu2, et c. P1 ‖ ii.] x. L ‖ Querendum] (c. *praem.* Mu1) est *add.* Ba Ba1 Ma Mu1 P1, Quasi credendum G, *om.* L ‖ cuius] quasi L, ubi dicitur *praem.* Mu2 ‖ et—fine *om.* C ‖ et c.] C. eadem q. eadem Ma ‖ in fine *om.* Mu1 ‖ fine] finem capituli A, episcopi *add. male* Ba, capituli *add.* Ba1 Ma Vp

⟨9.⟩ From a close relationship: understand this broadly.

⟨9.1.⟩ C.5 q.5 c.3.
⟨9.2.⟩ C.3 q.5 c.1 and c.2.
⟨9.3.⟩ C.35 q.6 c.1.
⟨9.4.⟩ C.16 q.2 c.1.

⟨10.⟩ From the consequence of a deed and from the preceding action.

⟨10.1.⟩ C.22 q.2–3 c.21: remember that [Jehu] killed the priests [of Baal].
⟨10.2.⟩ C.22 q.2–3 c.18.
⟨10.3.⟩ C.3 q.5 c.2.
⟨10.4.⟩ C.5 q.5 c.2 at the end.
⟨10.5.⟩ C.33 q.1 c.1, c.2.
⟨10.6.⟩ C.2 q.7 c.18 and c.24 at the end.

⟨10.7.⟩ C. eadem q. eadem Accusatio (C.2 q.7 c.15) "prius ad eos recurrat" et c. Si quis erga (C.2 q.7 c.16).

⟨10.8.⟩ C. xx. q. iii. Eos (C.20 q.3 c.3) in fine.

⟨11.⟩ Ex modo agendi.

⟨11.1.⟩ C. ii. q. vii. Accusatio quoque (C.2 q.7 c.15) "prius quam hec egerint lacerare."

⟨11.2.⟩ Q. eadem c. Si quis erga (C.2 q.7 c.16) et c. Si quis ab episcopo (C.2 q.7 c.20) "si nichil convitii."

⟨11.3.⟩ C. xxii. q. ii. Animadvertendum (C.22 q.2–3 c.2) "iudicium."

⟨11.4.⟩ C. eadem q. ultima Quotiens (C.22 q.5 c.21) "aut non ut convenit."

⟨11.5.⟩ D. xliii. Sit rector (D.43 c.1) in fine "quia si importunitas."

⟨11.6.⟩ D. xli Quisquis rebus (D.41 c.1) et c. Delicie (D.41 c.2) et c. Quod dicit (D.41 c.4).

⟨11.7.⟩ C. xxxii. q. iv. Origo (C.32 q.4 c.5).

⟨11.8.⟩ C. i. q. ii. Quam pio (C.1 q.2 c.2) "dum tamen omnis absit pactio."

⟨11.9.⟩ C. xi. q. i. Petimus (C.11 q.1 c.19) "servata forma discipline."

⟨11.10.⟩ C. eadem q. eadem Si qui clericorum (C.11 q.1 c.25).

10.7. *om. per totum* A ‖ C. eadem q. eadem] C. ii. q. vii. Ba Ba1 C G L Ma Mu1 P1 Mu2 Vp ‖ Accusatio] Accusantio *cum* n *exp.* G, Occasio L ‖ prius] ubi dicitur *praem.* Mu2 ‖ recurrat ad eos *tr.* C Mu1 P1 Vb ‖ et c. *om.* C, C. eadem q. eadem Ma, *rep.* P1 ‖ erga] *om.* L, "non semel sed sepissime" *add.* Ma, gra. Vb **10.8.** *om. per totum* A Ba C G L Ma Mu1 Mu2 P1 Vb **11.** *om. per totum* Ba1 P1 **11.1.** C.] arg. contra *praem.* Vp ‖ quoque *om.* A Ba Ba1 C L Ma Mu1 Mu2 P1 Vp ‖ prius] ubi dicitur *praem.* Mu2 ‖ egerint hec *tr.* C ‖ hec] hoc A Ba Ba1 G L Ma Mu1 ‖ egerint] egerit Ba1 ‖ lacerare *om.* Ma Mu1 P1 **11.2.** Q. eadem] et L P1, C. eadem *praem.* Ma, C. i. q. i. Mu1 ‖ Q.] arg. contra *praem.* Vp ‖ c. *om.* Ma Mu1 ‖ et *om.* Ma ‖ c.[2]] *om. L Ma* ‖ ab episcopo] *om. C Vp* ‖ si] sed Ma, ubi dicitur *praem.* Mu2 ‖ si nichil] siracu. Vp ‖ convitii] vicii A, *om.* C Vp, aut criminationis obiecerit *add.* Ma, coniugii Mu1 **11.3.** C. xxii. *del. et ins.* Mu1 ‖ C.] arg. pro *praem.* Vp ‖ q. ii. *om.* Ba1 L ‖ ii. *om.* C, iv. Mu1, i. Vp ‖ Animadvertendum] est *add.* A Ba Ba1 C G L Ma Mu1 Mu2 P1 Vp ‖ iudicium] ubi dicitur *praem.* Mu2 **11.4.** C. eadem] et L ‖ C.] arg. contra *praem.* Vp ‖ aut] autem Ba1, ubi dicitur *praem.* Mu2 **11.5.** D.] arg. contra *praem.* Vp ‖ xliii.] xliv. Mu2 ‖ Sit] Scit C, Si Mu1, c. *praem.* P1 ‖ fine] finem A C, capituli *add.* Ma ‖ quia—importunitas *om.* A Ba Ba1 C G L Ma Mu1 Mu2 P1 Vp **11.6.** D.] arg. contra *praem.* Vp ‖ Quisquis] c. *praem.* P1 ‖ rebus *om.* Mu1 ‖ et[1] c.[1] *om.* L ‖ c.[1] *om.* Ma ‖ Delicie] De licite Ba Ba1, "appetenter" *add.* Ma ‖ et[2]—dicit *om.* Ma ‖ et[2] c.[2] *om.* L ‖ Quod] Qui A C G L, Quo Mu1, Quid Mu2 ‖ dicit] "ardenter" *add.* A Ba Ba1 G P1 Vp, arderetur *add. male* C, videtur *add. male* L, ardentur *add. male* Mu1 **11.7.** C. xxxii. *om.* A ‖ C.] arg. contra *praem.* Vp ‖ xxxii.] xxxiii. Ba ‖ iv.] iii. G Mu2 ‖ Origo] quidem *add.* Ma, c. *praem.* P1 **11.8.** C.] arg. pro *praem.* Vp ‖ q. ii. *om.* L ‖ Quam] g. (*cum abbr. signo*) *corr.* P1 ‖ pio] ipsio A ‖ dum tamen omnis] divi cum causas L ‖ dum] dm *cum* m *exp. et corr.* A, ubi dicitur *praem.* Mu2 **11.9.** *om. per totum* A Ba C Ma Mu1 P1 Vb Vp ‖ servata] secundum naturam L, ubi dicitur *praem.* Mu2 **11.10.** *om. per totum* A Ba C Ma Mu1 P1 Vb Vp ‖ C. eadem q. eadem] et c. L

⟨10.7.⟩ C.2 q.7 c.15 and c.16.
⟨10.8.⟩ C.20 q.3 c.3 at the end.

⟨11.⟩ From the course of action.
⟨11.1.⟩ C.2 q.7 c.15.
⟨11.2.⟩ C.2 q.7 c.16 and c.20.
⟨11.3.⟩ C.22 q.2–3 c.2.
⟨11.4.⟩ C.22 q.5 c.21.
⟨11.5.⟩ D.43 c.1.
⟨11.6.⟩ D.41 c.1 and c.2 and c.4.
⟨11.7.⟩ C.32 q.4 c.5.
⟨11.8.⟩ C.1 q.2 c.2.
⟨11.9.⟩ C.11 q.1 c.19.
⟨11.10.⟩ C.11 q.1 c.25.

⟨IV. Circa intrinseci facti substantiam⟩

⟨1.⟩ Vidimus ex quibus locis circa extrinseca super incertis disputavimus. ⟨2.⟩ Restat ut despiciamus ex quibus locis circa intrinseca, id est voluntatem vel consensum eiusque accidentia, cum enim hec dubia sint, argumentemur. ⟨3.⟩ Cum de voluntatis vel consensus essentia dubitatur, aliquem consensisse vel econtra presumitur ex his causis:

⟨3.1.⟩ Ex perseverantia, vel longa mora eiusque contrario.
⟨3.2.⟩ Ex gravi mentis vel corporis calamitate eiusque contrario.
⟨3.3.⟩ Ex silentio eiusque contrario.
⟨3.4.⟩ Ex negligentia eiusque contrario.
⟨3.5.⟩ Ex coactione.
⟨3.6.⟩ Ex aliis exterioribus signis.

⟨4.⟩ Ex perseverantia vel diuturnitate eiusque contrario.
⟨4.1.⟩ C. xvii. q. ii. Consaldus (C.17 q.2–3 c.1) "mox se fieri."
⟨4.2.⟩ D. lxiii. Quanto (D.63 c.10) "consensum perdurare."
⟨4.3.⟩ C. ii. q. iii. Si quis iratus (C.2 q.3 c.5).
⟨4.4.⟩ C. i. q. iii. Si quis dator (C.1 q.3 c.2) "sed si perseverans."

IV.1. Vidimus] Circa intrinseca *praem.* Mu1 ‖ incertis] incerta L ‖ disputavimus *om.* C, disputatur L, disputemus Mu1, presumatur Mu2 **2.** iii. modus *praem. marg.* G ‖ Restat—ex *om.* A ‖ despiciamus] inspiciamus Mu1 Mu2 ‖ ex[1] *om.* P1 ‖ intrinseca] extrinseca P1, exintrinseca *cum* ex *exp.* Vp ‖ vel] seu G ‖ eiusque] eius actore P1, ei que Vp ‖ accidentia] accione *praem.* Ba Ba1 Ma, essentia *praem. et cum* a *exp. et corr.* e Mu2, accidere *praem.* G Vp ‖ enim *om.* A C G L Mu1 Mu2 Vp ‖ hec] circa *praem.* Vb ‖ sint] sit A, sunt Ba1 L Ma, *om.* P1 Vb ‖ argumentemur] argumentatur L Mu1, argumentetur Mu2, argumentamur Vb **3.** cum] itaque *add.* L ‖ consensu … voluntatis *tr.* L ‖ aliquem] aliquis C Vp, aliquid Vb ‖ consensisse] consenssisse *cum* s[1] *exp.* G, consessisse Vb **3.1.** vel *om.* A Ba Ba1 G Ma Mu1 Vp ‖ eiusque] eius C, et eius Vp **3.2.** *om. per totum* (*homoiotel.*) L ‖ gravi] gravis *cum* s *exp.* P1 ‖ vel] et A C Vp ‖ eiusque] et eius C Vp, eiusve G **3.3.** *om. per totum* (*homoiotel.*) L, *marg.* Mu1 ‖ eiusque] eiusve C, et eius Ba Ba1 G Ma Mu2 Vp **3.4.** *post § 3.5 tr.* Ba Ba1 L, *om. per totum* (*homoiotel.*) C P1, *marg.* Mu1 ‖ eiusque] et eius Ba Ba1 C Ma Mu2 Vp, eius Mu1 **3.5.** *post § 3.1 tr.* Vp ‖ coactione] actione Mu1 **3.6.** Ex] et Mu1, et *praem.* P1 ‖ aliis *om.* A ‖ signis exterioribus *tr.* P1 **4.** *om. per totum* Ba1 P1 ‖ perseverantia] severantia A ‖ vel *om.* Ma, et Vp ‖ diuturnitate] que *add.* L, longa morga Ma ‖ eiusque] eius *et ante* diuturnitate *tr.* L, eius Ma **4.1.** C.] pro *praem.* Mu1, arg. pro eo qui se fieri *praem.* Vp ‖ xvii.] xxii. Mu2 ‖ Consaldus] c. *praem.* Mu1 ‖ mox] ubi dicitur *praem.* Mu2 ‖ fieri se *tr.* Mu1 ‖ fieri] monachum *add.* Mu2 **4.2.** D.] contra *praem.* Mu1, arg. contra ea vel qui ele⟩ctus⟨ *praem.* Vp ‖ lxiii.] xliii. G, lxiiii. *cum* i.[1] *exp.* Vb ‖ Quanto] Quando Vb ‖ consensum] consensu Ba Ba1, contrario sensu Mu2 ‖ perdurare] perdurat L, perdurante Mu2 **4.3.** C.] pro *praem.* Mu1, arg. pro x. *praem. et cum* x. *exp.* Vp ‖ iratus] natus L, "sed permissio" *add.* Vp **4.4.** *post § 4.7 tr.* Mu1 P1, *om. per totum* A Ba Ba1 C G L Ma Mu2 Vp ‖ Si] c. *praem.* Mu1 ‖ sed] et Vb

⟨IV. On the substance of an intrinsic fact⟩

⟨1.⟩ We have seen from which topics we can dispute about the uncertainties of extrinsic facts. ⟨2.⟩ It remains to be seen from which topics we can adduce arguments about the intrinsic ones, i.e. the will or consent and its circumstances, when indeed they are doubtful. ⟨3.⟩ When there is uncertainty about the essence of will or consent, it is presumed that someone had consented to something or not from the following reasons:

⟨3.1.⟩ From persistence or long duration and its contrary.
⟨3.2.⟩ From a grave illness of mind or body and its contrary.
⟨3.3.⟩ From silence and its contrary.
⟨3.4.⟩ From negligence and its contrary.
⟨3.5.⟩ From duress.
⟨3.6.⟩ From other external signs.

⟨4.⟩ From persistence or long duration and its contrary.
⟨4.1.⟩ C.17 q.2–3 c.1.
⟨4.2.⟩ D.63 c.10.
⟨4.3.⟩ C.2 q.3 c.5.
⟨4.4.⟩ C.1 q.3 c.2.

⟨4.5.⟩ C. xxxiii. q. iii. d. i. Cogitatio (D.1 de pen. c.20), Quam si perseverantia (D.1 de pen. c.21).

⟨4.6.⟩ C. i. q. i. Constat (C.1 q.1 c.111) "si statim."

⟨4.7.⟩ C. xx. q. ii. Si in (C.20 q.2 c.1) et c. Puella (C.20 q.2 c.2).

⟨4.8.⟩ D. lxxxii. Presbiter (D.82 c.5) "si non in vitio perduraverit."

⟨4.9.⟩ C. ii. q. v. Quanto (C.2 q.5 c.8) in fine capituli.

⟨4.10.⟩ C. xxvii. q. ii. c. i. (C.27 q.1 c.1) "permanete."

⟨4.11.⟩ C. eadem q. eadem c. ii. (C.27 q.1 c.2) "permanete."

⟨4.12.⟩ C. xxxii. q. ii. Cum dicitur (C.32 q.2 c.12), Mulier (C.32 q.2 c.14) "statim."

⟨5.⟩ Ex gravi mentis vel corporis calamitate eiusque contrario.

⟨5.1.⟩ C. xvii. q. ii. Consaldus (C.17 q.2–3 c.1) "fervore passionis."

⟨5.2.⟩ C. xxxii. q. vii. Neque furiosus (C.32 q.7 c.26).

⟨5.3.⟩ C. xv. q. i. Aliquos (C.15 q.1 c.5) "eo quod non voluntate" et c. Illa (C.15 q.1 c.6).

⟨5.4.⟩ C. eadem q. eadem Sane (C.15 q.1 c.7).

⟨5.5.⟩ C. iii. q. ix. Indicas (C.3 q.9 c.14) "sane mentis."

4.5. *om. per totum* A Ma ‖ C.] pro *praem.* Mu1, arg. pro x. *praem et cum* x. *exp.* Vp ‖ xxxiii.] xxiii. Ba Ba1 C ‖ Cogitatio—perseverantia *om.* Mu2 ‖ Cogitatio] Cognatio Ba Ba1 C G L ‖ Quam si] Quasi Ba Ba1 Vp ‖ Quam] quod L Mu1 **4.6.** C.] pro *praem.* Mu1, arg. pro *praem.* Vp ‖ i. *om* Vp ‖ Constat] multos *add.* A Ba Ba1 C G Ma Vp, c. *praem.* Mu1 P1 ‖ si] ubi dicitur *praem.* Mu2 ‖ statim] constanti *cum* con *et* n² *exp. et corr.* G **4.7.** C.] pro et contra *praem.* Mu1, arg. pro et contra *praem.* Vp ‖ xx.] xxx. Ba Ba1 ‖ Si in] Sum Ba Ba1 G Vb Vp, faci L, *post* Puella *tr. et* qualibet *add.* Ma ‖ in] qualibet *add.* P1 ‖ et . *om.* Ma ‖ c. *om.* L ‖ Puella] "statim," "annum" *add.* Vp **4.8.** *post §4.12 tr.* G L, *om. per totum* A Ba Ba1 C Ma P1 Vp ‖ lxxxii.] lxxxi. L ‖ si—perduraverit] non percuti L, non peramaverit G ‖ si] ubi dicitur *praem. et* non *add.* Mu2 ‖ non *om.* Mu1 Vb ‖ perduraverit] perduravit Mu2 **4.9.** *om. per totum* A Ba C Ma Mu1 P1 Vb Vp ‖ C.] arg. *praem. marg.* G ‖ v.] iv. Mu2 ‖ Quanto] qtu *cum abbr. signo* G **4.10.** *om. per totum* A Ba C Ma Mu1 P1 Vb Vp **4.10.** *om. per totum* A Ba C Ma Mu1 P1 Vb Vp ‖ C. eadem q. eadem] et L ‖ c.] q. *praem. et exp.* G ‖ permanete *om.* Mu2 **4.12.** *om. per totum* Mu2 ‖ C.] pro et contra *praem.* Mu1, D. *exp. et corr.* C. P1, arg. pro et contra *praem.* Vp ‖ xxxii.] xxii. Ba Ba1, lxxxii. *cum* l *exp.* P1 ‖ Cum—statim *om.* Ma ‖ Mulier *om.* A Ba Ba1 C G L Vb Vp ‖ statim] statum L Mu1, "et tacuerit" *add.* Vp **5.** *om. per totum* Ba1 P1 ‖ Ex] arg. pro *praem.* Vp ‖ mentis] tantis A ‖ eiusque contrario *om.* Vp **5.1.** C.] arg. pro *praem.* Vp ‖ xvii.] xxxvi. C ‖ fervore] ubi dicitur *praem.* Mu2 **5.2.** *om. per totum* A ‖ C.] arg. pro *praem.* Vp ‖ xxxii.] xxxiii. Ba Mu2 ‖ furiosus] furtimus Ba **5.3.** C.] arg. pro *praem.* Vp ‖ xv.] xx. Mu2 ‖ Aliquos] Aliqui nos Mu1, a Mu2 ‖ eo—Illa *om.* Mu2 ‖ quod] qui C L ‖ non voluntate] noluerit L ‖ non] in Ba ‖ voluntate] voluntatem C ‖ et c.] C. eadem q. eadem Ma, et c. Sane (C.15 q.1 c.7) *praem.* Mu1 ‖ c. *om.* L ‖ Illa] cavenda *add.* Ma **5.4.** C. eadem q. eadem] et L, *om.* Ma Mu1, et c. P1 ‖ Sane] c. *praem.* Ba1, *om.* Mu2 **5.5.** *post §5.3 tr.* Mu2, *om. per totum* A Ba C Ma Mu1 P1 Vb Vp ‖ C.] x. *praem.* L ‖ ix.] xi. L ‖ Indicas] Indicans L ‖ sane] ubi dicitur *praem.* Mu2 ‖ mentis] tamen L

⟨4.5.⟩ D.1 de pen. c.20, c.21.
⟨4.6.⟩ C.1 q.1 c.111.
⟨4.7.⟩ C.20 q.2 c.1 and c.2.
⟨4.8.⟩ D.82 c.5.
⟨4.9.⟩ C.2 q.5 c.8 at the end of the chapter.
⟨4.10.⟩ C.27 q.1 c.1.
⟨4.11.⟩ C.27 q.1 c.2.
⟨4.12.⟩ C.32 q.2 c.12, c.14.

⟨5.⟩ From a grave illness of mind or body and its contrary.
⟨5.1.⟩ C.17 q.2–3 c.1.
⟨5.2.⟩ C.32 q.7 c.26.
⟨5.3.⟩ C.15 q.1 c.5 and c.6.
⟨5.4.⟩ C.15 q.1 c.7.
⟨5.5.⟩ C.3 q.9 c.14.

⟨6.⟩ Ex silentio eiusque contrario.

⟨6.1.⟩ D. liv. Si servus sciente et non contradicente (D.54 c.20) et c. Quis aut (D.54 c.11) "contradictione."

⟨6.2.⟩ C. xx. q. ii. Puella (C.20 q.2 c.2) et c. Si in qualibet minori (C.20 q.2 c.1).

⟨6.3.⟩ D. xxvii. Diaconus (D.27 c.1) "tacuerit."

⟨6.4.⟩ pro, contra: C. eadem q. eadem Cum dicitur (C.32 q.2 c.12).

⟨6.5.⟩ D. xxviii. Diaconi (D.28 c.8).

⟨6.6.⟩ C. xxxii. q. ii. Mulier (C.32 q.2 c.14) "et tacuerit," "contradixerit."

⟨7.⟩ Ex negligentia eiusque contrario.

⟨7.1.⟩ D. lxxxiii. Error (D.83 c.3) et Consentire (D.83 c.5).

⟨7.2.⟩ D. lxxxvi. Inferiorum (D.86 c.1) "negligentesque rectores."

⟨7.3.⟩ D. lxxxvi. Facientis (D.86 c.3) "culpam habet."

⟨7.4.⟩ C. ii. q. vii. Negligere (C.2 q.7 c.55).

⟨7.5.⟩ C. xxiii. q. iii. Qui potest (C.23 q.3 c.8).

⟨7.6.⟩ C. eadem q. viii. Preterea (C.23 q.8 c.12) in fine.

---

6. *om. per totum* Ba1 P1 ‖ eiusque] vel eius Ba **6.1.** D.] pro contra *praem.* Mu1, arg. contra et pro *praem.* Vp ‖ liv.] liii. G ‖ servus] servum L ‖ sciente—contradicente *om.* L ‖ sciente] scienti A Ba Ba1 C G ‖ et^1] vel Ba1 P1 ‖ non] sic A, *om.* C G Vp ‖ contradicente] contradicenti Ba Ba1 G ‖ et^2—contradictione *om.* Ma ‖ et c.] D. eadem Mu2 ‖ Quis] Quod A, Quos Ba Ba1, Si *praem.* C L Mu1, Qui ius P1 ‖ aut] ante A Ba G L ‖ contradictione] contradictionem A Ba1 G Vb Vp, conditione Ba, preeunte (ubi dicitur *praem.* Mu2, et *add.* P1) *add.* C Mu1 Mu2 P1 Vp, dttia L **6.2.** C.] pro contra *praem.* Mu1, arg. pro contra et contra *praem.* Vp ‖ Puella] c. *praem.* P1 ‖ et *om.* Ma ‖ c. *om.* L Ma ‖ Si in] Sui P1 ‖ in *om.* Ba1 G L ‖ qualibet in *tr.* Ba, quelibet G ‖ minori] mu. G L, *om.* Mu1 Mu2 P1, "mox" *add.* Vp **6.3.** *om. per totum* A ‖ D.] C. L, pro contra *praem.* Mu1, arg. pro et contra *praem.* Vp ‖ xxvi.] xvi. Ba Ba1 C G L, xxvi. Vb Vp ‖ tacuerit] "quod si in ordinatione" *praem.* Ma, tacuit G Mu1, ubi dicitur *praem.* Mu2, "et dixerit non posse" *add.* Vp **6.3.** *om. per totum* A Ba C G L Ma Mu2 P1 Vb Vp **6.5.** *om. per totum* Mu2 ‖ D.] arg. pro et contra *praem.* Vp ‖ Diaconi] "sane tacuerint" *add.* Ma, "protestati dicentes" "tacuerit" *add.* Vp **6.6.** *om. per totum* Ma ‖ C.] arg. pro et contra *praem.* Vp ‖ xxii.] xxxii. Ba Ba1 ‖ Mulier] Cum dicitur (C.32 q.2 c.12) A Ba Ba1 C G L Mu2 Vp, c. *praem.* Mu1 ‖ tacuerit] tacuit G ‖ contradixerit] et c. eo quod *praem.* Mu1, et c. "eo quod contradicerit" P1, scilicet in fine *add.* Vp **7.** *om. per totum* Ba1 P1 Vp **7.1.** D.—consentire] *rep.* Vp ‖ D.] contra *praem.* Mu1, arg. contra (et pro *add.* Vp) *praem.* Vp Vp$_1$ ‖ Error] c. *praem.* A Ba Ba1 G Vp, Errea L, Errori P1 ‖ et *om.* L Ma Mu2 ‖ Consentire] videtur *add.* Ma, c. *praem.* Mu1 P1, ubi dicitur *praem. cum* dicitur *interl.* Mu2 **7.2.** *om. per totum* A Ba C G L Ma Mu2 Vb Vp ‖ Inferiorum] c. *praem.* Mu1 *add.* Mu1 P1 **7.3.** *om. per totum* A Ma ‖ D. lxxxvi.] et c. P1 ‖ D.] contra *praem.* Mu1, arg. contra *praem.* Vp ‖ lxxxvi.] eadem Mu1 ‖ Facientis *om.* Ba Ba1 C G L Mu2 Vb, vel *praem. et post* culpam *tr.* Vp ‖ habet *om.* Ba Ba1 C G L Mu2 Vb Vp, etc. *add.* P1 **7.4.** C.] D. c. A, contra *praem.* Mu1, arg. contra *praem.* Vp ‖ vii.] iv. G L Mu2 ‖ Negligere] "cum possis" *add.* Ma, *om.* Mu2, c. *praem.* P1 **7.5.** C.] arg. contra *praem.* Vp ‖ xxiii.] xxxiii. L ‖ Qui potest *om.* Mu2 ‖ Qui] Quod (c. *praem.* P1) A P1, Quid Ba ‖ potest] obuiare *add.* Ma **7.6.** C. eadem] et Ba Ba1 L ‖ C.] contra *praem.* Mu1 ‖ eadem] xxiii. P1 ‖ Preterea] c. *praem.* Mu1 P1 ‖ fine] capituli *add.* Ma

⟨6.⟩ From silence and its contrary.

⟨6.1.⟩ D.54 c.20 and D.54 c.11.
⟨6.2.⟩ C.20 q.2 c.2 and c.1.
⟨6.3.⟩ D.27 c.1.
⟨6.4.⟩ For, against: C.32 q.2 c.12.
⟨6.5.⟩ D.28 c.8.
⟨6.6.⟩ C.32 q.2 c.14.

⟨7.⟩ From negligence and its contrary.

⟨7.1.⟩ D.83 c.3 and c.5.
⟨7.2.⟩ D. 86 c.1.
⟨7.3.⟩ D.86 c.3.
⟨7.4.⟩ C.2 q.7 c.55.
⟨7.5.⟩ C.23 q.3 c.8.
⟨7.6.⟩ C.23 q.8 c.12 at the end.

⟨7.7.⟩ D. xxiii. Pervenit (D.23 c.13).
⟨7.8.⟩ D. lxxxiv. c. i. (D.84 c.1).
⟨7.9.⟩ D. xliii. Multis (D.43 c.5).
⟨7.10.⟩ C. xxiv. q. iii. Qui negligunt (C.24 q.3 c.3).

⟨8.⟩ Ex coactione vel econtra.
⟨8.1.⟩ C. xxxiii. q. v. Notificasti (C.33 q.5 c.2) "licentiam extorsisse," "minis et terroribus."
⟨8.2.⟩ D. l. Presbiteros (D.50 c.32) "velud extra delictum."
⟨8.3.⟩ C. i. q. i. Constat multos vim passos (C.1 q.1 c.111).
⟨8.4.⟩ C. xxxi. q. iii. De neptis (C.31 q.2 c.3) "unus debet esse animus."
⟨8.5.⟩ C. xx. q. iii. Presens (C.20 q.3 c.4) "semper."
⟨8.6.⟩ C. xxxii. q. i. (C.32 q.1) universa capitula.

⟨9.⟩ Ex aliis exterioribus signis, puta ex fletu, clamore, fuga et similibus.
⟨9.1.⟩ C. xxxi. q. ii. Si verum (C.31 q.2 c.1) "flentem."
⟨9.2.⟩ C. xxxiv. q. i. Non satis (C.34 q.1–2 c.3) "et non clamaverit."
⟨9.3.⟩ C. xx. q. iii. Presens (C.20 q.3 c.4) "ab insequentibus."
⟨9.4.⟩ C. i. q. i. Constat (C.1 q.1 c.111) "rediit," "redierunt."

7.7. *om. per totum* A Ba C Ma Mu1 P1 Vb **7.8.** *om. per totum* A Ba C L Ma Mu1 P1 Vb Vp ‖ lxxxiv.] lxxxiii. Mu2 **7.9.** *ante §7.8 tr.* L, *om. per totum* A Ba C Ma Mu1 P1 Vb Vp ‖ xliii.] lxxxiv. L, liv. Mu2 ‖ Multis *om.* Mu2 **7.10.** *om. per totum* A Ba C L Ma Mu1 P1 Vb Vp **8.** *om. per totum* Ba1 P1 ‖ vel econtra] eiusque contrario Ma, et eius contrario Mu1 ‖ econtra] contra Mu2 **8.1.** C.] pro *praem.* Mu1, arg. pro *praem.* Vp ‖ v.] ii. Mu2 ‖ Notificasti licentiam] Notificantiam L ‖ Notificasti] c. *praem.* P1 ‖ licentiam] licentia A Mu2, *om.* Ma ‖ extorsisse *om.* A Ba Ba1 C G L Ma Mu1 Mu2 P1 Vp, exercuisse *cum* ercui *exp. et corr.* Vb ‖ minis] nimis L ‖ et terroribus *om.* L **8.2.** D.] pro *praem.* Mu1, arg. pro *praem.* Vp ‖ Presbiteros] c. *praem.* Mu1 ‖ velud] vidit Ba Ba1, vel de G, *om.* L, ubi dicitur vel Mu2, vel id est Vb ‖ extra delictum] "violenter attraherent" Mu2 **8.3.** C.] pro *praem.* Mu1, arg. pro *praem.* Vp ‖ Constat] c. *praem.* Mu1 ‖ multos *om.* L ‖ vim] ubi dicitur *praem.* Mu2 **8.4.** *post §8.6 tr.* Mu1 ‖ C.] pro *praem.* Mu1, arg. pro *praem.* Vp ‖ iii.] ii. Ba Ba1 Ma Mu1 P1 ‖ neptis] tue *add.* Ma ‖ unus *om.* Ba Ba1 P1 Vp, ubi dicitur *praem.* Mu2 ‖ animus *om.* L, et *praem.* Ma **8.5.** *om. per totum* A Ba C G Ma Mu2 P1 Vb ‖ C.] pro *praem.* Mu1, arg. pro *praem.* Vp **8.6.** *om. per totum* A Ba Ba1 C G L Ma Mu2 Vp ‖ C.] pro *praem.* Mu1 ‖ i.] v. P1, *om.* Vb ‖ capitula *om.* Mu1 **9.** *om. per totum* Ba1 P1 ‖ signis] si quis L ‖ puta *cum abbr. signo supra* a Ma ‖ ex *om.* C L ‖ fletu] fleti L ‖ clamore] clamorem L ‖ fuga *om.* L Vp ‖ et] vel L **9.1.** C.] arg. pro *praem.* Vp ‖ flentem] et renitentem *add.* Ma, ubi dicitur *praem.* Mu2, *om.* P1 **9.2.** C.] arg. pro *praem.* Vp ‖ xxxiv.] xxxiii. A ‖ q. i. *om.* Ba Ba1 C G L Vp ‖ i.] ii. Ma, i. et ii. Mu1 Mu2 P1 ‖ Non] c. *praem.* Mu1 ‖ et] ubi dicitur *praem.* Mu2 ‖ non *om.* L ‖ clamaverit] clamavit A, reclamaverit Ba C **9.3.** C.] arg. pro *praem.* Vp ‖ xx.] xxi. Mu2 ‖ Presens] c. *praem.* Mu1 P1 ‖ ab] demum *praem.* Mu1 P1, ubi dicitur *praem.* Mu2 **9.4.** C.] arg. *praem.* Vp ‖ q. i. *om.* Ba ‖ i. *om.* Ba1 ‖ Constat] c. *praem.* Mu1 ‖ rediit] reddunt C, reddiderat G, reddi L, ad ecclesiam *praem.* Ma, *om.* Mu1 P1, ubi dicitur *praem.* Mu2 ‖ redierunt *om.* A Ba Ba1 C G L Ma Mu2 P1 Vp

⟨7.7.⟩ D.23 c.13.
⟨7.8.⟩ D. 84 c.1.
⟨7.9.⟩ D.43 c.5.
⟨7.10.⟩ C.24 q.3 c.3.

⟨8.⟩ From duress or the contrary.
⟨8.1.⟩ C.33 q.5 c.2.
⟨8.2.⟩ D.50 c.32.
⟨8.3.⟩ C.1 q.1 c.111.
⟨8.4.⟩ C.31 q.2 c.3.
⟨8.5.⟩ C.20 q.3 c.4.
⟨8.6.⟩ C.32 q.1, the whole chapters.

⟨9.⟩ From other external signs, namely from weeping, clamor, escape, and similar things.
⟨9.1.⟩ C.31 q.2 c.1.
⟨9.2.⟩ C.34 q.1–2 c.3.
⟨9.3.⟩ C.20 q.3 c.4.
⟨9.4.⟩ C.1 q.1 c.111.

⟨9.5.⟩ D. l. Si quis diaconus (D.50 c.29) "nec compunctio."
⟨9.6.⟩ D. l. De his vero (D.50 c.34) in fine capituli.
⟨9.7.⟩ C. xxvii. q. i. Non aliqua (C.27 q.1 c.4) "ipse concubitus" etc.
⟨9.8.⟩ C. xxxii. q. v. Non solo (C.32 q.5 c.12).
⟨9.9.⟩ D. lxxiv. c. i. (D.74 c.1).

⟨v. Circa intrinseci facti qualitatem⟩

⟨1.⟩ Vidimus ex quibus locis quem voluisse vel consensisse, vel econtra, coniectare possimus. ⟨2.⟩ Sed quia contingit hoc bona quandoque vel mala intentione, fraude vel sinceritate fieri, et secundum hoc voluntatem vel consensum bonam vel malam iudicari, ex quibus locis hoc conspici valeat videamus. ⟨3.⟩ Itaque ex omnibus fere locis ex quibus facta extrinseca bona vel mala connicimus, etiam consensum et voluntatem probandam vel improbandam intelligimus. ⟨4.⟩ Ex quibus tamen aliquos repilogare volumus, ut concordantias, ex quibus hoc familiarius propendi valeamus, supponamus:

⟨4.1.⟩ Ex persona.
⟨4.2.⟩ Ex causa.
⟨4.3.⟩ Ex fine sive intentione.
⟨4.4.⟩ Ex debito vel indebito persone officio.

9.5. *om. per totum* A Ba C Ma Mu1 P1 Vb Vp ‖ quis] is L ‖ nec] ubi dicitur *praem.* L Mu2 9.6. *om. per totum* A Ba C Ma Mu1 P1 Vb Vp ‖ l.] i. L, eadem Mu2 ‖ De *om.* L ‖ his] ea L 9.7. *om. per totum* A Ba C Ma Mu1 P1 Vb Vp ‖ Non] nec G ‖ ipse] ubi dicitur *praem.* Mu2 ‖ etc. *om.* L 9.8. *om. per totum* A Ba C Ma Mu1 P1 Vb Vp ‖ Non] Nec G Mu2 9.9. *om. per totum* A Ba C Ma Mu1 P1 Vb Vp v.1. quem] quando C Vp, quam L, quid *add.* Vb ‖ voluisse] vel[1] consensisse *om.* Vb ‖ consensisse] concessisse A ‖ econtra] contrario Mu2, contradicere P1 ‖ coniectare] competere Ba Ba1 G Mu2 Vp, coniecture L, competitur P1 ‖ possimus] possumus G L Mu1 Mu2 P1 Vp 2. iv.us *praem. marg.* G ‖ quia] enim *add.* A, *om.* C ‖ hoc[1] *om.* Ba Ba1 Ma P1, hic L, hec G Mu2 ‖ bona quandoque] quandoque bona Mu1 ‖ bona *om.* P1 ‖ quandoque *post* vel mala *tr.* L ‖ vel[1] *om.* Ba1 C Ma Mu2 P1 Vp, *post* mala *tr.* G ‖ fraude] fraudis L Vp, et *praem.* Mu1 P1 ‖ sinceritate] necessitate Mu2 ‖ fieri] fidei P1 ‖ hoc[2] *om.* A ‖ vel[3]] et G L, *om.* P1 ‖ bonam … malam] bonum … malum C, bona … mala A Ba Ba1 G L Ma Mu1 Mu2 P1 Vp ‖ iudicari] iudicum Ba Ba1, videre L ‖ conspici] inspici Mu1 P1 3. ex[2] *om.* Ma ‖ facta *om.* G ‖ extrinseca] intrinseca Mu1 Mu2 P1 ‖ bona—etiam] etc. Vp ‖ vel[1]] sive Mu2 ‖ connicimus] communi A Vb, communis Ba Ba1, connimus Ma ‖ etiam] est Ba Ba1, et Mu2 ‖ consensum] consensu A Vb ‖ et] vel Mu2 ‖ voluntatem] voluntate A ‖ probandam … improbandam] improbandam … approbandam Mu2 ‖ probandam *om.* G, probanda L ‖ vel improbandam *om.* A ‖ improbandam] improbanda L 4. concordantias] concordantius Ba1 ‖ hoc *om.* P1 ‖ familiarius] facilius Mu2, *om.* P1 ‖ propendi] propendere Mu1 Vb ‖ valeamus] valeam Ba Ba1 Vp, valeat C G Ma Mu2, vale L, valeant P1 ‖ supponamus] supplicamus C, ad *praem.* L, ponamus P1 4.2. Ex] scilicet *praem.* Ba 4.3. fine] facto Ba ‖ sive] vel Ba1, sine C 4.4. persone *post* debit *tr.* Ba1

⟨9.5.⟩ D.50 c.29.
⟨9.6.⟩ D.50 c.34 at the end of the chapter.
⟨9.7.⟩ C.27 q.1 c.4.
⟨9.8.⟩ C.32 q.5 c.12.
⟨9.9.⟩ D.74 c.1.

⟨v. On the quality of an intrinsic fact⟩

⟨1.⟩ We have seen from which topics we could make a conjecture about whether or not someone had been willing or had given consent. ⟨2.⟩ But, since it happens that this is sometimes done with good or bad intention, with deceit or sincerity, and according to this will or consent may be judged either good or bad, let us see from which topics all of this may be considered. ⟨3.⟩ And so we can understand whether consent and will are to be approved or condemned from almost all the topics from which we can also infer whether the extrinsic facts are good or bad; ⟨4.⟩ Nevertheless, we want to summarize some of these in order to add some concordances from which we may be able to choose our topic in a more appropriate way:[2]

⟨4.1.⟩ From the person.
⟨4.2.⟩ From the cause.
⟨4.3.⟩ From the aim or intention.
⟨4.4.⟩ From the office, duly or unduly exercised by the person.

2 By 'concordances' (*concordantiae*), medieval jurists meant the parallel allegations: cf., for instance, Ioannes Bassianus, *Libellus de ordine iudiciorum*, ed. Nino Tamassia and Giovanni Battista Palmieri, BIMAE, 2:211–248, 220 § 69. The author of the *Perpendiculum*, however, uses the word to indicate the allegations both *pro* and *contra*, and more generally his brocards.

⟨4.5.⟩ Ex obedientia.

⟨4.6.⟩ Ex consequentia operis et actu precedenti, qui locus generalis est in omnibus iudiciis.

⟨5.⟩ Ex persona.

⟨5.1.⟩ D. lxxxviii. Fornicari (D.88 c.10).

⟨5.2.⟩ C. xi. q. iii. Absit (C.11 q.3 c.14).

⟨5.3.⟩ D. lxxxiv. c. i. ii. iii. (D.84 c.1, 2 et 3).

⟨5.4.⟩ Contra xxiii. q. viii. (C.23 q.8) omnibus premissis capitulis.

⟨5.5.⟩ C. xvii. q. vii. c. Quorumdam (?) et Quicumque recognoverit (C.16 q.7 c.4).

⟨5.6.⟩ C. ix. q. ii. Lugdunensis (C.9 q.2 c.10).

⟨5.7.⟩ C. xxiii. q. iv. Ea vindicta (C.23 q.4 c.51) "non est idoneus nisi," "ne odisse parvulum."

⟨5.8.⟩ D. xl. Non nos (D.40 c.1) "quis enim sanctum esse dubitet."

⟨5.9.⟩ C. xiv. q. v. Denique (C.14 q.5 c.10) "non est sacerdotale."

⟨5.10.⟩ D. l. Clericum qui (D.50 c.5) "Nam discreti."

⟨5.11.⟩ D. xcvii. Nobilissimus (D.97 c.3).

4.5 Ex *om.* Ba1 **4.6.** operis] corporis A ‖ actu] ex *praem.* Mu2 ‖ generalis] generale Ba1 ‖ omnibus] nominibus C ‖ iudiciis] dubiis A Ba Ba1 C G L Ma Mu1 Mu2 P1 Vp **5.** *om. per totum* Ba1 P1 ‖ persona] ut *add.* Mu1 **5.1.** D.] arg. pro et contra *praem.* Vp ‖ lxxxviii.] lxxxvi. L, lxxxiv. P1 ‖ Fornicari] c. *praem.* L, "hominibus" *add.* Ma, *om.* P1 **5.2.** *om. per totum* Ma Mu2 ‖ xi.] xii. A Vb ‖ q. iii.] qui A, quod G Vb ‖ Absit] c. *praem.* P1 **5.3.** D.] contra *praem.* Mu1 ‖ lxxxiv.] lxxxiii. Ba1 Ma P1 ‖ c. i. ii. iii. *om.* A Ba Ba1 C G L Mu2 Vp, Si quis episcopus fornicationem (D.83 c.1) D. eadem Nemo (D.83 c.2) Error (D.83 c.3) Quid prodest (D.83 c.4) Consentire (D.83 c.5) Ma, c. i. (*om.* P1) et (*om.* P1) ii. et iii. Mu1 P1 **5.4.** *om. per totum* A Ba Ba1 C G L Ma Mu2 Vp ‖ Contra] C. *add.* Mu1, C. P1 ‖ premissis] primis Mu1 P1 **5.5.** *post §5.6 tr.* L, *om. per totum* A C Mu1 P1 ‖ C.] et *praem.* Ba C G Vp ‖ xvii.] xi. L ‖ vii.] ultima L ‖ c.—recognoverit *om.* Mu2 ‖ c. *om.* L ‖ et *om.* Ma ‖ recognoverit *om.* L, Ex *add. male* Ma, recolo Vp **5.6.** *post §5 tr.* C ‖ C.] arg. pro *praem.* Vp ‖ ix.] xviii. L ‖ ii.] vii. L, i. Ma ‖ Lugdunensis] c. *praem.* L, c. Lundonensis P1, "sanctus" *add.* Vp **5.7.** C.] arg. pro et contra *praem.* Vp ‖ xxiii.] xvii. C ‖ iv.] iii. G ‖ Ea] † G, *om.* P1 ‖ vindicta] vindictione Ba, dicit G, tamen L ‖ non—nisi *om.* Ma ‖ non] ubi dicitur *praem.* Mu2 ‖ nisi—parvulum] vir C ‖ ne—parvulum] e *exp.* quid cuius Mu1, qui etc. P1 ‖ ne] qui Mu2, hoc *add.* Vp ‖ odisse] o⟩dium⟨ Mu2 ‖ parvulum] parvum (non est *add. male* G) Ba Ba1 G Vp, *om.* L Ma, s. Mu2 **5.8.** D.] arg. pro *praem.* Vp ‖ Non nos *om.* L ‖ Non] c. *praem.* Mu1 ‖ quis] qui Ba Ba1 Vp, ubi dicitur *praem.* Mu2 ‖ enim—esse *om.* P1 Vp ‖ enim *om.* A Ba C G L Ma Mu1 Vb ‖ esse A Ba Ba1 C G L Mu2 Vb ‖ dubitet] etc. *add.* Mu1, dubitat P1 **5.9.** *post §5.10 tr.* L ‖ C.] † Mu2, arg. pro contra *praem.* Vp ‖ xiv.] xi. L, xxiii. P1 ‖ Denique] c. *praem.* Mu1 ‖ non] ubi dicitur *praem.* Mu2 ‖ sacerdotale *ante* non est *tr.* G Mu2 ‖ est *om.* L **5.10.** D.] arg. pro et contra *praem.* Vp ‖ Clericum] c. *praem.* P1 ‖ qui—discreti *om.* A Ba C G L Mu1 Mu2, non convenit militibus ecclesie Ma ‖ qui *om.* Ba1 Vp ‖ Nam discreti *om.* Ba1 P1 **5.10.** *om. per totum* A Ba C L Ma Mu1 Mu2 P1 Vb Vp

⟨4.5.⟩ From obedience.

⟨4.6.⟩ From the consequence of a deed and of a previous act, which is a general topic in every judgement.

⟨5.⟩ From the person.

⟨5.1.⟩ D.88 c.10.

⟨5.2.⟩ C.11 q.3 c.14.

⟨5.3.⟩ D.84 c.1, 2, and 3.

⟨5.4.⟩ C.23 q.8 in all the following chapters.

⟨5.5.⟩ C.16 q.7 c.? and c.4.

⟨5.6.⟩ C.9 q.2 c.10.

⟨5.7.⟩ C.23 q.4 c.51.

⟨5.8.⟩ D.40 c.1.

⟨5.9.⟩ C.14 q.5 c.10.

⟨5.10.⟩ D.50 c.5.

⟨5.11.⟩ D.97 c.3.

⟨6.⟩ Ex causa ex qua vel per quam.

⟨6.1.⟩ C. xi. q. iii. Ira etiam sepe (C.11 q.3 c.68).

⟨6.2.⟩ C. xxiii. q. ultima c. ultimo (C.23 q.8 c.34).

⟨6.3.⟩ D. l. Eos (D.50 c.42).

⟨6.4.⟩ C. xxiv. q. ii. Sane super (C.24 q.2 c.3) "sed in Domini sui fide."

⟨6.5.⟩ D. l. Eum qui (D.50 c.46) et c. Si qua femina (D.50 c.43).

⟨7.⟩ Ex fine vel intentione sive ex causa propter quam.

⟨7.1.⟩ C. xi. q. iii. Qui recte iudicat (C.11 q.3 c.66).

⟨7.2.⟩ C. xxiii. q. v. Cum homo (C.23 q.5 c.19).

⟨7.3.⟩ C. xxii. q. iv. Si ad peccatum (C.22 q.4 c.20) "cum propterea" et c. Mulier (C.22 q.4 c.21).

⟨7.4.⟩ C. xxiii. q. iv. Ipsa pietas (C.23 q.4 c.24) "non quia coguntur sed quo coguntur."

⟨7.5.⟩ C. xxiii. q. v. De occidendis (C.23 q.5 c.8) "absit ut."

⟨7.6.⟩ C. xv. q. vii. c. Si quis tumidus (C.15 q.7 c.3).

⟨7.7.⟩ C. xv. q. i. Si quis non iratus (C.15 q.1 c.13).

---

6. *om. per totum* Ba1 P1 ‖ ex a Mu2 ‖ vel] et Mu1 ‖ per quam ... ex qua *tr.* A Ba C G L Mu1 Mu2 Vp, *om.* Ma ‖ per] prius A **6.1.** *post* §5.9 *rep.* L ‖ C.] arg. contra *praem.* Vp ‖ iii.] iv. Ma ‖ Ira] Ita (c. *praem.* Mu1 P1) Ba Ba1 G L Mu1 P1 Vb ‖ etiam] in A, et Ba Ba1 C G L Mu1 Vb, *om.* Vp **6.2.** C.] arg. contra arg. *praem.* Vp, arg. *praem.* C G ‖ xxiii.] xxxiii. Ba Ba1 ‖ ultima] vi. Ba ‖ c. ultimo *om.* Ma ‖ ultimo] velud *praem.* Ba **6.3.** D.] arg. pro arg. *praem.* Vp, arg. *praem.* C G ‖ l.] i. L ‖ Eos] "qui" *add.* Mu2, c. *praem.* P1 **6.4.** *rep.* G Vp ‖ xxiv.] xxiii. Vp ‖ ii. *om.* Ba1 Vp, iii. Vp_1 ‖ Sane *om.* Ba1 Vp_1, c. *praem.* P1 ‖ super] quod *praem.* Ba Mu1 P1 ‖ sed—fide *om.* Ba Mu2 ‖ sed in] tamen G_2 ‖ sed *om.* A C P1 Vp_1, si L ‖ Domini] Deum L ‖ sui fide *om.* G_1 L Vp, fide sui *tr.* Vp_1 ‖ fide] idem Ba1, atque servicio *add.* Ma Mu1 P1 **6.5.** D.] arg. pro et contra *praem.* Vp ‖ l.] i. L ‖ c. Si qua femina—Eum qui *tr.* Mu1 P1 ‖ Eum qui] Eos vero (D.50 c.42) Ma ‖ qui] quod A ‖ et c. *om.* Ma ‖ c. *om.* L **7.** *om. per totum* Ba1 P1 ‖ vel] sive Ma ‖ sive—quam *om.* Ma ‖ ex^2] et L **7.1.** C.] arg. contra *praem.* Vp ‖ Qui] Quod Ba Ba1 C ‖ recte] iuste P1 ‖ iudicat *om.* Ba P1, etiam C, ius Vb **7.2.** C.] arg. pro et contra *praem.* Vp **7.3.** *post* §7.6 *tr.* Ba Ba1 Ma, *post* §7.4 *tr.* Mu1 P1 ‖ C.] arg. pro *praem.* Vp ‖ xxii.] xxiv. G, xxvi. Mu2 ‖ iv.] iii. Vp ‖ Si ad] Sciat Ba Ba1 ‖ Si] c. *praem.* Mu1 ‖ cum—Mulier *om.* Mu2 ‖ et c.] C. eadem q. eadem Ma ‖ c. *om.* L **7.4.** *om. per totum* C Mu2 ‖ xxiii.] eadem P1 ‖ iv.] iii. G L ‖ Ipsa] c. *praem.* P1 ‖ pietas *om.* P1 ‖ sed—$coguntur^2$ *om.* Ma ‖ quo] qua Ba, quod G, quia L, quare Mu1 ‖ $coguntur^2$] attendat *add.* Mu1, attendant P1 **7.5.** *post* §7.7 *tr.* L ‖ xxiii.] xviii. Ba ‖ absit ut *om.* Mu2 ‖ ut] ea *add.* A Ba1 C G Ma Vp, *om.* Ba L, ea que propter bonum *add.* Mu1 P1 **7.6.** *om. per totum* A Ba C G L Ma Mu2 Vb Vp ‖ c. *om.* P1 **7.7.** *om. per totum* A Ma ‖ xv.] xvi. C ‖ q. i. *om.* Ba Ba1 C G Mu2 Vp ‖ Si] c. *praem.* Mu1 ‖ non iratus] tamen Ba Ba1 G L Mu2, "inde" (C.16 q.1 c.45) C ‖ non *interl.* Mu1, *om.* Vb Vp

⟨6.⟩ From the cause by which or for which something is done.

⟨6.1.⟩ C.11 q.3 c.68.
⟨6.2.⟩ C.23 q.8 c.34.
⟨6.3.⟩ D.50 c.42.
⟨6.4.⟩ C.24 q.2 c.3.
⟨6.5.⟩ D.50 c.46 and c.43.

⟨7.⟩ From the aim or intention, or from the cause for which something is done.

⟨7.1.⟩ C.11 q.3 c.66.
⟨7.2.⟩ C.23 q.5 c.19.
⟨7.3.⟩ C.22 q.4 c.20 and c.21.
⟨7.4.⟩ C.23 q.4 c.24.
⟨7.5.⟩ C.23 q.5 c.8.
⟨7.6.⟩ C.15 q.7 c.3.
⟨7.7.⟩ C.15 q.1 c.13.

⟨8.⟩ Ex debito vel indebito persone officio.

⟨8.1.⟩ C. xxiii. q. iii. Ea vindicta (C.23 q.4 c.51) "cui rerum ordine potestas."

⟨8.2.⟩ D. l. Clericum qui (D.50 c.5) "non convenit militem" et in "seculo per quod."

⟨8.3.⟩ C. xxiii. q. ultima Qui percutit malos (C.23 q.8 c.33).

⟨8.4.⟩ C. xv. q. i. Ut itaque (C.15 q.1 c.2) "de Lamech."

⟨8.5.⟩ C. xxiii. q. v. De occidendis (C.23 q.5 c.8) "nisi forte sit miles."

⟨8.6.⟩ C. eadem q. eadem Lex eterna (C.23 q.5 c.15).

⟨8.7.⟩ C. xiv. q. v. Dixit Dominus (C.14 q.5 c.12), Qui resistit (C.11 q.3 c.97).

⟨8.8.⟩ C. xxiii. q. iv. Ita plane sociatur (C.23 q.4 c.6) "malo."

⟨9.⟩ Ex obedientia.

⟨9.1.⟩ C. xxiii. q. v. Cum homo (C.23 q.5 c.19) "obediendi ordine," "sicut a carnifice."

⟨9.2.⟩ C. eadem. q. eadem Miles (C.23 q.5 c.13) et c. Lex eterna (C.23 q.5 c.15).

---

8. *om. per totum* Ba1 P1 ‖ Ex obedientia Ba **8.1.** *§ 8.1–2 post § 8.3 tr.* Mu1 P1 ‖ xxiii.] eadem Mu1 P1 xiii. Vb ‖ iii.] iv. A Ma Mu1 ‖ Ea] c. *praem.* Mu1 ‖ cui rerum] curr. *cum abbr. signo supra* r[2] C ‖ cui] circa Ba Ba1, vindicet *praem.* Ma, ubi dicitur *praem.* Mu2 ‖ ordine] ordinem Ba1 ‖ potestas] potestatis C, data (*om.* Mu1) est *add.* Ma Mu1 **8.2.** Clericum] c. *praem.* Mu1 ‖ qui] que A Mu1, quod C P1 Vp, *om.* Ma Mu2 ‖ non] ubi dicitur *praem.* Mu2 ‖ militem—quod *om.* Mu2 ‖ militem] in (uni Ba) eo Ba Ba1, et in ecclesie C, militibus ecclesie Ma, ecclesie *add.* Vp ‖ et—quod *om.* Ma ‖ et—seculo *om.* Mu1 P1 ‖ et *om.* A Ba1 C Vp, hec G ‖ quod] possint *add.* A Ba C G Vb Vp, possunt *add.* L, etc. *add.* P1 **8.3.** xxiii.] xxii. Vb ‖ ultima] v. Ba ‖ Qui] Quia A, Quicumque (c. *praem.* Mu1) Mu1 P1 ‖ percutit] parciet *cum abbr. signo* G, parcit Mu2 ‖ malos] malis Mu2 **8.4.** xv.] † Mu2 ‖ q.] † Mu2 ‖ i.] v. Ba, ii. L ‖ Ut itaque] vitaque A, utique Ba Ba1 C G L Mu2 Vp, ex premissis *add.* Mu1, ut ex premissis P1 ‖ de *om.* L ‖ Lamech] a malec Ma, Absit ut (C.11 q.3 c.14) ita Mu2 **8.5.** *post § 8.8 tr.* C P1, *om. per totum* Mu2 ‖ C.] B. *praem.* C ‖ xxiii.] eadem P1 ‖ De] c. *praem.* Mu1 ‖ forte *om.* Ma ‖ sit miles] similes A Ba Ba1 L Vb Vp ‖ sit] si C Mu1 ‖ miles] ut ea absit *add.* Ba Ba1, absit ut ea *add.* C G Ma Mu1 P1 Vp **8.6.** *om. per totum* A Ba C G L Mu1 Mu2 P1 Vb Vp **8.7.** *om. per totum* A Ba C G Ma Mu1 Mu2 P1 Vb Vp **8.8.** *om. per totum* L Mu1 ‖ C.] A. *praem.* C ‖ q. iv. *om.* Vp ‖ malo] malum Fr, *om.* P1 **9.** *om. per totum* Ba Ba1 P1 ‖ obedientia] inobedientia C **9.1.** xxiii.] xxiv. L, † Mu2 ‖ v.] quinta C ‖ Cum] c. *praem.* Mu1 ‖ obediendi] obedia Ba, hobedienda Ba1, *om.* Ma, ubi dicitur *praem.* Mu2 ‖ ordine—carnifice *om.* Ba Ma ‖ ordine] ideo Ba1, animo A C G L Mu2 Vb Vp ‖ sicut carnifice *om.* A Mu2 ‖ sicut] aut Ba1, ut C G L Vb Vp ‖ a *om.* L Vb **9.2.** *marg.* Mu1 ‖ Miles] Similes A Ba1 Ma Vb, Sileres Ba, Si *praem.* C Vp, Non (est *add.* Mu2) (C.23 q.5 c.11) *praem.* G L Mu2, c. *praem.* Mu1, Cum *praem.* P1 ‖ et] obedidiens *add. male* Mu1, *om.* Mu2, obediens *add.* P1 ‖ c. *om.* L Mu2

8.5. The letters A. and B. at the beginning indicate the right order of the allegations C **9.** The rubric is wrongly placed at v, 8 Ba

⟨8.⟩ From the office, duly or unduly exercised by the person.
⟨8.1.⟩ C.23 q.4 c.51.
⟨8.2.⟩ D.50 c.5.
⟨8.3.⟩ C.23 q.8 c.33.
⟨8.4.⟩ C.15 q.1 c.2.
⟨8.5.⟩ C.23 q.5 c.8.
⟨8.6.⟩ C.23 q.5 c.15.
⟨8.7.⟩ C.14 q.5 c.12, c.97.
⟨8.8.⟩ C.23 q.4 c.6.

⟨9.⟩ From obedience.
⟨9.1.⟩ C.23 q.5 c.19.
⟨9.2.⟩ C.23 q.5 c.13 and c.15.

⟨9.3.⟩ C. xxiii. q. i. Quid culpatur in bello (C.23 q.1 c.4) "quod sibi iubetur vel non esse."

⟨9.4.⟩ C. xiv. q. v. Dixit Dominus (C.14 q.5 c.12).

⟨9.5.⟩ C. xi. q. iii. Qui resistit (C.11 q.3 c.97).

⟨10.⟩ Ex consequentia operis actuque precedenti.

⟨10.1.⟩ C. xxxiii. q. i. Quod autem (C.33 q.1 c.1), Manifesta patet (C.33 q.1 c.2) "tunc hii."

⟨10.2.⟩ D. xlv. Et qui emendat (D.45 c.11) "dimittit ex corde," "verum etiam."

⟨10.3.⟩ C. xxiii. q. iv. Quid crudele (C.23 q.4 c.44) "nam eum nulla crudelitate."

⟨10.4.⟩ C. i. q. i. Constat (C.1 q.1 c.111).

⟨VI. Circa iuris vel scripture interpretationem⟩

⟨1.⟩ Iam nunc videamus de incerto quod circa iuris vel scripture interpretationem consistit. ⟨2.⟩ Cum itaque in iudiciis de canonis vel legis vel cuiuscumque autentice scripture interpretatione cum adversariis contendimus, illis pro se, nobis econtra, ut sepius evenit, pro nostra parte interpretantibus, inspi-

---

9.3. xxiii.] eadem Mu1 P1 ‖ Quid] c. *praem.* Mu1 P1 ‖ in bello *om.* L Mu1 Mu2 P1 ‖ quod] qui A C, ubi dicitur *praem.* Mu2 ‖ sibi *om.* L ‖ iubetur] iubeatur P1, videtur nil Vb ‖ vel—esse *om.* Mu2 ‖ vel *om.* Ba Ba1 C Vb Vp **9.4.** xiv.] xxiii. Ba, xxiv. Mu1 P1 Vp ‖ Dixit Dominus *post* § *9.3 rep.* B1 ‖ Dixit] c. *praem.* Mu1, Dicit G Mu2 ‖ Dominus] Moysen *add.* Ma **9.5.** C. xi. q. iii.] et c. A Ba C G Mu2 Vp, et L ‖ xi.] xxi. P1 ‖ Qui *om.* L, Quod P1 **10.** *om. per totum* Ba1 P1 ‖ consequentia] † Mu2 ‖ actuque] et actu Ma ‖ precedenti] precedentia L **10.1.** xxxiii.] xxiii. Ba P1 ‖ Quod] Qui A ‖ Manifesta—hii *om.* C ‖ Manifesta] manifeste L, ubi dicitur *praem.* Mu2 ‖ patet] pates A, pati Ba Ba1, ratio *add.* Mu1 P1 ‖ tunc hii *om.* L Mu2 ‖ tunc] contra G **10.2.** xlv.] xlvi. Ba Ba1 C G Mu2 Vb, xlvii. *cum* i.[2] *exp.* L, xlvii. Vp ‖ qui] quod Ba1 Ma Mu1, ubi Mu2 ‖ dimittit emendat *tr.* C ‖ dimittit] ubi dicitur † Mu2, amittit Vp ‖ verum etiam *om.* Ba Mu2 ‖ etiam] quam hii *add. male* L **10.3.** xxiii.] xxiv. L, † Mu2 ‖ iv.] iii. Ba Ba1 ‖ Quid] Qui A Mu2, c. *praem.* Mu1, Quod Ba1 P1 ‖ nam] est *add.* G, non L, *om.* Vp ‖ eum] cum A Ba Ba1 L Ma P1 Vp, cum *praem. male* Mu2 ‖ nulla] illa L ‖ crudelitate] credulitate G **10.4.** i.[2] *om.* G, ii. Vp **VI.1.** Iam] Nam A Ba, ⟩I⟨am Vb Vp ‖ de] quod *praem.* Ma ‖ quod] quoque A, quid Ba, qui C ‖ scripture *interl.* Vb ‖ interpretatione *om.* C

⟨9.3.⟩ C.23 q.1 c.4.
⟨9.4.⟩ C.14 q.5 c.12.
⟨9.5.⟩ C.11 q.3 c.97.

⟨10.⟩ From the consequence of a deed and of a previous act.
⟨10.1.⟩ C.33 q.1 c.1, c.2.
⟨10.2.⟩ D.45 c.11.
⟨10.3.⟩ C.23 q.4 c.44.
⟨10.4.⟩ C.1 q.1 c.111.

⟨VI. On the interpretation of the law or a document⟩

⟨1.⟩ Now let us see about the uncertainty that exists about the interpretation of the law or of a document. ⟨2.⟩ When we dispute in court against opponents about the interpretation of a canon, a law, or any authentic document, since it very often happens that they interpret it in their favor and we, conversely,

ciendum est utrum recens et specialis sit controversia, an etiam retro fuerit a sapientibus discordantibus sententiis attentata.

⟨3.⟩ Si recens et specialis est, recurrendum est ad ea que in constitutione legum observanda Isidorus dicit, D. iv. c. Erit autem (D.4 c.2). Diligenter prescrutanda sunt illius capituli singula elementa. ⟨4.⟩ Nam si ostenderis interpretationem adversarii ab aliquo illorum discrepare, probabis eum contra mentem legis latoris et sic male interpretari, cum omnia que ibi continentur in condenda lege legis lator inspexerit. ⟨5.⟩ Item, cum omnia que ibi ponuntur secundum magis et minus dicantur, probando tuam interpretationem predictis magis convenire quam suam, te melius interpretari probasti. ⟨6.⟩ Sic prosequere cum concordantiis. ⟨7.⟩ Talis enim debet esse:

⟨8.⟩ Honesta: quia per eam vita moderatur humana, ut supra capitulo proximo (D.4 c.1) et ante proximo (D.3 c.4).

---

2. v.us *praem. marg.* G ‖ itaque *post* in iudiciis *tr.* A ‖ de *om.* Ba Ma Mu1 Mu2, circa G, vel L ‖ canonis] canonum Ba Mu1 Mu2 P1, iuris G, canonum de nominis Ma ‖ legis] legum Ba Ma Mu1 Mu2 P1 ‖ cuiuscumque] cuiusque Ma Mu2 ‖ interpretatione] interpretationem A G Mu2, de *praem.* Ba Mu1 ‖ contendimus] ostendimus P1 ‖ econtra] hoc contra L ‖ ut sepius evenit *om.* Ma ‖ sepius] sepe L Mu1 ‖ et] vel L Vp ‖ specialis] nova L, nova vel *praem.* Mu1 ‖ sit *om.* P1 ‖ an] aut L, *om.* P1 ‖ retro *om.* C, raro L ‖ fuerit *post* sententiis *tr.* L, fuit G Mu2 ‖ a *rep. cum* a[1] *exp.* G ‖ discordantibus] et *praem.* L ‖ attentata] autenticata P1 3. Si] et *praem.* C ‖ est *ante* et specialis *tr.* L P1 ‖ recurrendum] recurrendus Ba ‖ que] quem L Vb Vp ‖ oservanda *post* dicit *tr.* L ‖ Isidorus *ante* in *tr.* L, *post* docet *tr.* C ‖ dicit] docet Ba C G Ma Mu1 Mu2 P1 Vp ‖ D.] supra *praem.* A Ba C G L Ma Mu1 P1 Vp ‖ c. *om.* L Ma P1 ‖ Erit] Erat A, Eum Vp ‖ autem] lex *add.* G, lex honesta *add.* Ma ‖ Diligenter] enim (arg. *praem.* Ba) *add.* Ba Mu1 Mu2, namque *add.* Ma, Distinguenter enim P1 ‖ elementa] verba P1 4. ostenderis] ostendes A, arg. *add. in medio* Ba, ostendis Mu1 ‖ adversarii] adversamur Vp ‖ aliquo] oblico Vp ‖ illorum] illarum Ba, eorum Mu1 Mu2 P1 ‖ discrepare] arg. *add.* Ba, disceptare Vp ‖ probabis] probabitur L, probandum Ma, probabilis *cum* is *exp. et cum* l *corr.* s Vb ‖ eum] eam L, exit Ma ‖ mentem] mente A, *om.* L ‖ latoris] dire *add.* Mu2 ‖ que *om.* P1 ‖ continentur] ponuntur Vp ‖ condenda] concedenda *cum* ce *exp.* Vp ‖ lege *om.* C Vp ‖ inspexerit] arg. *add.* Ba, inspexit G, intellexerit vel *praem.* L, vel intellexerit *add.* Mu1 5. ponuntur] continetur *praem. et exp.* Ba, dicuntur *add.* P1 ‖ magis] maius Mu2 ‖ dicantur] arg. *add. in medio* Ba ‖ probando tuam] probativam Ba ‖ probando] probanda L ‖ tuam] in ea Vp ‖ interpretationem] interpretatione Vp ‖ te] ut L ‖ interpretari] interpretante A, interpretantem L Vb 6. prosequere] prosequente Mu2 ‖ cum] nu *cum abbr. signo* L, cum *cum* us *abbr. signo* Mu1, *om.* P1, circa Vp ‖ concordantiis] constanciis Ma 7. *om. per totum* A C G L Ma Mu2 Vp, *add.* Vb[1] ‖ Talis] Salubris Mu2 ‖ esse debet *tr.* Mu1 8. Honesta *ante § 6 tr.* Mu1, Erit autem lex *praem.* Si ‖ eam] ea Ba L ‖ moderatur vita *tr.* Ma Mu1 ‖ vita] vitam A, via C Vp ‖ supra—proximo[2]] in duobus primis superioribus capitulis Si ‖ supra *om.* C ‖ ante proximo et proximo *tr.* L ‖ et ante proximo *om.* P1

---

8. From here and until v, 10, I have included in the collation the parallel gloss given by Simon de Bisignano, *Summa in Decretum*, v. *Erit autem lex honesta* to D.4 c.2, abbreviated with the *siglum* “Si,” in order to show clearly what stated above, pp. 73–74.

in ours, it should be examined whether the controversy is recent and specific, or whether it has already been dealt with before by wise men with differing opinions.

⟨3.⟩ If the controversy is recent and specific, one must resort to those principles which Isidore says ought to be observed in the establishment of the laws: D.4 c.2. Each element of that chapter should be carefully examined. ⟨4.⟩ Indeed, if you demonstrate that your opponent's interpretation differs from any of those elements, you will prove that his interpretation is contrary to the legislator's mind and is therefore wrong, because everything contained therein was carefully examined by the legislator when he made the law. ⟨5.⟩ Furthermore, since all that is stated there is said with a greater or lesser degree of probability, by proving that your interpretation of the aforesaid things is more appropriate than that of your opponent, you will have proved that you have interpreted better. ⟨6.⟩ Thus, continue with the concordances. ⟨7.⟩ The law in fact ought to be as follows:

⟨8.⟩ Righteous: because human life is governed through it, as is said in the penultimate chapter (D.4 c.1) and in the antepenultimate (D.3 c.4).

⟨9.⟩ Iusta: ut finaliter a naturali equitate non discrepet, alioquin irrita esset, ut in D. viii. c. Dignitate (D.8 d.p.c.1), arg. sunt omnia eiusdem distinctionis capitula.
⟨10.⟩ Possibilis: quia si impossibile preciperet, transgressio non imputaretur, arg. est in C. xxiii. q. iv. Nabuchodonosor (C.23 q.4 c.22), idem Vasis ire (C.23 q.4 c.23).
⟨11.⟩ Secundum naturam negotiorum, scilicet vel secundum bonos mores a natura procedentes, arg. in D. xxix. Regule (D.29 c.2) et D. viii. Que contra mores (D.8 c.2); ⟨12.⟩ vel secundum naturam hominum, quia "omnis ars naturam imitatur" (Phys. 2:2, 194a21–22), etc.
⟨13.⟩ Secundum consuetudinem: quia leges contraria consuetudine abrogantur, ut D. eadem Leges (D.4 c.3) et Hec etsi (D.4 c.6).
⟨14.⟩ Loco: quia in quibusdam locis quedam statui possunt, que in aliis non reciperentur, ut arg. in D. xxxi. Quoniam in Romani (D.31 c.13) et "hoc autem," et in c. Aliter (D.31 c.14).

---

9. ut[1]] si *add.* Vp ‖ a] vel C ‖ naturali] natali Ba, naturaliter C ‖ discrepet] discrepat Mu1, discordet Si ‖ esset] erit P1, *ante* irrita *tr.* Si ‖ ut in] arg. Si ‖ in *om.* A C L, infra Ba G Ma Mu2 P1 Vp ‖ viii.] ix. G ‖ c. *om.* Ba C G Mu1 Mu2 Si Vp, quia L, De P1 ‖ arg.] et L, ad idem Si ‖ sunt] supra L Ma Vp, valent Si ‖ distinctionis *om.* Vp ‖ capitula] c. A, *om.* Ba Ma **10.** Possibilis] Possibile P1 ‖ si] arg. *add.* Mu2 ‖ preciperet] precipet C ‖ transgressio] transgressioni A L Vb Vp, transgressionem Ba, transgressori Ma Mu1 ‖ non *om.* Ba C Mu2 Vp ‖ imputaretur] imputatur Ma, immutaretur G Mu2, evitaretur P1 ‖ arg.] et L ‖ est *om.* Ma Mu1 Si ‖ in] infra Ba G L Ma Mu2 P1 Si Vp ‖ C. *om.* Mu1 P1 ‖ iv.] iii. Mu2 ‖ Nabuchodonosor] c. *praem.* L ‖ idem—ire *om.* L P1 ‖ idem] scilicet de Ba **11.** negotiorum *om.* L ‖ scilicet *om.* G ‖ vel[1] *om.* L ‖ bonos *om.* Mu2, hos *praem.* Si ‖ procedentes] procedens Mu2 ‖ arg. in] et L ‖ arg. *om.* Ma ‖ in] infra Ba C G Ma Mu2, *om.* Mu1 P1 Si ‖ xxix.] xxxvii. Regula ix. A ‖ Regule] c. *praem.* Mu1 ‖ et *om.* P1 Si ‖ D.[2]—xxix. *ante* Regule *tr.* Ma ‖ viii.] ix. Ba C G Ma Mu2 P1 Vb Vp ‖ Que] Est A, c. *praem.* Mu1 ‖ mores[2]] bonos *praem. male* L ‖ omnis *om.* Mu2 **12.** naturam[1]] mores *praem.* A, *om.* C ‖ omnis *om.* G P1 ‖ etc. *om.* Ma Si **13.** abrogantur] approbantur G, abrogatur Vp ‖ ut *om.* Ma, infra *add.* Si ‖ D. eadem *om.* Ma ‖ eadem D. *tr.* A Ba C G L Mu1 Mu2 P1 Si Vp ‖ et] eadem *add.* A, *om.* Ba C G Ma Mu2 P1 ‖ Hec etsi] heresi L Mu1 ‖ etsi] et Vb **14.** Loco] Loca G ‖ statui] statuta Ba ‖ que] quis Vb ‖ in aliis] alibi Mu2 P1 ‖ aliis] locis *add.* L Si ‖ reciperentur] recipiuntur Mu2, recipientur Vp ‖ ut *om.* C Mu2 ‖ arg. in *om.* L ‖ arg. *interl.* Mu1, *om.* P1 ‖ in[3]] infra Ba C Ma Mu2 P1 Vp, *om.* Mu1 Si ‖ xxxi.] xxi. Ba, xxxv. Mu1, Ante triennium (D.31 c.1) *add.* Si ‖ xxxi.—Aliter *om.* P1 ‖ Quoniam in Romani] Quam viro C ‖ in Romani] raro L ‖ Romani] ordine *add.* Ma, Romanis Mu1, *om.* Si ‖ et[1]—c. *om.* Si ‖ et[1] *om.* Vp ‖ hoc] hec G Mu1 ‖ in *om.* A Ba C G L Ma Mu1 Mu2 Vp ‖ c. *om.* L ‖ Aliter] ut infra xxiii. *add.* Vp

⟨9.⟩ Just: so as not to differ from natural equity in the end, otherwise it will be invalid, as in D.8 d.p.c.1; all the chapters of the same distinction are arguments for this.
⟨10.⟩ Possible: because if it prescribed the impossible, the infringement would not be charged; an argument is in C.23 q.4 c.22, likewise c.23.
⟨11.⟩ In accordance with the nature of the affairs, namely in accordance with the good habits that arise from nature; arguments in D.29 c.2 and D.8 c.2; ⟨12.⟩ or in accordance with human nature, since "all art is an imitation of nature" (Phys. 2:2, 194a21–22), etc.[3]
⟨13.⟩ In accordance with custom, since laws are repealed by contrary custom, as in D.4 c.3 and c.6.
⟨14.⟩ Appropriate to the place: because in some places some laws may be laid down which are not adopted elsewhere, as in the arguments in D.31 c.13 and in c.14.

3 For a translation, see Aristotle, *Aristotle's Physics: Books I and II*, ed. and trans. William Charlton (Oxford: Clarendon Press, 1970).

⟨15.⟩ Tempori: quia omnia suis debent convenire temporibus, ut in C. xxiii. q. iv. Si ecclesia (C.23 q.4 c.42) "et omnia suis," et D. xxix. Sciendum (D.29 c.1), et C. i. q. vii. Necessaria (C.1 q.7 c.6), Quod pro (C.1 q.7 c.7).
⟨16.⟩ Necessaria: quia non nisi pro necessitate statui lex debet, ut D. xxix. c. Regule sanctorum patrum (D.29 c.2).
⟨17.⟩ Utilis: quia aliter onerosa esset et sic resecanda, licet non sit mala, ut arg. in D. xii. c. Omnia (D.12 c.12).
⟨18.⟩ Manifesta: et quantum ad verba vel saltim quantum ad sententiam, ne quid in captione contineat, id est fraude, ut arg. in C. xxxii. q. i. Dixit Dominus (C.32 q.1 c.2) "et quia poterat," et C. xiv. q. iii. Plerique (C.14 q.3 c.3) et in omnibus capitulis eiusdem questionis.
⟨19.⟩ Non privato commodo: quia multorum utilitas semper debet preponi, ut C. viii. q. ii. Dilectissimi (C.8 q.2 c.2).

---

15. *om. per totum* P1 ‖ Tempori] Tempore Mu1, Temporique Si ‖ omnia *ante* temporibus *tr.* Si ‖ debent (debeant *cum* a *exp.* Ma) suis *tr.* A Ma ‖ suis[1]] sua Vp ‖ temporibus convenire *tr.* Ma ‖ temporibus—xxiii. *om.* Vp ‖ ut] arg. C Vp, *om.* Ma ‖ in] infra Ba C G Mu2 Si, *om.* L Ma Mu1 ‖ C.[1] *om.* Ba C L Mu1 Vp ‖ iv.] iii. Ba C Vp ‖ et omnia[2] suis[2]] D. xii. c. Omnia (D.12 c.12) Ma ‖ omnia[2]] c. *praem.* G Mu2 ‖ suis[2]] sua *et* convenire temporibus *add.* Mu1 ‖ et[2] *om.* Ma Si, ut Mu1 ‖ Sciendum] Ex *praem.* Ba, c. *praem.* Ma Mu1 ‖ et[3] *om.* A G L Ma Si Vp ‖ Necessaria] c. *praem.* Mu1 ‖ Quod] Qui C, c. *praem.* G, et c. *praem.* Mu2 ‖ pro] remedio *add.* Ma Mu2, proprio Mu1 **16.** Necessaria—D. *om.* P1 ‖ non *om.* Mu2 Si ‖ pro] ex C ‖ lex statui *tr.* Ma Vp ‖ lex *om.* C ‖ ut] in *add.* A, infra Ma, infra *add.* Ba G Mu2 Vp ‖ xxix.] xxviii. A Ba C G Mu2 P1 Vp, † Vb ‖ c. *om.* C Mu1 P1 Si ‖ sanctorum patrum *om.* A Ba C G L Ma Mu1 Mu2 P1 Si Vp **17.** aliter] alia A C, *om.* Ba, alias Vp ‖ onerosa] onerasa *cum* a[1] *exp. et corr.* G ‖ sic] ita Mu1 ‖ resecanda] esset *add.* Mu2 ‖ licet—mala *om.* L Si ‖ non] † A, ita Vb ‖ ut arg.] et L ‖ ut *om.* C Ma ‖ arg. *om.* Mu1 Si ‖ in *om.* A L Ma Si, infra Ba C G Mu1 Mu2 P1 Vp ‖ xii.] xxii. *cum* x *exp.* A ‖ c. *om.* A Ba C G L Ma P1 Si Vp **18.** et[1] *om.* Ba Ma Mu1 Mu2 P1, vel Si ‖ ad verba *om.* C ‖ vel] et L, et *add.* Vb ‖ saltim] saltem A L Ma Mu1 P1 Si, santem *cum* n *exp. et corr.* l Mu2, *interl.* Vb ‖ ad[2] *om.* P1 ‖ ne] nec G ‖ quid] quis Ba, id G, qui Vp ‖ captione] cautione Mu1, captionem Si Vb ‖ id est] et in L, vel Mu2 P1, *om.* Si ‖ fraude] fraudo *cum* o *exp. Et corr.* G, fraudem L, vel fraudi P1, *om.* Si ‖ ut arg. in] et L ‖ ut *om.* A Ba C G Ma Mu1 Mu2 P1 Si Vp ‖ in[2]] est infra (et *add.* Ba) Ba G Mu2 Vp, *om.* C Si, infra Ma P1 ‖ C. *om.* Mu1 ‖ Dixit] Ait Fr, c. *praem.* Ma, Dicit P1 ‖ et[3]—questionis] Hinc collige—contineat Si ‖ et[3] *om.* Ma ‖ quia] quod G ‖ C.[2] *om.* P1 ‖ xiv.] xiii. L, xxxiv. Vb ‖ iii.] viii. P1 ‖ Plerique] Pluribus L Mu2 P1, c. *praem.* Ma, Pluribusque A Ba C G Vb Vp ‖ et—questionis] capitulis P1 ‖ eiusedm questionis] eiusdemque Ba ‖ questionis *om.* C L **19.** Non] Nec P1 ‖ preponi] private *add.* Si ‖ ut] in *add.* A, infra *add.* Ba G Ma Mu1 Mu2 P1 Si Vp ‖ C. *om.* Mu1 P1 ‖ vii.] vii. q. i. Scias frater (C.7 q.1 c.35) "nam plurimorum utilitas" *praem.* Mu1 ‖ Dilectissimi] "utilitati comuni" *add.* Mu1, et C. vii. q. i. Scias frater (C.7 q.1 c.35) Si

⟨15.⟩ Appropriate to the time: because all things should to be appropriate to their times, as in C.23 q.4 c.42 and D.29 c.1 and C.1 q.7 c.6, c. 7.
⟨16.⟩ Necessary: because a law should not be established, but by necessity, as in D.29 c.2.
⟨17.⟩ Advantageous: because otherwise it would be burdensome and so should be rejected, even if it were not bad, as in D.12 c.12.
⟨18.⟩ Clear: as much as the words, or at least the sentence, to ensure that it does not contain anything in deception, i.e. fraud, as in the arguments in C.32 q.1 c.2 and C.14 q.3 c.3, and in all the other chapters of the same *quaestio*.
⟨19.⟩ Not accommodated to some private individual, because the interest of the many should always be put first, as in C.8 q.2 c.2.

⟨20.⟩ Item si interpretationem adversarii alicui auctoritati adversari aliqua subtilitate probare poteris, obtinebis, quia in dubiis id sequendum est quod sanctorum regulis non est adversum, ut D. xiv. Sicut (D.14 c.1), et "qui vitio caret," ut ff. de legibus et consuetudine In ambigua (Dig. 1.3.19).

⟨21.⟩ Si vero recens non sit controversia, sed talis super quam retro sapientum contrarie manavere sententie preter predictas inspectiones, considera que sententia a maturioribus teneatur et hec prevalebit, arg. D. l. Domino. (D.50 c.28) in fine. ⟨22.⟩ Item considera que a pluribus et melioribus teneatur et hec prevalet. ⟨23.⟩ Cum autem plures ex una parte, graviores autem ex alia, paris auctoritatis erunt, ut arg. D. xix. In canonicis (D.19 c.6), arg. D. xx. De libellis (D.20 c.1) et c. De quibus (D.20 c.3), arg. D. ix. Noli (D.9 c.3), et Ego (D.9 c.5), et Noli frater (D.9 c.9). ⟨24.⟩ Item plurium sententia, quamvis non sint maioris auctoritatis, obtinebit, ut arg. D. lxv. c. ii. et iii. (D.65 c.2 et 3), D. lxxix. Si transitus (D.79 c.10).

---

20. si *ante* alicui *tr.* Ma ‖ interpretationem] interpretatione Ba L Ma Vp ‖ alicui—adversari *om.* (*homoiotel.*) Vp ‖ auctoritati] auctoritate Ba ‖ adversari] adversarii C L ‖ aliqua subtilitate] aliquo modo L, aliquo modo vel *praem.* Mu1, subtilitate aliqua *tr.* Mu2 ‖ probare *om.* A Ba G Ma Vp, ostendere (*et post* adversari *tr.* L) L Mu1, videns *et post* adversari *tr.* Mu2 ‖ subtilitate *om.* C ‖ poteris obtinebis] optinere poteris Mu2 ‖ obtinebis] obtinebit *cum* it *exp. et corr.* is Mu1 ‖ id—est[1]] idest A Ba C G L Mu1, id est *tr.* Ma ‖ id] idest Mu2 P1 Vp ‖ sequendum] sequende Ba, *om.* Vp ‖ ut *om.* Ma ‖ Sicut] Sacri L, quedam *add.* Mu1, Sic Mu2 ‖ qui] quod Ma Mu1 ‖ quae Mo ‖ vitio] incerto Ma ‖ ut[2]] et L ‖ ff.] c. P1 ‖ de *om.* A ‖ consuetudine] de contradictione Ba, constitutionibus Mu2 P1 ‖ ambigua] ambiguis L Ma, ambiguas Mu1 **21.** Si *om.* Vp ‖ recens non sit] recessint A, recessit Ba Vp ‖ non *om.* C Ma Mu2 P1 Vb, *ante* recens *tr. interl.* G ‖ sed] si A C ‖ super] supra Ma, semper P1 ‖ quam] qua C L, qualis P1 ‖ sapientum] sapientium Ma Mu1 Mu2 P1 ‖ contrarie *om.* A L Vb ‖ manavere] manaverunt C Mu1, manevere *cum* e[1] *exp. et corr.* G, remansere P1, *om.* A Vb Vp ‖ predictas] super dictas L, dictas Mu2 ‖ inspectiones] inspectione Vp ‖ considera] vidit L ‖ sententia] *om.* L, fraterna P1 ‖ a] que *praem.* A G ‖ maturioribus] maioribus et *praem.* Mu1, maioribus P1 ‖ teneatur] tenetur Ba Ma, teneantur L ‖ et *interl.* Vb ‖ hec] hac Mu1, hoc G L ‖ prevalebit] prevalebunt L ‖ arg.—fine *marg.* Vb ‖ arg.] et L ‖ Domino] sancto *add.* L Mu1 **22.** Item—prevalet *marg.* Vb ‖ que] sententia *add.* Mu1 ‖ a[1]] in Mu2 P1 ‖ et *om.* A C G Mu2 Vb Vp ‖ hec] hoc G, *om.* Mu2 ‖ prevalet] prevalebit Ma, prevaleat Mu2 **23.** plures] sunt *add.* Ba Ma Mu1 ‖ graviores—paris *om.* (*homoiotel.*) Vp ‖ autem[2] *om.* C L, aut Mu2 P1 ‖ alia] altera C Mu1 ‖ paris] parte C, pares Mu2, pars P1 ‖ auctoritatis] autoritates Vp ‖ erunt] erit Ba P1, essent Mu2 ‖ ut *om.* C Ma ‖ arg.[1]—arg.[3] *om.* L ‖ arg.[1] *om.* C G Ma Mu2 P1 ‖ xix.] xviii. Mu1 Mu2 P1 ‖ In canonicis—D. ix. *om.* Vp ‖ In] Infra G ‖ arg.[2]] et C, *om.* Ma ‖ et[2] c. *om.* Ma ‖ ix.] xi. L ‖ quibus] causis *add.* Ma ‖ arg.[3] *om.* Ma ‖ Noli[1]] c. *praem.* Mu1 ‖ et[3] *om.* Ma P1 ‖ Ego] solus *add.* Ma, c. *praem.* Mu1 ‖ et[4] *om.* Ma ‖ Noli[2]] c. *praem.* Mu1 **24.** sint] sit C G L Mu1 Mu2 P1 ‖ optinebit] obtinebis *et ante* auctoritatis *tr.* Ba, obtinebis Vp ‖ ut *om.* C G L Ma Mu2 ‖ arg. *om.* L P1 ‖ c. ii.] Non debet Ma, i. et ii. Mu1 ‖ et iii. *om.* Ma ‖ D.[2]] et *praem.* A Ba C G L Mu1 Mu2 Vp, et arg. *praem.* Ma ‖ lxxix.] lxxx. P1 ‖ Si] c. *praem.* Mu1 ‖ transitus] Papae in fine *add.* Ma

⟨20.⟩ Moreover, if you can prove by some subtlety that your opponent's interpretation is against some authority, you will prevail, for in matters of doubt one should follow what is not against the rules of the lawgivers, as in D.14 c.1, as in Dig. 1.3.19.

⟨21.⟩ If, however, a controversy is not recent, but one on which sages in the past have expressed conflicting opinions, then, apart from the abovementioned observations, pay attention to the opinion supported by the elders, and that will prevail; argument: D.50 c.28. ⟨22.⟩ Furthermore, pay attention to what is supported by the majority and by the best men, and this prevails. ⟨23.⟩ However, when the majority is on one side, but the most eminent men are on the other, they will have equal authority, as in the arguments D.19 c.6, D.20 c.1 and c.3, D.9 c.3 and c.5 and c.9. ⟨24.⟩ Moreover, the opinion of the majority will prevail, even if it has no greater authority, as in the arguments D.65 c.2 and 3, D.79 c.10.

⟨VII. De fide autem instrumentorum et attestationum⟩

⟨1.⟩ De fide autem instrumentorum et attestationum et quando aliquid deletum vel superscriptum sit, satis aperte in legibus continetur hoc, tamen adicere volumus, quia si in parte instrumenti vel attestationum mendatium reperitur, reliquum inutile redditur.

⟨2.⟩ Si in parte instrumenti vel ad testimonium mendatium reperitur, reliquum inutile redditur.

⟨2.1.⟩ C. iii. q. ix. Pura (C.3 q.9 c.17).
⟨2.2.⟩ D. ix. Si ad scripturas (D.9 c.7).
⟨2.3.⟩ C xxiii. Q. v. Quid ergo (C.23 q.5 c.6) "enim ad cetera."
⟨2.4.⟩ C. iii. q. x. Placuit (C.3 q.10 c.1).
⟨2.5.⟩ C. xii. q. ii. Monemus (C.12 q.2 c.18).
⟨2.6.⟩ C. ii. q. i. Inprimis (C.2 q.1 c.7) "talis ante non extitit."
⟨2.7.⟩ arg. de con. di. iii. Non oportet (D.3 de cons. c.8).
⟨2.8.⟩ arg. C. iii. q. v. Accusationes (C.3 q.5 c.7).

⟨3.⟩ Contra. ⟨3.1⟩ Pro contrario facit scriptura Origenis, Cypriani, Augustini, et multorum aliorum qui tam falsa quam vera scripserunt.

⟨3.2.⟩ D. ix. Negare (D.9 c.4) et c. Neque (D.9 c.10).

VII.1. autem] aut Ba, *om.* Vp ‖ et[1] attestationum[1] *om.* P1 ‖ et[1]] vel Ma ‖ attestationum[1]] testatorum A L, vel testamentorum *add.* Mu1, testamentorum Vb, attestatorium Vp ‖ et[2]—sit *post.* attestationum[2] *tr.* P1 ‖ et[2]] vel Ma ‖ quando] quem G ‖ aliquid] aliquem Vp ‖ super scriptum] inscriptum P1 ‖ sit *om.* C ‖ satis—attestationum[2] *post* sit *rep.* P1 ‖ aperte *post* continetur *tr.* P1 ‖ continetur] continebtus *cum* b *exp. et* us *corr.* ur Vp ‖ hoc] hec Ma ‖ quia] quod P1$_1$ ‖ si *rep.* A ‖ in *om.* A ‖ mendatium] mandatum Vp ‖ reperitur] repperiatur Ma, invenitur P1 ‖ reliquum] relicuum Ba ‖ redditur] efficitur C, reditur L, ut *add.* Ba Mu1 reperitur *praem.* Vp 2. *om. per totum* Ba Ma P1 ‖ Si] Item *praem.* C Vp ‖ ad testimonium] attestationum A C L Mu1 Mu2 Vp ‖ reperitur *om.* Vb ‖ redditur] efficitur C, dicitur L, ut *add.* Mu1 2.1. Pura] Pietas Ba, Puta (*cum* t *exp. et corr.* r) contra simplex L, Pauca Mu1, Puta G Vp 2.2. D.] arg. *praem.* C G Mu1 Vp ‖ ix.] xi. L ‖ Si] c. *praem.* Mu1 ‖ scripturas] scripturam Ba G L Ma Vp 2.3. *om. per totum* A Ba C G L Ma Mu1 Mu2 P1 Vb 2.4. C.] arg. *praem.* C G Mu1 Vp ‖ x.] v. Ba 2.5. C.] arg. *praem.* C G, arg. Mu1 ‖ Monemus] Manemus L 2.6. C.] arg. *praem.* C G Mu1 ‖ ante] antea A Ba C G L Ma Mu1 P1 Vb, alia Mu2 ‖ non *om.* C ‖ extitit] extiterit L, existat Mu2 2.7. *om. per totum* A Ba G L Ma Mu1 Mu2 P1 Vb Vp 2.8. *om. per totum* A C G L Mu2 P1 Vp ‖ arg. *om.* Ba Ma ‖ Accusationes] Accusatores Ba Ma Mu1 3. Contra *om.* Ba C Ma, Contrarium L Mu1 3.1. Pro contrario facit *om.* P1 ‖ contrario] contraria L ‖ facit *om.* A L Vb ‖ scriptura] scripturas Ba, facit *praem.* C Mu1 Mu2 Vp ‖ Cypriani] et *praem.* Ba ‖ et *om.* L ‖ aliorum multorum *tr.* Mu1 ‖ multorum] in A ‖ vera … falsa *tr.* Ba C G L Ma Mu1 Mu2 P1 ‖ scripserunt] dixerunt vel *praem.* Mu1 3.2. D.] arg. *praem.* A Ba G Ma Mu1 ‖ ix.] xi. L ‖ Negare] Negaret C, Negate L, c. *praem.* Mu1 ‖ et c. *om.* Ma ‖ et *om.* C

⟨VII. On the validity of documents and attestations⟩

⟨1.⟩ With regard to the validity of documents and attestations, and when something is deleted or overwritten, this is quite clearly contained in the laws, but we want to add it here anyway, because if a falsehood is found in any part of the document or attestations, the rest is made void.

⟨2.⟩ If a falsehood is found in any part of the document or attestations, the rest is made void.
⟨2.1.⟩ C.3 q.9 c.17.
⟨2.2.⟩ D.9 c.7.
⟨2.3.⟩ C.23 q.5 c.6.
⟨2.4.⟩ C.3 q.10 c.1.
⟨2.5.⟩ C.12 q.2 c.18.
⟨2.6.⟩ C.2 q.1 c.7.
⟨2.7.⟩ argument D.3 de cons. c.8.
⟨2.8.⟩ argument C.3 q.5 c.7.

⟨3.⟩ Against. ⟨3.1⟩ The writings of Origen, Cyprian, Augustine, and many others, who wrote both false and true things, make for the opposite.
⟨3.2.⟩ D.9 c.4 and c.10.

⟨3.3.⟩ C. i. q. i. Sacramenta (C.1 q.1 c.34) et c. Sicut ficti (C.1 q.1 c.35).
⟨3.4.⟩ De con. D. iv. Non in vobis (D.4 de cons. c.43).
⟨3.5.⟩ D. xxxvii. Si quid veri (D.37 c.13).
⟨3.6.⟩ De con. D. iv. Si non sanctificatur (D.4 de cons. c.72) in fine.
⟨3.7.⟩ C. iii. q. v. Accusatores (C.3 q.5 c.8).

⟨VIII. De re quam prelatus possedit⟩

⟨1.⟩ Item, quosdam titulos propter frequentem usum necessarios seorsum ponere volumus, quamvis ex superioribus intelligantur: scilicet an pro Ecclesia vel contra sit presumendum, cum de re quam prelatus possedit, eo vivente vel defuncto, cuius fuerit dubitatur.

⟨2.⟩ Hoc casu pro ecclesia presumitur.
⟨2.1.⟩ C. xii. q. i. Sint manifeste (C.12 q.1 c.21) "ut potestatem," "probantur."
⟨2.2.⟩ D. xxviii. De Siracusane (D.28 c.13) in fine capituli.
⟨2.3.⟩ C. xii. q. iii. Placuit (C.12 q.3 c.1) "nomine suo comparant."
⟨2.4.⟩ Q. eadem c. Quicumque (C.12 q.3 c.2) in fine capituli et c. Pontifices (C.12 q.3 c.3).

3.3. C.] arg. *praem.* G Mu1 ‖ i.[2]] v. L ‖ Sacramenta] c. *praem.* Mu1 ‖ et c. *om.* Ma ‖ c. *om.* L ‖ Sicut ficti] Si conficti L, Si fuerit (C.1 q.1 c.30) P1 ‖ ficti] fuit G, *om.* Mu2 **3.4.** *om. per totum* Ma ‖ De] arg. *praem.* G Mu1, D. Vb ‖ Non] c. *praem.* Mu1 ‖ Non in] Notum Vb **3.5.** D.] arg. *praem.* G Mu1 ‖ xxxvii.] xxvii. L, xxxviii. Mu2 ‖ Si] c. *praem.* Mu1 ‖ quid veri] quis C ‖ veri] veris Ba, verum C, *om.* G Mu2, novi L **3.6.** *om. per totum* A Ba L Ma Mu1 Vb Vp ‖ De] in *praem.* C, arg. *praem.* G ‖ in fine *om.* C **3.7.** *om. per totum* A C G L Ma P1 ‖ C.] arg. Mu1 ‖ Accusatores] "sacrus ingressus" *add.* Vp **VIII.1.** Item] Idem G ‖ titulos] articulos G P1 ‖ frequentem] sequentem P1 ‖ ex] et Ma ‖ intelligantur] intelligatur A, investigantur P1 ‖ scilicet *om.* P1 ‖ ecclesia] ecclesiam Ba, aliquo P1 ‖ vel econtra *post* presumendum *tr.* P1 ‖ vel[1]] an Ba L Ma ‖ de re] dote G ‖ possedit] possidebit C ‖ eo] ex *praem.* A ‖ fuerit] sit L ‖ dubitatur] dubitetur Ba Ma, et utrum heredibus possessoribus an ecclesie incumbat probatio *add.* C **2.** *om. per totum* C ‖ Hoc casu] Istis capitulis Ba, His capitulis Ma Mu1 ‖ ecclesia] de re qua prelatus possedit *add.* Ma ‖ presumitur *ante* pro ecclesia *tr.* Ma P1, contra prelatum vel eius heredes *add. gl. marg.* Vb **2.1.** C. *om.* Mu1 ‖ i.] ii. P1 ‖ potestatem] potestate A Ba L Mu2 P1 Vb Vp, habeat *add.* Mu1 ‖ probantur *om.* L Ma, probatur P1 **2.2.** *post* § *2.7 rep.* C ‖ xxviii.] xxvii. A G ‖ capituli *om.* Mu1, pontifices (*homoiotel.*) P1 **2.3.** C. *om.* P1 ‖ comparant] comparare Ba, et c. i. "invasionis crimine" *add.* C, comparat L, comparatur Mu1 **2.4.** Q. eadem] C. eadem *praem.* Ma, et Mu1 P1 ‖ Q.] et *praem.* Ba L C ‖ c.[1] *om.* C L Ma ‖ capituli—Pontifices *om.* P1 ‖ capituli *om.* C L ‖ et c.[2]] C. eadem q. eadem Ma ‖ Pontifices] "reliquerunt sacerdoti" *add.* Ma

⟨3.3.⟩ C.1 q.1 c.34 and c.35.
⟨3.4.⟩ D.4 de cons. c.43.
⟨3.5.⟩ D.37 c.13.
⟨3.6.⟩ D.4 de cons. c.72 at the end.
⟨3.7.⟩ C.3 q.5 c.8.

⟨VIII. On the possessions of a prelate⟩

⟨1.⟩ Moreover, we wish to provide some titles which, because of their frequent use, are particularly necessary, although they can be understood from the previous ones: namely, whether one should presume for or against the Church, when there is doubt about the possessions of a prelate, whether he is living or dead.

⟨2.⟩ In the following case, one should presume for the Church.
⟨2.1.⟩ C.12 q.1 c.21.
⟨2.2.⟩ D.28 c.13 at the end of the chapter.
⟨2.3.⟩ C.12 q.3 c.1.
⟨2.4.⟩ C.12 q.3 c.2 at the end of the chapter and c.3.

⟨2.5.⟩ C. eadem q. iv. Sacerdotes (C.12 q.4 c.1) “ad ecclesie nomen” et c. Presbiter (C.12 q.4 c.3).

⟨2.6.⟩ B. lib. iii. Investigandum (B.3 c.118).

⟨2.7.⟩ C. eadem q. ii. Illud (C.12 q.2 c.47) “si ad opus ecclesie et suo” et c. Non liceat (C.12 q.2 c.48).

⟨2.8.⟩ C. Arbitrium tutele, Si defunctus (Cod. 5.51.10).

⟨3.⟩ Contra.

⟨3.1.⟩ C. xii. q. i. Manifesta (C.12 q.1 c.20) “nullo modo possunt minui.”

⟨3.2.⟩ C. xvi. q. iii. Clerici (C.16 q.3 c.11) “dummodo pateat.”

⟨3.3.⟩ B. c. Investigandum (B.3 c.118).

⟨3.4.⟩ C. de donationibus inter virum et uxorem, l. Etiam. (Cod. 5.16.6).

⟨3.5.⟩ C. xv. q. v (C.15 q.5).

⟨3.6.⟩ ff. eodem Quintus Mutius (Dig. 24.1.51).

⟨3.7.⟩ C. xii. q. v. c. i. (C.12 q.5 c.1) “ut, si hoc constat, nullum ex his,” “que res possidet.”

⟨3.8.⟩ C. xii. q. iii. Quicumque (C.12 q.3 c.2) “ab alio percipere non poterit numerari.”

⟨3.9.⟩ C. eadem q. iv. Quicumque (C.12 q.4 c.2) “suos convictus.”

⟨3.10.⟩ C. Quorum bonorum. l. Constat (Cod. 8.2.3).

2.5. C. eadem] xii. Mu1 ‖ C. *om.* P1 ‖ iv.] iii. L ‖ ecclesie nomen *rep.* P1, *interl.* $P1_1$ ‖ et c. Presbiter] etc. L, *om.* Ma ‖ Presbiter et q. v. c. Fixum (C.12 q.4 c.4) *add.* Mu1 **27.6.** B.] d. *praem.* Mu1 ‖ l. iii.] liii. Vp ‖ iii.] iv. A L Mu1 P1 ‖ Investigandum] et c. Ut unus (B.3 c.121) et c. Ceterum (B.3 c.122) *add.* C, c. *praem.* Mu1, Investigando P1 **2.7.** *om. per totum* A Ba G L Ma Mu1 Mu2 P1 Vb Vp **2.8.** *post §3.13 tr.* C, *post §3.7 tr.* Vp ‖ *marg.* Vp ‖ C.] arg. *praem.* A G Mu1, *om.* Ba Ma ‖ Arbitrium] de arbitrio A Ba G L Ma Mu1 P1 Vb Vp ‖ tutele] tuto. L ‖ Si defunctus *om.* Vp **3.** *om per totum* Vp ‖ Contrarium] L Mu1 **3.1.** C. *om.* Mu1 P1 ‖ Manifesta] autem *add.* Mu1 ‖ nullo] nolo Ba ‖ minui possunt *tr.* Ma ‖ possunt] possint C Mu1 Vp ‖ minui] et *praem.* Ba, “ut in ecclesia dampnum” *add.* C, in *praem. et* et c. Ex hiis *add.* (C.12 q.1 c.22) Mu1, *om.* P1 **3.2.** Clerici] c. *praem.* Mu1 ‖ pateat] patent C, peccat G, parcat P1 **3.3.** *om. per totum* A Ba C G L Ma Mu1 Mu2 Vb Vp **3.4.** *§3.4–6 ante §3 tr.* C ‖ C.] arg. *praem.* A G Mu1 Vp ‖ de donationibus inter *om.* Ba ‖ donationibus] donatione P1 ‖ l. *om.* A Ba C G L P1, etiam *praem.* Vb **3.5.** *om. per totum* A Ba C G L Mu1 Mu2 P1 Vb Vp **3.6.** *om. per totum* A Ba G L Ma Mu1 P1 Vp ‖ ff. eodem] De C **3.7.** *post §3.8 tr.* C, *om. per totum* A G L Ma P1 ‖ xii.] eadem C ‖ c. *om.* C ‖ i.] Nulli C ‖ ut si hoc *om.* Ba Vp ‖ ut *om.* C ‖ nullum ex his *om.* Ba Vp ‖ nullum ex] de C ‖ possidet] post *et* c. Fixum (C.12 q.5 c.4) *add.* C, *om.* Mu2 Vb **3.8.** *om. per totum* A Ba G L Ma Mu1 Mu2 P1 Vb Vp **3.9.** *om. per totum* A G L P1 ‖ C. eadem] et Ba Mu1 Vb ‖ Quicumque] c. i. (C.12 q.4 c.1) in fine et *praem.* C ‖ suos *om.* C **3.10.** *om. per totum* A Ba G L Ma Mu1 Mu2 P1 Vb Vp

⟨2.5.⟩ C.12 q.4 c.1 and c.3.
⟨2.6.⟩ B.3 c.118.
⟨2.7.⟩ C.12 q.2 c.47 and c.48.
⟨2.8.⟩ Cod.5.51.10.

⟨3.⟩ Against.
⟨3.1.⟩ C.12 q.1 c.20.
⟨3.2.⟩ C.16 q.3 c.11.
⟨3.3.⟩ B.3 c.118.
⟨3.4.⟩ Cod.5.16.6.
⟨3.5.⟩ C.15 q.5.
⟨3.6.⟩ Dig. 24.1.51.
⟨3.7.⟩ C.12 q.5 c.1.
⟨3.8.⟩ C.12 q.3 c.2.
⟨3.9.⟩ C.12 q.4 c.2.
⟨3.10.⟩ Cod. 8.2.3.

⟨3.11.⟩ C. xii. q. iv. Sacerdotes (C.12 q.4 c.1) "equo iure."
⟨3.12.⟩ C. xxi. q. iii. Absit quicquam sinistrum (C.11 q.3 c.14).
⟨3.13.⟩ D. xciv. c. Valde (D.94 c.1) "de eius actibus dubitare."
⟨3.14.⟩ D. xl. c. i. (D.40 c.1) "eum dubitet."
⟨3.15.⟩ D. xxiv. (D.24).

⟨4.⟩ Ex prefato B. c., scilicet Investigandum (B.3 c.118), solutionem collige, ibi distinguitur an certum sit eum ante ordinationem habuisse propria, nec ne.

⟨IX.⟩ Quando presumptio non admittit probationem in contrarium

⟨1.⟩ Illud quoque notandum, quod presumptio alia iudicis, alia legis. Quando iudex ex facto presumit, si violenta sit presumptio, stabit ei nisi in contrarium probetur. ⟨2.⟩ Quando autem lex presumit, aut in suspenso relinquit ita quod nichil super presumpto constituit, quo casu probatio in contrarium admittitur; aut ita violenter presumit quod etiam super presumpto animadvertit. ⟨3.⟩ Quo casu probatio in contrarium non admittitur nisi lex hoc iudicaverit.

3.11. *om. per totum* A C G L Ma P1, *marg.* Vp ‖ C.—iv. *om.* Ba, et c. Mu1 Vb ‖ pro—vivere *om.* Vb ‖ Sacerdotes] pro persona *add.* Ba Mu2 Vp ‖ equo] ex quo Vp ‖ iure] vivere Ba Mu2 **3.12.** *om. per totum* A C G L Mu1 Mu2 P1 Vb, *marg.* Vp ‖ Absit—sinistrum *om.* Ma ‖ quicquam] quicumque Vp **3.13.** *om. per totum* A C G L Mu1 Mu2 P1 Vb ‖ xciv.] xliv. Ba ‖ Valde] De alde Vp ‖ eius] eo Vp ‖ actibus] artibus Vp ‖ dubitare] non *add.* Vp **3.14.** *om. per totum* A C G L Ma Mu1 Mu2 P1 Vb ‖ eum] esse Fr **3.15.** *om. per totum* A Ba C G L Mu1 Mu2 P1 Vb Vp **4.** Ex] et P1 ‖ B.—investigandum *om.* P1 ‖ B. c.] c. B. *tr.* A, c. brocardi Mu1 ‖ scilicet *om.* L Mu1 ‖ solutionem] solutio L ‖ ibi] enim *add.* Mu1 ‖ distinguitur] enim *praem.* Ba Ma, distinguit L ‖ eum] cum A ‖ ordinationem] ordines P1 ‖ habuisse] hiis Vp ‖ propria] propriam Ba, *om.* P1 ‖ nec] neque C **IX.** *om. per totum* P1, *rep.* Ma ‖ presumptio] probatio Ba ‖ probationem] probatione Ba, probatio Vp ‖ in contrarium *om.* Ma$_1$ **1.** Illud] Quorum quod Vp ‖ quoque] que *et ante* illud *tr.* P1 ‖ notandum] est *add.* Ba G L Mu1 ‖ Quando] enim *add.* Ba Mu1 ‖ iudex *post* ex facto *tr.* Ba Ma, *post* presumit *tr.* Mu1 ‖ stabit] stabiliter Ma, stabis Mu1 ‖ ei *om.* C L ‖ in contrarium *post* probetur *tr.* P1 ‖ probetur] propietur Ba **2.** aut[1]] vel P1 ‖ ita[1]] q. *praem. et exp.* Mu1 ‖ quod[1]—probatio *post* presumit[1] *rep.* Vp ‖ nichil super[1] presumpto[1]] super presumptionem nichil Mu1 ‖ nichil *om.* L, et iam Vp$_1$ ‖ admittitur *ante* probatio *tr.* L, *post* probatio *tr.* Mu1 ‖ aut[2]] vel P1 ‖ presumit[2]] presumitur P1 ‖ quod etiam] quia P1 ‖ super[2] presumpto[2]] sumpto C ‖ presumpto[2]] presumpta Ba, presumptio L, presumptione Mu1 ‖ animadvertit] penam statuit L, et penam statuit *add.* Mu1 **3.** Quo—admittitur *om.* Vp ‖ probatio *post* in[1] contrarium *tr.* C Vp ‖ nisi] et *praem.* Ba ‖ hoc[1] (hec L) lex *tr.* Ba C Ma Mu1 L P1, hec A, *om.* Vp ‖ iudicaverit] indicaverit A Vp

⟨3.11.⟩ C.12 q.4 c.1.
⟨3.12.⟩ C.11 q.3 c.14.
⟨3.13.⟩ D.94 c.1.
⟨3.14.⟩ D.40 c.1.
⟨3.15.⟩ D.24.

⟨4.⟩ Recall the solution from the above-mentioned chapter of Burchard, namely B.3 c.118: there is a distinction based on whether it is certain that the priest had possessions before ordination or not.

⟨IX.⟩ When a presumption does not admit evidence to the contrary

⟨1.⟩ It should also be noted that a presumption is made either by judge or by the law. When the judge presumes something from a fact, if the presumption is compelling, it remains valid until proven otherwise. ⟨2.⟩ When, on the other hand, it is the law that presumes, either it suspends judgement on condition that nothing is decided about what is presumed, in which case evidence to the contrary is admitted; or it presumes so compellingly that it also establishes the punishment on the basis of what is presumed.[4] ⟨3.⟩ In this case, evidence to the contrary is not admitted, unless the law so provided.

4 For the interpretation of '*animadvertere*', see Fiori, "Praesumptio," p. 95, which is also confirmed by the *lectio* given by L and Mu1.

⟨4.⟩ Queras hoc in:

⟨4.1.⟩ C. xi. q. i. Si qui clericorum (C.11 q.1 c.25) "nullis excusationibus labetur."

⟨4.2.⟩ D. liv. c. Fraternitatem (D.54 c.15) "sed ad sibi serviendum."

⟨4.3.⟩ D. lxxxvii. Si expositus (D.87 c.9) "sane."

⟨4.4.⟩ C. xi. q. iii. Cure (C.11 q.3 c.20) in fine capituli.

⟨4.5.⟩ C. xxxiii. q. i. Quod autem (C.33 q.1 c.1), Manifesta ratio (C.33 q.1 c.2) "periurii," "patet," "tunc hii."

⟨4.6.⟩ C. xxxiv. q. ii. Non satis (C.34 q.1–2 c.3) "quasi adulteram."

⟨4.7.⟩ C. xii. q. ii. Qui et humanis (C.12 q.2 c.24) "cum non potuerit."

⟨4.8.⟩ C. xxxii. q. ii. et iii. Extraordinaria (C.35 q.2–3 c.11).

⟨4.9.⟩ C. xxiii. Q. i. paratus (C.23 q.1 c.2) "nescire non."

⟨4.10.⟩ D. xvi. Quod dicitis (D.16 c.14) "non facile," "quia penes vos."

⟨4.11.⟩ ff. de historia sed et si pulli. § pro quo palam (?).

⟨4.12.⟩ D. xx. Si decreta (D.20 c.2) "incuria."

⟨4.13.⟩ C. i. q. i. Si qui a simoniacis (C.1 q.1 c.108).

⟨4.14.⟩ ff. de peculio Quotiens (Dig. 15.1.47).

⟨5.⟩ Contra.

⟨5.1.⟩ D. lxxxi. (D.81 c.20) et C. ii. q. v., capitulis Clericus solus, "ille deponatur," et c. Presbiter si (C.2 q.5 c.13).

---

4. Queras] Quamvis C Vp ‖ in^2 *om.* L Ma **4.1.** xi.] C. *praem.* C Vp ‖ q. i.] c. P1 ‖ qui] quid A, quis Ba, *om.* L Vp ‖ nullis] nullus C Vp ‖ excusationibus] excusantionibus *cum* n^1 *exp.* G ‖ labetur] habent A, *om.* L Ma **4.2.** liv.] lix. *cum* v. *exp.* Ma ‖ c. *om.* L Mu1 P1 ‖ sibi] cui Mu1 ‖ serviendum sibi *tr.* Ba Ma **4.3.** D. *om.* A ‖ lxxxvii.] lxxxvi. L ‖ sane] cave C qui post predictum tempus *add.* Ma **4.4.** Cure] sit omnibus *add.* Ma ‖ in fine capituli] "excusationis causa" Ma ‖ capituli *om.* Mu1 P1 **4.5.** C. *om.* Mu1 P1 ‖ i.] ii. P1 ‖ Quod] Qui Ba ‖ manifesta ratio] manifesto Ba, manifestato Vp ‖ ratio] ratione L, *om.* Ma ‖ periurii—hii *om.* P1 ‖ patet tunc hii *om.* A Ba C G L Ma Vp ‖ periurii *om.* Mu1 **4.6.** *om. per totum* Mu2 Vb ‖ C. *om.* Mu1 P1 ‖ xxxiv.] xxiii. C, xxxiii. Ma P1 ‖ ii.] i. A L Mu1 ‖ Non] c. *praem.* A C G, Que P1 ‖ quasi *om.* L P1, puniri *praem.* Ma ‖ adulteram] adultera L Mu1, adulterium P1 **4.7.** C. *om.* Mu1 P1 ‖ xii.] xiii. L ‖ Qui] Quod A G ‖ Qui et] Quod Vp ‖ humanis] inhumanis Vp ‖ cum non potuerit *om.* L ‖ potuerit] potuit Ba P1 Vb **4.8.** *om. per totum* A Ba C G L Ma Mu1 Mu2 P1 Vb **4.9.** *om. per totum* A Ba C G L Ma Mu1 Mu2 P1 Vb **4.10.** *om. per totum* A Ba C L Ma Vp ‖ xvi.] xvi. c. Velit Mu1 ‖ Quod dicitis *om.* Mu1 Vb ‖ dicitis] Sardicense *add.* G ‖ quia] quod Fr, capitulo Mu1 ‖ vos] tuos Mu1 **4.11.** *om. per totum* A Ba C L Ma Mu1 Mu2 Vb Vp ‖ ff.] contra P1 ‖ sed *om.* P1 **4.12.** *om. per totum* A Ba C L Ma Vp ‖ D.] arg. *praem.* G ‖ incuria] de *praem. male* Mu1, *om.* G P1 **4.13.** *om. per totum* A Ba C L Ma Mu1 Mu2 Vb Vp ‖ C.] arg. *praem.* G **4.14.** *om. per totum* A Ba C L Ma Mu1 Mu2 Vb Vp ‖ ff. *om.* P1 **5.** Contra] Econtra G, Contrarium L Mu1 **5.1.** et^1] eam *add.* Ba, *om.* C Ma Mu1 ‖ capitulis *om.* C Ma Mu1 ‖ Clericus—deponatur *post* lxxxi. *tr.* Ma Mu1 ‖ solus—deponatur *om.* L P1 ‖ solus] solet Ba ‖ ille] et *praem.* C ‖ deponatur] dixit Vp ‖ et^2 *om.* Ba Ma Mu1 Vp ‖ c.] cum C, *om.* L Ma Mu1 Vp ‖ Presbiter si] a plebe *add.* Ma ‖ si] solus *praem. et* illi de *add. male* L, *om.* P1

⟨4.⟩ You can examine this in:

⟨4.1.⟩ C.11 q.1 c.25.
⟨4.2.⟩ D.54 c.15.
⟨4.3.⟩ D.87 c.9.
⟨4.4.⟩ C.11 q.3 c.20 at the end of the chapter.
⟨4.5.⟩ C.33 q.1 c.1, C.33 q.1 c.2.
⟨4.6.⟩ C.34 q.1–2 c.3.
⟨4.7.⟩ C.12 q.2 c.24.
⟨4.8.⟩ C.35 q.2–3 c.11.
⟨4.9.⟩ C.23 q.1 c.2.
⟨4.10.⟩ D.16 c.14.
⟨4.11.⟩ ?
⟨4.12.⟩ D.20 c.2.
⟨4.13.⟩ C.1 q.1 c.108.
⟨4.14.⟩ Dig. 15.1.47.

⟨5.⟩ Against.

⟨5.1.⟩ D.81 c.20 and C.2 q.5 c.13.

⟨5.2.⟩ C. iii. q. ix. et C. xi. q. iii. c. Decrevimus (C.3 q.9 c.10), Rursus (C.11 q.3 c.36), Quicumque (C.11 q.3 c.37).

⟨5.3.⟩ C. xxxii. q. i. et C. xxxv. q. iii. c. Dicit Dominus (C.32 q.1 c.2), Extraordinaria (C.35 q.2–3 c.11).

⟨5.4.⟩ C. xii. q. iii. c. i. (C.12 q.3 c.1) "tamquam rerum."

⟨x. Explicit⟩

⟨1.⟩ Hec de presumptionibus, licet minus perfecte, scripsi, ut ex his peramplius et perfectius scrutandi materiam nanciscaris; ⟨2.⟩ nec tamen vera continet hoc perpendiculum, sed probabilia et apparentia propter exercitium disputandi, ut presentis instructionis beneficium oratorem potius quam iudicem instruat. ⟨3.⟩ Que autem concordantie in superioribus locis presumptionem pro aliquo vel contra aliquem faciant, tu ipse in singulis titulis diligenter attende; nam in uno eodemque titulo non una concordantia pro et contra, sed quedam pro, quedam contra presumptionem inducit, quam propter prolixitatem distinguere non curavi.

5.2. C.[1]—et *om.* P1 ‖ ix.] x. L ‖ et *om.* C Ma Mu1 ‖ c.—Decrevimus *om.* P1 ‖ c. *om.* C L Ma ‖ Decrevimus *post* ix. *tr.* (*et* in fine capituli *add.* Ma) Ma Mu1 ‖ Rursus] "nulla vox" *add.* Ma, Reursus Vp ‖ Quicumque] Quacumque Ba, C. eadem q. eadem *praem. et* "aditum audientie clausisse" *add.* Ma **5.3.** C.] et *praem.* P1 ‖ xxxii.] xxxiii. A L Vb ‖ i.] ii. C Vp, Dixit Dominus *add.* Mu1 ‖ et *om.* C Ma, *ante* Extraordinaria *tr.* Mu1 ‖ C.[2]–iii. *post* Dominus *tr.* Ma ‖ xxxv.] xxv. G ‖ iii.] iv. A L Vb ‖ c. *om.* Ba Ma P1 ‖ Dicit] Ait Fr, Dixit C Ma Vp ‖ Extraordinaria *ante* Dicit Dominus *tr.* L, ex ordinaria C **5.4.** xii.] xv. C ‖ iii.] iv. A L Vb ‖ c. i.] Placuit Ma ‖ c.] Q. *praem. et exp.* Vb ‖ i. *interl.* Vb ‖ rerum] dominicarum *add.* Ma **x.1.** Hec] Episcopi est ordinatio archidiaconi et ceterarum personarum *praem.* Vp ‖ presumptionibus] prescriptionibus P1 ‖ licet] et L ‖ his] ex *praem. et* et ex aliis *add.* Mu1 ‖ et perfectius] perfectiusque G P1 ‖ materiam] sentenciam C ‖ nasciscaris] nansciscaris *cum* s[1] *exp.* F **2.** vera *om.* Ma ‖ hoc] et *praem.* A ‖ probabilia] et *praem.* C F Vp ‖ et apparentia *post* exercitium *tr.* P1 ‖ oratorem] aratorem L ‖ ut[2]] nisi C ‖ presentis] a *praem.* Ma ‖ instructionis] instructoris F ‖ beneficium] beneficio Ma ‖ quam iudicem *post* instruat *tr.* Vp **3.** Que] Quod Mu1, Quam P1 ‖ concordantie] concordantieis *cum* is *exp.* Vp ‖ in superioribus] inferioribus Ba P1 ‖ presumptionem[1]—aliquem *om.* Ba ‖ presumptionem[1]] presumptionum F ‖ pro aliquo—tu ipse *om.* C ‖ faciant] faciunt A L P1 ‖ tu] et *praem.* P1 ‖ in singulis titutlis *post* diligenter *tr.* F ‖ titulis *om.* Ma ‖ nam] nec A L Vb ‖ in[3] *om.* P1 ‖ titulo *om.* A L Vb ‖ non *om.* L ‖ una] in *praem.* Ba ‖ pro et contra *om.* Vb ‖ pro[2]] presumptione *add.* F, aliquo *add.* P1 ‖ contra[2]] presumptionem *add.* F, aliquem *add.* P1 ‖ sed] si C ‖ quedam[1]—contra] quasdam Ma ‖ quedam[1] pro[3] *om.* Ba ‖ pro[3]] presumptione *add.* F, aliquo *add.* P1 ‖ contra[3]] aliquem *add.* P1 ‖ presumptionem[2]] presumpta Ba, presumptiones Ma, presumptione Vp ‖ inducit] inducitur F ‖ quam] quod Ba C G F Mu1 P1 Vp, quas Ma ‖ prolixitatem] probabilitatem P1 ‖ distinguere] distringere Ma

---

1. The rubric of the second borcard of part II has been wrongfully copied here Vp

⟨5.2.⟩ C.3 q.9 c.10, C.11 q.3 c.36, c.37.
⟨5.3.⟩ C.32 q.1 c.2, C.35 q.2–3 c.11.
⟨5.4.⟩ C.12 q.3 c.1.

⟨x. Explicit⟩

⟨1.⟩ I wrote this *Summula* on presumptions, though not perfectly, so that you may obtain from them material for a more extensive and perfect investigation; ⟨2.⟩ nevertheless, this plumb line does not contain the truth, but what is probable and discernible for the exercise of disputation, so that the benefit of this instruction may instruct the orator more than the judge. ⟨3.⟩ Moreover, in each title pay carefully attention yourself to which concordances in the previous topics may establish a presumption for or against someone; for in one and the same title there is not only one concordance both for and against, but some establish a presumption for and some against, which I did not care to distinguish because of the length.

Part II

⟨1.⟩ Introductis publica utilitate renuntiare non licet, etsi privatam utilitatem aliquatenus respiciant.

⟨1.1.⟩ D. xlv. Licet plerumque (D.45 c.4) "unde necesse est."

⟨1.2.⟩ C. x. q. i. c. ii. (C.10 q.1 c.2) "Quod factum."

⟨1.3.⟩ C. iii. q. iv. Alieni (C.3 q.4 c.1) "non possumus," "non permittimus."

⟨1.4.⟩ C. eadem q. v. Accusatores (C.3 q.5 c.2) "non possunt" et omnia capitula.

⟨1.5.⟩ C. xxx. q. ultima Iudicantem oportet (C.30 q.5 c.11).

⟨1.6.⟩ D. lxi Miramur (D.51 c.5) "nomen."

⟨1.7.⟩ C. de iureiurando propter calumniam l. ii. (Cod. 2.58.2).

⟨1.8.⟩ D. xxviii. De his quos (D.28 c.5) "auferre non possumus."

⟨1.9.⟩ C. iii. q. ix. Indicas (C.3 q.8 c.14) "credere non possumus."

⟨1.10⟩ C. vii. q. i. Quam periculosum (C.7 q.1 c.8) "in divinis."

⟨1.11.⟩ Contra.

⟨1.12.⟩ C. ii. q. vii. c. Nos si (C.2 q.7 c.41).

⟨1.13.⟩ C. eadem q. v. Mandastis (C.2 q.5 c.10) "licet evadere aliter" et c. Auditum (C.2 q.5 c.18).

⟨1.14.⟩ C. iii. q. ii. Si episcopus (C.3 q.2 c.8).

---

1. *§1—§1.13 om. per totum* P2 ‖ Introductis] Solutio: Sub speciale est in summo pontifice, scilicet ut possit renuntiare ius que introductus ob publica utilitate *praem.* Vp ‖ publica] comuni Ma ‖ utilitate] auctoritate A C L O Vb ‖ renuntiare] ab *praem.* Ma, et *praem. et post* licet *tr.* Vp ‖ privatam] publicam L ‖ utilitatem] voluntatem A, *interl. add.* m² Ma ‖ aliquatenus *om.* Ba, *interl.* Ma ‖ respiciant] ut *add.* Ba F, respiciunt L, respiciat P1 **1.1.** *§1.1—§1.11 om. per totum* O ‖ xlv.] xlxv. L ‖ licet *om.* L ‖ plerumque licet *tr. et post* unde *tr.* G P1 ‖ plerumque] presbiter L ‖ necesse est *post* xlv. *tr.* G P1 **1.2.** *om. per totum* A Ba C F G L Ma Mu1 P1 Vb **1.3.** iii.] iv. P1 ‖ Alieni] Alieni *cum* en *exp. et corr.* Alicui G P1 ‖ possumus] presumimus A L Vb ‖ non² *om.* Fr **1.4.** v.] eadem P1 ‖ Accusatores] esse *add.* Ma ‖ omnia] c. *cum abbr. signo* Ma ‖ capitula] copula Ba **1.5.** xxx.] xxxv. L ‖ ultima] vult A, v. L ‖ Iudicantem oportet] c. ultimo Ma ‖ Iudicantem] c. *praem.* Mu1 ‖ oportet *om.* L **1.6.** *om. per totum* A Ba C F G L Ma Mu1 P1 Vb **1.7.** propter calumniam] propterea (*et* dando *add.* Ma) A Ma Vb, dando *add.* Ba F **1.8.** *om per totum* A C G L P1 Vb ‖ quos *om.* Ma ‖ auferre] alle negare Ba, negare Ma Vp **1.9.** *om per totum* A C G L P1 Vb, *marg. add.* m² Ma ‖ Indicas] Indicans Ba Ma Vp, c. *praem.* Mu1 ‖ credere] ei Ba, proculdubio *add.* Fr, *om.* Mu1, hec Vp **1.10** *om. per totum* A Ba C F G L Ma Mu1 P1 Vb **1.11.** Contrarium L Mu1 **1.12.** c. *om.* L Ma P1 ‖ Nos *om.* Mu1 ‖ si] incompetenter *add.* G Ma P1 **1.13.** Mandastis] Mandasti Ba ‖ evadere aliter *om.* F ‖ et c.] C. eadem q. eadem Ma ‖ c. Auditum] D. c. Optantum (D.100 c.4) *add. et ante* C. *tr.* P1 ‖ c. *om.* L ‖ Auditum] Auderit A, Audierit Ba, est *add.* Mu1, Auditio Vb, Audent Vp **1.14.** *post §2 tr.* P1

 | DOI:10.1163/9789004713239_011

⟨1.⟩ It is not permissible to renounce rights introduced for the public good, even if they consider private interest to some extent.

⟨1.1.⟩ D.45 c.4.
⟨1.2.⟩ C.10 q.1 c.2.
⟨1.3.⟩ C.3 q.4 c.1.
⟨1.4.⟩ C.3 q.5 c.2 and all the chapters.
⟨1.5.⟩ C.30 q.5 c.11.
⟨1.6.⟩ D.51 c.5.
⟨1.7.⟩ Cod. 2.58.2.
⟨1.8.⟩ D. 28 c.5.
⟨1.9.⟩ C.3 q.8 c.14.
⟨1.10⟩ C.7 q.1 c.8.

⟨1.11.⟩ Against.

⟨1.12.⟩ C.2 q.7 c.41.
⟨1.13.⟩ C.2 q.5 c.10 and c.18.
⟨1.14.⟩ C.3 q.2 c.8.

⟨2.⟩ Episcopi est ordinatio archidiaconi et ceterarum personarum.

⟨2.1.⟩ D. lx. c. i. (D.60 c.1).

⟨2.2.⟩ D. lxxiv. Episcoporum (D.74 c.5).

⟨2.3.⟩ D. xxv. Perlectis (D.25 c.1) "perordinator," "que tamen auctoritate."

⟨2.6.⟩ Contra.

⟨2.7.⟩ D. xciii. Legimus in Ysaia (D.93 c.24).

⟨2.8.⟩ C. xii. q. ii. Alienationes (C.12 q.2 c.37) "personarum;" hoc trahitur ad utramquem partem.

⟨2.9.⟩ D. xxiv. Episcopus sine concilio (D.24 c.6).

⟨2.10.⟩ C. xvi. q. vii. Episcopus nullius (C.16 q.7 c.6) "absque presentia clericorum."

⟨3.⟩ De voluntate, opere et intentione. Animum, non opus, spectandum, remunerandum, puniendum.

⟨3.1.⟩ C. xi. q. iii. Quod predecessor (C.11 q.3 c.105) "spiritualiter servasse."

⟨3.2.⟩ C. xxiii. q. viii. Occidit (C.23 q.8 c.14).

⟨3.3.⟩ C. xxii. q. ii. Homines (C.22 q.2–3 c.3) "sed putat non pluisse," "nisi rea mens."

⟨3.4.⟩ Q. eadem Is autem (C.22 q.2–3 c.4) "ille mentitur, qui dicit verum" et c. Beatus (C.22 q.2–3 c.5).

---

2. *§2—§2.10 om. per totum* P2 ‖ *post §2.3 tr.* Vp ‖ Episcopi] Episcopus C ‖ ordinatio] ordinator C ‖ archidiaconi ordinatio *tr.* Vb ‖ ceterarum] aliarum F ‖ personarum] ut *add.* F **2.1.** *§2.1—§2.10 om. per totum* O ‖ lx.] xl. Ba Mu1, lv. L ‖ c. i.] primo Ba **2.2.** lxxiv.] lxxii. F, lxxiii. Vp ‖ Episcoporum] c. *praem.* F, in fine *add.* Ma, c. *praem. et* "quem legerit episcopus" *add.* Mu1, Episcopus Vb **2.3.** Perlectis] Perlectas A ‖ perordinator] perordinatorum G, perordinatio L, perordinata P1, ordinatio Vb ‖ que tamen] quantum G ‖ que] qua L ‖ tamen] tantum Ma ‖ auctoritate *om.* P1 **2.6.** *om. per totum* Vp ‖ Contrarium L Mu1 **2.7.** xciii.] lxxxiii. A L ‖ Legimus] Legitimus G ‖ in Ysaia *om.* Ma ‖ Ysaia] asia *praem.* G, diaconi eligunt *add.* Mu1 **2.8.** Alienationes] Alienationem P1, Alienations Vp ‖ personarum—partem *om.* Ma ‖ hoc trahitur] habeantur P1 ‖ utramquem] utraque Vp **2.9.** *om. per totum* A Ba C F G L Mu1 P1 Vb Vp **2.10.** *om. per totum* A Ba C F G L Mu1 P1 Vb Vp **3.** = 33 C, 22 O, 100 P1 ‖ *§3—§3.18 om. per totum* G ‖ De—intentione *om.* Ba C O P1 ‖ De voluntate *post* puniendum *tr.* F ‖ opere—intentione *om.* Vb ‖ opere] et *praem.* L Mu1 ‖ et *om.* Ma ‖ Animum] Animus F, Animi L ‖ non] ut *praem.* L ‖ puniendum remunerandum *tr.* C O P1 ‖ puniendum] et *praem.* Ma, plectendum Mu1 **3.1.** *§3.1—§3.18 om. per totum* O ‖ xi.] xv. Ma ‖ Quod] Qui A ‖ servasse] servare F P1, se *praem.* L, servasses Mu1 **3.2.** *om. per totum* P1 ‖ *post §3.5 tr.* C ‖ xxiii.] xxii. C ‖ Occidit] Finees *add.* F, Finees ad voluntatem personarum *add.* Mu1 **3.3.** Homines] c. *praem.* Mu1, Hominem P1 ‖ sed] si A Ba C F L P1 Vb Vp ‖ putat] putant L ‖ pluisse] punisse P1 ‖ nisi] ream linguam non facit *praem.* Ma ‖ rea] te a L ‖ mens] mes L **3.4.** Q. eadem] et C, C. eadem *praem.* Ma, et c. Mu1, *om.* P1 ‖ Is] non *praem. et exp.* L, His *cum* H *exp.* Vb ‖ et c.] C. eadem q. eadem Ma ‖ c. *om.* L ‖ Beatus] Paulus *add.* Ma Vb, Beati Vp

⟨2.⟩ The ordination of an archdeacon and other persons pertains to the bishop.

⟨2.1.⟩ D.60 c.1.
⟨2.2.⟩ D.74 c.5.
⟨2.3.⟩ D. 25 c.1.

⟨2.6.⟩ Against.

⟨2.7.⟩ D.93 c.24.
⟨2.8.⟩ C.12 q.2 c.37; this is drawn to both sides.
⟨2.9.⟩ D.24 c.6.
⟨2.10.⟩ C.16 q.7 c.6.

⟨3.⟩ Concerning will, deed, and intention. The mind, not the deed, is to be considered, rewarded, or punished.

⟨3.1.⟩ C.11 q.3 c.105.
⟨3.2.⟩ C.23 q.8 c.14.
⟨3.3.⟩ C.22 q.2–3 c.3.
⟨3.4.⟩ C.22 q.2–3 c.4 and C.22 q.2–3 c.5.

⟨3.5.⟩ D. l. Presbiteros (D.50 c.32) "extra delictum" et c. Quia te (D.50 c.38) et c. Eum qui (D.50 c.46).

⟨3.6.⟩ D. l. Quantum (D.50 c.48) "non agnoscitur perniciosa" et c. Hii qui (D.50 c.49) et c. Si duo (D.50 c.51).

⟨3.7.⟩ C. xxxii. q. v. infra xiii. capitulus continuus (C.32 q.8 c.13).

⟨3.8.⟩ C. xxxiv. q. ii. Si virgo (C.34 q.1–2 c.5).

⟨3.9.⟩ C. xv. q. i. Usque adeo (C.15 q.1 p.c.1).

⟨3.10.⟩ C. xxxiii. q. iii. D. i. c. Si propterea (D.1 de pen. c.29) et c. Sicut (D.1 de pen. c.83) et § Item (?).

⟨3.11.⟩ C. xiv. q. v. Scriptum est (C.14 q.5 c.11).

⟨3.12.⟩ Contra.

⟨3.13.⟩ D. l. Studeat (D.50 c.39) "voluntatem occidendi."

⟨3.14.⟩ D. eadem c. Eos (D.50 c.42) et c. Si qua (D.50 c.43) "si casu" et Si quis voluntarie (D.50 c.44) "si autem" et Qui saccum (D.50 c.45) "quamvis."

⟨3.15.⟩ D. eadem Quod factum (D.50 c.32?) et c. Sepe (D.50 c.50) "vel negligentia."

3.5. D.] p. *add.* Vp ‖ Presbiteros] Presbiter A Ba C P1 Vb, Presbiteri L, Presbiteri vel os Vp ‖ et^{1} c.^{1}] D. eadem Ma, *om.* P1 ‖ c.^{1} *om.* L ‖ te *om.* A Vb ‖ et^{2} c.^{2}] D. eadem Ma ‖ et^{2} *om.* P1 Vp ‖ c.^{2} *om.* L ‖ Eum] Eos F Ma, *om.* P1 **3.6.** D. l. *om.* Ma P1, et c. Mu1 ‖ agnoscitur] agnoscatur A Ba L, cognoscatur Vb ‖ perniciosa] vitiosa A Ba L Vb Vp, *om.* Ma ‖ et^{1} c.^{1}] D. eadem Ma, *om.* P1 ‖ c.^{1} *om.* Ba L ‖ qui] arg. *add.* C, *om.* F ‖ et^{2} c.^{2} *om.* Ma ‖ c.^{2} *om.* L **3.7.** *om. per totum* A F ‖ xxxii.] xxxiii. *cum* i.^{3} *exp.* Vp ‖ v.] viii. P1 Vb ‖ infra—capitulus *om.* P1 ‖ infra—continuus] omnibus capitulis Mu1 ‖ infra] in C L Vp, *om.* Ma Vb ‖ capitulus continuus] capitulis continuis Ba L Ma **3.8.** *om. per totum* A, *post §3.4 tr.* L ‖ xxxiv.] xxxiii. C L P1 ‖ q. ii. *om.* Ba F Mu1 ‖ ii.] iii. Ma, *vac.* P1 ‖ virgo] nesciens *add.* C P1 **3.9.** *ante §3.8 tr.* Vb ‖ xv.] xii. C ‖ Usque adeo] Si quis non iratus (C.15 q.1 c.13) F, Non est (C.15 q.1 c.10) Vb ‖ adeo] et *add.* Ma, et c. Merito (C.15 q.1 c.1) et omnibus sequentes capitulis *add.* Mu1 **3.10.** *om. per totum* Ma ‖ C. iii. *om.* P1 ‖ iii.] iv. Ba ‖ D. i. *om.* Ba ‖ i.] iii. Vp ‖ c.^{1} *om.* F L P1 ‖ et—Item *om.* Ba, Hinc vel inter. F ‖ et c.^{2} *om.* P1 ‖ c.^{2} *om.* L ‖ Sicut] Si cui Mu1 ‖ et § Item *om.* Mu1 ‖ § *om.* L **3.11.** xiv.] xxxiv. C P1 ‖ Scriptum] Sicut *praem. et exp.* C, c. *praem.* Mu1 **3.12.** Econtra Ba, Scriptum est L, Contrarium Mu1 **3.13.** Studeat] Si videat P1 ‖ voluntatem] voluntate A Ba C L Vb Vp, quoniam etsi *praem. et* non habuit *add.* Mu1 ‖ occidendi] occidere P1 **3.14.** D. eadem] et Ba F Mu1, *om.* P1 ‖ c.^{1} *om.* L Ma P1 ‖ Eos] qui *add.* Mu1 ‖ et c.] D. eadem F, *om.* Ma Vp ‖ c.^{2} *om.* C L P1 ‖ qua] quiam C, femina *add.* Mu1 ‖ si^{1} *om.* C Ma ‖ casu] visu Ba, *om.* Ma ‖ et^{2} *om.* F Ma ‖ Si^{2}] Su C, c. *praem.* Mu1 ‖ voluntarie—quamvis *om.* L, non sciant P1 ‖ voluntarie] voluntate Mu1 ‖ autem] non *add.* Mu1 ‖ et^{3}—quamvis *om.* A Ba C ‖ et^{3}] D. eadem F Ma Vp ‖ Qui] c. *praem.* Mu1 ‖ quamvis] quantum F, *om.* Ma Mu1 Vp **3.15.** D.—c. *om.* Ma ‖ D.—facum *om.* F Mu1 Vp ‖ D. eadem *om.* P1 ‖ Quod] Qui C P1 ‖ factum] factus P1, est *add.* Vb ‖ et c. *om.* Ba P1 ‖ c. *om.* L ‖ vel] qui L ‖ negligentia] negligentiam A L Vb, negligenti P1

⟨3.5.⟩ D.50 c.32 and c.38 and c.46.
⟨3.6.⟩ D.50 c.48 and c.49 and c.51.
⟨3.7.⟩ C.32 q.8 c.13.
⟨3.8.⟩ C.34 q.2 c.5.
⟨3.9.⟩ C.15 q.1 p.c.1.
⟨3.10.⟩ D.1 de pen. c.29 and c.83 and?
⟨3.11.⟩ C.14 q.5 c.11.

⟨3.12.⟩ Against.

⟨3.13.⟩ D.50 c.39.
⟨3.14.⟩ D.50 c.42 and c.43 and c.44 and c.45.
⟨3.15.⟩ D.50 c.32? and c.50.

⟨3.16.⟩ C. xxxi. q. iii. Si qui (C.31 q.3 c.un.) "excusati."
⟨3.17.⟩ C. xxxiii. q. iii. D. i. Cogitatio (D.1 de pen. c.20).
⟨3.18.⟩ C. xxxiii. q. iii. Hec autem verba (D.1 de pen. c.17) in i. pagina.

⟨4.⟩ Voluntas pro facto reputatur.
⟨4.1.⟩ C. xiv. q. v. Si quid invenisti (C.14 q.5 c.6).
⟨4.2.⟩ C. xxxiii. q. iii. Si cui (D.1 de pen. c.30) et c. Omnis iniquitas (D.1 de pen. c.25).
⟨4.3.⟩ Q. eadem Si quis cum telo (D.1 de pen. d.p.c.9).
⟨4.4.⟩ C. xxxii. q. v. Nec solo (C.32 q.5 c.12) et c. Qui viderit (C.32 q.5 c.13).
⟨4.5.⟩ Q. eadem Sicut enim (C.32 q.5 c.10).
⟨4.6.⟩ C. i. q. i. c. ii. (C.1 q.1 c.2).
⟨4.7.⟩ Contra.
⟨4.8.⟩ C. xxxi. q. i. Si qui (C.31 q.1 c.5).
⟨4.9.⟩ Supra conspice omnia que sunt in proximis titulis.
⟨4.10.⟩ C. xxii. q. ii. Is autem (C.22 q.2–3 c.4) "nec ideo illum."
⟨4.11.⟩ C. xv. q. i. Si quis non iratus (C.15 q.1 c.13).

3.16. *post §3.17 tr.* Ba Mu1, *post §3.18 tr.* C ‖ Si—excusati *om.* (*homoiotel.*) P1 ‖ qui] quis A L, parentes *add.* Ma ‖ excusati] excusari A L, erunt *add.* Ma Mu1, accusati Vp **3.17.** C. iii. *om.* (*homoiotel.*) P1 ‖ iii.] iv. Vp ‖ D.] c. Ba F ‖ Cogitatio] Cogitationis (D.1 de pen. c.14) et *praem. et* et c. i. (D.1 de pen. c.1) *add.* Mu1, *om.* Vb **3.18.** *om. per totum* Ma ‖ xxxiii.] xxx. P1 ‖ q. iii. *om.* Ba, D. i. § i. l. *add.* Mu1 ‖ Hec autem] Habeant Vp ‖ verba] que statuerit *add.* Mu1 ‖ in i. pagina *om.* Mu1 ‖ pagina] § L **4.** = 34 C, 23 O, 101 P1, 6 P2 ‖ *§4—§4.11 om. per totum* G ‖ Voluntas] Contrarium Mu1, Voluntates P2 ‖ reputatur] ut *add.* F, recipitur Ma, reputetur O, reputabitur P1, reputantur P2 **4.1.** *§4.1—§4.11 om. per totum* O ‖ xiv.] xxxiv. P1 ‖ v.] iv. L ‖ quid] qui Ba, quis P2, quod Vp **4.2.** iii.] D. i. *add.* Ma Mu1 ‖ Si cui] Scitum P1 ‖ cui] "non minus" *add.* Ma ‖ et c. *om.* Ma P1 ‖ c. *om.* L ‖ Omnis iniquitas *post §4.3 tr.* Ma **4.3.** *om. per totum* F P1 ‖ Q. eadem *om.* Ba P2, C. eadem D. eadem Ma, et § i. l. Mu1 ‖ Si quis] Is qui Fr **4.4.** xxxii.] xxxiii. L ‖ Nec—c. *om.* Ma ‖ Nec] Neque C ‖ et c. *om.* P1 ‖ c. *om.* L ‖ Qui] Quid A, Quod F P1 ‖ viderit] sicut illum *add.* F, *om.* P1 **4.5.** Q. eadem *om.* Ba L Ma Mu1 P2, et P1 ‖ enim] hunc Mu1, id P1 **4.6.** *post §4.7 tr.* Ma ‖ i.[1] *vac.* P1 ‖ q.] si quis *exp.* A ‖ ii.] i. P2 **4.7.** Econtra Ba P2, Contrarium L Mu1 **4.8.** *§4.8—§4.11 om. per totum* L ‖ xxxi.] xxxii. P1 ‖ i.] iii. (C.31 q.3 c.un.) C Ma Vb Vp, iv. P1 ‖ Si] c. *praem.* Mu1 ‖ qui] quis A C Mu1 P1 Vb **4.9.** Supra] vel infra *add.* F, Sibi P1 ‖ conspice] conspicere P1 ‖ omnia] cuncta Mu1 ‖ que] c. *praem. et exp.* F ‖ proximis] primis P1 ‖ titulis] capitulis F Ma, facilis *cum* fu *exp. et corr.* P2 **4.10.** *om. per totum* A C Ma P1 P2 ‖ C.] Item Vb ‖ xxii.] xxxii. Mu1, xxxiii. Vb ‖ ii.] v. Mu1, iii. Vb ‖ Is autem] c. Ille autem Mu1, Ille autem di. ii. *cum* di. ii. *exp. et corr. interl.* Vb ‖ nec—illum *om.* Mu1 Vb ‖ illum] ullum Fr **4.11.** *ante §4.10 tr.* Mu1, *add. alia* m^2 Vb, *om. per totum* A Ba C F Ma P1 P2 Vp

⟨3.16.⟩ C.31 q.3 c.un.
⟨3.17.⟩ D.1 de pen. c.20.
⟨3.18.⟩ D.1 de pen. c.17 in the first page.

⟨4.⟩ The will is to be considered as a deed.
⟨4.1.⟩ C.14 q.5 c.6.
⟨4.2.⟩ D.1 de pen. c.30 and c.25.
⟨4.3.⟩ D.1 de pen. d.p.c.9.
⟨4.4.⟩ C.32 q.5 c.12 and c.13.
⟨4.5.⟩ C.32 q.5 c.10.
⟨4.6.⟩ C.1 q.1 c.2.
⟨4.7.⟩ Against.
⟨4.8.⟩ C.31 q.1 c.5.
⟨4.9.⟩ Look above at all that is in the titles nearby.
⟨4.10.⟩ C.22 q.2 c.4.
⟨4.11.⟩ C.15 q.1 c.13.

⟨5.⟩ Intentio bona illicitum non prorsus excusat a culpa.

⟨5.1.⟩ C. xxii. q. ii. Is autem (C.22 q.2–3 c.4) “nec ideo ullum.”

⟨5.2.⟩ C. xiv. q. v. Forte (C.14 q.5 c.3).

⟨5.3.⟩ C. i. q. i. Non est putanda (C.1 q.1 c.27).

⟨5.4.⟩ C. xxxii. q. iv. Sic non sunt (C.32 q.4 c.10).

⟨5.5.⟩ C. xxii. q. ii. Si quelibet culpa (C.22 q.2–3 c.20).

⟨5.6.⟩ De con. D. iii. Perlatum (D.3 de cons. c.27).

⟨5.7.⟩ Contra.

⟨5.8.⟩ C. xxxii. q. iv. Dixit Sara (C.32 q.4 c.3) in fine.

⟨5.9.⟩ D. lxxiv. § Verum (D.74 d.p.c.6).

⟨5.10.⟩ C. xxiii. q. viii. Occidit Finees (C.23 q.8 c.14).

⟨5.11.⟩ C. xi. q. iii. Quod predecessor (C.11 q.3 c.105).

⟨6.⟩ Cum in re aliqua delinquitur, rei quantitas non spectatur ut intersit.

⟨6.1.⟩ C. xiv. q. ultima Fur autem (C.14 q.6 c.4) “non enim, quod.”

⟨6.2.⟩ C. xvii. q. iv. Quicumque (C.17 q.4 c.1) “vel exiguum.”

⟨6.3.⟩ Contra.

⟨6.4.⟩ B. l. xi. Si quis furtum (B.11 c.58).

---

5. = 15 C, 3 G P1, 11 O ‖ *§ 5—§ 5.11 om. per totum* P2 ‖ *om. per totum* L ‖ illicitum *post* excusat *tr.* A, *post* prorsus *tr.* Ba L Vb, illicita Ba F O ‖ prorsus non *tr.* O ‖ a culpa *om.* Mu1 ‖ culpa] ut *add.* F **5.1.** *§ 5.1—§ 5.11 om. per totum* O ‖ *post § 5.2 tr.* Ma ‖ C.] In *praem.* P1 ‖ xxii.] xxiii. C, xxxi. L ‖ Is] c. *praem.* Mu1, Michi P1 ‖ autem] qui mentitur *add.* Mu1 ‖ ullum] illum A Ba C F G L P1 Vb Vp, illius Ma, mendacium *add.* Mu1 **5.2.** *post § 4.9 rep.* F ‖ q. v. *om.* A Ba C G **5.3.** putanda] putandi Mu1 **5.4.** *om. per totum* Vb ‖ xxxii.] xxxiii. Ma, xxxiv. P1 ‖ iv.] iii. L ‖ Sic] Sicut Ba P1, c. *praem.* Mu1 ‖ sunt] fuerit P1 **5.5.** *post § 5.1 tr.* Mu1 ‖ *om. per totum* Ma ‖ C.—ii. *om.* Ba, et c. Mu1 ‖ Si—culpa *in § 5.1 post* illum *tr.* Ba ‖ quelibet] quemlibet Ba, qualibet L Mu1 ‖ culpa] a *praem. et exp.* P1 **5.6.** De con. *ante* Perlatum *tr.* Ma ‖ iii.] ii. Ma ‖ Perlatum] et D. c. Hii qui (?) et c. Si qui pereg. *cum abbr. signo add.* F **5.7.** Econtra Ba C, Contrarium L Mu1, rubrica *praem. marg.* Vb **5.8.** *post § 5.9 tr.* F ‖ xxxii.] xxxiii. A C Vb. xxxiii. *cum* i.[3] *exp.* Ma ‖ iv.] iii. F ‖ Dixit] c. *praem.* Mu1 ‖ fine] capituli *add.* Mu1 **5.9.** lxxiv.] lxxiii. A C F Ma Vb Vp, lxiii. Mu1, lxxxiii. P1 ‖ § *om.* Vb, *vac.* Vp **5.10.** C.] D. *exp. et corr.* Vb ‖ Occidit] c. *praem.* Mu1 ‖ Finees *om.* L, *in § 5.9 post* Verum *tr.* P1 **5.11.** *post § 9 tr.* P1 ‖ xi.] xv. A, xxi. Ba ‖ Quod] Qui (c. *praem.* Mu1) C Mu1 **6.** = 30 C, 19 O, 97 P1 ‖ *§ 6—§ 6.6 om. per totum* G P2 ‖ re aliqua] rem aliquam F ‖ quantitas] qualitas P1 ‖ non *om.* Mu1 ‖ spectatur] assignatur *praem. et exp.* Ba, inspectatur L ‖ ut intersit *om.* Vp ‖ ut] utrum A Mu1 O Vb Vp ‖ intersit] ut *add.* F, inter sic P1 **6.1.** *§ 6.1—§ 6.6 om. per totum* O ‖ xiv.] xiii. A Ba Vb, xvii. F, xxiv. P1 ‖ Fur] Furtum A, Fit L, c. *praem.* Mu1 ‖ enim *om.* P1 ‖ quod] qui Ba Vp, quam P1 **6.2.** *post § 14.6 rep.* P1 ‖ Quicumque] c. *praem.* Mu1 ‖ exiguum] exigui P1 $P1_1$ **6.3.** Econtra Ba, Contrarium L Mu1 **6.4.** *om. per totum* Ma P1 ‖ l. *om.* Vb ‖ furtum] forte Vp

⟨5.⟩ A good intention does not entirely excuse an unlawful act from guilt.
⟨5.1.⟩ C.22 q.2–3 c.4.
⟨5.2.⟩ C.14 q.5 c.3.
⟨5.3.⟩ C.1 q.1 c.27.
⟨5.4.⟩ C.32 q.4 c.10.
⟨5.5.⟩ C.22 q.2–3 c.20.
⟨5.6.⟩ D.3 de con. c.27.
⟨5.7.⟩ Against.
⟨5.8.⟩ C.32 q.4 c.3 at the end.
⟨5.9.⟩ D.74 d.p.c.6.
⟨5.10.⟩ C.23 q.8 c.14.
⟨5.11.⟩ C.11 q.3 c.105.

⟨6.⟩ When some wrongdoing is committed in a particular fact, the extent of the fact is not considered to make a difference.
⟨6.1.⟩ C.14 q.6 c.4.
⟨6.2.⟩ C.17 q.4 c.1.
⟨6.3.⟩ Against.
⟨6.4.⟩ B.11 c.58.

⟨6.5.⟩ C. i. q. i. Duces (C.1 q.1 c.23) v. "tantum obolorum."
⟨6.6.⟩ C. xvii. q. ultima Questi (C.17 q.4 c.41) "in sexcentum pedes."

⟨7.⟩ De consensu. Delinquentes et consentientes par pena comitatur.
⟨7.1.⟩ C. xvii. q. iv. Omnes ecclesie (C.17 q.4 c.5).
⟨7.2.⟩ C. i. q. i. Quisquis non exarserit (C.1 q.1 c.5) et c. Si quis episcopus (C.1 q.1 c.8).
⟨7.3.⟩ D. lxxxiii. c. i. (D.83 c.1), ii. (D.83 c.2), iii. (D.83 c.3), iv. (D.83 c.4), v. (D.83 c.5).
⟨7.4.⟩ C. xi. q. iii. Qui consentit (C.11 q.3 c.100).
⟨7.5.⟩ D. lxxxvi. Inferiorum (D.86 c.1) "ad nullos magis."
⟨7.6.⟩ D. eadem Culpam proculdubio facientis (D.86 c.3).
⟨7.7.⟩ C. ii. q. i. Notum (C.2 q.1 c.10) in fine.
⟨7.8.⟩ C. xxx. q. iii. Non oportet conscii simul (C.30 q.3 c.3).
⟨7.9.⟩ C. xxiii. q. viii. Preterea (C.23 q.8 c.12) et q. iii. Non inferenda (C.23 q.3 c.7).
⟨7.10.⟩ C. iii. q. iv. Consanguineorum (C.3 q.4 c.4).
⟨7.11.⟩ Contra.
⟨7.12.⟩ C. i. q. i. Quicquid invisibilis (C.1 q.1 c.101) "duobus mensibus."

6.5. Duces] Iudices A Ba C F L Ma P1 Vb Vp, c. *praem.* Mu1 ‖ ut—obolorum *om.* Mu1 ‖ ut *om.* F Ma ‖ tantum] quinque *praem.* Ma ‖ obolorum] ob ecclesiarum A, obolarum Ba, vobilorum *et ante* tantum *tr.* F, *ante* tantum *tr.* L, colorum Vb, obulorum *et ante* tantum *tr.* Vp **6.6.** xvii.] xvi. C ‖ ultima] iv. Mu1 ‖ Questi *om.* L, c. *praem. et* sunt *add.* Mu1 ‖ in] et Vp ‖ sexcentum] ex centum P1 ‖ pedes *om.* Ma Vb **7.** = 31 C, 20 O, 98 P1 ‖ *§7—§7.23 om. per totum* G P2 ‖ De consensu *om.* Ba C F Ma Mu1 P1 ‖ consensu pedis *add.* L ‖ Delinquentes et consentientes *post* comitatur *tr.* C O P1 ‖ Delinquentes] Delinquentis L ‖ par] per L, pura Vp ‖ pena] penam L **7.1.** *§7.1—§7.23 om. per totum* O ‖ iv.] ultima P1 ‖ Omnes] c. *praem.* Mu1 **7.2.** Quisquis] Si quis Vb ‖ non—c. *om.* P1 ‖ non *om.* L ‖ exarserit] exarsit C, arserit Fr, *om.* L ‖ et *om.* Ma ‖ c. *om.* L Ma ‖ episcopus] quicquid *add.* C, *om.* L **7.3.** lxxxiii.] lxxiii. F, lxxxi. P1 ‖ i. ii.] iv. Ba, *om.* Ma ‖ i.] ii. *del. et corr.* Mu1 ‖ ii.] et *praem.* A ‖ v.] et *praem.* Ma Mu1 Vp **7.4.** iii.] ii. P1 **7.5.** lxxxvi.] lxxxv. Ba ‖ Inferiorum] Interiorum Ba, c. *praem.* Mu1 ‖ magis] culpam producit *add.* Ma **7.6.** *post §7.7 tr.* Mu1 ‖ *om. per totum* Ma ‖ D. eadem] et F, *om.* P1 ‖ eadem] lxxxvi. Mu1 ‖ proculdubio facientis *om.* F ‖ proculdubio *ante* culpam *tr.* L ‖ facientis proculdubio culpam *tr.* Fr ‖ facientis *om.* A Ba L Mu1 Vb Vp, facientes P1 **7.7.** *post §7.10 tr.* Ma ‖ i.] ii. *cum* i.[2] *exp.* A L ‖ fine] et c. Inprimis (C.2 q.1 c.7) *add.* C **7.8.** *om. per totum* A L Ma Vb ‖ iii.] iv. P1 ‖ Non] c. *praem.* Mu1 ‖ conscii similis] consimilis Ba ‖ conscii] consu. C, consciis Fr, consil. P1 ‖ simul] similis C F P1 Vp **7.9.** *post §7.10 tr.* C, *post §7.7 tr.* Ma ‖ C.] C. xxx. q. ix. Interea (?) *praem.* Mu1 ‖ xxiii.] xxx. A L Vb, xxxiii. Ba F ‖ viii.] ix. Mu1, iv. P1 ‖ Preterea] Interea L, c. Propterea Mu1 ‖ et] C. xxx. Vb ‖ q. iii. *om.* L ‖ inferenda] est *praem.* C, in *praem.* Fr **7.10.** *post §7.11 tr.* Ma ‖ iii.] xiii. Mu1 ‖ iv.] iii. A L P1 Vb **7.11.** Econtra A Ba, Contrarium L Mu1 **7.12.** Quicquid] c. Quisquis Mu1 ‖ invisibilis] invisibiliter A, invisibile C, *om.* L

⟨6.5.⟩ C.1 q.1 c.23.
⟨6.6.⟩ C.17 q.4 c.41.

⟨7.⟩ About consent. Those who commit a crime and those who consent to it are subject to the same punishment.

⟨7.1.⟩ C.17 q.4 c.5.
⟨7.2.⟩ C.1 q.1 c.5 and c.8.
⟨7.3.⟩ D.83 c.1, c.2, c.3, c.4, c.5.
⟨7.4.⟩ C.11 q.3 c.100.
⟨7.5.⟩ D.86 c.1.
⟨7.6.⟩ D.86 c.3.
⟨7.7.⟩ C.2 q.1 c.10.
⟨7.8.⟩ C.30 q.3 c.3.
⟨7.9.⟩ C.23 q.8 c.12 and q.3 c.7.
⟨7.10.⟩ C.3 q.4 c.4.

⟨7.11.⟩ Against.

⟨7.12.⟩ C.1 q.1 c.101.

⟨7.13.⟩ C. ii. q. i. Notum (C.2 q.1 c.10) et c. ultimo (C.2 q.1 c.21).
⟨7.14.⟩ D. lxxxiii. c. i. (D.83 c.1), ii. (D.83 c.2) et iii. (D.83 c.3).
⟨7.15.⟩ C. xxxii. q. i. Si quis uxorem (C.32 q.1 c.4) "duobus annis."
⟨7.16.⟩ Q. eadem Si quis uxorem suam (C.32 q.1 c.6) "tres annos."
⟨7.17.⟩ D.xxxiii. c. ii. (D.33 c.2).
⟨7.18.⟩ C. ii. q. vii. Quod nec (C.2 q.7 c.32).
⟨7.19.⟩ C. xxxiii. q. viii. Preterea (C.23 q.8 c.12).
⟨7.20.⟩ B. ix. De his (B.9 c.32) "fautores," "iuxta modum."
⟨7.21.⟩ C. xxxv. q. iii. Si quis cum matre (C.35 q.2–3 c.5), "post penitentiam nubat" (C.35 q.2–3 c.6).
⟨7.22.⟩ C. xxvii. q. i. Devotam (C.27 q.1 c.27).
⟨7.23.⟩ D. lxxxvi. Facientes (D.86 c.3).

⟨8.⟩ His consentire dicitur qui cum possit prohibere non prohibet, impedire non impedit, et qui post coactionem cum possit non statim discrepat.
⟨8.1.⟩ D. xxvii. Diaconus (D.27 c.1).
⟨8.2.⟩ D. xxviii. Diaconi (D.28 c.8).
⟨8.3.⟩ D. lxxxiii. Error (D.83 c.3) et c. Consentire (D.83 c.5).
⟨8.4.⟩ D. lxxxvi. Culpam (D.86 c.3).
⟨8.5.⟩ C. ii. q. vii. Negligere (C.2 q.7 c.55).

7.13. *om. per totum* A Ba F L Ma Mu1 P1 Vb Vp **7.14.** *om. per totum* A Ba F L Ma Mu1 P1 Vb Vp **7.15.** i.] ii. C ‖ Si] c. *praem.* Mu1 ‖ annis *om.* Ba, anni L **7.16.** Q. eadem] et c. Mu1 P1 ‖ Q.] et *praem.* Ba Ma ‖ suam] scit *add.* Ba Mu1 P1, *om.* L, forte Ma ‖ tres] per *praem.* F, *om.* P1 ‖ annos] annis Mu1, *om.* P1 **7.17.** *om. per totum* A Ba F L Ma Mu1 P1 Vb Vp **7.18.** *om. per totum* A Ba F L Ma Mu1 P1 Vb Vp ‖ Quod] Qui Fr **7.19.** *om. per totum* A Ba F L Ma Mu1 P1 Vb Vp ‖ xxxiii.] xxiii. Fr **7.20.** B.] D. Ba Ma P1 ‖ ix.] liv. Ba, c. *add.* C F, l. *praem.* Mu1, xi. P1, xi. *cum* i. *exp. et corr.* Vp ‖ De his] Solis denis Ba Ma ‖ his] qui *add.* Mu1 ‖ fautores *om.* L, tutores Ma, factores P1 ‖ iuxta *cum* u *exp.* Ma ‖ modum] culpe *add.* F, *om.* Ma, med. *cum abbr. signo* Vp **7.21.** xxxv.] xxv. A Ba L Vb ‖ iii.] iv. A L Vb ‖ Si] c. *praem.* Mu1 ‖ cum matre] coniugem F ‖ post—nubat *om.* Ma ‖ penitentiam] penam P1 **7.22.** *om. per totum* A Ba F L Ma Mu1 P1 Vb Vp **7.23.** *om. per totum* A Ba F L Ma Mu1 P1 Vb Vp ‖ Facientes] Facientis Fr **8.** = 32 C, 21 O, 99 P1, 7 P2 ‖ *§8—§8.18 om. per totum* G ‖ His *om.* F Mu1 P2, Hic Vb ‖ consentire] prohibere L ‖ dicitur] videtur Ba F Mu1 P2 ‖ qui[1]] quod L Vp ‖ prohibere *om.* C O P1 ‖ non[1]] ut C, nec O P1 ‖ impedire—impedit *post possit tr.* C O, *ante* possit *tr.* P1 ‖ et *om.* A Ba F L Ma Mu1 P2 Vb Vp ‖ qui[2]] quod L Vp ‖ cum possit *om.* Ma ‖ possit] potest C O P1 ‖ discrepat] ut *add.* F, increpat Mu1 **8.1.** *§8.1—§8.18 om. per totum* O ‖ *om. per totum* A Ba C L Ma Mu1 P1 P2 Vb Vp **8.2.** *om. per totum* A Ba C L Ma Mu1 P1 P2 Vb Vp **8.3.** lxxxiii.] lxxiii. Ba ‖ Error] c. *praem.* Ba P2 Vp ‖ et *om.* Ma P1 ‖ c. *om.* L Ma P1 **8.4.** Culpam] Facientis proculdubio *praem.* Fr, Faciens *praem.* Mu1 **8.5.** C. ii.] q. vi. Legere anteriorum (Anteriorum legum Fr) (C.2 q.6 c.28), § Si adversus (C.2 q.6 p.c.29) *add.* F ‖ vii.] iii. Ba ‖ Negligere] c. *praem.* Mu1

⟨7.13.⟩ C.2 q.1 c.10 and c.21.
⟨7.14.⟩ D.83 c.1, c.2, and c.3.
⟨7.15.⟩ C.32 q.1 c.4.
⟨7.16.⟩ C.32 q.1 c.6.
⟨7.17.⟩ D.33 c.2.
⟨7.18.⟩ C.2 q.7 c.32.
⟨7.19.⟩ C.23 q.8 c.12.
⟨7.20.⟩ B.9 c.32.
⟨7.21.⟩ C.35 q.2–3 c.5, c.6.
⟨7.22.⟩ C.27 q.1 c.27.
⟨7.23.⟩ D.86 c.3.

⟨8.⟩ He is said to consent who, when able to forbid, does not forbid, and when able to prevent, does not prevent; and he who, after being compelled, does not immediately disagree when he can.
⟨8.1.⟩ D.27 c.1.
⟨8.2.⟩ D.28 c.8.
⟨8.3.⟩ D.83 c.3 and c.5.
⟨8.4.⟩ D.86 c.3.
⟨8.5.⟩ C.2 q.7 c.55.

⟨8.6.⟩ C. xxiii. q. iii. Qui potest (C.23 q.3 c.8) et Non inferenda (C.23 q.3 c.7).

⟨8.7.⟩ C. eadem q. eadem Ostendit (C.23 q.3 c.11).

⟨8.8.⟩ C. xxiii. q. viii. Preterea (C.23 q.8 c.12) "tamen, quia a te conprimi."

⟨8.9.⟩ C. xxxii. q. i. Mulier (C.32 q.2 c.14).

⟨8.10.⟩ C. xxxiv. q. ii. Non satis (C.34 q.1–2 c.3).

⟨8.11.⟩ C. i. q. i. Constat (C.1 q.1 c.111) "Ceterum, qui post mensem."

⟨8.12.⟩ D. liv. Si servus sciente (D.54 c.20).

⟨8.13.⟩ C. xx. q. ii. Si in qualibet (C.20 q.2 c.1) "non mox visam."

⟨8.14.⟩ C. xxii. q. v. Pueri (C.22 q.5 c.15).

⟨8.15.⟩ Contra.

⟨8.16.⟩ C. xxiii. q. iv. Ita plane (C.23 q.4 c.6) "illa duo."

⟨8.17.⟩ C. xi. q. iii. Quod predecessor (C.11 q.3 c.105) "communionis consensu."

⟨8.18.⟩ C. xx. q. ii. Puella (C.20 q.2 c.2) "At si annum et diem."

⟨9.⟩ Quod aliquorum consensu perfici debet, non nisi regulari eorum consensu perficitur.

⟨9.1.⟩ C. xviii. q. ii. Si quis abbas (C.18 q.2 c.15).

⟨9.2.⟩ D. xcii. c. penultimo (D.92 c.8).

⟨9.3.⟩ C. xii. q. ii. Quicumque (C.12 q.2 c.4).

8.6. *§ 8.6—§ 8.8 post § 8.14 tr.* F ‖ xxiii.] xxxiii. Qui pro C, xxxiii. P1, iv. Vb ‖ Qui] Quod Ba Ma, c. *praem.* Mu1 ‖ et] c. *add.* A C F, cum *add.* Ba, *om.* Ma P1 ‖ Non] c. *praem.* Mu1 P2 Vp ‖ inferenda] interferenda Ba, in *praem.* Fr **8.7.** *om. per totum* Mu1 ‖ C.—eadem² *om.* Ba P2, et c. F ‖ q.] c. L **8.8.** *post § 8.5 tr.* Mu1 ‖ C. xxiii.] et P1 ‖ xxiii.] xxiv. C ‖ tamen—conprimi *om.* L ‖ tamen] non Ma ‖ a te *om.* A Ba C F L Ma Mu1 P2 Vb Vp ‖ conprimi] et primi F, eum pri. P2, *primi add. interl. et exp.* Vp **8.9.** *om. per totum* A Ba C L Ma Mu1 P1 P2 Vb Vp **8.10.** *om. per totum* A Ba C L Ma Mu1 P1 P2 Vb Vp **8.11.** Ceterum *om.* L ‖ qui] quod Ba F ‖ post] prius F, possunt L ‖ mensem *om.* L **8.12.** *post § 8.3 tr.* F ‖ liv.] lxiv. *cum* v. *exp.* P2 ‖ sciente *om.* F L **8.13.** *post § 8.14 tr.* P1 ‖ Si] c. *praem.* Mu1 ‖ non—visam *om.* L ‖ mox] morum P1 ‖ visam] visum C P1 **8.14.** *post § 8.11 tr.* L ‖ xxii.] xx. C, xii. P1 ‖ v.] ii. L ‖ Pueri] c. *praem.* Mu1 **8.15.** *vac. cum signo* Ba, Contrarium L Mu1, Econtra P2 **8.16.** C. *om.* P1 ‖ xxiii.] xxiv. Mu1 ‖ illa] illi Mu1 P1 **8.17.** xi.] vi. P1 ‖ Quod] c. *praem.* F ‖ consensu communionis *tr.* Mu1 ‖ communionis] communis Ba, communioni F ‖ consensu] consentit F, consensus L P2 **8.18.** xx.] ii. Ba, xxi. L ‖ ii. *om.* P2 ‖ Puella] c. *praem.* Mu1, Puellam P2, Puolla Vp ‖ At] quod L, et P2 ‖ annum] an non A ‖ et diem] utilem P2 ‖ diem *om.* Vb **9.** = 13 C, 4 G P1, 8 P2 ‖ Quod] regulari *add.* Ba, Quando L ‖ perfici] fieri C O, profici Vp ‖ debet] habet C O, non *praem.* Ma ‖ nisi *rep.* Ba, sine P2 ‖ regulari] regula Vp ‖ eorum] in *praem.* Vp ‖ perficitur] perfici debet (ut *add.* F) Ba F P2 **9.1.** *§ 9.1—§ 9.11 om. per totum* O ‖ *post § 8.14 tr.* F ‖ xviii.] xix. A, xxi. L ‖ ii. *om.* L ‖ Si] c. *praem.* Mu1 **9.2.** D.] C. *exp. et corr. marg.* P2 ‖ penultimo] Si quis episcopus Mu1 **9.3.** *add. marg. inf.* P2 ‖ xii.] x. Ma, ii. Vb ‖ ii.] i. A ‖ Quicumque] Quodcumque P2

⟨8.6.⟩ C.23 q.3 c.8 and c.7.
⟨8.7.⟩ C.23 q.3 c.11.
⟨8.8.⟩ C.23 q.8 c.12.
⟨8.9.⟩ C.32 q.2 c.14
⟨8.10.⟩ C.34 q.1–2 c.3.
⟨8.11.⟩ C.1 q.1 c.111.
⟨8.12.⟩ D.54 c.20.
⟨8.13.⟩ C.20 q.2 c.1.
⟨8.14.⟩ C.22 q.5 c.15.

⟨8.15.⟩ Against.

⟨8.16.⟩ C.23 q.4 c.6.
⟨8.17.⟩ C.11 q.3 c.105.
⟨8.18.⟩ C.20 q.2 c.2.

⟨9.⟩ What ought to be accomplished by the consent of some, is not accomplished except by their regular consent.

⟨9.1.⟩ C.18 q.2 c.15.
⟨9.2.⟩ D.92 c.8.
⟨9.3.⟩ C.12 q.2 c.4.

⟨9.4.⟩ C. xxix. q. ultima Dictum (C.29 q.2 c.8) “per voluntatem.”
⟨9.5.⟩ C. eadem q. eadem Si quis ingenuus (C.29 q.2 c.4).
⟨9.6.⟩ C. xxxii. q. ii. Aliquando (C.32 q.2 c.7) “et si ab initio.”

⟨9.7.⟩ Contra.

⟨9.8.⟩ D. xxviii. De Siracusane (D.28 c.13).
⟨9.9.⟩ D. xxvii. Si vir (D.27 c.3) et c. Voventibus (D.27 c.4).
⟨9.10.⟩ C. xxvii. q. i. Nuptiarum (C.27 q.1 c.41).
⟨9.11.⟩ C. xxxii. q. ii. Solet queri (C.32 q.2 c.6) et c. Non omnis (C.32 q.2 c.12) “inter ingenuos.”

⟨10.⟩ Quod aliquorum consensu fieri debet, eorundem dissensu impeditur faciendum et dissolvitur factum.

⟨10.1.⟩ D. lxii. Nulla ratio (D.62 c.1).
⟨10.2.⟩ D. xcii. c. penultimo (D.92 c.8).
⟨10.3.⟩ D. li. Qui in aliquo (D.51 c.5) “quem nec clerus.”
⟨10.4.⟩ C. i. q. i. Ordinationes (C.1 q.1 c.113).
⟨10.5.⟩ D. xxiv. c. i. (D.24 c.1).
⟨10.6.⟩ D. lxiii. Obeuntibus (D.63 c.35).
⟨10.7.⟩ C. x. q. ii. Casellas (C.10 q.2 c.1).
⟨10.8.⟩ D. lxv. Non (D.65 c.2) “episcopus.”

9.4. *add. marg. inf.* P2 ‖ C.] arg. Mu1 ‖ xxix.] xxx. A Ba C F L Ma P2 Vb Vp, xxiv. G ‖ ultima] ii. Mu1 ‖ voluntatem] dominorum *add.* Ma **9.5.** *add. marg. inf.* P2 ‖ C.—eadem^{2}] et c. Mu1 P1 ‖ C.] arg. *praem.* A G **9.6.** *om. per totum* Vp, *rep. marg. inf.* P2 ‖ xxxii.] xxx. Vb ‖ Aliquando] c. *praem.* Mu1, Aliis $P2_1$ ‖ et] etc. $P2_1$ ‖ si—initio *om.* $P2_1$ ‖ si *om.* A Vb **9.7.** *om. per totum* Vp ‖ Econtra Ba C P2, Contrarium L Mu1 **9.8.** *om. per totum* Vp ‖ xxviii.] xxxiii. P1, xxxviii. P2 ‖ De] c. *praem.* Mu1 **9.9.** *om. per totum* Vp ‖ xxvii.] xxiv. P2 ‖ Si vir] Sunt P2 ‖ Si] c. *praem.* Mu1 ‖ vir] votum *add.* Mu1 ‖ et *om.* Ma ‖ c. *om.* L Ma ‖ Voventibus] Volentibus P2 **9.10.** *om. per totum* Vp ‖ xxvii.] xxiv. P2 ‖ q. i. *om.* C F Ma P2 **9.11.** q. ii. *add interl.* Mu1 ‖ queri] quando G ‖ et *om.* Ma ‖ c. *om.* L Ma P2 ‖ Non] Si Ba, Nos G, Tamen P2 ‖ omnis *om.* G, omnes P1 ‖ inter] et c. *praem.* F, § *praem.* P1 ‖ ingenuos] utrum F, geminos P1 ‖ ingenuos] et ideo *add.* Ba C Ma P2, et utrum et ux. *add.* F, ede. *add.* G, et de. *Vb*, ideorum *add.* Vp **10.** = 14 C, 5 G P1 ‖ *§10—§10.22 om. per totum* P2 ‖ Quod] Qui Ma ‖ consensus aliquorum *tr.* Ma ‖ fieri *om.* L, perfici Ma ‖ debet] habet O ‖ eorundem] eorum Ba F Ma, de eorum G P1 ‖ dissensu] dissensi L ‖ impeditur] impediatur C ‖ et—factum *om.* C ‖ factum] ut *add.* F, faciendum *praem. et exp.* P1 **10.1.** *§10.1—§10.22 om. per totum* O ‖ *§10.1 et §10.2 post §9.11 tr.* P1 ‖ lxii.] lxxii. Ba, lxi. Vb **10.2.** xcii.] xxii. P1 **10.3.** clerus] clericus A P1 **10.4.** Ordinationes] Multos P1 **10.5.** *post §10.1 tr.* C ‖ xxiv.] xxiii. Ba G Ma, xciii. F, xxxiv. P1 **10.6.** *§10.6 et §10.7 post §10.2 tr.* C ‖ lxiii.] lxxxiii. *cum* x.^{2} *et* x.^{3} *exp.* A, lxxiii. F, lxii. P1 ‖ Obeuntibus] episcopum *add.* Mu1 **10.7.** ii.] iii. Ba Ma Mu1 ‖ Casellas] Cassallas *cum* a^{2} *exp. et corr.* P1 **10.8.** *om. per totum* A Ba C F G L Ma P1 Vb Vp

⟨9.4.⟩ C.29 q.2 c.8.
⟨9.5.⟩ C.29 q.2 c.4.
⟨9.6.⟩ C.32 q.2 c.7.

⟨9.7.⟩ Against.

⟨9.8.⟩ D.28 c.13.
⟨9.9.⟩ D.27 c.3 and c.4.
⟨9.10.⟩ C.27 q.1 c.41.
⟨9.11.⟩ C.32 q.2 c.6 and c.12.

⟨10.⟩ What ought to be done with the consent of some is prevented by their dissent, and what has been done is dissolved.

⟨10.1.⟩ D.62 c.1.
⟨10.2.⟩ D.92 c.8.
⟨10.3.⟩ D.51 c.5.
⟨10.4.⟩ C.1 q.1 c.113.
⟨10.5.⟩ D.24 c.1.
⟨10.6.⟩ D.63 c.35.
⟨10.7.⟩ C.10 q.2 c.1.
⟨10.8.⟩ D.65 c.2.

⟨10.9.⟩ C. xii. q. ii. Alienationes (C.12 q.2 c.37) et c. Sine exceptione (C.12 q.2 c.52).

⟨10.10.⟩ C. xv. q. vii. Episcopus nullius (C.15 q.7 c.6).

⟨10.11.⟩ C. xxxiii. q. v. Quod Deo (C.33 q.5 c.4) et c. Manifestum (C.33 q.5 c.11) et c. Noluit (C.33 q.5 c.16).

⟨10.12.⟩ C. xx. q. ii. Puella (C.20 q.2 c.2).

⟨10.13.⟩ C. xxxi. q. ii. Si verum (C.31 q.2 c.1).

⟨10.14.⟩ ff. de re iudicata Sententiam (Dig. 42.1.15.1) aliud.

⟨10.15.⟩ Contra.

⟨10.16.⟩ C. xxxi. c. ultimo (C.31 q.3 c.un.).

⟨10.17.⟩ C. xxx. q. v. Aliter (C.30 q.5 c.1) et c. Qualis (C.30 q.5 c.4) et c. Sponsus (C.30 q.5 c.5).

⟨10.18.⟩ C. xxxii. q. ii. Non omnis (C.32 q.2 c.12) et c. Honorantur (C.32 q.2 c.13). ⟨10.19.⟩ Tenet tamen matrimonium contra istorum voluntatem contractum.

⟨10.20.⟩ ff. de decretis ab ordine faciendis Qui semel (Dig. 50.9.5).

⟨10.21.⟩ ff. ad municipales Municipes (Dig. 50.1.1), Quid maior (Dig. 50.1.19).

⟨10.22.⟩ ff. de re iudicata (Dig. 42.1) aliud etiam proferunt.

⟨11.⟩ Qui pretendit ignorantiam, eam probare debet.

⟨11.1.⟩ C. i. q. i. Si qui a simoniacis (C.1 q.1 c.108).

⟨11.2.⟩ C. vi. q. ultima c. ultimo (C.6 q.5 c.2).

⟨11.3.⟩ C. ix. q. i. Ordinationes (C.9 q.1 c.5) "nisi probare."

10.9. alienationes] alienationibus *cum* bus *exp. et corr.* A ‖ et *om.* Ma ‖ c. *om.* L Ma **10.10.** *post §10.13 tr.* C ‖ *rep.* Mu1 ‖ xv.] xvi. F Mu1$_1$ P1 Vb Vp ‖ vii.] vi. A Ba C F G L Mu1$_1$ P1 Vb Vp **10.11.** *post §11 tr.* F ‖ et^1 c.^{1} *om.* Ba Ma ‖ c.^{1}—c.^{2} *om.* F ‖ c.^{1} *om.* L ‖ et^2—Noluit *om.* L ‖ et^2 c.^{2} *om.* Ba Ma ‖ Noluit] Voluit C, Novit Vb **10.12.** *ante §10.3 tr.* C, *post §10.13 tr.* Ma ‖ xx.] xxx. F, xxi. L ‖ Puella] Puelle P1 **10.13.** *post §10.7 tr.* C ‖ verum] vera Vp **10.14.** *om. per totum* A Ba C F G L Ma P1 Vb Vp **10.15.** Econtra Ba, Contrarium L Mu1 **10.16.** *post §10.17 tr.* F ‖ C. *vac.* P1 ‖ xxxi.] xxxii. A, xxx. P1 ‖ c. ultimo] Clericus L **10.17.** et^1 c.^{1} *om.* F, C. eadem q. eadem Ma ‖ c.^{1} *om.* Ba L Vp ‖ Qualis] Qualiter Vp ‖ et^2 c.^{2} *om.* F Ma ‖ c.^{2} *om.* L **10.18.** et c. *om.* F Ma ‖ c. *om.* L ‖ Honorantur] Honoratum P1 **10.19.** istorum] eorum *et post* voluntatem *tr.* F, *post* voluntatem *tr.* L ‖ contractum] contra tantum L, contrarium Vp **10.20.** *om. per totum* A Ba C F G L Ma P1 Vb Vp **10.21.** *om. per totum* A Ba C F G L Ma P1 Vb Vp **10.22.** *om. per totum* A Ba C F G L Ma P1 Vb Vp **11.** = 6 A1 G, 26 C, 15 O, 6 *et* 80 *et* 88 P1, 9 P2 ‖ Qui] De ignorantia *praem.* A L O Vb Vp ‖ pretendit] allegat *et post* ignorantiam *tr.* P1$_1$ ‖ ignorantiam *om.* L ‖ eam] ante *praem.* G, de ea re *add.* L, *om.* Vp ‖ probare debet] probet P1$_1$ ‖ debet] ut *add.* F **11.1.** *§11.1—§11.12 om. per totum* O ‖ *post §11.3 tr.* P1$_1$ ‖ qui] quis A Ba C F L P1$_1$ P1$_2$ P2 Vb Vp **11.2.** *om. per totum* A Ba C F G L Ma Mu1 P1 P1$_2$ P2 Vb Vp **11.3.** ix.] xix. Vp ‖ Ordinationes] Ordinationem P1$_2$ ‖ nisi] non P1$_2$ ‖ nisi probare *om.* P1$_1$ ‖ probare] priori P2

⟨10.9.⟩ C.12 q.2 c.37 and c.52.
⟨10.10.⟩ C.15 q.7 c.6.
⟨10.11.⟩ C.33 q.5 c.4 and c.11 and c.16.
⟨10.12.⟩ C.20 q.2 c.2.
⟨10.13.⟩ C.31 q.2 c.1.
⟨10.14.⟩ Dig. 42.1.15.1.

⟨10.15.⟩ Against.

⟨10.16.⟩ C.31 q.3 c.un.
⟨10.17.⟩ C.30 q.5 c.1 and c.4 and c.5.
⟨10.18.⟩ C.32 q.2 c.12 and c.13. ⟨10.19.⟩ However, the marriage contracted against the will of those people holds.
⟨10.20.⟩ Dig. 50.9.5.
⟨10.21.⟩ Dig. 50.1.1, Dig. 50.1.19.
⟨10.22.⟩ Dig. 42.1.

⟨11.⟩ He who pleads ignorance must prove it.

⟨11.1.⟩ C.1 q.1 c.108.
⟨11.2.⟩ C.6 q.5 c.2.
⟨11.3.⟩ C.9 q.1 c.5.

⟨11.4.⟩ C. iv. q. v. Quisquis (C.4 q.5 c.1) "non potuisse occurrere probaverit."

⟨11.5.⟩ C. xxxiii. q. i. Quod autem (C.33 q.1 c.1) "si potest probare."

⟨11.6.⟩ C. xxxiv. q. ultima In lectum (C.34 q.1–2 c.6) "si ipse per securitatem."

⟨11.7.⟩ Contra.

⟨11.8.⟩ D. lxxxii. Proposuisti (D.82 c.2) "non probatur pervenisse," c. Plurimos (D.82 c.3).

⟨11.9.⟩ D. l. Quantum dicit iste Placidus (D.50 c.48).

⟨11.10.⟩ C. iii. q. ix. Indicas (C.3 q.9 c.14) "nec utrum sane mentis."

⟨11.11.⟩ C. xxix. q. ii. Si quis ingenuus (C.29 q.2 c.4) et c. Cuius rei (C.29 q.2 c.6).

⟨11.12.⟩ D. xxviii. Quia sunt culpe (D.28 c.10) "sed quoniam iste."

⟨12.⟩ Ignorantia etiam que est ex culpa vel in parte, excusat a culpa et pena.

⟨12.1.⟩ D. iv. Denique (D.4 c.6) "cecitati mentis," "cum venia."

⟨12.2.⟩ C. xv. q. i. Usque adeo (C.15 q.1 p.c.1) et q. eadem Illud (C.15 q.1 c.2) "nisi qui scit se."

11.4. *om. per totum* $P1_1$ ‖ C.] arg. *praem.* A C G ‖ Quisquis] c. *praem.* Mu1 ‖ non—occurrere] contra rem F, occurrere non voluisse, sed non potuisse Fr, occurre Mu1 ‖ probaverit] probavit A Vb, *om.* L Ma, conprobaverit *cum* con *exp.* Vp **11.5.** *om. per totum* $P1_1$, *add. marg.* P2, *ante §11.3 rep. et exp.* Vp ‖ C.] arg. *praem.* A A1 C G, *om.* P2 ‖ xxxiii.] xxxiv. P1 $P1_2$ Vp_1, *om.* P2 ‖ i.] v. $P1_2$ ‖ Quod] Qui G P1 Vb ‖ autem] aliter $P1_2$ ‖ si—probare *om.* (*homoiotel.*) A1, *om.* Vp_1 ‖ probare] § autem *add.* $P1_2$ **11.6.** *om. per totum* $P1_1$ ‖ C.—lectum *om.* (*homoiotel.*) A1 ‖ C. xxxiv.] et $P1_2$ ‖ xxxiv.] eadem P1 ‖ In] Ex $P1_2$ ‖ si ipse] supra P1 ‖ per securitatem] perseverantem A L Vb, severitatem *et* plurimos *add.* Ba **11.7.** *vac.* Vp ‖ Contrarium L Mu1, quod scilicet adversarius eam probet *add.* $P1_1$, Econtra P2 **11.8.** lxxxii.] lxx. A1, xxxii. L ‖ Proposuisti] quod *praem.* L Ma ‖ non—Plurimos *om.* $P1_1$ ‖ non—pervenisse *om.* P1 ‖ probatur] probat A ‖ pervenisse] venisse Ma ‖ c. *om.* L, D. eadem Ma, et *praem.* Mu1 P1 P2, et $P1_2$ ‖ Plurimos] Plurimas G, Populi omnes P2 **11.9.** *om. per totum* A Ba C F G L Ma Mu1 P1 $P1_2$ P2 Vb Vp **11.10.** iii.] vii. $P1_2$ ‖ Indicas] Indictas C, Indicans L Mu1, Hermannum *add.* $P1_1$ ‖ nec—mentis *om.* $P1_1$ ‖ nec utrum *om.* Ma ‖ nec] ne L P2 ‖ utrum] item $P1_2$, ut Vp ‖ sane] ante L, sacrum $P1_2$ ‖ mentis *om.* Ma $P1_2$ **11.11.** *om. per totum* $P1_1$ ‖ xxix.] xxxv. $P1_2$ ‖ ii.] ultima F ‖ ingenuus *om.* $P1_2$ ‖ et *om.* A1 Ma ‖ c. *om.* L Ma ‖ Cuius] h. *praem.* F, Eius G, Huius Mu1, Cur $P1_2$ **11.12.** *om. per totum* A Ba C G L Mu1 P1 $P1_1$ $P1_2$ P2 Vb Vp ‖ iste] coniugem diaconi asserit *add.* F **12.** = 27 C, 16 O, 94 P1 ‖ §12—§12.6 *post* §12.11 *tr.* Ba ‖ *§12—§12.11 om. per totum* G P2 ‖ Ignorantia] Ingno L ‖ etiam *om.* A L Mu1 P1 Vb ‖ ex culpa est *tr.* A ‖ est] esset L ‖ ex] a L ‖ vel *exp.* F ‖ in] ex O ‖ a culpa et pena] a pena et a culpa ut F ‖ et] vel L P1 ‖ pena] temporali *add.* C O P1 **12.1.** *§12.1—§12.11 om. per totum* O ‖ iv.] iii. L Vb ‖ Denique *rep.* A, c. *praem.* Mu1 ‖ mentis cecitati *tr.* Fr ‖ cum venia] convenia A, ascribendum est Ma, conveniat P1 **12.2.** *post §12.3 tr.* P1 ‖ adeo] ut non sit peccatum *add.* Ma ‖ et q. eadem *om.* Ba F P1 ‖ et] C. eadem Ma ‖ q. eadem *om.* Mu1 ‖ Illud] Illum relatum est Ma, relatum *add.* Mu1 ‖ qui] quod Ba, quis P1 ‖ scit] sit A ‖ se *ante* scit *tr.* L Mu1, *om.* Ma

⟨11.4.⟩ C.4 q.5 c.1.
⟨11.5.⟩ C.33 q.1 c.1.
⟨11.6.⟩ C.34 q.1–2 c.6.

⟨11.7.⟩ Against.

⟨11.8.⟩ D.82 c.2, c.3.
⟨11.9.⟩ D.50 c.48.
⟨11.10.⟩ C.3 q.9 c.14.
⟨11.11.⟩ C.29 q.2 c.4 and c.6.
⟨11.12.⟩ D.28 c.10.

⟨12.⟩ Ignorance, even if it is wholly or partly the result of guilt, excuses from guilt and punishment.

⟨12.1.⟩ D.4 c.6.
⟨12.2.⟩ C.15 q.1 p.c.1 and q.1 c.2.

⟨12.3.⟩ C. xxxii. q. v. Sicut (C.32 q.5 c.10).

⟨12.4.⟩ C. xv. q. vi. c. i. (C.15 q.6 c.1) iuxta finem, "qui per simplicitatem."

⟨12.5.⟩ C. xv. q. i. Inebriaverunt (C.15 q.1 c.9) "non tamen quantum" et c. Sane (C.15 q.1 c.7) "venia."

⟨12.6.⟩ Q. eadem Non est (C.15 q.1 c.10) et c. Aliquos (C.15 q.1 c.5) et c. Illa (C.15 q.1 c.6) et c. Si quis inaniens (C.15 q.1 c.12) "levior."

⟨12.7.⟩ Contra.

⟨12.8.⟩ C. xv. q. i. Ut itaque (C.15 q.1 d.p.c.2) "nec eum excusavit cecitatis."

⟨12.9.⟩ D. xxxv. Sexto die (D.35 c.8) "partus deterior."

⟨12.10.⟩ D. l. Sepe contingit (D.50 c.50) "omnino submitti."

⟨12.11.⟩ C. xxiv. q. i. Scisma quidem (C.24 q.1 c.34) "Sed nec illud."

⟨13.⟩ Invincibilis ignorantia facti prorsus excusat.

⟨13.1.⟩ C. i. q. iv. c. Quis locus ignorantie (C.1 q.4 c.2).

⟨13.2.⟩ C. eadem Placuit (C.1 q.4 c.3) "neque suo hoc iudicio" et c. Qui apud (C.1 q.4 c.4) "Non scire."

12.3. C. *om.* A ‖ xxxii.] xxxiii. *cum* i.^{3} *exp.* Vb ‖ Sicut] enim *add.* Mu1 **12.4.** *om. per totum* P1 ‖ c. i.] Si (a *add.* Mu1) sacerdotibus Ma Mu1 ‖ iuxta] in Ma Mu1 ‖ qui *om.* Mu1, quod Vp **12.5.** C.—i.] et c. P1 ‖ xv.] eadem Ma Mu1 ‖ i.] ii. Vp ‖ Inebriaverunt] Loth *add.* Mu1 ‖ non *om.* Mu1 ‖ tamen] tantum *add.* F, tantum Mu1 ‖ et c. *om.* L P1, C. eadem q. eadem Ma ‖ Sane] Si non Ba ‖ venia] et *praem.* L, vitandam ebrietatem Ma, non etiam aliquando *praem.* P1, *om.* Vb **12.6.** Q. c.^{3} *om.* P1 ‖ Q.—est *om.* Ma ‖ Q. eadem] et c. C *om.* Mu1 ‖ Q.] et *praem.* Ba F ‖ Non est] et c. *praem. et post* Illa *tr.* Mu1 ‖ et^{1} c.^{1} *om.* F ‖ c.^{1} *om.* L ‖ Aliquos] Aliquantos A Ba C F Vb Vp, Aliquanto L ‖ et^{2}] q. eadem *add.* F, *om.* Ma ‖ c.^{2} *om.* L Ma ‖ Illa] non potest *add.* Ma ‖ et^{3} c.^{3} *om.* Ba Ma ‖ c.^{3} *om.* L ‖ inaniens] insaniens A C, insanus F, insanies L ‖ levior *om.* L, ei penitentia imponenda est *add.* Ma **12.7.** *ante* §*12.1 tr.* Ba, *vac.* Vp ‖ titulum sequentem *add.* Ba, Contrarium L Mu1 **12.8.** C. *om.* P1 ‖ nec] neque Ba ‖ excusavit] excusat A Ba F L Mu1 Vb Vp ‖ cecitatis *in* §*11.9 post* rei *tr.* Ba, etas L, *om.* Ma, etc. Mu1, cecitas P1 Vb **12.9.** xxxv.] xxxvi. A Ba C L Ma P1 Vb Vp ‖ Sexto] Si ex toto Ba, c. *praem.* Mu1 ‖ die *om.* Vb ‖ partus] paxtus Ba ‖ deterior *om.* L **12.10.** Sepe] c. *praem.* Mu1 ‖ submitti] submittit P1 **12.11.** *om. per totum* F ‖ xxiv.] xxxiv. A ‖ Scisma] Similia Ba, c. *praem.* Mu1 ‖ quidem] quid A L, quod idem Ba Vp, quam C P1, siquidem Fr, *om.* Ma, si quis Mu1 ‖ Sed] Si Vb ‖ illud] aliud L, eis prodest *add.* Ma, de eis prodest *add.* Mu1 **13.** = 28 C, 17 O, 95 P1 ‖ §*13*—§*13.16 om. per totum* G P2 ‖ Invincibilis *post* facti *tr.* F, invincibilis *cum* in^{1} *exp.* Mu1 ‖ facti] factai *cum* a^{2} *exp.* A, *om.* P1 ‖ prorsus *om.* Ma, non *praem.* Vp ‖ excusat] ut *add.* F, *ante* invincibilis *tr.* P1 **13.1.** §*13.1*—§*13.16 om. per totum* O ‖ iv.] iii. F Vb ‖ c. *om.* Ba F ‖ Quis—ignorantie] i. et ii. Mu1 ‖ Quis] Qui Vp ‖ locus] secum Ba ‖ ignorantie] innocentiae Fr, ignominie L, ignorande A F Vb **13.2.** *om. per totum* A ‖ C. eadem *om.* Ba Ma P1, et c. Mu1 ‖ C.] Q. F Vp, et Q. L ‖ neque] eque Fr, nec Mu1 ‖ hoc] hic L Vb, *ante* suo *tr.* Ma ‖ et—scire *om.* L ‖ et c. *om.* Ma P1 ‖ Qui apud *om.* Vb ‖ Qui] Quod C F Mu1 P1 Vp ‖ Non scire *om.* Mu1 ‖ Non] dum *add.* Ma, dominus *add.* P1

⟨12.3.⟩ C.32 q.5 c.10.
⟨12.4.⟩ C.15 q.6 c.1.
⟨12.5.⟩ C.15 q.1 c.9 and c.7.
⟨12.6.⟩ C.15 q.1 c.10 and c.5 and c.6 and c.12.

⟨12.7.⟩ Against.

⟨12.8.⟩ C.15 q.1 d.p.c.2.
⟨12.9.⟩ D.35 c.8.
⟨12.10.⟩ D.50 c.50.
⟨12.11.⟩ C.24 q.1 c.34.

⟨13.⟩ Invincible ignorance of a fact completely excuses from culpability.

⟨13.1.⟩ C.1 q.4 c.2.
⟨13.2.⟩ C.1 q.4 c.3 and c.4.

⟨13.3.⟩ Q. eadem Quia presulatus (C.1 q.4 c.5) “sine consilio.”

⟨13.4.⟩ C. iii. q. ix. Indicas (C.3 q.9 c.14) “conpatiendum quam puniendum.”

⟨13.5.⟩ C. xv. q. i. Aliquos (C.15 q.1 c.5) “minime reos.”

⟨13.6.⟩ Illa (C.15 q.1 c.6) “nec enim frater furorem,” “si quis per inprudentiam.”

⟨13.7.⟩ C. eadem q. eadem Sane (C.15 q.1 c.7) “venia quidem.”

⟨13.8.⟩ D. l. Sepe (D.50 c.50) “insperatus occurrit.”

⟨13.9.⟩ C. xxxiv. q. i. Si virgo (C.34 q.1–2 c.5) “si semper nesciat” et c. Cum per bellicam (C.34 q.1–2 c.1).

⟨13.10.⟩ C. xxix. Si quis ingenuus (C.29 q.2 c.4) “et existimat.”

⟨13.11.⟩ Econtra. Invincibilis ignorantia facti non prorsus excusat.

⟨13.12.⟩ C. xv. q. i. Inebriaverunt (C.15 q.1 c.9) “culpandus est quidem.”

⟨13.13.⟩ C. eadem q. eadem Si quis insaniens (C.15 q.1 c.12) “levior ei penitentia.”

⟨13.14.⟩ C. i. q. v. Presentium (C.1 q.5 c.3) “suspensus.”

⟨13.15.⟩ C. xxxiv. In lectum (C.34 q.1–2 c.6) “penitentiam.”

⟨13.16.⟩ C. i. q. ultima Qui in qualibet etate (C.1 q.7 c.10).

13.3. Q. eadem *om.* Ba L P1, C. eadem *praem.* F Ma, et c. Mu1 ‖ Quia] Qui Vp ‖ presulatus] presulatum Ba ‖ sine consilio *om.* L ‖ sine] sive Fr ‖ consilio] concilio Ma Mu1 Vp **13.4.** ix.] xi. L ‖ Indicas] Indicans Ma ‖ conpatiendum] sit *add.* Fr, conpasci sciendum P1 **13.5.** C.] arg. Mu1 ‖ i. *vac.* Mu1, v. P1 ‖ Aliquos] c. *praem.* Mu1, Aliquando P1 ‖ minime reos *om.* L, humanos P1 **13.6.** *om. per totum* A Ba C F L Ma Mu1 Vb Vp **13.7.** *post § 13.8 tr.* C P1 ‖ C.—eadem[2] *om.* Ba F Ma P1, et Mu1 ‖ Sane] si non F ‖ venia quidem] neo. *Cum abbr. signo* L ‖ venia] eadem *praem.* P1 ‖ quidem] facta donantur Ma **13.8.** insperatus] imperatus C L **13.9.** *om. per totum* C ‖ q. i. *om.* A Ba C F Mu1 Vp ‖ i.] ii. Ma, *om.* Vb ‖ semper] per L ‖ et c.] C. eadem q. eadem Ma ‖ et *om.* Ba P1 ‖ c. *om.* L P1 ‖ per bellicam *om.* L ‖ bellicam] publicum Ba **13.10.** xxix.] xxxiv. A Ba C Vb, xxxi. L P1, xxxix. *cum* x.[3] *exp.* Mu1 ‖ Si] q. ii. *praem.* Ma Mu1, q. *praem.* Vb ‖ ingenuus] ingenitus P1 ‖ existimat] existimant P1 **13.11.** *vac.* Ma ‖ Econtra] Contra A C F P1 ‖ Invincibilis—excusat *om.* Ba C F ‖ Invincibilis—facti *om.* L, fori P1 ‖ Invincibilis *cum* In *exp.* Mu1 ‖ facti] fori P1 **13.12.** xv.] xxv. L ‖ culpandus] culpandum L Mu1 P1 Vp ‖ est *om.* A Ba C F L Mu1 P1 Vb Vp ‖ quidem *om.* Ma **13.13.** *post § 13.14 tr.* C ‖ C.—eadem[2] *om.* Ba F P1, et c. Mu1 ‖ insaniens] insani F, insanusies P1 ‖ levior] lervo Vp ‖ ei *om.* C, ea P1 ‖ penitentia] potentia Ba P1 **13.14.** *om. per totum* P1 ‖ *post § 13.16 tr.* F ‖ C. i.] et F ‖ v.] i. L ‖ suspensus] a sacerdotali *add.* Ma **13.15.** *om. per totum* P1 ‖ *ante § 13.12 tr.* F ‖ xxxiv.] xxx. c. iv. Ba, q. ii. *add.* F Ma, q. *add.* L Vb ‖ In] c. *praem.* Vp ‖ penitentiam] quidem *add.* Ma **13.16.** Qui] c. *praem.* Mu1 ‖ etate *om.* F L

⟨13.3.⟩ C.1 q.4 c.5.
⟨13.4.⟩ C.3 q.9 c.14.
⟨13.5.⟩ C.15 q.1 c.5.
⟨13.6.⟩ C.15 q.1 c.6.
⟨13.7.⟩ C.15 q.1 c.7.
⟨13.8.⟩ D.50 c.50.
⟨13.9.⟩ C.34 q.1–2 c.5 and c.1.
⟨13.10.⟩ C.29 q.2 c.4.

⟨13.11.⟩ Against. Invincible ignorance of a fact does not completely excuse from culpability.

⟨13.12.⟩ C.15 q.1 c.9.
⟨13.13.⟩ C.15 q.1 c.12.
⟨13.14.⟩ C.1 q.5 c.3.
⟨13.15.⟩ C.34 q.1–2 c.6.
⟨13.16.⟩ C.1 q.7 c.10.

⟨14.⟩ Iuris ignorantia eos qui ius scire tenentur nullatenus excusat.

⟨14.1.⟩ C. xii. q. ii. Nulli liceat (C.12 q.2 c.3) "inexcusabilis."

⟨14.2.⟩ D. xxxviii. Qui ea, que Dei sunt (D.38 c.10) et c. Si in laicis (D.38 c.3) "nec excusatione."

⟨14.3.⟩ D. xx. Si decreta (D.20 c.2).

⟨14.4.⟩ C. xxv. q. i. Omnia (C.25 q.1 c.12) et c. Hec consona (C.25 q.1 c.13).

⟨14.5.⟩ Contra.

⟨14.6.⟩ C. xxiv. q. i. Si quis dederit (C.24 q.1 c.41) "et nescit."

⟨14.7.⟩ D. lxxxvi. Tanta (D.86 c.24) "simplicitatem."

⟨14.8.⟩ D. lxxxii. Proposuisti (D.82 c.2) "his ignorantibus" et c. Plurimos (D.82 c.3).

⟨15.⟩ Vocem unius testis admittendam saltem ad presumptionem.

⟨15.1.⟩ D. lxxxvi. Tanta nequitia (D.86 c.24) "sed filius noster Ciriacus."

⟨15.2.⟩ C. xi. q. i. Quicumque (C.11 q.1 c.35).

⟨15.3.⟩ C. xx. q. iii. Presens (C.20 q.3 c.4) "sub testificatione."

⟨15.4.⟩ C. viii. q. iii. Talia (C.8 q.3 c.1) "cum hic filius noster."

⟨15.5.⟩ C. xvi. q. iii. Dilectio (C.16 q.3 c.7).

---

14. = 29 C, 18 O, 96 P1, 10 P2 ‖ *§14—§14.7 om. per totum* G ‖ Ignorantia iuris *tr.* Vb ‖ eos—tenentur *post* excusat *tr.* F ‖ qui] quod Ma ‖ ius *om.* F ‖ scire] sciverint L ‖ tenentur] ut *add.* F, *om.* L, debent P1 ‖ nullatenus] non F **14.1.** *§14.1—§14.8 om. per totum* O ‖ xii.] xxii. L ‖ Nulli] Nulla P2 ‖ inexcusabilis] propter quod *praem.* Mu1, que excusabilis P1 **14.2.** D.] C. F ‖ xxxviii.] xxxxix. F L P1 P2 ‖ ei] ea Vp ‖ et c. *om.* Ma ‖ c. *om.* L P1 ‖ Si in] Sine P1 ‖ in] non C, *om.* Vp ‖ nec excusatione *om.* A L Vb ‖ nec] non C P1 ‖ excusatione] excusationem C **14.3.** *om. per totum* A Ba C F L Ma Mu1 P2 Vb Vp **14.4.** xxv.] xxiv. F, xv. Mu1, xxiv. *cum* iv. *exp. et corr.* Vp ‖ i. *om.* L ‖ Omnia] Si in prima Ma, c. Prima (C.25 q.1 c.9) et c. *praem. et* decretalia *add.* Mu1 ‖ et c. *om.* L Ma ‖ c. *post* consona *tr.* F ‖ Hec] Hac Mu1 Vb ‖ consona] conscientia C **14.5.** Contrarium L Mu1, Econtra P2 **14.6.** q. i. *om.* P1 ‖ Si] c. *praem.* Mu1 ‖ dederit *om.* L, de extra P1 ‖ et] tunc A L Vb, *om.* F Mu1 ‖ nescit] dixit A L, contradicit (ignorantia *add.* Ba) *add.* Ba C F P1 P2 Vp, nec secus quod contra clericum Mu1, discit *add.* Vb **14.7.** *§14.7—§14.8 post §13.11 tr.* F ‖ *post §14.8 tr.* P1 ‖ Tanta] c. *praem. et* nequitia *add.* Mu1, s. *praem. et exp.* P2 ‖ simplicitatem] simplicitate A Ba F Mu1 Vp, quam *praem.* P1 **14.8.** lxxxii.] lxxii. A ‖ et. c.] D. eadem Ma ‖ c. *om.* L P1 ‖ Plurimos] ignorantes *add.* A C, Plurimis *et* ignorantes *add.* L, Quia aliquanti (D.82 c.4) "ignorantia" *add.* Ma Mu1 Vp, imponunt *add.* P1 **15.** = 7 G P1, 12 O, 11 P2 ‖ Vocem] Uxorem C ‖ saltem] aut *praem.* C, quo F, salteris Vp ‖ ad presumptionem] admittendam *cum* mittendam *exp. et corr.* Mu1 ‖ presumptionem] ut *add.* F **15.1.** *§15.1—§15.18 om. per totum* O ‖ *om. per totum* P1 ‖ lxxxvi.] lxxxv. P2 ‖ nequitia—Ciriacus *om.* L Vb ‖ sed—noster *om.* Ba C ‖ sed—Ciriacus *om.* A ‖ filius noster *om.* F G Mu1 P2 Vp ‖ Ciriacus] Ciriacum abbatem Mu1 **15.2.** xi.] ix. C ‖ Quicumque] Quecumque Ba, Te quidem Mu1 **15.3.** xx.] xii. A ‖ iii.] ii. P1 **15.4.** *post §15.5 tr.* Ba ‖ viii.] xiii. F Vb ‖ Talia *om.* P1 ‖ noster filius *tr.* Ma **15.5.** Dilectio] c. *praem.* Mu1

⟨14.⟩ Ignorance of the law excuses no one who is bound to know it.

⟨14.1.⟩ C.12 q.2 c.3.
⟨14.2.⟩ D.38 c.10 and c.3.
⟨14.3.⟩ D.20 c.2.
⟨14.4.⟩ C.25 q.1 c.12 and c.13.

⟨14.5.⟩ Against.

⟨14.6.⟩ C.24 q.1 c.41.
⟨14.7.⟩ D.86 c.24.
⟨14.8.⟩ D.82 c.2 and c.3.

⟨15.⟩ The testimony of one witness ought to be admitted at least to establish a presumption.

⟨15.1.⟩ D.86 c.24.
⟨15.2.⟩ C.11 q.1 c.35.
⟨15.3.⟩ C.20 q.3 c.4.
⟨15.4.⟩ C.8 q.3 c.1.
⟨15.5.⟩ C.16 q.3 c.7.

⟨15.6.⟩ C. xxxi. q. ii. Si verum (C.31 q.2 c.1) “ab ipso Iordane sacramentum.”

⟨15.7.⟩ D. xxviii. De Siracusane (D.28 c.13) “sicut filii nostri testificatione.”

⟨15.8.⟩ D. c. c. Optatum (D.100 c.4).

⟨15.9.⟩ C. xxiii. q. iv. Multiplices (C.23 q.4 c.27).

⟨15.10.⟩ Contra.

⟨15.11.⟩ C. vi. q. ii. Placuit (C.6 q.2 c.3) “quod illi soli non creditur.”

⟨15.12.⟩ C. xxxiii. q. ii. Admonere (C.33 q.2 c.8) “unius testimonio.”

⟨15.13.⟩ C. xxxv. q. vi. § Quod autem (C.35 q.6 d.p.c.11).

⟨15.14.⟩ B. l. vii. Ut omnis (B.7 c.17).

⟨15.15.⟩ C. xv. q. v. Presbiter (C.15 q.5 c.2).

⟨15.16.⟩ C. xxiii. q. iv. Forte (C.23 q.4 c.11).

⟨15.17.⟩ C. ii. q. iv. Placuit (C.2 q.4 c.1).

⟨15.18.⟩ C. iv. q. iii. Item iurisiurandi (C.4 q.3 p.c.3).

⟨16.⟩ Consuetudinis auctoritate defenditur, quod alias illicite fieri diceretur.

⟨16.1.⟩ D. lxiii. Agatho (D.63 c.21) “que solita” et c. Quia sancta (D.63 c.28) “nisi que antiqua.”

⟨16.2.⟩ C. xxxii. q. iv. Obiciuntur (C.32 q.4 c.7) “quod quando mos erat.”

15.6. xxxi.] xxxii. Mu1 ‖ q. ii. *om.* Mu1 ‖ ab ipso *om.* G P1 ‖ Iordane] ordine L, iordine Ma, Iordano Vb ‖ sacramentum] sacramenti Ba, *om.* L Ma **15.7.** xxviii.] xviii. A, xxix. P2 ‖ sicut] sic *add.* Ba C P2 Vp ‖ filii] filium L ‖ nostri] vestri Fr, *om.* L ‖ testificatione *om.* A Ba L Mu1 Vb **15.8.** *om. per totum* A Ba C F L Ma Mu1 P1 P2 Vb Vp **15.9.** *om. per totum* A Ba C F G L Ma Mu1 P1 P2 Vb **15.10.** Econtra C P2, Contrarium L Mu1 **15.11.** ii.] iii. (C.6 q.3 c.4) Vb ‖ quod … creditur *om.* A L Vb ‖ quod] que *cum* e *exp. et corr.* i P2 ‖ soli *post* creditur *tr.* Ma, *om.* Mu1 ‖ creditur] taliter C **15.12.** ii.] iii. P1 ‖ Admonere] Amonc Ba, Amonere Vb ‖ testimonio *om.* P1, C. xxxiii. q. ii. *add. et exp.* P2 **15.13.** *om. per totum* P2 ‖ xxxv.] xxv. G ‖ vi.] vii. L ‖ § *om.* A Ba ‖ Quod] Quidem Ba, Qui L **15.14.** *om. per totum* P2 ‖ B. *om.* L ‖ l. *post* vii. *tr.* G, *om.* Vb ‖ vii.] ii. Mu1 **15.15.** *post §15.17 tr.* Ma ‖ Presbiter] Presbiteri Vb **15.16.** xxiii.] xxiv. Ba ‖ iv.] iii. F **15.17.** *rep.* Vp ‖ iv.] iii. Ma Vb ‖ Placuit] c. *praem.* Mu1, Forte Vp_1 **15.18.** *om. per totum* A Ba C F L Ma Mu1 P2 Vb Vp ‖ iii.] ii. P1 ‖ iurisiurandi] iusiurandi G **16.** = 3 C O, 8 G P1 ‖ *§16—§16.20 om. per totum* P2 ‖ Consuetudinis—defenditur *post* diceretur *tr.* P1 ‖ defenditur] defendit Vp ‖ quod] quia C, qui Mu1 ‖ alias] vel C, aliter L ‖ fieri illicite *tr.* F, fieret Ma ‖ diceretur] dicentur C, ut *add.* F, *om.* Ma **16.1.** *§16.1—§16.20 om. per totum* O ‖ Agatho] Agathosa *cum* sa *exp.* L ‖ solita] solitam C, soluto *cum* u *et* o *exp. et corr.* solitam L ‖ et c. *om.* Ma ‖ et *om.* L ‖ que antiqua] quanti Ma ‖ antiqua] et c. Lectis (D.63 c.18) “ut mos est” *add.* G P1, ante quam L **16.2.** iv.] iii. G ‖ Obiciuntur] Iacob Mu1 ‖ quod *om.* C Ma Mu1, qui Vb ‖ quando] tempus *exp. et corr. interl.* G ‖ mos erat] moneantur Ba ‖ erat] erant Ma, peccatum non erat *add.* Mu1, *om.* P1

〈15.6.〉 C.31 q.2 c.1.
〈15.7.〉 D.28 c.13.
〈15.8.〉 D.100 c.4.
〈15.9.〉 C.23 q.4 c.27.

〈15.10.〉 Against.

〈15.11.〉 C.6 q.2 c.3.
〈15.12.〉 C.33 q.2 c.8.
〈15.13.〉 C.35 q.6 d.p.c.11.
〈15.14.〉 B.7 c.17.
〈15.15.〉 C.15 q.5 c.2.
〈15.16.〉 C.23 q.4 c.11.
〈15.17.〉 C.2 q.4 c.1.
〈15.18.〉 C.4 q.3 p.c.3.

〈16.〉 By the authority of a custom, that which would otherwise be considered illegal is defended.

〈16.1.〉 D.63 c.21 and c.28.
〈16.2.〉 C.32 q.4 c.7.

⟨16.3.⟩ D. l. Placuit (D.50 c.68) "ut penitentes," "aut si usus."

⟨16.4.⟩ C. x. q. iii. Nec numerus (C.10 q.3 c.5) "consuetudinem que" et § proximo (C.10 q.3 d.p.c.5).

⟨16.5.⟩ D. iv. Denique (D.4 c.6) "a tali consuetudine," "et ideo cum venia."

⟨16.6.⟩ D. xviii. Placuit (D.18 c.1).

⟨16.7.⟩ D. c. Prisca consuetudo (D.100 c.2).

⟨16.8.⟩ D. xvii. Multis (D.17 c.5) in fine.

⟨16.9.⟩ C. ix. Conquestus (C.9 q.3 c.9).

⟨16.10.⟩ D. xxiii. Quamquam (D.23 c.6) in fine.

⟨16.11.⟩ Econtra.

⟨16.12.⟩ C. xxxii. q. vii. Flagitia (C.32 q.7 c.13) "Que si omnes."

⟨16.13.⟩ D. c. Novit (D.100 c.3) "quod quoniam incongruum erat."

⟨16.14.⟩ C. i. q. iii. Si quis prebendas (C.1 q.3 c.15) "nec sub optentu."

⟨16.15.⟩ D. xii. Nos consuetudinem (D.12 c.8) "exceptis his qui ex."

⟨16.16.⟩ D. vii. Mala si consuetudinem (D.7 c.3) et sic usque in fine distinctionis.

⟨16.17.⟩ C. xvi. q. v. Consuetudo nova (C.16 q.5 c.1).

16.3. Placuit] c. *praem.* Mu1 ‖ ut *om.* Ma ‖ penitentes] penitenitentes Vb ‖ aut—usus *om.* Ma Mu1 P1 ‖ aut si] si necessitas aut Fr ‖ si] susa Ba, sus. C, filiis L, is G Vb Vp ‖ usus] inesse Ba, amet *add.* F, Samech C G Vb Vp, Lamech L **16.4.** Numerus] viris Ba C ‖ consuetudinem] consuetudinum A, infra *add.* Ba, consuetudine G P1 ‖ que—proximo *om.* A Ba L Mu1 ‖ que] quia P1 ‖ et *om.* Ma ‖ §] infra F, infra et *praem.* Vp ‖ proximo] et C. eadem q. ii. Precarie (C.10 q.2 c.4) *add.* G, et C. eadem Que *add.* P1 **16.5.** P1 ‖ D.] C. C ‖ iv.] iii. C ‖ Denique] c. *praem.* Mu1 ‖ cum venia] convenia A C G L Vp, convenia proximo Ba **16.6.** *om. per totum* A Ba C F L Ma Mu1 Vb Vp ‖ D.] s. in *praem.* P1 ‖ xviii.] xvii. P1 **16.7.** *om. per totum* A Ba C F L Ma Mu1 Vb Vp1 **16.8.** *om. per totum* A Ba C F L Ma Mu1 Vb Vp ‖ fine] capituli *add.* G **16.9.** *om. per totum* A Ba C F L Ma Mu1 Vb Vp ‖ C.] D. G ‖ ix.] Dixit P1 **16.10.** *om. per totum* A Ba C F L Ma Mu1 Vb Vp ‖ xxiii.] xxxii. P1 ‖ fine] capituli *add.* G **16.11.** *vac.* A Vb, Contra Ba C G F Ma P1, Contrarium L Mu1 **16.12.** xxxii.] xxxiii. L ‖ vii.] iv. Ma ‖ Flagitia *om.* F, Flagitio G, Flagitiosa L ‖ que si] quasi Ma ‖ omnes] omnis Ma **16.13.** c.] v. L ‖ Novit] c. *praem.* A G Mu1 Vp ‖ quod] quoniam C ‖ quoniam] quam Ma Mu1 Vp ‖ incongruum] congruum Vp ‖ erat] et contra *add.* Ba, et tunc *add.* C F G Ma P1 Vp **16.14.** Si *om.* A ‖ prebendas] fidelium Ma ‖ nec] neque A Ba C F G L Ma Vb Vp ‖ optentu] octentu consensu Ba, consuetudinis *add.* C F G Mu1 P1, optentuus Ma, consensu *add.* Vp **16.15.** *om. per totum* P1 ‖ xii.] xxi. G Ma ‖ Nos] Non A Ba G, Nosti Vp ‖ exceptis—ex *om.* C Vb ‖ exceptis] excepti Ma ‖ qui ex *om.* Ma Mu1, quies Vp **16.16.** *om. per totum* P1 ‖ D.—consuetudinem *om.* C Vb ‖ vii.] xii. Ma ‖ si *om.* Fr ‖ Mala] c. *praem.* Mu1 ‖ consuetudinem] consuetudo Fr ‖ et sic *om.* Ma ‖ sic] si L ‖ fine] finem G ‖ distinctionis] distinguit Ba **16.17.** xvi.] xvii. L ‖ v.] vi. A Ba C F G L Mu1 P1 Vb, vii. Vp ‖ Consuetudo] c. *praem.* Mu1 ‖ nova *om.* Ma

⟨16.3.⟩ D.50 c.68.
⟨16.4.⟩ C.10 q.3 c.5 and d.p.c.5.
⟨16.5.⟩ D.4 c.6.
⟨16.6.⟩ D.18 c.1.
⟨16.7.⟩ D.100 c.2.
⟨16.8.⟩ D.17 c.5.
⟨16.9.⟩ C.9 q.3 c.9.
⟨16.10.⟩ D.23 c.6.

⟨16.11.⟩ Against.

⟨16.12.⟩ C.32 q.7 c.13.
⟨16.13.⟩ D.100 c.3.
⟨16.14.⟩ C.1 q.3 c.15.
⟨16.15.⟩ D.12 c.8.
⟨16.16.⟩ D.7 C.3.
⟨16.17.⟩ C.16 q.5 c.1.

〈16.18.〉 D. xciii. Illud autem, quod pro utendis (D.93 c.22) "sed sola usurpatione."

〈16.19.〉 D. c. Contra morem (D.100 c.8) "quod si postremo nichil horum est."

〈16.20.〉 D. lxviii. Corepiscopi (D.68 c.5) in fine.

〈17.〉 In his postremis capitulis nota, karissime, quod quesisti. 〈17.1.〉 Cum enim de aliquarum rerum prescriptione agitur, inspiciendum est utrum communi iure talia a talibus possideri valeant, nec ne. 〈17.2.〉 Primo casu, sola longe usurpationis detentione currit prescriptio. 〈17.3.〉 Secundo, nequaquam. 〈17.4.〉 Exempli gratia: iura communia, scripta vel non scripta, prodita sunt, quibus laici predia et pecora, ecclesie decimas et primitias et prelati partem oblationum in subiectis ecclesiis ipsas quoque dioceses, possident. 〈17.5.〉 Ideoque tales talia prescribere possunt, ut C. xvi. q. iii. (C.16 q.3) et iv. (C.16 q.4) per totum, salvo eo quod de limitibus dicitur, C. eadem q. eadem Licet (C.16 q.3 c.5) et c. Inter memoratos (C.16 q.3 c.6).

〈17.6.〉 Econtra: nullum ius commune proditum est quo laici decimas vel primitias vel partem oblationum vel vasa mistica vel dispositionem ecclesiarum et similia possidere valeant, vel quo archiepiscopi pallio extra missarum sollempnia vel alii quam Romane ecclesie clerici mapulis

---

16.18. xciii.] xxiii. A ‖ Illud] c. *praem.* Mu1, Pervenit (D.93 c.21) et c. *praem.* Vb ‖ autem] que G ‖ quod—utendis *om.* Ma ‖ pro utendis] putendis F, potentis Mu1 ‖ utendis] intendis Ba, videndum P1 ‖ sola] solius L ‖ usurpatione *om.* Ba, subreptione Fr, penar. *cum abbr. signo* L **16.19.** c.] eadem A Ba ‖ morem] mortem G ‖ quod—est *om.* Ma ‖ quod] qui C ‖ nichil horum] nichilorum L, nullorum Mu1 ‖ horum] hortem G ‖ est *om.* G L Mu1 **16.20.** *om. per totum* A Ba C F G L Ma Mu1 Vb Vp **17.** = 4 C, 9 G P1 ‖ *§17—§17.9 om. per totum* O P2 ‖ *om. per totum* Ma ‖ In his *rep. post* postremis Ba ‖ postremis] extremis P1 ‖ capitulis *ante* postremis *tr.* G, *post* nota *tr.* P1 ‖ karissime] hec nonne *et post* quesisti *tr.* Ba, hoc est L, *post* quesisti *tr.* Mu1 P1 ‖ quod] que A, si *add.* Ba ‖ quesisti] quesistis L ‖ de *om.* A **17.1.** de *om.* A ‖ aliquarum] aliquorum L, *om.* Ma ‖ rerum *om.* Ma ‖ prescriptione] presumptione Vb ‖ agitur] agi G L Ma ‖ est[1] *om.* C ‖ utrum] an Ma ‖ valeant] valeantur L ‖ nec ne] an non Ma **17.2.** longe] longi Vp ‖ usurpationis] prescriptionis Mu1 ‖ currit] noverit L, currat Ma **17.3.** Secundo] vero P1 **17.4.** Exempli] Verbi L, Exemplum P1 ‖ iura] † *add.* L, iuxta Vb, nostra Vp ‖ gratia *om.* P1 ‖ communia] omnia P1 ‖ sunt *ante* prodita *rep.* Ba, *ante* prodita *tr.* Mu1 ‖ predia et] predicta Ma ‖ pecora ... predia *tr.* Vp ‖ pecora] possidere possunt episcopi ecclesias *add.* F Ma ‖ ecclesie] et *praem.* C Vb, *om.* F ‖ decimas *om.* P1 ‖ et[2] *om.* Ma ‖ et[3] *om.* Ma ‖ oblationum] obligationum C ‖ in[2]] vel Ba ‖ subiectis] subditis A Ba G ‖ ecclesiis] similibus in suis *praem.* Ba ‖ possident] possides F, *om.* Ma, possideri Vp **17.5.** Ideoque] Ideo quia G ‖ prescribere talia *tr.* P1 ‖ C.[1] *om.* Mu1 ‖ iii.] iv. P1 ‖ et[1]] c. P1 ‖ iv. ... iii. *tr.* F ‖ per totum] pretorium Vp ‖ per] et *praem.* F, vel G P1 ‖ eo *om.* C F G Ma P1 ‖ limitibus] liminibus Ba, militibus C G P1 ‖ dicitur] ut *add.* L ‖ eadem[1] *om.* Ma ‖ Licet] c. *praem.* Mu1 ‖ et[2] *om.* A Ma ‖ c. *om.* L

⟨16.18.⟩ D.93 c.22.
⟨16.19.⟩ D.100 c.8.
⟨16.20.⟩ D.68 c.5 at the end.

⟨17.⟩ In these last chapters, note, my dearest, what you have asked. ⟨17.1.⟩ For when it comes to the acquisitive prescription of certain things, it must be examined whether such things can be possessed by such persons by common right, or not. ⟨17.2.⟩ In the first case, acquisitive prescription runs only through the long detention of a usurped thing. ⟨17.3.⟩ In the second case, not at all. ⟨17.4.⟩ For example, common rights, whether written or unwritten, have been granted, by which laypeople possess lands and livestock, churches possess tithes and first-fruits, and prelates possess a portion of offerings in the churches subjected to them and even the dioceses themselves. Therefore, such persons can acquire such things by prescription, as throughout C.16 q.3 and q.4, except for what is said about boundaries, C.16 q.3 c.5, and c.6.

⟨17.6.⟩ Against: no common right has been handed down by which laypeople can possess tithes, or first-fruits, or a portion of offerings, or sacred vessels, or the disposal of churches, and similar things, or by which archbishops can use the pallium outside of solemn masses or anybody other than Roman Church clerics can use the maniples, or by

uti, vel quo simplices episcopi vel plebani sub se alios episcopos vel plebanos habere valeant. ⟨17.7.⟩ Ideoque in his et similibus prescriptio usurpationis locum habere non potest. ⟨17.8.⟩ Immo ad hoc ut retineantur, privilegium est necessarium, ut presignatis xciii. (D.93 c.22) et c. (D.100 c.8) D. capitulis continetur, et C. xvi. q. i. c. ultimo (C.16 q.1 c.68) et q. iii. § Potest etiam (C.16 q.3 d.p.c.15) et q. vii. Decimas (C.16 q.7 c.1). ⟨17.9.⟩ Prescriptio namque ius novum non creat, sed creatum avocat, ut C. xxxiii. q. v. Quod Deo pari (C.33 q.5 c.4) "numerus te nullus."

⟨18.⟩ Metus vel iussus principis vel cuiuscumque potentis irregulariter factum excusat.

⟨18.1.⟩ C. ii. q. i. Inprimis (C.2 q.1 c.7) "se metu iudicis."
⟨18.2.⟩ D. lxiii. Salonitane (D.63 c.24).
⟨18.3.⟩ D. xviii. Si episcopus (D.18 c.13).
⟨18.4.⟩ C. xii. q. ii. De rebus (C.12 q.2 c.22).

17.6. Econtra] Contra A L Vp ‖ commune *post* est *tr.* L ‖ est *om.* C ‖ vel[1]] et A L Vb, *om.* Ma ‖ vel[2]] et A L Vb, *om.* Ma ‖ partem] prelati *praem.* A L Vb ‖ vel[3] *om.* Ma ‖ vasa] masa *cum* m *exp. et corr.* Mu1 ‖ vel[4] *om.* Ma ‖ dispositionem *om.* L ‖ possidere] posteriore Vp ‖ quo[2]] quod G, *om.* P1 ‖ archiepiscopi] archiepiscopo Vp ‖ pallio] pallia P1 ‖ sollempnia] sollempnitatem Ma ‖ quam] quem Ma, quamvi Vp ‖ mapulis] manipulis C, in apul. *cum abbr. signo* Ma, mapulus Vp ‖ uti] utique Ba G Vp ‖ quo[3]] valeant *praem.* F. Ma, quod P1 ‖ simplices] supplices Ma **17.7.** et *om.* Ba Vp ‖ prescriptio] prescriptionis A F L Mu1 Vb Vp, vel *add.* C, prescriptionibus Ba Ma ‖ usurpationis] usurpatio A Ba C F L Ma Mu1 Vb Vp, usurpato G ‖ habere] habet et *praem.* Ba **17.8.** Immo] Uno Vp ‖ retineantur] retineatur Ba, retineant P1 ‖ est] ut *praem.* C ‖ necessarium] in contrarium Ma ‖ ut] in *add.* C, *rep.* L ‖ presignatis] predictis Ma, preassignatis *et ante* capitulis *tr.* Mu1, presignas Vp ‖ xciii.] xciv. F, xxiii. Ma, D. *praem.* Mu1 ‖ et[1] *om.* Ma P1 ‖ c.[1] *om.* C P1 ‖ D. *om.* F, De Ma ‖ et] c. Pervenit (D.93 c.21) et c. Illud (D.93 c.22) *praem.* Mu1 ‖ c.] Contra morem require erga et invenies predictas distinctiones *add.* Mu1 ‖ D. *ante* c. *tr.* Mu1 ‖ continetur *om.* Mu1 ‖ C. *om.* G ‖ i. *vac.* F ‖ iii.] iv. Ma ‖ Potest etiam] Pretium Ma ‖ Potest] non *praem.* Vb ‖ etiam *om.* F P1, et aliter Mu1 **17.9.** namque] enim P1 ‖ novum ius *tr.* G L P1 ‖ non] vero L ‖ creat] erat Ma Mu1 ‖ creatum] ad *praem. et exp.* A, *om.* C G P1 ‖ C. *om.* P1 ‖ v.] vi. Ba, ultima Ma ‖ Quod] Qui Ma ‖ pari *om.* Ba C F G L Ma P1 Vp ‖ numerus] iuris F, infra *praem.* Ma ‖ te] iste A, et Ba, tunc G ‖ nullus … numerus *tr.* Vb ‖ nullus] defendisset *add.* F, defendisset annorum *add.* L Mu1 Vb **18.** = 8 C, 10 G P1, 4 O, 12 P2 ‖ Metus vel] Metallus L ‖ vel[1]] et P2 ‖ iussus] ius F, iussu L ‖ principis] maioris *praem.* Ma ‖ vel[2]] et A Ba G P1 ‖ cuiuscumque] cuiusque Ba, cuius C, alicuius P2 ‖ potentis] potestatis F Ma P1 ‖ irregulariter] irregulariter *cum* ir *del.* F, regulariter P1, intelligla L, irrationabiliter Ma ‖ in *om* P1 ‖ excusat] ut *add.* F, inexcusat P1 **18.1.** *§18.1—§18.27 om. per totum* O ‖ se] si Ba L Mu1 P2 Vp, seu P1 ‖ iudicis *om.* P1, iudicem P2, mortis Vp **18.2.** lxiii.] lxiv. A Vb ‖ Salonitane] ita ex corde laxavi *add.* Ba Vp, c. *praem. et* ita ex corde relaxavi *add.* Mu1, ita ex corde *add.* P2 **18.3.** *in §18.2 ante* Salonitane *tr.* Ma ‖ D. xviii. *om.* Ma ‖ xviii.] xcviii. L, lxviii. *cum* l. *exp.* P2 ‖ Si] c. *praem.* Mu1 ‖ episcopus] metropolitanus "preceptione regia" *add.* Mu1, episcopo P2 **18.4.** *post §18.5 tr.* Mu1 ‖ De] c. *praem.* Mu1 ‖ rebus] illius concessio idest principis *add.* Mu1

which simple bishops or parish priests can have other bishops or parish priests under them. ⟨17.7.⟩ Therefore, in these and similar cases the acquisitive prescription of the usurped thing cannot take place. ⟨17.8.⟩ Rather, in order for these things to be kept, a specific privilege is necessary, as in the aforementioned chapters D.93 c.22 and D.100 c.8, and C.16 q.1 c.68, and q.3 d.p.c.15, and D.16 q.7 c.1. ⟨17.9.⟩ For indeed, an acquisitive prescription does not create a new right, but reclaims a right that is already created, as in C.33 q.5 c.4.

⟨18.⟩ Fear or an order of a ruler or of any powerful person excuses what is done irregularly.
⟨18.1.⟩ C.2 q.1 c.7.
⟨18.2.⟩ D.63 c.24.
⟨18.3.⟩ D.18 c.13.
⟨18.4.⟩ C.12 q.2 c.22.

⟨18.5.⟩ C. xi. q. i. Si tributum (C.11 q.1 c.27).

⟨18.6.⟩ C. xi. q. ultima Antecessor (C.11 q.3 c.104) et c. Quod predecessor (C.11 q.3 c.105) "principalem."

⟨18.7.⟩ C. xv. q. vi. Auctoritatem (C.15 q.6 c.2), C. iii. q. i. Redintegranda (C.3 q.1 c.3) "aut dolo" et q. ii. Si episcopus (C.3 q.2 c.8) "insidiis."

⟨18.8.⟩ C. xv. q. vi. Si a sacerdotibus (C.15 q.6 c.1).

⟨18.9.⟩ C. xiv. q. v. Dixit (C.14 q.5 c.12).

⟨18.10.⟩ C. xxiii. q. v. Miles (C.23 q.5 c.13).

⟨18.11.⟩ C. xxxi. q. ii. Lotharius (C.31 q.2 c.4) "metu," "admisisse."

⟨18.12.⟩ Contra.

⟨18.13.⟩ C. xi. q. iii. Iniustum (C.11 q.3 c.89).

⟨18.14.⟩ C. xxv. q. i. Omne (C.25 q.1 c.8).

⟨18.15.⟩ C. xxiii. q. ultima Convenior (C.23 q.8 c.21).

⟨18.16.⟩ C. ii. q. i. Scelus quod (C.2 q.1 c.21).

⟨18.17.⟩ D. lxiii. c. i. (D.63 c.1).

⟨18.18.⟩ D. xcvi. Duo sunt (D.96 c.10).

⟨18.19.⟩ C. ii. q. i. c. ultimo (C.2 q.1 c.21).

⟨18.20.⟩ C. xv. Auctoritatem (C.15 q.6 c.2).

⟨18.21.⟩ C. viii. q. iii. Artaldus (C.8 q.3 c.2) "post electionem."

⟨18.22.⟩ C. viii. q. iv. Nonne (C.8 q.4 c.1) "priusquam Salica."

⟨18.23.⟩ D. li. Qui in aliquo (D.51 c.5) "per gradus ecclesiasticos."

⟨18.24.⟩ D. lxii. Quanto (D.53 c.10) "sed quoniam eadem non fuit."

⟨18.25.⟩ D. li. Nullus invitis (D.61 c.13) "primum enim."

18.5. *post §18.6 tr.* C, *post §18.7 tr.* G P1 **18.6.** C. xi.] et F L Ma ‖ ultima] iii. Mu1 Vb, ii. P1 ‖ Antecessor] Antecessores P1 ‖ c. *om.* L ‖ Quod] Quid C, Quia P1, Qui P2 ‖ predecessor] de *praem. et exp.* A ‖ principalem] principale A Ba C F L Mu1 Vb Vp, principaliter G **18.7.** C.[1] *om.* P1 ‖ Auctoritatem] Auctoritate A, c. *praem.* Mu1 ‖ C.[2]—insidiis *om.* A C G L P1 ‖ i. *om.* F Vp ‖ Redintegranda] Reintegranda Ba F Vb, sunt *add.* Mu1 ‖ aut dolo *om.* Vb ‖ et *om.* Vp ‖ insidiis] que *praem.* Ba F Vp, inimicorum *add.* Ma Mu1 **18.8.** *om. per totum* A Ba C F G L P1 P2 Vp ‖ vi.] v. Ma ‖ Si] c. *praem.* Mu1 ‖ a *om.* Ma **18.9.** *om. per totum* A Ba C F G L Mu1 P1 P2 Vb Vp **18.10.** *om. per totum* A Ba C F G L Mu1 P1 P2 Vb Vp **18.11.** *om. per totum* A Ba C F G L Mu1 P1 P2 Vb Vp **18.12.** *post §18.6 tr.* P1 ‖ Contrarium L Mu1, Econtra P2 **18.13.** xi.] eadem P1 ‖ Iniustum] regio metu *add.* Ma, c. *praem.* Mu1, Iniustam P1 **18.14.** C. xii. q. ii. Monemus (C.12 q.2 c.18) L ‖ Omne] quod regio metu vel iussu *add.* Ma, c. *praem. et* regio metu *add.* Mu1, *rep. cum* Omne[1] *exp.* P1 **18.15.** Convenior] c. *praem.* Mu1 **18.16.** *om. per totum* A Ba C F G L Ma P1 P2 Vb Vp **18.17.** *om. per totum* Mu1 ‖ c. i. *vac.* P1 ‖ c. *om.* A, § Ba F G Ma P2 Vb Vp **18.18.** *om. per totum* A Ba C F G Ma Mu1 P1 P2 Vb Vp ‖ xcvi.] xciii. *male* L **18.19.** *om. per totum* Vp ‖ *post §18.26 tr.* Mu1 ‖ ii.] vi. G, xvi. P1 ‖ q. i. *om.* P1 ‖ i.] v. G ‖ ultimo] Iste P2 **18.20.** *om. per totum* A Ba C F G Ma Mu1 P1 P2 Vb Vp **18.21.** *om. per totum* A Ba C F G L Ma Mu1 P1 Vb Vp **18.22.** *om. per totum* A Ba C F G L Ma Mu1 P1 Vb Vp **18.23.** *om. per totum* A Ba C F G L Ma Mu1 P1 Vb Vp **18.24.** *om. per totum* A Ba C F G L Ma Mu1 P1 Vb Vp ‖ eadem] in *praem. et exp.* P2 **18.25.** *om. per totum* A Ba C F G L Ma Mu1 P1 Vb Vp

⟨18.5.⟩ C.11 q.1 c.27.

⟨18.6.⟩ C.11 q.3 c.104 and c.105.

⟨18.7.⟩ C.15 q.6 c.2, C.3 q.1 c.3, and q.2 c.8.

⟨18.8.⟩ C.15 q.6 c.1.

⟨18.9.⟩ C.14 q.5 c.12.

⟨18.10.⟩ C.23 q.5 c.13.

⟨18.11.⟩ C.31 q.2 c.4.

⟨18.12.⟩ Against.

⟨18.13.⟩ C.11 q.3 c.89.

⟨18.14.⟩ C.25 q.1 c.8.

⟨18.15.⟩ C.23 q.8 c.21.

⟨18.16.⟩ C.2 q.1 c.21.

⟨18.17.⟩ D.63 c.1.

⟨18.18.⟩ D.96 c.10.

⟨18.19.⟩ C.2 q.1 c.21.

⟨18.20.⟩ C.15 q.6 c.2.

⟨18.21.⟩ C.8 q.3 c.2.

⟨18.22.⟩ C.8 q.4 c.1.

⟨18.23.⟩ D.51 c.5.

⟨18.24.⟩ D.53 c.10.

⟨18.25.⟩ D.61 c.13.

⟨18.26.⟩ D. xviii. Quoniam quidem (D.18 c.7) “si quisquam princeps.”

⟨18.27.⟩ C. xxxvi. q. ii. Nullus (C.36 q.2 c.6) “aut regis beneficio.”

⟨19.⟩ Bene actum non infirmatur, etsi res in eum casum deveniat, a quo incipere non potuit.

⟨19.1.⟩ C. xxx. q. i. Ad limina (C.30 q.1 c.7).

⟨19.2.⟩ C. eadem q. eadem Nosse desideras (C.30 q.1 c.3) et c. Dictum (C.30 q.1 c.4).

⟨19.3.⟩ C. xxviii. Sic enim neque (C.28 q.1 c.9) “quoniam ergo.”

⟨19.4.⟩ C. xxxiv. q. i. In lectum (C.34 q.1–2 c.6).

⟨19.5.⟩ C. xxviii. q. ii. § Hinc distinguendum est (C.28 q.2 d.p.c.2).

⟨19.6.⟩ C. xxviii. q. ii. § Ecce impossibilitas (C.27 q.2 d.p.c.29).

⟨19.7.⟩ D. l. Clerico iaciente (D.50 c.37) et c. Quia te (D.50 c.38).

⟨19.8.⟩ D. lv. Si evangelica (D.55 c.13) “nam illi, cui erutus.”

⟨19.9.⟩ C. vii. q. i. Petisti (C.7 q.1 c.17) “nequaquam relinquas.”

⟨19.10.⟩ C. xxxii. q. vii. Hii, qui matrimonium (C.32 q.7 c.25) et c. Neque (C.32 q.7 c.26).

⟨19.11.⟩ C. eadem q. v. e. i. § furiosus (C.32 q.7 c.26).

⟨19.12.⟩ C. i. q. v. c. i. (C.1 q.5 c.1) “catholice ordinati sunt.”

⟨19.13.⟩ Contra.

18.26. *om. per totum* A Ba C F G P1 P2 Vp ‖ D. *om.* Vb ‖ Quoniam] c. *praem.* Mu1 ‖ quidem] quod Mu1 ‖ si—princeps *om.* L ‖ si *om.* Mu1 Vb **18.27.** *om. per totum* A Ba C F G L P1 P2 Vp ‖ Nullus] c. *praem.* Mu1 ‖ aut *om.* Mu1 Vb ‖ beneficio *om.* Vb **19.** = 9 C, 11 G P1, 5 O ‖ *§19—§19.18 om. per totum* P2 ‖ infirmatur] firmatur Vb ‖ etsi] etiamsi L ‖ res] reus Ba, *rep.* Ma ‖ deveniat] veniat A Mu1 Vb, incipiat Ba, devenerit F, veniet L ‖ a] in Mu1 ‖ a quo] aliquo C ‖ incipere non potuit] non possit incipere Ma ‖ non *rep.* G ‖ potuit] potest C P1, ut *add.* F, potest vel *praem.* O **19.1.** *§19.1—§19.18 om. per totum* O ‖ limina] olim legitime *add.* Mu1 **19.2.** C.—eadem[2] *om.* Ba F Ma, et c. Mu1 P1 ‖ Nosse] Nos esse A, Nolle P1 ‖ desideras *om.* L ‖ et c. *om.* Ba F, C. eadem q. eadem Ma ‖ c. *om.* L ‖ Dictum] est *add.* F Ma **19.3.** xxviii.] xxxii. L, q. i. *add.* Ma Mu1 ‖ enim *om.* A Ba F L Vb Vp ‖ neque quoniam] nequaquam P1 ‖ neque *om.* Ma Mu1 ‖ quoniam] vero *praem.* Mu1 **19.4.** q. i. *om.* A F G L Mu1 Vp, *vac.* C P1 ‖ i.] ii. Ma, *vac.* Vb **19.5.** *§19.5—§19.6 post §19.12 tr.* Mu1 ‖ *ante §19.4 tr.* Ba ‖ *om. per totum* F ‖ C.—ii. *om.* Ba L ‖ xxviii.] xxxviii. G ‖ q. ii. *om.* A C G Mu1 P1 Vp ‖ ii. *vac.* Vb ‖ Hinc] Hic A Ba Mu1 ‖ est *om.* P1 Vb **19.6.** xxviii.] xxviv. *cum* i.[4] *exp.* A, xxvii. Fr, xxv. Ma **19.7.** Clerico] c. *praem.* Mu1 ‖ iacente *om.* L Ma, iacenti Mu1 ‖ et c. *om.* Ma ‖ te] quasi obnoxium *add.* Ma **19.8.** illi cui] illicita F ‖ illi] isti L, ille P1 ‖ cui erutus] sciverunt G Vp ‖ erutus] erunt A Ba C G L, erit F, est *praem.* Ma, est oculus *add.* Mu1, *om.* Vb **19.9.** vii.] xxi. G, xi. P1 ‖ i.] iii. P1 ‖ Petisti] Petististi A ‖ relinquas] deli. F, relinquis Mu1 **19.10.** matrimonium *om.* F L, in *praem.* Mu1 ‖ et … Neque *om.* P1 ‖ et c. *om.* Ma ‖ c. *om.* G L ‖ Neque] et C. i. q. v. Catholice (C.1 q.5 p.c.1) *add.* Vb **19.11.** *om. per totum* A Ba C F G L Mu1 P1 Vb Vp **19.12.** *om. per totum* A Ba C F G L Ma P1 Vb Vp **19.13.** *vac. et ante §20 tr.* Mu1 ‖ Econtra C, Contrarium L Mu1 P1

⟨18.26.⟩ D.18 c.7.
⟨18.27.⟩ C.36 q.2 c.6.

⟨19.⟩ What is properly done is not invalidated, even if it changes into something from which the act could not have been started.
⟨19.1.⟩ C.30 q.1 c.7.
⟨19.2.⟩ C.30 q.1 c.3 and c.4.
⟨19.3.⟩ C.28 q.1 c.9.
⟨19.4.⟩ C.34 q.1–2 c.6.
⟨19.5.⟩ C.28 q.2 d.p.c.2.
⟨19.6.⟩ C.27 q.2 d.p.c.29.
⟨19.7.⟩ D.50 c.37 and c.38.
⟨19.8.⟩ D.55 c.13.
⟨19.9.⟩ C.7 q.1 c.17.
⟨19.10.⟩ C.32 q.7 c.25 and c.26.
⟨19.11.⟩ C.32 q.7 c.26.
⟨19.12.⟩ C.1 q.5 c.1.
⟨19.13.⟩ Against.

⟨19.14.⟩ C. vii. q. i. Qualiter (C.7 q.1 c.13) et c. Quamvis (C.7 q.1 c.14).
⟨19.15.⟩ C. eadem q. ii. c. ultimo (C.7 q.2 c.2).
⟨19.16.⟩ D. l. Miror (D.50 c.4).
⟨19.17.⟩ C. xxvii. q. ii. Quidam desponsavit (C.27 q.2 c.31).
⟨19.18.⟩ C. xxxii. q. vii. Qui dormierit (C.32 q.7 c.21) et c. Concubuisti (C.32 q.7 c.23).

⟨20.⟩ Quod contra leges factum est, per leges dissolvi meretur.
⟨20.1.⟩ C. de legibus et constitutionibus Non dubium est (Cod. 1.14.5pr.).
⟨20.2.⟩ C. xxvii. q. i. Ut lex continentie (C.27 q.1 c.40) et q. ii. Si quis uxorem (C.27 q.2 c.14).
⟨20.3.⟩ C. x. q. i. c. ii. (C.10 q.1 c.2) "corrigatur."
⟨20.4.⟩ D. x. Vide, fili karissime (D.10 c.10).
⟨20.5.⟩ C. xxv. q. ii. Imperiali (C.25 q.2 c.13).
⟨20.6.⟩ D. liv. Quis aut (D.54 c.11).
⟨20.7.⟩ D. xvii. Regula (D.17 c.2) "canonibus."
⟨20.8.⟩ C. xxxv. q. iii. Contradicimus (C.35 q.2–3 c.21).
⟨20.9.⟩ C. ii. q. vi. Quotiens episcopi (C.2 q.6 c.16) "quod si aliter."
⟨20.10.⟩ C. x. q. i. Sic quidam (C.10 q.1 c.2) "corrigatur."
⟨20.11.⟩ Econtra. Multa prohibentur que convalescunt ex post facto.

19.14. vii.] viii. P1 ‖ q.] et *praem.* Vp ‖ i.] eadem Ba, *vac.* G Vb, c. Vp ‖ Qualiter] Qualitas *cum* c. *praem. et* as *exp. et corr.* A, c. *praem.* G Mu1 ‖ et c. *om.* Ma ‖ c. *om.* L **19.15.** C. eadem] et Ba F Mu1 **19.16.** Miror] Minor A Ba C G Vp, c. *praem.* Mu1 **19.17.** xxvii. q. ii.] eadem q. ii. *exp. et corr. interl. cum* q. ii. *rep.* A ‖ xxvii.] xxviii. P1 ‖ Quidam] Qui Ma, c. *praem.* Mu1 **19.18.** et c. *om.* Ma ‖ c. *om.* L ‖ Concubuisti] Concubuit A Vb, Contula. L **20.** = 10 C, 12 G P1, 6 O ‖ *§20—§20.24 om. per totum* P2 ‖ *ante §20.12 tr.* Mu1 ‖ factum] factu L ‖ est *om.* L ‖ leges] legem Mu1 ‖ dissolvi] de issolvi A ‖ meretur] ut *add.* F, videtur L **20.1.** *§20.1—§20.24 om. per totum* O ‖ C.] Co. F ‖ et constitutionibus *om.* F ‖ constitutionibus] principum *add.* Mu1, institutionibus P1, q. i. Vp ‖ est dubium *tr.* C L ‖ dubium] etc. *add.* C ‖ est *om.* F Ma, *ante* dubium *tr.* P1 **20.2.** *om. per totum* A Ba C G L Ma Mu1 P1 Vb Vp **20.3.** *post §20.6 tr.* F ‖ *om. per totum* P1 ‖ C.] et *praem.* A Vp ‖ x.] ii. L ‖ i.] ii. L ‖ c. ii. *om.* L ‖ corrigatur] corrigantur Ba F L Vp, C. ii. q. i. corrigantur (C.2 q.1 p.c.10) Mu1 **20.4.** Vide] Vides F L Ma ‖ fili *om.* A Ba C G L Ma Vp ‖ karissime *om.* L Ma Mu1 P1 **20.5.** *post §20.9 tr.* F ‖ xxv.] xxxv. P1 **20.6.** *post §20.7 tr.* F ‖ aut] autem C L Mu1 **20.8.** *om. per totum* A Ba C G L Ma Mu1 P1 Vb Vp **20.9.** vi.] vii. Mu1 P1 ‖ episcopi *om.* L ‖ quod] qui Vb **20.10.** *om. per totum* A Ba C F G L Mu1 P1 Vb Vp **20.11.** *ante §21.1 tr.* Mu1 ‖ Econtra] Contra A Ba F Ma ‖ prohibentur] prohibet Ba ‖ que—facto] fieri etc. Ba ‖ que] cum Vp ‖ ex—facto *om.* L Mu1 ‖ ex *om.* Ma, et P1 ‖ post facto (factum Ma) *ante* convalescunt *tr.* Ma P1 ‖ facto] factum *cum* u *exp. et corr.* G, ut *add.* F

⟨19.14.⟩ C.7 q.1 c.13 and c.14.
⟨19.15.⟩ C.7 q.2 c.2.
⟨19.16.⟩ D.50 c.4.
⟨19.17.⟩ C.27 q.2 c.31.
⟨19.18.⟩ C.32 q.7 c.21 and c.23.

⟨20.⟩ What has been done against the laws deserves to be dissolved by the laws.
⟨20.1.⟩ Cod. 1.14.5pr.
⟨20.2.⟩ C.27 q.1 c.40 and q.2 c.14.
⟨20.3.⟩ C.10 q.1 c.2.
⟨20.4.⟩ D.10 c.10.
⟨20.5.⟩ C.25 q.2 c.13.
⟨20.6.⟩ D.54 c.11.
⟨20.7.⟩ D.17 c.2.
⟨20.8.⟩ C.35 q.3 c.21.
⟨20.9.⟩ C.2 q.6 c.16.
⟨20.10.⟩ C.10 q.1 c.2.
⟨20.11.⟩ Against. Many things are prohibited that become valid after the fact.

⟨20.12.⟩ D. liv. Ex antiquis (D.54 c.9) “si quis iam ex his presbiter” et c. Frequens (D.54 c.10) “prefinitus.”
⟨20.13.⟩ C. vii. q. i. Quia Frater (C.7 q.1 c.18).
⟨20.14.⟩ D. xxvii. Quidam (D.27 c.2) et c. Si vir (D.27 c.3).
⟨20.15.⟩ C. xxvii. q. i. Nuptiarum bonum (C.27 q.1 c.41) “nam,” “quia ipse nuptie.” ⟨20.16.⟩ Agit in illo capitulo Duobus modis dicitur fides (C.27 q.2 c.51).
⟨20.17.⟩ C. xx. q. iii. Constituit (C.20 q.3 c.5).
⟨20.18.⟩ D. lxxiv. Ubi ista (D.74 c.7).
⟨20.19.⟩ C. i. q. vii. Maximum (C.1 q.7 c.19).
⟨20.20.⟩ C. ii. q. i. Nemo episcopus (C.2 q.1 c.11).
⟨20.21.⟩ C. vii. q. i. Episcopus in diocesi (C.7 q.1 c.28) “altaris.”
⟨20.22.⟩ D. xlv. De Iudeis (D.45 c.5).
⟨20.23.⟩ C. xxii. q. iv. Inter cetera (C.22 q.4 c.22).
⟨20.24.⟩ C. xxxv. q. iii. De propinquis (C.35 q.2–3 c.3).

⟨21.⟩ Licitum est homini contra suum factum venire et mutare consilium.
⟨21.1.⟩ D. l. Penitentes (D.50 c.63).
⟨21.2.⟩ C. xii. q. i. Certe ego sum (C.12 q.1 c.18).
⟨21.3.⟩ C. xxxv. q. ix. Quod quis conmisit (C.35 q.9 c.3) et c. Apostolice (C.35 q.9 c.4).

20.12. Ex] c. *praem.* Mu1 ‖ si quis *om.* A ‖ his] ipsis A Ba C F G L P1 Vb Vp ‖ et c.] D. eadem Ma ‖ c.—prefinitus] si quias L ‖ prefinitus *post* quis *tr.* Ba, quem gradus *praem.* Ma, per sacerdotium non potest Mu1, *om.* P1 **20.13.** vii.] ix. F ‖ i.] ii. F **20.14.** *ante §20.13 tr.* F ‖ *om. per totum* C Vb ‖ xxvii.] xcvii. F ‖ Quidam] nubentes *add.* F Mu1 ‖ et c. *om.* Ma ‖ et—vir *om.* F ‖ c. *om.* L ‖ Si vir] Frater § Presumimus P1 ‖ vir] votum *add.* Ma **20.15.** bonum *om.* F L Ma Mu1 P1, *add. interl.* Vb ‖ nam] non Ba F L Mu1 Vp, *om.* P1 ‖ ipse nuptie *om.* L **20.16.** Agit—capitulo] et q. ii. Mu1 ‖ Agit *post* illo *tr.* A, Arg. Ma, Auget P1 ‖ capitulo] loco L ‖ fides dicitur *tr.* L Mu1 **20.17.** xx.] xxx. F, xii. L **20.18.** *post §20.22 tr.* F ‖ D. *vac.* Ma ‖ lxxiv.] lxxvii. Ba, lxxiii. Ma P1 ‖ Ubi ista *rep. in §20.14 ante* Constituit *et exp.* G ‖ ista] didicisti *add.* Ba, *om.* Mu1 **20.19.** *om. per totum* A Ba C G L Ma Mu1 P1 Vb Vp **20.20.** *om. per totum* A Ba C G L Ma Mu1 P1 Vb Vp **20.21.** diocesi] diocesis Ba ‖ altaris] alterius L, altaria Ma, consecratione *add.* Mu1 **20.22.** *post §20.14 tr.* F ‖ xlv.] xlx. *cum* x.^{2} *exp. et corr.* P1, lxv. Vp ‖ De] c. *praem.* Mu1 ‖ Iudeis] viduis Vp **20.23.** *post §20.23 tr.* F ‖ iv.] iii. L **20.24.** xxxv.] xxx. A, xxxi. P1 ‖ iii.] ii. et *praem.* Mu1 ‖ De] c. *praem.* Mu1 **21.** = 11 C, 13 G P1, 7 O, 2 P2 ‖ *om per totum.* Mu1 ‖ Licitum] Illicitum C ‖ factum suum *tr.* F L Ma P1 ‖ consilium mutare *tr.* Mu1 P2 Vb ‖ consilium] suum *praem.* Ba, suum ut *add.* F, in melius *add.* Ma, suum *add.* O **21.1.** *§21.1—§21.19 om. per totum* O ‖ *om. per totum* A Ba C G L Ma Mu1 P1 P2 Vb Vp **21.2.** xii.] xxii. F P2 ‖ ego sum *om.* L ‖ sum] suum A, ille *add.* Ma, *om.* P1 **21.3.** ix.] xi. L ‖ Quod] § L ‖ Quod quis] Quisquis (c. *praem.* Mu1) A Ba C Mu1 P1 Vb ‖ quis] qui P2 ‖ conmisit *om.* Ma, sancto P2 ‖ et c. *om.* Ma, non *praem. et exp.* P1 ‖ c. *om.* L ‖ Apostolice] sedis *add.* Ma

⟨20.12.⟩ D.54 c.9 and c.10.
⟨20.13.⟩ C.7 q.1 c.18.
⟨20.14.⟩ D. 27 c.2 and c.3.
⟨20.15.⟩ C.27 q.1 c.41. ⟨20.16.⟩ As it says in that chapter C.27 q.2 c.51.
⟨20.17.⟩ C.20 q.3 c.5.
⟨20.18.⟩ D.74 c.7.
⟨20.19.⟩ C.1 q.7 c.19.
⟨20.20.⟩ C.2 q.1 c.11.
⟨20.21.⟩ C.7 q.1 c.28.
⟨20.22.⟩ D.45 c.5.
⟨20.23.⟩ C.22 q.4 c.22.
⟨20.24.⟩ C.35 q.2–3 c.3.

⟨21.⟩ It is permitted for a person to go against their own deed and change their plan.
⟨21.1.⟩ D.50 c.63.
⟨21.2.⟩ C.12 q.1 c.18.
⟨21.3.⟩ C.35 q.9 c.3 and c.4.

⟨21.4.⟩ Q. eadem Veniam (C.35 q.9 c.5) et c. Sententiam (C.35 q.9 c.6) et c. Gregorius (C.35 q.9 c.7).

⟨21.5.⟩ C. xvii. q. ii. Consaldus (C.17 q.2–3 c.1).

⟨21.6.⟩ C. xxii. q. iv. Quod David (C.22 q.4 c.3) et c. Iuravit (C.22 q.4 c.4) et c. In malis (C.22 q.4 c.5) et c. Si aliquid (C.22 q.4 c.6).

⟨21.7.⟩ Q. eadem Inconmutabilis (C.22 q.4 c.9) et c. Magne (C.22 q.4 c.10) et c. Non semper (C.22 q.4 c.12) et c. Diffinitio (C.22 q.4 c.17).

⟨21.8.⟩ C. xxiii. q. vi. Vides (C.23 q.6 c.3) "in ea primitus."

⟨21.9.⟩ C. xx. q. iv. c. Monachum (C.20 q.4 c.3).

⟨21.10.⟩ C. xxxiii. q. v. Manifestum est (C.33 q.5 c.11).

⟨21.11.⟩ Contra.

⟨21.12.⟩ C. xii. q. ii. Monemus (C.12 q.2 c.18) "ita ut deinceps."

⟨21.13.⟩ C. xx. q. iii. Constituit (C.20 q.3 c.5) "perseverare cogantur."

⟨21.14.⟩ C. eadem q. eadem c. i. (C.20 q.3 c.1), ii. (C.20 q.3 c.2), iii. (C.20 q.3 c.3), et. q. iv. c. i. (C.20 q.4 c.1).

⟨21.15.⟩ C. xxvii. q. i. Nuptiarum (C.27 q.1 c.41) in fine capituli.

⟨21.16.⟩ C. eadem q. ii. Agathosa (C.27 q.2 c.21).

⟨21.17.⟩ C. xvii. q. ii. Nos novimus (C.17 q.2–3 c.2).

⟨21.18.⟩ C. xvi. q. quod a Iudei iam itaque presbiter constituit (C.17 q.4 c.31?).

⟨21.19.⟩ C. xvii. q. iv. Sunt qui opes (C.17 q.4 c.3).

21.4. Q. eadem] et Ba, et c. F Mu1 P1 P2, et *praem.* L, D. eadem *praem.* Ma ‖ Veniam—c.[1] *om.* Ma ‖ et[1] c.[1] *om.* Ba P2 ‖ Sententiam] Sententia F, Romane *add.* Ma ‖ et[2] c.[2] *om.* Ma P2 ‖ et[2] *om.* A P1 ‖ Gregorius] quartus *add.* Ma **21.5.** xvii.] xxvii. Mu1 ‖ q. ii. *om.* P1 ‖ Consaldus] Cosaldus Fr, mox se fieri *add.* Ma **21.6.** iv.] iii. P1 ‖ Quod] Qui A, Quia Ba ‖ David] dedit L, iuravit quod dedid *add.* Mu1, quidem Vp ‖ et[1]—malis *om.* A ‖ et[1] c.[1] *om.* F Ma ‖ c.[1] *om.* L ‖ et[2] c.[2] *om.* F Ma ‖ c.[2] *om.* L ‖ et[3] c.[3] *om.* F Ma ‖ c.[3] *om.* L ‖ aliquid] aliqui A, quis C, aliqua F, quid Ma, aliquem P1 **21.7.** Q. eadem] et c. Ba Mu1 P1 P2, *om.* F Ma ‖ et[1] c.[1] *om.* F Ma ‖ c.[1] *om.* L ‖ Magne] Magno P1 ‖ et[2] c.[2] *om.* Ba F Ma ‖ c.[2] *om.* L ‖ et[3]—Diffinitio *om.* P1 ‖ et[3] c.[3] *om.* Ba F Ma ‖ c.[3] *om.* L **21.8.** *om. per totum* A Ba C G L Ma Mu1 P1 P2 Vb Vp ‖ in ea] mea Fr **21.9.** *om. per totum* Vb ‖ iv.] iii. P1 P2 ‖ c. *om.* L P1 ‖ Monachum] Monachus A Ba C F G L Mu1 P1 P2 Vp **21.10.** xxxiii.] xxiii. L ‖ Manifestum] c. *praem.* Mu1 **21.11.** Econtra C P2, Contrarium L Mu1 **21.12.** xii.] xvi. L, xii. *cum* i.[1] *exp.* Vp ‖ ita *om.* G ‖ ut] aut F **21.13.** iii.] ii. P1 ‖ perseverare] perseverantem G ‖ cogantur] cogatur A Ba C F G L Mu1 P1 Vb Vp, *om.* P2 **21.14.** eadem c. *om.* P1 ‖ ii.] et *praem.* A ‖ iii.] iiii. *cum* i.[4] *exp.* A, et *praem.* L P1 ‖ q.[2] *om.* C P1 Vb ‖ iv.] iii. L ‖ c. i. *om.* C Vb ‖ i.] ii. *cum* i.[2] *exp.* L **21.15.** C.] contrari A ‖ Nuptiarum] bonum *add.* Ba C F G Mu1 P1 P2 Vp ‖ in—capituli *om.* Ma ‖ capituli *om.* C L P1 Vb **21.16.** *post § 22 tr.* P1 ‖ eadem] xxvii. P1 ‖ q. ii. Agathosa *rep in § 21.13 post* Nuptiarum Ma ‖ ii.] eadem P2 **21.17.** *om. per totum* A Ba C G L Mu1 P1 P2 Vb Vp **21.18.** *om. per totum* A Ba C G L Ma Mu1 P1 P2 Vb Vp **21.19.** *om. per totum* A Ba C G L Ma Mu1 P1 P2 Vb Vp

⟨21.4.⟩ C.35 q.9 c.5 and c.6 and c.7.
⟨21.5.⟩ C.17 q.2–3 c.1.
⟨21.6.⟩ C.22 q.4 c.3 and c.4 and c.5 and c.6.
⟨21.7.⟩ C.22 q.4 c.9 and c.10 and c.12 and c.17.
⟨21.8.⟩ C.23 q.6 c.3.
⟨21.9.⟩ C.20 q.4 c.3.
⟨21.10.⟩ C.33 q.5 c.11.

⟨21.11.⟩ Against.

⟨21.12.⟩ C.12 q.2 c.18.
⟨21.13.⟩ C.20 q.3 c.5.
⟨21.14.⟩ C.20 q.3 c.1, c.2, c.3, and q.4 c.1.
⟨21.15.⟩ C.27 q.1 c.41.
⟨21.16.⟩ C.27 q.2 c.21.
⟨21.17.⟩ C.17 q.2–3 c.2.
⟨21.18.⟩ C.17 q.4 c.31?
⟨21.19.⟩ C.17 q.4 c.3.

⟨22.⟩ Res inter alios acta aliis non preiudicat, nec factum unius aliis obesse vel prodesse consuevit.

⟨22.1.⟩ C. ii. q. v. Interrogatum est (C.2 q.5 c.24).

⟨22.2.⟩ C. i. q. iii. Nullius crimen (C.1 q.4 c.1) et c. Placuit (C.1 q.4 c.3) et c. Qui apud (C.1 q.4 c.4) et c. Quia (C.1 q.4 c.5).

⟨22.3.⟩ Q. eadem Iudei (C.1 q.4 c.7) et c. Iam itaque (C.1 q.4 c.8).

⟨22.4.⟩ C. xxiv. q. iii. Si habes (C.24 q.3 c.1).

⟨22.5.⟩ C. xi. q. ultima Quoniam multos (C.11 q.3 c.103).

⟨22.6.⟩ Contra.

⟨22.7.⟩ C. ii. q. v. Statuit (C.2 q.5 c.25).

⟨22.8.⟩ C. vi. q. i. Qui crimen (C.6 q.1 c.6).

⟨22.9.⟩ C. iii. q. xi. Neganda (C.3 q.11 c.1) et c. Non est (C.3 q.11 c.3).

⟨22.10.⟩ C. i. q. v. Quicumque (C.1 q.5 c.1).

⟨22.11.⟩ C. xxxii. q. iii. c. ultimo (C.32 q.3 c.un.).

⟨22.12.⟩ C. xv. q. iii. c. ultimo (C.15 q.4 c.3).

⟨22.13.⟩ C. xv. q. ultima Cum multe (C.15 q.8 c.3).

⟨22.14.⟩ C. i. q. vii. Qui in qualibet (C.1 q.7 c.10) et c. Tali (C.1 q.7 c.17).

⟨22.15.⟩ D. xxxv. c. penultimo (D.35 c.8), C. xxxii. q. v. Tunc salvabitur (C.33 q.5 c.7).

⟨22.16.⟩ De con. D. i. In sancta apostolica sede (D.1 de cons. c.41).

⟨22.17.⟩ C. i. q. iv. Ecclesia (C.1 q.4 c.11) "item pro peccato Achor."

---

22. = 12 C, 14 G P1, 8 O, 3 P2 ‖ *post §21.8 tr.* L ‖ acta] aucta G, gesta Ma, iudicata P2 ‖ aliis[1]] alii *et post* preiudicat *tr.* F, alii Ma ‖ nec—consuevit *om.* L ‖ nec] nisi Mu1 ‖ aliis[2]] alii F Ma ‖ prodesse—obesse *tr.* C F O P2, obest—prodest Ma ‖ consuevit] solet C O, ut *add.* F, consuerat G, *om.* Ma, convenit P1, const. P2 **22.1.** *§22.1—§22.17 om. per totum* O ‖ *§22.1 ... §22.6 om. per totum* (*homoiotel.*) P2 ‖ est *om.* F L Vb **22.2.** crimen *om.* L ‖ et.[1] c.[1]] *om.* F L Ma ‖ et.[2] c.[2] *om.* F Ma ‖ c.[2] *om.* P1 ‖ Qui] Quod A Ba C F ‖ et c. Quia *om.* F Ma ‖ c.[3] *om.* L ‖ Quia *in §22.3 ante* Inde *tr.* A, Quid Ba **22.3.** *om. per totum* F ‖ Q. eadem *om.* Ba Ma, et L, et c. Mu1 P1 ‖ Iudei] Inde (c. *praem.* A C) A C Vb, c. *praem. et* Videri *cum* er *exp. et corr.* G, Iudeis Mu1 ‖ et. c. *om.* Ba L Ma ‖ Iam *vac.* G, Nam P1 ‖ itaque *om.* A Mu1 **22.4.** xxiv.] xxxiv. F P1, xxiii. L ‖ q. iii. *om.* A C L Vp ‖ iii. *vac.* Ba G ‖ Si] c. *praem.* Mu1 ‖ habes] hanc F, haberis G, hominis P1 **22.5.** xi.] x. F ‖ q. ultima *post* multos *tr.* P1 ‖ ultima] iii. Mu1 ‖ Quoniam] c. *praem.* Mu1 **22.6.** Econtra A Ba, Contrarium Mu1 **22.7.** *post §22.5 tr.* Vp ‖ ii.—v.] Qui Ma ‖ v.] iii. Mu1 ‖ Statuit] c. *praem.* Mu1 **22.8.** vi.] vii. A Ba L P2 Vp ‖ i.] v. Vp ‖ Qui] Quod C F P2 **22.9.** xi. ... iii. *tr.* Mu1 ‖ xi.] ix. P1 ‖ et c. *om.* F Ma ‖ c. *om.* L ‖ est] credendum *add.* Ma Mu1 **22.10.** Quicumque] c. *praem.* Mu1, Quodcumque P2 **22.11.** xxxii.] xxxiv. A Ba C F G L Ma Mu1 O P1 P2 Vp, xxxiii. *cum* i.[3] *exp.* Vb ‖ iii.] v. Ba P2, iv. A C F G L Ma Mu1 O P1 Vp **22.12.** *om. per totum* A Ba C F G Ma Mu1 P1 P2 Vb Vp **22.13.** C.—ultima *rep.* A, *om.* (*homoiotel.*) P1 ‖ multe] in progeniem *add.* Ma **22.14.** vii.] ultima Mu1 ‖ Qui in] Nam P2 ‖ Qui] c. *praem.* Mu1 ‖ et—Tali *om.* L ‖ et c. *om.* Ba F Ma P2 ‖ et *om.* G Vp ‖ Tali] coniugio *add.* Ma, in ali P1 **22.15.** *om. per totum* A Ba C G L Ma Mu1 P1 P2 Vb Vp **22.15.** *om. per totum* A Ba C G L Ma Mu1 P1 P2 Vb Vp **22.15.** *om. per totum* A Ba C G L Ma Mu1 P1 P2 Vb Vp

⟨22.⟩ A transaction between others does not harm third parties, nor does the act of one usually benefit or harm others.

⟨22.1.⟩ C.2 q.5 c.24.

⟨22.2.⟩ C.1 q.4 c.1 and c.3 and c.4 and c.5.

⟨22.3.⟩ C.1 q.4 c.7 and c.8.

⟨22.4.⟩ C.24 q.3 c.1.

⟨22.5.⟩ C.11 q.3 c.103.

⟨22.6.⟩ Against.

⟨22.7.⟩ C.2 q.5 c.25.

⟨22.8.⟩ C.6 q.1 c.6.

⟨22.9.⟩ C.3 q.11 c.1 and c.3.

⟨22.10.⟩ C.1 q.5 c.1.

⟨22.11.⟩ C.32 q.3 c.un.

⟨22.12.⟩ C.15 q.4 c.3.

⟨22.13.⟩ C.15 q.8 c.3.

⟨22.14.⟩ C.1 q.7 c.10 and c.17.

⟨22.15.⟩ D.35 c.8, C.33 q.5 c.7.

⟨22.16.⟩ D.1 de con. c.41.

⟨22.17.⟩ C.1 q.4 c.11.

⟨23.⟩ Rati habitio et sequens consensus retro trahitur.

⟨23.1.⟩ C. i. q. i. Constat multos (C.1 q.1 c.111) "si statim," "rei sunt."

⟨23.2.⟩ D. lxiii. Salonitane (D.63 c.24) "ac si me auctore."

⟨23.3.⟩ C. xxviii. q. i. Non oportet (C.28 q.1 c.16). ⟨23.4.⟩ Hic consensus post fidem facit ut ab initio matrimonium intelligatur, cum non fuerit.

⟨23.5.⟩ C. xxix. q. i. "consensus alius precedens" (C.29 d.p.q.1).

⟨23.6.⟩ C. xxix. q. ii. Si quis ingenuus (C.29 q.2 c.4) "si voluerit."

⟨23.7.⟩ C. xxx. q. ii. Ubi non est consensus (C.30 q.2 c.un.), "ad tempus."

⟨23.8.⟩ C. eadem q. v. Aliter (C.30 q.5 c.1) "nisi voluntas."

⟨23.9.⟩ C. xxxi. q. ii. Si verum (C.31 q.2 c.1) "quod ceptum est perficere."

⟨23.10.⟩ C. eadem q. eadem De neptis (C.31 q.2 c.3) "persistit."

⟨23.11.⟩ C. xxxiv. q. i. Cum per bellicam (C.34 q.1–2 c.1) "ostendentes, sibimet."

⟨23.12.⟩ C. xvii. q. ii. Consaldus (C.17 q.2–3 c.1) "mox negavit."

⟨23.13.⟩ C. ultima q. ultima Tria (C.36 q.2 c.8) et c. Denique (C.36 q.2 c.9).

⟨23.14.⟩ Contra.

---

23. = 25 C, 14 O, 92 P1, 4 P2 ‖ *§23—§23.20 om. per totum* G ‖ et sequens] consequens L Ma ‖ retro trahitur] retrahitur C O ‖ trahitur] ut *add.* F **23.1.** *§23.1—§23.20 om. per totum* O ‖ multos *om.* F L Ma **23.2.** lxiii.] lxiv. *cum* i.[4] *exp.* A, lxi. L, xliii. P1 ‖ si me] sine L P1 Vp, fine Mu1, sine *cum* ne *exp. et corr.* Vb ‖ auctore] actore Mu1 P2 **23.4.** Hic] c. *praem. et exp.* A, Hec P1 ‖ consensus] sensus O Vb, *post* sit *tr. et* precedens *add.* P1 ‖ post fidem] possidere Ba P1 Vb Vp, *om.* Mu1, possideri P2 ‖ facit] fecit Ba, *om.* Ma P2 ‖ initio] inititio Ma ‖ matrimonium] meum L ‖ cum non fuerit] ut F, *om.* P2 ‖ fuerit] sit O Vb **23.5.** *om. per totum* F P1 Vb ‖ *post §23.9 tr.* Ma ‖ xxix.] xxxi. L, xxviii. P2 ‖ q. i.] § Ma ‖ consensus] est *add.* Fr ‖ alius consensus *tr.* Ba P2 Vp ‖ precedens] alius subsequens *add.* L **23.6.** C. xxix. *om.* Ba, et Mu1 P2 ‖ xxix.] eadem L, xxviii. P1 ‖ voluerit] valuerit A Ba C F L Ma P2 Vp **23.7.** Ubi—consensus *om.* Ba L ‖ non est consensus *om.* A C F Mu1 P1 P2 Vp ‖ consensus *om.* Ma ‖ ad] post quam venerit *praem.* Ma ‖ ad tempus] ad tempori F Vp, *post ubi tr. et del.* Vb ‖ tempus] turpi Ba P2 **23.8.** C.—v. *om.* Mu1 ‖ C. eadem *om.* Ba F P2, et P1 ‖ Aliter] e. *praem. et exp.* L ‖ nisi voluntas] non sit legitimum Ma ‖ nisi] nec A ‖ voluntas] voluptas C, do. *cum abbr. signo* F **23.9.** ii.] iii. F ‖ quod—est *om.* Ma ‖ quod *om.* P1 ‖ ceptum] acceptum A L Vb, *post* est *tr.* Mu1, exceptum P1 ‖ perficere] per fidem A Vb, voluerit *add.* Ba C Mu1, noluerit *add.* Ma, voluit *add.* P2, volunt *add.* Vp **23.10.** *om. per totum* P1 ‖ *post §23.12 tr.* Ma ‖ eadem[1]] xxxi. Ma ‖ q.] et D. Vp ‖ eadem[2]] ii. Ma ‖ De] c. *praem.* Mu1 ‖ persistit] in eadem voluntate *praem.* Ma **23.11.** bellicam] bella C ‖ ostendentes] ostendens P2 ‖ sibimet *om.* F Ma **23.12.** xvii.] xviii. P2, xxvii. Vp ‖ Consaldus] Cosaldus Fr ‖ negavit] se monachum *praem.* Fr, se fieri Ma, negat Vb **23.13.** ultima[1]] xxxvi. Ma ‖ q.] et *praem.* P1 ‖ ultima[2]] ii. Ma, iii. P2 ‖ Tria] legitima *add.* Ma, c. *praem.* Mu1, *om.* P2 ‖ et c. *om.* F Ma P1 **23.14.** Econtra A P2, Contrarium Mu1

⟨23.⟩ Ratification and subsequent agreement have a retrospective effect.

⟨23.1.⟩ C.1 q.1 c.111.

⟨23.2.⟩ D.63 c.24.

⟨23.3.⟩ C.28 q.1 c.16. ⟨23.4.⟩ This agreement after the conversion makes it understood that a marriage existed from the beginning, when there was none.

⟨23.5.⟩ C.29 d.p.q.1.

⟨23.6.⟩ C.29 q.2 c.4.

⟨23.7.⟩ C.30 q.2 c.un.

⟨23.8.⟩ C.30 q.5 c.1.

⟨23.9.⟩ C.31 q.2 c.1.

⟨23.10.⟩ C.31 q.2 c.3.

⟨23.11.⟩ C.34 q.1–2 c.1.

⟨23.12.⟩ C.17 q.2–3 c.1.

⟨23.13.⟩ C.36 q.2 c.8 and c.9.

⟨23.14.⟩ Against.

⟨23.15.⟩ D. xcii. Si quis episcopus vacans (D.92 c.8) "etiamsi populus."
⟨23.16.⟩ C. xi. q. i. Istud (C.11 q.1 c.20) "nullatenus potest," ergo nec sequenti consensu.
⟨23.17.⟩ C. vii. q. i. Episcopum de diocesi (C.7 q.1 c.25) "suadetur; manere."
⟨23.18.⟩ C. xxxi. q. i. Illud (C.31 q.1 c.3) "nolumus" et c. Relatum (C.31 q.1 c.4).
⟨23.19.⟩ C. xxxvi. c. ultimo (C.36 q.2 c.11) "postmodum conveniant."
⟨23.20.⟩ D. xvii. Regula (D.17 c.2) "nec poterit habere."

⟨24.⟩ Probatio facta in seculari iudicio, ecclesiastico iudici plenam fidem facit.
⟨24.1.⟩ C. ii. q. i. Multi (C.2 q.1 c.18) "sive seculari."
⟨24.2.⟩ C. xxiv. q. i. Quisquis pro (C.24 q.1 c.38) et c. Subdiaconus (C.24 q.1 c.39) "degradatus."
⟨24.3.⟩ C. xxiii. q. vii. Quicumque (C.23 q.7 c.1) "quisquis pro aliquo."
⟨24.4.⟩ Contra.
⟨24.5.⟩ C. xxiv. q. i. Ait (C.24 q.1 c.35), Aperte (C.24 q.1 c.36), Miramur (C.24 q.1 c.37).

23.15. *post §23.13 tr.* F ‖ xcii.] xiii. P2 ‖ vacans] ecclesia *add.* F ‖ etiamsi] etsi A L Vb, si Ma, et P1 ‖ popolus] populum Ba **23.16.** *marg.* P2 ‖ xi.] xxxi. L, i. P1 ‖ Istud] Illum F, Illud P1 ‖ ergo—consensu *om.* P1 ‖ sequenti] consequenti Ma **23.17.** *marg.* P2 ‖ vii.] xvii. P1 ‖ Episcopum] Episcopus Vp ‖ de *om.* A L ‖ diocesi] diocesis A, odio P1 ‖ suadetur] suadentur A, *om.* F, suadeatur Fr, suadent Mu1 ‖ manere *om.* F, inanere P2 **23.18.** Illud] vero *add.* Ma, c. *praem.* Mu1, Istud Vp ‖ nolumus] volumus C, enim *add.* Ma ‖ et c. *om.* Ma, enim P1 ‖ c. *om.* L ‖ Relatum] Relatam L **23.19.** xxxvi.] xxxv. P1 ‖ c.] q. L P2, q. ultima *praem.* Mu1 ‖ conveniant] coveniat A C L P2, conveniantur P1 **23.20.** *om. per totum* A Ba C L Ma Mu1 P1 P2 Vb Vp ‖ D.] C. *male* F ‖ habere poterit *tr.* Fr **24.** = 17 C, 13 O, 5 P2, 93 P1 ‖ *§24—§24.7 om. per totum* G ‖ in *om.* P2 ‖ iudicio seculari *tr.* Ma ‖ iudicio] iudici P2 ‖ iudici] in iudicio *et ante* ecclesiastico *tr.* Ma ‖ plenam *om.* P1 ‖ facit] facere C, ut *add.* F, *ante* fidem *tr.* P1 **24.1.** *§24.1—§24.7 om. per totum* O ‖ *post §23.19 tr.* P1 ‖ i. Multi] ultima C ‖ ii. … i. *tr.* F ‖ i.] ii. A Mu1 P1 P2 Vb Vp ‖ Multi] corriguntur *add.* Mu1 ‖ sive seculari] secularive P2 ‖ sive] sine A F L, si in Vp **24.2.** *om. per totum* P1 ‖ *post §24.3 tr.* F Ma ‖ xxiv.] xxxiii. L Vb ‖ Quisquis] c. *praem.* Mu1 ‖ pro *om.* L, aliquo *add.* Ma, aliquo apud *add.* Mu1 ‖ et c. *om.* F, C. eadem q. eadem Ma ‖ et *om.* L ‖ Subdiaconus] apud *praem.* Ba F P2 ‖ degradatus] degratatur *cum* ur *exp. et corr.* L **24.3.** xxiii.] xxvii. *cum* v. *exp. et corr.* P1 ‖ Quicumque] c. *praem.* Mu1 ‖ quisquis—aliquo *om.* L ‖ aliquo] aliquando P1 **24.4.** Contrarium Mu1, Econtra P2 **24.5.** *post §24.7 tr.* Mu1 ‖ xxiv.] xxxiii. L ‖ i.] ii. P2 ‖ Ait] Celestinus *add.* Ma, c. *praem.* Mu1 ‖ Aperte] et c. *praem.* Mu1 ‖ Miramur *om.* F, et c. *praem.* Mu1

⟨23.15.⟩ D.92 c.8.
⟨23.16.⟩ C.11 q.1 c.20.
⟨23.17.⟩ C.7 q.1 c.25.
⟨23.18.⟩ C.31 q.1 c.3 and c.4.
⟨23.19.⟩ C.36 q.2 c.11.
⟨23.20.⟩ D.17 c.2.

⟨24.⟩ A proof made in a secular court is valid in an ecclesiastical court.
⟨24.1.⟩ C.2 q.1 c.18.
⟨24.2.⟩ C.24 q.1 c.38 and c.39.
⟨24.3.⟩ C.23 q.7 c.1.
⟨24.4.⟩ Against.
⟨24.5.⟩ C.24 q.1 c.35, c.36, c.37.

⟨24.6.⟩ C. xi. q. i. Christianis (C.11 q.1 c.12) "servitutis addici," "per archidiaconem."

⟨24.7.⟩ C. xi. q. i. Si quis sacerdotum (C.11 q.1 c.18), ibi est autenticum quod sic incipit: "si vero."

⟨25.⟩ In minoribus ordinibus, meritis, virtutibus, vitiis, dampnum lucro non compensatur.

⟨25.1.⟩ C. xxxiii. q. v. c. i. (C.33 q.5 c.1) "non vult," "tali lucro."

⟨25.2.⟩ Q. eadem Quod Deo (C.33 q.5 c.4) "magis inobedientie" et in fine.

⟨25.3.⟩ C. eadem q. iv. c. penultimo (C.33 q.4 c.12) et ultimo (C.33 q.4 c.13).

⟨25.4.⟩ C. xiv. q. v. Forte aliquis (C.14 q.5 c.3), Inmolans (C.14 q.5 c.2).

⟨25.5.⟩ Q. eadem Neque enim (C.14 q.5 c.9) "ideo rapinam" et c. Denique (C.14 q.5 c.10).

⟨25.6.⟩ C. i. q. i. Non est putanda (C.1 q.1 c.27).

⟨25.7.⟩ C. xxii. q. ii. Primum capitale (C.22 q.2–3 c.8) proprie finem.

⟨25.8.⟩ Q. eadem Ne quis arbitretur (C.22 q.2–3 c.14).

⟨25.9.⟩ D. lv. Si evangelica (D.55 c.13) in fine capituli.

⟨25.10.⟩ Contra.

⟨25.11.⟩ C. xiv. q. v. Qui habetis aliquid de malo (C.14 q.5 c.14).

24.6. *om. per totum* C ‖ Christianis] Christianus F Mu1, Christiane P2 ‖ addici—archidiaconem] vidua et pauper P1 ‖ addici] adducti A Vb, adduci F, adducta L, adhuc P2, ad duo Vp ‖ per archidiaconem *om.* Ba Ma P2 ‖ per] et *praem.* Vp ‖ archidiaconem] archiepiscopum Mu1 ‖ per] et *praem.* F **24.7.** C.—i. *om.* P1 ‖ xi.] eadem Mu1 ‖ q. i. *om.* Ma ‖ i. *om.* C, eadem Mu1 ‖ ibi—sic] vel est adquisitio P1 ‖ autenticum] autem C ‖ quod] qui C, quii P2 ‖ sic] si Vp ‖ incipit] ancipit Ma ‖ si vero] quicumque P1 **25.** = 35 C, 24 O, 102 P1 ‖ *§ 25—§ 25.16 om. per totum* G P2 ‖ *om. per totum* Mu1 ‖ minoribus] moribus A Ma, omnibus F L, maioribus P1 ‖ ordinibus] ordininibus *cum* ni[1] *exp.* O ‖ vitiis *om.* A, iudiciis L ‖ dampnum] dandum L ‖ lucro] locus Ba, *om.* P1 ‖ non *exp.* F, sic P1 ‖ compensatur] ut *add.* F **25.1.** *§ 25.1—§ 25.16 om. per totum* O ‖ vult] Deus *add.* L Mu1 **25.2.** Q. eadem] et c. Mu1, *om.* P1 ‖ Q.] C. L Ma ‖ eadem] q. eadem *add.* Ma ‖ inobedientie] inobedienti C, inebe. P1 ‖ et in fine *om.* Ma P1 **25.3.** C. eadem] et P1 ‖ iv.] eadem Ma ‖ ultimo … penultimo *tr.* L ‖ ultimo] et § dictum in fine *add.* P1 **25.4.** Forte] c. *praem.* Mu1 ‖ aliquis] dedero Mu1 ‖ Inmolans *ante* Forte *tr.* Ma **25.5.** Q. eadem] et c. Mu1, *om.* P1 ‖ Q.] et *praem.* Ba, C. L, *om.* Ma ‖ Neque enim *om.* L ‖ enim *om.* Mu1, ei P1 ‖ ideo] in A C L Vb Vp ‖ rapinam—Denique *in § 25.2 post* fine *tr.* Ba ‖ rapinam] penitentiam P1, rapina Vp ‖ et *om.* Ba Ma ‖ c. *om.* L Ma **25.6.** i.[2]] eadem Ma **25.7.** xxii.] xxi. Ma ‖ Primum] c. *praem.* Mu1 ‖ capitale *om.* Mu1 **25.8.** Q. eadem] et L, et c. Mu1, *om.* P1 ‖ Q.] et *praem.* Ba, C. eadem *praem.* Ma **25.9.** Si] c. *praem.* Mu1 ‖ evangelica] invangelica A ‖ capituli *om.* A Ma P1 **25.10.** Contrarium Mu1 **25.11.** *post § 25.9 tr.* F ‖ Qui] c. Quod Mu1 Vp ‖ habetis] habeas *cum* habeat *praem. et exp.* C, habeas P1

⟨24.6.⟩ C.11 q.1 c.12.

⟨24.7.⟩ C.11 q.1 c.18, there it is authentic what begins like this: "if in truth."

⟨25.⟩ In minor orders, in merits, in virtues, and in vices, loss cannot be compensated by gain.

⟨25.1.⟩ C.33 q.5 c.1.

⟨25.2.⟩ C.33 q.5 c.4 and at the end.

⟨25.3.⟩ C.33 q.4 c.12 and c.13.

⟨25.4.⟩ C.14 q.5 c.3, c.2.

⟨25.5.⟩ C.14 q.5 c.9 and c.10.

⟨25.6.⟩ C.1 q.1 c.27.

⟨25.7.⟩ C.22 q.2–3 c.8 at the very end.

⟨25.8.⟩ C.22 q.2–3 c.14.

⟨25.9.⟩ D.55 c.13.

⟨25.10.⟩ Against.

⟨25.11.⟩ C.14 q.5 c.14.

⟨25.12.⟩ C. xxii. q. iv. § Sed cum his (C.22 q.4 d.p.c.22) et c. Innocens (C.22 q.4 c.23).

⟨25.13.⟩ C. xxii. q. ii. Si quelibet (C.22 q.2–3 c.20) et cuilibet.

⟨25.14.⟩ C. eadem q. iv. Quod David (C.22 q.4 c.3) et c. Iuravit (C.22 q.4 c.4) et in pluribus capitulis.

⟨25.15.⟩ D. xiv. c. i. (D.14 c.1) et ii. (D.14 c.2).

⟨25.16.⟩ C. xxxii. q. iv. Dixit Sara (C.32 q.4 c.3).

⟨26.⟩ Generali verbo non omnia continentur.

⟨26.1.⟩ D. ix. Quicumque (D.9 p.c.1) "primum," ergo invidus et infidelis.

⟨26.2.⟩ C. xi. q. iii. Si episcopus (C.11 q.3 c.4) "omnia" et c. Si quis episcopus (C.11 q.3 c.7) "omnes ab ecclesia."

⟨26.3.⟩ C. eadem q. eadem Si quis dampnatur (C.11 q.3 c.6) "omnes abici" et c. Si autem (C.11 q.3 c.11), "omnes ergo exempti."

⟨26.4.⟩ C. ii. q. i. Multi corriguntur (C.2 q.1 c.18) "non utique fornicariis."

⟨26.5.⟩ C. i. q. ultima Qui in qualibet (C.1 q.7 c.10).

⟨26.6.⟩ D. xii. Illa (D.12 c.11) "totum hoc genus."

⟨26.7.⟩ D. xviii. Propter ecclesiasticas (D.18 c.4) "quibus de omnibus causis."

⟨26.8.⟩ C. i. q. ultima c. Qui in qualibet (C.1 q.7 c.10).

25.12. xxii.] eadem Ma ‖ iv.] eadem Ma, v. Vp ‖ c. Innocens … § Sed cum his *tr.* Mu1 ‖ §—Innocens *om.* (*homoiotel.*) P1 ‖ et c. *om.* Ma ‖ et *om.* F ‖ Innocens] credit *add.* Ma **25.13.** *om. per totum* (*homoiotel.*) P1 ‖ xxii.] eadem Ma ‖ ii.] i. Ma ‖ Si] c. *praem.* Mu1 ‖ et *om.* Vp ‖ et cuilibet *om.* F Fr, culpa Ma ‖ et *om.* C Mu1 **25.14.** *post § 25.11 tr.* Ma ‖ C.—iv. *om.* (*homoiotel.*) P1 ‖ C. eadem] et Ba Mu1 ‖ iv.] iii. A ‖ Quod] Qui C, *om.* F, Quia L ‖ David] quidem Vp ‖ et[1]—Iuravit *om.* Ma ‖ et[1] *om.* A F ‖ c. *om.* F ‖ in *om.* L Ma Vp ‖ capitulis *om.* L, *ante* pluribus *tr.* Ma **25.15.** *om. per totum* F ‖ *post § 25.16 tr.* C Ma P1 ‖ xiv.] quod *add.* P1 ‖ et *om.* P1 Vb **25.16.** C.] D. Mu1, P1 ‖ xxxii.—iv.] liv. P1 ‖ iv.] iii. A Ba C G Mu1 Vb Vp, ii. F ‖ Sara *om.* Vb **26.** = 36 C, 25 O, 103 P1, 1 P2 ‖ *§ 26—§ 26.27 om. per totum* G ‖ Generali] Naturali L ‖ verbo] nomine C, *om.* O, *vac.* P1 ‖ omnia non *tr.* P2 ‖ non *om.* C ‖ continentur] comprehendi ut F, non *praem. et exp.* P1 **26.1.** *§ 26.1—§ 26.27 om. per totum* O ‖ ix.] xi. L P1 ‖ Quicumque] c. *praem.* Mu1 ‖ primum] premium Fr, primus Mu1, *om.* P2 ‖ et] vel Vp ‖ infidelis] infidelem P1 **26.2.** Si[1]] c. *praem.* Mu1 ‖ episcopus] episcopi L, quisquam *add.* Ma, episcopo P2 ‖ et c. *om.* F, C. eadem q. eadem Ma ‖ c. *om.* P1 ‖ omnes *om.* F, et quod *cum* et *exp.* P2, omnia Vp **26.3.** C.—eadem[2]] et c. Mu1, *om.* P1 ‖ C. eadem] et Ba P2, *om.* C F L Vb Vp ‖ quis] episcopus *add.* Fr ‖ dampnatur] dampnatus L ‖ abici] clerici dec. *cum abbr. signo* Ma ‖ et c. *om.* F P1, C. eadem q. eadem Ma ‖ omnes] ergo que sunt P1 **26.4.** i.] ii. A Ba C F L P2 Vb Vp ‖ utique] huius mundi Fr ‖ fornicariis *om.* L, fornicarunt Ma, fornicatoris Mu1, fornicarii P1 P2 **26.5.** *om. per totum* A Ba C F L Ma Mu1 P1 P2 Vp **26.6.** Illa *post* genus *tr.* L **26.7.** *om. per totum* A Ba C L Mu1 P1 P2 Vb Vp ‖ xviii.] viii. F ‖ quibus *om.* Ma ‖ de] his *add.* Ma ‖ causis *om.* Ma **26.8.** *om. per totum* A Ba C F L Ma P1 P2 Vb Vpa

⟨25.12.⟩ C.22 q.4 d.p.c.22 and c.23.
⟨25.13.⟩ C.22 q.2–3 c.20, 'any' and 'to any.'
⟨25.14.⟩ C.22 q.4 c.3 and c.4 and in many chapters.
⟨25.15.⟩ D.14 c.1 and c.2.
⟨25.16.⟩ C.32 q.4 c.3.

⟨26.⟩ Not all things are contained in a general word.
⟨26.1.⟩ D.9 p.c.1, therefore 'hostile' and 'faithless.'
⟨26.2.⟩ C.11 q.3 c.4 and c.7.
⟨26.3.⟩ C.11 q.3 c.6 and c.11.
⟨26.4.⟩ C.2 q.1 c.18.
⟨26.5.⟩ C.1 q.7 c.10.
⟨26.6.⟩ D.12 c.11.
⟨26.7.⟩ D.18 c.4.
⟨26.8.⟩ C.1 q.7 c.10.

⟨26.9.⟩ D. lxv. Mos aut (D.65 c.6) "parilis molis est."

⟨26.10.⟩ D. lxxx. Non debere (D.80 c.5).

⟨26.11.⟩ C. x. q. i. Quicumque (C.10 q.1 c.5) "omnia previdet."

⟨26.12.⟩ C. xii. q. i. Expedit (C.12 q.1 c.13) "omnium que." ⟨26.13.⟩ Illud omnis defectus more nature suscepit.

⟨26.14.⟩ Contra.

⟨26.15.⟩ D. xi. Catholica (D.11 c.8) "universali traditione maiorum nichilominus tota."

⟨26.16.⟩ C. xi. q. iii. Ad mensam (C.11 q.3 c.24) "omnem fidelem."

⟨26.17.⟩ D. xix. Si Romanorum (D.19 c.1) "dicendo vere omnia."

⟨26.18.⟩ D. lxvi. Si evangelica admonitio (D.55 c.13).

⟨26.19.⟩ C. iii. q. ix. Omnia (C.3 q.9 c.4).

⟨26.20.⟩ C. ix. q. iii. Cum simus (C.9 q.3 c.3) "omnes."

⟨26.21.⟩ C. x. q. i. Regenda (C.10 q.1 c.4) "unaqueque" et Quecumque (C.10 q.1 c.5).

⟨26.22.⟩ C. i. q. iii. Salvator (C.1 q.3 c.8) "non terminantem locum."

⟨26.23.⟩ C. i. q. i. Sunt nonnulli (C.1 q.1 c.114) "sed ab omni munere."

⟨26.24.⟩ In quedam extravaganti Senonensi archiepiscopo postquam ei simpliciter licet (JL 12293 = WH 944 = X. 1.29.5).

⟨26.25.⟩ C. xxxi. q. i. Deus (C.31 q.1 c.13) "non dicit primus vel secundus vel tercius" et C. xxiii. q. v. Si non licet (C.23 q.5 c.9) "non occides nichil deinde addito nec ipse utique," "videtur exceptus."

26.9. *om. per totum* A Ba C F L Ma Mu1 P1 P2 Vb ‖ aut] antiquus Fr ‖ molis] mos Fr **26.10.** *om. per totum* A Ba C F L Ma Mu1 P1 P2 Vb **26.11.** *om. per totum* A Ba C F L Ma Mu1 P1 P2 Vb **26.12.** *om. per totum* A Ba C F L Ma Mu1 P1 P2 Vb **26.13.** *om. per totum* A Ba C F L Ma Mu1 P1 P2 Vb **26.14.** *om. per totum* Vp ‖ Econtra A, Contrarium Mu1 **26.15.** *post §26.16 tr.* L ‖ universali] vel Ba L Vp, *om.* Ma Mu1 ‖ traditione] contraditione Ma ‖ maiorum—tota *om.* Ba P2 ‖ maiorum *om.* A C F L Mu1 P1 Vb ‖ tota] xi. *praem.* Ma, *om.* P1, toto Vb **26.16.** C.] eadem *add. et exp.* L ‖ omnem] omnes Vp ‖ fidelem] fideles Ma Vp **26.17.** *ante §26.14 tr.* C P1 ‖ xix.] xxi. L P1 ‖ Romanorum] Romatinorum *cum* ti *exp.* P1 ‖ dicendo] dicenda P1 ‖ vere *om.* A Ba C L Ma Mu1 P1 P2 Vb Vp, vero Fr **26.18.** *om. per totum* A C L Ma Mu1 P2 Vb ‖ admonitio] antique F, aliquem casuum *add.* Vp **26.19.** *om. per totum* A C Ma P1 ‖ ix.] viii. P2 **26.20.** *om. per totum* A Ba C F L Ma Mu1 P1 P2 Vb ‖ C.] Q. *male* Vp **26.21.** *om. per totum* A Ba C F L Ma Mu1 P1 P2 Vb ‖ i.] iii. *cum* ii. *exp.* Vp **26.22.** *om. per totum* A Ba C L P1 P2 Vp ‖ non—locum] indefinite loquentem (dicentem Fr) F, in fine Ma **26.23.** *om. per totum* A Ba C L Mu1 P1 P2 Vb Vp ‖ sed *om.* Ma ‖ munere] quomodo Ma **26.24.** *om. per totum* A Ba C L Mu1 P1 P2 Vb Vp ‖ In *om.* Ma ‖ quedam] quondam Ma ‖ simpliciter licet *om.* Ma **26.25.** *§26.25—§26.26 post §26.21 tr.* Vp ‖ *om. per totum* A Ba C L Mu1 P1 P2 Vb ‖ C.[1]—et *om.* Vp ‖ non] masculum *praem.* Ma ‖ vel—tercius *om.* Ma ‖ tercius] quartus Fr ‖ nichil—exceptus] scilicet est quod ait omnia occidit ei in manibus, ergo et sui ipsius traditor est Vp ‖ nichil] nec F ‖ addito] adiuto F ‖ utique *om.* F ‖ videtur] intelligatur Fr

⟨26.9.⟩ D.65 c.6.

⟨26.10.⟩ D.80 c.5.

⟨26.11.⟩ C.10 q.1 c.5.

⟨26.12.⟩ C.12 q.1 c.13. ⟨26.13.⟩ That assumed all the defects, following the example of nature.[1]

⟨26.14.⟩ Against.

⟨26.15.⟩ D.11 c.8.

⟨26.16.⟩ C.11 q.3 c.24.

⟨26.17.⟩ D.19 c.1.

⟨26.18.⟩ D.55 c.13.

⟨26.19.⟩ C.3 q.9 c.4.

⟨26.20.⟩ C.9 q.3 c.3.

⟨26.21.⟩ C.10 q.1 c.4 and c.5.

⟨26.22.⟩ C.1 q.3 c.8.

⟨26.23.⟩ C.1 q.1 c.114.

⟨26.24.⟩ In some extravagant decretal to the archbishop of Sens (JL 12293 = WH 944 = X. 1.29.5).

⟨26.25.⟩ C.31 q.1 c.13 and C.23 q.5 c.9.

1 The meaning of the sentence, which appears only in Vb, is not clear.

⟨26.26.⟩ In psalmo: “Omnia subiecisti” etc. (Ps 8:8), quod apostolicus exponens ait: “In eo enim quod omnia ei subiecit, nichil dimisit non subiectum ei” (Heb 2:8).

⟨26.27.⟩ D. lxi. Miramur (D.61 c.5) “in cuiusquam persona.”

26.26. *om. per totum* A Ba C F L Ma P1 P2 ‖ In—ait] Sed in epistola ad Ebreos Vp ‖ ei[1] *om.* Vp ‖ ei[1] omnia *tr.* Mu1 ‖ ei[2]] Idem super illum locum auctoritas ait quia in eo quod dixit omnia nichil d. non. *add.* Vp **26.27.** *om. per totum* A Ba C F L P1 P2 Vp

⟨26.26.⟩ In psalm: "Thou hast subjected all things" etc. (Ps 8:8), which the apostle explains in these words: "For in that he hath subjected all things to him, he left nothing not subject to him" (Heb 2:8).

⟨26.27.⟩ D.61 c.5.

Synoptic Table of the Brocards in Part II

Standard order	A	A1	Ba	C	F	G	L	Ma	Mu1	O	P1	P2	Vb	Vp
1	1		1	1	1	1	1	1	1	1	1		1	1
2	2		2	2	2	2	2	2	2	2	2		2	2
3	3		3	23	3		3	3	3	22	100		3	3
4	4		4	24	4		4	4	4	23	101	6	4	4
5	5		5	12	5	3	5	5	5	11	3		5	5
6	6		6	20	6		6	6	6	19	97		6	6
7	7		7	21	7		7	7	7	20	98		7	7
8	8		8	22	8		8	8	8	21	99	7	8	8
9	9		9	10	9	4	9	9	9	9	4	8	9	9
10	10		10	11	10	5	10	10	10	10	5		10	10
11	11	6	11	16	11	6	11	11	11	15	6, 80, 88	9	11	11
12	12		12	17	12		12	12	12	16	94		12	12
13	13		13	18	13		13	13	13	17	95		13	13
14	14		14	19	14		14	14	14	18	96	10	14	14
15	15		15	13	15	7	15	15	15	12	7	11	15	15
16	16		16	3	16	8	16	16	16	3	8		16	16
17	17		17	4	17	9	17	17	17		9		17	17
18	18		18	5	18	10	18	18	18	4	10	12	18	18
19	19		19	6	19	11	19	19	19	5	11		19	19
20	20		20	7	20	12	20	20	20	6	12		20	20
21	21		21	8	21	13	21	21	21	7	13	2	21	21
22	22		22	9	22	14	22	22	22	8	14	3	22	22
23	23		23	15	23		23	23	23	14	92	4	23	23
24	24		24	14	24		24	24	24	13	93	5	24	24
25	25		25	25	25		25	25	25	24	102		25	25
26	26		26	26	26		26	26	26	25	103	1	26	26

Part III

1 Critical Table of Contents

Group α

Manuscripts in which this group appears: A, G, L, Mu1, P1, and Vb.

α is a sequence of 26 brocards. The first 15 occur in a relatively standard order, while the last eleven are more heterogeneous. Vb contains only one brocard for this group, while in the others many of them are present. In the manuscripts A, G, L, Mu1, and P1, this group opens Part III. Manuscripts A and G consist only of this group, apart from the interpolation of a single brocard in the latter. In Mu1, almost half of the brocards are from α.

Notably, α contains two brocards that correspond to an equal number of *distinctiones* from the collection *"Hec sunt que suadent*:" α19 to no. 1 and α1 to no. 2.

1. Levius punitur qui commissum sponte confitetur, quam qui in iure convictus vel confessus est.
   1 A G L Mu1 P1 *om. per totum* Vb

   convictus] sponte *praem.* L vel *om.* L confessus … convictus *tr.* P1 confessus] consensus G, *om.* L est *om.* A Mu1

2. Quod a multis peccatis inultum est.
   2 G L Mu1 P1 *om. per totum* A Vb

   inultum] indultum L

3. Est honesta fornicatio.
   2 A, 3 G L P1 *om. per totum* Mu1 Vb

4. Propter alterum delictum, alium non debere puniri.
   3 A Mu1, 4 G L *om. per totum* P1 Vb

   alterum[1]] alterius L alium] alterum *male* A Mu1 G, alius L

5. Obest filio delictum patris et contra, et unius alteri.
   4 A Mu1, 5 G L *om. per totum* P1 Vb

   contra *om.* G et[2] *om.* A G alteri] alterius L

 | DOI:10.1163/9789004713239_012

6. Laicus nec gratis beneficium ecclesie habere potest.
5 A Mu1, 6 G L *om. per totum* P1 Vb

gratis] generalis L ecclesie *om.* Mu1

7. Solet plus timeri et observari quod specialiter permittitur quam quod generali sponsione continetur.
6 A Mu1, 7 G L *om. per totum* P1 Vb

et observari *ante* quam *tr.* G L et *om.* Mu1 observari *ante* quam *tr.* Mu1 quod[1]] quo A permittitur] permittatur G, probatur L quod[2] *om.* A generali] generaliter L sponsione *om.* L continetur] concutitur G, *om.* L

8. Eadem severitate voluntatem sceleris quam effectum puniri.
7 A Mu1, 8 G L, 4 P1 *om. per totum* Vb

Eadem] Ex *praem.* P1 sceleris *om.* L quam] qua G

9. Pro eventu rei quedam tolerantur.
8 A Mu1, 10 G, 9 L, 6 P1 *om. per totum* Vb

pro eventu] proventu A quedam] quodam A

10. Non videtur posse fieri quod iure fieri non potest.
9 A Mu1, 11 G, 10 L, 7 P1, 174 Vb

videtur] dicitur Vb posse *om.* L iure] de *praem.* P1 Vb

11. Non declinat penam qui mentem legis circumvenit.
10 A Mu1, 12 G, 11 L, 8 P1 *om. per totum* Vb

declinat] evitat P1 qui *rep.* L mentem] in etate L legis] cum declinat *add.* L

12. A contrario sensu non esse argumentum eliciendum.
11 A Mu1, 13 G, 12 L, 9 P1 *om. per totum* Vb

A *om.* G P1 esse] est P1 argumentum non esse *tr.* A eliciendum] eiciendum A

13. Gravius est dare consanguineis quam aliis.
12 A Mu1, 14 G, 10 P1 *om. per totum* L Vb

est *om.* Mu1

14. Quod preter formam vel contra formam fit, pro infecto habetur.
13 A L Mu1, 15 G, 11 P1 *om. per totum* Vb

contra … preter *tr.* Mu1 formam[2] *om.* P1 habetur] habent L

15. Facilius uni detrahitur et alii conceditur quam aliquid de novo constituatur.
14 A L Mu1, 16 G, 12 P1 *om. per totum* Vb

Facilius] Falcilius *cum* l[1] *exp.* Mu1 uni] viam L et *om.* L quam] quoniam L aliquid] alii L de novo *rep.* A

16. Arg. contra eos qui nova inveniunt et vetera vilipendunt.
17 G, 15 L Mu1 *om. per totum* A P1 Vb

Arg. *om.* L inveniunt] vilipendunt L

17. Cum aliquid prohibetur, id prohiberi videtur per quod venitur ad idem.
15 A Mu1, 18 G, 16 L, 13 P1 *om. per totum* Vb

Cum] Quando Mu1 aliquid] quid A, *om.* L prohibetur] prohibeatur A, prohibet L quod] quo A venitur] pervenitur A idem] ipsum P1

18. Arg.: maior habundans cautela non nocet exigi, speciale quandoque ubi speciale sufficeret.
19 G, 17 L, 83 P1 *om. per totum* A Mu1 Vb

Arg. *om.* P1 maior] super P1 maior] exigitur securitas *add.* G, interdum est † qui cautelas faciente *add.* L habundans] abendas L cautela] cautelam *cum* m *exp.* G exigi—sufficeret *om.* P1 exigi] arg. *praem.* G speciale[2]] generale G

19. Hec sunt cause que suadent ne spoliatus restituatur vel ordine iudiciario non observato spolietur.
20 G, 18 L, 17 Mu1 *om. per totum* A P1 Vb

ordine] ordinem L   iudiciario] diaconi L

Criminis infamia.

Cautela iacture.
Cautela] Cautele L

Coherentie ratio specialis.
Coherentie] Coherentio L

Malitie deprehensio.

Actio scandali.
Actio] Vitatio G

Defectus iudicii.

Delicti publicatio.

20. De mutatione et proprii nominis significatione.
22 G, 19 L, 18 Mu1   *om. per totum* A P1 Vb

et *om.* G   proprii] impropria G, propria Mu1   nominis] nominum G

21. Quod bene gestum est nullo superveniente delicto irritatur.
23 G, 20 L, 19 Mu1, 14 P1   *om. per totum* A Vb

nullo *om.* L   delicto superveniente *tr.* P1

22. Unius testimonium amittitur.
24 G   *om. per totum* A L Mu1 P1 Vb

23. Presumpcionem inducit.
25 G   *om. per totum* A L Mu1 P1 Vb

Contra.

24. Non esse precipitandam sententiam.
= 26 G, 21 L, 20 Mu1, 15 P1   *om. per totum* A Vb

precipitandam] precipitandand *cum* nd^2 *exp. et corr.* Mu1

25. Frustra ab alio quis exigit exibendum quod negat debitum.
= 27 G, 22 L, 21 Mu1, 16 P1 *om. per totum* A Vb

quis ab alio *tr.* P1 exibendum] exigendum *et ante* exigit *tr.* P1 quod] qui P1

26. Ubi culpa non deprehenditur, ad cautelam pena imponitur.
= 28 G, 23 L, 22 Mu1, 17 P1 *om. per totum* A Vb

Ubi] In L deprehenditur] est ibi P1 imponitur] impositur L

Contrarium.
om. per totum L Mu1 P1

Group β

Manuscripts in which this group appears: A1, Ba, C, F, G, L, Ma, Mu1, O, P1, P2, Vb, and Vp.

β is a sequence of seven brocards that is found in thirteen manuscripts. Ba, F, Ma, and O begin with the first brocard in this series, while A1 and P2 start with other brocards from this group. Although in most of the manuscripts the brocards are in the same sequence, in Vb some of them are divided into two different groups.

1. Principium spectandum.
8 A1, 1 Ba F Ma O, 5 C, 28 L, 23 Mu1, 85 P1, 6 P2, 20 Vb, 9 Vp *om. per totum* G

Principium] Initium Ma P1 spectandum] esse *praem.* C L, esse *add.* O, ut *add.* F

Contra.
Econtra Ba P2, Contrarium L Mu1 Vp, finem spectandum *add.* Ma, *om. per totum* O

2. Punitur qui alias esset excusandus vel misericorditer tollerandus, ne culpa per exemplum propagetur.
4 A1, 2 Ba F Ma O, 6 C, 29 L, 24 Mu1, 18 *et* 86 P1, 7 P2, 21 Vb, 10 Vp *om. per totum* G

vac. Mu1 Punitur] Punitus A1 qui] quod P1 P1$_1$, quis Vp alias] aliter L O esset] esse L excusandus *om.* F, de⟩pr⟨ecandus L vel *om.* F vel—tollerandus *om.* A1 C, tolerando *cum* o^2 *exp. et corr. us* P2 culpa] culpe F, quoquo modo *add.* Vb per] in C P1 exemplum] eius P1_1 propagetur] *post* culpa *tr.* A1, ut *add.* F, ageretur L, *ante* per *tr.* P1_1

Contra.
Contrarium L, *vac.* Mu1, *om. per totum* O, Econtra P2

3. Ordinis turbatio non irritat factum.
5 A1, 3 Ba F Ma O, 7 C, 30 L, 87 P1, 8 P2, 22 Vb, 11 Vp *om. per totum* G Mu1

irritat factum] inmitatur C irritat] mutat F O factum] ut *add.* F, *om.* P1

Contra.
Contrarium L, Econtra P2, *om. per totum* O

4. Hoc verbum sine personarum acceptione privilegia non excludit.
1 A1, 4 Ba F Ma O, 10 C, 31 L, 91 P1, 23 Vb, 12 Vp *om. per totum* G Mu1 P2

personarum *om.* C acceptione] exceptione A1, *ante* personarum *tr.* Ba, acceptatione C privilegia] privilegium P1 non excludit *ante* hoc *tr.* P1 excludit] ut *add.* F

5. Qui occasionem dampni dat, dampnum dedisse videtur.
2 A1, 5 Ba F Ma O, 8 C, 9 G, 32 L, 5 *et* 89 P1, 1 P2, 24 Vb, 13 Vp *om. per totum* Mu1

Qui] Quod Vp occasionem] accione A1, occasanem F dampnum] et *praem.* Ba videtur] ideoque tenetur *add.* A1 Ma O Vb Vp, ut F

Contra.
om. per totum Ba O P1, *vac.* P2, Contrarium L

6. Rationis est ubi maior culpa, maiori plectatur vindicta.
7 A1, 9 C, 6 F Ma O, 33 L, 90 P1, 10 P2, 41 Vb, 14 Vp *om. per totum* Ba G Mu1

Rationis—ubi *om.* Ma est *om.* Vp culpa *om.* C maiori—vindicta] magis est puniendi Ma plectatur] puniatur *et ante* maiori *tr.* C, multetur P1 vindicta] ut *add.* F, culpa *del. et corr.* O, pena P1

Contra minorem culpam gravius, contra maiorem levius puniri pro variis adiacentibus causis.

om. per totum P2 maiorem ... minorem *tr.* Ma Vb Vp maiorem] minorem *cum* i *exp. et corr.* ai Vp culpam *om.* F, *post* puniri *tr.* P1 gravius] maius L levius ... gravius *tr.* Ma Vb contra² *om.* F O Vp puniri *ante* levius *tr.* F pro— causis *om.* Vp adiacentibus *om.* Ma causis adiacentibus *tr.* Vb causis] ut *add.* F

7. Que statuta sunt ex causa, causam non excedunt, cum propter ficte penitentes statutum sit ne lapsi reparentur, tamen ubi fictio non est cessat edictum.

= 3 A1, 4 C, 7 F Ma O, 34 L, 84 P1, 42 *et* 66 Vb, 15 Vp *om. per totum* Ba G Mu1 P2

Que] Generaliter *praem.* Vb sunt *om.* Vp ex causa] *ante* statuta *tr.* C Vb_1, ob causam Vb causam] tantum L excedunt] excedant A1 L Vb Vp cum— edictum *om.* C Ma Vb_1 cum] nam A1 P1, ut que Vb propter] super L penitentes] generaliter *add.* F O Vp statutum *post* sit *tr.* F, sententia vel *praem.* P1, *om.* Vb sit] est A1 P1, *om.* Vb, ut velim *add.* Vp ne *ante* sit *tr.* F reparentur] resurgant A1 P1, reperientur L ubi] si A1, *om.* Vb, ut *cum* t *exp. et corr.* Vp fictio] factione Vb non est *om.* Vb cessat] locum non habet A1 P1

Sed cessante causa cessat edictum.

om. per totum O

Sed] Sic Vb_1 edictum] ut *add.* A1 L Vp

Causa edicti notatur.

om. per totum O

notatur] notatus F, nomine Ma

Contra.

om. per totum O, Contrarium Vb_1

A talibus causam habuerit edictum quod est omnibus generale.

om. per totum L O

causam *post* edictum *tr.* P1, causa Vp habuerit] habuit Ma P1 quod—generale *om.* Ma quod] quia P1 est *om.* Vp omnibus generale] generale in omnibus F Vb Vp

Group γ

Manuscripts in which this group appears: Ba, C, L, Ma, Mu1, O, P1, P2, Vb, and Vp.

γ is a group of eight brocards, strongly connected with δ. The two groups are found in the same manuscripts, and in the majority of them γ precedes δ. The two could be considered as part of the same tradition, but I divided them because in two manuscripts (P2 and Vb) the two sequences are separated.

1. Nec rite factum mutatur, nec rite susceptum amittitur, superveniente delicto aliquo vel alio impedimento.
= 11 C, 35 L, 69 Ma, 8 O, 19 P1, 11 P2, 43 Vb, 24 Vp *om. per totum* Ba Mu1

mutatur] imputatur O rite] recte Ma P2 amittitur] admittitur O, *om.* P1 P2 aliquo—impedimento *om.* L aliquo *om.* C Ma P1 Vp, *ante* delicto *tr.* P2 alio] nullo P1, *om.* P2

Contra.
Contrarium L, *om. per totum* O

2. Vitiose quesitum vel factum in bonos usus conversum desinit esse vitiosum.
= 12 C, 37 L, 70 Ma, 9 O, 21 P1, 12 P2, 45 Vb, 25 Vp *om. per totum* Ba Mu1

Vitiose—factum *om.* P1 quesitum] dictum Vb conversum—esse] *ante* in *tr.* P1 esse] in bonum *add. et exp.* P1, *om.* P2 vitiosum] quod fuit conversum P1, *om.* P2

Contra.
om. per totum O, Rubrica econtra Vp

3. Recte permittimus, optamus, facimus quod volumus, ut deterius deteriora declinemus.
= 13 C, 36 L, 71 Ma, 10 O, 20 P1, 44 Vb, 26 Vp *om. per totum* Ba Mu1 P2

Recte *om.* C L quod] que P1 volumus] nolumus C Vb Vp ut—declinemus *om.* P1 Vb ut] in O deterius *om.* C L deteriora *om.* Ma declinemus] devitemus Ma, declinamus O, dectinemus Vp

Contra.

Contrarium L, *om. per totum* O

4. Nichil interest dolo an vi quid factum esse dicatur.

= 14 C, 38 L, 72 Ma, 11 O, 22 P1, 13 P2, 46 Vb, 27 Vp *om. per totum* Ba Mu1

interest] interesse P2 dolo] cum *praem.* Ma, an *praem.* P1 an vi] anni C, animi Vp quid] quod L Vp, aliquid P2

Contra: multum interest.

om. per totum O Contra] Contrarium L, Econtra Ma, Rubrica econtra Vp multum interest *om.* C L P1 Vb

5. Confessio vel consensus ignavia adhibitus vel metu extortus pro nullo habetur.

= 11 Ba, 15 C, 39 L, 73 Ma, 12 O, 23 P1, 14 P2, 47 Vb, 28 Vp *om. per totum* Mu1

vac. Ba vel[1] consensus *om.* P2 ignavia] ignorantia P1 adhibitus] adhibetur O, d *exp.* adhibita P2 vel[2] *om.* P2 metu] metus P1, motu Vp extortus] exceptus O, extorta P2 nullo] nichilo P2

Contra.

vac. Ba, *om. per totum* O, Contrarium *cum signo* L, Contrarium P2, Econtra Ma, Rubrica econtra Vp

6. Non dicitur bonum nisi duret bonum, nec consensus vel voluntas nisi duret, sicut nec versum nisi duret versum.

= 16 C, 40 L, 74 Ma, 43 Mu1, 13 O, 24 P1, 15 P2, 48 Vb, 29 Vp *om. per totum* Ba

Non] Nec L, Rubrica *praem.* Vp dicitur] videtur P1 bonum[2] *om.* O P1 nec[1]] vel P1 vel voluntas *rep.* Ma vel] neque C, *om.* L, nec Mu1 nisi[2] duret[2] voluntas *tr.* L nisi[2]—versum[1] *om.* (*homoiotel.*) P1 sicut] sic Mu1 nec[2]] neque C versum[1]] ut dicitur Ma, dicitur O Vp

Contra.

Contrarium Mu1, *om. per totum* O, Rubrica econtra Vp

7. Nichil actum creditur vel irritari meretur, quod agitur pretermissis his que ad rei substantiam vel modum vel formam vel sollempnitatem exiguntur.

= 19 Ba, 17 C, 41 L, 75 Ma, 25 P1, 16 P2, 172 Vb, 30 Vp *om. per totum* Mu1 O

Nichil—vel[1] *om.* P1 Nichil] Nisi Ma agitur] agi Ma vel modum *om.* Ma Vp exiguntur] exigunt ut Ba, exigendam C, exigentur Ma

Rei substantia.
om. per totum P1 Ad substantiam C L, Esse Ma Vp

Forma.
om. per totum P1 Ad formam C L

Solempnis.
om. per totum P1 Sollempnitas Ba Ma P2 Vp, Ad sollempnitatem (ut *add.* L) C L

Modus et ordo.
om. per totum P1 Modus et ordo] Ad modum et ordinem C L, ordo modus Ma, et ordo modus Vp et ordo *om.* Ba

Contra.
om. per totum C L, *post γ8 tr.* Vp

Esse.
om. per totum C L P1 Vb Vp esse] rei *add.* Ba

Forma.
om. per totum C L P1 Vb Vp

Sollempnitas.
om. per totum C L P1 Vb Vp

Modus.
om. per totum C L P1 Vb Vp

8. Hic deest persona legitima nec irritatur.
= 18 C, 42 L, 31 Vp *om. per totum* Ba Ma Mu1 O P1 P2 Vb

Hic] Hec Vp deest] est Vp legitima persona *tr.* L nec] neque C

Forma.
om. per totum Vp

Sollempnitas.
om. per totum Vp

Modus.
om. per totum Vp

Group δ

Manuscripts in which this group appears: Ba, C, L, Ma, Mu1, O, P1, P2, Vb, and Vp.

δ is a small series of six brocards connected to γ. While the group is mostly found in a close sequence, in L some of the brocards are scattered and in Vb they are repeated twice.

1. Cui non licet quod minus est, nec id quod plus est licebit.
6 Ba, 19 C, 76 Ma, 14 O, 26 P1, 2 P2, 25 Vb, 32 Vp *om. per totum* L Mu1

Cui] Cum O licet] id *add.* Vb plus ... minus *tr.* P1 est] non *praem. et exp.* Vp nec] neque C id *om.* P1 licebit (licet C) *post* id *tr.* C Ma O Vp plus] maius C O est *om.* C

Contra.
Econtra P2 Vb, *om. per totum* O

2. Ex alterius persona quis consequi potest quod ex sua non consequeretur.
7 Ba, 20 C, 77 Ma, 15 O, 27 P1, 3 P2, 26 *et* 68 Vb, 33 Vp *om. per totum* L Mu1

Ex] Rubrica *praem.* Vb consequi] consequitur P2 potest *om.* P2 consequeretur] potest P1, consequi non possit P2

Contra.
Contrarium Ba Vb_1, *om. per totum* O, Econtra P2

3. Nec persone locive prerogativa, nec rei utilitas efficit, ut ius alterius minuatur vel contra iuris ordinem quicquam admittatur.
= 8 Ba, 21 C, 98 L, 78 Ma, 16 O, 28 P1, 4 P2, 27 *et* 70 Vb, 34 Vp *om. per totum* Mu1

Nec] Non Ba L Vb, Ne Ma persone *om.* C Ma P2 Vb, *ante* nec *tr.* L locive] loci C Ma P2 Vb, loci nec L P1 utilitas] utilia P1 efficit] efficiuntur P1 ut *om.*

L ius] nisi Ma minuatur] imminuatur P1, minuant Vp ordinem iuris *tr.* L quicquam] aliquid P2 admittatur] statuatur L, amittatur O, admittant Vp

Contra.
Contrarium Ba Vb_1, *om. per totum* L O P1, Econtra P2

4. Quedam honeste fieri possunt et debent que in pactione deducta de honestantur.
9 Ba, 22 C, 99 L, 79 Ma, 17 O, 29 P1, 28 Vb, 35 Vp *om. per totum* L Mu1 P2

et debent *om.* P1 pactione] pactionem C, pacationem L deducta] ducta Ma, de vita Vp de *om.* Vp honestantur] honestant (ut *add.* Ba) Ba L, vel sic *add.* Vb

Contra.
om. per totum L O, in eisdem canonibus pactio videtur admissa *add.* Vb

5. Frustra debitum exigit qui quod debet non impendit.
= 10 Ba, 23 C, 80 Ma, 41 Mu1, 18 O, 5 P2, 29 Vb, 36 Vp *om. per totum* L P1

6. Ammonitio semper debet precedere vindictam.
= 24 C, 25 L, 81 Ma, 40 Mu1, 19 O, 30 Vb, 37 Vp *om. per totum* Ba P1 P2

Ammonitio] In initio L, alio dicio *exp. et corr. interl.* Ma semper *om.* L precedere debet *tr.* O Vp

Contra.
om. per totum L O

Group ε

Manuscripts in which this group appears: C, F, L, Ma, Mu1, P1, Vb, and Vp.

ε is a large group of 48 brocards. In some manuscripts (C, F, L, and Ma) the group follows a relatively stable order, while in others (P1 and Vp) we find small series of scattered brocards connected to it. Finally, in Mu1 and Vp there are only a few brocards from this group.

4. 28 Vb has merged both the rubrics and the allegations of δ4 and θ1. Each of the two parts of 28 Vb has been collated separately under the two respective brocards.

1. Multa sunt licita que non nisi maioris licentia sunt facienda.
= 25 C, 16 F, 15 Ma, 43 L, 139 Vb *om. per totum* Mu1 P1 Vp

non *om.* L licentia maioris *tr.* F maioris] maiores L, maiori Ma facienda] ut *add.* F, concedenda Ma

2. Nec ratione probationis, nec utilitatis, nec perfectionis, ordo iuris mutandus est.
= 26 C, 44 L, 16 Ma *om. per totum* F Mu1 P1 Vb Vp

Nec] contra *praem.* L probationis] pro bonis C nec[1]] neque C utilitatis] utilitas L nec[2]] neque C ordo iuris] vel ordinis L

3. Scire presumitur quod agitur loco quo conversatur.
= 27 C, 18 F, 45 L, 17 Ma *om. per totum* Mu1 P1 Vb Vp

agitur] agi Ma loco] ex eo *praem.* L conversatur] versatur ut F

4. Qui non redarguit licentiam dare videtur.
= 28 C, 17 F, 46 L, 18 Ma *om. per totum* Mu1 P1 Vb Vp

non] nondum Ma videtur] ut *add.* F

5. Aliud dicitur et aliud significatur.
= 29 C, 20 F Ma, 47 L, 140 Vb *om. per totum* Mu1 P1 Vp

6. Cui prohibetur maius, prohibetur etiam minus.
= 30 C, 21 F Ma, 48 L *om. per totum* Mu1 P1 Vb Vp

Cui] Qui C minus … maius *tr.* L etiam *om.* F Ma, et L minus] ut *add.* F

Contra.

7. Episcopo iudicem et accusatorem esse non licet.
= 31 C, 22 F, 141 Vb *om. per totum* L Ma Mu1 P1 Vp

Episcopo] Episcopum F et *om.* F esse] fieri F non *om.* Vb, ut *add.* F

8. Multa licent que in stipulatione deducta non licent.
= 23 F, 22 Ma *om. per totum* C L Mu1 P1 Vb Vp

licent[1]] fieri licet F stipulatione] pactionem F deducta] deduci F licent[2]] licet F

Contra.

9. Alicuius absentia plus impedit quam eiusdem presentis contradictio.
= 32 C, 24 F, 23 Ma *om. per totum* L Mu1 P1 Vb Vp

eiusdem presentis *om.* Ma eiusdem] eius F contradictio] conditio ut F

10. Mentem canonis circumveniendam non esse, et perinde puniendum eum qui contra mentem facit ac si contra verba faceret.
= 33 C, 27 F, 24 Ma *om. per totum* L Mu1 P1 Vb Vp

Mentem—et *om.* Ma perinde] Eque Ma puniendum] puniendus Ma eum *om.* Ma facit *om.* Ma ac] et Ma si] qui Ma verba] verbum Ma faceret] ut *add.* F, facit Ma

11. Quod semel est verum, semper est verum, ut.
= 28 F, 25 Ma *om. per totum* C L Mu1 P1 Vb Vp

12. Iudices ex officio suo testes inutiliter testificaturos repellere debere.
= 34 C, 29 F, 26 Ma *om. per totum* L Mu1 P1 Vb Vp

testificaturos] testificatos Ma debere repellere *tr.* Ma debere] ut *add.* F

13. Iudex ex officio suo infames a testimonio repellere debere.
= 35 C, 30 F, 27 Ma *om. per totum* L Mu1 P1 Vb Vp

Iudex] Iudices C, Iudicem F suo *om.* Ma infames—debere] debet infames testes repellere Ma debere] ut *add.* F

14. Iudices ex officio suo locum provisuri in quo partes absque metu adesse possint.
= 36 C, 31 F, 28 Ma, 42 Mu1 *om. per totum* L P1 Vb Vp

Iudices—suo] Debet etiam Ma Iudices] Iudicem F provisuri] provisurum F, providere *et ante* locum *tr.* Ma, promissuri Mu1 absque metu *om.* C absque] sine Mu1 possint adesse (ut *add.* F) *tr.* F Ma

15. Quod alias facere tenetur specialiter, vel captione pecuniaria, vel iuratoria, vel cartule emissione, exequi compellitur. Captione pecuniaria, ut.

= 37 C, 32 F, 74 Vb *om. per totum* L Ma Mu1 P1 Vp

alias] alios C facere] quid *praem.* C, quis *praem.* F captione] cautione C vel iuratoria *om.* Vb exequi compellitur] verbi gratia F Captione] Cautione C pecuniaria[2]] pecunia et iura Vb

Cautione iuratoria.

om. per totum Vb Cautione] Captione F iuratoria] ut *add.* F

Cartule emissione, ut.

ut *om.* C

16. Iudicem ex officio suo absque cause cognitione expoliatum non debere restituere.

= 38 C, 3 F, 29 Ma, 75 Vb *om. per totum* L Mu1 P1 Vp

Iudicem—suo *om.* Ma absque—cognitione *post* restituere *tr.* Ma non *om.* Vb debere] debet Ma restituere] ut *add.* F

17. Alium plerumque ex persona alterius honoramus.

= 39 C, 34 F, 30 Ma, 76 Vb *om. per totum* L Mu1 P1 Vp

Alium plerumque] alterium *et ante* honoramus *tr.* Ma honoramus] honorii C, ut *add.* F

Contra.

om. per totum C F Ma

18. In libro regum, Salomone inter meretrices iudicante bonus dolus laudatur.

= 71 C, 31 Ma *om. per totum* F L Mu1 P1 Vb Vp

In—regum *om.* Ma Salomone] Salomon Ma iudicante] iudicans Ma bonus dolus] de bono dolo *et ante* Salomon *tr.* Ma laudatur *om.* Ma

19. Bonus dolus reprehensibilis non est, ut.

= 35 F *om. per totum* C L Ma Mu1 P1 Vb Vp

20. Ex agente presumitur.
= 40 C, 36 F, 32 Ma *om. per totum* L Mu1 P1 Vb Vp

agente] gente F Ma presumitur] ut *add.* F

21. Si aliquid de sollempnitate ecclesiastici officii relinquitur, quod sit pro infecto habetur.
= 41 C, 37 F, 33 Ma *om. per totum* L Mu1 P1 Vb Vp

relinquitur] relin- *praem. et exp.* C quod sit *om.* Ma habetur] abiectum C, ut *add.* F

22. Ex consuetudine testatoris posse presumi, ut.
= 38 F, 34 Ma *om. per totum* C L Mu1 P1 Vb Vp

consuetudine] inconsuetudine Ma testatoris] testatorum Ma posse presumi] presumitur Ma ut *om.* Ma

Contra, ut.

23. Rem in se illicitam imperio presidentis fieri licitam.
= 42 C, 39 F, 77 Vb *om. per totum* L Ma Mu1 P1 Vp

presidentis] presidentes C, possidentis F licitam] ut *add.* F

Contra.
om. per totum C F

24. Ratione incertitudinis totum posse exigi.
= 40 F, 35 Ma, 78 Vb *om. per totum* C L Mu1 P1 Vp

Incertitudinis] incertitudine Vb exigi] ut *add.* F

Contra.
Contrarium Vb

25. Quod quis ex sua persona habere non potest, per alium habere potest.
= 43 C, 36 Ma, 71 P1 *om. per totum* F L Mu1 Vb Vp

quis *post* persona *tr.* C ex] per P1 sua] suam P1 persona sua *tr.* Ma persona] personam P1 per] hoc *add.* C alium] extraneam P1 habere[2] *om.* P1

Contra.
om. per totum C Ma

26. Quod in dubiis, in meliorem partem interpretari debemus.
= 44 C, 41 F, 37 Ma, 39 Mu1, 73 P1, 79 Vb *om. per totum* L Vp

Quod in dubiis] Dubia Ma Quod] Nota *marg. praem.* F, *post* dubiis *tr.* P1 in meliorem partem *rep. et del.* Mu1, melius est P1 interpretari *om.* P1 debemus] debeamus (contra *add.* Vb) C Vb, ut *add.* Ma, amplectimur P1

Contra.

27. Ex eo solo quod quis non contradicit consentire videtur.
= 45 C, 42 F, 49 L, 38 Ma, 74 P1 *om. per totum* Mu1 Vb Vp

Ex—quis] Qui Ma eo] hec P1 solo] loco *corr.* solo L, ipso P1 quis *om.* L consentire videtur] consentit Ma videtur] ut *add.* F

Contra.
Eontra C P1

28. Factum alterius alteri non obest.
= 46 C, 43 F, 50 L, 39 Ma, 75 P1 *om. per totum* Mu1 Vb Vp

Factum] Quod *praem.* P1 obest] ut *add.* F, obsit P1

Contra.

29. Quod si ecclesiasticus patronus aliquid exigat, etiam nomine pensionis simoniam sit.
= 47 C, 44 F, 51 L, 40 Ma, 44 P1, 92 Vb, 41 Vp *om. per totum* Mu1

Quod *om.* Ma, et *add.* Vp aliquid] nomine *add.* Ma exigat] exigerit C F, exegerit L, exigit Vb etiam *om.* C F nomine pensionis *post* patronus *tr.* C nomine *om.* F Ma Vb pensionis *post* aliquid *tr.* F Ma, *post* patronus *tr.* Vb simoniam] ex delicto *praem.* Vb, simonia P1 sit] fit F, est Ma, quia pactum contra ius nullius est momenti *add.* P1, sapit *et* quia pactum contra ius nullius est momenti *add.* Vb

Contra, scilicet quod non sit.
om. per totum P1 Contra] Contrarium L scilicet—sit *om.* C L Ma

30. Quod si clericus aliquid aquisierit inuendo de bonis ecclesie forsitan in remuneratione impensi obsequii sui decessit, ab intestato si vero nullo herede esse debeat.
= 45 P1, 42 Vp *om. per totum* C F L Ma Mu1 Vb

aquisierit] adquiscerit Vp forsitan *vac.* P1 nullo] non P1 herede] querendum P1 esse] est P1 debeat] quid sit clerici P1

Contra.

31. Propter mutabilitatem mundanarum rerum ecclesia mutari non debet, ut.
= 48 C, 46 F, 41 Ma, 30 Mu1, 176 Vb *om. per totum* L

Propter—rerum *om.* Ma Propter] Quod ad C F mutabilitatem] necessitatum C, necessitatem F rerum] multiplicitatem C, mutabilitatum F non debet] non debere *et ante* mutari *tr.* Ma ecclesia] Dei *add.* C F debet] debeat C F ut *om.* C Ma

32. Quod delictum persone non sit convertendum in dampnum ecclesie.
= 49 C, 45 F, 52 L, 42 Ma, 47 P1, 93 Vb *om. per totum* Mu1 Vp

Quod *om.* L Ma non—convertendum *post* ecclesie *tr.* P1 sit convertendum] redundat Ma sit] est L ecclesie *om.* F

Contra.
om. per totum F L Ma P1

33. Quod qui armantur contra patres ipso iure infames.
= 50 C, 47 F, 53 L *om. per totum* Ma Mu1 P1 Vb Vp

qui *om.* L contra] adversus F patres] presbiteros *add.* L ipso iure] questione L infames] sint *add.* F, fuerint *add.* L

34. Quod prelatus invitis subditis quod canonicis regulis permittitur facere possit.
= 51 C, 48 F, 54 L, 94 Vb *om. per totum* Ma Mu1 P1 Vp

---

33. In F the brocard is without allegations and has been merged with ε36 F.

invitis] invitus L subditis] sudditis *cum* d[1] *exp. et corr.* b F canonicis] canones L facere] faciendum F possit] sit F, possunt L

35. Si sacerdos res ecclesie vendidit, eas recuperando ab accusatione se non liberat.
= 52 C, 49 F, 55 L, 43 Ma, 95 Vb *om. per totum* Mu1 P1 Vp

ecclesie res *tr.* C L vendidit] vendiderit C L, distrahat F eas *om.* Ma recuperando] reddendo Ma se *ante* ab *tr.* Ma accusatione] accusatore F, excusatione L, exatione Ma liberat] liberet Vb

Contra.

36. Si sacerdos permiserit matrimonium consanguineos contrahere, illud accusare non possit.
= 53 C, 50 F, 56 L, 44 Ma, 96 Vb *om. per totum* Mu1 P1 Vp

permiserit] permiserint F consanguineos *ante* permiserint *tr.* F, consanguineo *et ante* matrimonium *tr.* Ma matrimonium *om.* L contrahere] coniungi C illud] matrimonium C, eos Ma, et *praem.* Vb non possit accusare *tr.* C L accusare] accusari F possit] potest (ut *add.* F) F Ma

Contra, scilicet quod possit.
scilicet—possit *om.* C L Ma possit] ut *add.* F

37. Plus valet quod in veritate agitur, quam quod simulate concipitur.
= 54 C, 51 F, 45 Ma, 97 Vb *om. per totum* L Mu1 P1 Vp

in veritate *om.* Ma concipitur] ut *add.* F

Contra.
om. per totum C F Ma

38. Nota: quod si aliquis fecerit quod in se ipso pium est, eo ipso contra ipsum presumitur.
= 55 C, 52 F, 57 L, 98 Vb, 2 Vp *om. per totum* Ma Mu1 P1

aliquis] quis C ipso *om.* C L pium] contra canones Vb eo] pro F contra *om.* F, in Vb ipsum] eum Vp presumitur] ut *add.* F, presumendum sit Vp

39. Testes esse cogendos ad testimonium dicendum.
= 1 C, 53 F, 105 L, 46 Ma, 99 Vb, 3 Vp *om. per totum* Mu1 P1

Testes] Nota *praem.* F, Quod *praem.* Vp esse cogendos] cogi possunt Vp testimonium *om.* L dicendum] ut *add.* F, deferre L, *om.* Vb

Contra.
Contrarium L, *om. per totum* Vp

40. Clericus ad testimonium cogi potest habita distinctione: in civili causa compellitur, dummodo levis causa non sit, in criminali vero testificari non.
= 2 C, 54 F, 111 L, 47 Ma *om. per totum* Mu1 P1 Vb Vp

Clericus ad testimonium *om.* L cogi potest *om.* F, *ante* ad *tr.* Ma habita distinctione *om.* F Ma levis] levi L non[1]] minime *et post* sit *tr.* L testificari *om.* C L, testificatur Ma non[2]] nullo modo *et ante* testificatur *tr.* Ma, potest *add.* F

41. Quod aliquid probandum multum temporis est necessarium.
= 3 C, 55 F, 106 L, 48 Ma, 100 Vb *om. per totum* Mu1 P1 Vp

Quod *om.* Ma aliquid] ad aliquam C, aliquem F Ma, ad *praem.* L probandum] comprobandum C F multum] inusitatum Vb est] sit F necessarium] ut *add.* F

42. Quod ecclesia ex hoc solo quod lapis benedictus ibi ab episcopo positus est, numquam vendi possit.
= 56 C, 56 F L, 49 Ma, 59 P1, 101 Vb *om. per totum* Mu1 Vp

Quod] Qui L ex hoc solo] eo ipso L ex *om.* Ma ibi—episcopo *om.* P1 ibi *rep.* C, † *praem.* Vb ab] a Vb positus est *om.* Vb est *om.* F numquam] nisi quam L, nonnumquam Ma possit] ut *add.* F, potest *et ante* vendi *tr.* Ma

Contra.
om. per totum P1 Contra] Contrarium L, quod vendi possit *add.* Vb

43. Quod pro sola suspitione quis possit condempnari nisi contrarium probetur, ut.
= 57 C, 57 F L, 50 Ma, 61 P1, 102 Vb *om. per totum* Mu1 Vp

Quod *om.* Ma pro *om.* P1 suspitione (presumptione P1) sola *tr.* L Ma P1 sola *om.* C suspitione] susceptione C quis possit condempnari] dampnatur quis Ma probetur contrarium *tr.* Ma P1 contrarium] in *praem.* F P1 ut *om.* C L Ma

Contra.

44. Quod ab initio non valet tractu temporis convalescit.
= 58 C, 58 F L, 51 Ma, 70 P1 *om. per totum* Mu1 Vb Vp

ab initio] a principio Ma valet] valuit L tractu] contractu C F Ma P1 convalescit] ut *add.* F, non convaluit L

Contra.
Contra] ut *add.* F

45. Quod consentienti et facienti par pena debeatur.
= 59 F, 52 Ma, 76 P1 *om. per totum* C L Mu1 Vb Vp

Quod *om.* Ma pena] non *add.* P1 debeatur] ut *add.* F, debetur Ma

Contra.

46. Quod si clericus post uxorem habuit concubinam, a sacro ordine non sit repellendus.
= 59 C, 60 F, 61 L, 53 Ma, 78 P1, 103 Vb *om. per totum* Mu1 Vp

Quod si *om.* Ma clericus] qui *add.* Ma uxorem] uxore F Vb habuit] habuerit F L concubinam] concubinium *et post* uxorem *tr.* L a—repellendus *om.* C a] et *praem.* L sacro ordine] conversione P1 non *om.* Ma sit] est F Ma repellendus] prohibendus ut F

Contra.
om. per totum P1

47. Quod inordinate constitutum est a summo pontifice, a suo successore mutari potest.
= 61 F P1, 54 Ma, 104 Vb *om. per totum* C L Mu1 Vp

Quod *om.* Ma inordinate] ordinate Ma, *om.* Vb constitutum] factum *et ante* a² *tr.* P1 est *om.* Ma P1 a summo pontifice] ab uno potenti Vb a²] vel *praem.*

Ma successore suo *tr.* P1 mutari] immutari *et post* potest *tr.* P1 potest] ut *add.* F, non *praem.* Ma

Quod ordinate constitutum est a summo pontifice, a suo successore mutari non potest.

om. per totum P1 Quod—potest] Contra Ma ordinate *om.* Vb a summo pontifice] ab uno potenti Vb mutari] immutari F potest] ut *add.* F

48. Quod si factum fuerit contra canones, pontifex non potest dispensare.
= 60 C, 62 F, 62 L, 55 Ma *om. per totum* Mu1 P1 Vb Vp

Quod *om.* Ma fuerit *om.* L pontifex *om.* Ma dispensare *ante* non (ut *add.* F) *tr.* F Ma

Group ζ

Manuscripts in which this group appears: Ba, C, F, L, Ma, O, P1, P2, Vb, and Vp.

ζ is a series of twelve brocards. In many of the manuscripts it is in relation with δ and ε. In Ma and partly in Vb, the sequence is repeated twice, while in L it is divided into two different groups.

1. Infirmum est quod ab eo qui infirmus est corpore vel mente vel etate permittitur.
= 61 C, 8 F, 8 *et* 82 Ma, 20 O, 31 P1 Vb, 16 Vp *om. per totum* Ba L P2

rep. Vp quod] qui Vp eo—est[2]] infirmo Ma eo] aliquo O mente ... corpore *tr.* C vel[1] *om.* Ma vel[2] *om.* Ma permittitur] promittitur ut F

2. Mitius agitur cum occulte peccantibus vel extra iudicium confitentibus, quam cum in crimine deprehensis vel convictis vel in iure confessis.
= 62 C, 9 F, 9 *et* 83 Ma, 21 O, 32 P1 Vb, 17 Vp *om. per totum* Ba L P2

rep. Vp agitur] agi Ma_1, Vp_1 peccantibus] penitentibus P1 vel[1]—confitentibus *om.* P1 vel[1]] quam F quam—confessis] ut F, *om.* Ma cum[2] *om.* Vp vel[2]—confessis *om.* Vp_1 in *om.* Ma_1

3. Articulus necessitatis prorsus excusat vel saltim penam relevat, nisi ad cautelam aliquid fiat.
= 63 C, 10 F, 100 L, 84 Ma, 22 O, 33 P1 Vb, 18 Vp *om. per totum* Ba P2

Articulus—penam *post* fiat *tr.* P1 excusat] equitas non est equistas *praem.* F saltim] saltem F O penam] minuit *add.* P1 nisi] ut F, saltem *add.* L fiat] ut *add.* F

Contra.
om. per totum F L Ma O P1 Vb Vp

4. In detestatione criminis plurima, contra citraque iuris ordinem inveniuntur admissa.
= 64 C, 12 F, 101 L, 10 *et* 85 Ma, 23 O, 34 P1 Vb, 19 Vp *om. per totum* Ba P2

detestatione] detestationem C Vp plurima] multa Ma contra] contraria C P1 Vb citraque] citra C, *om.* L, curaque Ma_1 admissa] ut *add.* F, *om.* L

Contra.
om. per totum C F Ma O P1 Vb Vp

5. Interdum deliquenti in odium alterius subvenitur.
= 65 C, 63 L, 11 *et* 86 Ma, 24 O, 35 P1 Vb, 20 Vp *om. per totum* Ba F P2

Interdum] In destetatione *praem.* P1 delinquenti] debiti quanti L, delinquendi Ma_1 in odium] odio Ma, non Ma_1 subvenitur] subvertitur L

6. Aliquando humanis precibus tollerari potest quod esset irritandum.
= 66 C, 13 F, 102 L, 12 *et* 87 Ma, 25 O, 36 P1 Vb, 21 Vp *om. per totum* Ba P2

Aliquando *om.* Ma, Quod *praem.* Vp humanis] humanius Vb precibus *om* C Vb tollerari] toleratur Ma potest *om.* Ma esset] alias *praem.* Ma, etiam Ma_1 irritandum] irritum F, imitandum L, inhibendum P1

Contra.
om. per totum C F Ma P1 Vb Vp

7. Accidit quandoque ut comuni duorum opere alter obligatur delicto vel contractu, alter vero non.
= 67 C, 15 F, 64 L, 13 *et* 88 Ma, 26 O, 37 P1 Vb, 22 Vp *om. per totum* Ba P2

Accidit—ut *om.* Ma Accidit] Accidere Ma_1 quandoque] quando L, aliquando P1 ut] in P1 duorum *om.* Ma alter[1]] in ius L obligatur] obligetur F L Vb, obliget Vp vel contractu *om.* C L vel] alter non *praem. et exp.* F contractu] contracto F vero non] minime L non] ut *add.* F non alter[2] *tr.* Vp

8. Nonnunquam preceptionis verbum pro permissione vel suasione accipitur.
= 68 C, 14 F, 14 *et* 89 Ma, 27 O, 38 P1 Vb, 23 Vp *om. per totum* Ba L P2

Nonnunquam] Quandoque Ma verbum perceptionis *tr.* Ma preceptionis] verbum perceptum communiter *exp. et corr.* F pro *om.* Vp vel] ac Ma suasione] persuasione P1 accipitur] ut *add.* F, *post* permissione *tr.* Ma, accusatur P1

9. Cum aliqua inter se consequentiam habent uno probato reliquum probatum intelligitur.
= 69 C, 65 L, 90 Ma, 28 O, 39 P1 Vb, 38 Vp *om. per totum* Ba F P2

consequentiam *ante* inter *tr.* O Vb reliquum] reliquo Vp intelligitur] intelligatur P1

10. Tam lege divina quam humana bonus dolus admittatur.
= 14 Ba, 70 C, 66 L, 91 Ma, 29 *et* 31 O, 40 *et* 71 Vb, 40 P1, 9 P2, 39 Vp *om. per totum* F

lege] leges O_1 Vb_1, et de *praem.* Vp divina ... humana] principum ... canones sacerdotum O_1 Vb_1 divina lege *tr.* O humana] lege *praem.* C bonus dolus] bonum dolum O_1 Vb_1, dolus bonus *tr.* P2 admittatur] admittunt O_1 Vb_1, admittitur P1 P2

Contra.
om. per totum C L Ma O O_1 P2 Vp

11. ⟩*vacat*⟨
= 12 Ba, 167 Vb *om. per totum* C F L Ma O P1 Vp P2

Contra.

12. Ob delictorum emendationem et cum constantiam interpretantur canones non esse quod est.
= 13 Ba, 103 L, 92 Ma, 30 O, 168 Vb, 40 Vp *om. per totum* C F P1 P2

---

11. In Ba, this brocard lacks the rubric. In Vb, the allegations at the beginning of fol. 7ra pertain to a different brocard from the last one on fol. 6^{vd}. This different brocard, that I have numbered as 167, starts in the middle of the allegations, because between 6^{vd} and 7ra there was at least one lost folio, which contained its rubric. It corresponds to Ba's brocard 12, as can be deduced from the allegations of the *contrarium*, that are identical.

cum] animi Ba Ma O interpretantur] interpretari tantum Vb est] ut *add.* Ma O Vp

Propter predictas causas interpretantur canones esse quod non est.
Propter] Non potest *praem.* Ba predictas] easdem *et post* causas *tr.* L interpretantur] interpretatur O canones] omnes L, canon O esse] contra Vp non *ante* esse *tr.* L est] ut *add.* Ba Ma O

In odium culparum interpretantur canones non esse quod est, ut.
In] Econtra *praem.* Ba Ma Vp interpretantur] non *praem.* Vp quod est] quam darum L ut *om.* L Vb

Propter proximam predictam causam interpretantur canones non esse quod est.
= 19 *et* 92 Ma, *om. per totum* O

Propter—causam *om.* Ma proximam—causam] idem non L proximam] proxime Ba Ma_1 Vp predictam] dictum Ba, dictam Ma_1 Vp interpretantur canones *post* est *tr.* Ma interpretantur] intepretatur Ba canones] ea L non *post* quod *tr.* Ba L Vp est] ut *add.* Ma_1

Group η

Manuscripts in which this group appears: C, F, L, Ma, Mu1, and Vb.

η is a series of 18 brocards. In most of the manuscripts this group follows ε.

1. Quod reus non teneatur respondere ad causam, nisi prius litteris noverit quid ei opponatur.
= 72 C, 64 F, 67 L *om. per totum* Ma Mu1 Vb

teneatur] tenetur L ad causam *om.* L

2. Quod ieiunium possit quis redimere.
= 73 C, 63 F, 56 Ma *om. per totum* L Mu1 Vb

Quod *om.* Ma ieiunium] officium F possit] posse Ma quis *om.* Ma redimere] ut *add.* F, redimi denario uno Ma

1. In F, the brocard is without allegations and has been merged with η3.

3. Quam penam patiatur qui non ratione sed presbiteris in causa contendit.
= 74 C, 65 F, 57 Ma *om. per totum* L Mu1 Vb

Quam] Que sit Ma penam] pena Ma patiatur—sed *om.* Ma presbiteris] proprii F, *post* litigantium *tr.* Ma in] sui F contendit] contenditur ut F, litigantium Ma

4. Si presbiteri vel diaconi falsum testimonium dixerint, qualiter puniendi sunt.
= 75 C, 66 F, 58 Ma *om. per totum* L Mu1 Vb

presbiteri ... diaconi] presbiter ... diaconus Ma vel *om.* F dixerint] dixerit *et ante* testimonium *tr.* Ma qualiter—sunt *om.* Ma sunt] ut *add.* F

Contra.
om. per totum C F

5. Non semper quicumque pellitur ab accusatione, pellitur a testimonio; immo, debet extorqueri veritas.
= 76 C, 67 F, 59 Ma, 105 Vb *om. per totum* L Mu1

semper *om.* Ma pellitur[1]] repellitur C pellitur[2] a] et C Ma testimonio] testificatione C F immo—veritas] ut F, *om.* Ma debet] ab eo *add.* C veritas extorqueri *tr.* C

Contra.
om. per totum F Vb

6. Quod responsioni per vim extorte creditus.
= 77 C, 60 Ma *om. per totum* F L Mu1 Vb

Quod *om.* Ma creditus] creditur Ma

Contra.

7. Omnibus clericis prohibitum est possessiones aliorum conducere et negotiari.
= 78 C, 68 F, 61 Ma *om. per totum* L Mu1 Vb

Omnibus *om.* Ma conducere] conductu Ma negotiari] ut *add.* F

Contra, ut.
om. per totum C ut *om.* Ma

8. Quod magis dampnandus est qui errorem defendit quam qui errat.
= 79 C, 69 F, 62 Ma *om. per totum* L Mu1 Vb

Quod *om.* Ma errat] ut *add.* F

9. Quod sacerdotes templum debeant ornare.
= 80 C, 70 F *om. per totum* L Ma Mu1 Vb

Contra.
Contra] ut *add.* F

10. Quotiens quis contra canones facit, eo ipso adversus ipsum presumitur.
= 81 C, 72 F *om. per totum* L Ma Mu1 Vb

adversus] contra F presumitur] ut *add.* F

11. Irritatur aut tolerabile ne culpa propagetur in exemplum.
= 82 C, 71 F *om. per totum* L Ma Mu1 Vb

aut] alias F in exemplum] exemplo ut F

12. Auget peccatum sublimitas peccantium.
= 83 C, 73 F, 68 L, 63 Ma, 106 Vb *om. per totum* Mu1

peccantium] ut *add.* F

Contra.
om. per totum C F L Ma

13. Auget peccatum reiteratio peccati.
= 84 C, 74 F, 69 L, 64 Ma, 45 Mu1, 107 Vb

reiteratio] iteratio C Ma, mutatio Mu1 peccati *om.* Ma

14. Erudicior quandoque digniori proponitur.
= 85 C, 70 L, 65 Ma *om. per totum* F Mu1 Vb

digniori quandoque *tr.* L quandoque *om.* Ma

15. Immoderatus usus quod erat excusabile reddit inexcusabile.
= 86 C, 75 F *om. per totum* L Ma Mu1 Vb

inexcusabile] ut *add.* F

16. Quemlibet criminosum licet, nondum de crimine dampnatum a testificatione posse repelli.
= 87 C, 94 L, 66 Ma, 108 Vb *om. per totum* F Mu1

Quemlibet *om.* Ma nondum de crimine] non credendum L, *om.* Ma dampnatum] dampnatus Vb a testificatione] a testimonio *et post* repelli *tr.* C L a *rep.* Ma

Contra.
om. per totum C L Ma

17. Contrarius sensus decreti pro decreto habeantur.
= 88 C, 71 L, 67 Ma, 110 Vb *om. per totum* F Mu1

Contrarius] Contra Ma habeantur] habetur L Ma

Contrarium.
Contra C L

18. Multa iuste rogantur que iuste effectui non mancipantur.
= 89 C, 68 Ma, 44 Mu1, 109 Vb *om. per totum* F L

iuste] iniuste C Mu1 non *om.* C Mu1 mancipantur] emancipantur Ma

Group ϑ

Manuscripts in which this group appears: Ba, C, L, O, P1, P2, and Vb.

θ is a small group of four brocards. They are usually near ζ or γ.

1. Multa possunt recte fieri de quibus tamen non potest pacisci ut fiant.
15 Ba, 32 O, 41 P1, 15 P2, 28 *et* 72 Vb *om. per totum* C L

1. 28 Vb has merged both the rubrics and the allegations of δ4 and θ1. Each of the two parts of 28 Vb has been collated separately under the two respective brocards.

fieri recte *tr.* Ba tamen *om.* Vb_1 potest] licet P1 P2 pacisci] pascisci Ba ut fiant *om.* P2

Contra: in eisdem casibus pactio videtur admissa.
om. per totum P1 Contra] Econtra Ba O in—admissa *om.* Ba casibus] canonibus Vb pactio] pacta P2

2. Quanto aliquid favorabilius habetur et difficilius factum solvitur, tanto difficilius factum editur, cum an factum sit ambigitur.
= 16 Ba, 90 C, 73 L, 34 O, 73 *et* 169 Vb *om. per totum* P1 P2

favorabilius—et *om.* L favorabilius] est vel *add.* Vb_1 factum[1] *om.* L solvitur] solverit L tanto—editur] solvitur Ba, credatur C, *om.* Vb factum[2]—ambigitur] id ratum et firmum esse dicitur L factum[2] *om.* O editur] ceditur O ambigitur] ambiges Ba

3. Quod non potest ecclesia, corrigit secularis potestas.
= 17 Ba, 91 C, 42 P1, 17 P2, 33 O, 67 *et* 170 Vb *om. per totum* L

vacat *add. interl.* Vb corrigit] corrigere Ba P2 Vb_1, corrigere *praem.* P1 potestas secularis *tr.* P2

Contra
Econtra Ba, *om. per totum* P1 Vb

4. Sicut peccat qui in verbum canonis incidit, ita qui incidit in eius sententiam.
= 18 Ba, 92 C, 35 O, 43 P1, 18 P2, 171 Vb *om. per totum* L

verbum canonis] canones P1 verbum] verba C incidit[1]] incidet Vb ita] peccat *add.* Vb in eius sententiam *post* qui[2] *tr.* Ba incidit[2] *om.* C P2, incidet Vb

Group ϰ

Manuscripts in which this group appears: Mu1 and Vb.

ϰ is a sequence of eight brocards that appears only in Mu1 and Vb. In the latter it precedes δ, while in the former it is between mixed brocards.

1. Ab exemplis summi pontificis potest efficaciter argumentari.
= 31 Mu1, 177 Vb

summi] sumi Vb   pontificis *om.* (*homoiotel.*) Vb   argumentari] ut *add.* Mu1

Contra.
Contrarium Mu1

2. Licita consuetudo violari non debet, ut.
= 32 Mu1, 178 Vb

3. Qui incidit in canonem date sententie, ab aliquo nisi a summo pontifice absolvi non potest.
= 33 Mu1, 179 Vb

incidit] incidet Mu1   potest] debet ut Mu1

4. Que publice fiunt nemini licet ignorare.
= 34 Mu1, 180 Vb

ignorare] ut *add.* Mu1

5. Incorrigibiles clerici per seculares debent opprimi potestates.
= 35 Mu1, 182 Vb

Contra.
Contrarium Mu1

6. Primo in ecclesia ordinatus, priorem locum debet habere.
= 36 Mu1, 183 Vb

priorem] primum Mu1

7. Pro sequentia precedentia intelliguntur.
= 37 Mu1, 184 Vb

vac. Mu1

8. Si quis pro aliquo testimonium dicit in alia causa, contra eum debet admitti.
= 38 Mu1, 185 Vb

vac. Mu1

Contra.
om. per totum Mu1

Group λ

Manuscripts in which this group appears: L, Mu1, Vb, and Vp.

λ is a group of twelve brocards, basically shared only by L and Vb, but with two brocards present also in Mu1 and Vp.

1. Non vult Dominus lucro aliquo dampnum compensari.
= 78 L, 85 Vb *om. per totum* Mu1 Vp

2. Ubi plurima faciunt pro aliquo quam contra aliquem vel vice versa, paucitas cedit pluralitati.
= 80 L, 84 Vb *om. per totum* Mu1 Vp

vice versa] econtra L

3. Ubi aliquis excomunicatur, culpa precedentem non auditur.
= 81 L, 86 Vb *om. per totum* Mu1 Vp

excomunicatur] excusetur L

4. Plus valet quod agitur, quam quod verbis vel scripto concipitur.
= 83 L, 87 Vb, 1 Vp *om. per totum* Mu1

agitur] in veritate *praem.* Vp quam] quem L quod *om.* L verbis vel scripto] simulate Vp vel *om.* L concipitur] ut *add.* L, concipit Vp

5. Plus valet quod in opinione quam quod in veritate consistit.
= 84 L, 88 Vb *om. per totum* Mu1 Vp

valet quod *om.* L quam] quem L

6. Quod sibi insufficiens videtur, si alterius aminiculo utatur vires, fortitur.
= 86 L, 89 Vb *om. per totum* Mu1 Vp

Quod] Qui L

7. Utile vitiatur pro inutile.
= 87 L, 29 Mu1, 90 *et* 175 Vb *om. per totum* Vp

vitiatur *post* inutile *tr. et* ut *add.* Mu1 Vb_1

Contra.
Contrarium Mu1, *om. per totum* L Vb

8. Consensus delinquentum quibus aliquid videtur commissum non excusat delictum.
= 88 L, 149 Vb *om. per totum* Mu1 Vp

delinquentum] delinquentium L commissum] commissus L

9. Simplicitas operatur quandoque indulgentiam.
= 92 L, 91 Vb *om. per totum* Mu1 Vp

indulgentiam] ceditur L

10. Illiteratos non debere promoveri.
= 93 L, 80 Vb *om. per totum* Mu1 Vp

debere non *tr.* L

Illiteratos promotos posse tollerari.

11. Negligentem puniri.
= 95 L, 81 Vb *om. per totum* Mu1 Vp

12. Quod fieri non debet si factum fuerit ratum manet.
= 108 L, 82 Vb *om. per totum* Mu1 Vp

Contrarium.
Contra Vb

Group μ

Manuscripts in which this group appears: P1 and Vb.

μ is a series of eight brocards present only in P1 and Vb.

1. Episcopum que promiserit, consensu clericorum teneri persolvere.
= 104 P1, 1 Vb

Episcopum] Episcopus P1 que *om.* P1 promiserit] promisit se soluturum promisit pro fundo suo necessario *et post* clericorum *tr.* P1 consensu] assensu P1 clericorum] suorum *add.* P1 teneri] tenetur P1 persolvere] ad solvendum *et ante* tenetur *tr.* P1

Sine consensu clericorum episcopum non teneri.
om. per totum P1

2. Episcopus pro utilitate ecclesie cum consensu clericorum obligatus, eis postea renuntiantibus de ipsorum licite se liberat.
= 106 P1, 2 Vb

marg. Vb cum *om.* P1 renuntiantibus] renitentibus P1 ipsorum] prebendis *add.* P1

Contra.

3. Qui consentit delinquenti, eundem post accusare non potest.
= 107 P1, 3 Vb

delinquenti] alicui *praem.* P1 post] postea P1

Contra.

4. Qui virginem quam prius corrupit postea in uxorem duxit, ad sacros ordines promoveri non potest.
= 108 P1, 4 Vb

prius *om.* P1 corrupit] cognovit P1 promoveri] ascendere P1

Contra.

5. Valeat privilegium super ecclesia de manu laici ab alio prelato in cuius territorio est susceptum.
= 109 P1, 49 Vb

super ecclesia *post* laici *tr.* P1 in cuius] quam eius † Vb susceptum] suscepta P1

Contrarium.

6. Valeat ad predictam ecclesiam tenendam xxx. annorum prescriptio.
= 110 P1, 50 Vb

Contrarium.

7. Coactus uxorem ducere cogendus est eam retinere.
= 111 P1, 5 *et* 51 Vb

cogendus *om.* P1 est] † *add.* Vb_1 eam *om.* P1

Contra.
om. per totum P1, Contrarium Vb_1

8. Testes non nisi de visis testimonium ferre.
= 112 P1, 6 Vb

visis] et auditis *add.* P1 ferre] possunt *add.* P1

Econtra: scilicet sufficere de auditu.
om. per totum P1

2 Synoptic Table of the Brocards in Part III

Standard order	A	A1	Ba	C	F	G	L	Ma	Mu1	O	P1	P2	Vb	Vp
α1	1					1	1		1		1			
α2						2	2		2		2			
α3	2					3	3				3			
α4	3					4	4		3					
α5	4					5	5		4					
α6	5					6	6		5					
α7	6					7	7		6					
α8	7					8	8		7		4			
α9	8					10	9		8		6			
α10	9					11	10		9		7		174	
α11	10					12	11		10		8			
α12	11					13	12		11		9			
α13	12					14			12		10			
α14	13					15	13		13		11			

(*cont.*)

Standard order	A	A1	Ba	C	F	G	L	Ma	Mu1	O	P1	P2	Vb	Vp
α15	14					16	14		14		12			
α16						17	15		15					
α17	15					18	16		16		13			
α18						19	17				83			
α19						20	18		17					
α20						22	19		18					
α21						23	20		19		14			
α22						24								
α23						25								
α24						26	21		20		15			
α25						27	22		21		16			
α26						28	23		22		17			
β1		8	1	5	1		28	1	23	1	85	6	20	9
β2		4	2	6	2		29	2	24	2	18, 86	7	21	10
β3		5	3	7	3		30	3		3	87	8	22	11
β4		1	4	10	4		31	4		4	91		23	12
β5		2	5	8	5	9	32	5		5	5, 89	1	24	13
β6		7		9	6		33	6		6	90	10	41	14
β7		3		4	7		34	7		7	84		42, 66	15
γ1				11			35	69		8	19	11	43	24
γ2				12			37	70		9	21	12	45	25
γ3				13			36	71		10	20		44	26
γ4				14			38	72		11	22	13	46	27
γ5			11	15			39	73		12	23	14	47	28
γ6				16			40	74	43	13	24	15	48	29
γ7			19	17			41	75			25	19	172	30
γ8				18			42							31
δ1			6	19				76		14	26	2	25	32
δ2			7	20				77		15	27	3	26, 68	33
δ3			8	21			98	78		16	28	4	27, 70	34
δ4			9	22			99	79		17	29		28	35
δ5			10	23				80	41	18		5	29	36
δ6				24			25	81	40	19	30		30	37
ε1				25	16		43	15					139	
ε2				26			44	16						
ε3				27	18		45	17						
ε4				28	17		46	18						
ε5				29	20		47	20					140	
ε6				30	21		48	21						
ε7				31	22								141	
ε8					23			22						

(*cont.*)

Standard order	A	A1	Ba	C	F	G	L	Ma	Mu1	O	P1	P2	Vb	Vp
ε9				32	24			23						
ε10				33	27			24						
ε11					28			25						
ε12				34	29			26						
ε13				35	30			27						
ε14				36	31			28	42					
ε15				37	32								74	
ε16				38	33			29					75	
ε17				39	34			30					76	
ε18				71				31						
ε19					35									
ε20				40	36			32						
ε21				41	37			33						
ε22					38			34						
ε23				42	39								77	
ε24					40			35					78	
ε25				43				36		71				
ε26				44	41			37	39	73			79	
ε27				45	42		49	38		74				
ε28				46	43		50	39		75				
ε29				47	44		51	40		44			92	43
ε30										45				44
ε31				48	46			41	30				176	
ε32				49	45		52	42		47			93	
ε33				50	47		53							
ε34				51	48		54						94	
ε35				52	49		55	43					95	
ε36				53	50		56	44					96	
ε37				54	51			45					97	
ε38				55	52		57						98	2
ε39				1	53		105	46					99	3
ε40				2	54		111	47						
ε41				3	55		106	48					100	
ε42				56	56		58	49		59			101	
ε43				57	57		59	50		61			102	
ε44				58	58		60	51		70				
ε45					59			52		76				
ε46				59	60		61	53		78			103	
ε47					61			54		63			104	
ε48				60	62		62	55						
ζ1				61	8			8, 82		20	31		31	16

(*cont.*)

Standard order	A	A1	Ba	C	F	G	L	Ma	Mu1	O	P1	P2	Vb	Vp
ζ2				62	9			9, 83		21	32		32	17
ζ3				63	10		100	84		22	33		33	18
ζ4				64	12		101	10, 85		23	34		34	19
ζ5				65			63	11, 86		24	35		35	20
ζ6				66	13		102	12, 87		25	36		36	21
ζ7				67	15		64	13, 88		26	37		37	22
ζ8				68	14			14, 89		27	38		38	23
ζ9				69			65	90		28	39		39	38
ζ10			14	70			66	91		29, 31	40	9	40, 71	39
ζ11			12										167	
ζ12			13				103	19, 92		30			168	40
η1				72	64		67							
η2				73	63			56						
η3				74	65			57						
η4				75	66			58						
η5				76	67			59					105	
η6				77				60						
η7				78	68			61						
η8				79	69			62						
η9				80	70									
η10				81	72									
η11				82	71									
η12				83	73		68	63					106	
η13				84	74		69	64		45			107	
η14				85			70	65						
η15				86	75									
η16				87			94	66					108	
η17				88			71	67					110	
η18				89				68		44			109	
θ1			15							32	41	16	28, 72	
θ2			16	90			73			34			73, 169	
θ3			17	91						33	42	17	67, 170	
θ4			18	92						35	43	18	171	
κ1									31				177	
κ2									32				178	
κ3									33				179	
κ4									34				180	
κ5									35				182	
κ6									36				183	
κ7									37				184	
κ8									38				185	

(*cont.*)

Standard order	A	A1	Ba	C	F	G	L	Ma	Mu1	O	P1	P2	Vb	Vp
λ1							78						85	
λ2							80						84	
λ3							81						86	
λ4							83						87	1
λ5							84						88	
λ6							86						89	
λ7							87		29				90, 175	
λ8							88						149	
λ9							92						91	
λ10							93						80	
λ11							95						81	
λ12							108						82	
μ1											104		1	
μ2											106		2	
μ3											107		3	
μ4											108		4	
μ5											109		49	
μ6											110		50	
μ7											111		5, 51	
μ8											112		6	

3 List of other brocards that occur only in a single manuscript

The brocards in this last list have not been included in any of the previous groups because they appear in a single manuscript, often interspersed between other groups. They have been listed under the *siglum* of their manuscript and numbered according to it.

A

16. In quibus in verbo †.

A1

7. ⟩*vacat*⟨

Ba

20. ⟩*vacat*⟨

21. ⟩*vacat*⟨

C

93. Duarum ecclesiarum clerici, communicantes omnia que habebant in possessionibus et que habuerant in oblationibus, videntur molendinum quod unius illarum ecclesiarum presbiter possidebat communicare.

et *om. male.* C

94. Quod absque consensu et conniventia eorum fit ad quos spectat, irritum habetur si factum fuerit.

si *rep.* C

95. Pena tamdiu.

F

11. Sententia propter peccatum magis presumitur pro eo qui publice peccat.

peccatum *om. male* F

19. Non esse quod est, interpretantur, ut.

25. Modicum tempus accipitur iv. mensium.

26. Modicum tempus xxx. dierum, ut.

G

21. In dubiis equitatem sequendam.

---

95. These are, obviously, the incipit words of a brocard which the author knew by heart, so he merely noted here its first words, as a mnemonic aid for himself.

L

24. Licet quid non exprimatur, tamen tacite actum intelligitur.

26. Nichil interest ab initio dolum committatur, an ex post facto.

27. In pari causa, melior est conditio possidentis.

possidentis] pro bibertis *cum* b[1] *corr.* l L

Contrarium.

72. Prius iudicari debet secundum allegationes quam secundum conscientiam, ut.

74. Cum frater hoc dubitatur, unde non sufficit, si favore pretendatur, ut in matrimonio vel alia re consimili que favorabilis est, ut.

75. In re dubia vel obscura vel ubi sententiarum videtur esse diversitas, id preiudicat quod sacre scripture non obloquitur, ut potiori et antiquiori et plurium auctoritate, vel maiori immutanter pietate.

76. Quid auctoritate ecclesiastica non potest corrigi, necesse est severitate seculari coherceri, ad leges enim imperatorum tamquam ad supremum subsidium est recurrendum, ut.

Contrarium.

77. De sententia.

79. Ex eo quod verisimile est et frequentius solet contingere, sepe presumptio nascitur, et ideo aliquid umquam quandoque super eo constituitur, ut.

umquam] unus *male* L

82. Uno prohibito, alium prohibitum intelligi. Et uno concesso, alium concessum intelligi.

85. Re pristina a me redita, pristina via restituitur. Et cessante culpa cessat effectus culpe, ut.

via] viam *male* L effectus *om. male* L culpe] † *add.* L

89. Ubi res inlicita committitur, quantitas rei non inspicitur.

inlicita] inlicitas *male* L

90. Tantum valet multitudinis consensus, ut interdum vim eandem habeat quod conservatur a pluribus et quod a gravioribus.

91. Quod in extraneum alicui negatur, in sue conditionis hominem quandoque conceditur.

96. Quod addicitur licet, bonum totum decolorat.

97. Ex alterius conscientia † quod ex sua non consequitur.

104. Quod ab initio est voluntarium, ex post facto est necessarium.

107. Cum dubitatur de facto prelati, presumendum est illum factum licitum esse, nisi evidentia sit malum esse.

licitum *om. male* L esse[2] *om. male* L

Contrarium.

109. Cum de re cuius sit dubitatur, pro ecclesie presumitur.

110. Quedam sunt que, licet sint bona vel licita, ex causis tamen concurrentibus reperiuntur prohibita.

111. Sicut vice versa, quedam, licet minus licita quidem regulariter facta invenimus, inspectis circumstantiis tollerari.

quidem] qui *male* L

Mu1

26. Leges Romane in causis ecclesiasticis vel aliorum hominum locum non habent.

27. Quod uni conceditur, videtur alteri concedendum, nisi specialitas meretur, ut.

28. Propter favorem testium vel aliorum non debet eis fides adhiberi, nisi verba videantur asserere, ut.

46. Quod reprobanda sit permissio, habetur.

O

36. Omnes monachi, cum propriam voluntatem non habeant, tenentur prelatis suis in omnibus bonis obedire.

37. Concessio tenet cum a maiori et digniori parte facta fuerit. In omnibus enim ecclesiasticis negociis optinere solet sententia plurimorum.

38. Non licet presbitero super unum altare in una die duas missas canere.

P1

46. Quod si dubium est de rebus defuncti cuius sint, an ecclesie an defuncti, utrum honus probationis pertineat ad heredes defuncti quod pertinent ad eos.

Contra.

48. Quod episcopus gravamen seu servile officium quandoque clericis imponere non possit.

49. Nota: que fuerint ratione temporis, prohiberi.

50. Quod si mulier despoliata est pro viro et recessit quando potuit, consensisse non videtur.

videtur] vnr *cum* n *exp. et abbr. signo corr.* P1

51. Episcopus, licet ex usu servile servicium habuerit a clericis, ab eis per usum petere non potest.

52. Si episcopus non est electus sollempniter, non debet esse episcopus.

est] de *praem. et exp.* P1

53. Episcopus cogatur eum ordinare quem populus elegit vel clerus.

Contra.

54. Episcopus nec honores, nec dignitates, nec sententiam dare potest sine consilio clericorum.

55. Si quis id quod tenetur per peccuniam facit, crimen simonie incurrit.

56. Ad aliquem probandum multum tempus desideratur.

57. Ex ecclesiis annui reditus haberi possunt.

58. Simulationem non prodesse sed obesse i. s. quod cogetur quod incepit quis adimplere.

Contra.

60. Penitentia non excusat sacerdotem a depositione.

Contra.

62. Quod maior pars fecit, per aliam non potest immutari.

64. Quod ante litem contestatam non sunt cuncta restituenda possessori.

Contra.

65. Per hoc quod infinite dicitur, colligitur universalitas, ita ut tam ea que dicta sunt quam ea que sunt dicenda intelliguntur.

infinite] infinete *cum* e[1] *exp. et corr* P1

66. Quod si testis inter multa mala aliquod bonum reperiatur, ei testandum sit.

Inter *om. male* P1

Contra.

67. Quod si aliquis ipso iure excommunicatus sit, eius iudicium non sit timendum.

Contra.

68. Ea que a pluribus et gravioribus tenuntur, sunt proponenda eis que a paucioribus et minoris auctoris tenentur.

69. Si quid alias a pluribus, alias a gravioribus observatur, in auctoritatis probabilitate servetur.

71. Quod argumenta pro loco sunt accipienda.

Contra.

72. Ex seculari iudicio, ecclesiasticum sit sumendum.

seculari] a *praem. male* P1

77. Laici excommunicandi sunt, nisi dederint decimas et primitias seu oblationes usuorum et mortuorum.

79. Quicumque privatur officio, et beneficio.

Privatur quis officio, nec beneficio.

Privatur quis beneficio, nec officio.

81. Ignorantia crassa et supina neminem excusat.

82. Publice facti ignorantia non excusat.

105. Discentientibus quibus, non remanet obligatus.

Vb

7. Occultum hereticum non consecrare.

Contra.

8. Convictum de heresi et reconciliatum, alium de heresi accusare posse.
8 *et* 52 Vb

Convictum] Convictus Vb_1 reconciliatum] ecclesie reconciliatus Vb_1 posse] potest Vb_1

Contra.
Contrarium Vb_1

9. Deficientem in probatione minoris criminis, ad accusationem maioris admitti.
9 *et* 53 Vb

Deficientem] † Vb_1 probatione] probationem Vb_1 criminis] † Vb_1 accusationem] † Vb_1 maioris *ante* ad *tr.*Vb_1 admitti] admittitur Vb_1

Contrarium.
om. Vb

10. Monacos ad decimas prestandas teneri.

Contra.

11. Monasterium egredienti, pristina bona esse restituenda.

Contra.

12. Licitum esse sacramentum clericorum quo se astringunt in electione episcopi, ne extraneus eligatur.
12 *et* 55 Vb

Esse] est Vb_1 sacramentum] iuramento Vb_1 clericorum *om.* Vb_1 astringunt *om.* Vb_1 in electione] spectat electio *et post* episcopi *tr.* Vb_1 episcopi] ad quos *praem.* Vb_1 extraneus] ab eis *praem.* Vb_1

Contra.

Contrarium Vb_1

13. Electionem et consecrationem episcopi irritandam quam cetus eligentium invitis aliis intronizari.

Contra.

14. Culpa non existente, secundum humanitatis rationem equales esse.

15. Qui de gradu cecidit, eius esse conditionis cuius fuerat ante gradum.

15 *et* 65 Vb

Qui] Hec clerici debeat causas agere vel iudicare *praem.* Vb_1 esse] est *et post* conditionis *tr.* Vb_1

16. Delinquentes episcopum excommunicare posse.

17. Sacramentum non prestandum esse, ne fiat quod fieri veremur.

18. Tacentem sibi preiudicium facere.

18 *et* 57 Vb

Tacentem] Qui tacet Vb_1 facere] facit Vb_1

19. Quod sine communi consensu eorum ad quos spectat fit, nullius esse momenti.

Contra.

53. Commoneri debet quis antequam accusetur.

56. Ex suspitione nemo est iudicandus.

Contrarium.

58. Iuramentum clerici factum laico sine superioris auctoritate, illicitum fore iudicandum.

59. Leges mundanas iure canonum tenendas.

Leges forenses sacri canones non admittunt.

60. Qui delinquentem non manifestat, tenetur.

delinquentem] delinquente *male* Vb manifestat] manifestant *cum* n^2 *exp.* Vb

61. Omnis pontificalis † ad apostolicam sedem restoratur.

62. Non est alienum quod licite possidetur.

63. Presumptionem valere.

64. Convictus quid exigisse solvit quadruplum.

69. Pactum a donatore insertum ne res ecclesiastica alienetur non valet post, quia videtur contra can⟨o⟩nes insertum.

83. Negligenti immo subvenitur tamen in alio.

111. A seculari iudice ad ecclesiasticum iudicem non est appellandum.

Contra.

112. Multa in odium actorum reprobari non debent.

reprobari] reprobatur *male* Vb

Contra.

113. Episcopum non posse repellere a populo vel patrono electum non iusta causa.

114. Sacrilegium non incurri et si clericus feriatur inornate incedens.

115. Obnoxium alicui ad religionem non posse transire, nisi primo persolverit.

116. Licitum conditionem in omni generalitate subaudiri.

117. Verberari debere qui penam canonicam non valet sustinere.

118. Imperatorem appellationis potestatem habere.

Contra.

119. Decimas reddendas absque minoratione.

Contra.

Personale beneficium ad consequentiam trahi non posse *praem. et exp. cum* 'vacat' *signo* Vb

120. Personale beneficium ad consequentiam trahi non posse.

Contra.

121. Seculares potestates ad ecclesiam tuendam teneri.

122. Aliquem post mortem iudicari non posse.

Contra.

123. In quo peccat, aliquem debere puniri.

124. Quod sacris canonibus non diffinitur, ab aliquo diffiniendum non esse.

Contra.

125. Prelatum non teneri de peccato subditorum, si pro eo non stet quominus corrigantur.

126. Canones proniores ad absolvendum quam ad condempnandum.

127. Ad omnia porrigitur ius ubi querit ratio iuris.

ubi] non *male* Vb querit] que *male* Vb

128. Clericum hereditatem petere non posse.

Contra.

129. Aliquem in causa sua testificari posse.

Contra.

130. Non presumi illicitum quod fit ab uno auctore.

Contra.

131. Pro qualitate meritorum faciendum esse distributionem stipendi.
25 Mu1, 131 Vb

Pro *om.* Mu1 qualitate] qualitatem *et post* meritorum *tr.* Mu1 meritorum] Iuxta personarum et *praem.* Mu1 faciendum esse] fieri debet Mu1 distributionem] distributio Mu1 stipendi] prebendarum Mu1

Contra.
om. per totum Mu1

132. Ecclesiam non debere dampnari pro aliquorum discordia.

133. Qui ratione preterite conversationis vel facti suspectus habetur, nec ipse recipi, nec ei reddendum est sine magna cautela quod petit.
133 *et* 212 Vb

†.

134. Nota: penam unam aliam non excludere.
134 et 213 Vb

Nota *om.* Vb_1 penam unam] una pena Vb_1 aliam *post* excludit *tr. et* ut *add.* Vb_1 excludere] excludit Vb_1

Contra.
om. per totum Vb_1

135. Secundum allegata iudicari debere.
72 L, 135 *et* 214 Vb

iudicari] iudicandum Vb_1 debere] videtur Vb_1

Contra.

136. Qui non facit quod facere debet, contra id facere videtur.

facere] non *male* Vb

137. Quod uni conceditur, filiis eius omnibus concessum intelligitur.

eius] de ca. *male* Vb

Contra.

138. Causa scandali vitandi aliquid esse obmittendum vel faciendum.

142. Multa bona prestantur unitis.

Contra.
rep. Vb

143. Qui tenet officium, teneat et beneficium et econverso.

Contra.

144. Nullus in aliqua ecclesia extraneus eligatur, si dignus in ea inveniatur.

Contra.

145. Quod favore alicuius introductum est, non est in eius lesionem retorquendum.

146. Quod iuris est in aliquo, idem in contrario.

in] mediorum *cum* ediorum *exp. et* m *corr.* (*homoiotel.*) Vb

147. Quod iuris est mediorum ad infima, adest superiorum ad media.

148. Quod sacramentum admitti non potest.

Contra.

150. Propter cautelam futuri periculi debet aliquid ad presens prohiberi.
150 *et* 186 Vb

151. Cum canones de rigore et alii ex dispensatione loquuntur, secundum rigorem iudicari debet.
151 *et* 196 Vb

de] ex Vb_1 loquuntur] locuntur Vb_1

152. Abstinendum est non solum a malo, sed etiam a spe mali.
152 *et* 199 Vb

spe] spem *male* Vb, specie Vb_1

153. Sepe aliquid irritatur ad iniuriam facientis.
153 *et* 202 Vb

154. Equitas et mansuetudo rigori preferetur.

preferetur] prefertur Vb

Contra: rigor servandus est.

155. Licitum est a contrario sensu argumentari.

156. Si pro te admittis, et contra te admittere debes.

te] irate *cum* ira *exp.* Vb

Contra.

157. Quandoque simulate acta vel ludicre, tamquam seria facta reputantur.

Contra.

158. Licite se ulciscitur provocatus.

Contra.

159. Statim, idest infra v. 'dies,' 'menses' proximos. Quandoque accipitur pro 'anno' et pro 'die.'

infra] insfra *cum* s *exp.* Vb proximos] pro *male* Vb

'Et' pro 'vel,' et e converso 'vel' pro 'et.'
Et—vel[1] *post* die *tr. male* Vb e *om. male* Vb pro] et[2] *praem. et exp.* Vb

160. Arg. quod quis per se non potest, potest tantum per alium.

161. Quod quis facere tenetur, per alium explicare non valet.

162. Presertim maxime quandoque ponuntur expositorie pro i.

163. Prelatus potest sibi subditos pena pecuniaria punire.

pena] penam *male* Vb

164. Non debet pars a toto discedere.

165. Arg. contra dissimulatores.

166. Nemini permittitur contra suum factum venire.

Contra.

Vel predecessoris sui.

Contrarium.

173. Quod semel bonum diffinitum est, nulla novitate potest mutare.

181. Quod fit contra leges, firmum esse non debet.

187. Una persona duarum personarum locum in iudicio videtur posse tenere, ut.

Contra.

188. Privilegium speciale ad consequentiam non trahitur, nec beneficium personale personam transgreditur, ut.

Contra.

189. Factum predecessoris successorem non ligat.

Contra.

190. Pro se aliquis testificari videtur, ut.

Contra.

191. Per exteriora indicia, interiora deprehenduntur.

192. Non licet superiori electum refutare, nisi ei aliquid opposuerit.

193. Sicut reprehensibile est penitus non facere quod debetur, sic reprehendendum est si in faciendo mora ingeritur.

194. Validum est argumentum quod a contrario sensu trahitur, ut.

195. Excusatur aliquis auctoritate maioris.

Contra.

197. Ratione facientis presumitur aliquid esse bonum.

198. Potest aliquis cogi tam ad ordinem quam ad dignitatem.

200. Imputatur ei qui sua culpa in necessitatem devenit.

Imputatur] Imputantur *male* Vb

201. Lapsi post personam restitui debent.

203. Non licet alicui exponere vel excipere quod in canone non invenitur expressum.

Contra.

204. Sumitur argumentum ex improprietate sermonis pro aliquo et contra aliquem.

205. Non sufficit ut aliquorum consensus sit concors, sed etiam canonicus.

206. Honestas preces subditi prelatus implere tenetur.

207. Citius quam potest iudex tenetur liti debitum finem imponere.

208. Quedam irritari debent, ne in exemplum mali, mali retineant.

209. Imperator ab apostolico gladii potestatem consequitur.

Contra.

210. Recte potest aliquis cogi ad accusandum, etiam ad deferendum testimonium veritati.

Contra.

211. Mucro anathematis dicitur tantum episcopo pertinere.

212. Habitu sine voce loquimur, et interdum simulatis operibus sine voce mentimur.

215. Propter inopiam probationum minus idonei testes recipiendi.

Contra.

216. Qui alias canonice puniri non potest, subiciatur verberibus.

217. Non tenet ab renuntiatio, nisi in manu prelati fiat, ut.

218. Non licet prelato excomunicato rem ecclesie alienare, ut.

219. Causa vitandi scandali sunt aliqua omittenda, ut.

220. Clerici, quia filiis Levi successerunt, paternam hereditatem petere non possunt.

Contra.

221. In confirmatione et consecratione archiepiscopi, consensus Romani pontificis desideratur, ut.

222. Cui minus non conceditur nec maius, et cui maius conceditur et minus, et cui principale et accessorium, ut.

223. Non cogitur subditus aliquid dare prelato, nisi probet per canones hoc sibi deberi, ut.

224. Consanguinitatis ratio contra aliquem sinistram generat presumptionem.

225. Prelati gravius sunt puniendi quam subditi, ut.

Contra.

226. Aliquis obligatus ere alieno vel alio debito, ad aliquam religionem transire non potest, ut.

Aliquis] Aliquos *cum* o *corr.* Vb ere] here *male* Vb

227. Testimonium de auditu recipitur.

Contra.

228. Propter similitudinem dicitur interdum aliquid esse 'crimen' quod non est.

229. Que per coactionem fuerint, non imputantur.

Contra.

230. Extrinseca peccantis merita et preterita conversatio dispensationem inducunt.

231. Iterata delicta gravius sunt punienda.

232. Tenentur principes ecclesiam etiam materiali gladio defendere, ut.

233. In quolibet promisso conditio 'si licita' intelligitur.

si *om. male* Vb

234. Iudex pro causa tractanda securum locum providere tenetur.

Contra.

235. Subditorum malitia prelato corrigenti non imputatur.

236. Ibi quis puniri debet in quo loco peccavit.

loco *om. male* Vb

237. Mitius animadvertitur in peccata multorum.

Vp

4. Nota quod si sacramentum necessitate quidem interveniente adimplere non poterit, non sit reus periurii, ut.

quidem] quod *male* Vp

5. Nota quod ex subsequenti operis presumitur contra aliquem et pro aliquo.

6. Nota quotiens aliquid rogando mandatum fieri totum impune, illud dimitti potest.

7. Quod si quis obligatus fuerit aliqua obligatione, ut sacramento vel alia, dare non teneatur, si ille cui promiserit suscipere voluit.

8. Quod ex auditu solo testimonium suscipiendum non est, ut.

Quod] Qui *cum* ui *exp. et corr.* Vp

43. Quod si omnes clerici fuerint in culpa etiam in faciendo eorum delictum, in dampnum ecclesie converti debeat.

44. Et similiter per vim deposita sit, si non recessit cum recedere potuit, consensisse videtur.

CHAPTER 4

Appendix: Other Texts Inserted into the *Perpendiculum*

1 Texts inserted into Several Manuscripts

1.1 *The* distinctio "Ad movendum varie iudicem"

Manuscripts in which this text appears: G, L, Mu1, P1, Vb, Vb_1, and Vb_2.

⟨1.⟩ Ad movendum varie iudicem.
⟨2.⟩ Delicto coram iudice manifestato aliquando allegantes delinquenti volumus implorare veniam. ⟨3.⟩ Aliquando contra ipsum volumus exasperare vindictam. ⟨4.⟩ Aliquando assidentes iudici iustitie ordine equitatis suadere volumus normam. ⟨5.⟩ Aliquando lesum inducere ut remittat gratis offensam.

⟨6.⟩ In primo casu.
⟨6.1.⟩ D. xlv. Licet plerumque (D.45 c.4) et c. Licet nonnunquam (D.45 c.6).
⟨6.2.⟩ C. xxxv. q. ix. Veniam (C.35 q.9 c.5) "sollicitos."
⟨6.3.⟩ D. xlv. Recedite (D.45 c.16).
⟨6.4.⟩ C. xxiii. q. iv. Duo (C.23 q.4 c.35) "nulli claudenda est."
⟨6.5.⟩ D. l. Ponderet (D.50 c.14) et c. Ut constitueretur (D.50 c.25).
⟨6.6.⟩ C. xxvi. q. vii. Alligant (C.26 q.7 c.12).
⟨6.7.⟩ C. xi. q. iii. Nemo (C.11 q.3 c.41).
⟨6.8.⟩ D. lxxxvi. Non satis (D.86 c.14).

---

1. *om. per totum* P1 ‖ varie] vario modo Vb_1 **2.** manifestato] manifeste L, manifesto P1 Vb_1 ‖ aliquando *om.* L ‖ delinquenti *post* veniam *tr.* P1, *the text ends here* Vb_1 ‖ veniam implorare veniam *tr.* L Mu1 **3.** volumus *ante* contra *tr.* L ‖ exasperare] implorare P1 ‖ vindictam] iudicium vel *praem.* G **4.** assidentes] existentes L ‖ ordine] ordinem G Vb Vb_2 ‖ equitatis] et *praem.* G Vb, equitatisque P1 ‖ volumus suadere *tr.* P1 ‖ normam] formam L **5.** inducere] iudicem G P1, in iudi Vb ‖ ut *rep.* G ‖ remittat] emittat Vb_2 ‖ offensam *om.* P1 **6.** casu] sic *add.* P1 **6.1.** et *om.* Vb ‖ c. *om.* L Vb_2 **6.2.** *post §3.5 tr.* Vb ‖ xi.] viii. L Mu1 ‖ Veniam] v. *add.* L Mu1 P1 ‖ sollicitos] sollicitas L, *om.* Vb_2 **6.3.** xlv.] lxv. P1 ‖ Recedite] Accedite L, Recidite inquiunt Mu1 **6.4.** *ante §3.6 tr.* Vb ‖ xxiii.] xxiv. G ‖ q. iv. *om.* G ‖ iv.] iii. Mu1 P1 ‖ Duo] c. *praem.* Mu1 ‖ nulli] et *praem.* L, nonnulli P1 ‖ est *om.* P1 Vb_2 **6.5.** *post §3.6 tr.* G, *ante §3.3 tr* Vb_2 ‖ Ponderet] Pondus P1 ‖ et c. *om.* L Vb_2 ‖ Ut *om.* P1 ‖ constitueretur] constituere P1 **6.6.** C.] D. G ‖ xxvi.] xvi. Mu1 ‖ vii.] v. G, vi. Vb_2 **6.7.** Nemo] c. *praem.* P1 Vb_2 **6.8.** *post §4 tr.* Vb ‖ Non] c. *praem* Mu1 Vb_2

 | DOI:10.1163/9789004713239_013

⟨7.⟩ In secundo casu.
⟨7.1.⟩ D. xlv. Et qui emendat (D.45 c.11).
⟨7.2.⟩ C. xxiii. q. iv. Duo (C.23 q.4 c.35) "nulli peccatori laxanda."
⟨7.3.⟩ D. l. c. i. (D.50 c.1) et ii. (D.50 c.2) et c. Postquam (D.50 c.11) et c. Absit (D.50 c.26) et c. Si quis prepostera (D.50 c.27).
⟨7.4.⟩ C. xxiii. q. iv. Est iniusta (C.23 q.4 c.33) in fine.
⟨7.5.⟩ D. xciii. Pervenit ad nos (D.93 c.21).
⟨7.6.⟩ C. xxi. q. ii. Placuit (C.21 q.2 c.2).
⟨7.7.⟩ C. xxxv. q. ix. Loci (C.35 q.9 c.2).

⟨8.⟩ In tertio casu.
⟨8.1.⟩ C. xi. q. iii. Summopere (C.11 q.3 c.70).
⟨8.2.⟩ C. ii. q. i. c. i. (C.2 q.1 c.1) et c. Deus (C.2 q.1 c.20).
⟨8.3.⟩ C. xxx. q. v. c. ante penultimo (C.30 q.5 c.9) et penultimo (C.30 q.5 c.10) et ultimo (C.30 q.5 c.11).
⟨8.4.⟩ D. xlv. Disciplina (D.45 c.9) et c. Omnis qui (D.45 c.10) et c. Sunt nonnulli (D.45 c.14) et c. Vera (D.45 c.15).
⟨8.5.⟩ D. lxxxvi. Odio (D.86 c.2).
⟨8.6.⟩ C. xxiv. q. iv. Duo (C.23 q.4 c.35).
⟨8.7.⟩ C. i. q. ultima Exigunt (C.1 q.7 c.18) et c. Etsi illa (C.1 q.7 c.23).
⟨8.8.⟩ D. xiv. Sicut (D.14 c.1).
⟨8.9.⟩ D. xxviii. Quia sunt culpe (D.28 c.10).

---

7. casu *om.* L Mu1 Vb$_2$ **7.1.** xlv.] xl. G ‖ Et] c. *praem.* G Mu1 **7.2.** *post* §*7.3 tr.* Vb, *rep.* Vb$_2$ ‖ xxiii.] xxxiii. L Mu1 ‖ iv.] iii. G ‖ Duo] Domino L ‖ peccato] peccatori G L Vb Vb$_2$ ‖ laxanda] relaxanda Fr, *om.* L Mu1 Vb, claudenda est Vb$_2^1$ **7.3.** i. et ii.] iii. Vb ‖ et^1 ii.] Duo P1 ‖ et^1 c.^{1} *om.* L P1 ‖ c.^{2} *om.* L ‖ et^3—prepostera *om.* Vb ‖ et^3 c.^{3} *om.* P1 ‖ et^4 *om.* Mu1 P1 ‖ c.^{3} *om.* L P1 ‖ quis] quid *cum* d *exp. et corr.* L ‖ prepostera] ds *cum* d *exp.* L, parte P1, potest Vb$_2$ **7.4.** *post* §*7.5 tr.* P1 ‖ *om. per totum* G ‖ C—iv. *om.* Vb ‖ iv.] i. P1 ‖ Est *om.* L ‖ in fine *om.* P1 ‖ fine] capitulo *add.* Vb$_2$ **7.5.** *post* §*4.7 tr.* Vb ‖ D] C G ‖ xciii.] C. Mu1 ‖ Pervenit] c. *praem.* L Mu1 Vb$_2$ ‖ ad nos *om.* L P1 ‖ nos *om.* Vb **7.6.** xxi.] xvi. Vb$_2$ ‖ Placuit] c. *praem.* Vb$_2$ **7.7.** q. *om.* Vb ‖ ix.] xi. P1 Vb ‖ Loci] c. *praem.* L Mu1, c. Loqui Vb$_2$ **8.** *om. per totum* Vb ‖ casu *om.* L Mu1, casus *cum* s^2 *exp.* P1 **8.1.** *om. per totum* Vb ‖ Summopere] Summo opere Vb$_2$ **8.2.** *post* §*8.3 tr.* Mu1, *om. per totum* Vb ‖ et *om.* P1 ‖ c.^{2} *om.* L **8.3.** *om. per totum* Vb ‖ xxx.] xxv. P1 ‖ v.] ultima P1 ‖ ante penultimo … penultimo] penultimo … ante penultimo *tr.* P1 ‖ et penultimo *om.* G Vb$_2$ ‖ ultimo … penultimo *tr.* L ‖ et^2 *om.* Vb$_2$ **8.4.** *om. per totum* Vb ‖ xlv.] lxlv. *cum* l^1 *exp.* P1 ‖ Disciplina] Disciplinam L ‖ c.^{1} *om.* L Vb$_2$ ‖ et^2—nonnulli *om.* Vb$_2$ ‖ et^2 c.^{2}] D. eadem L, enim P1 ‖ nonnulli *om.* L ‖ c.^{3} *om.* L **8.5.** *om. per totum* Vb ‖ Odio] c. Ordo Vb$_2$ **8.6.** *om. per totum* Vb ‖ xxiv.] xxxiv. L, xxviii. P1 ‖ Duo] c. *praem.* Vb$_2$ **8.7.** *om. per totum* Vb ‖ ultima] vii. P1 ‖ Exigunt] Exigere G ‖ et. c. *om.* L ‖ Etsi illa] Sulla L ‖ Etsi] Etiamsi G P1, ce si Vb$_2$ ‖ illa] olla P1 **8.8.** *om. per totum* Vb ‖ xiv.] xvii. Mu1, xxiii. P1 ‖ Sicut] Si cuius Mu1, c. *praem.* Vb$_2$ **8.9.** *om. per totum* G L Mu1 Vb Vb1 Vb2

⟨9.⟩ In quarto casu.
⟨9.1.⟩ D. xlv. Tria sunt (D.45 c.12) et c. Due sunt (D.45 c.13).
⟨9.2.⟩ D. xc. c. i. (D.90 c.1) et ii. (D.90 c.2) et iii. (D.90 c.3) et c. Placuit (D.90 c.9).
⟨9.3.⟩ In oratione dominica: "dimitte nobis" etc.
⟨9.4.⟩ In evangelio: "Serve, nequam quia noluisti misereri conservi tui, exigam a te universum debitum" (Mt 18:32–34).

⟨10.⟩ Casus tamen remittere non cogi nisi oblata satisfactione, ut:
⟨10.1.⟩ D. xc. Si quis contristatus (D.90 c.10).
⟨10.2.⟩ C. xxiii. q. iv. Si illic (C.23 q.4 c.29).

1.2 *The Gloss* "In multis"

Manuscripts in which this text appears: A, G, L, Mu1, and P1.

⟨1.⟩ In multis iuris articulis deterior est conditio feminarum quam masculorum: ff. de statu hominum, In multis (Dig. 1.5.9), etc.
⟨2.⟩ Verbi gratia, in: iurisdictione; arbitrio; tutele, cure susceptione; tabularum depositione; intercessione; adoptione; testamentaria testificatione; accusatione; delatione, ut ff. de iure fisci, Deferre (Dig. 49.14.18pr); procuratione; magistratus susceptione; postulatione:
⟨3.⟩ ff. de tutelis l. ultima (Dig. 26.1.18).
⟨4.⟩ ff. de fide instrumentorum l. ultima (Dig. 22.4.6).
⟨5.⟩ ff. de regulis iuris l. ii. (Dig. 50.17.2).
⟨6.⟩ ff. de iudiciis Cum § Non autem (Dig. 5.1.12.2).
⟨7.⟩ In Inst. de adoptionibus, Femine (Inst. 1.11.10).

---

9. casu *om.* L Mu1 Vb **9.1.** xlv.] xliii. Vb ‖ Tria] c. *praem.* L Mu1 ‖ et *om.* P1 Vb ‖ c. *om.* L P1 ‖ Due] Duo Mu1 **9.2.** xc.] xciii. P1 ‖ et[1]. *om.* L P1 Vb Vb_2 ‖ et[2]—Placuit *om.* P1 ‖ et[2]. *om.* Vb Vb_2 **9.3.** dimitte] ut *praem.* G Vb Vb_2, dimittit L, usque *praem.* P1 ‖ nobis *om.* Vb ‖ etc] et Vb_2 **9.4.** misereri] miseri L, *post* tui *tr.* P1 ‖ debitum] tuum *add.* Vb_2 **10.** Casus] Leso G, Lesus P1 Vb Vb_2 ‖ tamen *om.* Vb_2 ‖ remittere *ante* nisi *tr.* G P1 Vb ‖ cogi] cogitur Mu1 P1 ‖ oblata satisfactione] ut remiserat dationem L ‖ ut *om.* P1 **10.1** *om. per totum* P1 ‖ *post §7.2 tr.* Vb ‖ xc.] xx. G L ‖ contristatus] const. L, contristaverit Vb **10.2** xxiii.] xxiv. G L Mu1 Vb_2
1. *§1—§3 post §13 tr.* G ‖ iuris] et variis Mu1, *om.* P1 ‖ ff.] ut *praem.* G, ut infra *praem.* P1 ‖ statu] statutis P1 ‖ In[2] multis[2]] Inter litis L ‖ verbi] ubi L **2.** in *om.* P1 ‖ arbitrio] arbitrii A G L P1, arbitrarii Mu1 ‖ cure] iure A, cause L ‖ tabularum] tabulorum Mu1 ‖ depositione] depositum est G ‖ intercessione *om.* P1 ‖ adoptione *om.* P1 ‖ delatione] In *praem.* G P1 ‖ ut *om.* A ‖ ff.] infra G, infra *praem.* P1 ‖ de iure fisci *vac.* P1 ‖ Deferre] l. *praem.* G, l. differentie P1 ‖ procuratione] pro cautione G, pro tutore Mu1 ‖ postulatione] ut L **3.** ff.] ut infra *praem.* P1 **4.** ff.] et *praem.* L ‖ fide instrumentorum *male* fideiussoribus A G L Mu1 P1 **5.** D. i. l. v. P1 ‖ ff.] et *praem.* L **6.** iudiciis] viduis Mu1 ‖ Cum] pretor *add.* G P1 **7.** *om. per totum* P1 ‖ In *om.* A, Infra G ‖ adoptionibus] aptionibus A, adeptionibus G, acceptionibus Mu1

⟨8.⟩ In Inst. de ordine testamenti § Testes (Inst. 2.10.6).
⟨9.⟩ C. de arbitris, Sancimus (Cod. 2.55.6).
⟨10.⟩ ff. ad senatus consultum Velleianum, l. i. (Dig. 16.1.1) § Verba (Dig. 16.1.2.2).
⟨11.⟩ ff. de postulando l. i. § Secundo (Dig. 3.1.1.5).
⟨12.⟩ ff. de procuratoribus, Neque (Dig. 3.3.54pr).
⟨13.⟩ ff. de accusationibus, Qui accusare (Dig. 48.2.8).

2 Texts Inserted into G and P1

2.1 Brocardum e iure civilis

⟨1.⟩ Punitur quod factum iure non tenuit.
⟨2.⟩ ff. ad senatus consultum Turpillianum l. i. § Accusationem (Dig. 48.16.1.10).
⟨3.⟩ ff. ad legem Corneliam l. Si quis (Dig. 48.8.10).
⟨4.⟩ C. de sacrosanctis ecclesiis Iubemus § Sane (Cod. 1.2.14.3).
⟨5.⟩ ff. ad legem Iuliam de adulteriis Eum que (Cod. 9.9.18).
⟨6.⟩ C. si quacumque preditus dignitate (Cod. 5.7.1).
⟨7.⟩ Non punitur quod factum iure non tenuit.
⟨8.⟩ ff. quod quisque iuris l. i. § ultimo (Dig. 2.2.1.2).
⟨9.⟩ C. si mancipium ita fuerit alienatum, ut l. Ea (Cod. 4.57.5).

2.2 Distinctio de denuntiatione

⟨1.⟩ Denuntiatio:
⟨2.⟩ inducit dolum, ut ff. que in fraudem creditorum l. Ait pretor § i. (Dig. 42.8.1.1), ii. (Dig. 42.8.1.2);
⟨3.⟩ inducit malam fidem, ut C. de rei vindicatione Si fundum (Cod. 3.32.17);
⟨4.⟩ inducit accusationem, ut C. de negotiis gestis l. ultima (Cod. 2.18.24);
⟨5.⟩ impedit faciendum, irritat factum, ut ff. de operis (Dig. 39.1.0);
⟨6.⟩ inducit interpretationem, ut c. de plus petitionibus (Cod. 3.10.0).

---

8. *om. per totum* P1 ‖ In *om.* A, Infra G ‖ ordine *om.* G ‖ testamenti] testator G, testa. te. L ‖ Testes] Testis A, Teste G 9. C.] ff. A, S. P1 ‖ Sancimus] Sanctimus 10. *§10—§13 om. per totum* P1 ‖ consultum *vac.* G ‖ Velleianum *om.* A ‖ § u. *om.* G L 11. *om. per totum* A L Mu1 ‖ Secundo *male* ii. G P1 12. de *om.* A ‖ procuratoribus *vac.* G 3. longa in primis *add.* G 4. ecclesiis] et c. P1 7. *om. per totum* P1 8. iuris *om.* P1 9. mancipium] mancipius P1 ‖ ita *om.* P1 1. denuntiatio] denominatio P1 2. in fraudem] infimi. G ‖ i. ii.] iii. G 4. gestis *om.* P1 5. de *om.* P1 ‖ operis] novi *add.* P1 6. interpetationem] interruptionem P1

Bibliography

1 Primary Sources

1.1 *Manuscripts*

Aschaffenburg, HB, Perg. 26.

Barcelona, ACA, Cugat 55. Available at https://pares.mcu.es/ParesBusquedas20/catalogo/show/2345617. Accessed 2022 Oct 06.

Bamberg, SB, Can. 17 (P.I.11).

Cambridge, Pembroke College, 101.

Cambridge, Trinity College, B.1.29. Available at https://mss-cat.trin.cam.ac.uk/Manuscript/B.1.29/UV. Accessed 2024 Sep 01.

Fulda, HLB, 100 D. 10. Available at https://fuldig.hs-fulda.de/viewer/image/PPN440858038/1/LOG_0000/. Accessed 2022 Oct 06.

Grenoble, BM, 391 (1) Rés.

Leipzig, UB, 975, *Collectio Lipsiensis*. Available at https://digital.ub.uni-leipzig.de/object/viewid/0000004966. Accessed 2024 Jan 20.

Leipzig, UB, Rep. II 117. Available at https://www.digital.ub.uni-leipzig.de/object/viewid/0000013705. Accessed 2022 Oct 06.

Luxembourg, BNL, 139, *Brocarda Argumentum quod voluntas*.

Madrid, BNE, 421. Available at https://bdh-rd.bne.es/viewer.vm?id=0000012327. Accessed 2022 Oct 06.

Munich, BSB, Clm. 7622.

Munich, BSB, Clm. 8013. Available at https://www.digitale-sammlungen.de/en/view/bsb00092543. Accessed 2022 Oct 06.

Munich, BSB, Clm. 28175. Available at https://www.digitale-sammlungen.de/en/view/bsb00106853. Accessed 2024 Sep 01.

Oxford, University College, 117.

Paris, BNF, lat. 1566, *Collectio Parisiensis secunda*. Available at https://gallica.bnf.fr/ark:/12148/btv1b532472042. Accessed 2024 Jan 20.

Paris, BNF, lat. 4720A. Available at https://gallica.bnf.fr/ark:/12148/btv1b10722354w. Accessed 2022 Oct 06.

Paris, BNF, lat. 14606. Available at https://gallica.bnf.fr/ark:/12148/btv1b90666086. Accessed 2022 Oct 06.

Rome, Biblioteca Casanatense, 1105, *Distinctiones "Tria sunt que faciunt."*

Vatican City, BAV, Borgh. 261, *Notabilium fragmenta Borghesiana*. Available at https://digi.vatlib.it/view/MSS_Borgh.261. Accessed 2022 Oct 06.

Vatican City, BAV, Borgh. 287. Available at https://digi.vatlib.it/view/MSS_Borgh.287. Accessed 2022 Oct 06.

Vatican City, BAV, Chigi E.VII.218. Available at https://digi.vatlib.it/view/MSS_Chig.E.VII.218. Accessed 2022 Oct 06.

Vatican City, BAV, Pal. lat. 653. Available at https://digi.vatlib.it/view/bav_pal_lat_653. Accessed 2022 Oct 06.

Vienna, ONB, Cvpl. 2157, Pilius de Medicina, *Libellus Disputatorius*. Available at https://digital.onb.ac.at/RepViewer/viewer.faces?doc=DTL_3595012. Accessed 2022 Oct 06.

1.2 *Printed primary sources*

Accursius. *Glossa ordinaria ad Digestum vetus*. In *Pandectarum, seu digestorum Iuris Ciuilis*, ed. Nicolaus Bevilacqua. Venice: Bevilacqua, 1569.

Aristotle. *Categories and De Interpretatione*. Edited and translated by John Ackrill. Oxford: Clarendon Press, 1963.

Aristotle. *De sophisticis elenchi*. Edited by Bernard G. Dod. Leiden: Brill, 1975.

Aristotle. *Physica*. Edited by Fernand Bossier and Jozef Brams. Leiden: Brill, 1990.

Aristotle. *Aristotle's Physics: Books I and II*. Edited and translated by William Charlton. Oxford: Clarendon Press, 1970.

Atto of Vercelli. *Polipticum quod appellatur Perpendiculum*. Edited and translated by Giacomo Vignodelli, 2 vols. Florence: SISMEL-Edizioni del Galluzzo, 2019.

Augustine. *Confessionum libri XIII*. Edited by Luc Verheijen (Aurelii Augustini opera), 1:1. Turnhout: Brepols, 1981.

Augustine. *De doctrina Christiana*. Edited and translated by R.P.H. Green. Oxford: Clarendon Press, 1995.

Augustine. *De utilitate agendae poenitentiae*. PL 39:1549–1560.

Azo. *Glosse preaccursiane alle istituzioni: Strato azzoniano*. Edited by Severino Caprioli et al., 2 vols. Rome: Istituto Storico Italiano per il Medio Evo, 1984–2004.

Bartholomaeus Brixiensis. *Casus decretorum*. Edited by Nikolaus Kessler. Basel: Kessler, 1489.

Bernardus Papiensis. *Bernardus Papiensis Faventini episcopi Summa decretalium*. Edited by Ernst A.T. Laspeyres. Regensburg: Manz, 1860.

Bertrandus Metensis. *Bertrandus Metensis de regulis iuris*. Edited by Severino Caprioli. Perugia: Università di Perugia, 1981.

Boethius. *In Ciceronis Topica*. Edited and translated by Eleonore Stump. Ithaca, New York: Cornell University Press, 1988.

Böhmer, Justus Henning, ed. *Corpus Iuris Canonici*, 2 vols. Halle: Orphanotropheus, 1747.

Brundage, James A. "The Quaestiones of Rotbertus Modicipassus in a Barcelona Manuscript." *Studies in Medieval Culture* 5 (1975): 87–95.

Brundage, James A. "Some Canonistic Quaestiones in Barcelona." *Manuscripta* 15 (1971): 67–76.

Burchard of Worms. *Burchardi Wormatiensis ecclesiae episcopi decretorum libri XX: Ergänzter Neudruck der Editio princeps Köln 1548*. Edited by Gérard Fransen and Theo Kölzer. Aalen: Scientia Verlag, 1992.

Cicero. *De inventione*. Edited and translated by Harry M. Hubbell. Cambridge, Massachusets: Harvard University Press/London: Heinemann, 1949.

Cicero. *Topica*. Edited and translated by Wilhelm Friedrich (M. Tullii Ciceronis scripta quae manserunt omnia) 1:2. Leipzig: Teubner, 1912.

Caprioli, Severino, ed. *Modi arguendi: Testi per lo studio della retorica nel sistema del diritto comune*. Spoleto: Centro Italiano di Studi sull'Alto Medioevo, 2006.

Coppens, Christian, ed. "Libellus de ordine iudiciorum." In *Voortschrijdend Procesrecht. Ein historische Verkenning*, ed. C.H. van Rhee, F. Stevens, and Ernest Persoons, 219–295. Leuven: Universitaire Pers Leuven, 2001.

Crabbe, Pierre, ed. *Concilia omnia tam generalia quam particularia*, 2nd ed., 1. Cologne: Quentel, 1551.

de Libera, Alain. *César et le Phénix: Distinctiones et sophismata parisiens du XIIIe siècle*. Pisa: Scuola Normale Superiore, 1999.

Dreves, Guido Maria, Clemens Blume, and Henry Marriott Bannister, eds. *Analecta hymnica*, 55 vols. Leipzig: Fues's Verlag/Reisland, 1886–1922.

Ebbesen, Sten. "Anonymi Parisiensis Compendium Sophisticorum Elenchorum: The Upsala Version." *Cahier de l'Institut du Moyen Age grec et latin* 66 (1996): 253–312.

Ebbesen, Sten, and Yukio Iwakuma. "Compendium Sophisticorum Elenchorum (ms. Paris BN 4720A)," *Cahiers de l'Institut du Moyen-Âge Grec et Latin* 60 (1990): 47–112.

Ebbesen, Sten. "Paris 4720A: A 12th Century Compendium of Aristotle's Sophistici Elenchi." *Cahier de l'Institut du Moyen Age grec et latin* 10 (1973): 1–20.

Elliot, Michael D., ed. *Wigorniensis D (Barlow 37)*. Available at http://individual.utoronto.ca/michaelelliot/manuscripts/texts/transcriptions/wigorniensisD.pdf. Accessed 2020 Aug 28.

Fitting, Hermann, ed. *Summa Codicis des Irnerius*. Berlin: Guttentag, 1894.

Fransen, Gérard. "Canonistica minora." In *Xenia iuris historiae G. van Dievoet oblata*, ed. Fred Stevens and Dirk Van den Auweele, 33–54. Leuven: Katholieke Universiteit Leuven, Faculteit der Rechtsgeleerdheid, Afdeling Romeins Recht en Rechtgeschiedenis, 1990. Reprinted in Gérard Fransen, *Canones et Quaestiones: Évolution des doctrines et système du droit canonique*, 1.1:625–646. Goldbach: Keip, 2002.

Fransen, Gérard. "États différents d'une même Question disputée." *ZRG Kan. Abt.* 68 (1982): 136–152. Reprinted in Gérard Fransen, *Canones et Quaestiones: Évolution des doctrines et système du droit canonique*, 1.2:215–231. Goldbach: Keip, 2002.

Fransen, Gérard. "États différents d'une même Question disputée." *ZRG Kan. Abt.* 74 (1988): 141–167.

Fransen, Gérard. "Le mariage simulé: Deux questions disputées au XIIe siècle." In

Études de droit et d'histoire: Mélanges mgr. H. Wagnon, 531–541. Leuven: Bibliotheque Centrale de l'U.C.L., 1976. Reprinted in Gérard Fransen, *Canones et Quaestiones: Évolution des doctrines et système du droit canonique*, 2:305–315. Goldbach: Keip, 2002.

Fransen, Gérard. "Quaestiones Aschaffenburgenses." BMCL 16 (1986): 71–86. Reprinted in Gérard Fransen, *Canones et Quaestiones: Évolution des doctrines et système du droit canonique*, 1.2:355–370. Goldbach: Keip, 2002.

Fransen, Gérard. "Quaestiones Barcinonenses breves." BMCL 15 (1985): 31–49. Reprinted in Gérard Fransen, *Canones et Quaestiones: Évolution des doctrines et système du droit canonique*, 1.2:335–353. Goldbach: Keip, 2002.

Fransen, Gérard. "Quaestiones decretales dans un manuscrit espagnol." In *Sine invidia communico: Opstellen aangeboden aan Prof. Dr. A.J. de Groot*, ed. Paul L. Nève and Emile Christian Coppens, 2nd ed., 81–102. Nijmegen: Gerard Noodt Instituut, Katholieke Universiteit Nijmegen, 1987. Reprinted in Gérard Fransen, *Canones et Quaestiones: Évolution des doctrines et système du droit canonique*, 1.2:313–333. Goldbach: Keip, 2002.

Fransen, Gérard. "Les 'Questiones' des canonistes: Essai de dépouillement et de classement (I)." *Traditio* 12 (1956): 566–592. Reprinted in Gérard Fransen, *Canones et Quaestiones: Évolution des doctrines et système du droit canonique*, 1.2:1–27. Goldbach: Keip, 2002.

Fransen, Gérard. "Les 'Questiones' des canonistes II." *Traditio* 13 (1957): 481–501. Reprinted in Gérard Fransen, *Canones et Quaestiones: Évolution des doctrines et système du droit canonique*, 1.2:29–49. Goldbach: Keip, 2002.

Fransen, Gérard. "Les 'Questiones' des canonistes III." *Traditio* 19 (1963): 516–531. Reprinted in Gérard Fransen, *Canones et Quaestiones: Évolution des doctrines et système du droit canonique*, 1.2:51–66. Goldbach: Keip, 2002.

Fransen, Gérard. "Les 'Quaestiones Neapolitanae'." BMCL 6 (1976): 29–46. Reprinted in Gérard Fransen, *Canones et Quaestiones: Évolution des doctrines et système du droit canonique*, 1.2:197–214. Goldbach: Keip, 2002.

Fransen, Gérard. "Questiones Lemovicenses II." *ZRG Kan. Abt.* 76 (1990): 156–171. Reprinted in Gérard Fransen, *Canones et Quaestiones: Évolution des doctrines et système du droit canonique*, 1.2:411–426. Goldbach: Keip, 2002.

Fransen, Gérard. "Les questions disputées de Maitre S." In *Satura Roberto Feenstra sexagesimum quintum annum aetatis complenti ab alumnis collegis amicis oblata*, ed. Johan Albert Ankum, Johannes Emil Spruit, and Felix B.J. Wubbe, 331–343. Fribourg: Éditions universitaires, 1985. Reprinted in Gérard Fransen, *Canones et Quaestiones: Évolution des doctrines et système du droit canonique*, 1.2:299–311. Goldbach: Keip, 2002.

Fransen, Gérard. *Summa 'Elegantius in iure divino' seu Coloniensis*. Vatican City: BAV, 1986.

Friedberg, Emil, ed. *Die Canones-Sammlungen zwischen Gratian und Bernhard von Pavia*. Leipzig: Tauchnitz, 1897.

Friedberg, Emil, ed. *Quinque compilationes antiquae nec non collectio canonum Lipsiensis ad librorum manu sciptorum fidem recognovit et adnotatione critica*. Leipzig: Tauchnitz, 1882.

Gandulphus. *Magistri Gandulphi Bononiensis sententiarum libri quatuor*. Edited by Johannes Wilhelm von Walter. Vienna: Aemilius Haim, 1924.

García y García, Antonio, ed. *Constitutiones Concilii quarti Lateranensis una cum Commentariis glossatorum*. Vatican City: BAV, 1981.

Gillmann, Franz. "Die Dekretglossen des Cod. Stuttgart. hist. f. 419." AKKR 107 (1927): 192–250. Reprinted in *Gesammelte Schriften zur klassischen Kanonistik von Franz Gillmann*, ed. Rudolf Weigand, 1:3–70, no. 14. Würzburg: Echter, 1988.

Gratian. *Decretum magistri Gratiani Editio Lipsiensis secunda post Aemilii Ludovici Richteri curas ad librorum manu scriptorum et editionis Romanae fidem recognovit et adnotatione critica instruxit Aemilius Friedberg*. Edited by Emil Friedberg. Leipzig: Tauchnitz, 1879.

Gregory the Great. *Moralia in Iob*. Edited by Marc Adriaen. Turnhout: Brepols, 1979.

Gregory the Great. *Registrum epistularum: Libri I–VII*. Edited by Dag Norbeg. Turnhout: Brepols, 1982.

Gross, Carl, ed. *Incerti auctoris Ordo judiciarius, pars summae legum et Tractatus de praescriptione: Nach einer Göttweiger* (*Stiftsbibliothek, saec.12. ex.*) *und einer Wiener* (*Hofbibliothek, saec.13. ex.*) *Handschrift*. Innsbruck: Verlag von Wagner'schen Universitäts-Buchhandlung, 1870.

Guillelmus Durantis. *Repertorium aureum corpore iuris canonici*. Rome: Schencbecher, 1474.

Guillelmus Durantis. *Speculum iuris*, 2 vols. Basel: apud Ambrosium et Aurelium, 1574; reprinted Aalen: Scientia-Verlag, 1975.

Honorius of Kent. *Magistri Honorii Summa 'De iure canonico tractaturus'*. Edited by Rudolf Weigand, Peter Landau, Waltraud Kozur, Stephan Haering, Karin Miethaner-Vent, and Martin Petzolt, 3 vols. Vatican City: BAV, 2004–2010.

Hugh of St Victor. *Hugonis de Sancto Victore Didascalicon De studio legendi. A Critical Text*. Edited by Charles H. Buttimer. Washington, D.C.: The Catholic University Press, 1939.

Isidore of Seville. *Etymologiarum sive Originum*. Edited by Wallace M. Lindsay. Oxford: Clarendon Press, 1911.

Isidore of Seville. *The Etymologies of Isidore of Seville*. Edited and translated by Stephen A. Barney, Jennifer Beach, W.J. Lewis, Oliver Berghof, and Muriel Hall. Cambridge: Cambridge University Press, 2006.

Iulianus. *Iuliani Epitome Latina Novellarum Iustiniani*. Edited by Pietro Fiorelli and

Anna Maria Bartoletti Colombo. Florence: Università degli studi di Firenze, Dipartimento di teoria e storia del diritto, 1996.

Jaffé, Philippe, Samuel Löwenfeld, Ferdinand Kaltenbrunner, and Paul Eward, eds. *Regesta pontificum Romanorum*, 2 vols. Leipzig: Veit, 1885–1888.

Krüger, Paul, ed. *Corpus Iuris Civilis, II, Codex Iustinianus*. Berlin: Weidmann, 1877.

Mansi, Giovanni Domenico, ed. "Appendix Concilii Lateranensis." In *Sacrorum Conciliorum nova et amplissima collectio*, ed. Giovanni Domenico Mansi, 22:248–453. Florence/Venice: Zatta, 1778.

McLaughlin, Terence P., ed. *The Summa Parisiensis on the Decretum Gratiani*. Toronto: Pontifical Institute of Mediaeval Studies, 1952.

Mommsen, Theodor, and Paul Krüger, eds. *Corpus Iuris Civilis, I, Institutiones et Digesta*. Berlin: Weidmann, 1868.

Palmieri, Giovanni Battista, and Augusto Gaudenzi, eds. *Bibliotheca Iuridica Medii Aevii. Scripta anecdota glossatorum*, 2nd ed., 2 vols. Bologna: Ex aedibus Angeli Gandolphi Typis Societatis Azzoguidianae, 1913–1914.

Palmieri, Giovanni Battista, ed. *Quaestiones dominorum Bononiensium: Collectio Parisiensis*, BIMAE, 1: 235–264.

Palmieri, Giovanni Battista, ed., *Wernerii Summa Institutionum cum glossis Martini, Bulgari, Alberici aliorumve*, BIMAE, 1, *Additiones*: 1–208.

Peter of Blois. *Petri Blesensis opusculum de distinctionibus in canonum interpretatione adhibendis, sive ut auctor voluit 'Speculum iuris canonici.'* Edited by Gottlieb Reimer. Berlin: Reimer, 1837.

Peter Lombard. *Libri sententiarum*. PL 192:519–964.

Pilius de Medicina. *Libellus Pylei Disputatorius: Liber Primus*. Edited by Jürgen Meyer-Nelthropp. PhD dissertation: University of Hamburg, 1958.

Placentinus, *Placentini Summa Codicis*. Edited by Nicolaus Rhodius. Mainz: Ivo Schoeffer, 1536; reprinted Turin: Bottega d'Erasmo, 1962.

Placentinus. *Placentini Summa Institutionum*. Edited by Nicolaus Rhodius. Mainz: Schoeffer, 1535; reprinted Turin: Bottega d'Erasmo, 1973 (CGJC 1:1).

Pseudo-Damasus. *Die "Summa de ordine iudiciario" des Magister Damasus*. Edited by Ludwig Wahrmund. Innsbruck: Wagner, 1926; reprinted Aalen: Scientia Verlag, 1962.

Quintilianus. *Institutio Oratoria*. Edited and translated by Harold E. Butler, 2. Cambridge, Massachusetts: Harvard University Press, 1921.

Rabanus Maurus. *De rerum naturis*. PL 111:9–612.

Rainerius Perusinus. *Die Ars Notariae des Rainerius Perusinus*. Edited by Ludwig Wahrmund. Innsbruck: Wagner, 1917.

Richter, Emil Ludwig, and Emil Friedberg, eds. *Decretalium Collectiones: Decretales Gregorii p. IX*. Leipzig: Tauchnitz, 1881.

Rogerius. *Catalogus prescriptionum*. In *Octavum volumen tractatuum e variis iuris inter-*

pretibus collectorum. Lyon: Regnault, 1549; reprinted Turin: Bottega d'Erasmo, 1970 (CGJC 5:6).

Rufinus. *Die Summa magistri Rufini zum Decretum Gratiani*. Edited by Johann Friedrich von Schulte. Giessen: E. Roth, 1892.

Schoell, Rudolf, and Wilhelm Kroll, eds. *Corpus Iuris Civilis, III, Novellae*. Berlin: Weidmann, 1895.

Schulte, Johann Friedrich von, ed. *Der ordo iudiciarius des Codex Bambergensis P I II, Wiener SitzB. 70*. Vienna: Gerold, 1872.

Simon de Bisignano. *Summa in Decretum Simonis Bisinianensis*. Edited by Pier V. Aimone-Braida. Vatican City: BAV, 2014.

Société des Bollandistes, ed. *Bibliotheca hagiographica Latina antiquae et mediae aetatis*, 2 vols. Bruxelles: Société des Bollandistes, 1898–1901.

Stephen of Tournai. *Die Summa über das Decretum Gratiani*. Edited by Johann Friedrich von Schulte. Giessen: E. Roth, 1891.

Tamassia, Nino, and Giovanni Battista Palmieri, eds. *Iohannis Bassiani Libellus de ordine judiciorum*. BIMAE, 2:229–248.

Tancred of Bologna. *Ordo iudiciarius*. Edited by Friedrich Bergmann. In *Pillii, Tancredi, Gratiae libri de iudiciorum ordine*, ed. Friedrich Bergmann, 82–314. Göttingen: Vandenhoeck et Ruprecht, 1842.

Victorinus, Gaius Marius. *Commenta in Ciceronis Rhetorica*. Edited by Thomas Riesenweber. Berlin: De Gruyter, 2013.

Viora, Mario, ed. *Corpus Glossatorum Juris Civilis*, 11 vols. Turin: Bottega d'Erasmo, 1966–1973.

Wallinga, Tammo. *The Casus Codicis of Wilhelmus de Cabriano*. Frankfurt am Main: Klostermann, 2005.

Weigand, Rudolf. "Die Glossen des Johannes Faventinus zur Causa 1 des Dekrets und ihr Vorkommen in späteren Glossenapparaten." AKKR 157 (1988): 73–107.

Weigand, Rudolf. "Die Glossen des Simon von Bisignano." AKKR 161 (1992): 362–395.

Weigand, Rudolf. *Die Glossen zum Dekret Gratians*, 2. Rome: Libreria Ateneo Salesiano, 1991.

Weigand, Rudolf, Peter Landau, Waltraud Kozur, Stephan Haering, Karin Miethaner-Vent, and Martin Petzolt, eds. *Summa 'Omnis qui iuste iudicat' sive Lipsiensis*, 5 vols. Vatican City: BAV, 2007–2018.

Weigand, Rudolf. "W.-Glossen zum Dekret Gratian." In *Ministerium Iustitiae: Festschrift für Heribert Heinemann zur Vollendung des 60. Lebensjahres*, ed. André Gabriels and Heinrich J.F. Reinhardt, 151–159. Essen: Ludgerus-Verlag, 1985.

Yukio, Iwakuma. "Two more Instantia Texts: An edition." *Zinbun* 24 (1989): 13–88.

2 Secondary Sources

Andrés, Gregorio de. "Catálogo de los manuscritos de la biblioteca del Duque de Uceda." *Revista de archivos, bibliotecas y museos* 78 (1975): 5–40.

Ashdowne, Richard K., David R. Howlett, and Ronald E. Latham, eds. *Dictionary of Medieval Latin from British Sources*. Oxford: Oxford University Press, 2018. Available at http://logeion.uchicago.edu. Accessed 2021 Sep 14.

Austin, Greta. *Shaping Church Law Around the Year 1000. The Decretum of Burchard of Worms*. Farnham: Ashgate, 2009.

"Bamberg, Staatsbibliothek Bamberg, Msc.Can.17." In *Handschriften Portal*. Available at https://resolver.staatsbibliothek-berlin.de/HSP0004E4F500000000. Accessed 2024 Jan 20.

Barlow, Frank. "Apulia, Simon of." In *ODNB*. Published online: May 24, 2007. DOI: 10.1093/ref:odnb/94380.

Bauch, Andreas. *Das theologisch-aszetische Schrifttum des Eichstätter Bischofs Philipp von Rathsamhausen (1306–1322)*. Eichstätt: Verlag der Katholischen Kirche in Bayern, 1948.

Bellomo, Manlio. "'Factum' e 'ius': Tra le certezze e i dubbi del pensiero giuridico medievale." *RIDC* 6 (1996): 21–45. Reprinted in Manlio Bellomo, *Medioevo edito e inedito*, 2:63–89. Rome: Il Cigno Galileo Galilei, 1997.

Bellomo, Manlio. *I fatti e il diritto tra le certezze e i dubbi dei giuristi medievali (secoli XIII–XIV)*. Rome: Il Cigno Galileo Galilei, 2000.

Bellomo, Manlio. "Legere, repetere, disputare: Introduzione ad una ricerca sulle 'quaestiones' civilistiche." In Manlio Bellomo, *Aspetti dell'insegnamento giuridico nelle Università medievali. Le 'quaestiones disputatae,'* 13–81. Reggio Calabria: Parallelo 38, 1974. Reprinted in Manlio Bellomo, *Medioevo edito e inedito*, 1:53–97. Rome: Il Cigno Galileo Galilei, 1997.

Bellomo, Manlio. "Una nuova figura intellettuale: il giurista." In *Il secolo XI: Una svolta?*, ed. Cinzio Violante and Johannes Fried, 237–256. Bologna: Il Mulino, 1993. Reprinted in Manlio Bellomo, *Medioevo edito e inedito*, 2:5–21. Rome: Il Cigno Galileo Galilei, 1997.

Belloni, Annalisa. *Le questioni civilistiche del secolo XII*. Frankfurt am Main: Klostermann, 1989.

Berman, Harold J. *Law and Revolution*, 2 vols. Cambridge, Massachusetts: Belknap Press, 1983–2003.

Bernards, Matthäus. "Zur Überlieferung mittelalterlicher theologischer Schriften: Neue Handschriften." *Recherches de théologie ancienne et médiévale* 19 (1952): 327–336.

Bertram, Martin. "Rodoicus Modicipassus und der Praecentor von Sens. Wer war der Verfasser der Dekretsummen 'Omnis qui iuste iudicat' (Lipsiensis), 'Et est sciendum' und des Ordo iudiciarius 'Olim edebatur'?" *Mittelalter: Interdisziplinäre Forschung und Rezeptionsgeschichte* 3 (2020): 120–153.

Bertram, Martin. "Simon of Apulia: Randbemerkungen zu der Edition der Dekretsumme des Simon von Bisignano." *Mittelalter: Interdisziplinäre Forschung und Rezeptionsgeschichte* 18 (2017): 1–27.

Bettetini, Andrea. "Giovanni da Faenza (Johannes Faventinus)." In *DBGI*, 1:1013–1014.

Bischoff, Bernhard. *Die Abtei Lorsch im Spiegel ihrer Handschriften*, 2nd ed. Lorsch: Laurissa, 1989.

Bohácek, Miroslav. "Un manuscrit intéressant du 'Compendium' de Werner von Schussenried." *Traditio* 18 (1962): 472–482.

Boureau, Alain. *L'Empire du livre: Pour une histoire du savoir scolastique (1200–1380)*. Paris: Belles Lettres, 2007.

Boureau, Alain. *La loi du royaume: Les moines, le droit et la construction de la nation anglaise (XIe–XIIIe siècles)*. Paris: Belles Lettres, 2001.

Brasington, Bruce. "'A Minor Literary Genre': Examination of Selected 12th Century Canonistic Argumenta/Notabilia." In *Proceedings of the Fifteenth International Congress of Medieval Canon Law: Paris, 17–23 July 2016*, ed. Florence Demoulin-Auzary, Nicolas Laurent-Bonne, and Franck Roumy, 1159–1173. Vatican City: BAV, 2022.

Brasington, Bruce. *Order in the Court: Medieval Procedural Treatises in Translation*. Leiden: Brill, 2016.

Brett, Martin. "English Law and Centres of Law Studies in the Later Twelfth Century." In *Archbishop Eystein as Legislator: The European Connection*, ed. Tore Iversen, 87–102. Trondheim: Tapir, 2011.

Brundage, James A. and Melodie H. Eichbauer, *Medieval Canon Law*, 2nd ed. London: Routledge, 2023.

Buchner, Jürgen. *Die Paleae im Dekret Gratians: Untersuchung ihrer Echtheit*. Rome: Pontificium Athenaeum Antonianum, 2000.

Buchthal, Hugo. "A School of Miniature Painting in Norman Sicily." In *Late Classical and Medieval Studies in Honour of Albert Mathias Friend jr.*, ed. Kurt Weitzmann, Sirarpie der Nersessian, George H. Forsyth, Jr., Ernst H. Kantorowicz, and Theodor E. Mommsen, 312–339. Princeton, New Jersey: Princeton University Press, 1955.

Caillemer, Exupère. "Le droit civil dans les provinces anglo-normandes au XIIe siècle." *Mémoires de l'Académie nationale des Sciences, Arts et Belles-Lettres de Caen* 1883 (1883): 157–226,

Calasso, Francesco. *Medio Evo del diritto: I. Le fonti*. Milan: Giuffrè, 1954.

Cambridge Dictionary, s.v. "presumption." Available at http://dictionary.cambridge.org/dictionary/english/presumption. Accessed 2021 January 25.

Carbasse, Jean-Marie. "L'ordo iudiciorum Sapientiam affectant omnes." In *Confluence des droits savants et des pratiques juridique. Actes du colloque de Montpellier (12–14 décembre 1977)*, 15–36. Milan: Giuffrè, 1979.

Condorelli, Orazio. "A proposito della Summa in Decretum di Simone da Bisignano edita da Pier V. Aimone Braida." *BMCL* 32 (2015): 37–55.

Condorelli, Orazio. "Note su formazione e diffusione delle raccolte di quaestiones disputatae in diritto canonico (secoli XII–XIV)." In *Juristische Buchproduktion im Mittelalter*, ed. Vincenzo Colli, 395–430. Frankfurt am Main: Klostermann, 2002.

Conrat, Max. *Geschichte der Quellen und Literatur des römischen Rechts im früheren Mittelalter*. Leipzig: Hinrichs, 1891.

Conte, Emanuele. "Il Digesto fuori dal Digesto." In *Interpretare il Digesto: Storia e metodi*, ed. Antonio Padoa-Schioppa and Dario Mantovani, 277–298. Pavia: IUSS Press, 2014.

Conte, Emanuele. *Diritto comune: Storia e storiografia di un sistema dinamico*. Bologna: Il Mulino, 2009.

Conte, Emanuele. "La France dans une 'Europe juridique'? La relation à l'Italie au 12ème siècle." *RSDI* 94, no. 2 (2021): 17–37.

Conte, Emanuele. "Lapse of Time in Medieval Laws: Procedure, Prescription, Presumptions, Custom." In *Limitation and Prescription: A Comparative Legal History*, ed. Harry Dondorp, David Ibbetson, and Eltjo J.H. Schrage, 69–90. Berlin: Duncker & Humblot, 2019.

Conte, Emanuele. "Ordo iudicii et regula iuris: Bulgarus et les origines de la culture juridique (XIIe siècle)." In *Frontières des savoirs en Italie à l'époque des premières universités*, ed. Joel Chandelier and Aurelien Robert, 157–176. Rome: École française de Rome, 2015.

Conte, Emanuele. "Piacentino." In *DBI* 83 (2015). Available at https://www.treccani.it/enciclopedia/piacentino_(Dizionario-Biografico)/. Accessed 2022 Jul 31.

Conte, Emanuele. "Pillio da Medicina." In *DBI* 83 (2015). Available at https://www.treccani.it/enciclopedia/pillio-da-medicina_(Dizionario-Biografico)/. Accessed 2022 Jul 31.

Conte, Emanuele. *Servi medievali: Dinamiche del diritto comune*. Rome: Viella, 1996.

Conte, Emanuele, and Sara Menzinger. *La Summa Trium Librorum di Rolando da Lucca (1195–1234): Fisco, politica, scientia iuris*. Rome: Viella, 2012.

Conte, Emanuele. "Verona 1187. Pillius and the Monks of Canterbury." Under publication in the *Studies in Honour of Anne Duggan*.

Cortese, Ennio. "Alle origini della scuola di Bologna." *RIDC* 4 (1993): 7–49. Reprinted in Ennio Cortese, *Scritti*, 2:1095–1137. Spoleto/Rome: Centro italiano di studi sull'alto Medioevo/Il Cigno Galileo Galilei, 1999.

Cortese, Ennio. "Bassiano (Bosiano, Boxiano), Giovanni." In *DBGI*, 1:191–193.

Cortese, Ennio. *Il diritto nella storia medievale*, 2. Rome: Il Cigno Galileo Galilei, 1995.

Cortese, Ennio. "Lex, aequitas, utrumque ius nella prima civilistica." In *Lex et iustitia nell'utrumque ius: Radici antiche e prospettive attuali; Atti del 7. Colloquio inter-*

nazionale romanistico-canonistico (12–14 maggio 1988), ed. Americo Ciani and Giovanni Diurni, 95–119. Vatican City: Libreria Editrice Vaticana, 1989. Reprinted in Ennio Cortese, *Scritti*, 2:1019–1043. Spoleto/Rome: Centro italiano di studi sull'alto Medioevo/Il Cigno Galileo Galilei, 1999.

Cortese, Ennio. *La norma giuridica: Spunti teorici nel diritto comune classico*. Milan: Giuffrè, 1964; reprinted Rome: Senato della Repubblica, 2020.

Cortese, Ennio. "Piacentino." In *DBGI*, 2:1568–1571.

Cortese, Ennio. "Pillio." In *DBGI*, 2:1587–1590.

Cortese, Ennio. *Il Rinascimento giuridico medievale*, 2nd ed. Rome: Il Cigno Galileo Galilei, 1996.

Cortese, Ennio. "Rogerio." In *DBGI*, 2:1716–1717.

Coxe, Henry O. *Catalogus codicum MSS. qui in collegiis aulisque Oxoniensibus hodie adservantur*, 1. Oxford: E Typographeo Academico, 1852.

Cuena Boy, Francisco. "Presunciones (DCH)." *Max Planck Institute for European Legal History Research Paper Series*, 2018–06 (2018): 1–25.

Curtius, Ernst R. *European Literature and the Latin Middle Ages*. Translated by Willard R. Trask. New York: Pantheon Books, 1953.

Dahan, Gilbert. "L'Exégèse de l'histoire de Caïn et Abel du XIIe au XIVe siècle en Occident: Textes." *Recherches de théologie ancienne et médiévale* 49 (1982): 21–89.

Dalbrenta, Daniele Velo. *Brocardica: Una introduzione allo studio e all'uso dei brocardi. Principi di filosofia forense*. Milan: Franco Angeli, 2007.

Daneu Lattanzi, Angela. "Due sconosciuti manoscritti di epoca normanna." In *Atti del Convegno Internazionale di Studi Ruggeriani (Palermo 21–25 aprile 1954)*, ed. Società siciliana per la storia patria, 1: 303–316. Palermo: Scuola linotypografica Boccone del povero, 1955.

De Concilio, David. "Imputer l'intention dans les procédures romano-canoniques. Réflexions sur la théorie des présomptions autour du Concile du Latran IV." In *Intention, imputation, responsabilité Autour du concile du Latran IV*, ed. I. Rosier-Catach, R. Eckert, C. Grellard, and C. Leveleux-Teixeira. Rennes: Presses Universitaires de Rennes, forthcoming.

De Concilio, David. "Moneta e cultura giuridica: Un brocardo di Azzone nella costruzione del diritto pecuniario medievale." *TvR* 87 (2019): 384–426.

De Concilio, David. "Soggettività e qualificazione del fatto. L'indagine del factum intrinsecum tra diritto e teologia nel XII secolo: due casi di studio e spunti per una ricerca." *Historia et Ius* 22 (2022), paper 9: 1–42. Reprinted in *Tra diritto e religione. Dialoghi e influenze nella storia giuridica*, ed. Marta Cerrito and Francesco Di Chiara, 27–71. Rome: Historia et Ius, 2023.

De Concilio, David. *Via Brocardica: The Development of Brocards and the Western European Legal Tradition (c. 1160–c .1215)*, 2 vols. PhD dissertation: University of St Andrews, 2022.

Deeters, Walter. *Die Bambergensisgruppe der Dekretalensammlungen des 12. Jahrhunderts*. PhD dissertation: University of Bonn, 1956.

De Fraja, Valeria. "Le prime fonti di Gioacchino da Fiore Libri e intellettuali nel Regno di Sicilia." *BISM* 116 (2014): 93–129.

de Libera, Alain. "Bulletin d'Histoire de la Logique Médiévale." *Revue des Sciences philosophiques et théologiques* 76 (1992): 640–666.

De Rijk, Lambertus Marie. *Logica Modernorum: A Contribution to the History of Early Terminist Logic*, 2.1. Assen: Van Gorcum, 1967.

De Rijk, Lambertus Marie. *Some Earlier Parisian Tracts on Distinctiones Sophismatum*. Nijmegen: Ingenium Publishers, 1988.

Derolez, Albert. *The Palaeography of Gothic Manuscript Books: From the Twelfth to the Early Sixteenth Century*. Cambridge: Cambridge University Press, 2003.

Di Chiara, Stefano. *Memoria per la consecrazione dei vescovi di Sicilia da tenersi presente nelle attuali circostanze che rendono pericoloso e difficile l'accesso al Sommo Pontefice*. Palermo: Nella Stamperia Reale, 1813.

Dolezalek, Gero. "Zur Datierung des Kommentars 'De regulis iuris' von Bertrandus Metensis." *Ius Commune* 11 (1984): 31–36.

Donatuti, Guido. "Le 'praesumptiones iuris' come mezzi di svolgimento del diritto sostanziale romano." *Rivista di Diritto Privato* 3, no. 1 (1933): 161–206. Reprinted in Guido Donatuti, *Studi di diritto romano*, 1:487–532. Milan: Giuffrè, 1976.

Donatuti, Guido. "Le praesumptiones iuris in diritto romano (loro origine)." *Annali della Facoltà di giurisprudenza della R. Università di Perugia*, 42 (1931): 1–112. Reprinted in Guido Donatuti, *Studi di diritto romano*, 1: 421–486. Milan: Giuffrè, 1976.

Dondorp, Harry, David Ibbetson, and Eltjo J.H. Schrage, eds. *Limitation and Prescription: A Comparative Legal History*. Berlin: Duncker & Humblot, 2019.

Dondorp, Harry. "Limitation and Prescription in Justinian's Corpus Iuris Civilis." In *Limitation and Prescription: A Comparative Legal History*, ed. Harry Dondorp, David Ibbetson, and Eltjo J.H. Schrage, 43–68. Berlin: Duncker & Humblot, 2019.

Dondorp, Harry. "Prescription and Limitation in Medieval Canon Law." In *Limitation and Prescription: A Comparative Legal History*, ed. Harry Dondorp, David Ibbetson, and Eltjo J.H. Schrage, 91–124. Berlin: Duncker & Humblot, 2019.

Dossey, Leslie. *Peasant and Empire in Christian North Africa*. Berkeley: University of California Press, 2010.

Duggan, Charles. "English Canonists and the 'Appendix Concilii Lateranensis'." *Traditio* 18 (1962): 459–468.

Duggan, Charles. *Twelfth-century Decretal Collections and Their Importance in English History*. London: Athlone Press, 1963.

Ebbesen, Sten. "Ancient Scholastic Logic as the Source of Medieval Scholastic Logic." In *The Cambridge History of Later Medieval Philosophy*, 1, *From the rediscovery of Aristo-*

tle to the disintegration of Scholasticism, 1100–1600, ed. Norman Kretzmann, Anthony Kenny, Jan Pinborg, and Eleonore Stump, 101–127. Cambridge: Cambridge University Press, 1982.

Errera, Andrea. "Aristotele, i "Topica" e la scienza giuridica medievale." *Angelicum* 85, no. 1 (2008): 341–362.

Errera, Andrea. *Il concetto di scientia iuris dal XII al XIV secolo: Il ruolo della logica platonica e aristotelica nelle scuole giuridiche medievali.* Milan: Giuffrè, 2003.

Errera, Andrea. "The Role of Logic in the Legal Science of the Glossators and Commentators." In *A Treatise of Legal Philosophy and General Jurisprudence*, 7, *The Jurists' Philosophy of Law from Rome to the Seventeenth Century*, ed. Peter Stein and Andrea Padovani, 79–156. Dordrecht: Springer, 2007.

Evans, Gillian R. *Law and Theology in the Middle Ages.* London: Routledge, 2002.

Falmagne, Thomas, and Luc Deitz. *Die Echternacher Handschriften bis zum Jahr 1628 in den Beständen der Bibliothèque Nationale de Luxembourg sowie der Archives diocésaines de Luxembourg, der Archives nationales, der Section historique de l'Institut grand-ducal und des Grand Séminaire de Luxembourg*, 2. Wiesbaden: Harrassowitz, 2009.

Faucon, Maurice. *La librairie des papes d'Avignon: Sa formation, sa composition, ses catalogues, 1316–1420; D'après les registres de comptes et d'inventaires des archives vaticanes*, 2. Paris: Thorin, 1886–1887.

Fernández Pomar, José María. "La colección de Uceda de la Biblioteca Nacional: Nueva edición del catálogo de manuscritos." *Helmántica* 27 (1976): 475–518.

Ferrini, Contardo. "Le presunzioni in diritto romano." *Rivista italiana per le scienze giuridiche* 14 (1892): 258–294. Reprinted in *Opere di Contardo Ferrini*, ed. Emilio Albertario, 3:417–451. Milan: Hoepli, 1929.

Fiori, Antonia. "Praesumptio violenta o iuris et de iure? Qualche annotazione sul contributo canonistico alla teoria delle presunzioni." In *Der Einfluss Der Kanonistik auf die Europäische Rechtskultur*, 1, *Zivil- und Zivilprozessrecht*, ed. Orazio Condorelli, Franck Roumy, and Mathias Schmoeckel, 75–106. Cologne: Böhlau Verlag, 2009.

Fiori, Antonia. "Sicardo da Cremona." In *DBGI*, 2:1859–1860.

Fitting, Hermann. *Juristische Schriften des früheren Mittelalters.* Halle: Buchhandlung des Waisenhauses, 1876.

Fitting, Hermann. "Ueber die Entstehung des Zeichens ff für die Digesten." *Zeitschrift für Rechtsgeschichte* 12 (1876): 300–301.

Forcellini, Egidio, Giuseppe Furlanetto, Francesco Corradini, and Josephus Perin, eds. *Lexicon totius Latinitatis*, 6 vols, 2nd ed. Padua: Typis Seminarii, 1940.

Fournier, Paul, Edmond Maignien, and Auguste Prudhomme. *Catalogue général des manuscrits des bibliothèques publiques de France: Départements*, 7, *Grenoble*. Paris: Éditions du Centre national de la recherche scientifique, 1889.

Fowler-Magerl, Linda. *Ordines Iudiciarii and Libelli De Ordine Iudiciorum* (*From the Middle of the Twelfth to the End of the Fifteenth Century*). Turnhout: Brepols, 1994.

Fowler-Magerl, Linda. *Ordo iudiciorum vel ordo iudiciarius: Begriff und Litteraturgattung*. Frankfurt am Main: Klostermann, 1984.

Fraher, Richard M. "Conviction According to Conscience: The Medieval Jurists' Debate Concerning Judicial Discretion and the Law of Proof." *Law & History Review* 7 (1989): 23–88.

Fransen, Gérard. *Canones et Quaestiones: Évolution des doctrines et système du droit canonique*, 2 vols. Goldbach: Keip, 2002.

Fransen, Gérard. "Manuscrits canoniques (1140–1234) conservés en Espagne." *RHE* 48 (1953): 224–234. Reprinted in Gérard Fransen, *Canones et Quaestiones: Évolution des doctrines et système du droit canonique*, 1.1:13–37. Goldbach: Keip, 2002.

Fransen, Gérard. "Manuscrits canoniques conservés en Espagne (II)." *RHE* 49 (1954): 152–156. Reprinted in Gérard Fransen, *Canones et Quaestiones: Évolution des doctrines et système du droit canonique*, 1.1:25–29. Goldbach: Keip, 2002.

Fransen, Gérard. "Les questions disputées dans les facultés de Droit." In *Les questions disputées et les questions quodlibétiques dans les facultés de Théologie, de Droit et de Médecine*, ed. Bernardo Carlos Bazàn, John W. Wippfel, Gérard Fransen, and Danielle Jacquart, 223–277. Turnhout: Brepols, 1985. Reprinted in Gérard Fransen, *Canones et Quaestiones: Évolution des doctrines et système du droit canonique*, 1.2:243–297. Goldbach: Keip, 2002.

Fransen, Gérard. "La structure des 'Quaestiones disputatae' et leur classement." *Traditio* 23 (1967): 516–534. Reprinted in Gérard Fransen, *Canones et Quaestiones: Évolution des doctrines et système du droit canonique*, 1.2:151–169. Goldbach: Keip, 2002.

Gallo, Cajo-Domenico. *Annali della Città di Messina Capitale del Regno di Sicilia: Dal giorno di sua fondazione sino a tempi presenti*, 2. Messina: Gaipa, 1758.

Gama, Raymundo. "Presumptions and Fictions: A Collingwoodian Approach." In *Legal Fictions in Theory and Practice*, ed. Maksymilian Del Mar and William Twining, 347–366. Cham: Springer, 2015.

Garvin, Joseph N. "Magister Udo: A Source of Peter of Poitiers' Sentences." *The New Scholasticism* 28 (1954): 285–298.

Garvin, Joseph N. "The Manuscripts of Udo's Summa super Sententias Petri Lombardi." *Scriptorium*, 16 (1962): 376.

Genka, Tatsushi. "The Distinctiones Tria consideranda sunt in electione in the Oxford, Bodleian MS Barlow 37." *BMCL* 36 (2019): 275–297.

Genka, Tatsushi. "Die Hallenser Handschrift ULB Ye 20 52 im Licht der Überlieferung der Summa Permissio quedam zum Dekret Gratians." In *Rechtshandschriften des deutschen Mittelalters: Produktionsorte und Importwege*, ed. Patrizia Carmassi and Gisela Drossbach, 147–165. Wiesbaden: Harrassowitz, 2015.

Genzmer, Erich. "Vorbilder für die Distinctionen der Glossatoren." In *Acta Congressus*

Iuridici Internationalis VII *saeculo a decretalibus Gregorii* IX *et* XIV *a Codice Iustiniano promulgatis*, 2:345–358. Rome: Libraria Pont. Inst. Utriusque Iuris, 1935.

Giuliani, Adolfo. "Civilian Treatises on Presumptions, 1580–1620." In *The Law of Presumptions: Essays in Comparative Legal History*, ed. Richard H. Helmholz and W. David H. Sellar, 21–71. Berlin: Duncker & Humblot, 2009.

Giuliani, Alessandro. *Il concetto di prova: Contributo alla logica giuridica*. Milan: Giuffrè, 1961.

Giuliani, Alessandro. "L'ordo iudiciarius medioevale." *Rivista di diritto processuale* 43 (1988): 598–614.

Giuliani, Alessandro. "Osservazioni sulla procedura nel metodo dialettico: dalla tradizione aristotelica a quella medievale." In *L'educazione giuridica. 6. Modelli storici della procedura continentale; 2. Dall'ordo iudicarius al codice di procedura*, ed. Alessandro Giuliani and Nicola Picardi, 27–32. Napoli: Ed. Scientifiche Italiane, 1994.

Glorieux, Palémon. "Répertoire des Maîtres en théologie de Paris au XIIIe siècle." *Études de philosophie médiévale* 17–18 (1933): 1933–1934.

Gouron, André. "L'auteur et la patrie de la Summa Trecensis." *Ius Commune* 12 (1984): 1–38.

Gouron, André. "Autour de Placentin à Montpellier: Maître Gui et Pierre de Cardona." In *Mélanges G. Fransen*, ed. Stephan Kuttner and Alfons M. Stickler, 1:337–354. Rome: Libreria Ateneo Salesiano, 1976.

Gouron, André. "Aux racines de la théorie des présomptions." RIDC 1 (1990): 99–109. Reprinted in André Gouron, *Droit et coutume en France aux* XII*e et* XIII*e siècles*, no. VII. Aldershot: Variorum, 1993.

Gouron, André. "Canon Law in Parisian Circles Before Stephan of Tournai's Summa." In *Proceedings of the Eighth International Congress of Medieval Canon Law: San Diego, University of California at La Jolla, 21–27 August 1988*, ed. Stanley Chodorow, 497–503. Vatican City: BAV, 1992.

Gouron, André. "La diffusion des premiers recueils de Questions Disputées: Des civilistes aux canonistes." In *Studia in honorem eminentissimi cardinalis Alphonsi M. Stickler*, ed. Rosalio Castillo Lara, 157–169. Rome: Libreria Ateneo Salesiano, 1992.

Gouron, André. *Droit et coutume en France aux* XII*e et* XIII*e siècles*. Aldershot: Variorum, 1993.

Gouron, André. "Une école de canonistes anglais à Paris. Maître Walter et ses disciples (vers 1170)." *Journal des savants* 1 (2000): 47–72. Reprinted in André Gouron, *Pionniers du droit occidental au Moyen Âge*, no. VI. Aldershot/Burlington: Variorum/Ashgate, 2006.

Gouron, André. "Une école ou des écoles? Sur les canonistes français (vers 1150–vers 1210)." In *Proceedings of the Sixth International Congress of Medieval Canon Law: Berkeley, California, 28 July–2 August 1980*, ed. Stephan Kuttner and Kenneth Pennington, 223–240. Vatican City: BAV, 1985. Reprinted in André Gouron, *Pionniers du droit occidental au Moyen Âge*, no. VIII. Aldershot/Burlington: Variorum/Ashgate, 2006.

Gouron, André. "L'élaboration de la 'Summa Trecensis'." In *Sodalitas: Scritti in onore di Antonio Guarino*, ed. Vincenzo Giuffrè, 8:3684–3689. Napoli: Jovene, 1985.

Gouron, André. *Études sur la diffusion des doctrines juridiques médiévales*. London: Variorum, 1987.

Gouron, André. *Juristes et droits savants: Bologne et la France médiévale*. Aldershot\Brookfield: Variorum\Ashgate, 2000.

Gouron, André. "Notes sur les collections de quaestiones reportatae chez les civilistes du XIIe siècle." In *Xenia iuris historiae G. van Dievoet oblata*, ed. Fred Stevens and Dirk Van den Auweele, 55–66. Leuven: Katholieke Universiteit Leuven, Faculteit der Rechtsgeleerdheid, Afdeling Romeins Recht en Rechtgeschiedenis, 1990. Reprinted in André Gouron, *Droit et coutume en France aux XIIe et XIIIe siècles*, no. VI. Aldershot: Variorum, 1993.

Gouron, André. *Pionniers du droit occidental au Moyen Âge*. Aldershot/Burlington: Variorum/Ashgate, 2006.

Gouron, André. "Placentinus 'Herold' der Vermutungslehre?" In *Festschrift zum 65. Geburtstag und zur Emeritierung von Professor Dr. Hans Kiefner: Herausgegeben von Freunden, Kollegen und Mitarbeitern*, ed. Ulrike Brüning and Thomas Hoeren, 90–103. Münster: Institut für Kirchenrecht, 1994. Reprinted in André Gouron, *Juristes et droits savants: Bologne et la France médiévale*, no. VIII. Aldershot: Variorum, 2000.

Gouron, André. "'Primo tractavit de natura actionum Geraudus'. Studium bononiense, glossateurs et pratique juridique dans la France méridionale." In *Chiesa, diritto e ordinamento della societas Christiana nei secoli XI e XII: Atti della nona Settimana internazionale di studio; Mendola, 28 agosto–2 settembre 1983*, 202–215. Milan: Vita e Pensiero, 1986. Reprinted in André Gouron, *Droit et coutume en France aux XIIe et XIIIe siècles*, no. I. Aldershot: Variorum, 1993.

Gouron, André. "Qui a écrit l'ordo 'Olim edebatur'?" *Initium* 8 (2003): 64–84. Reprinted in André Gouron, *Pionniers du droit occidental au Moyen Âge*, no. XIII. Aldershot/Burlington: Variorum/Ashgate, 2006.

Gouron, André. "Qui était l'énigmatique maître G?" *Journal des savants* 3–4 (1990): 269–289. Reprinted in André Gouron, *Droit et coutume en France aux XIIe et XIIIe siècles*, no. XIV. Aldershot: Variorum, 1993.

Gouron, André. *La science juridique française aux XIe et XIIe siècles: Diffusion du droit de Justinien et influences canoniques jusqu'à Gratien*. Milan: Giuffrè, 1978.

Gouron, André. "Le traité 'De actionum varietate', la version du manuscrit de Barcelone (A.C.A. San Cugat 55) et la 'Glossa Coloniensis' aux institutes (manuscrit de Cologne H.A. W 328)." *Initium* 2 (1997): 373–390. Reprinted in André Gouron, *Pionniers du droit occidental au Moyen Âge*, no. II. Aldershot/Burlington: Variorum/Ashgate, 2006.

Green-Pedersen, Niels Jørgen. *The Tradition of the Topics in the Middle Ages: The Commentaries on Aristotle's and Boethius' "Topics."* Munich: Philosophia Verlag, 1984.

Grellard, Christophe. "L'erreur invincible et le problème sceptique à la fin du Moyen Age." In *Irrtum—Error—Erreur*, ed. Andreas Speer and Maxime Mauriège, 39–52. Berlin: de Gruyter, 2018.

Grellard, Christophe. *La possibilità dell'errore: Pensare la tolleranza nel Medioevo*. Canterano: Aracne, 2020.

Grellard, Christophe. "Que m'est-il permis d'ignorer? La foi, l'ignorance et les limites acceptables de l'orthodoxie." In *Genèses antiques et médiévales de la foi*, ed. Christophe Grellard, Philippe Hoffman, and Laurent Lavaud, 429–449. Paris: Institut d'études Augustiniennes, 2020.

Grellard, Christophe. "Systèmes de pensées et de croyances médiévaux." *Annuaire de l'École pratique des hautes études (EPHE), Section des sciences religieuses* 125 (2018): 293–300.

Grosse, Rolf. "Entre cour et cloître: Saint-Victor et les Capétiens au XIIe siècle." In *L'école de Saint-Victor de Paris: Influence et rayonnement du Moyen Âge à l'époque moderne*, ed. Dominique Poirel, 79–100. Turnhout: Brepols, 2010.

Halm, Karl, Georg von Laubmann, and Wilhelm Meyer. *Catalogus codicum latinorum Bibliothecae Regiae Monacensis*, 1.3. Munich: Bibliotheca regia, 1873.

Hardy, Thomas D. *Descriptive Catalogue of Materials Relating to the History of Great Britain and Ireland: to the End of the Reign of Henry VII*, 2. London: Longman, 1862.

Hartmann, Wilfried, and Kenneth Pennington, eds. *The History of Medieval Canon Law in the Classical Period, 1140–1234: from Gratian to the Decretals of Pope Gregory IX*. Washington, D.C.: The Catholic University of America Press, 2008.

Haskins, Charles H. "England and Sicily in the Twelfth Century." *The English Historical Review* 26, no. 103 (1911): 433–447.

Hausmann, Regina. *Die Historischen, Philologischen und Juristischen Handschriften der Hessischen Landesbibliothek Fulda bis zum Jahr 1600. B 1–25, C 1–18.68, D1–48. Beschrieben von Regina Hausmann*. Wiesbaden: Harrassowitz, 2000.

Helmholz, Richard H. "The Law of Presumptions and the English Ecclesiastical Courts." In *The Law of Presumptions: Essays in Comparative Legal History*, ed. Richard H. Helmholz and W. David H. Sellar, 137–151. Berlin: Duncker & Humblot, 2009.

Helmholz, Richard H., and W. David H. Sellar. "Presumptions in Comparative Legal History." In *The Law of Presumptions: Essays in Comparative Legal History*, ed. Richard H. Helmholz and W. David H. Sellar, 9–18. Berlin: Duncker & Humblot, 2009.

Hoffmann, Hartmut, and Rudolf Pokorny, *Das Dekret des Bischofs Burchard von Worms: Textstufen—frühe Verbreitung—Vorlagen*. Munich: Monumenta Germaniae Historica, 1991.

Hofmann, Josef, and U. Hermann Hauke. *Die Handschriften der Stiftsbibliothek und der Stiftskirche zu Aschaffenburg*. Aschaffenburg: Geschichts- und Kunstverein, 1978.

Hohmann, Hanns. "Presumption in Legal Argumentation: From Antiquity to the Middle Ages." In *Proceedings of the Ontario Society for the Study of Argumentation Conference, 3 (1999): Argumentation at The Century's Turn; held at Brock University*, ed. Hans v. Hansen, Christopher W. Tindale, and Elmar Sveda. Available online at https://scholar.uwindsor.ca/ossaarchive/OSSA3/papersandcommentaries/28/. Accessed 2022 Aug 01.

Hohmann, Hanns. "Presumptions in Roman Legal Argumentation." In *Proceedings of the Ontario Society for the Study of Argumentation Conference,* 4 *(2001): Argumentation and its Applications; University of Windsor, May 17–19, 2001*, ed. Hans v. Hansen, Robert C. Pinto, Christopher W. Tindale, J. Anthony Blair, and Ralph H. Johnson, 1–14. Available online at https://scholar.uwindsor.ca/ossaarchive/OSSA4/papersandcom mentaries/61/. Accessed 2022 Aug 01.

Hohmann, Hanns. "Rhetoric in Medieval Legal Education: Libellus Pylei Disputatorius." *Disputatio* 4 *Discourses of Power: Grammar and Rhetoric in the Middle Ages* (1999): 59–73.

Höhl, Norbert. *Die Glossen des Johannes Faventinus zur Pars I des Decretum Gratiani: Eine literargeschichtliche Untersuchung*. PhD dissertation: Universität Würzburg, 1987.

Höhl, Norbert. "Wer war Johannes Faventinus? Neue Erkenntnisse zu Leben und Werk eines bedeutendsten Dekretisten des 12. Jahrhunderts." In *Proceedings of the Eighth International Congress of Medieval Canon Law: San Diego, University of California at La Jolla, 21–27 August 1988*, ed. Stanley Chodorow, 189–203. Vatican City: BAV, 1992.

Holopainen, Toivo J. *Dialectic and Theology in the Eleventh Century*. Leiden: Brill, 1996.

Holtzmann, Walther. *Studies in the Collections of Twelfth-century Decretals*. Edited by Christopher R. Cheney and Mary G. Cheney. Vatican City: BAV, 1979.

Holtzmann, Walther. "Walther Holtzmann Kartei." In *Stephan Kuttner Institute of Medieval Canon Law*. Available at https://www.kuttner-institute.jura.uni-muenchen.de/. Accessed 2021 Aug 7.

Hunt, Tony. *Teaching and Learning Latin in Thirteenth-century England*, 1. Cambridge: D.S. Brewer, 1991.

Imperia, Vincenzo Roberto. *I vescovati nella Sicilia normanna (secc. XI–XII): Potestà normative e competenze giurisdizionali in un territorio multiculturale*. Palermo: Palermo University Press, 2022.

Inventario general de manuscritos de la Biblioteca Nacional, 1. Madrid: Ministerio de Educación Nacional, 1953.

Isola, Lisa. *Venire contra factum proprium: Herkunft und Grundlagen eines sprichwörtlichen Rechtsprinzip*. Frankfurt am Main: Peter Lang GmbH, Internationaler Verlag der Wissenschaften, 2017.

Jaeger, C. Stephen. *The Envy of Angels: Cathedral Schools and Social Ideals in Medieval Europe, 950–1200*. Philadelphia: University of Pennsylvania Press, 1995.

James, Montague Rhodes. *A Descriptive Catalogue of the Manuscripts in the Library of Pembroke College, Cambridge*. Cambridge: Cambridge University Press, 1905; reprinted 2009.

Jamison, Evelyn. "Alliance of England and Sicily in the Second Half of the 12th Century." *Journal of the Warburg and Courtauld Institutes* 6 (1943): 20–32.

Jasper, Detlev. "Burchards Dekret in der Sicht der Gregorianer." In *Bischof Burchard von Worms. 1000–1025*, ed. Wilfried Hartmann, 167–198. Mainz: Selbstverlag der Gesellschaft für Mittelrheinische Kirchengeschichte, 2000.

Juncker, Josef. "Die Summa des Simon von Bisignano und seine Glossen." ZRG *Rom. Abt.* 15 (1926): 326–500.

Kaiser, Wolfgang. *Die Epitome Iuliani: Beiträge zum römischen Recht im frühen Mittelalter und zum byzantinischen Rechtsunterricht*. Frankfurt am Main: Klostermann, 2004.

Kalb, Herbert. *Studien zur Summa Stephans von Tournai: Ein Beitrag zur kanonistischen Wissenschaftsgeschichte des späten 12. Jahrhunderts*. Innsbruck: Universitätsverlag Wagner, 1983.

Kantorowicz, Hermann. *Einführung in die Textkritik: Systematische Darstellung der textkritischen Grundsätze für Philologen und Juristen*. Leipzig: Dieterich, 1921.

Kantorowicz, Hermann. "The Quaestiones Disputatae of the Glossators." *TvR* 16 (1939), 1–67. Reprinted in Hermann Kantorowicz, *Rechtshistorische Schriften*, 137–185. Karlsruhe: C.F. Müller, 1970.

Kantorowicz, Hermann. *Studies in the Glossators of the Roman Law: Newly Discovered Writings of the Twelfth Century*. Cambridge: Cambridge University Press, 1938.

Kaser, Max. *Das römische Zivilprozessrecht*, 2nd ed. Munich: Beck, 1996.

Kautz, Michael. "Vatikan, Biblioteca Apostolica Vaticana, Pal. lat. 653. Manuscript description." In *Bibliotheca Laureshamensis—digital: Virtual Monastic Library of Lorsch*, ed. Alexandra Büttner and Michael Kautz. Heidelberg, 2014. Available online at https://digi.ub.uni-heidelberg.de/sammlung51/werk/pdf/bav_pal_lat_653.pdf. Accessed 2019 Jul 19.

Kempshall, Matthew. *Rhetoric and the Writing of History, 400–1500*. Manchester: Manchester University Press, 2014.

Kéry, Lotte. *Gottesfurcht und irdische Strafe: Der Beitrag des mittelalterlichen Kirchenrechts zur Entstehung des öffentlichen Strafrechts*. Cologne: Böhlau, 2006.

Kéry, Lotte. "Non enim homines de occultis, sed de manifestis iudicant. La culpabilité dans le droit pénal de l'Église à l'époque classique." RDC 80 (2003): 311–336.

Kessler, Peter-Josef. "Untersuchungen über die Novellen-Gesetzgebung Papst Innozenz IV (I)." ZRG *Kan. Abt.* 31 (1942): 142–320.

Klemm, Elisabeth. *Die romanischen Handschriften der Bayerischen Staatsbibliothek*, 3.2. Wiesbaden: Reichert, 1988.

Krämer, Sigrid. *Handschriftenerbe des deutschen Mittelalters*, 2. Munich: Beck, 1989.

Kunstmann, Friedrich. "Über den ältesten Ordo iudiciarius mit Rücksicht auf Magistri Ricardi Anglici ordo iudiciarius …" *Kritische Überschau der deutschen Gesetzgebung und Rechtswissenschaft* 2 (1854): 10–29.

Kuttner, Stephan, and Eleanor Rathbone. "Anglo-Norman Canonists of the Twelfth Century. An Introductory Study." *Traditio* 7 (1949): 279–358. Reprinted in Stephan Kuttner, *Gratian and the Schools of Law. 1140–1234*, no. VIII. London: Variorum, 1983.

Kuttner, Stephan. "Annual Report." *Traditio* 16 (1960): 531–533.

Kuttner, Stephan. "Annual Report." *Traditio* 19 (1963): 509–516.

Kuttner, Stephan. "Bertram of Metz." *Traditio* 13 (1957): 501–505.

Kuttner, Stephan. "The Decretal Presbiterum (JL 13912)—A Letter of Leo IX." *BMCL* 5 (1975): 133–135.

Kuttner, Stephan. "General Report." *Traditio* 12 (1956): 557–559.

Kuttner, Stephan. "An Interim Checklist of Manuscripts." *Traditio* 11 (1955): 439–448.

Kuttner, Stephan. "An Interim Checklist of Manuscripts (III)." *Traditio* 13 (1957): 467–471.

Kuttner, Stephan. *Kanonistische Schuldlehre von Gratian bis auf die Dekretalen Gregors IX: Systematisch auf Grund der handschriftlichen Quellen dargestellt.* Vatican City: BAV, 1935.

Kuttner, Stephan. "Die Konstitutionen des ersten allgemeinen Konzils von Lyon." *Studia et documenta historiae et iuris* 6 (1940): 70–131. Reprinted in Stephan Kuttner, *Medieval Councils, Decretals and Collections of Canon Law: Selected Essays*, no. XI. London: Variorum, 1980.

Kuttner, Stephan. "Notes on Manuscripts." *Traditio* 17 (1961): 533–534.

Kuttner, Stephan. "Notes on the Presentation of Text and Apparatus in Editing Works of the Decretists and Decretalists." *Traditio* 15 (1959): 452–464.

Kuttner, Stephan. "Notes on the Roman Meeting, on Planning and Method." *Traditio* 11 (1955): 431–439.

Kuttner, Stephan. "Réflexions sur les brocards des glossateurs." In *Mélanges Joseph de Ghellinck*, 2:767–792. Gembloux: J. Duculot, 1951. Reprinted in Stephan Kuttner, *Gratian and the Schools of Law. 1140–1234*, no. IX. London: Variorum, 1983.

Kuttner, Stephan. "Retractationes IX." In Stephan Kuttner, *Gratian and the Schools of Law. 1140–1234*, 39–43. London: Variorum, 1983.

Kuttner, Stephan. *Repertorium der Kanonistik (1140–1234): Prodromus corporis glossarum.* Vatican City: BAV, 1937.

Kuttner, Stephan. "Rodoicus ou Rotbertus Modicipassus (Parvipassus)." In *DDC* 7 (1965): 701–702.

Kuttner, Stephan. "The Third Part of Stephen of Tournai's Summa." *Traditio* 14 (1958): 502–506.

Labandeira, Eduardo. *Las presunciones en derecho canónico*. Pamplona: Universidad de Navarra, 1967.

Lambert, A. "Blois (Pierre de)." In DDC 2 (1937): 925–926.

Landau, Peter. "Der Dekretglossenapparat Et est sciendum–ein Werk des Kanonisten Rodoicus Modicipassus." *RIDC* 24 (2013): 19–26.

Landau, Peter. "Die Dekretsumme 'Tractaturus magister' und die Kanonistik in Reims in der zweiten Hälfte des 12. Jahrhunderts." *ZRG Kan. Abt.* 131 (2014): 132–152.

Landau, Peter. "Die Entstehung der systematischen Dekretalensammlungen und die europäische Kanonistik des 12. Jahrhunderts." *ZRG Kan. Abt.* 65 (1979): 120–148.

Landau, Peter. "Gerard Pucelle und die Dekretsumme Reverentia sacrorum canonum: Zur Kölner Kanonistik im 12. Jahrhundert." In *Mélanges en l'honneur d'Anne Lefebvre-Teillard*, ed. Bernard D'Alteroche, Florence Demoulin-Auzary, Olivier Descamps, Breandán Ó Buachalla, and Franck Roumy, 623–638. Paris: Éditions Panthéon-Assas, 2010.

Landau, Peter. *Die Kölner Kanonistik des 12. Jahrhunderts: Ein Höhepunkt der europäischen Rechtswissenschaft*. Badenweiler: Bachmann, 2008.

Landau, Peter. "Lehrbuch contra Fälschung: Die Bamberger Anfänge der europäischen Strafrechtswissenschaft und die Würzburger Güldene Freiheit." *Deutsches Archiv für Erforschung des Mittelalters* 62, no. 2 (2006): 505–536.

Landau, Peter. "Master Peter of Louveciennes and the Origins of the Parisian School of Canon Law around 1170." In *Proceedings of the Fourteenth International Congress of Medieval Canon Law: Toronto, 5–11 August 2012*, ed. Joseph Goering, Stephan Dusil, and Andreas Their, 379–394. Vatican City: BAV, 2016.

Landau, Peter. "The Origins of Legal Science in England in the Twelfth Century: Lincoln, Oxford and the Career of Vacarius." In *Readers, Texts and Compilers in the Earlier Middle Ages: Studies in Medieval Canon Law in Honour of Linda Fowler-Magerl*, ed. Martin Brett and Kathleen G. Cushing, 165–182. London: Routledge, 2017.

Landau, Peter. "The Origin of the Regula iuris 'Quod omnes tangit' in the Anglo-Norman School of Canon Law during the Twelfth Century." *BMCL* 32 (2015): 19–35.

Landau, Peter. "Rodoicus Modicipassus—Verfasser der Summa Lipsiensis?" *ZRG Kan. Abt.* 92 (2006): 340–354.

Landau, Peter. "The School of Canon Law in Cologne during the 12th Century." In *Proceedings of the Thirteenth International Congress of Medieval Canon Law: Esztergom, 3–8 August 2008*, ed. Peter Erdö and Szabolcs Anzelm Szuromi, 431–435. Vatican City: BAV, 2010.

Landau, Peter. "Simon von Bisignano, Sikard von Cremona und die Mainzer Kanonistik der Barbarossazeit: Zur Biographie des Simon von Bisignano und zur Forschungsgeschichte." *BMCL* 28 (2008): 119–144.

Landau, Peter. "Vorgratianische Kanonessammlungen bei Dekretisten und in frühen Dekretalensammlungen." In *Proceedings of the Eighth International Congress of*

Medieval Canon Law: San Diego, University of California at La Jolla, 21–27 August 1988, ed. Stanley Chodorow, 93–116. Vatican City: BAV, 1992.

Landau, Peter. "Walter von Coutances und die Anfänge der anglo-normannischen Rechtswissenschaft." In *Panta Rei: Studi dedicati a Manlio Bellomo*, ed. Orazio Condorelli, 3:183–204. Rome: Il Cigno Galileo Galilei, 2004.

Lang, Albert. "Rhetorische Einflüsse auf die Behandlung des Prozesses in der Kanonistik des 12. Jahrhunderts." In *Festschrift Eduard Eichmann zum 70. Geburtstag dargebracht von seinen Freunden und Schülern*, ed. Martin Grabmann and Karl Hofmann, 69–97. Paderborn: Schöningh, 1940.

Lang, Albert. "Zur Entstehungsgeschichte der Brocardasammlungen." *ZRG Kan. Abt.* 31 (1942): 106–141.

"Latin 4720A." In *Archives et manuscrits de la Bibliothèque Nationale de France*. Available at http://archivesetmanuscrits.bnf.fr/ark:/12148/cc63589v. Accessed 2019 Oct 6.

"Latin 14606." In *Archives et manuscrits de la Bibliothèque Nationale de France*. Available at https://archivesetmanuscrits.bnf.fr/ark:/12148/cc75357s. Accessed 2019 Oct 6.

Lefebvre, Charles. "Pierre de Blois." In *DDC* 6 (1957): 1472.

Lefebvre-Teillard, Anne. "Du Décret aux décrétales: L'enseignement du droit canonique au sein de l'école parisienne (fin XIIe–début XIIIe s.)." In *Les débuts de l'enseignement universitaire à Paris (1200–1245 environ)*, ed. Jacques Verger and Olga Weijers, 319–328. Turnhout: Brepols, 2013.

Legendre, Pierre. "Miscellanea Britannica." *Traditio* 15 (1959): 491–497.

"Leipzig, Universitätsbibliothek Leipzig, Rep. II 117 (Leihgabe Leipziger Stadtbibliothek)." In *Handschriften Portal*. Available at https://resolver.staatsbibliothek-berlin.de/HSP00051F2C00000000. Accessed 2024 Jan 20.

Leitschuh, Friedrich, and Hans Fischer. *Katalog der Handschriften der Königlichen Bibliothek zu Bamberg*, revised ed. Wiesbaden: Harrassowitz, 1966.

Lemaitre, Jean-Loup, and Françoise Vielliard. "La Liève de la confrérie des premières chandelles à Limoges." *Bulletin de la Société archéologique et historique du Limousin* 129 (2001): 45–113.

Lévy, Jean-Philippe. *La hiérarchie des preuves dans le droit savant du Moyen-Âge depuis la renaissance du droit romain jusqu'à la fin du XIVe siècle*. Paris: Librairie du Recueil Sirey, 1939.

Lewis, Charlton T., and Charles Short, eds. *A Latin Dictionary*. Oxford: Oxford University Press, 1879, reprinted 1933.

Litewski, Wiesław. *Der römisch-kanonische Zivilprozeß nach den älteren ordines iudiciarii*, 1. Kraków: Wydawnictwo Uniwersytetu Jagiellonskiego, 1999.

Loewenthal, L.J.A. "For the Biography of Walter Ophamil, Archbishop of Palermo." *The English Historical Review* 87, no. 342 (1972): 75–82.

Loschiavo, Luca. "Ottone da Pavia." In *DBGI*, 2: 1475.

Loschiavo, Luca. "Lo studio e l'insegnamento del ius civile nel secolo XII." In *Pietro Lom-*

bardo: Atti del XLIII Convegno storico internazionale. Todi, 8–10 ottobre 2006, 89–121. Spoleto: Fondazione Centro italiano di studi sull'alto Medioevo, 2007.

Loschiavo, Luca. "Rogerio." In *DBI* 88 (2017). Available at https://www.treccani.it/enciclopedia/rogerio_(Dizionario-Biografico)/. Accessed 2023 May 10

Lottin, Odon. "Le Premier commentaire connu des Sentences de Pierre Lombard." *Recherches de théologie ancienne et médiévale* 11 (1939): 64–71.

Lottin, Odon. *Psychologie et morale aux XIIe et XIIIe siècles*, 6 vols. Louvain/Gembloux: César/Duculout, 1946–1960.

Loud, Graham A. "Il regno normanno-svevo visto dal regno d'Inghilterra." In *Il Mezzogiorno normanno-svevo visto dall'Europa e dal mondo mediterraneo: Atti delle tredicesime giornate normanno-sveve; Bari, 21–24 ottobre 1997*, ed. Giosuè Musca, 175–195. Bari: Dedalo, 1999.

Maier, Anneliese. *Codices burghesiani Bibliothecae Vaticanae*. Vatican City: BAV, 1952.

Maier, Anneliese. "Die Handschriften der 'Ecclesia Sidonensis'." In *Ausgehendes Mittelalter: Gesammelte Aufsätze zur Geistesgeschichte des 14. Jahrhunderts*, ed. Anneliese Maier and Agostino Paravicini Bagliani, 3, 281–287. Rome: Edizioni di storia et letteratura, 1977.

Maleczek, Werner. "Die Urkunden des päpstlichen Legaten Guido, Kardinalpriester von S. Lorenzo in Lucina, aus den Jahren 1265 bis 1267 (Legation nach Skandinavien und Deutschland)." *Archiv für Diplomatik, Schriftgeschichte, Siegel- und Wappenkunde* 56 (2010): 65–150.

Markgraf, Hermann. "Über die Legation des Guido, tit. s. Laurentii in Lucina presbyteri cardinalis, von 1265–1267." *Zeitschrift des Vereins für Geschichte (und Alterthum) Schlesiens* 5 (1863): 65–106.

Martin, Jean-Marie. "L'immigrazione normanna, inglese e francese nel regno normanno di Sicilia." In *Studi in onore di Salvatore Tramontana*, ed. Errico Cuozzo, 281–289. Ariano Irpino: Elio Sellino, 2003.

Martín Avedillo, José-Antonio. "Estado actual de la investigación sobre el canonista Ambrosius." In *Proceedings of the Third International Congress of Medieval Canon Law: Strasbourg, 3–6 September 1968*, ed. Stephan Kuttner, 101–111. Vatican City: BAV, 1971.

Martín Avedillo, José-Antonio. "La 'Summa super titulis decretalium' del canonista Ambrosius." *ZRG Kan. Abt.* 54 (1968): 57–94.

Martínez Diez, Gonzalo. "Tres lecciones del siglo XII del Estudio general de Palencia." *AHDE* 61 (1991): 391–449.

McIlroy, David. "Christianity, mens rea and the boundaries of criminal liability." In *Christianity and Criminal Law*, ed. Mark Hill, Norman Doe, Richard H. Helmholz, and John Witte, Jr, 116–132. London: Routledge, 2020.

Menzinger, Sara. "Finzioni dei canoni: Natura, realtà e finzione nella canonistica del XII secolo." *Reti Medievali Rivista* 21 (2020): 203–241. Published online: March 29, 2020. DOI: 10.6092/1593-2214/6727.

Menzinger, Sara. *Finzioni del diritto medievale*. Macerata: Quodlibet, 2023.

Menzinger, Sara. "Legal Profession." In *A Cultural History of Law in the Middle Ages*, ed. Emanuele Conte and Laurent Mayali, 2:125–139. London: Bloomsbury Academic, 2019.

Menzinger, Sara. "Riflessioni sul rapporto tra autore e testo nella produzione giuridica medievale." *Historia et ius* 11 (2017): paper 23: 1–18.

Meyer, Christoph. *Die Distinktionstechnik in der Kanonistik des 12. Jahrhunderts: Ein Beitrag zur Wissenschaftsgeschichte des Hochmittelalters*. Leuven: Leuven University Press, 2000.

Morris, Colin. *The Discovery of the Individual, 1050–1200*. Toronto: University of Toronto Press, 1972.

Motzenbäcker, Rudolf. *Die Rechtsvermutung im kanonischen Recht*. Munich: Zink, 1958.

Müller, Hubert. *Der Anteil der Laien an der Bischofswahl: Ein Beitrag zur Geschichte der Kanonistik von Gratian bis Gregor IX*. Amsterdam: B.R. Grüner, 1977.

Murano, Giovanna. "Chi ha scritto le interpretationes hebraicorum nominum?" In *Etienne Langton, prédicateur, bibliste, théologien*, ed. Louis-Jacques Bataillon, Nicole Bériou, Gilbert Dahan, and Riccardo Quinto, 353–371. Turnhout: Brepols, 2010.

Naumann, Robert. *Catalogus librorum manuscriptorum qui in Bibliotheca Senatoria civitatis Lipsiensis asservantur*. Grimma: Gebhardt 1838.

Nicolini, Ugo. *Pilii Medicinensis quaestiones sabbatinae: Introduzione all'edizione critica*. Modena: Università degli studi, 1933.

Nörr, Knut Wolfgang. "Die Kanonistische Literatur." In *HQLR*, 1:365–381.

Nörr, Knut Wolfgang. "Die Literatur zum gemeinen Zivilprozess." In *HQLR*, 1:383–400.

Nörr, Knut Wolfgang. "Ordo Iudiciorum und Ordo Iudiciarius." *Studia Gratiana* 11 (1967): 327–343. Reprinted in Knut Wolfgang Nörr, *Iudicium est actus trium personarum: Beiträge zur Geschichte des Zivilprozessrechts in Europa*, 3–17 (Goldbach: Keip, 1993).

Nörr, Knut Wolfgang. *Zur Stellung des Richters im gelehrten Prozess der Frühzeit: Iudex secundum allegata non secundum conscientiam iudicat*. Munich: Beck, 1967.

OED, s.v. "presumption." Available at www.oed.com/view/Entry/150903. Accessed 2021 January 25.

Otte, Gerhard. *Dialektik und Jurisprudenz: Untersuchungen zur Methode der Glossatoren*. Frankfurt am Main: Klostermann, 1971.

Ouy, Gilbert. *Les manuscrits de l'abbaye de Saint-Victor: Catalogue établi sur la base du répertoire de Claude de Grandrue (1514)*, 2. Turnhout: Brepols, 1999.

Palacký, František. *Über Formelbücher, zunächst in Bezug auf böhmische Geschichte*. Prague: Kronberger und Řiwnač, 1842.

Panofsky, Erwin. *Gothic Architecture and Scholasticism*. Latrobe: Archabbey Press, 1951.

Papp Kamali, Elizabeth. *Felony and the Guilty Mind in Medieval England*. Cambridge: Cambridge University Press, 2020.

Pasciuta, Beatrice. "La costruzione del genere nel diritto medievale: norme e dottrina." *RSDI* 95 (2022): 1–21.

Pennington, Kenneth, and Wolfgang P. Müller. "The Decretists: The Italian School." In *HMCLCP*, 121–173.

Pennington, Kenneth. "Learned Law, Droit Savant, Gelehrtes Recht: The Tyranny of a Concept." *Syracuse Journal of International Law and Commerce* 20: (1994): 205–215.

Pescatore, Gustav. *Beiträge zur mittelalterlichen Rechtsgeschichte*, 2. Berlin: Prager Verlag, 1889.

Pfändtner, Karl-Georg, and Stefanie Westphal. *Die Handschriften des 13. und 14. Jahrhunderts der Staatsbibliothek Bamberg: Mit Nachträgen von Handschriften und Fragmenten des 10. und 12. Jahrhunderts*, 2. Wiesbaden: Harrassowitz, 2015.

Poggioli, Peter A. *From Politician to Prelate: The Career of Walter of Coutances, Archbishop of Rouen, 1184–1207*. PhD dissertation: Johns Hopkins University, 1984.

Poirel, Dominique. "'Apprends tout': Saint-Victor et le milieu des Victorins à Paris, 1108–1330." In *Lieux de savoir*, ed. Christian Jacob, 1: 302–322. Paris: Albin Michel, 2007.

Poirel, Dominique. "Reading and Educating Oneself in the 12th: Hugh of Saint-Victor's Didascalicon." In *A Companion to Twelfth-Century Schools*, ed. Cédric Giraud, 113–140. Leiden: Brill, 2020.

Quaglioni, Diego. *La giustizia nel medioevo e nella prima età moderna*. Bologna: Il Mulino, 2004.

Radding, Charles, and William Clark. *Medieval Architecture, Medieval Learning: Builders and Masters in the Age of Romanesque and Gothic*. New Haven/London: Yale University Press, 1994.

Rand Schmidt, Kari Anne. *The Index of Middle English Prose: Handlist XVIII; Manuscripts in the Library of Pembroke College, Cambridge and the Fitzwilliam Museum*. Cambridge: D.S. Brewer, 2006.

Robertson, Durant W. jr. "A Note on the Classical Origin of 'Circumstances' in the Medieval Confessional." *Studies in Philology* 43, no. 1 (1946): 6–14.

Rosell, Francesc x. Miguel. "Catàleg dels llibres manuscrits de la Biblioteca del Monestir de Sant Cugat del Vallès existents a l'Arxiu de la Corona d'Aragó." *Butlletí de la Biblioteca de Catalunya* 8 (1928–1932): 143–240.

Rosemann, Philip W. *The Story of a Great Medieval Book: Peter Lombard's Sentences*. Peterborough, Ontario: Broadview Press, 2007.

Sánchez-Gil, Antonio. *La presunzione di validità dell'atto giuridico nel diritto canonico*. Milan: Giuffrè, 2006.

Savigny, Friedrich Carl von. *Geschichte des römischen Rechts im Mittelalter*, 4, 2nd ed. Heidelberg: Mohr, 1850; reprinted Aalen: Scientia-Verlag, 1986.

Schlauch, Margaret. "Literary Exchange Between Angevin England and Sicily." *Romanic Review* 14 (1923): 168–188.

Schneider, Élisabeth. "L'interprétation des termes d'homme ou de personne en droit savant, source d'inégalité." *Droit et cultures* 69 (2015): 89–112.

Schulte, Johann Friedrich von. "De criminalibus causis (aus dem Bamberger Codex P. I. II)." In *I. Constitutio Constantini ad Ablavium. II. De criminalibus causis: Festschrift zur Feier des 22. Dezember 1888, an welchem vor 50 Jahren Geheimerat Prof. Dr. Bernhard Windscheid in Bonn zum Doctor iuris utriusque promoviert wurde …*, ed. Johann Friedrich von Schulte, 7–15. Bonn: Universitäts-Buchdruckerei von Carl Georgi, 1888.

Schulte, Friedrich von. "Über die Summa Legum des Codex Gottwicensis Nr. 38 aus dem XII. Jahrhundert." *Sitzungsberichte der philosophisch-historischen Klasse der kaiserlichen Akademie der Wissenschaften in Wien* 57 (1868): 433–460.

Schwaibold, Matthias. *Brocardica 'Dolum per subsequentia purgari': Eine englische Sammlung von Argumenten des römischen Rechts aus dem 12. Jahrhundert*. Frankfurt am Main: Klostermann, 1985.

Schwaibold, Matthias. "Wer sucht, der findet." *Rechtshistorisches Journal* 4 (1985): 202–214.

Šebánek, Jindrich. "Die Urkunden des päpstlichen Legaten Guido im Codex Diplomaticus et Epistolaris Regni Bohemiae." In *Palaeographica, diplomatica et archivistica: Studi in onore di Giulio Battelli*, 2:135–143. Rome: Edizioni di Storia e Letteratura, 1979.

Seckel, Emil. *Distinctiones glossatorum: Studien zur Distinktionen-Literatur der romanistischen Glossatorenschule*. Berlin: Verlag von Otto Liebmann, 1911.

Seckel, Emil. "Ueber neuere Editionen juristischer Schriften aus dem Mittelalter I." *ZRG Rom. Abt.* 21 (1900): 212–338.

Seipp, David J. "Presumptions in Early English Common Law." In *The Law of Presumptions: Essays in Comparative Legal History*, ed. Richard H. Helmholz and W. David H. Sellar, 117–136. Berlin: Duncker & Humblot, 2009.

Sharpe, Richard. "Reconstructing the Medieval Library of Bury St Edmunds: The Lost Catalogue of Henry of Kirkstead." In *Bury St Edmunds: Medieval Art, Architecture, Archaeology and Economy*, ed. Antonia Gransden, 204–218 (London: British Archaeological Association, 1998).

Smith, Lesley. *The Glossa Ordinaria: The Making of a Medieval Bible Commentary*. Leiden: Brill, 2019.

Souter, Alexander, ed. *A Glossary of Later Latin to 600 A.D.* Oxford: Clarendon Press, 1949.

Southern, Richard W. "The Necessity for Two Peters of Blois." In *Intellectual Life in the Middle Ages: Essays Presented to Margaret Gibson*, ed. Lesley Smith and Benedicta Ward, 103–118. London: Hambledon Press, 1992.

Southern, Richard W. "The Place of England in the Twelfth -Century Renaissance." *History. The Journal of the Historical Association* 45 (1960): 201–216. Reprinted in Richard W. Southern, *Medieval Humanism and Other Studies*, 158–180. Oxford: Blackwell, 1970.

Southern, Richard W. *Scholastic Humanism and the Unification of Europe*, 2 vols. Oxford: Blackwell, 1995–2001.

Speciale, Giuseppe. "Studio sui notabilia del codice Assisi 220." *Quaderni catanesi di studi classici e medievali* 17 (1987): 157–214.

Spinella, Barbara Maria Rita. *La Cattedrale di Santa Maria di Messina nei documenti dell'Archivio Ducale Medinaceli di Toledo (1282–1412)*. PhD dissertation: University of Catania, 2013.

Stein, Peter. "The Digest Title 'De diversis regulis iuris antiqui' and the General Principles of Law." In *Essays in Jurisprudence in Honor of Roscoe Pound*, ed. Ralph A. Newman, 1–20. Westport: Greenwood Press, 1962.

Stelzer, Winfried. *Gelehrtes Recht in Österreich: Von den Anfängen bis zum frühen 14. Jahrhundert*. Vienna: Böhlaus, 1982.

Stelzer, Winfried. "Die Summa Monacensis ('Summa Inperatorie maiestati') und der Neustifter Propst Konrad von Albeck." *Mitteilungen des Instituts für Österreichische Geschichtsforschung* 88 (1980): 94–112.

Stevenson, Enrico. *Codices Palatini Latini Bibliothecae Vaticanae*, 1. Rome: Ex Typographeo Vaticano, 1886.

Stickler, Alfons M. "Iter Helveticum." *Traditio* 14 (1958): 475–477.

Stickler, Alfons M. "Ordines judiciarii." In *DDC* 6 (1957): 1132–1143.

Stickler, Alfons M. "Sacerdotium et Regnum nei decretisti e nei primi decretalisti: Considerazioni metodologiche di ricerca e testi." *Salesianum* 15 (1953): 5–42.

Stölzel, Adolf. "Nochmals die Abkürzung ff für die Abkürzung D." *Zeitschrift für Rechtsgeschichte* 13 (1878): 399–400.

Stump, Eleonore. *Dialectic and Its Place in the Development of Medieval Logic*. Ithaca, NY: Cornell University Press, 1989.

Stump, Eleonore. "Topics: Their Development and Absorption into Consequences." In *The Cambridge History of Later Medieval Philosophy*, 1, *From the rediscovery of Aristotle to the disintegration of Scholasticism, 1100–1600*, ed. Norman Kretzmann, Anthony Kenny, Jan Pinborg, and Eleonore Stump, 273–299. Cambridge: Cambridge University Press, 1982.

Summerlin, Danica. *The Canons of the Third Lateran Council of 1179: Their Origins and Reception*. Cambridge: Cambridge University Press, 2019.

Taliadoros, Jason. *Law and Theology in Twelfth-century England: The Works of Master Vacarius (c. 1115/1120–c .1200)*. Turnhout: Brepols, 2007.

Tedesco, Anna. "Juan Francisco Pacheco v duca di Uceda, uomo politico e mecenate tra Palermo, Roma e Vienna nell'epoca della guerra di successione Spagnola." In *La pérdida de Europa : la guerra de sucesión por la Monarquía de España*, ed. Antonio Alvarez-Ossorio Alvariño, Bernardo José García García, and Virginia León Sanz, 491–550. Madrid: Fundación Carlos de Amberes, 2007.

Tessera, Miriam Rita. "Dalla liturgia del Santo Sepolcro alla biblioteca di Sidone: Note sulla produzione libraria latina di Oltremare nel secolo XII–XIII." *Aevum* 79, no. 2 (May–August 2005): 413–415.

Thomas, Yan. "Fictio legis. L'empire de la fiction romaine et ses limites médiévales." *Droits* 21 (1995): 17–63.

Thomson, Rodney M. *A Descriptive Catalogue of the Medieval Manuscripts owned by Pembroke College, Cambridge*. Cambridge: Brewer, 2022.

Thomson, Rodney M. "England and the Twelfth-Century Renaissance." *Past & Present* 101 (1983): 3–21.

Todescan, Franco. *Diritto e realtà: Storia e teoria della fictio iuris*. Padua: CEDAM, 1979.

Turner, Ralph V. "Coutances, Walter de." In *ODNB* 13 (Oxford, 2004): 712–714.

Turner, Ralph V. "Les Anglo-Normands et la Sicilie." *Études Normandes* 35, no. 3 (1986): 39–60.

Vallerani, Massimo. "I fatti nella logica del processo medievale: Note introduttive." *Quaderni Storici* 36 (2001): 665–693.

van de Wouw, Hans. "Brocardica Dunelmensia." *ZRG Rom. Abt.* 108 (1991): 234–278.

van de Wouw, Hans. "Gandulphus von Bologna." In *LexMA* 4 (1989): 1105.

van de Wouw, Hans. "Notes on the Aschaffenburg Manuscript Perg. 26." *BMCL* 3 (1973): 97–107.

Vignodelli, Giacomo. *Il filo a piombo: Il Perpendiculum di Attone di Vercelli e la storia politica del regno italico*. Spoleto: Fondazione Centro italiano di studi sull'alto Medioevo, 2011.

Wei, John C. *Π-group (P-group)*. Available at https://web.archive.org/web/20210415052423/https://sites.google.com/site/repertoriumiuriscanonici/home/gratian/p-group. Accessed 2024 May 29.

Wei, John C. "Gratian's Decretum in France and Halberstadt." In *Rechtshandschriften des deutschen Mittelalters: Produktionsorte und Importwege*, ed. Patrizia Carmassi and Gisela Drossbach, 363–383. Wiesbaden: Harrassowitz, 2015.

Weigand, Rudolf. *Die bedingte Eheschließung im kanonischen Recht*, 1. Munich: Max Hueber, 1963.

Weigand, Rudolf. "Die Dekretanhänge in den Handschriften Heiligenkreuz 44, Pommersfelden 142 und München 28175." *BMCL* 13 (1983): 1–25.

Weigand, Rudolf. "The Development of the Glossa ordinaria to Gratian's Decretum." In *HMCLCP*, 55–97.

Weigand, Rudolf. "Fälschungen als Paleae im Dekret Gratians." In *Fälschungen im Mittelalter: Internationaler Kongress der Monumenta Germaniae Historica, München, 16.–19. September 1986*, ed. Detlev Jasper, 2:301–318. Hannover: Hahnsche Buchhandlung, 1988.

Weigand, Rudolf. "Die frühen kanonistischen Schulen und die Dekretabbreviatio Omnebenes." AKKR 155 (1986): 72–91.

Weigand, Rudolf. “Paleae und andere Zusätze in Dekrethandschriften mit dem Glossenapparat Ordinaturus Magister.” AKKR 159 (1990): 448–463.

Weigand, Rudolf. “The Transmontane Decretists.” In *HMCLCP*, 174–210.

Weimar, Peter. “Argumenta brocardica.” *Studia Gratiana* 14 (1967): 91–123.

Weimar, Peter. “Die legistische Literatur der Glossatorenzeit.” In *HQLR*, 1:129–260.

Weimar, Peter. “Die legistische Literatur und die Methode des Rechtsunterrichts der Glossatorenzeit.” *Ius Commune* 2 (1969): 43–83.

Weimar, Peter. “Johannes Bassianus.” In *LexMA* 5 (1991): 556–557.

Weimar, Peter. “Otto Papiensis.” In *LexMA* 6 (1993): 1585.

Weimar, Peter. “Pilius, Bologneser Zivilrechtslehrer (um 1150—nach 1207).” In *LexMA* 6 (1993): 2159

Whitman, James Q. *The Origins of Reasonable Doubt: Theological Roots of the Criminal Trial*. New Haven: Yale University Press, 2008.

Winroth, Anders. “Law Schools and Legal Education.” In *The Cambridge History of Medieval Canon Law*, ed. Anders Winroth and John C. Wei, 262–284. Cambridge: Cambridge University Press, 2022.

Winroth, Anders. “Law Schools in the Twelfth Century.” In *Mélanges en l'honneur d'Anne Lefebvre-Teillard*, ed. Bernard D'Alteroche, Florence Demoulin-Auzary, Olivier Descamps, Breandán Ó Buachalla, and Franck Roumy, 1057–1064. Paris: Éditions Panthéon-Assas, 2010.

Winroth, Anders. “Sankt Gallen, Stiftsbibliothek, 673 in Context: Twelfth-Century Transformations and Abbreviations of Gratian's Decretum.” In *Creating and Sharing Legal Knowledge in the Twelfth Century: Sankt Gallen, Stiftsbibliothek, 673 and Its Context*, ed. Stephan Dusil and Andreas Thier, 221–241. Leiden: Brill, 2022.

Witt, Ronald G. *The Two Latin Cultures and the Foundation of Renaissance Humanism in Medieval Italy*. Cambridge: Cambridge University Press, 2012.

Woo, B. Hoon. “Augustine's Hermeneutics and Homiletics in De doctrina Christiana.” *Journal of Christian Philosophy* 17 (2013): 97–117.

Wunderlich, Agathon. “Beiträge zur Literaturgeschichte des Prozesses im 12 u. 13. Jahrhundert.” *Zeitschrift für geschichtliche Rechtwissenschaft* 2 (1842): 92–98.

Zimmerman, Michael J., and Ben Bradley. “Intrinsic vs. Extrinsic Value.” In *The Stanford Encyclopedia of Philosophy (Spring 2019 Edition)*, ed. Edward N. Zalta. Available at https://plato.stanford.edu/archives/spr2019/entries/value-intrinsic-extrinsic/. Accessed 2021 Aug 29.

Index to Part 1 of the Book

Modern Authors

Names and Subjects

Index to Prolegomena and Manuscript Descriptions

Modern Authors

Names and Subjects

Index to the *Perpendiculum* (Parts I–III) and the Appendix

Part I–II

Part III and Appendix

Index to Legal Sources

Index to Incipits of the Brocards (Parts II and III)

Index to Manuscripts

www.ingramcontent.com/pod-product-compliance
Lightning Source LLC
Chambersburg PA
CBHW071336230926
51849CB00002B/408
9789004712751